CRIMINOLOGY

CRIMINOLOGY

A Canadian Perspective

SECOND EDITION

RICK LINDEN, GENERAL EDITOR

UNIVERSITY OF MANITOBA

HARCOURT BRACE JOVANOVICH CANADA INC.

TORONTO   MONTREAL   ORLANDO   FORT WORTH   SAN DIEGO   PHILADELPHIA
LONDON   SYDNEY   TOKYO

Canadian Cataloguing in Publication Data

Main entry under title:

Criminology

2nd ed.
Includes bibliographical references and index.
ISBN 0-03-922790-1

1. Criminology - Canada.   I. Linden, Rick.

HV6807.C75 1992   364.971   C91-094482-2

Editorial Director: Heather McWhinney
Acquisitions Editor: Sheila Malloch
Developmental Editor: Lorraine Doherty
Director of Publishing Services: Steve Lau
Editorial Manager: Liz Radojkovic
Editorial Co-ordinator: Sandra L. Meadow
Production Manager: Sue-Ann Becker
Production Assistant: Sandra Miller
Copy Editor: Cy Strom
Interior Design: The Brookview Group
Cover Design: Dave Peters
Typesetting and Assembly: Bookman Typesetting Co.
Printing and Binding: John Deyell Company Limited

Cover art: "Three in Sorrow," Jack Bush, 1947. Copyright, Jack Bush Heritage Corp. Reproduced with permission.

∞ This book was printed in Canada on acid-free paper.

1 2 3 4 5   96 95 94 93 92

To Christopher, who gave so much and asked so little

PREFACE

Upon publication, the first edition of *Criminology: A Canadian Perspective* received an enthusiastic welcome from professors and students who had been frustrated by the absence of a Canadian text in this field. The success of this text has prompted the publication of the second edition. This book is intended as a text for a one-term course in introductory criminology. While the book deals extensively with theories of crime causation (which have largely been developed elsewhere), its purpose is to provide students with information about crime in Canada. Over the last two decades, the discipline of criminology has grown from a few widely scattered faculty members to a large community of academics, researchers, practitioners, and students. The second edition of *Criminology: A Canadian Perspective* continues to reflect their work.

Part I provides some of the basic information about crime: the sources of criminal law; the legal elements of crime; the sources of information about crime; and the social correlates of criminal behaviour. A new chapter, "Women and Crime," has been included. This part provides the student with the background necessary to assess the theories of crime causation presented in Part II. In this part, all of the major theories are covered, including biological, psychological, and sociological explanations. In Part III many of the most serious and frequent types of crime are discussed.

The many different theories proposed to explain criminality are continually being revived and revised. Often the popularity of a particular theory owes as much to ideological commitment and academic fashion as it does to the explanatory power of the theory. As a result of this unresolved diversity, the pages of many texts are littered with the bodies of straw men, set up only to be sacrificed to the author's favourite approach. All of the major perspectives have merit, and can be most effectively presented by someone who is well informed and sympathetic. The advantage of a multiple-authored text is that each approach is given a fair chance.

ACKNOWLEDGEMENTS

It has become traditional for authors to thank families for not making demands, and spouses, or close friends, both for moral support and for those unspecified but essential services that writing seems to require. Since my wife and children had already reached their tolerance limit with my work schedule, I decided that I couldn't just disappear into my office and reappear two years later with a book. Thus it is to them that I again owe my wise decision to get help from the friends and colleagues who co-authored this text. For the time

I did spend writing, I thank for their support Olive, Brad, Chris, Robin, Shawn, T.J., Amanda.

Working with the people at Harcourt Brace Jovanovich has been a delightful experience. Tony Luengo and Tessa McWatt provided me with a great deal of help on the first edition of this text, and I have enjoyed working with a new team, including Heather McWhinney, Sheila Malloch, Lorraine Doherty, and Sandra Meadow, on the second edition. Special thanks to the reviewers who gave us good advice: Bill Avison, Thomas Bernard, Augustine Brannigan, Tullio Caputo, Sange de Silva, Karlene Faith, Thomas Gabor, Colin Goff, Jim Hackler, Sheilagh Hodgins, Carl Keane, Gail Kellough, Michael Petrunik, Vincent F. Sacco, Les Samuelson, Bernard Schissel, Phillip C. Stenning, and Austin T. Turk.

Finally, I would like to thank each of the authors who contributed to the book. I appreciate your enthusiastic response to revision suggestions and your efforts to meet deadlines. I continue to enjoy and learn from your articles.

Individual authors wished to make the following acknowledgements:

J. Evans and A. Himelfarb (Chapter 3)—"The authors wish to thank the Canadian Centre for Justice Statistics for their assistance."

T.F. Hartnagel (Chapter 4)—"The financial assistance of the Ministry of the Solicitor General of Canada through its grant to the Criminology Research Centre, University of Alberta, is gratefully acknowledged. Marianne Nielson provided research assistance."

J.C. Hackler (Chapter 9)—"The author would like to thank the Ministry of the Solicitor General for the contributions grant and their support in completing this chapter."

D.J. Koenig (Chapter 13)—"The author wishes to thank SSHRC for a grant that assisted the research on which this chapter drew."

R.R. Corrado (Chapter 15)—"I want to thank Garth Davies for his assistance in revising this chapter."

PUBLISHER'S NOTE TO STUDENTS AND INSTRUCTORS

This textbook is a key component of your course. If you are the instructor of this course, you undoubtedly considered a number of texts carefully before choosing this one as the one that would work best for your students and you. The authors and publishers spent considerable time and money to ensure its high quality, and we appreciate your recognition of this effort and accomplishment. Please note the copyright statement.

If you are a student, we are confident that this text will help you to meet the objectives of your course. It will also become a valuable addition to your personal library.

Since we want to hear what you think about this book, please be sure to send us the stamped reply card at the end of the text. Your input will help us to continue to publish high-quality books for your courses.

CONTRIBUTORS

Tullio Caputo	Carleton University
Elizabeth Comack	University of Manitoba
Raymond R. Corrado	Simon Fraser University
David N. Cox	Simon Fraser University
John Evans	Ministry of the Solicitor General
James C. Hackler	University of Alberta
John Hagan	University of Toronto
Timothy F. Hartnagel	University of Alberta
Alexander Himelfarb	Ministry of the Solicitor General
Ronald Hinch	Guelph University
Sheilagh Hodgins	Université de Montréal and Centre de Recherche Philippe Pinel
Daniel J. Koenig	University of Victoria
Rod Kueneman	University of Manitoba
Graham Parker	Osgoode Hall Law School, York University
Ronald Roesch	Simon Fraser University
Rodney T. Stamler	Lindquist Avey MacDonald Baskerville and Company
Robert A. Stebbins	University of Calgary

CONTENTS

PART I: CRIME AND SOCIETY

CHAPTER 1
THE ORIGINS AND ROLE OF LAW IN SOCIETY   3
Rod Kueneman

Introduction   3
Patterns of Human Social Organization   4
Small-Scale Society   5
Dispute Settlement in Small-Scale Society   9
The Transformation from Small-Scale Society to the State   14
Modern State Systems   18
Summary   31
Bibliography   32
Further Reading   34

CHAPTER 2
CRIME, LAW, AND LEGAL DEFENCES   37
Graham Parker

Introduction   37
Sources of Criminal Law   38
A Definition of Crime   38
The Relativity of Crime   39
Classification of Crimes   42
General Principles of Criminal Liability   42
The Defences to a Criminal Charge   45
A Slightly Different View of the Criminal Law   48
The History of Criminal Law as a History of Proof
  and Procedure   48
The Problem of Theory   51
Summary   55
Bibliography   56
Further Reading   56

CHAPTER 3
COUNTING CRIME   57
John Evans and Alexander Himelfarb

Introduction   57
Statistics on the Criminal Justice System   61
How Much Crime?   65
Official Statistics: Canadian Uniform Crime Reports   68

Victimization Surveys   79
Victimization Surveys and the UCR   85
Self-Report Studies   86
Summary: The Future of Crime and Criminal Justice Statistics   87
Bibliography   88
Further Reading   89

CHAPTER 4

CORRELATES OF CRIMINAL BEHAVIOUR   91
Timothy F. Hartnagel

Correlates Defined   91
Age   92
Sex   97
Race   106
Social Class   113
Summary   120
Bibliography   121
Further Reading   125

CHAPTER 5

WOMEN AND CRIME   127
Elizabeth Comack

Working for Change: Violence against Women   127
Feminism in the Academy: Explaining Women's Criminality   147
Summary   158
Bibliography   159
Further Reading   162

PART II: EXPLANATIONS OF CRIME

CHAPTER 6

EARLY THEORIES OF CRIMINOLOGY   165
Tullio Caputo and Rick Linden

Introduction   165
The Classical School   166
The Statistical School   171
Lombroso and the Positive School   172
Biological Theories in the Early Twentieth Century   176
Summary   180
Bibliography   181
Further Reading   182

CHAPTER 7

BIOLOGICAL FACTORS IMPLICATED IN THE
DEVELOPMENT OF CRIMINAL BEHAVIOURS   185
Sheilagh Hodgins

The Role of Biological Factors in the Development of Behaviour   185
Obstacles to Research on the Role of Biological Factors
 Implicated in Crime   186
Generalizing Results from One Society to Another   186
Biological States and Factors Directly Related to
 Criminal Behaviour   187
Biological Factors Indirectly Related to Criminal Behaviour   188
Two Theories of the Role of Biological Factors in Determining
 Criminal Behaviour   199
Biological Factors Implicated in Psychopathy   200
Major Mental Disorder   203
Alcohol and Drug Abuse and Dependence   204
Conclusion   204
Summary   205
Bibliography   207
Further Reading   212

CHAPTER 8

PSYCHOLOGICAL PERSPECTIVES ON CRIMINALITY   213
David N. Cox and Ronald Roesch

Psychoanalytic Theory   215
Theories of Moral Development   217
Antisocial Personality   224
Crime and Mental Illness   229
Summary   232
Bibliography   232
Further Reading   236

CHAPTER 9

STRAIN THEORIES   239
James C. Hackler

The Structural-Functionalist Foundations   239
Opportunity Structures   244
Empirical Evidence for the Theory of Illegitimate
 Opportunity Structures   249
Assessing Functionalist and Opportunity Theories   254
Heuristic Uses of Strain Theory   256
Policy Implications   260
Conclusion and Summary   262

Bibliography   263
Further Reading   265

CHAPTER 10

CONFLICT AND MARXIST THEORIES   267
Ronald Hinch

Cultural Conflict Theories   267
Group Conflict Theory   270
Weberian Conflict Theory   272
Marxist Theories   277
Conclusion   287
Summary   287
Bibliography   288
Further Reading   291

CHAPTER 11

INTERACTIONIST THEORIES   293
Robert A. Stebbins

The Deviant Career   294
Socialization into Crime   306
Limitations   307
Implications   309
Summary   310
Bibliography   311
Further Reading   313

CHAPTER 12

SOCIAL CONTROL THEORY   315
Rick Linden

Theories of Social Disorganization—Durkheim, Thrasher, and
  Shaw and McKay   315
Early Social Control Theories—Reiss, Nye, and Reckless   318
Hirschi and the Social Bond   321
Family Relationships   323
Schooling   325
Religiosity   326
Female Criminality   328
Criticisms of Social Control Theory   329
Policy Implications of Control Theory   338
The Schools and Social Policy   341
The Need for Social Change   343
Summary   343
Bibliography   344
Further Reading   348

PART III: PATTERNS OF CRIMINAL BEHAVIOUR

CHAPTER 13
CONVENTIONAL CRIME   351
Daniel J. Koenig

The Lifestyle/Exposure, Routine Activities Approach   351
Patterns of Specific Crimes   355
Murder and Other Criminal Homicides   355
Assaultive Behaviours   359
Robbery   370
Break and Enter   374
Other Offences   376
What Can Be Done?   378
Summary   383
Bibliography   384
Further Reading   387

CHAPTER 14
ORGANIZED CRIME   389
Rodney T. Stamler

What Is Organized Crime?   389
Who Is Involved in Organized Crime?   394
Major Crime Groups in Canada   394
The Nature of Organized Crime Activity   405
The Nature of Consensual Crime Activity   408
Money Laundering Schemes   409
Controlling Organized Crime   413
National Criminal Laws and Procedures   415
International Co-operation   415
Summary   416
Bibliography   416
Further Reading   417

CHAPTER 15
POLITICAL CRIME IN CANADA   419
Raymond R. Corrado

Multiple Perspectives on Political Crime in Canada   419
The Conceptualization of Political Crime   419
Examining Political Crime in Canada   422
Theoretical Perspectives on Political Crime   423
Examples of Political Crime in Canada and
   Theoretical Interpretations   427
Corruption in the Political Process   439

Summary   446
Bibliography   447
Further Reading   449

CHAPTER 16
WHITE-COLLAR AND CORPORATE CRIME   451
John Hagan

Class, Crime, and the Corporations   451
White-Collar Crime and the Social Organization of Work   456
White-Collar Crime and Legal Sanctions   462
Summary   468
Bibliography   469
Further Reading   472

INDEX   475

P A R T I

CRIME AND SOCIETY

This part provides some of the basic information about crime: the origins of our criminal law; the legal elements of crime; the sources of information about crime; and the social correlates of criminal behaviour.

In Chapter 1, we learn how our system of law has developed as we have evolved from simple hunting and gathering societies to modern industrial societies. With the increased complexity and growth of modern societies comes the need for a formal legal system to maintain order. We also learn why some social harms are defined as illegal, while others are not.

The legal elements of a crime are *actus reus* (the physical element) and *mens rea* (the mental element). These are discussed in Chapter 2, along with defences available to an accused, a history of criminal procedure, and an outline of the social factors affecting the definition of specific types of crime.

We cannot systematically study crime unless we can measure it. Chapter 3 details some of the ways we count crime, such as official government statistics, victimization surveys, and self-report surveys. None of these methods is completely adequate; you will learn the strengths and weaknesses of each.

Before we can explain a phenomenon such as crime, we must know something about the way it is distributed demographically. In Chapter 4, a number of correlates of crime are discussed including age, sex, race, and social class. In recent years, there has been an increased recognition of the importance of looking at the issue of women and crime. Because of this, Chapter 5 considers this correlate in more depth. The explanations of crime discussed in Part II may be judged according to how well they account for these regularities.

CHAPTER 1

THE ORIGINS AND ROLE OF LAW IN SOCIETY

By Rod Kueneman

INTRODUCTION

*T*here have been disputes in all forms of human society. Every human group has developed some mechanisms for restoring social order. In our lives today, the law takes a prominent place in this restoration process. As of 1986, the Law Reform Commission of Canada noted, the Canadian federal state had created in excess of 90 000 laws. But not all communities have relied on formally enacted laws which are enforced by the power of a state apparatus. As we shall see, this pattern has emerged rather late in human history.

Throughout most of human existence, we lived in small hunting and gathering communities. Co-operation, mutual aid, and kinship within these communities were the essential means of preserving harmony and the restoration of order. The absence of a centralized power structure meant that these communities had to rely on these different mechanisms to keep the peace. One of the tasks of this chapter is to show how these different dispute-settlement mechanisms can be understood within their social context. As patterns of societal organization changed, different forms of dispute settlement emerged. The general role of dispute settlement processes in all societies is the restoration of order. Nevertheless, the nature of these different social orders and the groups who have received the most benefit from order within them have changed to a considerable extent. As we shall see, dispute-settlement processes are intimately involved in the structuring of social relationships.

Crime is the subject of this text. It is important to realize that crime does not exist in all societies. A crime is a violation of a law, and not all societies have had formulated laws. While each society has had to develop a moral order, complete with stated expectations for acceptable behaviour, not all societies have developed laws to restrain their members. The formulation of law requires the existence of a central body such as a state which formulates law and enforces compliance with it. This is not only a matter of semantics. For much of human history, social order was facilitated by other means. It is equally important to note that criminal law, as we know it, has not been part of the social fabric for most of human history. Harms between individuals were resolved by various forms of redress in societies without a state. Even in societies with a state apparatus, many disputes are regulated by civil law. Under civil law, the state adjudicates between the parties to the dispute in an effort to repair the damage. Criminal law comes into existence at the point when the state declares itself to be the injured party for certain types of infractions. In its narrowest sense, criminology is concerned with this limited subset of laws and social infractions. But in order to understand the broad question of social order, it is important to see criminal law within a historical and social context that considers the full spectrum of dispute-settlement practices.

Finally, it is important to reflect on the human condition. The human animal does not have instincts. In place of the instincts that order so much of the lives of other animals, human beings must fashion their collective stability by way of culture. While sharing common emotional, intellectual, and motivational attributes, humans have produced an amazing variety of solutions to the problems they have faced. Equipped with a powerful imagination, members of our species have introduced both inspiring and terrifying innovations to their communities. This human imagination has contributed to the development of human culture. But it is also a principal source of instability, which has threatened to erode, weaken, and destroy the social fabric that had already been created. Humans have the ability to create disputes and to upset social arrangements. Law and other forms of dispute settlement are at the heart of our efforts to limit and to recover from the harm that is inflicted. Although there are many differences between societies, each social order must be recognized as a response to the need to construct a moral, or at least a legal, order.

It will not be possible here to provide a detailed description and analysis of the vast array of human cultures. Instead, our inquiry will be guided by a reconstruction of human history into two basic patterns of social organization.

PATTERNS OF HUMAN SOCIAL ORGANIZATION

The variety of human cultures has been classified in many different ways. Lenski emphasized the mode of production used by societies. He developed the following classification: hunting and gathering, pastoral, horticultural, agricultural, and industrial. This chapter will focus on the hunting and gathering and the industrial forms because they provide the greatest contrast with respect to dispute-settlement practices.

The hunting and gathering society has been a dominant form of social order in the history of the human species. For example, Michalowski (1985) argues that humans have lived in small-scale societies for the vast majority of the time that we have been in existence.

Acephalous [headless, leaderless] societies were the only type of human community for 30,000 of the 40,000 years since the evolution of modern humans. It is also highly probable that archaic humans had been living in acephalous social arrangements for the preceding 200,000 years. Acephalous societies are small, economically cooperative and relatively egalitarian societies with simple technology and division of labor based mainly upon age and sex. Stratification in terms of differential access to material goods and political power does not exist. While these societies lack rulers or governments with the power to command, direct and correct the behavior of others, acephalous societies are generally characterized more by order and cooperation than by chaos and competition.

Some of these societies did change their mode of production and were transformed into pastoral and horticultural forms. Under certain conditions, some of them were further transformed into agricultural and industrial societies. The hunting and gathering form, however, persisted in many parts of the world into this century. It was eventually destroyed by contact with the Western world.

The change in the mode of production to the pastoral or horticultural form created new possibilities for patterns of social organization which were inchoate and rudimentary when first introduced. These new patterns slowly and inexorably transformed some human cultures and are now visible in modern industrial society. The emergence of surplus, stratification, technological innovations, social power, and large populations has made possible the growth of the industrially based social system (Newman, 1983).

The rest of this chapter will outline the basic characteristics of the dominant social forms and will show how the dispute-settlement processes used in these different settings were a part of the social fabric. It will become clear that the discussion of custom, law, and dispute settlements must be couched within a social context in order to understand how each functions to settle the troubles that spring up in all human societies.

SMALL-SCALE SOCIETY

In this section, the general characteristics of small-scale societies will be described as a prelude to a discussion of their typical practices for settling disputes. Although such attributes are not present in all small-scale societies, they do appear in virtually all hunting and gathering societies and hence are useful as "ideal types" for the purposes of analysis.

VULNERABILITY WITHIN NATURE

Without underestimating the often harsh realities of the small-scale society or succumbing to the propensity to romanticize it, there is no question that such communities were characterized by a strong collective solidarity. Whether living in the high arctic, on the plains, or under the tropical rain forests, hunters and gatherers were well aware that they were part of a natural ecosystem that had forces that they could not control. They were aware of their individual vulnerability and realized that their collective life was an exercise in mutual survival. The co-operative, mutual-aid character of these societies was not accidental. The willingness to work as a community was predicated on an awareness of the desperate situation that humans faced in coping with nature.

The absence of a developed technology to soften the grip of nature on the group actually aided in the control of individuality. The impossibility of surviving without the assistance of the group strengthened the group's solidarity. The powerful role of ancestors in such societies is understandable, since they were believed to be the only sources which could control nature. The spiritual and ritual life of these communities helped to calm the anxiety of their members and simultaneously to establish cultural expectations. Commitment to community life was both existentially and culturally desirable.

THE NEED FOR SELF-RESTRAINT

Hunting and gathering groups were small communities of approximately 50 members who had closely related kin ties. In these small face-to-face communities, social networks were dense and were characterized by a high degree of social visibility. The mutual-aid character of such social relationships meant that there was the expectation of continuity of relationships over time. The absence of a complex division of labour made it necessary for each individual in the group to fulfil a number of roles with other members. This diffuseness of roles continuously reminded the group of the value of each member and placed a premium on co-operation, since each member was intimately involved with other members. Continuous interaction with other members of the group provided each member with feedback from others concerning the acceptability of certain types of behaviour and created a climate for the development of common norms and the cultivation of a consensus.

In such close and intimate quarters, members were reluctant to offend each other because of their mutual interdependence. Each member learned to cultivate personal restraint and the control of impulse in order to prevent the breakdown of a working order. Colson (1974) shows how these social circumstances fostered the development of forbearance, the avoidance of disputes, the sharing of resources, and the tolerance of human foibles. She relates how the Tonga of Zambia attempted to sidestep controversial issues and were reluctant to allow others to drag them into disputes. The Tonga's social structure worked against the outbreak of violence, the fear of attack by sorcerers, or other forms of retaliation. This contributed to the development of self-restraint.

Colson also reminds us that it is not that these people lacked "occasion for quarrels and hostility but they learn that they must control their hostility, their greed, and their envy if they are to survive" (61). Such communities could easily punish any individual who consistently went his or her own way.

The self-restraint that members exercised stemmed not only from the close, intimate, and friendly ties that are a product of common life, but also out of the fear of reprisal and the desire to keep hostilities from surfacing and disturbing the business of living. Brant (1990), a Mohawk psychiatrist, emphasized the need for the principles of non-interference, non-competitiveness, and emotional restraint in order to suppress the emergence of conflict. Ross (1989), a Crown attorney in northern Ontario, relates in the accompanying insert how the principle of emotional restraint still operates in some remote Ojibway communities.

One such rule requires that grief, anger and sorrow be quickly buried. They should not be expressed, for that only serves to burden the person who hears. They should not be explored or indulged privately, for doing so results in a lessened capacity to contribute the fullest energy, attention and skills which the hunter-gatherer society needed to maintain survival. Expressions of anger or criticism would serve only to create friction, a dangerous luxury to a people who required the maximum cooperation of all. Even the *thinking* of critical thoughts about others was to be avoided. Quite simply, the past was the past, and its negative parts were to be buried and forgotten as quickly as possible....

While such overt observances of these rules are declining, it remains a central tenet of life in many communities that it is wrong to speak of your hurts and angers and criticisms, wrong to indulge your private emotions. Instead, you bury and you carry on, resisting the backwards glance. I recall one teenage rape victim who refused to testify when her assailant finally came to trial more than a year after the event; her reason was simply that he should have paid his penalty by now and be getting on with his life. For her, it was simply too late to put him through it. The past was the past.

Asking a Native accused to explain what it was that aggravated him to such a degree that he attacked his victim is the subject of a special constraint, already referred to, which forbids the criticism of others.

Source: Rupert Ross. "Leaving Our White Eyes Behind: The Sentencing of Native Accused." [1989] 3 *Canadian Native Law Reporter* 1 at 4.

MUTUAL DEPENDENCE

Living in a subsistence economy, where little or no surplus could be generated, created the necessity for the group to share the fruits of a day's hunting or foraging. Typically, the spoils were distributed in such a way as to ensure that everyone received an equal and adequate share, regardless of the extent and nature of each one's contribution. In such a distribution system there may have been collective scarcity if food was not found, but there was never poverty in the sense that some ate while others went hungry. Though a member was not expected to love everyone else, each one was expected to care for all members of the community. This ensured that all members would be cared for in the nonproductive times of their life such as childhood and old age, and during times of sickness. This bond of mutual dependence helped to keep greed and the desire for advantage in check.

A COMMUNITY OF BELIEF

The structure of small-scale society fostered both moderation and compassion, which acted as powerful curbs to egotism. A shared system of customs and patterns of behaviour in domestic, economic, and political life grew out of the personal and interpersonal accommodations that were required of such intimate social actors. There is no question that this type of society was coercive; there was virtually no freedom of belief. One's location in the kinship system established basic duties, obligations, rights, and privileges. Failure to meet obligations jeopardized one's relationship with many members of the group and, especially, with one's immediate kin. The notion of collective responsibility which was prevalent in such communities made kin groups accountable for the behaviour of their members. The positive dimension of community membership was that throughout the life cycle, the customary ways provided meaning for members. This sense of purpose helped foster commitment to community beliefs and practices.

THE ABSENCE OF SURPLUS, STRATIFICATION, AND THE STATE

The life of the hunters and gatherers was an exercise in co-operative living. The inability to produce or to keep large amounts of food on hand meant that food gathering was a regular activity that included all able-bodied members. The division and distribution of foodstuffs to all community members underscored the understanding that everyone had a right to the fruits of this collective activity; they were a group possession to be shared by all. The need to move regularly acted to limit the amount of personal belongings a person could accumulate, and since each member had access to the same raw materials, there was little difference in the individuals' limited possessions. The possibility of generating any significant surplus under these conditions was limited. In richer environments such as Canada's west coast, where surpluses were sometimes possible, the practices of potlatch and ritual offerings to the spirits in an effort to secure continued bounty helped to level out any possibility of material advantage. Small-scale society, then, acted as a brake on the human tendency to secure an advantageous individual position. By identifying one's "self" with the interests of the entire group, the individual self so familiar to our society was superseded by a social or collective self-concept.

The absence of surplus was a strong force which suppressed the emergence of economic stratification and any form of state-like structure or political institution. Small-scale societies have been characterized as acephalous (without a head) because there was no distinct source of social power or authority independent of the collective will. The only form of power available to special individuals in such societies was influence. Influence was based on status derived from hunting skill, sex, wisdom, or generosity, and not on differential access to and accumulation of material resources. Social status was a group property, not a personal attribute. The members of the group could give it and take it away. Hoebel (1973) comments on the position of the Inuit headman:

> The headman possesses no fixed authority; neither does he enter into formal office. He is not elected, nor is he chosen by any formal process. When other men accept his judgement and opinions, he is headman. When they ignore him, he is not.

Thus, if an esteemed individual became arrogant or tried to force others to comply in ways that were deemed inappropriate, the special status was removable. All aspects of group life worked in a systematic fashion to control and limit the will of the individual in the best interests of the group. This is the type of society to which Tönnies (1887) applied the term *Gemeinschaft*, where human beings "remain essentially united in spite of all separating factors."

DISPUTE SETTLEMENT IN SMALL-SCALE SOCIETY

The major goal of dispute settlement in small-scale societies was to restore harmonious relations between parties who could not interact because of some conflict. It was essential that problems be settled in mutually agreeable ways for all involved parties as quickly as possible, so as not to impede group life. The absence of an independent political institution meant that disputants typically had to resolve their differences without the assistance of an adjudicator (Gulliver, 1979). Community pressure was applied to the parties in a dispute to meet and to bring an end to the discord. Each party had to give and to receive information from the other in order to learn of the other party's needs and expectations. In a series of such educational exchanges, an attempt was made to move toward a mutually agreeable outcome and the restoration of harmonious interaction.

This type of approach to discord led to a general airing of all the issues that created friction between the parties. This ensured that an effort was made to keep the conflict from escalating and to lead the discordant parties to a mutually satisfying conclusion to their problem. Resolving trouble involved a face-to-face encounter with a well-known disputant, almost invariably a kinsman. This required the active participation of both offender and victim. Potential troublemakers had to recognize that, at some point, they would have to confront those whom they had directly harmed, rather than some abstract system of justice and a victim who was a stranger. Inside this general framework there was some variation in the types of disputes and the form of the settlement practices.

TYPES OF DISPUTES AND THEIR SETTLEMENT

Newman (1983) provides rich detail concerning the types of disputes which arose in hunting and gathering society. Most disputes among hunting and gathering peoples concerned women. Because women were valuable producers, adultery, failure to honour marriage agreements, and the taking of a woman by an enemy caused serious disruptions. While not necessarily considered the property of their fathers or husbands, there was an interest in controlling women as valuable resources to the kin system. Other causes of conflict involved such acts as improper food distribution, asymmetrical gift exchange, laziness, stinginess, theft, and murder. Theft was an infrequent offence among nomadic foragers, owing to the relative absence of property. Murders were relatively infrequent and almost always resulted from disputes concerning women. Because of the emergence of the notion of property among sedentary food collectors, however, there was a greater incidence of theft and disputes over the use of land in those societies.

The primary method of redress in small-scale society was self- or kin-based redress. Other methods, used less frequently, were advisor or mediator systems.

Self- or Kin-Based Redress

The range of responses available in self- or kin-based redress included public criticism, shaming rituals, temporary ostracism, expulsion from the group, blood feuds, and reprisal killings. Some sedentary food gatherers also developed a scale of fines for certain types of infractions. This list in no way exhausts the full range of responses that were employed, but it does encompass those used most frequently. Less harsh methods were often employed initially, and only when they failed were more punitive responses called forth. In some instances, a disputant may simply have chosen to leave the group and join another on a temporary or permanent basis.

The injured party had to initiate the dispute process because there was no centralized authority. This does not mean that the victim was free to do whatever he or she chose to an offender. The society had customary expectations about the appropriateness of different reprisals. Too harsh a response could evoke group disapproval and sanctions. For example, among the Aranda of Australia, the socially defined punishment for adultery included cuts around the shoulder blades of the offending man inflicted by the cuckolded husband during hot pursuit of the offender. If the cuts were too deep and exceeded the standard of acceptable punishment, however, he stood to forfeit his wife. Among the Mataco of South America, if the reprisal was considered to be more serious than the original offence, the initial offence was expunged and the offender became the injured party. An individual could lose the support of his or her family by retaliating too vigorously. It is important to emphasize here that self-redress is a regulated social process. The image of small-scale societies as violent and constantly feuding is inaccurate. The ordered interdependence which was the hallmark of such social formations did not allow for anarchy when wrongs were redressed. While it is true that disputes did escalate into blood feuds and cycles of revenge killings, even these proceeded in an orderly fashion. Furthermore, small-scale society had a body of custom that was coupled with the fear of reprisal which acted as a brake on such escalation by defining an appropriate level of redress for various offences.

Clearly defined notions of right and wrong behaviour existed in spite of the absence of third-party authority figures. It should be noted that formalized civil or criminal law was not present or necessary for these small, kin-based communities to restore order. If an individual violated a custom, he or she suffered the consequences. His or her kin did not provide protection from legitimate retaliation. If the punishment was too harsh or unfairly exacted, a retaliation was initiated and conflict continued until both sides were satisfied with the resolution of the situation. An exchange of gifts often signalled the end to hostilities.

Advisor Systems

The advisor system is really only an extension of the self-redress method of dispute settlement because it was once again ultimately the victim or kin who would enforce any retaliation. Disputants approached advisors, who tended to be men who were distinguished warriors, hunters, or speakers. They were mature, although not always the eldest men of the community, and were regarded as public repositories of wisdom about customs and rituals. In general, they were not selected because of hereditary birthright.

The process of dispute settlement was activated when one or both parties sought out one of these high-status figures. They were not required to turn to this third party, but it was expected that they would do so. Each party presented its case, and after considering the facts, the advisor recommended what should be done. He interpreted the case with respect to custom and it was his role to ensure that the social group's conception of appropriate behaviour was protected. He was a moral authority, but he could not enforce compliance. He could, however, attempt to influence disputants with sham-ing rituals and his ability to make compelling arguments. Among some groups, the advisor could take a more active role by indicating which side his own kin group would back in the event of a reprisal. Here, too, the advisor could not direct his kin group, but only report its position with reference to the dispute. The advisor was, essentially, a communication link between parties and attempted to co-ordinate a settlement without violence. An advisor gained status by being able to settle disputes without the outbreak of revenge activity. A demonstrated ability to resolve disputes peacefully strengthened his moral authority. If the advisor overstepped his bounds and tried to make his authority too exacting, the community would stop using him in his capacity of advisor.

Thus, the advisor system was still firmly controlled by the community. The emergence of the advisor, and his moral authority, were still a matter of esteem and respect—this was not a position based on the social or material power of a social group such as a family. It is true that some kin groups "supplied" more advisors than other groups, but a successful resolution required the satisfaction of both parties to the dispute as well as a general satisfaction with the role as enacted by the advisor.

Most hunting and gathering societies relied on self-redress; a smaller proportion developed an advisor system.

In general, the dispute-settlement processes used by small-scale societies were designed to restore social integration and harmony. These societies tried to surround and contain problems involving members of the community and sought to resolve them through compromise and reconciliation. Each member was tied to other members for a variety of social purposes. The discord created by disputants interfered with these other positive and necessary ties. These people simply could not afford to have long-standing anger and discord. As Ross (1989) points out in the insert shown here, traditional Inuit and Ojibway dispute-settlement mechanisms provide a poignant contrast to the assumptions of the Canadian criminal justice system.

The practice in one Inuit village was to call the entire village together, and to put the actual event forward as a *hypothetical* event which might happen some time in the future. All people, including the miscreant and his victim, were required to put forward their views as to how things might be handled peacefully and properly were the situation ever to arise. There was no blaming, no pointing of fingers, no requirement of explanation, nor was there ever any discussion, much less imposition, of either punitive or restitutionary response. At an Ojibway Reserve in my district similar dynamics governed. While the miscreant and his victim were summoned before an Elders Panel, there was never any discussion of what had happened and why, of how each party felt about the other or of what might be done by way of compensation. Nor was there any imposition of punishment. Each party was instead provided with a counselling Elder who worked privately to "cleanse his spirit." When both counselling Elders so signified by touching the peace pipe, it would be lit and passed to all. It was a signal that both had been "restored to themselves and to the community." If they privately arranged recompense of some sort, that was their affair. As far as the community was concerned, the matter was over. While I have not learned what the private counselling did consist of, I have been told that it did not involve retrieval and re-examination of the past in either its factual or emotional facets. It concentrated upon the future, and its spiritual component was central.

As a footnote, such ethics also cast the behavior of native victims in a very different light. Refusal or reluctance to testify or, when testifying, to give anything but the barest and most emotionless recital of events, may of course have been prompted by fear of the accused, by fear of the court, by love for and forgiveness of the accused or by any other such "sensible" reason (including the possibility, of extreme rarity in my experience, that they are uncomfortable because they are lying). Another reason, culturally foreign to us, could be that giving testimony face to face with the accused is simply considered wrong. It was not part of the traditional processes described above, where in fact every effort seems to have been made to *avoid* such direct confrontation. I recall one Indian woman who repeated her entire story of abuse to me in vivid detail before going into court and then asked me to do whatever I could to have the court send her very dangerous assailant to jail for as long as possible. Ten minutes later she took the witness stand and absolutely refused to say anything of an accusatory nature. When such witnesses regularly ask why they have to repeat their stories in court when they have already to "us" (meaning the police and the Crown), I have come to suspect that it is more than fear or embarrassment at work. I suspect instead that it is perceived as ethically wrong to say hostile, critical, implicitly angry things about someone *in their presence*, precisely what our adversarial trial rules have required.… In fact, we have taken this legal challenge into our daily lives, exhorting each person to open up with the other, to be honest and up front, to get things off our chests, etc., all of which are, to traditional native eyes, offensive in the extreme. When they refuse to follow the exhortations of our rules, we judge them as deficient in rule-obedience or, worse still, rule-less. In our ignorance we have failed to admit the possibility that there might be rules other than ours to which they regularly display allegiance, an allegiance all the more striking because it is exercised in defiance of our insistent pressures to the contrary.

Source: Rupert Ross. "Leaving Our White Eyes Behind: The Sentencing of Native Accused." [1989] 3 *Canadian Native Law Reporter* 1 at 5–6.

On the whole, small-scale society had considerable success in avoiding the outbreak of serious trouble. Each member of the community was able to exercise some measure of control over others and so power remained diffuse. As a community, members were able to deal with discord in such a way that victim and offender could once again enter into harmonious interaction after a mutually agreeable settlement of a dispute had been made. While anger, a desire for revenge, and the penchant to blame other people may be universal human tendencies, small-scale societies were effective in muting these dispositions because of the high degree of interdependence they exhibited. Social relations were regulated by custom rather than by law and were based on values shared by all members of the society.

THE TRANSFORMATION FROM SMALL-SCALE SOCIETY TO THE STATE

Within the last 6000 to 8000 years, most hunting and gathering societies have been transformed into pastoral, horticultural, agricultural, and industrial societies, either as a result of their own development or the invasion of an outside culture. The transformation from some small-scale societies to state societies will be outlined in this section, along with the way in which this transformation affects the dispute-settlement process.

THE SLOW EMERGENCE OF SOCIAL POWER

Hunting and gathering communities were long able to resist any aspirations to autonomy and power by their members. While positions of influence did exist for those who made special contributions to the group, this status was not consolidated by greater access to material resources. Influential members still had to be responsive to the opinions, expectations, and judgements of the rest of their community in order to retain their special status.

At some point, the mutuality of tribalism was ruptured. The emergence of the concept of property slowly and progressively created social power for families and individuals. Privately owned land and livestock meant that the more fortunate members of the community were in a position to generate a surplus (Newman, 1983). This surplus increasingly gave them and their progeny the ability to rely less on the community for their survival. Under such circumstances, some communities began to define women as property, not only to secure control of their labour, but also their reproductive capacities.

New modes of production and technological innovations not only increased the ability to create a greater surplus, they also steadily moved humans out of direct contact with nature into an increasingly artifactual environment. The sense of smallness and vulnerability to nature which kept hunters and gatherers humble and mindful of their ancestors was replaced with a sense of mastery of nature and an attentiveness to the new sources of power to be found in the community. Chiefs, deified rulers, kings, parliaments, and ultimately, financial magnates reflect the reorientation of humans toward social power sources. Slowly, human behaviour would be refashioned under the control of this new form of social order. Some people would have greater access to material power and would use that advantage to increase their ability to control the circumstances of their lives. This momentous change would not bode well for less powerful groups or the natural environment.

THE EVOLUTION OF INEQUALITY

The power constellation of small-scale society was that of the community as a whole which moved against the interests of individuals or factions when their undertakings were viewed as a serious threat to the good of the group. New forms of power inaugurated important changes. The emergence of surplus, stratification, and the basis for factional power gave rise to the development of the state in rudimentary form. The role of mediators, elders' councils, restricted councils, and then chieftainships shows the slow, yet progressive, development and consolidation of a social form of power independent of the community as a whole.

In small-scale society, each individual was expected to discharge his or her obligations directly to other community members. Slowly, the social elites were able to redirect this exchange to consolidate and to enhance their position in the changing social order. The goods that had been readily available to all members in a simple economy of sharing became distributed in patterns that reflected the stratified nature of pastoral, horticultural, agricultural, and industrial orders. These new modes of production made it increasingly possible for powerful groups and individuals to extract surplus value from those who turned to them in order to make a living. The ability to have other people help generate their personal wealth greatly accelerated the formation of stratified inequality. Less powerful segments in society found it increasingly difficult to resist those social forces which were compromising their interests.

Ultimately, the state would emerge in agricultural society and it would champion and represent the interests of the powerful. The growing size, technological sophistication, and complexity of social systems gave rise to the need for large bureaucracies and a class of officials whose personal interests would become fused with those of the state. Human history was firmly established on a course that would generate hitherto unseen levels of surplus, poverty, and social inequality. The interests of whole groups of individuals were devalued and subordinated to the interests of powerful factions and the state. The equality of condition in small-scale society had been replaced by a class system rife with disparities.

The dispute-settlement practices that emerged with these different social forms and the types of offences committed in such societies reflected the basic changes in social structure that have been outlined in this section. Attention will now be focused on the dispute process and the changes that took place that created law as it exists today.

TRANSFORMATION IN THE FORMS OF DISPUTE SETTLEMENT

As societies changed their form, social relationships became complex and the types of disputes that arose in these societies changed. For example, with the emergence of private property, theft became possible. The concepts of rent and the violation of contracts became grounds for disagreement. When individuals began writing wills, problems emerged concerning appropriate or disputed inheritance. The emergence of contracts and wills contributed to the need for more codified conventions and a body of civil law. Finally, the emergence of surplus meant that disputes could be settled by the payment of various types of fines to compensate the party who had been wronged. For example, under Anglo-Saxon law, if a woman was raped, a compensatory fee was paid to either her husband or father, depending on who exercised the rights of ownership over her at the time of the offence. The fee was not paid directly to the woman herself, as she was not considered to be the person who had been wronged by the act (Clark and Lewis, 1977).

Increased productive capacity resulted in disputes concerning property, accompanied by increasingly complex legal codifications to deal with them. The creation of chiefdoms, and eventually states, was accompanied by the emergence of offences such as treason, slander, and libel, and in general, the possibility for criminal law as defined as offences against the Crown. Failure to pay taxes or work on public projects all became offences and a source of litigation. In this section, some of the basic features of mediator systems, elders' councils, chieftainships, and paramount chieftainships will be examined. These are the dominant structural elements in dispute settlement that distinguish societies that lie between small-scale societies and state systems.

Mediator Systems

Under the advisor system, as described earlier, disputants were not required to seek out a third party to settle a dispute. Under the mediator system, there was strong social pressure to seek out such third parties, and it was not considered socially acceptable to seek self-redress unless mediation had failed. Mediators generally had more authority than advisors. However, they were unable to impose binding verdicts and could only suggest compromises. Social pressure to reach a compromise was strong. When disputes were resolved successfully, the mediator gained financially by receiving a larger fee and the promise of more business. Mediators were chosen from wealthy families and had a longer tenure than advisors. Members of wealthy families were selected as mediators because of their authoritative position and the greater strength and prestige of their family. While the family of the mediator would not directly enter the dispute to enforce the mediator's recommendations, a disputant could ill afford to damage his or her relationship with such powerful community members.

Elders' Councils

Elders' councils performed legal, political, economic, and administrative functions. They were a significant development and a correlate of centralization in social life. Disputants were required to submit their dispute to these councils, whose verdicts were binding. There were often several levels of councils, including local and regional councils with different powers; for example, one level would hear appeals. The membership in these councils was representative of the influential segments of the society. The members of the council may have included all married males, or the oldest male in each family. In all instances, each family was represented and hence membership was basically democratic. Participation was not contingent upon wealth, although there was a clear sex bias. Eventually, most men in the community would have occasion to sit on the elders' councils.

Council procedures were marked by a high degree of formality. This is uncharacteristic of the forms of dispute settlement discussed so far. Formal language, recourse to precedents, and rules of conduct all marked the seriousness of the occasion. The conclusions of these councils carried considerable weight because they were made by a representative group of elders who were charged with the duty of determining a dispute in the best interests of the community. Community pressure dictated the obligation to accept the judgement of the council. If an individual was recalcitrant, the council could enlist local men to threaten the offender and deprive him or her of property, or direct the kinsmen of the victim to retaliate. This was the only type of self-redress that was available in these systems.

Chieftainships

A chief was the highest political authority in the community and was recognized as having the ultimate power in settling disputes. The chief's decisions were binding, although others may have been required to enforce them. Chieftainships tended to be based on heredity, or supernatural knowledge. Chiefs were primarily rich men from influential families. They also were expected to display oratorical skills, wisdom, and knowledge of customary ways. Chiefs usually served on a permanent basis and held office through their productive years, either voluntarily relinquishing it when they judged themselves incapable of continuing or being overthrown by rebellions when they fell from popularity. Chiefs often had the right to select their successor, although this was contingent upon community approval.

Chieftainships made possible a formalization and institutionalization of the legal system. The chief was able to intervene in a dispute without being requested to do so and heard appeals if more informal attempts to settle a dispute failed. Chiefs had the power to order executions, beatings, public reprimands, and economic sanctions such as fines and destruction or confiscation of property. No form of self-redress was allowed unless the approval of the chief had been secured. Considerable power was placed in the hands of the chief, although he often consulted community members prior to making a decision.

Paramount Chieftainships

Paramount chieftainship was a form of social order that took a significant step away from the participatory and democratic features of other models. Paramount chieftainships were much like royal kingdoms. They were based on hereditary aristocracies and drew together a large number of communities or villages that retained some level of local autonomy. Paramount chieftainships were complex, hierarchical structures. The chief was surrounded with retainers and nobles who performed judicial and administrative tasks. Many such chieftainships had a "civil service" recruited from the ranks of royalty to handle daily affairs. This apparatus allowed a more formal and structured legal system to develop. In this way the paramount chief was able to extend control over a large geographical region and a sizeable population.

The paramount chief held court in a capital city—and the paramount chief's court also served as the highest court of justice. District or circuit courts were used as a first resort to settle disputes, but more serious cases came under the jurisdiction of the paramount chief who had the final authority to make binding decisions. In many societies, the chief had an advisory council made up of royalty. However, the final decision in settling cases rested with the chief, who had a full range of options available.

The transformations of the hunting and gathering social form and the attendant dispute-settling processes are dramatic when considered in this comparative framework. But the changes occurred so gradually that the historical actors barely noticed them. Once the checks on the accumulation of wealth and power that bound small-scale society together were undercut, there seemed to be an inevitable chain of events that led to the emergence of a state system. Some of the reasons for this steady and cumulative development have been discussed in general terms. In the next section of this chapter, the modern state system will be examined in greater detail. Implicit in this analysis will be a comparison of modern social and legal structures with those of small-scale society.

MODERN STATE SYSTEMS

The full emergence of the state in the past 3000 or 4000 years has created a rich and complex social tapestry. We will sketch the essential changes in social-power constellations that transformed land-based feudalism into the modern capitalist state. The historical case of England provides the basis for the analysis of the emergence of law in Western democratic states. This focus is clearly appropriate when seeking to understand the legal system in North America. The analysis of law in state systems in other historical circumstances is beyond the scope of this chapter.

FROM TRIBALISM TO FEUDALISM

The primary basis for social order prior to feudalism was tribal kinship. In this social order, military leaders had already begun to emerge in a class system where conquered individuals became followers who were tied to their leaders with reciprocal obligations (Jeffrey, 1969; Kennedy, 1976). A patchwork of local fiefdoms under the control of local lords began to develop. The invasions of England, especially the Norman Invasion, accelerated the full development of a feudal order. In essence, feudalism was a social system based on the tenure of land, which was the dominant form of capital in an agrarian mode of production. The use of land was granted to the vassal in return for military service or, in later years, for rent. The lord had obligations to protect and provide food for the vassal in hard times. This relationship, while based on subjection, had a quasi-familial tone. Land was not a commodity that was for sale. The right to use the land was controlled by the lord. A vassal could only lose the right to land use for neglect of the land or failure to meet obligations.

No central power existed in the early period of feudalism. Social order was maintained through the kinship system as well as the developing land tenure system, in which each individual was eventually required to have a lord. In tribal times, blood feuds were the primary dispute-settlement mechanism. In medieval England, the secure emergence of local fiefdoms resulted in intervention by the local lord who had the authority to administer a variety of different sanctions. As feudalism developed, and the notion of collective responsibility was replaced with that of individual responsibility, money settlements and fines were used to settle serious disputes, with the exception of those committed by outlaws who were slain without fear of reprisal. By the year 871, feuds could be resorted to only if other forms of compensation had been requested and denied. Compliance with such standards was through local custom, since no centralized source of power had emerged to enforce them. Local lords were not willing or able to become involved in all disputes. For example, only the rape of wealthy, propertied virgins would typically secure the involvement of the powerful lords who protected them (Brownmiller, 1975).

Once these Anglo-Saxon lords were able to consolidate some power in England they began to develop a body of law to deal with disputes. Under this system, trial by ordeal was the means to establish guilt or innocence for those disputants who could not find some other way to settle a dispute. The pattern is clear; kin-based dispute settlement practices were being continuously undermined and replaced by feudal lords and their laws.

THE EMERGENCE OF THE CENTRALIZED STATE

With the success of the Norman Invasion, King William declared himself the "supreme landlord" of all England, so that all individuals who held land held his land. Over the succeeding centuries, the English kings slowly expanded and consolidated their power over the feudal landscape. Harms committed in disputes between individuals increasingly were seen to harm the *mund* or the king's region. As a result, compensation was paid to kings, lords, and bishops, rather than to kinship groups. Originally, the King's Peace referred to his ability to protect his own person, but, as Jeffrey argues, the development of the central state meant that " ... gradually it was extended to include the king's court, army, servants, hundred-court, and finally the four main highways of England." The Norman kings saw themselves as the injured party when a crime was committed since the harm was against their peace. Since some crimes were now against the Crown, criminal law became a reality. The Crown replaced the victim as the injured party and compensation to the victim's family was replaced by punitive fines which were payable to the Crown.

This trend continued, as the king could enforce his increased claims to sovereignty with force. A central authority had emerged in England to replace the authority of feudal lords. Henry II introduced a system of royal courts and a system of royal writs. Thus, common law came into existence as the law of the Crown available to all individuals. As Jeffrey (1969) has stated, "the family was no longer involved in law and justice. The State was the offended unit, and the State was the proper prosecutor in every case of crime." The pivotal role that law and the courts played in this undertaking to consolidate centralized political and economic power is of primary significance. But before this matter is considered, an additional major factor must be introduced.

THE RISE OF THE MERCHANT CLASS

Merchants were originally a despised and marginal group of traders. In times of feudal obligations and chivalry, their usurious behaviour was subjected to ridicule. In a society ordered by feudal taxes and customary reciprocal obligations, there was only a marginal place for them. Most goods were transferred according to feudal obligations and, as a consequence, there was very little trade or barter. Trade consisted primarily of luxury goods (silks, spices, and jewellery) and, because of this, there was little need for laws to regulate commerce.

Feudal lords and the church were opposed to trade, as it weakened social stability. As they were the primary beneficiaries of feudal arrangements, feudal lords and the church were not interested in establishing a social group which would operate outside of the feudal structure. Artisans and merchants banded together in towns along trade routes and often came into conflict with feudal lords and monarchs. These town and city dwellers co-swore oaths of mutual aid in their revolt against feudalism. The more powerful oath-bound groups demanded of their lord that the trading and manufacturing functions be separated from the body of feudal life and placed outside feudal relationships. Tigar and Levy (1977) outline some of the demands of these communes.

> Typically the commune—a collection of several dozen to several hundred artisans, lords' officials, minor clerics, peasants, runaway serfs, and others—demanded rights within the territory of the city, including the right to hold a regular market, free of tolls, and a periodic fair to which merchants from afar might come unhindered. They demanded the right to regulate the work of artisans within the city walls. And they generally wished it understood that serfs who made it to the city gates were free upon entry, or after a period of residence. More than anything else, this

last condition reflected a general dissolution of feudal obligations working in favor of all within the city.

Up to this time, the right of individuals to make their own rules had only been granted to monasteries. The resistance to these demands by the feudal structure is understandable.

The church increasingly supported the towns and communal cities against feudal lords, who eventually became supportive of cities in return for regular tax revenues. Cities began to arise in the reign of King John (1199–1216) and, although they were situated on land controlled by feudal lords, they fell under the jurisdiction of the Crown. A new basis for social relationships had emerged. With the recognition of an individual's right to exist as he or she wished came a different type of connection, one based on commerce instead of feudal obligations. This new form would eventually destroy feudal relationships.

THE COALITION OF MERCHANTS AND MONARCHS

William the Conqueror had established a state apparatus when he made all nobles take an oath to establish him as their feudal overlord. With this came the power to create laws to govern the kingdom, royal officials to protect the king's interests, and royal courts to dispense the king's justice. This state apparatus was superimposed on feudalism. While feudalism was dominant, the king used the state apparatus to defend the common interests of feudal lords. However, the breakdown of feudal obligations and the feudal tax system also meant a loss of revenue for the Crown, which needed to find new ways to finance war and the state. This was accomplished by going outside the feudal system to negotiate loans with merchants, using land as collateral. The king wanted his power consolidated and needed political support and financial assistance, while the merchants wanted a unified and safe trading area (Chambliss, 1969; Hall, 1969a). The state was to become the vehicle which would be used by the Crown and its merchant allies to defeat the resistance that impeded the development of the new social order. In return for their support, Henry VIII conceded that Parliament would have control over tax revenues and the legislative function. Thus, the state, which was staffed with the bourgeois class, would become the mechanism for change by statute. Laws would be passed by Parliament.

The merchants would benefit from this new arrangement because they were able to gain greater access to land. The feudal lords' losses in war brought the merchants the land that the lords had put up as collateral for loans. When Henry VIII expropriated church land, over one-sixth of the land in England was removed from its connection to feudalism. Henry sold this land to friends and allies for whom he created peerages with seats in the House of Lords. This action more than doubled his revenue, placed a large block of land outside of feudal control, and made this land available for the money market. As the feudal system declined, many lords were tied into feudal land arrangements of rent, which were driving them into financial ruin. Eventually, their lands also were freed of feudal ties and became part of the commodity market to be bought and sold as private property in the interest of profit. Henry VIII also gave his support to the Statute of Wills, which made most land in England transmittable by will. The role of the Crown had changed from that of shared owner of land under feudalism to that of land regulator via the state, which was becoming a separate and sovereign entity.

The labour of vassals, which had been tied to the land under feudalism, was freed from the land, as were the lords. In addition, much of the land which had been controlled by the church was also made available as commons for serfs to graze their animals. However, the new owners enclosed a great deal of this land for wool production and thoroughly disrupted the lives of the commoners. The right of commoners to hunt, fish, and gather wood on their lord's manor were extinguished under the new property relations. The Black Act of 1723 increased the number of offences for which the courts could impose the death penalty. These harsh measures were seen as necessary to encourage the common people to abandon these feudal practices (Thompson, 1976). The new land regulations displaced the rural workforce, which then became the new workforce of the factories which were made possible by technological innovation.

These fundamental changes contributed to the increased importance of commerce and money. The close and personal ties of fealty and its reciprocal duties and obligations were being eclipsed by the abstract and anonymous transactions of money in commercial enterprise. The growth of banking institutions, the use of paper currency, and other instruments of credit created new occasions for theft on the part of trusted third parties. The famous Carrier's Case of 1473 made it clear that the law of theft would need to be refined in order to prevent intermediaries from keeping goods put in their possession for transport (Hall, 1952). International trade, which was spurred by Britain's colonial empire, also necessitated an expansion and refinement of the concept of theft. Hall (1969b) recounts how the law governing embezzlement was enacted to make theft of paper money and commercial bonds a crime. Transactions between anonymous parties would henceforth be regulated by law, because of the absence of customary ties between them.

The role of law and the place of lawyers would figure prominently in the regulation of the new social relationships. In order to chart the consolidation of state power within the context of law, it is essential to study the activities of various interest groups with respect to commerce and contract law. The consolidation of a new form of social life based on contract was achieved within the context of commerce and the rise of the bourgeois class.

COMMERCE, CONTRACTS, AND THE PRIMARY ROLE OF LAW

The growth of commerce, spurred by the industrial revolution and the expansion of trade, required greater uniformity and enforceability of trading arrangements. Towns, cities, and even nation states realized that a system of law, and a court system to apply it, would be essential if trade was to stabilize and grow. The volume of trade, its growing impersonality, the practice of joint ventures, and the long distances involved in trade created the need for a mechanism to secure the interests of traders. Legal contracts, which had existed since Roman times, became the dominant mechanism which would tie social relationships together in the new social order. Tönnies (1887) argued that the *Gesellschaft* (i.e., the modern society) came to exist as a superior power to enforce the terms set out in the contracts of the merchants and capitalists. Lawyers grew in number and importance as new contract forms were developed to meet the increasingly complex trade arrangements of the time. Contracts, which had been private agreements, now became widely used to bind together individuals in the new social order. This new reliance on contract required changes in the court structure. In the feudal era, common law had developed to settle disputes. This law was applied in seigneurial and church courts, and in the king's court.

The king sought to consolidate power, and found that great inroads could be made into common law by throwing his support behind merchant law in support of the merchant class. In return for taxes and loans, the Crown placed the power of the state behind the laws of commerce and enforced these laws. The merchant class supported the legislative and judicial power of the Crown in exchange for the development of legal mechanisms which would further strengthen their class position, increase their fortunes, and consolidate their power. The law and lawyers had been guaranteed a primary role in the new industrial, capitalist mode of production. The bourgeois had helped to strengthen the power of the monarch, in order to be protected by his state apparatus. The king's support of merchant law as the law of the land helped to stabilize the necessary social and legal conditions for commerce.

The power of the nation state was solidified around the interests of commerce. The role of custom and kinship was eroded. The basis for the new social order was predicated on law, in the realm of both commercial and criminal activity. While the primary interest of this chapter is criminal law, it is important to track the rise of the institution of law in the modern state—and this was primarily within the context of merchant interests.

The merchant class had supported the aspirations of the Crown because they needed a stable and modified system in order to conduct their affairs. However, once the land had been redistributed, and feudal village life had been disrupted, the bourgeois became interested in forming a new alliance so as to curb the Crown's ability to restrict trade. Tigar and Levy (1977) document the new alliance with common law lawyers.

THE CONSOLIDATION OF BOURGEOIS ASCENDANCE

Contracts under merchant law were enforced in merchant courts, as well as in chancery and admiralty courts. Common lawyers realized that the portion of law that they administered was shrinking with the decline of the landed nobility. Some of them were eager to have merchant law enforced in their courts. The bourgeois were supportive of such a development, as it would make them less dependent on the king and his special courts. Common law lawyers made a concerted effort to make their courts more receptive to bourgeois legal principles. By 1600, an alliance between the common lawyer and the bourgeois was finding success in introducing the bourgeois theory of contract into common law courts. A conflict between the Crown and the merchant class ensued, as the Crown wanted to control merchant activity through the monarch's court and the bourgeois wanted to evade the Crown's attempts at controlling trade by having matters handled through the common law courts.

The merchant class gained a strong hold on the Parliament as the landed aristocracy's power waned. Parliament used its control over tax revenues in its efforts to limit the king's control of trade. This conflict was resolved in the English Civil War of 1642–48 by a reduction in the power of the monarchy and the establishment of the bourgeois-controlled Parliament as the sole source of political control.

Peasants and workers were not represented in this early Parliament. The modern state developed under the influence of the bourgeois. The rise of the labour movement would come later, but as Miliband (1969) has convincingly displayed in his book *The State in Capitalist Society*, the power of organized labour has never managed to match that of organized business. Whatever advances have been made in democratizing the state apparatus, it remains a political and legal structure to protect the interests of property. In the arena of modern political life, various interest groups bring pressure on the state to protect their interests under the rule of law.

STATE, LAW, AND INTEREST GROUPS

As the structures of feudalism declined, the state became the dominant institution which regulated social order and settled disputes. The state extended its authority over specific geopolitical boundaries and sought to order human activity via the rule of law. State decisions were backed up by military and police organizations. The state stood as the superior force behind the contractual arrangements of business and property in order to ensure that the terms of these agreements were observed. The interests of business are central to the modern state, as business activity and industrial manufacturing contribute the largest proportion of Gross National Product. The viability of modern, industrial nations has become intimately tied to the success of capitalist undertakings because these enterprises dominate the national economy. Structural Marxists assert that the modern state's principal purpose is to ensure that capitalist accumulation is protected because the future of the state is so closely tied to corporate capitalism.

In this context, the law has become the dominant means to regulate human affairs. Legislation and administrative directives are the legal apparatus which create the bases of modern nation states. Property, commerce, real estate, labour, and contractual agreements are all regulated by law. Municipalities and corporations are governed by law. The protection of the environment is regulated by law. Disputes over person and property are handled through family, civil, and criminal law. In short, the law is the principal means whereby human activity is prohibited, permitted, or required. The state and the law are intimately meshed in the creation of the modern social order.

As shown in earlier sections, the merchant class was quite successful in promoting and protecting its interests as it helped shape the nature of the state and the law. But business interest groups are not the only types of groups that approach the state to promote their interests. A variety of cultural, ethnic, minority, class, economic, and political interest groups lobby the state in order to promote their own interests. The modern state has become a vehicle sought after by a plethora of groups, each seeking certain guarantees and protections. The heterogeneous nature of modern societies and the antagonistic relationships between various groups ensures that the state cannot promote the interests of all groups. Choices need to be made. Given the nature of electoral politics, the state is under some pressure to promote the values and interests of the majority and of powerful minorities in order to maintain legitimacy and popularity. In the remainder of this chapter, several examples will be reviewed to provide some insight into the range of interest groups seeking to influence the content and role of law in modern society. Given the sheer volume of law, and the complexity of modern society, this review is meant only to be illustrative of the role of law in modern society.

REGULATION BY LAW

Some authors argue that the law reflects the values of the majority of the population. Other authors analyze various laws to show that powerful minority interests have shaped the content of the law. There is no reason to conclude that only one of these positions is correct. It is clear that some legal enactments reflect the values of the majority and are an instance of "double institutionalization," as argued by Bohannan (1968). It is also clear that Diamond (1971) was correct when he criticized Bohannan, since other laws clearly do not reflect the values of the majority, but reflect the values of powerful minorities. The significant impact of powerful interests on the content of law is a topic which is subject to much debate. In this section, examples that support both points of view will be discussed.

Consensus and the Law

Under some circumstances, there is broadly based consensus about limiting certain forms of behaviour. There is general consensus regarding laws that seek to protect individuals from common assault in public places, breaking and entering, or theft of property from their residence. There is also considerable agreement about what constitutes serious crime. Rossi and Waite

(1974) replicated the earlier work of Sellin and Wolfgang (1964) on the ranking of seriousness of crimes and came to the following conclusion: "The norms defining how serious various criminal acts are considered to be, are quite widely distributed among blacks and whites, males and females, high and low socio-economic levels, and among levels of educational attainment." (237). This basic consensus about what constitutes crime against person and property should not be understated.

Interest Groups and the Law

Most of the research on law, however, shows the operation of interest groups. Hagan and Leon (1977) and Platt (1969) show the operation of various "moral entrepreneurs" who were part of a child saving movement, and show the responsiveness of the state in creating legislation and a separate juvenile court. West and Snider (1985) have also documented the operation of interest groups here, but expand the argument by suggesting that their motives were not only to save children but also to deal with an excess labour supply.

Research on drug legislation also shows the state responding to various forms of pressure. Becker (1963) attempts to demonstrate that drug legislation in the United States was the result of the efforts of a civil servant, Harry Anslinger, who was primarily a moral entrepreneur. Dickson (1968) further argues that this bureaucrat was able to use his access to government services not only to foster particular moral objectives, but possibly also to save his organization and help it expand. The research of Shirley Small (1978) into Canadian narcotics legislation suggests that strong racist sentiments against Orientals were a motivating force in the push for drug laws. Comack (1985) suggests that these anti-Oriental sentiments were grounded in labour disputes which, instead of being handled in class terms, were being handled in racial terms.

Graham's (1976) analysis of amphetamine legislation clearly demonstrates the operation of special interests. In spite of strong support from the American public and the president, attempts to change the Federal Drug Administration's control of amphetamine production failed because of pressure from the powerful drug companies. A legislative remedy would have gone a long way in promoting the common good with regard to this significant problem, but the power of a sizeable lobby stifled the attempted changes. This fact was hidden from public view.

The analysis of the history of rape legislation (Brownmiller, 1975; Clark and Lewis, 1977; Kinnon, 1981) shows that such laws were enacted to protect the transmission of property in the male line of descent. Fathers used rape laws to avoid transferring property to men of whom they disapproved but who had taken their daughters by bride capture. They also sought compensation for the reduction of bride price that they suffered because their daughters had lost virginal status. Husbands wanted to secure control over their wives' reproductive capacity to ensure that they transferred their property to their own sons. Women and children became the property of the man of the household, and the act of rape became an offence against the husband. Over time, and as the result of concerted feminist activity, the act of sexual assault has been reconceptualized as a crime against the woman who has been victimized and in some jurisdictions, including Canada, the husband can now be prosecuted for the rape of his wife. This, of course, means that women are having some success in having themselves redefined as persons and not merely as the property of their fathers or husbands.

Research conducted on anti-combines legislation in Canada also provides the kind of evidence which demonstrates the operation of class-based interest groups in the framing of the law. Smandych (1985) outlines the confrontation that was brewing in the 1880s between labour and capital. The Knights of Labour movement specifically focused on the monopolistic nature of industrial capitalism and demanded the elimination of combines. A Royal Commission was established and it submitted its report in the same year that the first anti-combines legislation was enacted. But as Goff and Reasons (1978) point out, the wording of the statute was weakened in comparison with proposals in preliminary drafts. So, the statute appeared to constrain capital interests when, in fact, it hardly did so. More changes to this statute in the 1970s further liberalized the circumstances under which mergers were permissible. Thus, not only was the state unwilling to champion the interests of organized labour in the legislation, but as Goff and Reasons, and Snider (1980) have shown, the Act has been applied only to small firms in Canada. In spite of the evidence of higher prices under conditions of oligopoly, and in spite of protest by organized labour, the Canadian government has been unwilling to regulate the larger corporations in order to make Canada competitive in the international market. The government appears to be afraid of the loss of investor confidence and the flight of capital.

The history of occupational health and safety legislation is also very instructive. Friedman and Ladinsky (1980) trace the changes in the law governing industrial accidents and relate that, initially, employers were held responsible for injuries to workers under tort law, even if such injury resulted from the negligence of another employee. But this doctrine of *respondeat superior* was slowly replaced by the fellow-servant rule, which did not allow an employee to sue the employer in case of injury unless harm was caused by the employer's personal misconduct. This move effectively prevented thousands of lawsuits in the United States, but the large number of accidents generated a continuing series of cases. Pressure was exerted by workers and their unions and, in some jurisdictions, legislation was introduced to exclude the application of the fellow-servant rule. Workers' compensation schemes were proposed, but employers showed little interest in them until judges began awarding damages to employees. The compensation legislation which was finally enacted was based on a compromise position. Employers and employees would both contribute to the cost of the program, which would guarantee the injured employee compensation based on statutory schedules. However, the employer would be protected from the bulk of civil liability litigation, because employee claims would be handled by an administrative agency instead of by the courts.

While this compensation program has been more or less acceptable to workers and owners, Walters (1983) shows how the Ontario government has undertaken changes in occupational health and safety legislation in an effort to reduce the cost of running its health care system. It has been estimated that $1.4 billion is added to the health care system's bill every year because of industrial accidents. Here is an interesting case of the state enacting legislation not to promote or protect the interests of any specific interest group, but rather to reduce its own deficit.

These examples demonstrate that the process of law creation is heavily influenced by various interest groups and the pressure that they bring to bear on the state. It seems quite clear that the state often does find itself in situations where it can make decisions based on the wishes and interests of the majority. At other times, it finds itself hard pressed to effectively regulate some of the special-interest groups.

THE FAILURE TO REGULATE: THE ECLIPSE OF THE STATE?

There is growing concern among some analysts that transnational corporations have amassed so much economic power that they are getting beyond the control of nation states. Ermann and Lundman (1982) show that, between the 1890s and the 1920s, changes in U.S. incorporation legislation made possible the unprecedented accumulation and concentration of economic power in the form of the corporation. The decisions which allowed corporations to persist beyond a finite life expectancy and to amass large amounts of capital have created large economic organizations which threaten to eclipse the power of the state. Veltmeyer (1987) has used World Bank data to show that 46 of the top 100 largest economies in the world are transnational corporations. These corporations are expanding at two to three times rates of growth of national economies. The scale of such organizations gives them considerable power to resist the efforts of nation states to regulate them. These corporations can, and do, bring considerable pressure to bear on national governments. If a government is too restrictive in its regulatory policies, a transnational corporation can relocate operations in another country with laws more to its liking. The ability to have a serious impact on employment levels, investment patterns, and the GNP gives the transnational corporation considerable clout. It is clear that corporations are responsible for behaviour which is harmful to various other interest groups. It is also clear that these harms are not being effectively controlled by the state and the rule of law. The following examples help make the point.

Victims of Avoidable Harms

Reasons et al. (1981) recount numerous instances where Canadian workers are needlessly exposed to risks in the workplace which result in injury and death. Many of these dangers are known to employers and are avoidable, leading Reasons et al. to suggest that these casualties are "victims without crimes" and that such injuries should be conceptualized as "assaults" on the worker. Stone (1975) recounts cases of corporate actions involving injury which would have resulted in criminal trials, and possibly death sentences, had they been committed by individuals. Dowie (1977) reports that the design problems of the Ford Pinto that resulted in passenger injury and death were known by the auto manufacturer, that these problems could have been addressed by cost-effective measures, and that the corporation chose not to make the improvements. Internal Ford memos reveal that the costs of design changes were compared to the costs of potential litigation for death, dismemberment, and injury, and that the company decided to put Pinto passengers at risk. It is hard to conceive of the death and injury created by the Pinto as accidental when such injury and death was anticipated and could have been avoided. It could be argued that these deaths were homicides and that such harmful behaviour ought to come under the control of the Criminal Code. Ford was, in fact, charged with homicide for one of the Pinto accidents, but was acquitted by an Indiana jury.

Branan (1980) makes a similar case against Ford for continuing to produce automobiles with automatic transmissions which were known to slide out of park into reverse, in some instances crippling or killing persons behind them. A Ford engineer came up with a design improvement that would have solved the problem at a cost of three cents per car, but Ford rejected the improvement so as not to admit it had a design defect for fear that it would be an invitation to lawsuits. Consequently, instead of making the necessary changes in 1972 when the problem was discovered, Ford continued to manufacture thousands of cars with faulty transmissions until 1980. It has been estimated that there have been more than 60 deaths, 1100 injuries, and over 3700 accidents as a result of this defect. An accident is, by definition, an "unforeseen or unintentional happening." This was not the case here, since Ford clearly foresaw, and could have avoided, these serious harms. The modern consumer-citizen is not being protected under the rule of law from dangerous corporate misbehaviour.

The courts could move in the direction of holding corporations and their managers accountable for harms such as the one that took place in Cook County, Illinois. On July 1, 1985, three former executives of a silver-recycling plant were convicted of murder and each received a sentence of 25 years in prison and a fine of $10 000 for the death of an employee. The company had exposed workers to cyanide gas by intentionally concealing warnings of hazards from immigrant workers. These murder convictions are believed to be the first in the United States of corporate officials in a job-related death.

But to date, governments have not pursued a vigorous policy of bringing such corporate harms under the appropriate sections of the Criminal Code. This case turned out to be a rarity and not a harbinger of greater corporate accountability.

Finally, Brodeur (1985) has provided a detailed analysis of problems associated with the asbestos industry in the United States and Canada. It has come to light that the industry had been aware of the health hazards related to the inhalation of asbestos particles since the 1930s but that it withheld this information from workers and did not take steps to improve the safety of the workplace. Asbestos firms have been flooded with lawsuits in which courts have been finding them responsible for the resultant illnesses and deaths and have awarded victims sizeable punitive damages. In 1982, the Johns-Manville Corporation, with assets of more than $2 billion, filed for bankruptcy in the United States in an effort to escape paying the damages assessed for its harmful business practices. The U.S. government is under considerable corporate pressure to grant this request. However, it is also faced with pressure to hold corporate citizens accountable to the same laws that ordinary citizens are bound to obey. It appears that the government is considering a compensation system which would award a fixed sum of money to affected workers, who would then lose their right to seek damages through the courts. It remains to be seen whether the most powerful nation state in the world is prepared to hold a major corporation responsible under the law for its reckless and harmful behaviour.

Transnational corporations exist to make profits for investors. The pursuit of profit has often been maximized by reckless and dangerous behaviour. The growing evidence of the serious harm to employees, customers, and the environment that has resulted suggests that a very powerful set of human actors are currently operating beyond the control of law. The ability of corporations to make decisions to relocate their firms to new geographic, economic, and legal locations to evade regulation continues to cause serious harm and disruption to employees and to local and national economies. The state has remained unwilling to step in and regulate the use of private economic resources when they disrupt or undermine the well-being of other citizens. It is questionable whether decisions that are good for business interest groups should be allowed to proceed unchecked by state intervention when it can be demonstrated that they cause serious harm to other interest groups. At present, many such harms cannot be brought to the courts for remedy because the state has not defined them as disputes or crimes. It may be asked whether the modern state has truly established the rule of law when serious sources of harm escape regulation and control. In some important ways the *de jure* power of the state has been superseded by the *de facto* power of the modern corporation. The law cannot function to restore order in areas of social life where the state does not establish its jurisdiction. The absence of protection from the raw economic power of corporations places individuals, and perhaps even humanity, in harm's way.

SUMMARY

In this chapter, the changing forms of social order have been traced from early, small-scale societies to the complex arrangements of the modern era. Small communities based on self-restraint and mutual dependence were transformed into large industrial states where social life is controlled by political and economic power. Societies that based their order on customary beliefs have been eclipsed by those that are organized according to differential access to surplus and the resultant stratification. As can be seen in the accompanying comparison of legal concepts, the very nature of societal response to transgressions reflects a fundamental difference in social organization.

COMPARISON OF LEGAL CONCEPTS

EURO-CANADIAN	TRADITIONAL NATIVE INDIAN/INUIT
• Laws formulated by elected representatives	• Laws formulated by the community through tradition and consensus
• Laws tied to man-made economy and therefore complex and numerous	• Laws tied to the natural environment; only a few universally condemned actions in Native Indian/Inuit customary law
• Protestant Ethic and Christianity the moral foundation of the law	• Traditional Native Indian/ Inuit religions the foundation of Native Indian/Inuit codes of behaviour
• Personal offences seen as transgressions against the state as represented by the monarch	• Personal offences seen as transgressions against the victim and his/her family; community involved only when the public peace is threatened
• Law administered by representatives of the state in the form of officially recognized or operated social institutions	• Law usually administered by the offended party—i.e., the family, clan, or tribe, through a process of mediation or negotiation

- Force and punishment used as methods of social control

- Individualistic basis for society, and the use of the law to protect private property

- Arbitration and ostracism usual peacekeeping methods

- Communal basis for society; no legal protection for private property; land held in trust by an individual and protected by the group

Source: Christie Jefferson (1983). "Conquest by Law: A Betrayal of Justice in Canada." Unpublished paper.

The nature of dispute settlement has undergone a dramatic transformation from the small-scale society, where every member had direct access to the process of redress, to the present era, where not everyone can afford the costs of seeking a remedy through the courts. Furthermore, some serious harms are not currently subsumed under the law and, without a crime, there are few alternatives available for victims to seek redress. The concentration of social power has seen the emergent state come to play a central role in the dispute-settlement process. Since Tudor times, the administration and control of the legal process has been the prerogative of the state. While the interests of all members formed the basis of customary practice in small-scale communities, the interests of the merchant class have been given a special place in law in Western industrial societies. The modern state has not extended protection to all interest groups under the law. The heterogeneous nature of contemporary society and inherent conflicts of interest of various groups make this impossible. Nevertheless, there is growing pressure on the state to regulate the business practices of transnational corporations when they cause serious harm to human beings and the natural environment. However, some argue convincingly that nation states lack the ability, or the will, to regulate such powerful organizations, which have come to dominate the social landscape in the past 50 years. It remains very much an open question whether the state and its legal system are up to the task of bringing these behemoths back under the rule of law.

BIBLIOGRAPHY

Becker, Howard. (1963). "Moral Entrepreneurs." In *The Outsiders.* New York: Free Press.

Bohannan, Paul. (1968). "Law." In *The International Encyclopedia of the Social Sciences.* New York: Macmillan Co.

Branan, Karen. (1980). "Running in Reverse." *Mother Jones* 5 (5) (June).

Brant, Clare C. (1990). "Native Ethics and Rules of Behaviour." *Canadian Journal of Psychiatry* 35 (August):534–39.

Brodeur, Paul. (1985). "The Asbestos Industry on Trial." In *The New Yorker* (June 10, June 17, June 24, July 1).

Brownmiller, Susan. (1975). *Against Our Will: Men, Women and Rape.* New York: Simon and Schuster.

Chambliss, William. (1969). "The Law of Vagrancy." In Chambliss (ed.), *Crime and the Legal Process.* New York: McGraw-Hill.

Clark, Lorenne, and Debra Lewis. (1977). *Rape: The Price of Coercive Sexuality.* Toronto: The Women's Press.

Colson, Elizabeth. (1974). *Tradition and Contract: The Problem of Order.* Chicago: Aldine Publishing.

Comack, Elizabeth. (1985). "The Origins of Canadian Drug Legislation: Labelling versus Class Analysis." In Thomas Fleming (ed.), *The New Criminologies in Canada: State, Crime and Control.* Toronto: Oxford University Press.

Diamond, Stanley. (1971). "The Rule of Law versus the Order of Custom." *Social Research* 38 (Spring):42–72.

Dickson, Donald. (1968). "Bureaucracy and Morality: An Organizational Perspective on a Moral Crusade." *Social Problems* 16 (2) (Fall).

Dowie, Mark. (1977). "Pinto Madness." *Mother Jones* 2 (8) (Sept./Oct.).

Ermann, M. David, and Richard Lundman. (1982). *Corporate Deviance.* New York: Holt, Rinehart and Winston.

Friedman, Lawrence and Jack Ladinsky. 1980. "Social Change and the Law of Industrial Accidents." In William Evan (ed.), *The Sociology of Law.* New York: Free Press.

Goff, Colin, and Charles Reasons. (1978). *Corporate Crime in Canada.* Scarborough: Prentice-Hall.

Graham, James. (1976). "Amphetamine Politics on Capital Hill." In William Chambliss (ed.), *Whose Law, What Order?* New York: Wiley.

Gulliver, P.H. (1979). *Disputes and Negotiations: A Cross-Cultural Perspective.* New York: Academic Press.

Hagan, John, and Jeffrey Leon. (1977). "Rediscovering Delinquency: Social History, Political Ideology and the Sociology of Law." *American Sociological Review* 42 (August).

Hall, Jerome. (1952). *Theft, Law, and Society.* (2nd ed.). Indianapolis: Bobbs-Merrill.

——— . (1969a). "Theft, Law and Society: The Carrier's Case." In William Chambliss (ed.), *Crime and the Legal Process.* New York: McGraw-Hill.

——— . (1969b). "Crime and the Commercial Revolution." In Donald Cressey and David Ward (eds.), Delinquency, Crime and Social Process. New York: Harper and Row.

Hoebel, E. Adamson. (1973). *The Law of Primitive Man.* New York: Atheneum Press.

Jeffery, Clarence Ray. (1969). "The Development of Crime in Early English Society." In William Chambliss (ed.), *Crime and The Legal Process.* New York: McGraw-Hill.

Kennedy, Mark. (1976). "Beyond Incrimination: Some Neglected Facets of the Theory of Punishment." In William Chambliss (ed.), *Whose Law, What Order?* New York: Wiley.

Kinnon, Dianne. (1981). *Report on Sexual Assault in Canada.* Report to the Canadian Advisory Council on the Status of Women.

Michalowski, Raymond. (1985). *Law, Order and Crime.* New York: Random House.

Miliband, Ralph. (1969). *The State in Capitalist Society.* London: Quartet Books.

Newman, Katherine. (1983). *Law and Economic Organization: A Comparative Study of Preindustrial Societies.* London: Cambridge University Press.

Platt, Anthony. (1969). *The Child Savers: The Invention of Delinquency.* Chicago: University of Chicago Press.

Reasons, Charles, Lois Ross, and Craig Paterson. (1981). *Assault on the Worker.* Toronto: Butterworths.

Rossi, Peter, and Emily Waite. (1974). "The Seriousness of Crimes: Normative Structure and Individual Differences." *American Sociological Review* 39 (April):224–37.

Sellin, Thorsten and Marvin Wolfgang. (1964). *The Measurement of Delinquency.* New York: Wiley.

Small, Shirley. (1978). "Canadian Narcotics Legislation, 1908–1923: A Conflict Model Interpretation." In W. Greenaway and S. Brickey (eds.), *Law and Social Control in Canada.* Scarborough: Prentice-Hall.

Smandych, Russell. (1985). "Marxism and the Creation of Law: Re-Examining the Origins of Canadian Anti-Combines Legislation 1890–1910." In Thomas Fleming (ed.), *The New Criminologies in Canada: State, Crime and Control.* Toronto: Oxford University Press.

Snider, Laureen. (1980). "Corporate Crime in Canada." In Robert Silverman and James Teevan (eds.), *Crime in Canadian Society.* (2nd ed.). Toronto: Butterworths.

Stone, Christopher. (1975). *Where the Law Ends: Social Control of Corporate Behavior.* New York: Harper and Row.

Sutherland, Edwin. (1950). "The Diffusion of Sexual Psychopath Laws." *American Journal of Sociology* (September).

Thompson, Edward P. (1976). *Whigs and Hunters: The Origin of the Black Act.* New York: Pantheon Books.

Tigar, Michael, and Madeleine Levy. (1977). *Law and the Rise of Capitalism.* New York: Monthly Review Press.

Tönnies, Ferdinand. (1887). *Community and Society.* New York: Harper Books.

Veltmeyer, H. (1987). *Canadian Corporate Power.* Toronto: Garamond Press.

Walters, Vivienne. (1983). "Occupational Health and Safety Legislation in Ontario: An Analysis of Its Origins and Content." *Canadian Review of Sociology and Anthropology* 20(4) (November).

West, Gordon and Laureen Snider. (1985). "A Critical Perspective on Law in the Canadian State: Delinquency and Corporate Crime." In Thomas Fleming (ed.), *The New Criminologies in Canada: State, Crime and Control.* Toronto: Oxford University Press.

FURTHER READING

Chambliss, William, and Robert Seidman. (1982). *Law, Order, and Power.* (2nd ed.). Reading, MA: Addison-Wesley. Using a critical conflict perspective, the authors compare state and stateless societies with respect to dispute settlement. Primary emphasis is placed on the state system, the rule of law, and the role of social power in modern class-based social systems.

Clinard, Marshall, and Peter Yeager. (1980). *Corporate Crime.* New York: Free Press. The authors trace the development of the modern corporation and analyze the relationship it has with the modern state. They discuss the issues of anti-trust legislation and corporate attempts at political corruption through bribes and foreign payoffs. The oil, auto, and pharmaceutical industries get special scrutiny. The issue of corporate social responsibility, the role of business ethics, and corporate criminal liability are all part of this work's skilful expansion of a critical area of study.

Friedman, Wolfgang. (1972). *Law in a Changing Society.* (2nd ed.) New York: Columbia University Press. This text traces legal change in a number of types of law, including contract, tort, insurance, criminal, family, and public law. The state, economic power, and corporate power are all examined for the part they have played in legal change. The changing place of the individual within modern law receives attention, as does the changing scope of international law.

Glendon, Mary Ann. (1981). *The New Family and the New Property.* Toronto: Butterworths. The author traces the basic changes in the nature of the family and its declining role in modern life. The cohesiveness of kinship is being replaced with legal bonding. The use of legal bonding is also traced in the realm of occupations where changes in law are transforming the obligations of employers to employees. Legal ties are being strengthened to replace the loss of social cohesiveness; the author discusses pitfalls and possibilities of this approach to social cohesion.

Nader, Laura, and Harry Todd (eds.). (1978). *The Disputing Process—Law in Ten Societies.* New York: Columbia University Press. After a lengthy introduction which discusses the disputing process in its many dimensions, this collection presents the accounts of dispute settlement in a wide variety of cultural settings. This reader is an excellent enticement to the rich anthropological literature on the human animal in its various cultural forms.

Synder, Francis. (1981). "Anthropology, Dispute Processes and Law: A Critical Introduction." *British Journal of Law and Society* 8 (2) (Winter). This review article examines current anthropological studies of law and dispute processes. It provides an excellent overview of major work and attempts to assess the value of these contributions for the development of social theories of law. It is an excellent article which will help a newcomer get his or her bearings.

CHAPTER 2

CRIME, LAW, AND LEGAL DEFENCES
By Graham Parker

INTRODUCTION

*T*he criminal law consists of three broad areas:

1. The General Principles of Criminal Liability

On what basis does society consider a person liable, responsible, blameworthy, or guilty? The criminal law is based on the Judeo-Christian ethic of free will and therefore persons will be found guilty only if they acted intentionally or recklessly. They may still be considered innocent if they have defences such as insanity, intoxication, self-defence, or mistake of fact.

2. The Definition of Offences

At first glance, it might be thought easy to define antisocial acts such as murder, sexual assault, robbery, or theft. However, the law has some difficulty defining with any exactitude the acts that come within these offence categories.

3. Rules of Evidence and Criminal Procedure

The task of the criminal law is not completed until the accused is declared by the fact-finder to be guilty. The trial is carried out according to the rules of evidence and criminal procedure. The bases for these rules are the presumption of innocence, the burden of proof being on the prosecution, and procedural fairness.

A crime can be defined as any form of human activity that the law defines as a crime. The criminal law is a closed system. It is not the only way to describe deviant behaviour but, in this chapter, crime will be described in legal terms. The legal elements of crime and the defences available to an accused will be discussed.

SOURCES OF CRIMINAL LAW

When Britain established colonies in Canada, English criminal law was applied. Since 1763, this has also been true in Quebec. At the time of Confederation, the federal Parliament was given power to make criminal laws. This decision ensured that the law governing crime would be uniform throughout the country. Canada's 1892 Criminal Code was the first codification of criminal law in what is now the Commonwealth. That Code closely followed a systematic body of law that had been drafted in England but never adopted there. So, the 1892 Code was not really a home-grown product, although it did recognize some crimes specific to Canada, such as those relating to lumber, railroads, and fencing frozen ponds.

The Canadian Criminal Code is not an all-inclusive body of law; judges are often required to consult and apply principles of the common law, a body of case precedents and custom accumulated since the 12th century.

The common law can now only be used to define defences. The courts cannot create new offences. The effect of the Charter of Rights on the definition of offences is already being felt where the appeal courts have decided that the very broad and sometimes vague description of crimes has unduly prejudiced the accused.

A DEFINITION OF CRIME

In some ways, law is a form of myth. Compared with the great religious writings, fairy tales, and Greek, Roman, Norse, and Inuit myths, the law may seem shallow and silly. It does, however, have one advantage over those other sources of human history. The law can be enforced. If people do not believe in the sanctity of private property or the value of human life, the state will soon persuade society of the importance of law and order by charging people with theft or murder. Sometimes, the law tries to control human behaviour where there are competing mythologies. Adultery was a crime in the 19th century. Adult consensual homosexual behaviour was a crime until a couple of decades ago. In the 19th century, the criminal law made criminals of workers who tried to strike for higher wages. In the 20th century, the law has prosecuted corporations that have shown monopolistic tendencies. Some citizens are in favour of freedom of expression, while others wish to curtail it using the law of obscenity. One drug, alcohol, is lawful despite the high social costs connected with it, while another drug, cannabis, is banned, and dealing in it can attract very serious punishment.

It must be remembered that the definition of crime is very simple. Crime is any form of human behaviour designated by the law as criminal and subject to a penal sanction.

THE RELATIVITY OF CRIME

The average Canadian, no doubt, believes that anyone knows what a crime is. Unfortunately, the law is not quite that clear. The most serious crime on the crime calendar is treason. Yet, what would be considered treasonous behaviour? Treason, along with the crimes of sedition and criminal libel, is not easily defined. While it is easy to define treason if an accused assassinates or tries to assassinate a head of state, it is a very different situation if an accused is merely a critic of a regime. Is it treason or sedition to suggest that the administration of a country is corrupt, inefficient, or merely wrongheaded? There is no obvious answer. George Washington and V.I. Lenin were successful traitors. On the other hand, Louis Riel, William Lyon Mackenzie, and Louis Papineau were not merely critics of society, but were considered criminals.

HOMICIDE—LAWFUL AND UNLAWFUL

Homicide is as ambiguous as treason. Some of the defences to murder will be examined later in this chapter. In the past, when most males went about armed with swords or knives and a sense of male dignity, the law of self-defence developed. The same rules of self-defence apply today. In the past, self-defence relied on swordplay (retreat to the wall and so forth, as recorded in all those Hollywood swashbuckling movies) and had little relevance to today's long-range and high-velocity firearms. Murder could also be reduced to manslaughter if the accused was provoked, and provocation usually consisted of physical violence. There was one exception where nonviolent provocation could provide a partial defence to murder—if a husband found his wife in the act of adultery. In many societies, at least until recent years, this partial defence was only available to males, thereby perpetuating the double standard. The moral relativity of murder can also be seen in superior orders as a defence. Most frequently, the courts have convicted the accused, treating the law of war as clear and the accused as a moral leper who has distorted that law.

SEXUAL CRIME AND SEXUAL MANNERS

The average citizen, particularly if female, would consider that there should be no difficulty in defining sexual assault and other forms of illegal sexual activity. The history of sexual offences provides a true reflection of male attitudes toward women. Only recently has the law decided that a husband can be convicted of raping or sexually assaulting his wife. Until the middle of the 19th century, the age of consent was twelve years. At that time, females, particularly unmarried poor girls, were looked upon as chattels. Sexual predators acted with impunity after a girl reached puberty. Today, the age of sexual consent is sixteen (or even higher in some instances). However, the word *consent* has caused difficulties. Rape no longer exists as a crime. It has been replaced by sexual assaults of three degrees of seriousness, depending upon the violence used. The violent sexual attack on a female does not cause definitional problems, but there are legally ambiguous situations where sexual manners are involved. For example, if Doug meets Veronica in a bar, touches her on a nonerogenous zone such as the elbow, and also makes a comment perceived by Veronica as a sexual affront, has Doug committed a sexual assault? Technically, he could have.

MORALITY AND CRIME

The law is at its most relative in those crimes where there are very diverse views of morality. Someone trafficking in marijuana may be given a sentence of fifteen years, but a person who uses his or her automobile recklessly, killing three people, may be given fifteen months. The law tries to make a clear statement about moral values. The prosecution kept charging Dr. Morgentaler with abortion offences, but juries continued to acquit him. In this case, opposing moral forces are at work in an ambiguous and controversial situation. Laws against homosexuality have been reformed in the last three decades so that private adult, consensual behaviour is no longer a crime. However, sexual acts between two eighteen-year-olds of the same gender continue to be a crime, while they would not be if one were male and the other female. Prostitution itself is not a crime, but there is an elaborate apparatus, largely unsuccessful, to control public manifestations of prostitution. The law tolerates relatively explicit sex in TV videos but school boards try to remove Margaret Laurence's novels from the senior high school curriculum. This dichotomy of law and morals is not susceptible to easy solutions for the very reason that, in a democracy, highly divergent views must be respected. Whatever might be the "correct" view about the state trying to control the moral behaviour of its citizens, a strong argument can be made that the criminal law is too crude and punitive an instrument to control acts that are, at best, only marginally harmful to anyone but the accused. In other words, they are looked upon as crimes without victims.

PROPERTY OFFENCES

"Thou shalt not steal" is one of the Ten Commandments, and theft, or larceny, is one of the oldest crimes. One would imagine that the law would be clear and simple in regard to this crime, and yet it is a complete morass. If a rogue takes an individual's goods when that individual is not looking and the goods are given up unwillingly, it is obvious that theft has been committed. The law ran into trouble when the rogue was the individual's clerk or servant and had been allowed to have possession of the goods, even though they were not given with the intent that the clerk or servant pawn them. The law had trouble dealing with this problem because the owner of the goods voluntarily gave the servant possession. The essence of theft is the invasion of possession. The servant had possession with permission, so the law developed a legal fiction that the owner of the goods only gave limited rights to the servant. The servant was guilty of larceny because he or she exceeded those rights. The same problem might arise when a clerk in a bank pockets money rather than putting it in the till. The law invented the crime of embezzlement to plug this particular hole.

FALSE PRETENCES

Donald goes into a store and persuades Victoria, the storeowner, that he is Dougald. Victoria accepts a cheque and Donald leaves with Victoria's goods. Donald is later found not guilty of larceny because Victoria had given Donald property in the goods and larceny is only an invasion of possession. Eventually, the law invented the crime of false pretences to cover this situation. If this sounds like an antiquarian problem, consider a recent case. Jane pulled into a gas station and had a litre of oil and ten litres of gasoline put in her car. She left without paying and was charged with larceny. She was acquitted because she had not merely obtained possession in the oil and the gas, but property in those goods had passed to Jane because the oil and gas could not be regained intact from the engine or the gas tank. This case makes little sense because the accused was obviously dishonest. There was no conviction because the law is very technical and makes a distinction between the legal concepts of possession and property. As stated earlier, a crime is any form of deviance so defined by the law.

The Law Reform Commission of Canada examined these anomalies and despaired of the chaotic state of the law. It deplored the technicalities of the law and suggested that "anyone who dishonestly deals with the goods of another shall be guilty of an offence." What does "dishonestly" mean? The Law Reform Commission maintained that everyone knows what is dishonest, although that statement seems open to question.

FRAUD

The Commission found it necessary to make special rules for the relatively modern crime of fraud, but these rules are not very instructive. How does one differentiate between the bumble-headed entrepreneur who makes stupid business decisions and the sharp rogue? In both instances, the customers lost money, but one person was mostly foolish and a little knavish, while in the other case the proportions were reversed. Is this a suitable subject for criminal law or should such a case be left to consumer protection laws and licensing agencies? Where does advertising hype end and dishonesty start? One could realize the difficulty of formulating laws against fraud if one asked the average citizen to draft laws defining criminal dishonesty (as opposed to excusable evasion) in relation to student loan applications, filing of income tax returns, or the sale of used cars.

PUBLIC WELFARE OFFENCES

There is a large number of people one may not want to call criminals, but whose behaviour makes everyday life annoying, dangerous, or unhygienic.

These might include used car dealers who turn back odometers, restaurateurs who have cockroach-infested kitchens, drivers who park on major arteries at rush hour, factory owners who have unsafe machinery, or dog owners who allow their pets to befoul the pavement. Should such persons be automatically guilty (or absolutely liable) without the prosecution having to prove criminal intent, or *mens rea?* The courts have decided that the legislatures may pass laws imposing absolute liability if the statutory language clearly describes liability without fault. However, if the language is ambiguous or if there are severe penalties, such as deprivation of liberty or loss of livelihood, then the offender should not be convicted unless it can be demonstrated that there was lack of due diligence on the part of the accused, i.e., that he or she did not take particular care to avoid infraction of the law.

CLASSIFICATION OF CRIMES

Crimes were originally divided by English law into the categories of felonies and misdemeanours. Felonies were more serious crimes and, until the 19th century, resulted in execution (or mutilation or banishment) and the confiscation of the felon's property by the Crown. Misdemeanours were less serious crimes and were punished by fine or imprisonment. All the classic crimes— such as murder, robbery, piracy, rape, and theft—were felonies. This classification has been abandoned. Today, the classification divides crime into indictable and summary offences. The two categories divide crimes on the basis of the seriousness of the criminal behaviour, the amount of punishment that may be inflicted for the crime, and the type of tribunal that can hear the case. The maximum penalty on a summary offence is six months' imprisonment or a $2000 fine, or both. Some of the more serious indictable offences are tried by the more senior courts, sometimes with a jury.

GENERAL PRINCIPLES OF CRIMINAL LIABILITY

While criminal procedure has lost its religious qualities, the substantive criminal law (the definitions of the offences) is very much based on the Judeo-Christian ethic. The law judges the accused on the ability to choose freely between right and wrong. If an individual willingly commits a crime, then the law says that individual deserves to be punished. Modern psychological and sociological views of crime have little relevance to the way in which the law defines crime and determines guilt (although those disciplines do make some contribution to the sentencing process).

COINCIDENCE OF *MENS REA* AND *ACTUS REUS*

The legal elements of a crime are *actus reus* (the physical element) and *mens rea* (the mental element). These elements must be coincident. The law does not usually punish anyone for merely having evil thoughts. Similarly, if a person performs a physical act without meaning or intending to do so, that act is not criminal. For example, David has always hated Victor and has been heard to make death threats against him. David would like to see Victor dead. While driving home one night, David's car collides with a taxi in which Victor, by sheer coincidence, is a passenger and Victor dies. David's *mens rea* about Victor's life is not sufficient to convict him because the *actus* was not *reus* (blameworthy) but was merely accidental.

VARIOUS TYPES OF *MENS REA*

We apply moral standards, and even quantitative blameworthiness, to our everyday dealings. If, on an isolated occasion, a child spills his or her milk at the dinner table, a parent may patiently wipe it up and console the child by saying that it was obviously an accident. If the child manages to spill the milk at every other meal, the parent may tell the child that he or she is being careless and may have to be punished so that the child will be more careful in the future. If the child spills milk at every meal, the parent may apply punishment on every occasion—even though the parent has long ago decided that punishment does not deter the child's milk spilling (and even though the child protests "I didn't mean to spill it"). The child does not intend to spill milk, and the thoughtful (and loving) parent may decide that the method of milk distribution must change. The punishment system obviously does not work, and the parent may have serious reservations about punishing a child whose behaviour is not intentional. A merely careless actor does not foresee the harm that will be caused and is, therefore, not deterred. When careless behaviour becomes habitual, is that behaviour still only careless?

The criminal law system is based on desert and blameworthiness. A person will only be convicted of a crime if he or she intended to commit the act or was reckless in committing it. The criminal law does not consider it appropriate to punish those who merely commit acts accidentally or negligently.

Imagine other cases where the milk spilling is not habitual. During a particular meal, there has been great acrimony between parent and child, and as an act of defiance, the child pours milk on the floor. The parent says, "You did that deliberately." The child has acted intentionally, and the parent has no hesitation in applying punishment.

On another occasion, the child is sitting at one end of the table and a brother is sitting at the other. The child decides to throw a dinner roll at the brother. In front of the brother is a glass of milk. The roll-thrower realizes that there is a risk that the glass might be hit instead of the sibling, but decides to take the risk. The milk is spilled and the parent who witnessed the event will not listen to protestations of innocence based on the fact that the milk-spiller did not really want to knock over the glass. The parent says, "You saw the danger and you still threw the roll; therefore, you were reckless."

Finally, imagine a situation where a child has been exceptionally mischievous during the meal. The parent is fully aware of the child's past reputation for spilling milk. Before leaving the room, the parent notices that the child has been gradually moving a glass of milk toward the edge of the table. The glass is now on the very edge. Soon after leaving the room, the parent hears a crash and returns to the table to discover that milk is spilled on the floor. The parent immediately accuses the milk-spiller of deliberately spilling the milk, although there is no direct proof of it. Guilt is inferred from the surrounding circumstances. The parent may have developed an unhealthy preoccupation with the evils of milk spilling or has an unfair bias against this particular milk-spiller. The child may have intentionally spilled the milk, or may have been unlucky in that he or she wanted to keep the glass on the table but misjudged the balancing trick. A vengeful sibling may have jolted the table, causing the glass to fall. The parent knows none of these facts from eyewitness evidence. There may be other witnesses to the event, more or less sympathetic to the alleged milk-spiller, who may confirm or refute the parent's inferences.

A child, of course, does not incur criminal liability, and one hopes that parents do not treat milk spilling as a serious domestic crime. However, these incidents are fairly accurate metaphors for accident, negligence, gross (or criminal) negligence, intention, recklessness, and imputed intent in the criminal law. The first two are not tests of responsibility or blameworthiness in law. The last three are descriptions of *mens rea*. Gross (or criminal) negligence is a strange hybrid. In the milk-spilling incidents, the parent's attitude toward responsibility will depend on many factors: his or her philosophy of child raising; the size of the family; the incidence of milk spilling; his or her educational level; the age of the child; and the mental and physical health of the child. Many of these factors can be transposed into the public's attitudes toward alleged criminals (who commit acts a little more serious than spilling milk).

The appeal courts of Canada have recently shown a preference for subjective rather than objective *mens rea*. This means that the standard of guilt should be based on what the accused believed, thought, or intended rather than some more punitive external test based on what "the reasonable person" would have thought in such circumstances. These cases have seriously challenged and, in many instances, overturned the idea of "constructive crime" which is based on objective *mens rea*.

CRIMES OF POSSESSION AND THE LAW OF ATTEMPT

There are many instances in the Code where the Crown does not have to prove the full *mens rea* and *actus reus* of an offence. Typically, these are possession offences—possession of stolen goods, counterfeiting equipment, burglary tools, or automobiles with defaced serial numbers. These crimes are similar to the crime of attempt, where the Crown has to prove that if the accused had not been stopped, they would have completed the crime. In many instances, the accused may have had an evil intent (*mens rea*) but may not have done anything close to an evil act (*actus reus*).

These are known as inchoate (or incomplete) crimes. The law's rationale is that prevention is better than cure. A similar and very significant crime is conspiracy, which simply consists of two or more persons agreeing to commit a crime, even though the crime is never actually committed.

> **EXAMPLE OF THE LAW OF ATTEMPT AND IMPOSSIBILITY**
>
> Can you be convicted of attempted murder if you shoot into your enemy's bed when he is not there although you think he is? Can you be convicted of attempted pickpocketing if you are caught with your hand in someone else's pocket which happens to be empty? The answer is "yes" on both occasions.

THE DEFENCES TO A CRIMINAL CHARGE

In most defences, such as self-defence, the accused says, "Yes, I committed the act but I have an explanation that will show I lacked criminal intent." Mistake, as a defence, is different. When asked to respond to the charge, the accused says, "No, I am not guilty of that particular offence because I mistakenly believed I was doing something quite different."

MISTAKE

The defence is restricted to mistake of fact. Ignorance of the law is not a good excuse for committing a criminal act, because everyone is presumed to know the law. The defence of mistake of fact results in acquittal because the court treats the facts as the accused mistakenly perceived them.

Example
Beaver had a friend who was a narcotics trafficker. The friend persuaded Beaver to carry out a fraudulent "drug" transaction; he was told the package would not contain heroin, but a harmless (and lawful) white powder. The victim turned out to be an undercover RCMP officer. Beaver was charged with possession of heroin because the package did contain narcotics. Beaver argued that he should have been acquitted because he honestly believed that the package contained nothing unlawful. (*R. v. Beaver*, 1957)

The *Beaver* decision was a crucially important one because the Supreme Court of Canada gave a very subjective rule of *mens rea* in relation to mistake of fact in this case. Beaver was acquitted because he had an honest belief based on reasonable grounds. The standard of honest belief was based on Beaver's perception, not some exterior objective standard such as "Would the ordinary

citizen have believed what Beaver believed?" In effect, the *Beaver* case decided
that criminal guilt should depend upon personal responsibility.

There are difficulties, however, when an accused's mistake does not result
in his or her believing that he or she was committing a lawful act, but simply
a different kind of unlawful act. For instance, what if Beaver honestly believed
he was not selling heroin, but it turned out the white powder was, in fact,
cocaine? The courts have had difficulty with cases like this and have usually
denied the accused a defence of mistake of fact.

Mistake of fact has recently caused difficulty in the crime of sexual assault
(previously called rape). In *Pappajohn,* the accused claimed that he honestly
believed that the woman involved was consenting to sexual intercourse. The
woman denied this. The court applied the *Beaver* rule. The decision in
Pappajohn does not mean that men will be acquitted of rape if they tell
cock-and-bull stories. An accused's story must be based on reasonable evidential grounds. Pappajohn's conviction was upheld by the Supreme Court of
Canada.

Other defences to criminal charges are of the "Yes, I committed the act
but I have an explanation" variety. Most of these defences have arisen in the
case of murder where, until this century, the only punishment was the death
penalty. Judges and juries have sought ways to mitigate the punishment for
murder.

PROVOCATION AND INTOXICATION

The defences of provocation and intoxication are only partial. They reduce
murder to the lesser crime of manslaughter. Most of the defences to the charge
of murder are the law's concession to human nature. If the accused was
uncontrollably provoked to kill in the heat of passion by a victim's assault or
by a victim's verbal insults, then the law will allow a partial defence. If the
accused was so drunk that he or she could not form the necessary *mens rea,*
then, again, a homicide would be reduced to manslaughter.

SELF-DEFENCE, COMPULSION, AND NECESSITY

When a person acts in self-defence, the law will accept that as a legal defence,
for it recognizes that it is natural for persons to react to save their own lives.
In theory, the defences of compulsion and necessity apply, although they are
seldom successfully used in practice. If you are forced at gunpoint to drive
the getaway car at a bank robbery, you will be acquitted because the compulsion caused you to act involuntarily. You were not acting with free will and,
therefore, are not legally accountable for the crime. Similarly, a person would
be acting under the lawful power of necessity if, during some crisis such as a
fire or a flood, he or she broke into a warehouse to obtain life-saving or
emergency equipment.

When policemen kill in the course of carrying out their duties, such behaviour will be legally justified as long as the officers acted reasonably and used no more force than necessary. A related "defence" is superior orders. Should Adolf Eichmann have been able to claim that he was only carrying out orders when he took part in the Final Solution—the killing of Jews during the Second World War? Was Lieutenant Calley justified (and, therefore, not a murderer) when he helped kill Vietnamese villagers? His explanation was that he had been ordered to do so because the U.S. Army believed that the villagers were harbouring Vietcong insurgents. Both Eichmann and Calley were convicted. The law in Canada is unclear.

INSANITY AND AUTOMATISM

The purest defence of all is insanity. The law says, "If you are mentally ill at the time of the crime, if you did not know what you were doing or did not know it was legally wrong, then you are not blameworthy. You are not responsible." At least in theory, that is the way it is supposed to work. The insanity defence is a legal test, not a psychiatric diagnosis. Psychiatrists give evidence of insanity, but judges only use such expertise within the narrow confines of the legal test. There seems to be an unwritten rule that if the accused are more bad than mad, then they are denied the insanity defence. One need only think of the monstrous mass murderers of the last few decades. Without exception, all of them were convicted of murder rather than found not guilty on grounds of legal insanity.

AUTOMATISM

Occasionally, the law allows a defence of automatism. In this instance, the accused are quite sane but commit an act without free will because they are automatons. This condition could be a result of sleepwalking, epilepsy, brain tumour, or some other physical condition that causes the accused to act involuntarily. This defence is more often found in detective stories and soap operas than in real life, although there has been a recent successful defence of somnambulism in Ontario.

CONSENT

Finally, there is the defence of consent. Persons charged with murder or wounding cannot justify their behaviour by claiming that the victim wanted to be killed or hurt. On the other hand, in property and sexual offences, consent is of the essence. Sex with consent is merely fornication if the parties were both willing. If I am found in possession of your property, it is a complete defence to a charge of theft if I show that you consented to lend me the book or videotape. Consent is a difficult and ambiguous concept when violence in sports and aggressive medical procedures are concerned.

A SLIGHTLY DIFFERENT VIEW OF THE CRIMINAL LAW

So far, the black-letter law—the law in the books—has been examined. People think they know what murder and theft are; they learned right and wrong at their parent's knee. It is also thought that people are convicted only when they really intended to commit a criminal act. According to the crime shows on television, people have always had fundamental civil rights—the presumption of innocence, the right to remain silent, the right against self-incrimination, protection against illegal arrests, protection against unreasonable searches and other illegal police behaviour, the right to counsel, the right to make full answer and defence, and the right to appeal against conviction.

An examination of the criminal law that limits itself to a bunch of textbook definitions and the idealistic rhetoric of civil liberties would provide a very incomplete and distorted picture. Instead, the criminal law must be placed in its historical and social setting. A lawyer who merely knows the letter of the law and is ignorant of its history would be a mere plumber.

THE HISTORY OF CRIMINAL LAW AS A HISTORY OF PROOF AND PROCEDURE

When lawyers and judges congregate and indulge in self-congratulation, they like to give the impression that the English common law has always been perfect and vastly superior to all other systems. These people will maintain that English liberties were enshrined in the Magna Carta of 1215 and have triumphantly survived for more than 750 years. It is true that these fundamental rules included a guarantee against arbitrary imprisonment and the right to confront one's accuser. On the other hand, many of the procedural protections that are now taken for granted—such as the right to counsel, witnesses giving evidence for the defence, the accused being able to give evidence on oath, the provision of free legal aid, and the right to appeal a conviction—did not come into existence until the 19th century or later.

EARLY PROCEDURE

The history of the criminal law is a history of procedure. The definitions of the classic crimes (homicide and so on) have mostly remained static for the obvious reason that a killing is a killing. But procedure, the manner of deciding whether the accused is guilty, has been very sensitive to official attitudes toward superstition and religion.

Until the end of the medieval period, the courts were not very concerned with definitions of crime or with the presumption of the accused's innocence.

Instead, the court was confronted with a suspect and it was the court's duty to ensure that the court was right and that the prisoner confessed his or her guilt. When the court did not hear the evidence of independent witnesses, and the facts were not tried by an impartial jury of strangers, the trial was more like a town meeting. It was conducted at the local level, in the tribe, village, or small community where everyone knew everybody else's business. All members concerned with the crime were summoned to provide the court with their personal knowledge of the events surrounding the crime. In such a circumscribed environment they knew what goods were missing, who had been fighting whom, and who was a likely arsonist or rapist. At that stage, there was little difference between a witness and a juror. The major concern of the court was to convince itself that the right person was charged. If there were insufficient witnesses, or the accused did not admit guilt, it was necessary to obtain either a confession or a clear manifestation that the prisoner was indeed guilty. Both methods had strong religious overtones. At this time, the sacred and the secular were clearly interrelated in a society where everyone professed religion. Religion and superstition were often synonymous. The court did not want to execute persons who had not made confessions because their immortal souls would be in jeopardy. If an accused refused to plead either guilty or not guilty, the judge would order the prisoner to be taken away and "pressed" under the process of *peine forte et dure*. The prisoner would be tortured by having increasing weight placed on his or her chest until he or she confessed or died.

METHODS OF PROOF

Trial by Ordeal

A more dramatic illustration of the role of religion in the criminal law is seen in methods of proof. Many of these rituals were supervised by both priest and judge. This is most obvious in the so-called trial by ordeal, although it was not so much a trial as a method of proof. The suspect would be required to carry a red-hot iron for a specified distance, to walk barefoot through hot coals, to swallow the eucharist, or to plunge a hand into boiling water to retrieve a pebble. If the suspect's wound did not show signs of recovery within a specified time it was a sure sign of divine displeasure and a clear indication of the suspect's guilt. Similar appeals to supernatural sources are found in the cases of water tests for witches. It was believed that water, being a pure substance, would reject a witch as a disciple of the Devil. Of course, the non-witch sometimes drowned, but that was a hazard of the judicial lottery.

Trial by Battle

Trial by battle had religious connotations and, once again, the deity would smile upon the righteous party and the guilty party would be vanquished.

This method of proof, reminiscent of medieval jousting, was never very popular. However, there are recorded instances of trial by battle in colonial America and in the anachronistic English case of *Ashford v. Thornton* in the 19th century.

EXAMPLE OF TRIAL BY BATTLE

Ashford came before the judges and accused Thornton of murder. He accused Thornton of raping and killing Ashford's sister. Thornton pleaded not guilty and said, "I am ready to defend the charge with my body." By this, he meant that he was prepared to have trial by battle. Thornton expressed this by taking off his glove and throwing it on the floor. If a battle took place, and if Ashford won the fight, then Thornton would be hanged (if he survived the battle). If Thornton won, then he would be acquitted. The court was taken unawares because it thought that trial by battle had been abolished. It had not been used for many decades. Yet, in 1818, trial by battle still legally existed. The rest of the story is an anticlimax. Ashford asked for time and he came back to court after a few days and announced that he would not fight. Therefore, Thornton went free. (*Ashford v. Thornton*, 1818)

TRIAL BY JURY AND THE LAW OF EVIDENCE

Trial by ordeal disappeared in the 13th century because the Pope maintained that it represented superstition rather than religion. Its replacement was trial by jury, although many centuries passed before the jury took its present form. Indeed, the early jury had few of the qualities of the impartial panel of strangers that make up a jury today. The early jury was more a collection of witnesses who had some knowledge of the alleged crime and who provided evidence, rather than judging the facts of the case for guilt or innocence. The criminal trial has always had some of the qualities of a morality play. Until the 16th century (and the time of the Reformation in England), the trial had strong religious overtones. The presumption of innocence was subordinated to the need for a confession. The accused was often not represented. There was no emphasis on giving the benefit of the doubt to the prisoner in cases of factual ambiguity. In contrast, the modern trial is a very secular affair. The modern trial is much more concerned with facts and only those facts admissible within narrow evidential guidelines. So, the classic question asked of criminal lawyers—"How can you defend one you know is guilty?"—is an irrelevant one. The lawyer's response must be: "I am not interested in the moral guilt of my client. He or she is only guilty when the trier of fact (judge or jury) reaches that conclusion on admissible evidence that would exclude hearsay, hunch, gossip, and innuendo that might have been important and relevant in a medieval trial." In other words, the modern criminal trial is concerned with proof, not truth, although it is hoped that they will usually coincide.

From the viewpoint of the 20th century, one may have difficulty realizing what important changes came about when the accused could give evidence, when counsel could defend the accused (even though he or she was unable to pay for such services), and when the principles of criminal law and procedure could be classified and amplified in appeal courts. The criminal trial continues to be a theatre, though with little emphasis on superstition. The trial is rather artificial because the evidential rules are stylized forms of the truth and the definitions of crime are wrapped in legalese.

The adoption of the Charter of Rights has meant, so far, that the procedural aspects of the criminal law have now become much more important than its substantive or definitional side. The history of the methods of proof in criminal law has been examined at some length because it shows so clearly the validity of Henry Sumner Maine's famous dictum that "the history of the law is found in the interstices [crevices] of procedure." The present importance of procedural law (with its emphasis on human rights, fundamental fairness, and the necessity that public officials act in a proper manner) is only history repeating itself. This is not the place to go into the procedural niceties now being questioned on the basis of the Charter. In any case, such debate would be premature and endless. Suffice it to say that substantial change is occurring.

THE PROBLEM OF THEORY

THE LAW AS A CLOSED SYSTEM

Behavioural and social sciences make little contribution to the definition of crime. The criminal law is based on notions of blameworthiness and guilt that owe nothing to Freud, Jung, or the sociological theories of deviance. These notions are based on the Judeo-Christian ethic. Persons "deserve" punishment if they are acting voluntarily in committing a crime and are not suffering from the few disabilities recognized by law as a defence for their crimes (such as youth or a legal definition of insanity). The law is diametrically opposed to the behavioural scientist who might describe (and excuse or explain) criminal behaviour as behaviour that is conditioned by the social environment or motivated by the subconscious of the criminal. The law is a closed system that is governed by its own peculiar logic, and sometimes by a moral stance that is incomprehensible to social workers, psychologists, or conflict model theorists.

LEROY POWELL: LEGAL TRADITION VERSUS SOCIAL THEORY

An excellent illustration of the problem of theory is the case of Leroy Powell, a hopeless alcoholic who had been arrested more than 100 times for public drunkenness. On one occasion, his lawyer claimed that Powell should not be convicted because there was evidence from experts on alcoholism that the accused was powerless to resist the urge to drink and, therefore, lacked *mens rea*. The majority of the U.S. Supreme Court denied this argument on two levels, one theoretical and the other pragmatic. The court said that on any given day, Powell made a conscious voluntary decision to start drinking. Therefore, at the start of his binge, Powell made a free choice to drink. The court ignored the arguments of the experts and treated *mens rea* as a purely legal concept backed up by centuries of judicial precedent. The court also decided that to recognize this defence would undermine the whole theoretical basis of the criminal law. If the court were to recognize alcoholism as a defence, why should the law not also find a lack of *mens rea* if the accused had an underprivileged childhood or was a member of an oppressed minority? Instead, the law adhered to the centuries-old notions of free will and Judeo-Christian morality. The court also had a more pragmatic reason for denying Powell's defence. It argued that the accused would be no better off, considering his condition, if he were found not guilty and committed to a treatment centre instead of a prison. Finally, the court pointed out that alcoholism was very difficult to define and, even with a conservative definition of the disease, there simply were not enough institutions and skilled workers to treat all the alcoholics in the United States.

THE LAW AS PRAGMATIC PREDICTOR

The last observation in the Powell case contains an important truth. While behavioural scientists and social theorists may criticize the law for its conservatism, it must be remembered that the law, in practice, does not have the luxury of merely thinking about some utopian solution to be applied in the next millennium. Lawyers and judges are forced to deal with urgent problems, and they must predict the outcome of those problems. Their solutions must reflect several conflicting values—practical political considerations, civil liberties, social mores, and the need to use language with some precision. No one is suggesting that the law has done an exemplary job of this.

CRIME CONTROL

The Code has many sections where the law is primarily interested in a perceived but unproved notion that these laws will deter antisocial behaviour. If a person is found in possession of housebreaking tools, counterfeiting equipment, or stolen goods, the law will convict the criminal without subjective proof of intent, and the courts will attribute blame to the victim unless the accused personally provides proof of innocence. These are known as "reverse onus" clauses. They have given the Canadian Criminal Code a strong crime-control philosophy (although a few of these clauses have been successfully attacked as unconstitutional under the Charter of Rights).

THE RELATIONSHIP OF LAW AND MORALS

Comment was made earlier in this chapter that law and morals should probably be clearly separated. The enlightened view is that the criminal law should not be used to control behaviour as long as that behaviour does not cause damage to any other person. While this viewpoint is gaining support, there is no question that the criminal law will continue to make moral judgements. This should not come as a surprise because human beings make moral judgements about all aspects of social behaviour.

MORAL JUDGEMENTS VERSUS LEGAL JUDGEMENTS

The courts also apply moral judgements in an indirect fashion. They may convict an accused based on the social attitudes prevalent toward his or her crime and the victim involved. The victim may have been a police officer and the accused may have been a heroin trafficker. Or, they may acquit an accused despite obvious factual guilt because he or she was "more sinned against than sinning." The most obvious cases of this type are those where the accused has been a battered wife who finally lost patience with her abusive spouse or where the victim had been grossly unfaithful to the accused. The trier of fact is applying moral standards in judging such cases that are much broader than the conventional defence of self-defence or the partial defence of provocation. A purist would say that the question of motive in such cases is irrelevant and data relating to the personality of the victim or the hardships previously suffered by the accused should be excluded on the strict rules of evidence.

PROOF AND TRUTH

In real life, a skilled defence lawyer is able to inject facts into the morality play that is called the trial. Moral (or, at least, political) values are clearly built into the laws of evidence. The law takes the view that the accused is presumed innocent until found otherwise. The burden of proof is on the prosecution. The rules of evidence dictate that fairness to the accused should always be given precedence over admissibility of evidence. It may well be true that the accused is a rather nasty person, or has had 50 previous convictions for dishonesty or violence. However, the courts will not usually admit this evidence because the prejudice that such evidence evokes overrides its relevance.

ILLEGALLY OBTAINED EVIDENCE

In the past, the Canadian courts have taken a remarkably tolerant view of illegally obtained evidence. The police may conduct an unlawful search and obtain evidence pointing to the accused's guilt. The courts have taken the cynical view that the police had a hunch that the accused was probably guilty, so the police were correct in proving it by the use of evidence obtained by misconduct. Action may be taken against the police for their misconduct, but the evidence they collect is still admissible in a trial. This type of action loses sight of the fact that the criminal trial should be concerned with "Proof" by admissible evidence according to the rules of the game, rather than "Truth" arrived at by questionable and unfair methods. The Charter of Rights has curtailed the use of much of this illegally obtained evidence.

CRIMINAL LAW VERSUS SOCIAL AND PENAL POLICY

Perhaps some of these problems already discussed could be solved by a revised criminal code which contains clear statements of penal philosophy. For instance, the technical legal definitions could be downplayed. It might be said, in agreement with social scientist Barbara Wootton, that in the majority of criminal cases people know, even before the trial starts, that the accused committed the act. Therefore, most of our efforts in a criminal case could be made in order to find out the psychological and social needs of the accused and make the most appropriate disposition of the case. The legal philosopher H.L.A. Hart, and others, such as C.S. Lewis, are critical of this approach. First, the moral disapproval of the community must be expressed in finding the accused guilty. Second, the law should be based on desert—that is, only those who of their own free will choose to do wrong should be punished. Third, it is contrary to the conventional notions of civil liberties for a person to be subject to therapy and treatment because people are just as "unfree" in a hospital as in a prison. (Hart would also add that he has serious doubts about the efficacy of the behavioural sciences.)

The criminal law has shown a disdain for penal theory; but then, it might be asked whether criminologists have given very useful information on the aetiology of crime, the efficacy of deterrence, or prognoses of dangerousness. The drafters of criminal laws might justly ask how these data, even if valid (which is doubtful), can be translated into definitions of crimes. The Criminal Code does take penal theory into consideration, but only in the most crude, superficial, and nonempirical fashion. Most frequently, laws are defined by political exigency and public pressure. There are few indications that much rational thought is devoted to such definitions.

Finally, even if criminologists could provide hard evidence as to the causes of crime, if the penologists could explain what punishments are effective, if the moralists could agree on which acts need to be defined as crimes (rather than subjected to re-education, therapy, or social reform), if civil libertarians could provide the perfect balance between public good and individual interest, the problem of language would remain. How can all these concepts be described in plain language, free of ambiguity and controversy? If that state of perfection is reached, the law courts and all the law schools may be shut down.

SUMMARY

The criminal law of Canada is based on English law but is in a codified form. Canada's Criminal Code of 1892 was the first in what is now the Commonwealth.

The basic elements of a crime are *actus reus* (based on the fundamental tenet that the prosecution must prove, beyond a reasonable doubt, that the accused committed an act) and *mens rea* (the mental element founded on the Judeo-Christian ethic of free will). The mental element consists of intention, recklessness, and, occasionally, negligence. Usually the *mens rea* will be a subjective test, based on what the accused intended in committing a crime.

The defences to crime are, appropriately, grounded in human infirmity—mistake of fact, self-preservation, passion, and overwhelming circumstances such as superhuman forces or overbearing human agency. Insanity is the best example of the negation of liability based on psychic irresponsibility.

Black-letter law provides the base, but does not envisage the spirit, of the law. The history of the law must be understood to appreciate this.

The history of the criminal law is a history of procedure. The most obvious manifestations of civil liberties—right to counsel, presumption of innocence, and so on—are very recent. Previously, the influence of religion ensured that confession and indications of guilt were more important than procedural safeguards.

The definition of crime is simple. Crime consists of those forms of human behaviour that are so defined by the law. Crime is a relative term. It is not easy to define murder, sexual assault, or dishonesty. Moral, political, and social considerations affect the definitions.

The relationship between law and morals is an uneasy one. The best counsel may be that an act should not be a crime unless it harms another party. In other words, acts committed that do not involve victims should not be regarded as crimes.

The criminal law is interested in Proof (based on intricate rules of evidence protecting the accused) and not Truth (based on hunch and innuendo). The law is a closed system and takes little cognizance of the social and behavioural sciences.

BIBLIOGRAPHY

Ashford v. Thornton (1818), 1 B. & Ald. 405, 106 E.R. 149 (K.B.).
Beaver v. R., [1957] S.C.R. 531, 26 C.R. 193.
Pappajohn v. R., [1980] 2 S.C.R. 120, 14 C.R. (3d) 243.
Powell v. Texas (1968), 392 U.S. 514.

FURTHER READING

All four of the following books deal with criminal law in Canada.

Fletcher, George. (1978). *Rethinking Criminal Law.* Boston: Little, Brown and Company.

Hall, Jerome. (1971). *General Principles of the Criminal Law.* Indianapolis: Bobbs Merrill.

Parker, Graham. (1986). *Introduction to Criminal Law.* (3rd ed.). Toronto: Methuen.

Stuart, Don. (1982). *Canadian Criminal Law: A Treatise.* Toronto: Carswell Publishers.

CHAPTER 3

COUNTING CRIME

By John Evans and Alexander Himelfarb

> *"The government are very keen on amassing statistics. They collect them, raise them to the n'th power, take the cube root and prepare wonderful diagrams; but you must never forget that every one of these figures comes in the first place from the village watchman, who puts down what he damn pleases."*
>
> Sir John Stamp
> Inland Revenue Dept.
> England, 1896–1919

INTRODUCTION

*T*his chapter is about statistics on crime and criminal justice. Those who have tried to understand crime have, over the last century, relied heavily on statistical descriptions of criminal behaviour, criminals, and the criminal justice response. What we know about crime, then, is limited by the quality, coverage, reliability, and validity of the statistics.

Social statisticians' first concern was coverage—how does one get statistical descriptions of crime phenomena? As the official sources of statistics have increased, and as creative methodologies for data collection have advanced, the questions of reliability and validity have become the most pressing. In simple terms, are the methods and techniques involved in gathering statistics strong enough that anyone following the procedures would produce the same counts? And do the statistics collected count what they purport to count?

Let us say that you wished to test some theory or other on what causes crime. For example, what aspects of community create pressures to greater criminality? Further, let us say that your theory predicts more crime per capita in big cities than in small towns. You are then going to need statistical data on the amount of crime in these two types of setting. How do you get these counts? You could consult police statistics. Police gather vast amounts of information on suspects, incidents, arrests, and charges. These are the data most often used by criminologists to test their ideas; however, there have always been problems with reliance on police statistics. Police are supposed to follow a uniform set of rules (known as Uniform Crime Reporting Rules) in recording criminal incidents or calls for service. Yet it has been discovered that different police departments often use different rules for recording their information. In fact, individual police officers exercise a good deal of discretion in what they decide to record and how they record it. There may be doubts, then, about the reliability of the statistics derived from police records. Second, there is perhaps an even more fundamental problem. Are suspects criminals? Are those arrested and charged criminals? Are all incidents that are recorded actual crimes, and are these incidents a complete count of crimes? Do the data provide a valid count of crime?

A particular difficulty arises in crime counts because as reliability of the crime count increases, validity decreases. While the police certainly never detect or become aware of all crimes, and despite enormous problems of reliability, their counts of crime are likely to be a far more valid reflection of the amount of criminal behaviour than are counts of convictions or counts of prisoners. The criminal justice system operates as a funnel: only some fraction of incidents result in a police record of a criminal incident; only a portion of recorded incidents result in suspects identified; only a portion of suspects are arrested or charged; only a portion of charges result in conviction; and only a portion of convictions result in incarceration. The further you go into the system, the more confident you can be that the count is accurate and reliable, and that it is a decreasingly valid representation of all criminal behaviour. This is particularly the case given the strong likelihood that there are built-in biases, that some crimes (and some criminals) are more likely than others to be reported and to result in arrest, charge, conviction, and a sentence to incarceration. The further you go into the system, the more obvious it becomes that you are counting something about how the system itself operates; you are counting official decisions about crime and criminals. To put this another way, statistical descriptions of the prison population may provide valid indicators of how a society and its criminal justice system respond to crime. These descriptions, however, do not provide a valid measure of crime.

How have criminologists handled these problems? For a long time they acknowledged the problems and then, when they needed data, they pretended the problems away. Kaplan's "law of the hammer" holds that if you give a small boy a hammer he discovers that everything needs pounding. Similarly, social scientists have often been accused of letting their methods, or statistics that were most readily available, dictate their theories. Social scientists will often find out what they are able to discover most easily, and build their theories around this limited information. Much of the history of criminology—the development of positivist criminology, theories of social disorganization and social pathology, and the various opportunity theories of crime—discussed elsewhere in this text was built upon a rather uncritical acceptance of official sources of statistics. Many early criminologists, for example, used prisoners to study the differences between criminals and noncriminals. Some

BREAK AND ENTER OFFENCES PROCESSED THROUGH
THE CANADIAN CRIMINAL JUSTICE SYSTEM

All Break and Enter: Offences reported and not reported to the police.

Reported: About 2 out of 3 break and enters are thought to be reported to the police.

Actual: The police assess slightly over 9 out of 10 offences as actual.

Charged: For about every 8 offences that occur, 1 person is charged.

Prosecuted: For about every 20 offences that occur, 1 person is prosecuted

Convicted: For about every 23 offences that occur, 1 person is convicted.

Sentenced: For about every 43 offences that occur, 1 person is sentenced to either a prison or penitentiary.

Note: This diagram illustrates the processing of break and enter offences through various stages in the criminal justice system. Data are approximations.

Source: Solicitor General Canada. (1984). *Reported and Unreported Crimes.* Canadian Urban Victimization Survey, Bulletin No. 2; Solicitor General Canada.(1981). *Selected Trends in Canadian Criminal Justice.* Reproduced with permission of the Minister of Supply and Services Canada, 1991.

used police records of arrest or charge; some used court records. These criminologists rarely asked the questions, Are all criminals equally likely to get arrested? To be charged? To be put in prison? Even when criminologists recognized the limits of the available information, they used these unreliable and often invalid measures because this was all they had.

In the sixties and the seventies, a number of sociologists and criminologists focused their attention on the systematic biases of past theories built on official records. Official records, new theories suggested, showed us how the criminal justice system operated to create crime and criminals. The statistics revealed information about the police, about the courts, and about whom they selected for their attention and worst punishments. Arrest, charge, and conviction were parts of a formal labelling process, a ceremony of degradation, in which a person was formally stigmatized. These labelling or social reaction theories asked why certain people were more often selected for this process and studied the consequences for these people of being labelled and stigmatized. The same bodies of "crime statistics" that had been used to describe the behaviour of criminals were now being used to describe the official agents of social control.

More recently, particularly in Canada and Britain, criminologists are increasingly becoming polarized. Many seem to be returning to the conservative criminology of the past, to the acceptance of official records as a reasonable indicator of crime, and focusing on explaining crime for the purpose of controlling it. Others, influenced by some variant of the "new" or "critical" criminology, see crime statistics as simply part of the government's control mechanism, a way of characterizing the crime problem, a means of self-justification, and a reflection of more fundamental structural inequalities.

Are crime statistics whatever one makes of them? Are statistics simply a resource to tell lies or support one's own favoured position? Yes, sometimes. But they need not be. Theories about crime and facts about crime are built simultaneously, are mutually dependent, and shape one another. Theory without facts is indistinguishable from ideology; facts without theory are often implicit ideology; statistical facts without theory are numerology, often bent to ideological ends. Theorists and policy makers have often been guilty of using statistics to their own ends, using crime counts to show that we were going through a crime wave, or using the same counts to show how we were living through a wave of repression. We live in an age where numerical values have a certain magic and a power to convince us, to make arguments seem true. Statistics can be dangerous if we do not have the tools to consider them critically.

For example, imagine that you read, in some credible source, that violence in Canadian society has risen by 100 percent over the past decade. Before you set off to explain this "fact," before you turn your home into a fortress, you should ask: Just what is being counted as violence? Crimes? Some crimes? Political dissent? Violence by the state? Domestic violence? What theory or ideological assumptions have guided this choice of "fact"? And, how good are the facts? How well and consistently have they been counted? Are they reliable and valid?

What have social scientists and policy makers done about the lack of good crime information? Over twenty years ago, the American sociologist Ned Polsky (1967) argued that our understanding of crime would never be significantly furthered if we relied on statistical data. He was concerned that sociologists and criminologists relied too heavily on remote sources of information; they remained too distant from the criminals they wished to understand. He advocated field research through which social scientists live among and learn from the criminals themselves. Not surprisingly, few have followed Polsky's lead. Rather, most have worked to improve the quality of statistics based on official sources, to specify the valid uses of these statistics, and to develop innovative methodologies to complement official data and to fill gaps. Despite the problems, criminological theory and criminal justice policy remain heavily dependent on statistics about crime and the criminal justice system.

One might distinguish three broad types of criminal justice statistics: statistics about crime and criminals; statistics about the criminal justice system and its response to crime; and statistics about perceptions of crime and criminal justice. Theory and policy require statistics about the decisions of those who break the law, about the decisions of those who maintain it, and about what people think of all of this. For the most part, statistics on the criminal justice system are the most developed.

STATISTICS ON THE CRIMINAL JUSTICE SYSTEM

The criminal justice system produces an enormous amount of raw data in the form of police reports and records, the recorded decisions of prosecutors and judges, the administrative records of prisons and penitentiaries, and the recorded decisions of parole boards and probation and parole services. One might then assume that Canada has a sophisticated system of statistics on the criminal justice system. This is not entirely the case.

FROM RECORDS TO STATISTICS

Administrative records are not statistics. Records are about individual cases and are intended primarily to help practitioners make decisions about these individual cases. Statistics are aggregated; they are about what is common among individual cases. Statistics are meant to provide information about larger questions: planning and evaluation, policy and program development, and theory building and testing. While good records are the base, the conversion of records into statistics requires a number of conceptual decisions. The potential clients or users of the statistics must decide what it is they want to know and how they plan to use the information. Statistical systems should be built to address the enduring theoretical and policy concerns.

Specifically, the following issues must be addressed before records can be converted into statistics: unit of count, levels of aggregation, definitions, data elements, and counting procedures.

(A) Unit of count—consensus about what it is that we are counting.
In the course of their everyday activities the police, for example, may count many different things: suspects, offences, charges, or calls for service. Typically, they work with occurrences; an occurrence may involve several offenders, several victims, and several offences. The unit we wish to count in a statistical system will depend on whether we are trying to learn something about police workload or productivity, or whether we are seeking to learn something about crime or victims. Recently, for example, there has been a growing awareness among policy makers and criminologists that victims have been an ignored unit of count.

Some units of count are specific to a particular sector. For example, the prison sector can count inmates; the court sector, convictions; and the police, suspects. Some units, however, are common, or at least allow one to track offenders or incidents through the system from charge to disposition. Decisions about units of count, then, must be sensitive to the key theoretical and policy questions, and, whenever possible, allow comparability among sectors.

(B) Levels of aggregation—consensus about how to combine data.
A crucial decision, particularly in a federated state such as Canada, is the level at which we want our statistics. For example, do we want to combine police records for a city? Do we want to combine statistics for an entire province? Or region? Or the nation? To the extent that we want to generalize our theories or develop or evaluate national policies, we are likely to want national statistics. But several criminologists have warned that the further you move from those who produce the data and the more you try to combine data from different sources, the more questionable is the result. They prefer the richer and more detailed information available from local police to the abstracted, less complete data available about national policing.

That Canada has a single Criminal Code makes the goal of national statistics more realistic than in a country such as the United States with its many criminal codes. On the other hand, the constitutional split between the Canadian federal government with its criminal code responsibilities and the provincial and territorial governments, who have prime responsibility for the administration of criminal justice, has made the development of national statistics extremely difficult.

(C) Definitions—consensus about how to define what is being counted.
While the Criminal Code provides a common set of definitions for counting crime, there remains a good deal of discretion about when an incident of crime is truly an incident, or even what, for example, constitutes "inmate." If one

wishes to count inmates, should one count those who are temporarily absent, or those on remand, or those in community correctional facilities, or those assigned to mental institutions? Common definitions are essential. This is not merely a technical issue. Depending on how the terms are defined, you can inflate or deflate the statistics; you can make it appear that crime is higher or lower, or that there are more or fewer prisoners. When presented with statistics, it is always important to ask how the units have been defined.

(D) Data elements—consensus about what specific information should be collected.
While the police will need certain kinds of information to help them in their investigative activities, this information will be far more detailed than, and sometimes quite different from, what is needed as aggregated statistics. Similarly, the police in one jurisdiction may, for their own good reasons, maintain records quite different from those of other police departments. The information needs of the Montreal Urban Community police will differ from those of the Saanich, British Columbia, police. As understandable as this is, it is extremely difficult to build aggregated statistics out of different types of records which may be incompatible.

One of the greatest obstacles to the development of statistical systems is the difficulty in convincing practitioners to collect information for which they do not see immediate or practical benefits. Social scientists and policy makers will generally want information on socio-economic and demographic characteristics such as sex, age, employment and income, and ethnic background. This information may appear irrelevant for operational purposes. The determination of data elements must be informed by both theory and policy concerns. The tension between the practical and immediate needs of local officials who actually produce data, and the theoretical and policy needs of those who wish to use data, is a perennial problem in the production of statistics.

(E) Counting procedures—consensus on how to count units and elements.
If an offender goes on a break-and-enter spree and hits a half-a-dozen houses in an evening, how many offences should be counted—six or one? Or if, during a break and enter, an offender is confronted by the home owner and assaults him or her, is this one or two offences? If one, which offence should be counted? If we agree that the most serious should be counted, how do we determine seriousness?

The most influential work on developing a scale of seriousness remains that of Sellin and Wolfgang (1964). They conducted surveys, including some in Canada, to develop a seriousness scale based on public perceptions of the seriousness of various offences. The scale demands more information about the offence than simply its criminal code designation. While in general terms their findings confirm the more formal way of determining seriousness through the Criminal Code itself (i.e., looking at the penalty structure), their scale demands information about the nature of the offence. Canadian studies

(Akman and Normandeau, 1967) have confirmed the reliability and validity of Sellin and Wolfgang's approach but it has not been routinely incorporated into our crime statistics.

CANADIAN CRIMINAL JUSTICE STATISTICS

The questions or issues of unit of count, levels of aggregation, definitions, data elements, and counting procedures are at the base of much of the technical and critical literature on criminal justice statistics. Within Canada, attempts to answer these questions have traditionally been the responsibility of our national statistical service, Statistics Canada. More recently, the federal and provincial governments have created a national institute, The Canadian Centre for Justice Statistics, a satellite of Statistics Canada, governed by a board of directors of senior officials responsible for justice.

The major difficulty confronting the Canadian Centre is getting agreement on priorities such as whose needs should be met. Crime statistics are used by different people and for different purposes. Criminologists and researchers want to build and test theories. Policy makers and analysts want to identify problems and develop and test solutions. Administrators and program managers want to plan and run their operations and to monitor and evaluate their programs. Each will have different statistical needs. Moreover, statistics can be used as statistical indicators, a measure of the state of health of the nation, and as performance indicators, a measure of the effectiveness and efficiency of the components of the criminal justice system. Most important, statistics serve the public interest by keeping people informed and providing some measure of public accountability. Good statistics are important, but they are important in different ways for different users.

As the present time, Canada has reasonably good national data on criminal justice inputs such as resources and expenditures. The data are far weaker when it comes to outputs such as incidents, arrests, charges, convictions, and dispositions. In fact, there have been no national statistics on court decisions since 1973. Like those of most Western countries, Canada's statistics regarding corrections are probably the best. We can give a fairly accurate count of the number of prisoners in Canada and some information on their social characteristics. Despite some difference in counting from province to province, Canada can produce a reasonably accurate description of its inmate population. This can be quite useful for projecting future inmate population and for planning future facilities and services. It can also, when linked to other data, be useful for developing correctional policy. For example, how much are we using incarceration and are we doing so in the most useful and appropriate ways?

Data on prisoners, however, do not tell us much about crime and criminal behaviours; they tell us about the criminal justice system. The confusion comes when people equate "criminal" and "prisoner." Some people are more likely to be caught; some people are more likely to be charged; some people are more likely to be convicted; and some people are more likely to be sentenced to prison or to penitentiary. We know too much about how people get selected for incarceration to assume that prison statistics tell us very much about crime.

But what can such data show? Figure 3.1 shows the growth in number of those incarcerated in Canadian penitentiaries between 1950 and 1990.* In this period the penitentiary population more than doubled and from 1971 to 1986 moved up rather rapidly. Obviously, these figures are important for administrative and planning purposes. But do these figures tell us something about growing crime in Canada? No. Do they tell us something about harsher or more punitive sentencing practices? No. In fact, if we look at the rate of incarceration (per 100 000 Canadians) we see that much of the growth in penitentiary population can be accounted for by the growth of the Canadian population (Figure 3.2).

International comparisons, as difficult and problematic as such comparisons are, show Canada to be a nation which incarcerates at a much higher rate than most Western European nations and at a lower rate than the United States. Some have argued that this is proof that Canada is too punitive, that too many people are being put behind bars, and put there for too long. Others have argued that it simply means that Canada has more serious crime than many other nations. The debates flourish. Canadian statistics do not provide the answers, only indications of where problems may exist.

To make sense of these statistics for policy and research purposes, we would need statistics on convictions and sentences, on admissions and releases, and on the rates of crime and police clearance. Unfortunately, Canada does not have national data on convictions and sentences and has not had such data for almost twenty years. This is, in large part, a result of the difficulties in resolving the kinds of issues discussed in this chapter in a country which has shared jurisdiction for criminal justice between the federal and provincial governments. If we are to answer the pressing problems of how best to co-ordinate efforts of crime prevention and control, these gaps will have to be filled. In other words, the ultimate goal of a program of criminal justice statistics is to provide statistical data bases which can be linked to one another to answer these more complex questions. Because Canada lacks such an integrated program, many important theoretical and policy issues can only be answered partially or speculatively. Nowhere is this clearer than in our inability to count crime.

HOW MUCH CRIME?

It should come as no surprise that criminologists have had difficulty counting crime. By its very nature crime is typically a secretive activity. When people commit their crimes they try to avoid becoming part of the count of criminals.

---

* Note that this includes only inmates who have received sentences of two years or more. Those who are sentenced to less than two years serve their time in provincial institutions, not federal penitentiaries.

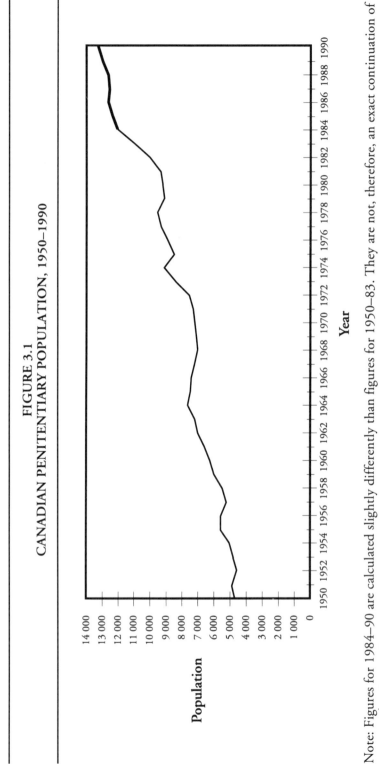

FIGURE 3.1
CANADIAN PENITENTIARY POPULATION, 1950–1990

Note: Figures for 1984–90 are calculated slightly differently than figures for 1950–83. They are not, therefore, an exact continuation of the time-series.

Source: Ministry of the Solicitor General, Correctional Service of Canada, Operational Information Services; Adult Correctional Services in Canada, Catalogue No. 85-211. Reproduced with permission of the Minister of Supply and Services Canada, 1991.

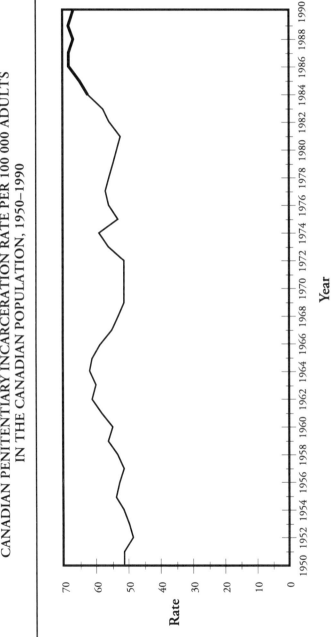

FIGURE 3.2
CANADIAN PENITENTIARY INCARCERATION RATE PER 100 000 ADULTS
IN THE CANADIAN POPULATION, 1950–1990

Note: Figures for 1984–90 are based on a different source than figures for 1950–83. Slight discrepancies may therefore be present.

Source: Ministry of the Solicitor General, Correctional Service of Canada, Operational Information Services; Adult Correctional Services in Canada, Catalogue No. 85-211. Reproduced with permission of the Minister of Supply and Services Canada, 1991.

(They do not want to become a statistic!) The "best" crime is one that no one knows about, and no criminal justice system will ever be able to ferret out all the crimes and criminals. Some crimes are harder to detect than others and some criminals harder to apprehend and convict. Criminologists have long recognized that the major problem of counting crime is the so-called "dark figure" of crime that remains unreported, unrecorded, and largely unknown. In response to the problem, criminologists have developed a variety of approaches to count crime, or at least to describe crime patterns and trends. They have tried to rationalize and improve official statistics, but they have also developed approaches that do not depend on official counts of crime. In the next section we shall look at official statistics, victimization surveys, and self-report studies as data sources about crime.

OFFICIAL STATISTICS: CANADIAN UNIFORM CRIME REPORTS

Despite all the expressed concerns, we have for the most part relied upon official counts of the amount of crime. Until just over twenty years ago we were dependent on local police records collected for police purposes and handled differently in each locale. For over two decades now, Canada has had in place a system called the Canadian Uniform Crime Reports, designed to provide uniform, comparable, and national statistics. Just what this system counts has been the subject of an almost endless debate within criminology.

While the Canadian Uniform Crime Reports drew heavily from a similar system in the United States, it arguably represents something of an improvement over the American system. First, as we have indicated, common crime classifications and definitions are somewhat easier to arrive at in Canada than in other countries since Canada operates under a common criminal code. Second, the coverage of police departments is far more complete in Canada than in the United States. But both systems share some fundamental problems. Some of these problems can be corrected by further improvements to the Uniform Crime Report System; some of the problems are more fundamental, are built into all official statistics.

Let us first look at the problems that could be corrected, indeed are being corrected in both Canada and the United States. A number of studies (Nettler, 1974; Silverman and Teevan, 1975; Silverman, 1980; DeSilva and Silverman, 1985) have documented some of the problems in the recording and scoring rules and how these rules are applied. Specifically, the studies have examined the implications of the "seriousness rule" which holds that only the most serious crime is scored in an incident involving multiple crimes. The concerns are threefold: first, this rule deflates the total crime count, since less serious crimes are not counted separately; second, it inflates serious crimes as a proportion of the total; and third, the way in which seriousness is scored is problematic, for not enough qualitative data about the crimes are recorded to use a sophisticated scale of seriousness.

Concerns have also been expressed that the crime categories used are too general, allowing too many different kinds of acts to be recorded in the same way. For example, thefts and attempted thefts are recorded under the same category.

Furthermore, as previously indicated, it is not always entirely clear just what it is we want to count. In Canada, the count of crimes includes violations of the Criminal Code, violations of other federal and of provincial statutes, and violations of some municipal by-laws. Many of these criminal and quasi-criminal laws are fairly remote from what most Canadians think of as crime. When most people think of crime, when they worry about or fear crime, they are thinking about particular offences; they are not thinking about the Criminal Code and the full panoply of behaviours legally defined as criminal. When we seek to count crime we are invariably stuck with a complex mix of these two sets of definitions. For this reason, gross counts of crime may be very misleading. For example, in 1969 the Ouimet report pointed out that total convictions for all criminal offences in Canada increased by a frightening 2500 percent between 1901 and 1965. The report added, however, that 98 percent of the increase was for summary convictions—less serious crime— particularly traffic offences. With the report of the gross crime counts alone, most people would no doubt have had horrific visions of violent predators preying on innocent victims, rather than the more accurate vision of careless motorists abusing each other and pedestrians. For these reasons, UCR programs count offences within particular offence categories. Table 3.1 shows the major offence categories selected for the crime statistics programs in Canada.

Another oft-cited problem is that the Canadian UCR treats property crimes and personal crimes differently. Several property crimes, even if they involve different victims, may be recorded as a single offence if they are considered to be part of the same incident. This is not the case for personal offences. DeSilva and Silverman (1985) provide not only a detailed account of the problems but also a description of what the Canadian Centre for Justice Statistics proposes to do to remedy these problems, in what they describe as the possible future of police statistics. The question remains, however, of whether the new improved Canadian UCR will provide us with an accurate count of crime or even a reasonable indicator of crime and crime trends. Can official statistics ever tell us about total crime? Are official statistics only useful for understanding the criminal justice system?

We might have discussed the Canadian UCR under the heading of criminal justice statistics because these official data may tell us more about police activities than about crime. "Official violations" statistics are, in part, a product of policy decisions within the criminal justice system, that is, decisions about which criminal infractions deserve the most police attention and resources. Furthermore, crime statistics are the product of individual police decisions made in the exercise of police discretion about what crimes are serious enough to attend to, record, and pursue. In fact, the ways in which police and police departments apply crime recording and scoring procedures

TABLE 3.1
MAJOR CATEGORIES FOR WHICH CRIMES
KNOWN TO THE POLICE ARE RECORDED

CANADA

Crimes of Violence:

Homicide
- Murder 1st and 2nd degree
- Manslaughter
- Infanticide

Attempted Murder

Assault
- Assault level 1
- Assault with weapon or causing bodily harm level 2
- Aggravated assault level 3
- Unlawfully causing bodily harm
- Discharge firearm with intent
- Police
- Other peace or public officers
- Other assaults

Abduction
- Abduction of person under 14
- Abduction of person under 16
- Abduction contravening custody order
- Abduction no custody order

Sexual Offences
- Aggravated sexual assault
- Sexual assault with weapon
- Sexual assault
- Other sexual offences

Robbery
- Firearms
- Other offensive weapons
- Other robbery

Property Crimes:

Breaking and Entering
- Business premises
- Residence
- Other break and enter

Theft Motor Vehicles
- Automobiles
- Trucks
- Motorcycles
- Other motor vehicles

Theft over $200
- Bicycles
- From motor vehicles
- Shoplifting
- Other thefts over $200

Theft $200 and Under
- Bicycles
- From motor vehicles
- Shoplifting
- Other thefts $200 and under

Have Stolen Goods

Frauds
- Cheques
- Credit cards
- Other frauds

TABLE 3.1 (*continued*)

CANADA

Other Criminal Code Offences:

Prostitution
• Bawdy house
• Procuring
• Other prostitution

Gaming and Betting
• Betting house
• Gaming house
• Other gaming and betting offences

Offensive Weapons
• Explosives
• Prohibited weapons
• Restricted weapons
• Other offensive weapons

Other Crimes
• Arson
• Bail violation
• Counterfeiting currency
• Disturbing the peace
• Escape custody
• Indecent acts
• Kidnapping
• Public morals
• Obstruct public or peace officer
• Prisoner unlawfully at large
• Trespass at night
• Wilful damage private
• Wilful damage public
• Other Criminal Code offences

Federal Statutes:

Addicting, Opiate-like Drugs
• Possession—heroin, cocaine, other drugs, cannabis
• Trafficking—heroin, cocaine, other drugs, cannabis
• Importation—heroin, cocaine, other drugs, cannabis
• Cultivation—cannabis

Controlled Drugs
• Trafficking

Restricted Drugs
• Possession
• Trafficking

Other Federal Statutes
• Bankruptcy Act
• Canada Shipping Act
• Customs Act
• Excise Act
• Immigration Act
• Juvenile Delinquents Act
• Other federal statute offences

Provincial Statutes:
• Liquor Acts
• Securities Act
• Other provincial statutes

Municipal By-Laws

Source: Statistics Canada. (1984). *Canadian Crime Statistics*, Catalogue No. 85-205.

reflect to some extent the policing style and policy of the particular police department. Combining or comparing statistics from different departments is highly problematic (Silverman, 1980).

Police statistics are also shaped by public perceptions, concerns, and fears. The police are very much dependent on the accounts of victims and witnesses. That is to say, victims and witnesses must recognize an act as a criminal justice matter, must believe it to be of sufficient seriousness to warrant a report to the police, and must believe that reporting the act is worthwhile—all this before the police make their decisions about how to respond to and record an act. (See, for example, Shearing, 1984.)

Official crime statistics, then, are shaped by both common sense and legal definitions of what constitutes crime. These statistics reflect the decisions of many people, not simply the behaviours of criminals. Official counts of crime will change as legal definitions change, as common-sense definitions change, and as the priorities of agents of law enforcement change. For example, if Parliament made premarital sex illegal, we could well expect a rather sharp increase in crime. Would this be reflected in official crime counts? To the extent that there are no direct victims to bring these offences to police attention, the answer is probably "no." Much would depend on the priority attached to enforcement of this offence.

Consider two less hypothetical examples. As official statistics reveal to us increasing rates of family violence, theoretical explanations of the crisis in the nuclear family abound. But has the incidence truly increased, or have Canadians, within and outside of the criminal justice system, become increasingly intolerant of such behaviour and more willing to bring such incidents to police attention? Have police become more sensitive to the seriousness of the problem and more likely to record the incidents as crimes? In other words, has the incidence increased or have the definitions and reporting and recording behaviours changed?

Similarly, official statistics show a decline in cannabis-related offences. It may be that use of cannabis has declined in Canada. It may be that the priorities of law-enforcement agencies have shifted, perhaps toward trafficking and importation and the use of "harder" drugs. Not coincidentally, offences involving cocaine and other harder drugs have shown some increase over the past few years.

What, then, can the Canadian UCR tell us? From the inception of the Uniform Crime Reports in 1962, the total Criminal Code offence rate more than tripled from 2771 offences per 100 000 Canadians to 9903 in 1990. Figure 3.3 shows the trend line during this period.

During this period, both violent and property crime rates increased steadily. Violent crimes, however, were consistently a very small proportion of total crimes, about 7 percent as opposed to the more frequent property crimes, 50 percent of the total (Figure 3.4(A) and (B)). Those who work with crime statistics generally refer to crime rates when they wish to take into account the size of the population. The crime rate is simply the number of incidents for every 100 000 Canadians (Table 3.2). Reference to rate, then,

FIGURE 3.3
TOTAL CRIMINAL CODE OFFENCES, RATE PER 100 000 CANADIANS, 1962–1990

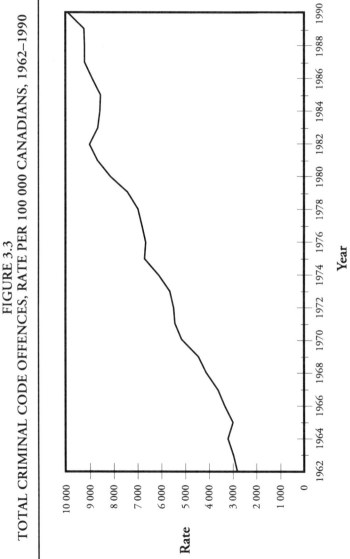

Source: Statistics Canada. *Crime and Traffic Enforcement Statistics*, Annual Catalogue No. 85-205.

TABLE 3.2
SELECTED CRIME OFFENCES, CANADA, 1989 AND 1990

	1989		1990 (PRELIMINARY)	
	NUMBER	RATE PER 100 000 POPULA-TION	NUMBER	RATE PER 100 000 POPULA-TION
Homicide[1]	657	2.51	654	2.47
Attempted Murder	829	3	910	3
Sexual Offences[2]	30 430	116	31 522	118
Assault[3]	190 364	726	206 956	778
Robbery	25 709	98	28 051	106
Break and Enter	349 164	1332	378 822	1425
Theft Motor Vehicle	100 336	383	113 369	426
Theft—Over and Under $1000	845 843	3226	907 601	3414
Cannabis	40 740	155	38 847	146

[1]Includes first- and second-degree murder, manslaughter, and infanticide.
[2]Includes sexual assault.
[3]Non-sexual assault.

Source: Uniform Crime Reporting Survey preliminary data release *Juristat* 11(9).

rather than incidence, makes sure that comparisons from jurisdiction to jurisdiction, or over time, do not reflect differences in population size rather than differences in criminal behaviour.

Violent crimes are relatively rare. In 1990, Canada had 654 homicides (a rate of 2 per 100 000 Canadians), about 1 percent of total violent crimes. Violent crimes continue to be about 7 percent of total offences. In fact, the category "violent offences" includes robberies, which are judged to have had the potential for violence, even if no violence, as most Canadians would understand it, occurred. The presence of a weapon, even if the weapon was not used, and even if no injury occurred, would include the incident in the violent crime count.

Things seem to be getting better. Although crime has been rising since 1962, the rate of growth has been decelerating. (See Table 3.3 and Table 3.4)

Despite these general trends, some crime problems seem to be getting worse. One example of this is sexual assault (rape, prior to recent legislative

FIGURE 3.4(A)

VIOLENT CRIMES, RATE PER 100 000 CANADIANS, 1962–1990

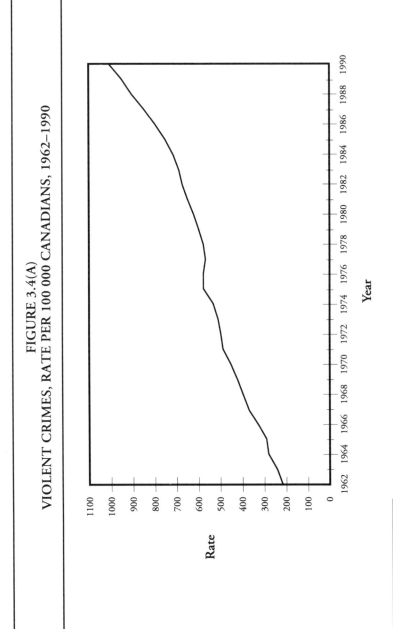

Source: Statistics Canada. *Crime and Traffic Enforcement Statistics*, Annual Catalogue No. 90-205.

FIGURE 3.4(B)
PROPERTY CRIMES, RATE PER 100 000 CANADIANS, 1962–1990

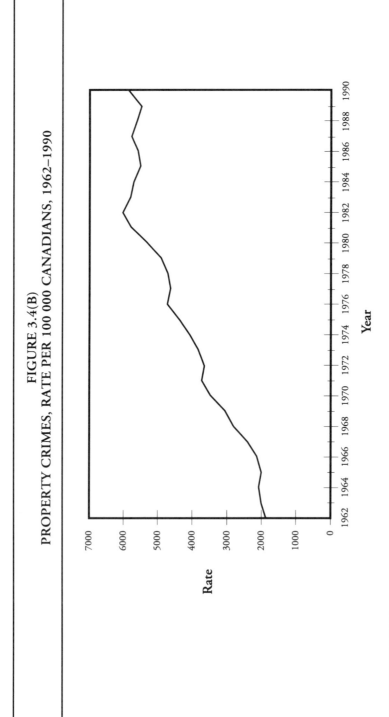

Source: Statistics Canada. *Crime and Traffic Enforcement Statistics*, Annual Catalogue No. 90-205.

TABLE 3.3
ALL CRIMINAL OFFENCES—BY MAJOR CATEGORIES, CANADA, 1985–1990

	1985		1986		1987		1988		1989		1990[1]	
	NO.	RATE	NO.	RATE	NO.	RATE	NO.	RATE	NO.	RATE	NO.	RATE
Total Violent Offences	189 822	749	204 917	801	219 381	856	232 699	898	248 922	950	269 118	1 012
Total Property Offences	1 408 717	5 555	1 448 550	5 660	1 468 591	5 731	1 458 821	5 630	1 445 748	5 514	1 560 308	5 869
Other Crimes	575 636	2 270	624 282	2 439	675 586	2 636	700 899	2 705	736 688	2 810	803 107	3 021
Total Criminal Code	2 174 175	8 574	2 277 749	8 901	2 363 558	9 224	2 392 419	9 233	2 431 428	9 274	2 632 533	9 903
Narcotic Control Act	43 803	173	53 348	208	58 384	228	57 879	223	65 576	250	58 725	220
Food & Drug Act	3 096	12	2 903	11	3 274	13	2 478	10	2 306	9	4 687	18
Other Federal Statutes	38 915	153	40 251	157	40 344	157	37 265	144	40 373	154	32 441	122
Total Federal Statutes	96 120	379	96 502	377	102 002	398	97 622	377	108 255	413	95 853	361
Provincial Statutes	359 559	1 418	381 354	1 490	380 692	1 486	366 138	1 413	361 467	1 379	350 528	1 319
Municipal By-Laws	94 454	372	102 600	401	109 258	426	101 628	392	98 973	377	102 095	384
All Offences	2 724 308	10 743	2 858 205	11 169	2 955 510	11 534	2 957 807	11 415	3 000 123	11 443	3 181 009	11 966

[1]Preliminary figures.
Rates may not add to totals due to rounding. Rates are calulated per 100 000 population.

Source: Statistics Canada. *Crime and Traffic Enforcement Statistics*, Annual Catalogue.

TABLE 3.4
SELECTED CRIME OFFENCES IN NUMBERS AND RATES
PER 100 000 POPULATION FOR CANADA AND THE U.S.A.—1989

	CANADA		U.S.A.	
	NO.	RATE	NO.	RATE
Murder	657	3	21 500	9
Robbery	25 709	98	578 326	233
Burgulary (B&E)	349 164	1 332	3 168 170	1 276
Theft & Possession of Stolen Goods[1]	973 845	3 714	9 437 242	3 802
Fraud & Forgery	122 739	468	not available	

[1]Includes motor vehicle theft.

Note: Because police methods of recording and offence definitions differ between nations, these figures cannot be used for comparison. They are given as an indication of the levels of crime in each country.

Sources: Statistics Canada. *Canadian Crime Statistics,* Catalogue No. 85-205; U.S. Department of Justice. *Uniform Crime Reports—Crime in the United States.*

changes), which has shown a rapid increase over the past years. Other examples include offences related to hard drugs.

But what can we say given all the cautions with which we began this chapter? How much crime remains hidden to the police? Which crimes? How much do police recording practices shape the UCR figures? How much do these practices change over time? Are these data useless? The answer to the last question is No. For example, the homicide statistics collected by the Canadian Centre for Justice Statistics probably give us a pretty complete and consistent count of homicides in Canada. It is also probable that certain other offences that are of high priority within the criminal justice system, and which victims are likely to report, are relatively well captured by the UCR program. Motor vehicle theft is probably the best example of this type of offence. In sum, we can probably learn something about crime from these data, but we are not sure how much.

We can be more confident that if police departments across Canada are recording and reporting crimes relatively consistently, then the UCR data give us a picture of law enforcement in Canada, of what crimes the police are processing. For example, recent changes in police policy limit police discretion in laying charges when handling domestic violence incidents. This policy has produced more official incidents of such assaults, reflecting changes in police practice if not changes in criminal behaviour.

Some optimists would argue that the UCR gives an indication of trends in crime. The less optimistic say No: there is too much we do not know about victim reporting behaviour, about the exercise of police discretion in deciding what is criminal and what is not, about police recording and reporting practices, and about the nature and seriousness of the offences captured by UCR. Out of these concerns have emerged attempts to develop other ways of counting crime. The most important of these is the victimization survey.

VICTIMIZATION SURVEYS

In 1982, the Ministry of the Solicitor General of Canada, with the assistance of Statistics Canada, conducted a large-scale victimization survey in seven major cities: Greater Vancouver, Edmonton, Winnipeg, Toronto, Montreal, Halifax-Dartmouth, and St. John's. The development of this survey profited from earlier Canadian work by Courtis (1970), Waller and Okihiro (1978), and a large body of American work admirably presented in Edison Penick and Owens (1976). Victimization surveys are based on the idea of going straight to the people to ask them to indicate whether they have been victims of acts which the Criminal Code defines as criminal; to describe the nature and consequences of their victimization experiences; to describe the criminal justice response; to indicate whether victims or others brought the incidents to official attention, and, if not, why not; and to indicate their perceptions and attitudes about crime and criminal justice in Canada.

In Canada, the methodology employed was a random sample of city residents sixteen years of age or older, interviewed by telephone on their victimization experiences within the calendar year preceding the interview. More than 61 000 interviews were conducted overall. On the basis of these interviews, statistical estimates were made for each of the cities surveyed.

Not all crimes can be captured through this survey method. One need not be a methodologist to recognize that murder cannot be included in such a survey. Nor can the range of consensual crimes for which there are no direct victims—drug use, gambling, and the like. These crimes are nowhere captured very well, not through official data, nor through victimization surveys. Similarly, those crimes designed to keep victims unaware that they have been victimized cannot be well captured in victimization surveys (or official data sources). Fraud, embezzlement, employee pilferage, price fixing, and the wide range of consumer, corporate, and white-collar crimes were not included in the survey. The eight categories of crime included were sexual assault, robbery, assault, break and enter, motor vehicle theft, theft of household property, theft of personal property, and vandalism. A full account of the methodology can be found in Catlin and Murray (1979), Solicitor General Canada (1983, 1984a, 1984b, 1985a, 1985b, 1985c, 1986), Evans and Leger (1978), and Skogan (1981).

For the calendar year 1981, the survey uncovered more than 700 000 personal victimizations (sexual assault, robbery, assault, and theft of personal property), and almost 900 000 household victimizations (break and enter, motor vehicle theft, theft of household property, and vandalism). Remember that these figures apply only to the seven cities surveyed and only to those sixteen years of age and over. Of the incidents identified, fewer than 42 percent had been reported to the police or had otherwise come to police attention. Recognizing that the victimization survey cannot capture all of that "dark" figure missed by the UCR, the survey data do reveal that many more Canadians are victimized by crime than is revealed by official statistics.

As most would guess, a large proportion of the unreported crime is relatively trivial, the kinds of incidents that most of us would not expect the police to devote time or resources to. For example, a few dollars stolen by somebody within the household, a toy stolen from the porch, or an umbrella stolen from a restaurant are the kinds of common incidents rarely reported. Nonetheless, as Table 3.5 and Table 3.6 show, more serious incidents may often go unreported. For example, about two-thirds of the women who had been sexually assaulted did not report the incident to the police. In explaining their decisions, many of the women indicated concern about the attitudes of those within the criminal justice system as being an inhibiting factor. Women

TABLE 3.5
NUMBER OF INCIDENTS OF SELECTED TYPES AND
PROPORTION NOT REPORTED TO POLICE

TYPE OF INCIDENT	ESTIMATED INCIDENTS	PERCENT- AGE OF ESTIMATED INCIDENTS	PERCENT- AGE UN- REPORTED	PERCENT- AGE REPORTED
Sexual Assault	17 200	1	62	38
Robbery	49 300	3	55	45
Assault	285 700	18	66	34
Break and Enter	227 400	14	36	64
Motor Vehicle Theft	40 600	3	30	70
Household Theft	417 300	26	56	44
Personal Theft	349 900	22	71	29
Vandalism	213 100	13	65	35
TOTAL	1 600 500	100	58	42

Source: Ministry of the Solicitor General. (1982). Canadian Urban Victimization Survey. Reproduced with permission of the Minister of Supply and Services Canada, 1991.

TABLE 3.6
REASONS GIVEN FOR FAILURE TO REPORT INCIDENTS TO THE POLICE BY OFFENCE CATEGORY

	SEXUAL ASSAULT	ROBBERY	ASSAULT	BREAK & ENTER	MOTOR VEHICLE THEFT	HOUSEHOLD THEFT	PERSONAL THEFT	VANDALISM	TOTAL	%
Nothing Taken	33	47	28	42	51	8	6	28	179 000	19
Police Couldn't Do Anything	52	54	51	58	57	64	64	69	564 000	61
Fear Revenge	33	10	11	3	**	1	2	2	40 000	4
Protect Offender	16	9	16	5	**	3	5	3	60 000	6
Too Minor	26	56	63	65	56	71	62	73	606 000	66
Inconvenience	**	33	24	20	19	26	24	25	224 000	24
Personal Matter	27	22	29	8	**	7	13	6	123 000	13
Reported to Another Official	**	**	7	7	**	7	27	4	109 000	12
Negative Attitude of Police	43	14	12	7	**	7	5	6	75 000	8
Overall % Unreported	62	55	66	36	30	56	71	65		
Number Unreported	11 000	27 000	185 000	81 000	12 000	227 000	243 000	136 000	921 000	58

**The actual count was very low (10 or fewer); therefore, extreme caution should be exercised when interpreting this percentage.
Note: Columns do not add to 100 percent since respondents could indicate more than one reason for failure to report any one incident. Numbers may not add to totals given due to rounding.

Source: Ministry of the Solicitor General. (1982). Canadian Urban Victimization Survey. Reproduced with permission of the Minister of Supply and Services Canada, 1991.

assaulted by people they knew indicated fear of revenge as one of the reasons they failed to report. Table 3.6 presents the major reasons for failing to report to the police.

Where incidents produced great financial loss to the victim, reporting was far more likely, even more likely than for those incidents which resulted in pain or injury but no loss. As concluded by the Solicitor General Canada (1984b) study: "For many, it would seem, reporting crimes is less an act of justice (or even revenge) than a far more utilitarian act—seeking redress, recompense or recovery."

The survey data confirm many of the concerns about official sources of crime data. Some crimes are more likely to come to police attention than others. Some categories of victims are more likely to report their victimizations and some categories of offenders (for example, family members) are less likely to be reported. In general, it is only through such knowledge that we can begin to understand the UCR data and the dark figure of crime.

Because victimization surveys are based on victims' perceptions and experiences, and because they collect information about the victims of crime, they are useful in identifying those categories of people most at risk of criminal victimization. For example, Figure 3.5 and Figure 3.6 show that, contrary to the conventional wisdom, the risk of victimization is lowest for older Canadians, especially those 65 years of age or older. While we already know that women are far more likely than men to be victims of sexual assault, the survey data also show that women are more likely to be victims of personal theft, and less likely to be victims of other personal offences. In fact, the victimization data provide a profile of the victim of crime which explodes many popular myths. The typical victim of crime is young, single, male, not employed full-time, and living an active social life. In particular, the number of evenings spent outside the home is one of the best predictors of whether one will have been victimized or not (Table 3.7).

TABLE 3.7
INCIDENT RATES PER 1000 POPULATION BY AVERAGE
NUMBER OF EVENING ACTIVITIES OUTSIDE THE
HOME PER MONTH

EVENING ACTIVITIES	SEXUAL ASSAULT	ROBBERY	ASSAULT	PERSONAL THEFT
1–9	2	5	21	34
10–19	3	6	38	54
20–29	4	10	59	88
30 or more	5	20	119	118

Source: Ministry of the Solicitor General. (1982). Canadian Urban Victimization Survey. Reproduced with permission of the Minister of Supply and Services Canada, 1991.

FIGURE 3.5
PERSONAL VIOLENT OFFENCE VICTIMIZATION RATES
PER 1000 POPULATION BY AGE CATEGORY

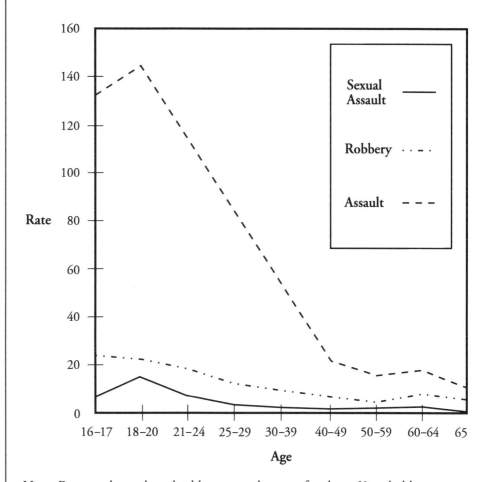

Note: For sexual assault and robbery, actual counts for those 60 and older were
      very low (10 or fewer); therefore, extreme caution should be exercised
      when interpreting these rates.

Source: Ministry of the Solicitor General. (1982). Canadian Urban Victimization Survey.
        Reproduced with permission of the Minister of Supply and Services Canada, 1991.

Perhaps most important, victimization surveys allow us to go beyond
merely counting incidents. They provide data on the costs of victimization,
on the financial losses, on the physical injuries, and on the concern and fear
victimization may produce. In addition, these data allow the exploration of
various dimensions of seriousness. Clearly, victimization hits some harder

FIGURE 3.6
PERSONAL THEFT VICTIMIZATION RATES
PER 1000 POPULATION BY AGE CATEGORY

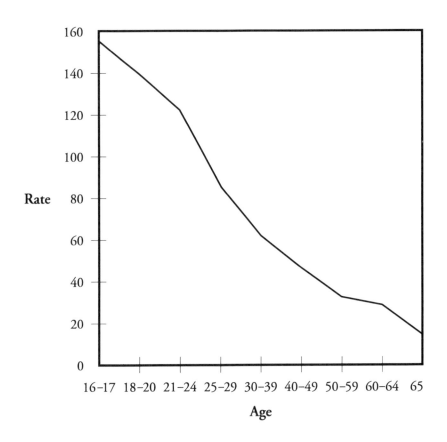

Source: Ministry of the Solicitor General. (1982). Canadian Urban Victimization Survey.
        Reproduced with permission of the Minister of Supply and Services Canada, 1991.

than others. When victimized, women and elderly people suffer most. Their fear is greatest. There is little wonder that women and the elderly fear crime in a way that might be described as disproportionate to their risk of victimization. Even those women and elderly people who had not been victimized were likely to express fear of crime, an expression of their vulnerability and perhaps a realistic understanding of the consequences of crimes for them when they do occur.

Victimization surveys try to gauge the kinds of activities people engage in to avoid victimization. In 1981, most people were not actively involved in organized crime-prevention efforts. Those most fearful of crime apparently withdrew from the social supports that might have helped them deal with their fear and cope with the aftermath of victimization if it did occur. This and similar studies have shown that fear does not lead to constructive action, and may in itself be a problem to be addressed by the criminal justice system. An accurate portrayal of crime in Canada through better methods of counting crime and better crime statistics can help to minimize fears based on myth and media.

Victimization surveys are particularly useful to help us monitor people's perceptions, concerns, and fears about crime and criminal justice. Effective criminal justice policies and programs and relevant criminological theories must address the subjective side of crime and address people's everyday fears and concerns. The fear of crime can be as great a problem as crime itself, and public disenchantment with criminal justice and the agencies of control provides not only an indicator of serious problems, but a significant challenge to criminal justice.

Victimization surveys cannot measure all crimes. They are dependent on the vagaries of human memory and are subject to the kinds of criticisms levelled against any survey. Victimization surveys are dependent on respondents' ability not only to recall incidents and their details, but also to place the incidents correctly in time. We know that respondents are fallible. And, as Skogan (1978) suggests, well-educated, articulate respondents are more likely than others to talk to interviewers and to give rich and full accounts of their victimization experiences, thus perhaps biasing the data. There is reason as well to be cautious about interpreting data on domestic and sexual assaults which have been collected through surveys. Respondents may well be reluctant to discuss such experiences with an interviewer. Also, the methodology is still relatively young. Special methodologies will be needed to get at, for example, rural victimization and victimization of Native Canadians. Special methodologies are required to get at white-collar crime, consensual crime, and what has come to be called enterprise crime—organized crime and the crimes of organizations and the state. More is required on the psychological and emotional impact of victimization (Solicitor General Canada, 1986). Only through replications of the survey will trends emerge.

Despite the limitations, these data provide us with the opportunity to go beyond counting incidents and to gain some understanding of what it is we are counting. The data are an important, perhaps essential, complement to other sources of crime statistics.

VICTIMIZATION SURVEYS AND THE UCR

Despite the obvious temptation, UCR data and victimization data do not lend themselves to direct comparison. Although they are designed to use the same categories of crime, they generate separate data bases. The data are based on different populations and different assumptions. Over time, however, victimization data should allow us to contextualize the UCR. How much of the change in official crime data can be attributed to changes in reporting patterns or police priorities? What is the nature and seriousness of the crimes being counted in the UCR? What do the trends mean about people's attitudes toward crime and the criminal justice system? Significantly, the UCR program is itself being revised to include more data about the victims of the offences reported (DeSilva and Silverman, 1985). Despite these qualifications, recent U.S. comparisons of UCR and victimization data have emphasized important areas of convergence. The two data sources reveal similar general trends and "social maps" of criminal victimization.

It would appear that UCR and victimization surveys can confirm and complement one another. Each is especially useful for particular kinds of questions. Many important criminal justice policies and theories deal with crimes which produce no direct victims (public drunkenness, prostitution, and gambling—typically called consensual crimes) and, therefore, cannot be addressed by victimization surveys. Consensual crimes are of particular interest for police planning and policy because such a large proportion of arrests result from such crimes. Perhaps the most serious problem with victimization surveys as the major source of crime data is their cost. Because crime is relatively rare and unevenly distributed, sample sizes must be large—especially if the intent is to generalize from these samples to the national level. Some combination of improved official statistics and episodic victimization surveys would appear to be the likely solution to this problem.

SELF-REPORT STUDIES

Yet another approach to generating data on the nature and distribution of crime is the self-report study. For the most part, these studies emerged out of a belief that there were systematic biases in police data. A number of sociologists, drawing particularly on the seminal work of Short and Nye (1958), have asked adolescents to report on their own acts in violation of the law. These data have generally been taken as corroborating the view that there are systematic biases in official statistics, that the number of crimes known to the police is far smaller than the number actually committed, that certain kinds of crimes are far more likely to be captured in police data, and that certain offenders, particularly lower-class offenders, are more likely to find their way into police records.

Because self-report studies supposedly avoid these biases, they have been particularly important in research and theory on the aetiology of crime and delinquency, particularly the relationship between social class and crime. For a long time, these studies were not very carefully scrutinized. They were perceived as such a significant breakthrough that few questions were asked. A major work to determine the reliability of self-report studies was carried out by Hindelang, Hirschi, and Weis (1981). They concluded that the self-report method does demonstrate that people are willing to report crimes, both those known and not known to officials, and that respondents' reports are internally consistent. A difficulty arises in that it appears that different populations answer self-report questions in different ways. Lower-class males and black males, in the United States study, are more likely to under-report their own criminal behaviour than are middle-class white males. Similarly, in Canada, Fréchette and LeBlanc (1979, 1980) confirm that while self-report studies do uncover much hidden delinquency and raise questions about the biases in official statistics which show the preponderance of lower-class crime, previous self-report studies have also masked the fact that lower-class crime is typically more serious and persistent.

There are two related problems here. First, it would appear that those who are typically law-abiding are more likely to report completely their occasional infractions than are the more committed delinquents to report their more serious and frequent infractions. Second, differences between official statistics of delinquent behaviour and self-report data may reflect not simply biases in official data, but biases in the self-report methodology as well. The official data are likely to include more serious offences and self-report data are more likely to include more minor infractions.

A number of other more technical problems regarding, for example, sampling—the difficulty in getting "hard-core criminals" in a sample, disagreements about which offences to select and which produce the most reliable and valid data, and which scoring procedures best suit the uses of the data—are given full discussion in Hindelang, Hirschi, and Weis (1981). While self-report studies are never likely to be an instrument for counting crimes, recent methodological refinements have enhanced their potential for addressing fundamental questions about crime and the correlates of crime.

SUMMARY: THE FUTURE OF CRIME AND CRIMINAL JUSTICE STATISTICS

The importance of good statistics for planning, policy making, and administration has long been recognized within the criminal justice system. Out of this recognition and concern emerged, in 1981, The Canadian Centre for Justice Statistics, with a mandate to collect national statistics. The existence of the Canadian Centre is a recognition—in a country with shared jurisdiction for criminal justice—of the importance of developing national commitment and national strategies for producing and sharing criminal statistics. The concept of the Centre is still evolving; however, the commitment to national statistics has been given concrete form.

The new information technology holds great promise for improving the official records which form the basis for most criminal justice statistics on prisons, on courts, and on police. Canada is virtually alone among Western nations in its lack of national court data on convictions and sentences, so crucial for understanding how our criminal justice system is working. Perhaps the new commitment and the new technology will allow us to fill these gaps. It is only through a nationally co-ordinated effort that we can avoid the danger of developing incompatible systems in each province (or worse, municipality) that feed many different criminal justice systems and inhibit the continued development of a co-ordinated national system of justice.

The methods for counting crimes are still in their formative stages. Some, like the UCR, will be derived from official records (designed in accordance with UCR rules) and will, therefore, suffer the limitations of all such official statistics. Nevertheless, recent advances in police management information systems and crime classification systems hold great promise for providing us with a measure of calls for police service, police case loads, and police activity. Other methods, like the victimization surveys, will draw on people's experiences and will, therefore, suffer the limitations of all such surveys. Significant progress has been achieved in Canada in the development and refinement of victimization surveys and, perhaps to a lesser extent, self-report studies.

How much crime is there in Canada and what are the trends? Is it awful and getting worse? Do we have cause for alarm? Are things okay and getting better? Do we have cause for complacency? Depending on your bias and prejudices, the state of the art allows you to find some evidence and numbers to justify either extreme. But, with the improvements in our knowledge about crime and the development of new methodologies, we are coming to recognize the complexity of the questions. When taken together, the UCR and the victimization surveys encourage neither alarm nor complacency. Overall, there is certainly less serious crime than most Canadians assume based on media accounts and the high visibility of sensational incidents. At the same time, we are starting to uncover some particular kinds of serious incidents which have, for too long, remained hidden. Sexual assault and family violence are two important examples. Much more work is needed. Only through an integrated program of criminal justice statistics, recognizing the limits of any one source of information, will we be able to build powerful theories of crime and sound policies and programs for crime prevention and control.

BIBLIOGRAPHY

Akman, D., and A. Normandeau. (1967). "The Measurement of Crime and Delinquency in Canada: A Replication Study." *British Journal of Criminology* 7:129–49.
Catlin, G., and S. Murray. (1979). "Report on Canadian Victimization Survey Methodological Pretests." Ottawa: Statistics Canada.
Courtis, M.C., assisted by I. Dussuyer. (1970). "Attitudes to Crime and the Police in Toronto: A Report of Some Survey Findings." Toronto: Centre of Criminology, University of Toronto.
de Silva, S., and R.A. Silverman. (1985). "New Approaches to Uniform Crime Reporting in Canada." Paper presented at the annual meeting of the American Society of Criminology, San Diego (November).

Edison Penick, B.K., and M.E.B. Owens (eds.). (1976). *Surveying Crime.* (Report of the Panel for the Evaluation of Crime Surveys submitted to the Law Enforcement Administration). Washington, DC: National Academy of Science.

Fréchette, M., and Marc LeBlanc. (1979). "La délinquance cachée à l'adolescence." *Inadaptation juvénile* Cahier 1. Montreal: Université de Montréal.

Hindelang, M.J., T. Hirschi, and J.G. Weis. (1979). "Correlates of Delinquency." *American Sociological Review* 44:995–1014.

Nettler, G. (1974). *Explaining Crime.* New York: McGraw-Hill.

Sellin, T., and M.E. Wolfgang. (1964). *The Measurement of Delinquency.* New York: Wiley.

Shearing, Clifford D. (1984). "Dial-A-Cop: A Study of Police Mobilization." Report for the Centre of Criminology, University of Toronto.

Short, J., and F. Nye. (1958). "Extent of Unrecorded Juvenile Delinquency: Tentative Conclusions." *Journal of Criminal Law, Criminology and Police Science* 49:296–302.

Silverman, R.A. (1980). "Measuring Crime: More Problems." *Journal of Police Science and Administration* 8(3):265–74.

Silverman, R.A., and J. Teevan. (1975). *Crime in Canadian Society.* Toronto: Butterworths.

Skogan, W. (1978). "Review of Surveying Crime." *Journal of Criminal Law and Criminology* 69:139–40.

———. (1981). "Issues in the Measurement of Victimization." Washington, DC: U.S. Department of Justice, Bureau of Justice Statistics.

Solicitor General Canada. (1983). "Victims of Crime." Canadian Urban Victimization Survey. Ottawa: Solicitor General Canada.

———. (1984a). "Reported and Unreported Crimes." Canadian Urban Victimization Survey. Ottawa: Solicitor General Canada.

———. (1984b). "Crime Prevention: Awareness and Practice." Canadian Urban Victimization Survey. Ottawa: Solicitor General Canada.

———. (1985a). "Female Victims of Crime." Canadian Urban Victimization Survey. Ottawa: Solicitor General Canada.

———. (1985b). "Cost of Crime to Victims." Canadian Urban Victimization Survey. Ottawa: Solicitor General Canada.

———. (1985c). "Criminal Victimization of Elderly Canadians." Canadian Urban Victimization Survey. Ottawa: Solicitor General Canada.

———. (1986). "Household Property Crimes." Canadian Urban Victimization Survey. Ottawa: Solicitor General Canada.

Waller, I., and N. Okihiro. (1978). *Burglary: The Victim and the Public.* Toronto: University of Toronto Press.

FURTHER READING

Fréchette, M., and Marc LeBlanc. (1980). "Pour une pratique de la criminologie: configurations de conduites délinquantes et portraits de délinquants." *Inadaptation juvénile* Cahier 5. Montreal: Université de Montréal. Fréchette and LeBlanc's monograph provides not only rich data and insights on delinquency but also a good illustration of the use of self-report studies.

Silverman, R.A., and J. Teevan. (1980). *Crime in Canadian Society.* Toronto: Butterworths. This integrated anthology brings together some of the major Canadian work in criminology and has excellent chapters on statistical and methodological issues in counting crime.

Skogan, W. (1981). "Issues in the Measurement of Victimization." Washington, DC: U.S. Department of Justice, Bureau of Justice Statistics. Skogan's monograph on victimization surveys, one of many he has written in this area, is the most readable and exhaustive account of the potential and limits of this approach to counting crime. His discussion is based largely on the American experience.

Solicitor General Canada. (1983). "Victims of Crime." From the Canadian Urban Victimization Survey. Ottawa: Solicitor General Canada. This, the first in a series of bulletins, provides a brief overview of the major findings and methodology of the first large-scale Canadian victimization survey conducted in 1982.

Waller, I., and N. Okihiro. (1978). *Burglary: The Victim and the Public.* Toronto: University of Toronto Press. This influential study of burglary in a Canadian city did a great deal to promote an understanding of crime from the victims' and public's perspective.

CHAPTER 4

CORRELATES OF CRIMINAL BEHAVIOUR
By Timothy F. Hartnagel

CORRELATES DEFINED

A correlate is a phenomenon that accompanies another and is related in some way to it. Correlates of crime refer, then, to those phenomena that are associated with criminal activity. While a list of such phenomena would include any number of conditions, this chapter will limit itself to social conditions correlated with crime. Before turning to the details of these selected and specific correlates, the concept of correlation itself should be briefly considered.

Correlation refers to a relationship between at least two phenomena that are related, or occur or vary together. For example, some criminologists have claimed that delinquent behaviour is correlated with physique or body type. They claim that adolescent males with an athletic, muscular body build commit more delinquent acts than those whose physique is lean and fragile. Other criminologists have shown that crime, at least of some types, occurs more frequently in larger cities than in smaller towns and rural areas. They argue that city size and crime vary together. These examples give measurements on two variables (for example, city size and crime) for a number of individuals or aggregates (for example, cities). The task is to determine whether and how these two sets of measurements go together—that is, whether and how they're correlated. Discovering such correlations or relationships is an important first step for any scientific discipline such as criminology. Thus, a good deal of the early work in criminology was devoted to the task of identifying and describing the correlates of crime.

Having identified and described a correlate of crime—a relationship—it's natural to want to know why it exists. How might this relationship be explained? What might have produced it?

One explanation for a correlation or relationship between two variables is causal. The concept of causation has been debated a good deal by philosophers and social scientists. At the very least, the idea of causation has proven to be a useful way of thinking about the natural and social world. A causal explanation refers to the inference that a change in one variable results from or is produced by change in another variable. A common mistake is to confuse correlation with causation and so to infer that one variable causes another from the fact that they are correlated. However, correlation means only that two variables are related. They are associated or go together, but change in one does not necessarily produce a change in the other. Criminologists are frequently interested in establishing causal explanations. They are not usually satisfied, for example, with knowing that poverty and crime are correlated; they want to know if crime results from poverty and if it does, how? However, it would be a mistake to conclude from their correlation alone that poverty causes crime. So, correlation between two variables is a necessary first step toward causal explanation but is not in itself sufficient for inferring such an explanation.

Human beings have a tendency to simplify their perceptions of the world. This tendency can lead to a distortion of the understanding of correlates and causes. There is a temptation to assume that an effect can have only one cause that is both necessary and sufficient. There is also the temptation to assume that causes must be perfectly correlated with their effects, and that no other variables are necessary for interpreting how the cause operates or for specifying the particular conditions or circumstances under which it has its effect(s) (Hirschi and Selvin, 1966). But reality is substantially more complicated than this, and it would be wise to develop the habit of thinking of crime as the consequence of multiple causes which combine in complicated ways to produce their effects. Nettler (1982) uses the image of a dense web to communicate the meaning of this view of causation. He describes this as a multiplicity of tightly packed causes which interact strongly and nonuniformly. As selected correlates of crime are examined, then, the urge to reach hasty conclusions concerning the causal character and significance of these correlations should be resisted.

AGE

PEAK AGES FOR CRIME

Without much exaggeration, crime can be said to be a young man's game. To put this into more technical terms, age and sex are strong correlates of criminal behaviour. Any number of criminologists have singled out these two variables for their strong relationship with crime. For example, Sutherland and Cressey (1970) state that sex status is of greater importance in differentiating criminals from noncriminals than any other trait, and that statistics from a variety of years and jurisdictions uniformly indicate a higher prevalence of crime among young persons compared with other age groups.

Official crime data from the United States (Federal Bureau of Investigation, 1989) indicate that the general pattern is for arrests to increase from early to late adolescence and then to decline gradually with increasing age. Just under half (47 percent) of all arrestees in 1988 were below age 25; 30 percent were below age 21 and 16 percent below the age of 18. The largest percentage of all arrests occurred among those 18 years of age (4.9 percent). So, as Empey has stated (1982), the younger age categories are overrepresented among all arrestees compared to their proportion of the total U.S. population.

These patterns vary somewhat for different types of crime. For crimes of violence, 45 percent of all arrestees in the United States in 1988 were below age 25; 28 percent were below 21 and 15 percent were below 18. However, for property crime, 61 percent were below age 25, 47 percent below 21, and 32 percent below 18 years of age. Violent crimes seem to peak later in age than property crimes and decline more slowly with age. In fact, the peak age for property crime arrests was 13–14, compared to the peak age of 18 for violent crime (Federal Bureau of Investigation, 1989). And there are certain specific crimes—for example, gambling and drunkenness—that don't conform to this general pattern of an early peak followed by decline with increasing age. So although arrest rates typically decline with age after an initial rise in adolescence, different crimes peak at different ages and some crime rates decline more slowly with increasing age (Steffensmeier et al., 1989).

Canadian crime data paint a somewhat similar picture. The median age on admission to custody for all inmates sentenced to provincial correctional institutions in 1988–89 was 27 years, which is considerably younger than the median age of the Canadian adult population, 40 years (Statistics Canada, 1989a). No official data are available on the age of persons charged, so court statistics for persons convicted of indictable offences must be relied upon. These were last published for 1973 and do not include data from Quebec or Alberta. Table 4.1 shows these age-specific conviction rates for three categories of crime, taken separately for males and females for selected age categories. The general pattern is for the conviction rates to rise with increasing age to 18–19 and then to decline as the age categories increase. Clearly, the highest rates of conviction occur among those 19 and under. This holds for males and females with one exception. Among females, the highest rate of conviction for violent crimes against the person occurs in the ages 20–24. In most instances, the peak ages for these conviction rates are 18 to 19. The only other exception is for crimes against property with violence, where the peak age for males is 16–17. These figures, no doubt, understate the amount of crime actually committed, particularly in the younger age categories, since these categories are less likely to be processed through the criminal justice system and since, until recently, some provinces treated those under 18 as juveniles. Concerning juveniles, West (1984) recently remarked that from one-third to one-half of serious Criminal Code offences known to the police in recent years were committed by juveniles (ages 7 to 16), though juveniles constitute only about 20 percent of the population.

TABLE 4.1

RATES OF CONVICTION FOR INDICTABLE OFFENCES PER 1000 000 PERSONS, BY SEX AND
SELECTED AGE CATEGORIES, CANADA (EXCEPT QUEBEC AND ALBERTA), 1973

OFFENCES	AGE GROUPS										
	16–17		18–19		20–24		25–29		All Ages 16+	
	M	F	M	F	M	F	M	F	M	F
Against Persons	47.6	4.4	144.6	8.2	137.1	9.6	83.6	5.9	67.1	4.7
Against Property with Violence	488.3	11.9	483.4	16.4	224.7	8.5	87.0	2.2	126.1	4.0
Against Property without Violence	795.4	179.1	985.1	232.8	575.8	163.5	291.5	123.3	345.7	108.9
Total Criminal Code	1438.3	211.7	1841.9	277.8	1116.6	205.6	572.9	143.6	635.7	128.4

Source: Rates calculated from Statistics of Criminal and Other Offences, 1973, using intercensal estimate of population by sex and age.

Tepperman (1977) calculated historical Canadian conviction rates for indictable offences for males by age categories and concluded that such rates have shown a shift in recent years toward the younger ages. Between 1950 and 1966 the rate of conviction for males 16–17 increased by 50 percent, while for older age categories the conviction rate increased only marginally or declined. Tepperman also pointed out that the conviction rate for serious offences for young people has progressively increased since 1891 as their entrance into adult status has been delayed and they have become increasingly concentrated in schools, enhancing their sense of belonging to a distinctive youth culture.

Self-report data also support the age-crime relationship, though such research has generally limited its attention to juveniles and is, therefore, of only limited usefulness for examining the full range of the age-crime relationship. Empey (1982) concludes that the self-report results from a national survey of adolescents in the United States by Ageton and Elliott only partially agree with the official data concerning age and crime. Ageton and Elliott's results suggest that the peak ages for youthful crime are somewhat younger than the official data indicate, with the highest incidence for many property and violent offences occurring between the ages of 13 and 15. Juvenile diversion programs and a hesitancy to formally process adolescents through the criminal justice system may play some role in explaining the higher peak ages in official data on arrests and convictions. Osgood et al. (1989) compared offence rates based on arrests and on self-reports and found that both methods show substantial declines from ages 17 through 23 for virtually all offences, with the major exception of arrests for assault.

Canadian self-report research in Montreal by LeBlanc (1983) found that in a sample of adolescents aged 12 to 18, self-reported delinquency increased progressively until age 16 or 17 and then diminished, though this pattern varied with the nature of the delinquency. Serious delinquency tended to diminish with increasing age while drug and status offences increased. Similarly, Fréchette (1983) found delinquency to be closely linked with age in his sample of male wards of the Montreal Social Welfare Court. Seventy-five to 80 percent of his respondents reduced or stopped their delinquency during the second half of their adolescence. However, he found an abrupt and substantial rise in criminal activity with the onset of adulthood. Fifteen to 20 percent of his initial sample of respondents had an adult record for serious crime.

One self-report study that surveyed a representative sample of respondents aged 15 and above in the United States investigated "criminal propensity," or the likelihood of an individual engaging in four different types of criminal acts (Rowe and Tittle, 1977). The results of this study were consistent with the official data in showing a negative relationship between age and a self-estimate of the probability of engaging in crime. The proportion of individuals admitting the possibility of committing one of these crimes declined from the youngest to the oldest age category for both male and female respondents.

MATURATIONAL REFORM

To conclude this discussion on age and its relation to crime, the ways in which criminologists have attempted to explain this correlation should be briefly noted. Factors such as bias in the criminal justice system in favour of the very young or the much older offender, increased skill in avoiding detection with advancing age, and the decline in physical strength and agility associated with aging have all been mentioned as possible causes. However, the social position of youth in urban, industrial society has been seen as the major contributor to "maturational reform," or the rapid decline in crime as adolescents move into young adulthood. Various authors have argued that adolescence is a time of transition, a period between childhood and adulthood, and that the ambiguities and marginality of the social position of youth in modern societies create a variety of tensions and problems, of which crime is but one example (Nettler, 1984). Adolescents tend to be excluded from participation in adult roles such as marriage, work, and adult leisure activities. At the same time, they experience emancipation from the constraints and demands of childhood, and are encouraged to aspire to adult status (Bloch and Niederhoffer, 1958; West, 1984). As Nettler (1984:217) remarks, " … structures of modern states encourage crime and delinquency. They lack institutional procedures for moving people smoothly from protected childhood to autonomous adulthood." But, as youth move into the adult ages and their social status and integration increase, the personal costs of crime to the individual also increase—they now have more to lose—while at the same time crime becomes somewhat redundant to their improved social position. Youth acquire added stakes in conforming behaviour (Briar and Piliavin, 1965) as they occupy social roles and acquire material goods that would be jeopardized by criminal behaviour. They become more socially integrated into relationships, groups, and organizations and, therefore, more dependent upon the social rewards of conformity (Rowe and Tittle, 1977). New rewards and costs associated with their new adult status replace those that sustained delinquency in adolescence; new satisfactions replace those previously provided by delinquency (Trasler, 1980).

Greenberg (1979) has offered the most elaborate version of this type of explanation. He argues that adolescents in North American society are particularly vulnerable to the expectations and evaluations of their peers because of the increased age segregation resulting from the exclusion of young people from adult work and leisure activity. At the same time, money is necessary for participation in this youth culture, but the deterioration of the teenage labour market has resulted in adolescents being less able to finance their costly social life. Greenberg regards theft as a way of financing participation in activities with peers in the absence of legitimate sources of income. With increasing age, both the dependence on peers and the lack of legitimate sources of funds are reduced for many of these young people; consequently, theft declines. Greenberg also discusses how the extended requirements for schooling restrict adolescent autonomy and how public humiliation of some students by teachers undermines self-esteem and produces embarrassment before peers. This can result in nonutilitarian crime, such as vandalism and violence, as an attempt to assert independence and enhance self-esteem before a sympathetic audience of peers. These motivations to crime are removed when young people leave the restrictive and sometimes degrading school setting. Greenberg also claims that the cost of crime for youth through legal penalties increases as they progress from early to later adolescence, as do opportunities for establishing stakes in conforming behaviour, particularly employment. These social controls, or costs, increase with age and, therefore, also contribute to the decline in crime.

Hirschi and Gottfredson (1983) have subjected this, and other, attempts to explain the age-crime relationship to a close examination, and found them lacking. They present evidence that the relationship of age to crime has been similar in earlier historical times and in other types of society. Thus, they challenge the premise that the nature of modern, urban, industrialized society is crucial for explaining this age-crime correlation. They also point out that Greenberg's attempt at explanation is really a combination of strain and external-control theories and, therefore, subject to the logical and empirical limitations of each. Hirschi and Gottfredson cite research suggesting that the effects of age on crime do not depend on such life-course events as leaving school, finding gainful employment, entering upon marriage, and so forth: "Age affects crime whether or not these events occur" (1983:580). These findings undermine the maturational reform type of explanation. Greenberg (1985) has responded that Hirschi and Gottfredson's arguments rest on faulty logic and misstatements of the empirical evidence, while Steffensmeier et al. (1989) claim that over time the age-crime distribution peaks earlier and becomes progressively steeper so that recent offenders are younger and less variable in age than in 1940. So, although the correlation of age with crime is one of the most undisputed facts of criminology, its interpretation and explanation remain open to a good deal of debate.

SEX

SEX DIFFERENCES AND CRIME TRENDS

As has already been indicated, sex is highly correlated with crime. The crime rate for men greatly exceeds the rate for women. The U.S. Uniform Crime Reports for 1988 show that males 18 and over comprised 70 percent of all arrestees, while in Canada, in 1988, adult males constituted 82 percent of adults charged with Criminal Code offences. Over 80 percent of the young persons appearing in youth courts are male (Statistics Canada, 1990).

This sex difference in crime varies somewhat by type of crime. In the United States, males comprised 79 percent of the arrestees for the seven Index (serious) crimes in 1988 and 89 percent of those arrested for violent crime, but 76 percent of those arrested for property crimes. These same data indicate that larceny/theft was the crime for which females were most often arrested, constituting 20 percent of all female arrests and 78 percent of female arrests for Index crimes. In arrests for fraud, sexual equality is approached (Nettler, 1984). Furthermore, there are a few offences, such as prostitution and infanticide, which are distinctively female. Again, Canadian data are similar (see Figure 4-1). Males made up 90 percent of the adults charged with violent crime in 1988, 77 percent for property crime, and 86 percent for other crimes, while females constituted only 10 percent, 23 percent, and 14 percent, respectively. Violent crime in particular, then, is correlated with maleness.

Victim survey data from the United States parallel the official data by showing that for a variety of personal and household crimes, the sex of the predominant majority of offenders as indicated by the victims, for the years 1972–76, was male (Hindelang, 1979). For example, in 1976 males constituted 96 percent of the offenders for robbery, 92 percent for aggravated assault, 86 percent for simple assault, 95 percent for burglary, and 94 percent for auto theft. The highest percentage of female offenders (17 percent) from these data in 1976 occurred for the crime of larceny (theft). Over this limited time period of four years, it was in this type of property crime that the greatest increase—from 14 percent to 17 percent—in female participation in crime occurred, with the greatest growth in the subcategory of larceny of unattended property. The Canadian Urban Victimization Survey (Johnson, 1986) estimated that males represented 90 percent of the perpetrators of robbery and assault in 1981, a figure reasonably similar to that provided by the official data on males charged with these same two offences (95 percent).

Self-report research with juveniles has generally substantiated this sex difference in delinquency, though the gap is not as great as in the official data on adults. Hagan (1985a) noted that the sex ratio in a number of self-report surveys conducted in the United States in the 1970s showed males exceeding females in self-reported delinquency by more than 2 to 1 compared to the 1975 official arrest ratio of 3.72 to 1 for those younger than 18. From a study in the Toronto metropolitan area conducted early in 1979, Hagan, Gillis, and Simpson (1985) reported strong gender effects on self-reported "common" delinquent behaviour, such as minor theft and aggression. On average, males scored 2.28 points higher on their delinquency scale than did females, with the greatest differences occurring for the offences of taking cars and fighting. Yet LeBlanc's (1983) research in Montreal showed a much smaller gap between male and female delinquency (3 to 1) than the official statistics indicated (8 or 10 to 1). This may, at least in part, reflect differences in police handling of juvenile offenders. Gomme, Morton, and West (1984) carried out a self-report study among senior elementary and junior high school students in a small rural-urban school district in southern Ontario and found that for all offences but running away from home, the mean frequencies on self-reported delinquencies were significantly higher for males. The mean sex ratio for the respondents reporting any delinquency involvement was 1.19 to 1 for juvenile status offences, but 1.34 to 1 for serious criminal offences. In particular, males exhibited a greater propensity for damaging property and engaging in interpersonal aggression. However, females were fairly frequently

FIGURE 4.1
RATIO OF PERSONS REPORTED CHARGED BY SEX AND
OFFENCE GROUP, CANADA, 1988

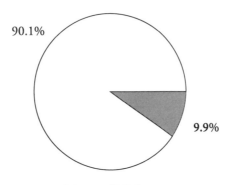

90.1%

9.9%

Crimes of Violence

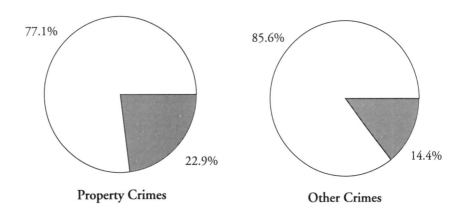

77.1%

22.9%

85.6%

14.4%

Property Crimes

Other Crimes

Adult Male

Adult Female

Source: *Canadian Crime Statistics.* (1988). Ministry of Supply and Services.

involved in theft offences, with a sex ratio of about 1.1 to 1, though less than 2 percent of females reported ever being involved in major thefts (compared with 10 percent of males) and only 9 percent reported involvement in even medium-serious thefts (compared with 20 percent of males). Compared with official data, then, these self-report results demonstrate a somewhat greater similarity in the types of delinquent acts committed by males and females. But Hindelang et al. (1979) have argued that sex differences found in self-report studies are highly contingent upon the content of the specific items asked. They concluded that once the typically limited seriousness of these items is taken into account, apparent discrepancies between self-report and official data prove to be illusory; they don't measure the same domain of behaviour.

These official statistics and self-report studies are static and don't give any indication of historical trends. For instance, it is *possible* that sex differences in crime have varied over the years such that at certain times females may have approached equality with males in a broad spectrum of offences. In fact, some criminologists have argued that a new female criminal has arisen in recent years (Adler, 1975). Not only has the participation of women in crime increased, but they have moved into areas of lawbreaking that were formerly the exclusive domain of men. The data on trends through time in the criminality of men and women should be considered, then, to see whether the gap between them has expanded and/or narrowed over the years.

The Uniform Crime Reports for the United States (Federal Bureau of Investigation, 1989) show that between 1979 and 1988 arrests of males increased by 18.9 percent while female arrests increased 37.4 percent. Arrests of males for violent crime increased 23.1 percent and for property crime 8.4 percent, while female arrests for violent crime jumped 41.5 percent, with female arrests for property crime climbing by 22.3 percent. Table 4.2 presents the rates of adults charged in Canada, by sex, for the years 1968, 1978, and 1988. Over the twenty years, the rate for all Criminal Code offences for males increased by 88 percent while for females the increase was 261 percent. Females increased from 9 percent to 17 percent of adults charged with Criminal Code offences. For violent crime, the rate at which males were charged increased by 142 percent and for females 365 percent. For property crime, the increase for males was 78 percent and for females 316 percent. So, the increases for females have greatly exceeded those for males over this recent twenty-year period. However, a quick glance down the two columns of rates for 1988 will reveal that large absolute differences remain, with the male rates greatly exceeding those for females. Furthermore, 86 percent of the increase between 1968 and 1988 in the number of females charged with Criminal Code offences was for nonviolent offences. In 1968 only 10 percent of all women charged were charged for violent crimes, while 52 percent were charged for property crimes. By 1988 women charged for violence had increased to 13 percent of all women charged, while 60 percent were now charged with property crime.

TABLE 4.2
RATE OF ADULTS CHARGED[1] BY SEX PER 100 000 POPULATION[2]
FOR SELECTED CRIMINAL CODE OFFENCES,
1968, 1978, 1988, CANADA

	1968		1978		1988	
	M	F	M	F	M	F
Homicide	2.4	0.3	4.4	0.7	3.2	0.5
Robbery	26.6	1.6	49.7	3.6	42.6	4.1
Crimes of Violence	270.5	15.0	372.6	34.8	653.3	69.8
Break and Enter	157.6	3.4	308.3	12.9	279.2	12.9
Theft over[3]	82.4	8.5	77.2	11.3	43.1	7.8
Theft under[4]	175.0	49.7	369.5	186.8	438.8	215.3
Frauds	105.0	12.8	177.8	53.8	215.1	76.0
Property Crimes	639.7	79.2	1120.3	281.5	1140.5	329.1
Criminal Code	1443.4	152.0	2375.0	415.0	2714.8	549.4

[1] Source: 1968 – Dominion Bureau of Statistics. (1969). *Crime Statistics.* Ottawa: Queen's Printer. 1978 – Statistics Canada. (1980). *Crime and Traffic Enforcement Statistics.* Ottawa: Minister of Supply and Services. 1988 – Statistics Canada. (1989). *Canadian Crime Statistics.* Ottawa: Minister of Supply and Services.

[2] Sources of population estimates: 1968 – Dominion Bureau of Statistics. (1970). *Estimates of Population by Marital Status, Age and Sex, Canada and Provinces 1968.* Ottawa: Dominion Bureau of Statistics. 1978 – Statistics Canada. (1980). *Estimates of Population by Marital Status, Age and Sex for Canada and the Provinces, June 1, 1977 and 1978.* Ottawa: Minister of Supply and Services. 1988 – Statistics Canada. (1988). *Postcensal Annual Estimates of Population by Marital Status, Age, Sex and Components of Growth for Canada, Provinces and Territories, June 1, 1988.* Ottawa: Minister of Supply and Services.
1968 males = 10 409 900; females = 10 334 100
1978 males = 11 674 100; females = 11 808 500
1988 males = 12 784 600; females = 13 138 700

[3] 1968 – Theft over $50; 1978 – Theft over $200; 1988 – Theft over $1000.

[4] 1968 – Theft $50 and under; 1978 – Theft $200 and under; 1988 – Theft $1000 and under.

A number of researchers have examined and attempted to interpret trends in male and female contribution to crime. Rita Simon (1975) was one of the earliest contributors to this literature with her examination of U.S. arrest data over some twenty years. She concluded that the pattern of male and female criminality was fairly stable from 1953 to 1972, with the major exception being a substantial increase in the proportion of female arrests for theft, forgery, fraud, and embezzlement. The proportion of females arrested for violent crime hadn't increased over these years, nor had their arrests for the traditional female crimes, such as prostitution and child abuse. Overall, by 1972, 1 in 6.5 arrests were of women; they accounted for 30 percent of arrests for larceny, fraud, and embezzlement, and 25 percent of arrests for forgery. Larceny (theft) went from 1 female in every 7 arrests in 1953 to 1 in every 3 by 1972. However, women still constituted only 15.3 percent of all arrests in 1972, up from 10.8 percent in 1953. Simon interpreted these crime trends as a reflection of the movement toward greater sexual equality, particularly via increased female labour force participation, which offers women greater opportunities as well as increased pressures for criminal behaviour.

Hagan (1985), drawing upon data from Steffensmeier (1978), calculated that in the United States the ratio of male to female arrest rates for a property crime index declined from 9.43 to 1 in 1960 to only 3.93 to 1 by 1975. A similar decline in the sex ratio occurred for a number of specific property crime rates. Steffensmeier (1978) concluded that the largest increase occurred in female arrests for larceny/theft and that *relative* to males, female property crime rates have increased. However, he also emphasized that since the female base rate, or starting point, is so low, small absolute changes get magnified into large percentage gains when, in fact, the *absolute* differences between male and female crime rates have generally increased and remain substantial. Steffensmeier et al. (1979) also examined trends in violent crime and found that although the level of female violence had increased, so had the male rate such that the relative difference between the sexes remained about the same from 1960 to 1977. However, the absolute gap widened for each violent offence so that violent crime remained overwhelmingly a male phenomenon.

There have been some similar investigations of male-female differences in crime trends in Canada. The report of the Canadian Committee on Corrections (1969) showed that during the 1950s the ratio of male to female offenders fluctuated between 13 to 1 and 17 to 1. However, from 1960 to 1966 the male-female ratio decreased steadily to 7 to 1 (in 1966), primarily because of an 80 percent increase in the female conviction rate for theft. Similarly, the sex ratio for charges for theft under $50 went from about 8 to 1 in 1960 to 3 to 1 by 1966. Giffen (1976) calculated the sex ratio of persons convicted of indictable offences for the years 1956 and 1966 and found that the ratio of male to female rates was 16 to 1 in 1956 and 7 to 1 in 1966, "showing a considerable but rapidly declining male superiority in getting into trouble with the law" (1976). The female rate increased 293 percent while the male rate rose only 28 percent. Yet the rate for both sexes combined increased only 36 percent, which is due to the much higher male rates (482 and 615) compared to female rates (30 and 88) for 1956 and 1966 respectively. There are interesting differences by age between the sexes. For males, the greatest increase in rates was among the younger age categories, while a high rate of increase was found at all ages for women. But again, a large part of the increase in *total* rates between 1956 and 1966 was due to the high-risk younger men. Similar to the U.S. research reported was Giffen's finding that men were much more likely than women to be convicted of violent crimes and that simple theft accounted for a majority of female convictions and for most of the increase in their total conviction rate.

Tepperman (1977) examined longer-term trends in the conviction rates of males and females in Canada (see Figure 4.2). These rates show some convergence in recent years, similar to the convergence observed during the two world wars of this century. Tepperman suggested that the pressures toward sexual equality of recent years are similar to those experienced during the world wars and that these pressures exerted an influence toward equalization of conviction rates. However, variation in the scale used for the rates in Figure 4.2 makes more precise comparison unwise.

Fisher (1986) has replicated Steffensmeier's U.S. research with Canadian data on trends in persons charged by sex between 1962 and 1978. Similar to Steffensmeier's conclusions, she found a narrowing of the relative gap between males and females in property crime charge rates, with the greatest increases in the rate at which females are charged with petty property crime—the crimes with which women have traditionally been associated. However, the absolute gap widened for all property crimes except theft over

---

FIGURE 4.2
RATES OF CONVICTION FOR INDICTABLE OFFENCES PER 100 000 PERSONS AGED 16 AND OVER, BY SEX, CANADA, 1891–1971

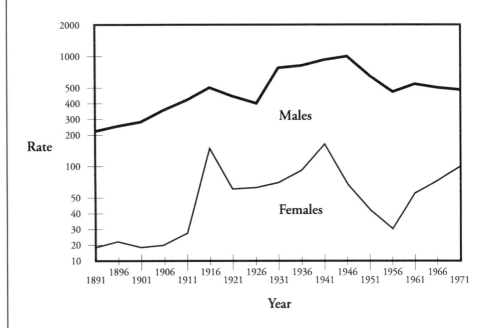

Source: L. Tepperman. (1977). *Crime Control.* McGraw-Hill Ryerson.

$200, such that female property crime levels continue to lag behind those of males, despite large increases in the rate at which females are charged for property crime. The relative gap between the sexes in violent crime remained about the same while the absolute gap widened. Violent crime remains predominantly the domain of males. Fisher also documented the much lower base rates (1962) for females. Therefore, large percentage increases can easily result from relatively small absolute increases in female crime. Fisher's Canadian results are generally quite comparable to those of Steffensmeier for the United States, though the Canadian crime rates for both men and women are lower, particularly for violent crime.

Conclusions about trends in female crime that are based on official data sources, such as arrest rates or charge rates, are vulnerable to the claim that such official data reflect changes in the response to female crime by the criminal justice system as much as or more than they do real changes in criminal behaviour. Therefore, it would be desirable to have trend data from alternative sources, such as self-report research. But self-report data are generally very time-bound, having been conducted in a particular location at a given point in time, and are, therefore, limited in their usefulness for examining trends in crime. However, Smith and Visher (1980) analyzed 44 different self-report and official data studies that reported on the relationship between sex and deviance and found that the year the data were gathered was an important factor in explaining the magnitude of the sex-deviant behaviour correlation. They found that this correlation has been decreasing in size over time—meaning less gender disparity in deviant behaviour—and has declined more rapidly according to self-report studies than to research based on official sources of data. This narrowing of the gap is mainly for minor acts of deviance rather than for serious criminal behaviour, and more for youths than for adults. There was also some indication of increased rates of female delinquency in Canada in the 1970s in the previously discussed self-report research of Gomme et al. (1984), since the sex ratio for comparable offences was 1.34 to 1, smaller than the ratio of 1.67 to 1 reported by Linden and Fillmore (1981) for Edmonton in 1965.

These various data on sex differences and crime trends lead to the conclusion that sex, like age, remains strongly correlated with criminal behaviour. Males are much more involved in criminal acts than females. However, women have increased their rate of participation in the less serious forms of property crime, particularly small thefts and fraud, with which women have been associated in the past through shoplifting and credit fraud.

ROLE CONVERGENCE?

Criminologists have offered various explanations for the sex difference in criminal involvement, as well as for the changes in female participation in crime through time. Early theories of female criminality emphasized biological and psychological factors (Smart, 1976). Some claimed that sex differences in criminality were illusory and resulted from the greater cunning and deceitfulness of women, as well as from their preferential treatment by the police and the courts (Pollak, 1950). More recently, greater emphasis has been placed on the importance of socially structured differences in gender roles. This line of reasoning argues that males and females are subjected to differing expectations and demands regarding appropriate behaviour, as well as being subject to different mechanisms of social control. Boys are socialized to greater independence and risk taking and are, therefore, freer to experiment with deviant conduct (Hagan et al., 1979). Girls, on the other hand, are rewarded for compliance and dependence and so have fewer opportunities to experiment with delinquency. The traditional division of labour between the sexes, with women facing greater restriction to the private sphere in the domestic roles of wife and mother, further limited women's opportunities to engage in many forms of criminal conduct. The more public role of men, on the other hand, not only provided more opportunities for certain crimes, it also exposed them, to a much greater extent, to the formal social controls of the criminal justice system (Hagan et al., 1979).

Changes in gender role expectations should have consequences on the actual behaviour of males and females, including their criminal behaviour. More specifically, the convergence hypothesis suggests that as the social roles of the sexes become more equal or begin to converge, differences in their criminal behaviour should diminish (Nettler, 1984; Fox and Hartnagel, 1979). In one version of this thesis, Simon (1975) suggested that recent increases in property crimes committed by women could be attributed to the expansion of employment opportunities for women. This apparent emancipation of women from domestic roles may bring with it increased opportunities to commit property crime as well as subjecting women to greater pressures for achievement, which may create pressures or strains toward crime (Merton, 1938). Fox and Hartnagel (1979) tested the role convergence hypothesis by examining the relationship between changes in the Canadian conviction rate for females from 1931 to 1968 and three measures of women's changing gender role. Women's participation in the labour force over these same years and the rate at which females were granted postsecondary degrees were used as measures of the convergence of gender roles, while the total fertility rate indicated the degree of persistence of women's domestic role. The convergence hypothesis was generally supported by this analysis, particularly for the female conviction rate for theft. As the female labour force participation rate and the rate at which females were granted postsecondary degrees increased and the fertility rate declined, the female conviction rate for theft increased. However, the authors note that they were unable to introduce measures to control for an alternative hypothesis. Changes in the treatment of females by the police or courts may better account for any changes in the female conviction rate. Less preferential treatment for women by the criminal justice system could explain rising female crime rates.

Other criminologists have questioned the role convergence hypothesis. Steffensmeier (1980), for example, has argued that most of the increase in female property crime is for the traditional female crimes of petty theft and fraud. These crimes are more related to the traditional female domestic roles of shopper and consumer. He questioned the degree to which gender roles have really changed by pointing to women's restricted labour market participation. Most women work in jobs with limited access to illegitimate opportunities. Furthermore, women still have primary responsibility for home and childcare. "Female experiences are not moving beyond traditional roles, either legitimate or illegitimate" (1980:1102). As Holly Johnson (1987) has reminded us, the high proportion of women offenders charged with theft or fraud (54 percent of all Criminal Code charges against women in 1988) is consistent with women's traditional role as consumers and, increasingly, as low-income, semi-skilled, single parents. Further, Box and Hale (1984) have argued that the role convergence hypothesis should logically imply that female emancipation should lead to a reduction in the formerly female-dominated crimes such as shoplifting. They found some limited evidence in their British data that deteriorating economic conditions experienced by women, rather than female emancipation, were related to increases in female crime. Also, an admittedly weak measure of change in the treatment received by women from the police had a significant impact on female conviction rates. Further research on this topic should include attention to possible changes in the way the criminal justice system processes women.

RACE
OVERREPRESENTATION OF CANADIAN NATIVE PEOPLE IN THE CRIMINAL JUSTICE SYSTEM

Overrepresentation of Native people in the Canadian criminal justice system is widely recognized (LaPrairie, 1983). A survey, *Indian Conditions*, carried out by the Ministry of Indian Affairs and Northern Development (1980) points out that while Canadian Indians and other Natives are estimated to constitute 3 to 3.5 percent of the total population of Canada, they represent about 9 percent of the penitentiary population nationally, and upwards of 40 percent of the jail and penitentiary population in the Prairies and the North. Figure 4.3 shows the distribution of Natives as a percentage of Provincial populations and as a percentage of inmates of federal penitentiaries and provincial correctional institutions for 1971. Clearly, overrepresentation of Natives in prisons is widespread. This overrepresentation is particularly characteristic of British Columbia, the Prairie provinces, and the North. For Saskatchewan, Hylton (1982) found that male treaty Indians over fifteen were 37 times more likely and male nonstatus Indians were 12 times more likely to be admitted to a provincial correctional centre in 1976–77 than male non-Natives of comparable age. The corresponding figures for Native females were 131 times and 28 times more likely. For those same years, 64 percent of all male admissions and 85 percent of all female admissions were of Indian ancestry. In Alberta, Hagan (1974) reported that offenders of Native background were incarcerated at a rate in excess of 4 times their representation in

FIGURE 4.3
NATIVES IN PRISON, 1971

Natives as % of Provincial Population

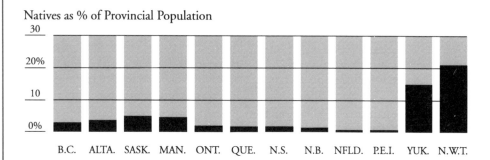

Natives as % of Prison Population

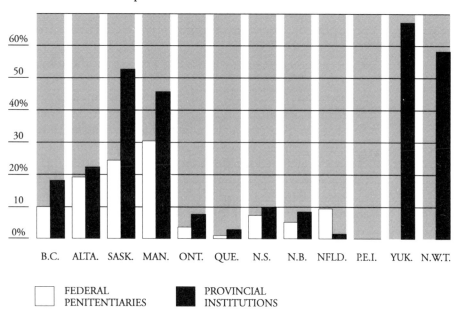

Source: Indian Conditions, 1980. Minister of Indian Affairs and Northern Development,
        Catalogue No. R32-45/1980E.

the general population. In 1981, Natives made up only 2 percent of Ontario's
population but accounted for 8 percent of the total male admissions and 17
percent of the total female admissions to the correctional system (Jolly, 1982).
These prison data probably underestimate the extent of Native overrepresentation (Task Force on Aboriginal Peoples in Federal Corrections, 1989).
There is only limited evidence, however, concerning the overrepresentation

of Natives at the earlier stage of arrest (Bienvenue and Latif, 1974), with Indians having a greater involvement in the more minor types of crime, particularly liquor violations.

Data presented by Havemann et al. (1985) reveal the persistence of Native overrepresentation throughout the decade of the 1970s. By 1988–89, Native offenders accounted for approximately 19 percent of all sentenced admissions to provincial correctional institutions and 13 percent of warrant of committal admissions to federal custody, up from 15 percent and 9 percent, respectively, in 1982–83 (Statistics Canada, 1989). A report from the Solicitor General Canada (1988) found that the overrepresentation of Natives in federal institutions in the Prairie region increased from 27.6 percent in 1980 to 32.2 percent in 1987, and in the Pacific region from 9.4 percent to 12.2 percent. The recent report of the Task Force on Aboriginal Peoples in Federal Corrections (1989) concluded that the rate of growth of the Native offender population has exceeded that of the general inmate population since at least 1982–83.

In a recent survey (Correctional Service of Canada, 1985) of the Native population in federal institutions —which contain inmates convicted of more serious offences—the largest percentage of Native inmates was doing time for robbery as their major offence (22 percent), followed by break and enter (16 percent), assault (15 percent), manslaughter (12 percent), and murder (11 percent). But Mikel (1979/80) reported that for federal institutions the types of offences committed by Native inmates differed only slightly from those of non-natives. Assault, theft, and homicide were more frequent for Natives. The Law Reform Commission report, *The Native Offender and the Law* (1974), concluded that Native offenders in provincial institutions were usually involved in less serious crimes than non-Native offenders, with many incarcerated for violations of provincial and municipal statutes, such as liquor and vehicles legislation. In fact, the Commission found that a large number of Native offenders are sent to jail for nonpayment of fines. In 1970/71, 57.4 percent of all Natives admitted to Saskatchewan jails—one-third of all admissions—were admitted for nonpayment of fines. The Commission also concluded that federal (Criminal Code) offences committed by Native offenders are more likely to be offences against the person; that Native women constitute a much greater proportion of the female prison population than do Native men of the male prison population; and that directly or indirectly, much, if not most, Native crime is associated with the use of alcohol.

Hagan (1985b), using data from a survey of offenders admitted to Ontario correctional institutions during 1979 and 1980, also discovered variation in the overrepresentation of Natives for specific offences and variation between the sexes. The total Native crime rate for those years was 4.5 times the non-Native rate. But crimes against persons and property were more than 3 times the non-Native rate, while alcohol offences were 16 times greater. He also found that the ratio of Native to non-Native crime rates was greater among women than among men and that the Native crime rates peak later (ages 25 to 35) than do the non-Native rates (ages 19 to 24). With increasing age, the differences between Native and non-Native crime rates increased faster for women. Therefore, older Native women are particularly overrepresented, which Hagan suggested reflects their extremely disadvantaged position in Canadian society.

EXPLANATIONS OF NATIVE OVERREPRESENTATION

There is disagreement among criminologists on the causes of this overrepresentation of Native people in the Canadian criminal justice system. LaPrairie (1983) has identified three possible explanations: the offenders' behaviour, namely that Natives commit a disproportionate amount of criminal acts and/or commit serious acts to which the public and the criminal justice system are more likely to respond; intentional or unintentional discrimination against Native people by agents of the criminal justice system; and social inequality and segmentation among groups in society. This third explanation encompasses both of the previous ones by seeing both higher crime rates and criminal justice system discrimination as reflections of these fundamental cleavages in society.

Verdun-Jones and Muirhead (1979/80) distinguish further between the cultural and structural explanations. The former emphasizes the lack of certain traits in Native culture that are valued by the dominant white culture. This creates barriers to the assimilation of Native people into the dominant culture. James (1979), while claiming that the core values of Native and white cultures may be essentially the same, argues that there is conflict in the ways in which these values are expressed behaviourally in society. "Native values are placed under stress by the pressures of expressing them acceptably in a complex urban society" (1979:455). For example, James suggests that the sharing of material possessions among Natives implies a potentially reciprocal action rather than a permanent transfer of ownership. However, when such sharing of belongings is practised without permission in the dominant culture, it is called theft. The Native Counselling Services of Alberta (1982) has identified a number of areas of conflict between Native and non-Native cultures related to the legal system, and has suggested that many Native people have only a limited understanding of the dominant Canadian legal and justice system. So, cultural explanations emphasize conflicting values. The overrepresentation of Natives results from the imposition of a somewhat alien set of values and rules on Native culture, as well as from the higher rate of commission by Natives of acts called crime by Canadian law but regarded as normative or expected behaviour in the context of Native culture.

Structural explanations of Native overrepresentation emphasize the economically and socially dependent position of Natives in Canadian society. Thus, Hylton (1982) claims that the overrepresentation of Native people is a symptom of the underlying social and economic inequality of Canadian society, while LaPrairie (1983) states that the suggestion of a link between the living conditions of Natives and their overrepresentation in the criminal justice system is compelling. She views overrepresentation as an effect of structural disadvantage. She documents examples of such disadvantage with comparisons between Natives and non-Natives in federal penitentiaries. Only 12 percent of Native inmates compared to 26 percent of non-Native inmates had more than a grade nine education; 31 percent of Native inmates but only 19 percent of non-Native inmates had either no education or education of only grade six or less. The Métis and Non-status Indian Crime and Justice Commission report (1978) also attributed the high rate of Native imprisonment to their deprived social situation, illustrated by the report's findings from a survey of Native inmates in federal penitentiaries. Fifty-seven percent of the inmates said they were unemployed at the time of their offence; 49 percent had spent time in skid row areas of cities; and 49 percent had less than a grade nine education. More recently, the final report of the Task Force on Aboriginal Peoples in Federal Corrections (1989) concluded that any reduction in Native crime must address the correlated socio-economic conditions among Natives which, compared to other Canadians, are discouraging. Generally, Natives continue to have a lower average level of education, fewer marketable skills, a higher rate of unemployment, an infant mortality rate twice the national rate, a higher degree of family instability, and a rate of violent death three times the national average. Native inmates, then, are even more disadvantaged in some respects than other inmates.

Verdun-Jones and Muirhead (1979/80), moreover, argue that the structurally deprived position of Natives in contemporary Canadian society is rooted in a history of exploitation by the dominant white society through what was, in essence, a colonial system based on the fur trade. From this perspective, the criminal justice system functions today primarily to control subjugated groups such as Natives—to keep them in their dominated, powerless position—in order to protect the interests of the dominant, powerful segment of society. This dominant segment of society is comprised of the white majority generally and, more particularly, its leading, economically powerful segments. The criminal justice system, and the state generally, is seen by these authors as an agent of the economically powerful who control the underclasses. The criminal justice system mirrors the socio-economic organization and operation of society. Hence, overrepresentation of Natives within the criminal justice system is merely a reproduction of the basic socio-economic inequalities present in the surrounding society. Furthermore, the criminal justice system functions to support and maintain that structure of inequality. Structural explanations, then, regard higher Native crime rates as a product of the social and economic oppression of Natives by the dominant white society. The majority of Natives are kept poor and dependent and this breeds crime, violence, and other social disorders to which the criminal justice system responds, thereby furthering Natives' exploitation by the existing system of inequality.

Some criminologists have suggested that criminal justice system agents actively discriminate against Native people and other minorities in their discretionary enforcement of the criminal law. Such "biased discretion"

(Havemann et al., 1985) or selective enforcement would, then, help account for the observed overrepresentation of Natives in the criminal justice system. Several Canadian research studies that investigated this hypothesis of differential treatment by the criminal justice system included race as a variable in their analysis. The most relevant of these studies for the present discussion is no doubt Hagan's (1974) research in five Alberta correctional institutions. He examined the sentences received by Indian and Métis inmates, who were represented at least four times as often among newly incarcerated offenders as among the general population. Hagan discovered that Natives were primarily charged with minor offences and, as a result, received shorter sentences. Incarceration resulting from failure to pay a fine was nearly twice as common for Natives as for non-Natives. Almost two-thirds of Native inmates were serving sentences resulting from such default. Race, therefore, played no *direct* role in influencing the overrepresentation of Natives in these institutions. The sentences imposed conformed to legal requirements and reflected the disproportionate involvement of Natives in minor offences, particularly involving alcohol abuse, for which they received a fine. It was a subsequent failure to pay this fine, which could, of course, reflect their disadvantaged socio-economic circumstances, that in turn produced a good deal of the Native overrepresentation in these Alberta institutions. In a subsequent analysis, Hagan (1977) found that Indians were more likely to be sent to jail in default of fine payments in rural than in urban Alberta communities, a finding he attributed to the trend toward greater uniformity of treatment in the more bureaucratic urban criminal justice system.

Several other studies have examined the hypothesis of selective enforcement against Native people in different parts of the criminal justice system. Hagan (1977), for example, found that probation officers in rural jurisdictions in Alberta were more likely to recommend more severe sentences for Native offenders in their pre-sentence reports, without the justification of legally relevant considerations such as prior record, seriousness of offence, or number of charges. But Boldt et al. (1983) found no racial effect on pre-sentence recommendations in the Yukon. In general, Hagan (1975a, 1975b) failed to discover evidence of differential treatment due to race itself in pre-sentence recommendations or sentencing, though probation officers took a dimmer view of Native defendants' prospects for success on probation which, in turn, affected their sentence recommendations and the final disposition of the case by the judge. But judges characterized by Hagan as less concerned about the maintenance of a conservative notion of "law and order" used part of their discretion to sentence Native defendants more *leniently* (Hagan, 1975c). Research on parole decision making by Demers (1978) supported Hagan's conclusion that Native candidates were less likely to receive favourable recommendations from parole officers. This was probably due to a variety of factors, but indirectly produced racial inequality in parole release decisions made by the Parole Board, which is dependent upon parole officers for information and advice. Wynne and Hartnagel (1975) found evidence from a study of Crown prosecutors' files that Natives were less likely than whites to successfully engage in plea bargaining, though this depended upon certain conditions, such as being represented by defence counsel and the presence of repetitious counts and/or multiple charges in the indictment. Unfortunately, there is little evidence on how the police exercise their discretion with respect to Native people. It has been suggested that in cities Native people may tend to attract police attention by their physical appearance and/or location in the run-down, skid row areas (Canadian Corrections Association, 1967). Natives may have a greater public visibility, particularly when drinking, and this may result in more frequent arrests (Bienvenue and Latif, 1974). Some criminologists (Giffen, 1966; Greenaway, 1980) have even argued that the police "find" crime where they look for it, at least with respect to public-order type offences such as public drunkenness. Therefore, police initiative and discretion in seeking out the poor and disadvantaged may be implicated to some extent in the higher frequency of Native arrests for certain types of crime. However, there is little evidence to support the claim that the agents of the criminal justice system actively and directly discriminate against Canadian Native people.

THE ROLE OF ALCOHOL

Alcohol abuse has had a severe impact on Native people. The survey *Indian Conditions* (1980) estimated that between 50 and 60 percent of Indian illnesses and deaths are alcohol related. Havemann et al. (1985) have reviewed a number of Canadian studies which identify alcohol as a major contributor to the crimes Native people commit. This contribution can be direct, through the violation of liquor laws, as well as indirect, as when other crimes are committed under the influence of alcohol. A survey of Native inmates in Ontario (Irvine, 1978) found that 38 percent had been convicted of specific alcohol offences, while 86 percent admitted that alcohol was involved in the crimes for which they were incarcerated. The survey of federal penitentiary inmates by the Métis and Non-status Indian Crime and Justice Commission (1978) found that only 10 percent of the Natives committed the major charge resulting in their imprisonment with no alcohol or drug involvement. Thirty percent had been taking both alcohol and drugs, while the greatest proportion (48 percent) committed their offence under the influence of alcohol alone. Hagan's (1974) study in Alberta correctional institutions discovered that 48 percent of the Indian and Métis offenders had drinking problems, compared to 25 percent of non-Native offenders. Bienvenue and Latif (1974) showed that Indians were most overrepresented in arrests for liquor violations. Finally, Finkler (1982) reported that alcohol was a factor in at least 63 percent of the offences for which inmates were admitted to Northwest Territories institutions from 1968 to 1980.

However, the link between alcohol abuse and Native criminality is not well understood or agreed upon. Some have suggested that heavy drinking has become a regular, normal occurrence within some Native communities, associated with family and group activities and, therefore, accorded a good deal of tolerance (Brody, 1971; Jensen, Stauss, and Harris, 1977). Highly visible group drinking may be socially accepted and expected, without the development of corresponding informal social controls to regulate or limit the extent of such drinking. An additional possibility is that alcohol abuse and its associated criminal consequences may be a response to, or reaction against, the poverty and deprivation experienced by so many Native people. Alcohol may provide some respite, however temporary, from their oppressive life circumstances, whether on reserves, in impoverished rural areas, or in the city slums. Havemann et al. (1985) expand on this argument by linking alcohol and involvement with the criminal justice system with the social impact of the underdevelopment of Native communities. They argue that alcohol is used as a means to modify moods and escape real-life situations; that it is a way for Native people to manage the alienation created by the destruction of their culture and the economic exploitation of their land and resources for the benefit of southern Canada and the corporate structure. Thus, these authors locate the use of alcohol by Native people and their consequent overrepresentation in the criminal justice system in the structure of socio-economic relations between Native people and the dominant white society, rather than in some disease model or other individualistic-type explanation which ends up blaming the victim.

This short review of what is currently known concerning the relationship of Canadian Native people to crime and the criminal justice system suggests that Canadian criminology needs to devote more of its research effort to this topic (LaPrairie, 1990). While it is clear that Native people are overrepresented in the criminal justice system, the reasons for such overrepresentation remain in doubt. Furthermore, little research has been done in Canada on the ways in which crime may be produced by the relations between indigenous Native society and culture and the dominant white society and its culture.

SOCIAL CLASS

CONFLICTING EVIDENCE?

Few issues have been in greater dispute among criminologists in recent years than the correlation between social class and criminal behaviour. Thus, Gordon (1976), for example, regards the crime or delinquency relationship with socio-economic status as one of the most thoroughly documented, while Tittle and Villemez (1977) conclude that the purported relationship between class and criminality is problematic; Tittle et al. (1978) refer to such a relationship as a myth. Hindelang et al. (1979) state that illusions of discrepancies in the research evidence abound, while Braithwaite (1981) concludes from his review of over 100 studies that class is one of the very few correlates of criminality which is persuasively supported by a large body of empirical evidence. Clearly, this is a controversial question among criminologists and there are disagreements over what the research literature reveals.

Official data appear to support an inverse or negative relationship. Those arrested, convicted and/or incarcerated are more likely to come from lower socio-economic categories of the population as indexed by such variables as income, education, or occupational status. Tittle and Villemez (1977) report that of the 23 studies on this relationship they could locate that used official police or court data, 65 percent found a negative relationship, while another 8 percent detected class variation in crime but only for some subcategories of individuals. Twenty-six percent of these studies found no consistent class variation. Of course, these official records may underestimate the amount of crime committed by those in the higher socio-economic positions. Nettler (1984) states that official statistics on serious crimes from a variety of countries show that people with less money, lower occupational status, and less schooling are disproportionately represented. But it could be immediately asked: what qualifies as a serious crime? Some would argue that bank embezzlement, for example, is at least as serious as bank robbery or that corporate crimes are more seriously harmful than many of the crimes typically committed by lower-class individuals.

Additional evidence, using official crime statistics, on the class-crime relationship comes from the long history of research on poverty, economic inequality, and crime. While the argument that crime is one of a number of undesirable consequences of poverty can be traced far back into antiquity, the first empirical research examining the relationship between poverty and crime can be found in the mid-19th century work of Guerry and of Quetelet in Europe (Vold and Bernard, 1986). Anticipating later developments, this early work showed that wealthier provinces had higher property crime rates and suggested that the greater opportunities for theft and other property offences offered by these wealthier regions might explain this unexpected pattern. Quetelet also suggested that great inequality between wealth and poverty in the same place, rather than absolute poverty, might be a critical factor. While poverty refers to the lack of that level of income necessary for mere survival, economic inequality signifies the size of the income gap between those who have the least income and those who have the most income (Vold and Bernard, 1986).

Since this early research, criminologists have continued to analyze and interpret various data relating economic conditions and crime at different levels of ecological aggregation ranging from city neighbourhoods to nation states. Summarizing this large body of research is complicated by this variation in the unit of analysis, as well as by such factors as varying measurement of poverty and inequality, the inclusion of a variety of crime types, and the use of differing sets of control variables. However, there appears to be some consensus that the degree of economic inequality rather than the amount of poverty is the more important variable (Braithwaite, 1979; Box, 1987; Vold and Bernard, 1986). More specifically, nations with greater economic inequality have higher homicide rates, particularly under conditions of political democracy (Krahn et al., 1986). Cross-national comparisons of property crime rates are more inconsistent, perhaps as a result of the effect of varying opportunities for property crime in different nations (Stack, 1984). Economic inequality and crime rates, with the possible exception of homicide, are fairly strongly and consistently related in studies of U.S. cities and Standard Metropolitan Statistical Areas, but less so at the level of states. So this body of work suggests that the degree of contrast between economic classes—poverty amidst affluence—is more strongly correlated with rates of crime than the proportion of the population in the poorest class.

Evidence from self-report research seems to challenge this conclusion of a negative relationship between class and criminal behaviour. It was Short and Nye's (1957) use of the self-report measurement of delinquency which stimulated much of the later debate concerning the class and delinquency correlation, since they reported no relationship between self-reports of delinquency and parental socio-economic status. However, they did find a moderately strong relation between social class and incarceration in a training school. Fifty percent of the institutionalized boys studied came from the lowest socio-economic status category, compared to only 13 percent of the high school boys. But Hindelang et al. (1979) have shown how Short and Nye overestimated the strength of the relationship between official delinquency and socio-economic status, since the institutionalized boys did not constitute a representative sample. Tittle and Villemez's (1977) review of 26 studies using the self-report technique to investigate the class and crime relationship found that 50 percent reported no significant relationship.

Their own self-report study among adults showed social class to be largely unrelated to criminality, though this conclusion is limited by the fact that they only inquired about six criminal acts with a restricted range of seriousness. Tittle et al. (1978) examined 35 studies where the relationship between a measure of individual class position and a measure of crime or delinquency was reported and found, on average, only a very slight, negative correlation (–.09). Moreover, this conclusion didn't appear to vary in the presence of different conditions such as type of offence, age, sex, or race, the specific indicator of socio-economic status used, and so forth. The two exceptions to this, however, were type of data (official or self-report) and the decade in which the study was conducted. Tittle et al. (1978) claim that studies using official data show a more marked negative correlation (average of –.25) than do those based upon self-report data (–.06). They argue that the average correlation between class and crime or delinquency showed a steady decline in strength from the 1940s (–.73) to the 1970s (–.03), a trend they believe is largely the result of a decline in the relationship between class and official measures of crime, since the correlation for self-report measures remained relatively constant and low. However, others (Clelland and Carter, 1980) have pointed out that none of the 1970s research reviewed by Tittle et al. (1978) involved adults. In fact, prior to the 1970s, only six studies of adult crime and social class were included in their review. In any event, Tittle et al. interpret these findings as a reflection of changes in the way in which criminal justice agencies deal with members of the various social classes. Their interpretation implies that the true correlation between class and crime "has remained consistently near zero and has only appeared to be greater because official data reflected biases in the law enforcement process which have now been ameliorated" (1978:652). Of course, any number of researchers have attempted to account for the apparent discrepancy between self-report versus official measures of delinquency in their relationship to socio-economic status by examining the hypothesis of official discrimination against lower-class adolescents in the enforcement of the law (see Nettler, 1984 for a review of many of these studies). However, once legally relevant factors such as serious-ness of the offence and prior record of the suspect or accused are taken into account, the evidence for such class bias in law enforcement is weak and is, therefore, unlikely to substantially affect the official statistics.

Two more recent studies that used the self-report technique found a negative relationship between class and crime, once certain refinements in measurement and analysis were introduced. Elliott and Ageton's (1980) research, which involved a national sample with a fairly large number of respondents, and a self-report measure covering the full range of delinquent and criminal acts with a true measure of frequency, discovered class differ-ences on an overall delinquency scale as well as for predatory crimes against persons, but not for other types of offences. Lower-class respondents reported close to four times as many predatory crimes against persons (for example, assault and robbery) as did middle-class respondents. But these differences are largely the result of the high-frequency offenders. Lower-class youth are found disproportionately among high-frequency offenders; they reported more than one-and-a-half times as many offences overall as middle-class youth in the high-frequency category, and nearly three times as many predatory crimes against persons. So, Elliott and Ageton seem to have demonstrated a behavioural basis for the class differences observed in the official data, since the more frequent and serious offenders are more likely to be arrested and the class differences in self-reported delinquency are greater at the high end of the frequency continuum and for serious, predatory crimes. The second study, by Thornberry and Farnworth (1982), followed a sample of respondents from early adolescence to young adulthood. They collected information on both self-reported and official criminal involvement, along with several measures of the social status of both the respondents and their families of origin. Both the self-report and official measures of delinquency were only weakly related to social status, while a strong inverse relationship between status and crime was found for adults, particularly blacks, with both measures. The strongest relationship between status and crime occurred when official measures were used. Furthermore, different measures of status produced different results. Educational attainment of the respondents and their job instability, rather than their occupation or income, were the status dimensions most related to criminality. Thornberry and Farnworth suggest that the relatively weak correlation between status and crime in much of the previous research may have resulted from focusing upon occupational position as the measure of status and from failing to focus separately upon adult blacks, the subcategory for which the relationship is strongest. These two studies, then, support the conclusion of a negative correlation between social class and crime under certain conditions, specifically for more serious offences and among more frequent and adult offenders, particularly those most disadvantaged educationally, racially (blacks), and in terms of employment status. However, Tittle and Meier (1990) concluded from a review of recent evidence concerning twelve hypothesized specifying conditions that a class/delinquency relationship that varies under certain conditions cannot be sustained.

There is comparatively little Canadian research on the class and crime relationship. The studies that do exist illustrate some of the same problems and apparently conflicting conclusions as discussed. Bell-Rowbotham and Boydell (1972) looked at the official data concerning the characteristics of persons convicted of indictable offences and found both educational and occupational status related to such convictions. Those with no schooling had much higher rates of conviction for virtually all of the more serious offences, while those with some education beyond high school had the lowest rates, except for homicide. However, there are some crimes—fraud is an example (Giffen, 1965)—for which those with more education had the highest rates, probably as a result of the opportunities available to those with white-collar occupations. But to the extent that educational attainment can be taken as a measure of socio-economic status, these data generally support the negative correlation between class and crime. Similarly, Bell-Rowbotham and Boydell (1972) also conclude that the lower-status occupational groups tend to have the highest conviction rates, though they caution that there is a significant amount of information missing from these data. West (1984) has also noted that a study by Byles in Toronto found that working-class juveniles were five times more likely to be arrested than middle-class juveniles and that about 90 percent of Ontario training school inmates were from working-class backgrounds. West goes on to argue that, although official delinquency is largely a working-class phenomenon, officially defined delinquents are not representative of all those who commit delinquencies.

Canadian self-report studies raise the same issues as the U.S. studies discussed. In an early study, Vaz (1966) collected data from boys in five high schools in four different communities, the largest with a population of only 100 000. The boys were asked to report on a limited set of delinquent acts (robbery, rape, and gang fighting, for example, were not included) and it is doubtful, as Vaz himself states, that the lower–socio-economic–status boys were representative, since they came from schools in middle-class neighbourhoods. For the large majority of comparisons Vaz made, there were no significant differences in reported delinquency by socio-economic status. In fact, none of the delinquent acts were committed most frequently by these lower–socio-economic–status boys. Similarly, LeBlanc (1975) found no difference in the self-reported delinquency of adolescents from working-class areas compared to those from upper-class neighbourhoods, using a standard set of self-report delinquency items, even though adolescents from the working class neighbourhoods were more likely to be officially labelled as delinquent by the police. Gomme's (1985) analysis of self-reported delinquency among younger adolescents (grades seven to ten) in a small urban centre in southern Ontario found no direct relationship between socio-economic status, measured by father's occupation, and participation in delinquent behaviour. But in a study in New Brunswick, Tribble (1972) concluded that the higher the status of the father's occupation, the lower was the probability that the son would be involved in delinquency. Furthermore, among the delinquents, the higher the status the fewer the number of offences reported. None of these Canadian studies, however, compare with the best of the recent U.S. studies in terms of sample size, representativeness, and inclusion of a full range of delinquent or criminal acts comparable in seriousness to those found in the official statistics.

RECONCILING THE APPARENT CONFLICTS

There are several methodological and substantive issues in the research on class and crime which, once understood, should help clarify and, one hopes, reconcile the apparently conflicting conclusions of different studies. First of all, most of these studies of the relationship between class and crime are not very representative of the population at large, and this severely limits the degree to which one can generalize from them. Almost all of this research has focused upon juveniles rather than adults, and more specifically upon white male adolescents in small towns to medium-sized cities (Elliott and Ageton, 1980; Tittle et al., 1978). Poor adults in large cities—precisely those many criminologists would expect to have higher crime rates—have been very underrepresented in the research on socio-economic status and crime (Clelland and Carter, 1980). Recent research by Hagan and McCarthy (1990) has suggested that the use of self-report surveys administered for convenience to school populations has diverted attention from street youth who experience current class conditions that are more likely to cause serious delinquency.

Second, serious crime is a relatively rare event, so rare that the victimization surveys in the United States spend a large amount of money to draw a sample of the general population large enough to identify sufficient numbers of crime victims to make comparisons with the official data. The typically small sample sizes, restricted time frame, and crude measurement of frequency of crime commission in self-report studies make it extremely difficult to identify class differences in serious crime, given its low prevalence in the general or adolescent population (Hindelang et al., 1979).

Third, it is inappropriate to compare most self-reports with official data on crime, since they only rarely refer to the same domain of conduct (Hindelang et al., 1979). The usual set of self-report items is weighted in favour of less serious acts, particularly those trivial acts for which middle-class adolescents report higher prevalence (Elliott and Ageton, 1980). So, the typical self-report delinquency scale overlaps only in part with the crimes in official statistics, particularly those predatory, interpersonal crimes most often officially reported. Therefore, one should be cautious about generalizing from the failure to find class differences in the self-reports of the less serious forms of delinquency to *any* conclusion concerning predatory criminal acts by adults.

Fourth, it should be recognized that official statistics are limited and give only a partial picture of the class distribution of crime. In particular, official data are notorious for understating the frequency of certain crimes, some of which are characteristically committed with greater frequency by members of the middle class (for example, occupationally related theft) and representatives of the powerful segments of society (such as consumer fraud). So, official statistics distort the true relationship between class and crime, since the crimes of higher-status persons may be less visible (Nettler, 1984) and, therefore, less likely to come to the attention of the official agents of social control. And, of course, class position may also influence the likelihood of official intervention (Tittle and Villemez, 1977), particularly for those crimes more typically committed by those higher in status.

Criminologists have not paid sufficient attention to the many meanings and measures of class. Class position has most often been equated by criminologists with occupational status or prestige, at least for purposes of measurement. Class is thereby reduced to a handful of occupational categories, such as blue-collar, white-collar, or professional/managerial. These categories lump together some quite diverse positions in the labour market on questionable grounds, while at the same time excluding those not in the labour force, such as the unemployed. In much of the self-report research, only two classes are recognized: middle class and working class. Even these are usually measured only in terms of occupational status. This type of conceptualization and measurement ignores the definition of social class as a position in relation to the means of production, and at least implicitly downplays the significance of power in relation to class.

Some criminologists have questioned these conventions (Clelland and Carter, 1980) and others have proposed alternative conceptualizations. For example, Quinney (1977) argues for the adoption of a Marxist orientation with a focus upon the relative surplus population of a capitalist economy as the locus for much of the conventional personal and property crime. Those most marginal to the labour market—rather than those in less skilled occupations, with less education, or fewer financial resources—are, from this perspective, most at risk for turning to conventional, predatory crime. This is precisely the population segment typically ignored in criminological research on class and crime, partly because this segment is difficult for researchers to locate and survey (Clelland and Carter, 1980), and partly on account of the fuzzy thinking that has characterized much of the empirical research on this topic. Quinney also identifies a second category of crime in capitalist society: the crimes of domination. These include offences committed by members of the so-called ruling class, such as violations of human rights not currently defined as crimes, as well as illegal acts engaged in by government authorities and law enforcement officials. These crimes of domination most often go undetected and/or unpunished, and hence rarely appear in official statistics. Quinney, and others, argue that the negative correlation between class and crime found in such statistics only applies to the crimes of the underclass, or marginalized, segment of the population. So, class position may be related to crime in something of a curvilinear fashion—high crime at both the bottom and the top of the class hierarchy—depending on how one defines and measures both class position and criminal behaviour. In fact, Tittle et al. (1978) have gone so far as to suggest that it is *only* at the extremes of the class hierarchy that class is a significant factor in crime in a mass society with a mass culture such as that found in North America. It's a bit paradoxical, then, that these same authors conclude their paper by stating that criminology should shift away from class-based theories. Rather, what seem to be required "are class-based theories which explain why certain types of crime are perpetrated disproportionately by the powerless, while other forms of crime are almost exclusively the prerogative of the powerful" (Braithwaite, 1981:49).

SUMMARY

Correlates of crime are those phenomena that are associated with or related to criminal behaviour. Discovering a correlate of crime is only the first step in explaining it. The temptation to infer that a correlate of crime is necessarily a cause of it must be resisted.

Four correlates of crime were reviewed in this chapter: age, sex, race, and social class. Crime is strongly correlated with age and sex. Young males are disproportionately involved in criminal behaviour. Overall, age and crime are negatively correlated. Crime decreases with increasing age. However, the shape of this relationship is curvilinear as crime increases during adolescence to a peak in late adolescence/early adulthood, and then systematically decreases with increasing age.

Sex is strongly related to crime. Males are much more criminal than females, particularly for violent crimes against persons and property. However, women have increased their rate of participation in the petty forms of property crime, such as small thefts and fraud. Differences in the socialization experiences of males and females and variations in the behaviour expected of them by society during a particular historical period no doubt contribute to these differences in criminal behaviour. As their socialization and gender role expectations change, one should expect to see some effects in the behaviour of males and females, including their criminal behaviour.

Canadian Native people are greatly overrepresented in our criminal justice system. This is most evident when looking at the statistics on the population composition of various types of correctional institutions. Alcohol plays a major role in the crimes of Native people and, directly or indirectly, contributes to this overrepresentation. Both cultural and social structural explanations have been given for the disproportionate involvement of Native people in crime, as has the hypothesis of biased enforcement of white man's law. However, Canadian criminology has not devoted much research attention to date toward explaining this correlation.

Finally, the seemingly conflicting evidence on the relationship between class position and criminal behaviour was examined. Some criminologists conclude that at least a moderate negative correlation exists between these two variables. Others argue for different shapes to the relationship and some deny any correlation. Once certain distinctions are made, however, particularly concerning the meaning and measurement of crime and social class, it seems best to conclude with Gibbons (1982) that the correlation has the shape of a bimodal curve. That is, the crime rate seems to be highest both at the bottom and the top of the class structure.

BIBLIOGRAPHY

Adler, F. (1975). *Sisters in Crime.* New York: McGraw-Hill.

Bell-Rowbotham, B., and C.L. Boydell. (1972). "Crime in Canada: A Distributional Analysis." In C.L. Boydell, C.F. Grindstaff, and P.C. Whitehead (eds.), *Deviant Behavior and Societal Reaction.* Toronto: Holt, Rinehart and Winston.

Bienvenue, R.M., and A.H. Latif. (1974). "Arrests, Disposition and Recidivism: A Comparison of Indians and Whites." *Canadian Journal of Criminology and Corrections* 16(2):105–16.

Bloch, H.A., and A. Niederhoffer. (1958). *The Gang.* New York: Philosophical Library.

Boldt, E.D., L.E. Hursh, S.D. Johnson, and K.W. Taylor. (1983). "Presentence Reports and the Incarceration of Natives." *Canadian Journal of Criminology* 25:269–76.

Box, S. (1987). *Recession, Crime and Punishment.* London: Macmillan Education Ltd.

Box, S., and C. Hale. (1984). "Liberation/Emancipation, Economic Marginalization, or Less Chivalry." *Criminology* 22(4):473–97.

Braithwaite, J. (1979). *Inequality, Crime, and Public Policy.* London: Routledge.

———. (1981). "The Myth of Social Class and Criminality Reconsidered." *American Sociological Review* 46:36–57.

Briar, S., and I. Piliavin. (1965). "Delinquency, Situational Inducements and Commitments to Conformity." *Social Problems* 13:35–45.

Brody, H. (1971). *Indians on Skid Row.* Ottawa: Information Canada.

Campbell, D.T., and J.C. Stanley. (1963). *Experimental and Quasi-Experimental Designs for Research.* Chicago: Rand McNally.

Canadian Committee on Corrections. (1969). *Toward Unity: Criminal Justice and Corrections.* Ottawa: Queen's Printer.

Canadian Corrections Association. (1967). *Indians and the Law.* Ottawa: Canadian Corrections Association.

Chilton, R., and A. Spielberger. (1971). "Is Delinquency Increasing? Age Structure and the Crime Rate." *Social Forces* 49(3):487–93.

Clelland, D., and T.J. Carter. (1980). "The New Myth of Class and Crime." *Criminology* 18(3):319–36.

Cline, H.F. (1980). "Criminal Behavior Over the Life Span." In O.G. Brim and J. Kagan (eds.), *Constancy and Change in Human Development* (pp. 641–74). Cambridge, MA: Harvard University Press.

Correctional Service of Canada. (1985). *Native Population Profile Report.* Ottawa: Correctional Service of Canada.

Demers, D.J. (1978). "Discretion, Disparity and the Parole Process." Unpublished Ph.D. dissertation, University of Alberta.

Easterlin, R.A. (1980). *Birth and Fortune.* New York: Basic Books.

Elliott, D.S., and S. Ageton. (1980). "Reconciling Differences in Estimates of Delinquency." *American Sociological Review* 45(1):95–110.

Empey, L. (1982). *American Delinquency.* Homewood, IL: The Dorsey Press.

Farrington, D.P. (1986). "Age and Crime." In M. Tonry and N. Morris (eds.), *Crime and Justice* (pp. 189–250). Chicago: University of Chicago Press.

Federal Bureau of Investigation. (1989). *Crime in the United States, 1988.* Washington, DC: Superintendent of Documents.

Finkler, H.W. (1982). "Corrections in the Northwest Territories 1967–81, with a Focus on the Incarceration of Inuit Offenders." *Canadian Legal Aid Bulletin* 5(1):25–38.

Fisher, J. (1986). "Canadian Trends in Selected Female Crimes." Unpublished M.A. thesis, University of Alberta.

Fox, J., and T. Hartnagel. (1979). "Changing Social Roles and Female Crime in Canada." *Canadian Review of Sociology and Anthropology* 16(1):96–104.

Fréchette, M. (1983). "Delinquency and Delinquents." In R.R. Corrado et al. (eds.), *Current Issues in Juvenile Justice* (pp. 49–60). Toronto: Butterworths.

Gibbons, D.C. (1982). *Sociology, Crime and Criminal Behavior.* Englewood Cliffs, NJ: Prentice-Hall.

Giffen, P.J. (1965). "Rates of Crime and Delinquency." In W.T. McGrath (ed.), *Crime and Its Treatment in Canada.* Toronto: Macmillan.

———. (1966). "The Revolving Door." *Canadian Review of Sociology and Anthropology,* 3(3):154–66.

———. (1976). "Official Rates of Crime and Delinquency." In W.T. McGrath (ed.), *Crime and Its Treatment in Canada.* Toronto: Macmillan.

Gomme, I.M. (1985). "Predictors of Status and Criminal Offences among Male and Female Adolescents in an Ontario Community." *Canadian Journal of Criminology* 27(2):147–59.

Gomme, I.M., M.E. Morton, and W.G. West. (1984). "Rates, Types, and Patterns of Male and Female Delinquency in an Ontario Community." *Canadian Journal of Criminology* 26(3):313–23.

Gordon, R.A. (1976). "Prevalence: The Rare Datum in Delinquency Measurement and Its Implications for the Theory of Delinquency." In M.W. Klein (ed.), *The Juvenile Justice System* (pp. 201–84). Beverly Hills: Sage.

Greenaway, W.K. (1980). "Crime and Class: Unequal Before the Law." In J. Harp and J.R. Hofley (eds.), *Structured Inequality in Canada* (pp. 247–65). Scarborough: Prentice-Hall.

Greenberg, D. (1979). "Delinquency and the Age Structure of Society." In S.L. Messinger and E. Bittner (eds.), *Criminology Review Yearbook* (pp. 586–620). Beverly Hills: Sage.

———. (1985). "Age, Crime, and Social Explanation." *American Journal of Sociology* 91:1–21.

Hagan, J. (1974). "Criminal Justice and Native People." *Canadian Review of Sociology and Anthropology* Special Issue (August):220–36.

———. (1975a). "The Social and Legal Construction of Criminal Justice." *Social Problems* 22(5):620–37.

———. (1975b). "Parameters of Criminal Prosecution." *Journal of Criminal Law and Criminology* 65(4):536–44.

———. (1975c). "Law, Order and Sentencing." *Sociometry* 38(2):374–84.

———. (1977). "Criminal Justice in Rural and Urban Communities." *Social Forces* 55(3):597–612.

———. (1985a). *Crime, Criminal Behavior, and its Control.* New York: McGraw-Hill.

———. (1985b). "Toward a Structural Theory of Crime, Race and Gender: The Canadian Case." *Crime and Delinquency* 31(1):129–46.

Hagan, J., A.R. Gillis, and J. Simpson. (1985). "The Class Structure of Gender and Delinquency." *American Journal of Sociology* 90(6):1151–78.

Hagan, J., and B. McCarthy. (1990). "Streetlife and Delinquency." Paper presented to American Society of Criminology.

Hagan, J., J. Simpson, and A.R. Gillis. (1979). "The Sexual Stratification of Social Control." *British Journal of Sociology* 30:25–38.

Hartnagel, T.F. (1978). "The Effect of Age and Sex Compositions of Provincial Populations on Provincial Crime Rates." *Canadian Journal of Criminology* 20(1):28–33.

Havemann, P., K. Couse, L. Foster, and R. Matonovich. (1985). *Law and Order for Canada's Indigenous People.* Regina: Prairie Justice Research, School of Human Justice, University of Regina.

Hindelang, M.J. (1979). "Sex Differences in Criminal Activity." *Social Problems* 27(2):143–56.

Hindelang, M.J., T. Hirschi, and J.G. Weis. (1979). "Correlates of Delinquency." *American Sociological Review* 44(6):995–1014.

Hirschi, T., and M. Gottfredson. (1983). "Age and the Explanation of Crime." *American Journal of Sociology* 89(3):552–84.

Hirschi, T., and H. Selvin. (1966). "False Criteria of Causality in Delinquency Research." *Social Problems* 13(3):254–68.

———. (1967). *Delinquency Research.* New York: The Free Press.

Hylton, J.H. (1982). "The Native Offender in Saskatchewan." *Canadian Journal of Criminology* 24(2):121–31.

Indian and Northern Affairs Canada. (1980). *Indian Conditions.* Ottawa: Minister of Indian Affairs and Northern Development.

Irvine, M.J. (1978). *The Native Inmate in Ontario.* Toronto: Ministry of Correctional Services, Province of Ontario.

James, J.T.L. (1979). "Toward a Cultural Understanding of the Native Offender." *Canadian Journal of Criminology* 21(4):453–62.

Jensen, G.F., J.H. Stauss, and V.W. Harris. (1977). "Crime, Delinquency, and the American Indian." *Human Organization* 36(3):252–57.

Johnson, H. (1986). *Women and Crime in Canada.* Ottawa: Solicitor General Canada.

———. (1987). "Getting the Facts Straight." In E. Adelberg and C. Currie (eds.), *Too Few To Count* (pp. 23–46). Vancouver: Press Gang Publishers.

Jolly, S. (1982). "Natives in Conflict with the Law." *Correctional Options* 2(1):83–96.

Krahn, H., T.F. Hartnagel, and J.W. Gartrell. (1986). "Income Inequality and Homicide Rates." *Criminology* 24:269–95.

LaPrairie, Carol P. (1983). "Native Juveniles in Court." In T. Fleming and L.A. Visano (eds.), *Deviant Designations* (pp. 337–50). Toronto: Butterworths.

———. (1990). "The Role of Sentencing in the Overrepresentation of Aboriginal People in Correctional Institutions." *Canadian Journal of Criminology* 32:429–40.

Law Reform Commission of Canada. (1974). *The Native Offender and the Law.* Ottawa: Information Canada.

———. (1975). "Upper Class vs. Working Class Delinquency." In R.A. Silverman and J.J. Teevan Jr., *Crime in Canadian Society* (pp. 102–18). Toronto: Butterworths.

LeBlanc, M. (1983). "Delinquency as an Epiphenomenon of Adolescence." In R.R. Corrado et al. (eds.), *Current Issues in Juvenile Justice* (pp. 31–48). Toronto: Butterworths.

Lee, G.W. (1984). "Are Crime Rates Increasing? A Study of the Impact of Demographic Shifts on Crime Rates in Canada." *Canadian Journal of Criminology* 26(1):29–41.

Linden, R., and C. Fillmore. (1981). "A Comparative Study of Delinquency Involvement." *Canadian Review of Sociology and Anthropology* 18(3):343–61.

Lindsay, P.H., and P.A. Walpole. (1978). "Crimes of Violence and the Female Offender." In M. Gammon (ed.), *Violence in Canada* (pp. 40–50). Toronto: Methuen.

Maxim, P.S. (1985). "Cohort Size and Juvenile Delinquency." *Social Forces* 63(3):661–81.

Merton, R. (1938). "Social Structure and Anomie." *American Sociological Review* 3:672–82.

Métis and Non-Status Indian Crime and Justice Commission. (1978). *Report.* Ottawa: Minister of Supply and Services.

Mikel, D. (1979/1980). "Native Society in Crisis." *Crime and Justice* 7/8(1):32–41.

Minister of Indian Affairs and Northern Development. (1980). *Indian Conditions.* Ottawa: Government of Canada.

Native Counselling Services of Alberta. (1982). "Native People and the Criminal Justice System." *Canadian Legal Aid Bulletin* 5(1):55–63.

Nettler, G. (1982). *Explaining Criminals.* Cincinnati: Anderson Publishing.

———. (1984). *Explaining Crime.* New York: McGraw-Hill.

Osgood, D.W., P.M. O'Malley, J.G. Backman, and L.D. Johnston. (1989). "Time Trends and Age Trends in Arrests and Self-Reported Illegal Behaviour." *Criminology* 27:389–417.

Pollak, O. (1950). *The Criminality of Women.* Philadelphia: University of Pennsylvania Press.

Quinney, Richard. (1977). *Class, State and Crime.* New York: David McKay Company.

Rowe, A.R., and C.R. Tittle. (1977). "Life Cycle Changes and Criminal Propensity." *The Sociological Quarterly* 18:223–36.

Rutter, M., and H. Giller. (1983). *Juvenile Delinquency.* New York: The Guilford Press.

Sagi, P.C., and C.F. Wellford. (1968). "Age Composition and Patterns of Change in Criminal Statistics." *Journal of Criminal Law, Criminology and Police Science* 59(1):29–36.

Short, J.F., Jr., and F.I. Nye. (1957). "Reported Behavior as a Criterion of Deviant Behavior." *Social Problems* 5:207–13.

Simon, R.J. (1975). *Women and Crime.* Lexington, MA: D.C. Heath.

Smart, C. (1976). *Women, Crime and Criminology.* London: Routledge and Kegan Paul.

Smith, D.A., and C.A. Visher. (1980). "Sex and Involvement in Deviance/Crime." *American Sociological Review* 45(4):691–701.

Solicitor General Canada. (1988). *Correctional Issues Affecting Native Peoples.* Ottawa: Solicitor General Canada.

Stack, S. (1984). "Income Inequality and Property Crime." *Criminology* 22:229–57.

Statistics Canada. (1976). *Homicide in Canada.* Ottawa: Department of Supply and Services.

———. (1989a). *Adult Correctional Services in Canada.* Ottawa: Minister of Supply and Services.

———. (1989b). *Canadian Crime Statistics,* 1988. Ottawa: Minister of Supply and Services.

———. (1990). "Sentencing in Youth Courts, 1984–85 to 1988–89." *Juristat* 10 (January).

Steffensmeier, D. (1978). "Crime and the Contemporary Woman." *Social Forces* 57(2):566–83.

———. (1980). "Sex Differences in Patterns of Adult Crime, 1965–77." *Social Forces* 58(4):1080–1108.

Steffensmeier, D.F., E.A. Allan, M.D. Harer, and C. Streifel. (1989). "Age and the Distribution of Crime." *American Journal of Sociology* 94:803–31.

Steffensmeier, D., R.H. Steffensmeier, and A.S. Rosenthal. (1979). "Trends in Female Violence, 1960–1977." *Sociological Focus* 12(3):217–27.

Sutherland, E., and D. Cressey. (1978). *Criminology.* New York: J.P. Lippincott.

Task Force on Aboriginal Peoples in Federal Corrections. (1989). *Final Report.* Ottawa: Minister of Supply and Services.

Tepperman, L. (1977). *Crime Control.* Toronto: McGraw-Hill Ryerson.

Thornberry, T.P., and M. Farnworth. (1982). "Social Correlates of Criminal Involvement." *American Sociological Review* 47(4):505–18.

Tittle, C.R., and R.F. Meier. (1990). "Specifying the SES/Delinquency Relationship." *Criminology* 28:271–99.

Tittle, C.R., and W.J. Villemez. (1977). "Social Class and Criminality." *Social Forces* 56(2):474–502.

Tittle, C.R., W.J. Villemez, and D.A. Smith. (1978). "The Myth of Social Class and Criminality." *American Sociological Review* 43(5):643–56.

Trasler, G. (1980). "Aspects of Causality, Culture, and Crime." Paper presented at the 4th International Seminar at the International Centre of Sociological, Penal and Penitentiary Research and Studies, Messina, Sicily.

Tribble, Stephen. (1972). "Socio-Economic Status and Self-Reported Juvenile Delinquency." *Canadian Journal of Criminology and Corrections* 14:409–15.

Vaz, Edward. (1966). "Self-Reported Delinquency and Socio-Economic Status." *Canadian Journal of Criminology and Corrections* 8:20–27.

Verdun-Jones, S.N., and G.K. Muirhead. (1979/80). "Natives in the Canadian Criminal Justice System." *Crime and Justice* 7/8(1):3–21.

Vold, G.B., and T.J. Bernard. (1986). *Theoretical Criminology.* New York: Oxford University Press.

Wellford, C.F. (1973). "Age Composition and the Increase in Recorded Crime." *Criminology* 11:61–70.

West, W.G. (1984). *Young Offenders and the State.* Toronto: Butterworths.

Wolfgang, M. (1961). "A Sociological Analysis of Criminal Homicide." *Federal Probation* 23(1):48–55.

Wynne, D.F., and T.F. Hartnagel. (1975). "Race and Plea Negotiation." *Canadian Journal of Sociology* 1(2):147–55.

FURTHER READING

Braithwaite, J. (1981). "The Myth of Social Class and Criminality Reconsidered." *American Sociological Review* 46:36–57. A comprehensive survey of the evidence concerning the relationship between social class and criminality which concludes that the evidence for such a relationship is persuasive.

Cline, H.F. (1980). "Criminal Behavior over the Life Span." In O.G. Brim and J. Kagan (eds.), *Constancy and Change in Human Development* (pp. 641–74). Cambridge, MA: Harvard University Press. A review of what longitudinal studies and official arrest statistics reveal concerning criminal behaviour throughout the life span.

Farrington, D.P. (1986). "Age and Crime." In M. Tonry and N. Morris (eds.), *Crime and Justice* (pp. 189–250). Chicago: University of Chicago Press. A detailed analysis of the age-crime relationship using aggregate and individual level data, cross-sectional as well as longitudinal methods, that attempts to disentangle prevalence from incidence rates and reviews the ages of onset and termination of criminal careers, as well as considering a number of explanations for why crime varies with age, and various policy implications.

Giffen, P.J. (1976). "Official Rates of Crime and Delinquency." In W.T. McGrath (ed.), *Crime and Its Treatment in Canada.* Toronto: Macmillan. Official Canadian crime statistics and several of their correlates are reviewed.

Hagan, J. (1974). "Criminal Justice and Native People: A Study of Incarceration in a Canadian Province." *Canadian Review of Sociology and Anthropology* Special Issue (August):220–36. The overrepresentation of Natives in a prison system is studied, with an examination of sentences and forfeiture of fines.

Hindelang, M.J., T. Hirschi, and J.G. Weis. (1981). *Measuring Delinquency.* Beverly Hills: Sage. A detailed discussion of the issues involved in measuring delinquency officially and with self-reports, and an examination of the alleged discrepancies in the correlates of delinquency produced by these measures.

Smith, D.A., and C.A. Visher. (1980). "Sex and Involvement in Deviance/Crime: A Qualitative Review of the Empirical Literature." *American Sociological Review* 45(4):691–701. An empirical analysis of how the relationship between sex and deviance, particularly over time, depends upon various characteristics of a given study and its sample.

Tittle, C.R., W.J. Villemez, and D.A. Smith. (1978). "The Myth of Social Class and Criminality: An Empirical Assessment of the Empirical Evidence." *American Sociological Review* 43(5):643–56. An assessment of 35 studies examining the correlation between social class and crime/delinquency, with a sceptical conclusion.

Verdun-Jones, S.N. and G.K. Muirhead. (1979/80). "Natives in the Canadian Criminal Justice System." *Crime and Justice* 7/8(1):3–21. An overview of Canadian research on Natives and the criminal justice system that calls for the development of a more comprehensive and integrated theoretical framework.

CHAPTER 5

WOMEN AND CRIME

By Elizabeth Comack

*L*ike other academic disciplines, criminology has been a male-centred enterprise. Despite the use of generic language like "criminals," "defendants," or "delinquents," most of criminology has really been about what *men* do. As a consequence, women as both offenders and victims have been rendered invisible in much criminological inquiry. As offenders, women's small numbers relative to men have typically been used to justify or rationalize this neglect. Women now constitute only 15 percent of those charged with Criminal Code offences in Canada. As victims, violence against women was traditionally not a major area of concern. Official statistics on crime indicated that offences like rape were relatively infrequent, and victim surveys reported young males to be the group most at risk from crime.

However, over the past two decades there has been a growing awareness of the subject of women and crime. This has come about largely through the efforts of the women's movement. The women's movement has used a range of social and political activities to publicize and to work toward changing the subordinate position which women as a group occupy in Canadian society, and has developed a body of theory that is distinctly feminist in its orientation. The net effect of these two developments within the women's movement has been to move women from the periphery to the centre of criminological inquiry. In this chapter, each of these developments will be discussed to clarify the kinds of issues and questions which are now commanding criminologists' attention. The first part of the chapter will focus on women as victims of violence, as this issue has been a central concern of the women's movement over the last twenty years. In the second part, the attention will shift to women as offenders—more specifically, to the explanations of women's crime traditionally offered in the discipline and the emergence of a feminist criminology which challenges these explanations.

WORKING FOR CHANGE: VIOLENCE AGAINST WOMEN

While its organizational forms, constituencies, strategies, and issues of concern have varied, the women's movement has been united around the goal of improving the condition and quality of women's lives. One of the first issues to be addressed by the movement was the provision of support to women who had been victimized by rape. Beginning in the early 1970s, rape crisis centres were established across the country. With their establishment came the recognition that the incidence of rape far exceeded what was reported in the official crime statistics. In the early 1980s, for example, the Canadian Advisory Council on the Status of Women (CACSW) estimated that one in every five Canadian women will be sexually assaulted at some point in her life, and one in every seventeen will be the victim of forced sexual intercourse. Yet only one in ten sexual assaults was ever reported to the police (Kinnon, 1981).

THE CULTURAL CONSTRUCTION OF RAPE

The recognition that sexual assault was widespread throughout the society led to investigations of the reasons why women did not report the offence, of their treatment by the criminal justice system when they did report it, and of the limitations inherent in the existing laws. In particular, recognition was given to the cultural construction of rape, which takes the form of certain myths or misconceptions about rape. These myths constitute a set of beliefs about the nature of the act itself and stereotypical images of "true" rape victims and offenders that have become part of the public discourse. They have not only been internalized by many of the victims, who believed that they were in some way responsible for the violence, but also found their way into the law and legal practice. To many observers, it appeared to be the victim rather than the offender who was on trial. Given their pervasiveness, it is worth examining some of these myths in detail (see also Morris, 1987; Gunn and Minch, 1988).

"Rape Is Impossible"

According to this myth, anatomically and physiologically, a woman cannot be forced into sex, and a man cannot "fight and copulate" at the same time. Such a belief is reflected in sayings like "you can't thread a moving needle" or "a woman with her skirt up can run faster than a man with his pants down." This ignores the element of physical coercion and the effects of fear and threats on the victim. It also presumes that victims and offenders are equal when, in fact, victims can be as young as six months and as old as 90 years (CACSW, 1985).

"Women Want To Be Raped"

This belief suggests that a woman who has been raped must have either consciously or unconsciously "asked for it," either by her dress or by her behaviour (hitchhiking, going to bars). As Allison Morris (1987) notes, to say that women want to be raped presumes that female sexuality is inherently masochistic, that is, that women somehow enjoy being victimized. It also ignores or at least neutralizes the actions of the offender. According to the

CACSW, in one-quarter of the incidents where a rape occurred, the assailant had made a legitimate initial contact with the victim (such as requesting information or posing as a maintenance person). Studies have also found that 82 percent of rapes were planned in advance by the assailant (Medea and Thompson, 1974:31). The absurdity of the claim that women "ask for it" is revealed when we apply this same logic to victims of robbery.

"WAS HE ASKING FOR IT?"

In 1975, *Harper's Weekly* carried the following item in response to an American Bar Association finding that few rapists are punished for their crime. The article asks us to imagine a robbery victim undergoing the same sort of cross-examination that a rape victim does.

"Mr. Smith, you were held up at gunpoint on the corner of First and Main?"

"Yes."

"Did you struggle with the robber?"

"No."

"Why not?"

"He was armed."

"Then you made a conscious decision to comply with his demands rather than resist?"

"Yes."

"Did you scream? Cry out?"

"No. I was afraid."

"I see. Have you ever been held up before?"

"No."

"Have you ever given money away?"

"Yes, of course."

"And you did so willingly?"

"What are you getting at?"

"Well, let's put it like this, Mr. Smith. You've given money away in the past. In fact you have quite a reputation for philanthropy. How can we be sure you weren't contriving to have your money taken by force?"

"Listen, if I wanted — "

"Never mind. What time did this holdup take place?"

"About 11 p.m."

"You were out on the street at 11 p.m.? Doing what?"

"Just walking."

"Just walking? You know that it's dangerous being out on the street that late at night. Weren't you aware that you could have been held up?"

"I hadn't thought about it."

"What were you wearing?"

"Let's see — a suit. Yes, a suit."

"An expensive suit?"

"Well — yes. I'm a successful lawyer, you know."

"In other words, Mr. Smith, you were walking around the streets late at night in a suit that practically advertised the fact that you might be a good target for some easy money, isn't that so? I mean, if we didn't know better, Mr. Smith, we might even think that you were **asking** for this to happen, mightn't we?"

Source: *Harper's Weekly.* (1975).

"Rape Is a Sexual Act"

To say that rape is a sexual act suggests that a man has "uncontrollable urges" that cannot be halted once a woman has "turned him on." It excuses the offender for his actions (he simply got "carried away" or was "just trying to give her a good time"), and ignores the violent nature of the act. The CACSW (1985a) reports that 62 percent of victims of assault involving forced sexual intercourse are physically injured in the attack; 9 percent are severely beaten; 12 percent are threatened with a weapon; 70 percent experience verbal threats. Indeed, several writers have argued that men who rape are not motivated by sex, but by anger and power; their aim is to control, to degrade, and to humiliate (Brownmiller, 1975; Messerschmidt, 1986). The following account by a rapist demonstrates this point:

> Rape gave me the power to do what I wanted to do without feeling I had to please a partner or respond to a partner. I felt in control, dominant. Rape was the ability to have sex without caring about the woman's response. I was totally dominant. (cited in Scully and Marolla, 1985:259)

"No Means Yes"

Women are the "sexual gatekeepers" in our society. The dating game is one where the women hold the "prize" that men attempt to "win" (Morris, 1987:169). Following this, sex comes to be viewed as an obligation in return for economic expenditure. In marriage, it is a husband's prerogative. Such cultural beliefs, which essentially legitimize rape, are learned by both males and females at an early age. Indeed, one study of 1700 grades six to nine students in Rhode Island found that 51 percent of the boys and 41 percent of the girls said a man has the right to force a woman to kiss him if he has spent "a lot of money" (defined by twelve-year-olds as $10 to $15) on her; 65 percent of the boys and 57 percent of the girls in grades seven through nine said it is acceptable for a man to force a woman to have sexual intercourse if they have been dating for more than six months; and 87 percent of the boys and 79 percent of the girls said rape is acceptable if a couple is married (*The Globe and Mail*, 3 May 1988). Given these views, a man is "expected" to make sexual advances, and a woman to be "coy" and "flirtatious": when she says no, she really means yes.

"If 'Yes' to One, Then 'Yes' to All"

Since the key issue in rape trials is whether the victim actually consented to the act, the trial often is focused on the victim's credibility and moral character. Chaste women, either virgins or monogamous wives, are considered to be more credible victims than those who have had prior sexual experiences, especially prostitutes. According to this reasoning, if a woman has had sexual relations in the past, who is to say she did not consent to the act in question? This good girl/bad girl dichotomy also implies that women who engage in sexual behaviour lie more frequently than those who do not (Morris, 1987), or that consenting to one man automatically means consenting to all.

"Women Cannot Be Trusted"

This myth suggests that women are inherently untrustworthy. They will make false accusations and engage in selective recall to blackmail an unfaithful lover, excuse their curfew violation, or account for an unwanted pregnancy. It follows that men accused of rape must be given the benefit of the doubt beyond the obligatory "innocent until proven guilty" which all accused persons are afforded by law. For example, prior to 1976, Canadian law made corroborative evidence mandatory in rape trials. The accused could not be found guilty in the absence of evidence (such as cuts and bruises) which would support the testimony of the victim. As well, under the doctrine of recent complaint, which was in force until 1983, it was assumed that a victim who complained at the first reasonable opportunity was more credible than one who complained some time after the rape had taken place.

"The Act of Rape Has Little Impact on the Victim"

Unless there is severe physical violence against the woman, it is assumed that the rape will not have long-term effects. In their examination of sentencing reports, the Metro Toronto Action Committee on Violence Against Women and Children (METRAC) found that judges frequently remark that the victim has suffered no long-lasting trauma, even in what might seem to be alarming circumstances. One 1986 report noted that the victim was urinated on and assaulted with a bathroom plunger. The sentencing report commented that the victim, who was a prostitute, "suffered no lasting psychological injury." In another case of a man convicted of sexually assaulting his step-daughter and daughter over an eight-year period, the judge commented: "There is no evidence of lasting impact on the children." METRAC (1988) contrasts such statements with studies indicating that sexual assault survivors experience psychological consequences which are usually severe and long-lasting.

"Rapists Are 'Abnormal' "

This belief suggests that men who rape comprise an isolated group in society that is psychologically different from the majority of males. However, it is not supported by the evidence. For example, in a series of surveys of male university students on North American campuses, Neil Malamuth (1981) asked: If you knew you could get away with it would you

- a. force a woman into sexual acts against her will;
- b. commit rape; or
- c. do neither?

One-third of the respondents said "no" to *a* but "yes" to *b*; one-third said "yes" to *a* and *b*; and one-third answered *c*. In effect, *two-thirds* of the sample reported that they would commit rape. Attributing rape to the actions of a small, disturbed minority in society effectively lets men as a group off the hook. It either becomes an isolated problem for psychologists and psychiatrists to deal with, or is narrowly defined as a "women's issue." A recent incident at Queen's University in Kingston, Ontario, exemplifies the need to address the widespread and pervasive nature of such cultural attitudes toward rape. After the student council launched an anti-rape campaign which used the slogan "No means no," students in one of the male residences responded with signs bearing some slogans of their own, all in the spirit of a "good joke": "No means more beer," "No means tie me up," and "No means kick her in the teeth."

BEING A WOMAN IS NO JOKE

A good deal has been said and written about the controversy over some sexist jokes that began to circulate at Queen's University in Kingston, Ont., after the student council launched an anti-rape campaign.

The campaign slogan is "No means no." Perhaps not surprisingly, students in one men's residence responded with signs bearing some slogans of their own, including "No means more beer" and "No means harder." What did come as a surprise was the attention generated by what was seen to be a harmless prank.

I am no longer a student—not even a Queen's graduate—but I know I am affected by the events that have taken place there. No one could seriously suggest that reading signs like this would cause male students to go out, ply a woman with alcohol and force her to have sex. Still, such hijinks have a darker side.

Far from being forgotten as childish pranks and left behind on graduation, the attitudes the signs reflect will be impressed upon everyone who reads them and carried far beyond the bounds of campus.

Every day, life at work, at home and on the street is made more difficult for women by the fact that most people we deal with, at some level, are looking at us with attitudes influenced by a world that has permitted a statement such as "No means harder" to be regarded as a joke.

It is rarely obvious. It's not that I think men, when annoyed, say to themselves, "That woman needs a good rape to keep her quiet." But I know that in many cases, my experience, qualifications and efforts are regarded as irrelevant because society dictates that women be thought of primarily in terms of their gender.

It's hard to describe how difficult it can be to do my job when the person I'm talking to leads off the conversation by saying, "I had no idea they'd send someone pretty."

Of course, it's not very common; of course, you can turn it off with a shrug or a joke or a blank stare in return. But it wastes time and it's so unfair. Unfair because before women can even begin to do the job their male colleagues do, they have to go through stupid games just to reach the same starting point.

And that's just the problems faced with strangers. In a previous job, I used to go back to my own office and deal with some of the worst sexism I have encountered anywhere. There was only one woman in management and yet male managers were heard to say the place was being overrun by women.

It wasn't exactly a feminist, or even a tolerant, environment. Women who complained about sexism were called "the thought police," while some of our male colleagues keep pornography in their desks and indulged themselves with it on company time.

We were accused of having no sense of humor when we didn't find jokes about wife-beating funny. We were even told that forming a woman's group was divisive — although the man who said so didn't see sexism as divisive.

If it is bad at work, though, it only gets worse out in the streets.

Women know what it's like to have to walk past a crowd of teen-agers after dark and try to ignore their jeers and threats.

Women know what it's like to have total strangers comment on their physical appearance or stare at their breasts before bothering to meet their eyes — if they bother at all.

Women know what it's like to face this day after day. And that's why there's no such thing as harmless fun when it comes to reinforcing sexist attitudes toward women.

Once, when I was talking to a man who had been making rape jokes, I finally found a way to get through to him by telling him to imagine he was Jewish and had to listen to someone say, "I'm going to throw you in the oven if you don't shape up."

I suggested the Jew would not actually believe he was about to be gassed — but he would still feel threatened, degraded and hurt.

Well, 50 years ago, people did talk to Jews that way. Lots of people still do. But that doesn't make it harmless fun, it doesn't mean anti-semitism is a figment of the imagination and it doesn't mean it should be tolerated.

We know the cost of anti-semitism; it was six million dead and millions more suffering around the world. We know there will probably never be a holocaust against women.

But unless jokes such as those being made at Queen's are put in their proper perspective, women will never have a hope of escaping from economic discrimination or physical abuse or even the small, daily indignities that degrade us — and degrade all the men who perpetuate them.

Source: Jane Coutts. "Being a woman is no joke." *The Globe and Mail* 8 November 1989:A7.

Clearly, the more prevalent such myths and misconceptions about sexual assault are, the more far-reaching will be their consequences. For offenders, they can translate into less chance of detection, higher acquittal rates, and lighter sentences. Studies have shown that most rapists do not even believe they have done anything wrong (Clarke and Lewis, 1977; Messerschmidt, 1986). For victims, rape myths can mean a "double victimization." Victims not only endure the humiliation and degradation inherent in the act itself, but may experience further humiliation if they choose to report the case to the authorities. Also, since cultural beliefs suggest rape is the woman's fault, victims may feel responsible for their own victimization. For women generally, the cultural construction of rape can produce feelings of fear and vulnerability that impose restrictions on their daily activities. A 1989 study by Linda MacLeod, for example, found that 56 percent of urban Canadian women feel unsafe walking alone in their neighbourhoods after dark, compared with 18 percent of Canadian men (*The Globe and Mail*, 11 October 1989).

THE OLD RAPE LAW

These myths and misconceptions were very evident in the old rape legislation. Prior to 1983, the law defined a rape to have occurred when "[a] male person has sexual intercourse with a female person who is not his wife, (a) without her consent, or (b) with her consent if the consent (i) is extorted by threats or fear of bodily harm, (ii) is obtained by impersonating her husband, or (iii) is obtained by false and fraudulent representations as to the nature and quality of the act" (s. 143). Under this legal definition, rape was a "gendered" offence, since the offender was presumed to be male and the victim female. The focus was on the sexual nature of the act, in that penetration was necessary in order for a rape to have occurred. Under this legislation, husbands could not be charged with raping their wives. The key element in establishing the guilt of the accused in rape cases was consent. If there was reasonable doubt that the woman's claim of lack of consent was true, then the accused could not be held culpable. As a consequence, the focus of the trial rested on the credibility of the victim. Her moral character came under the scrutiny of the court in the attempt to determine whether she could be believed when she said she did not consent. Defence lawyers were permitted to ask questions about the past sexual history of the victim, and both the corroboration requirement and the doctrine of recent complaint were in effect. At the same time, however, as with all other offences, the accused could not be compelled to testify at all.

Given the specific nature and focus of the rape law, it became common practice for the police, as the first contact point in the criminal justice system, to differentiate between those victims who were "credible" and those who were not. For example, Clark and Lewis (1977) found that the Metropolitan Toronto Police classified a large percentage of cases as "unfounded," not because they believed that a rape had not occurred, but because they believed the case would be difficult to prosecute. The growing awareness of the nature and extent of violence against women, coupled with an increasing recognition of the deficiencies in the law and legal practice, led to pressures for legislative reform from women's groups across the country. These efforts resulted in the passage of new legislation.

THE NEW SEXUAL ASSAULT LEGISLATION

In January of 1983, the old rape law was repealed and in its place three new categories were added to the offence of assault: sexual assault (s. 246.1); sexual assault with a weapon, threats to a third party, and bodily harm (s. 246.2); and aggravated sexual assault (s. 246.3). Under this new legislation, the offence was "degenderized," husbands could now be charged with sexually assaulting their wives, and penetration was no longer a necessary element. Limitations were placed on the ability of the defence to ask questions about the past sexual history of the victim, the corroboration requirement was dropped, the requirement of recent complaint was removed, and there was provision for a publication ban on any disclosure of the identity of the complainant. In combination, these changes were designed to redress the apparent gender inequities in the law and to reduce the trauma experienced by the victim during the trial in an attempt to encourage the reporting of cases. While an improvement over the previous rape law, the new sexual assault legislation has been the subject of a number of criticisms.

For one, by framing the law in gender neutral terms, the intent was to eliminate sexual discrimination from the Criminal Code by suggesting that sexual assault can be committed by either a male or female upon either a male or female victim (Ruebsaat, 1985). Several writers, however, have opposed this de-genderization of the offence on the grounds that such neutrality masks the reality of rape in our society: it is overwhelmingly men who commit rape on women.

The concern with reducing the trauma of the trial for victims is reflected in changes to the evidentiary rules. Witnesses in criminal trials for other offences, for example, are not likely to be questioned as to their private sex lives or to be required to explain why they did not immediately report the offence. Nor is their testimony presumed untrustworthy if uncorroborated by other evidence (Boyd and Sheehy, 1989:264). As Hinch (1985:37) notes, however, because consent is still very much a key issue in sexual assault cases, the removal of both the doctrine of recent complaint and the corroboration requirement "place a great deal of pressure on the victim. The victim's testimony and character *may* now become even more important than it has ever been. (emphasis added)" As well, although limitations have been imposed on the introduction of evidence that pertains to the past sexual history of the complainant, section 246.6 allows the defence to introduce evidence of the prior sexual activity between the victim and the accused, and judges have the discretion to allow certain evidence of the victim's sexual activity with persons other than the accused on the same occasion. The concern raised here is that the victim will be denied the opportunity to say that on this occasion and with this person consent was not given. In the same vein, the new legislation enshrines the defence of "honest but mistaken belief." In determining the presence or absence of consent, if the judge "is satisfied there is sufficient evidence which if believed by the jury would constitute an offence," he or she is required to "instruct the jury when reviewing all evidence relating to the determination of the honesty of the accused's belief, to consider the presence or absence of reasonable grounds for that belief" (s. 244.4). Critics argue that this element works to the detriment of the victim. As Hinch (1985:39) has commented: "The victim, who has not consented to the attack, is being asked to accept that, because someone else misinterpreted, misunderstood, or otherwise was unable to understand her lack of consent, her refusal to give consent is virtually irrelevant."

One of the main objectives of the legislative reform was to shift the focus away from the sexual nature of the act and make its violent nature the main point of concentration. Thus, while the old rape law was included under Part IV of the Criminal Code, "Sexual Offences, Public Morals and Disorderly Conduct," the new sexual assault legislation is included under Part VI, "Offences Against the Person and Reputation." One of the difficulties with the new legislation, however, is the absence of a clear definition of what constitutes a sexual as opposed to a common assault. In the absence of a statutory definition, it has been left to the courts to determine what comprises a sexual assault.

In *R. v. Chase*, one of the first major cases dealt with under the new law, a New Brunswick court adopted a narrow biological definition of sexual assault and ruled that, in order for an assault to be sexual, there had to be genital contact. The case involved the forcible touching of a 15-year-old girl's shoulders and breasts by a 40-year-old male neighbour. The court held that these actions were not sexual and found the accused guilty of common assault only. According to the New Brunswick Court of Appeal, the forcible touching of the complainant's breasts was not a sexual assault, as breasts were only a "secondary sexual characteristic" and not a primary sexual organ. The court reasoned that without this distinction, forcible touching of a man's beard (also a "secondary sexual characteristic") could be construed as a sexual assault. As Ruebsaat notes, "the problem with this approach is that it does not correspond to how men and women experience reality. For women the touching of breasts is generally experienced as a sexual act. Furthermore ... beard pulling is not a social problem whereas breast grabbing or pinching is. The theoretical equating of the two acts, therefore, is misleading" (Ruebsaat, 1985:5).

In *Alderton*, however, the Ontario Court of Appeal adopted a more subjective approach and focused on the intention of the accused. The court held that a sexual assault included "an assault committed with the intention of having intercourse with the complainant without her consent. It also included an assault committed for the purpose of sexual gratification" (Ruebsaat, 1985:9). In this particular case, the accused broke into the complainant's apartment and jumped onto her bed, forcing her back into the pillows. He then held her down with one hand covering her mouth and nose, at which point she managed to escape. This was deemed to be a sexual assault by the court. While stating a potentially broader definition than *Chase*, *Alderton* has also been criticized in that it still concentrates primarily on the sexual, instead of the violent, nature of the assault. As well, emphasis on the sexual motivation of the assailant has been deemed to be problematic in that sexual violence may also be motivated or intended to exercise control, or to degrade and humiliate the victim (Ruebsaat, 1985:9–10).

When *Chase* was subsequently heard by the Supreme Court in 1987, the appeal court decision was overturned. The Supreme Court held that breasts were indeed sexual, and defined sexual assault as an assault "committed in circumstances of a sexual nature, such that the sexual integrity of the victim is violated" (cited in Boyle, 1991:104). Under this definition, all of the circumstances are relevant—"the part of the body touched; the nature of the contact; the situation, words, and gestures; the intent of the person committing the act" (Boyle, 1991:104). In its ruling, then, the Court has recognized that, while sexual gratification may be a relevant motivating factor, not all sexual assaults are committed for the purpose of sexual gratification. Yet, as Boyle comments, while the Supreme Court decision is helpful, questions remain as to the meaning of *sexual* and thus the scope of the offence. She queries: "Is sexual assault a deviant, *violent* form of sexual activity, or are violence and sex so intermingled in our society that any form of violence against women could conceivably be seen as sexual?" (Boyle, 1991:104).

Related to this, Carol Smart (1989) has offered an analysis of law that calls attention to both the legal method by which the courts arrive at decisions of guilt or innocence and the manner in which sexuality (and hence, rape) has been construed. Similar to our discussion of the cultural construction of rape, Smart describes our culture as "phallocentric": it gives priority to the masculine experience and meaning of sexuality. "Sexuality is comprehended as the pleasure of the Phallus, and by extension the pleasures of penetration and intercourse—for men.... Female pleasure is assumed to either coincide with the male definition or to be beyond understanding" (Smart, 1989:28). Smart makes the point that this phallocentrism is embedded in the law itself. When cases are tried in court, a finding of guilt or innocence rests very much on the issue of consent/nonconsent of the victim. Yet this dichotomy of consent/nonconsent fails to adequately reflect a woman's experience: "A woman may agree to a certain amount of intimacy, but not to sexual intercourse. In the legal model, however, consent to the former is consent to full intercourse" (Smart, 1989:34).

Smart is also critical of efforts to redefine rape by simply shifting the focus from "sex" to "violence," in that by doing so, we fail to confront the larger problem of phallocentrism. As she notes, "The problem about calling rape violence is that it attempts to avoid male sexuality. Yet male sexuality, and its prerogatives, are precisely what rape, and the rape trial, are about" (1989:44). Thus, to the extent that consent remains a key issue, and that the violence is framed in phallocentric terms, "the trial remains a denial of women's experience" (1989:46).

The extent to which the sexual assault legislation will be able to offer both women and men equal protection and treatment under the law and thereby dispel the kinds of myths and misconceptions that have traditionally surrounded the act of rape will require attention to the very structure of law and the extent to which it merely reflects—or challenges—the cultural construction of rape. In addition, meaningful reform of the law will also depend upon the willingness of key personnel within the criminal justice system to meet the legislative objectives intended by the reform. In this regard, recent comments made by members of the judiciary would appear to indicate that the traditional cultural construction of rape is still very much alive and well. During a 1984 case involving a man charged with sexual assault, a Manitoba provincial court judge told a Crown attorney "he would have to have grown up in a vacuum not to know women often at first resist sexual advances only to give in to their instincts eventually" (*Winnipeg Free Press*, 14 April 1990). The same judge, in sentencing a man who pointed a shotgun at his ex-girl-friend and threatened her for almost an hour, stated: "...the trouble with women is you can't live with them and you can't live without them. But I can tell you from 60-odd years' experience, there isn't any woman worth the trouble you got yourself into" (*Winnipeg Free Press*, 14 April 1990). A Northwest Territories judge told a reporter that sexual assaults in the North cannot be treated in the same light as those in southern Canada. He was quoted as saying that the average southern rapist is more violent and victimizes "a dainty co-ed," while the northern rapist tends to be a drunk who "comes along and sees a pair of hips and helps himself" when a woman has passed out (*The Globe and Mail*, 22 December 1989). In January of 1989, a Quebec judge, during an assault and weapons trial, interjected in an argument over a point of law and said: "Rules are like women, they are made to be violated." A lawyer involved in the case responded: "Exactly." (*The Globe and Mail*, 12 February 1990).

INCIDENT WITH "SEXUALLY AGGRESSIVE" TOT NETS MAN PROBATION

The Canadian Press

VANCOUVER — A man who admitted a sexual incident with a three-year-old girl has been given a suspended sentence because the judge found the victim was "sexually aggressive."

Because of the "unusual circumstances," county court Judge Peter van der Hoop distinguished the case from those sexual-assault cases involving children where the B.C. Court of Appeal has said an intermittent sentence, or a suspended sentence, is inappropriate.

"You have been convicted on a charge of touching with a part of your body for sexual purposes the body of a three-year-old girl," the judge told Delbert Leeson, 33.

"The circumstances are unusual in part because it appears that this three-year-old girl was sexually aggressive. It seems to me that that is an aspect of this case that may be deserving of investigation but that is not under my control."

"It is, however, a factor that I think can and should be taken into consideration here on sentencing."

A second factor the judge considered was that Leeson was "under the influence of alcohol to a fair extent at the time," and the judge said he was satisfied Leeson was also suffering from fatigue.

Leeson was placed on probation for 18 months and directed to take alcohol counselling and to "make all reasonable efforts to obtain and keep employment."

Crown prosecutor Ron Kockx said an appeal was not being considered "at this point."

The case was "somewhat unique in that the judge was stuck with facts related by the accused and with no other evidence." Kockx, who spoke to sentence but did not conduct the prosecution at the recent trial, said Thursday.

The girl's mother, who asked Leeson to babysit one night in September 1988, testified that her daughter sometimes masturbated by rubbing herself against people.

Leeson made a videotape statement to police that was entered at trial and was the basis for the conviction.

In it, Leeson said the girl rubbed herself against him, grabbed his crotch and undressed herself. He said he was concerned as to how she had learned such behavior, but admitted he did not stop her immediately and became aroused.

Source: The Canadian Press. Reprinted with permission.

Judicial discretion in the implementation of the sexual assault legislation has recently been raised as an issue in light of a Supreme Court decision in August of 1991. In a 7 to 2 majority ruling, the Supreme Court struck down section 246.6 of the Criminal Code. Known as the "rape shield" provision, section 246.6 was included in the 1983 reform with the aim of preventing a victim's sexual conduct from being used to discredit her testimony. The Supreme Court ruled that, while laudable in its intent, the provision goes too far and could deny the accused the right to a fair trial, as enshrined in section 7 and section 11(d) of the Canadian Charter of Rights and Freedoms. The decision came as a result of applications to the court relating to two separate cases: *Seaboyer* and *Gayme*.

Seaboyer was charged with the sexual assault of a woman with whom he had been drinking in a bar. The judge at the preliminary inquiry refused to allow the accused to cross-examine the complainant on her sexual conduct on other occasions. The accused contended that he should have been permitted to cross-examine as to other acts of sexual intercourse that may have caused bruises, and other aspects of the complainant's condition that the Crown had put to evidence. Such evidence, it was argued, might be relevant to consent, as it might provide other explanations for the physical evidence offered by the Crown to explain the use of force against the complainant.

In the *Gayme* case, the complainant was fifteen, the accused eighteen. They were friends. The Crown alleged that the accused sexually assaulted the complainant at the accused's school. The defence, relying on the defences of consent and honest belief in consent, contended that there was no assault and that in fact the complainant was the sexual aggressor. In pursuing this defence at the preliminary inquiry, the accused sought to cross-examine and present evidence on prior and subsequent sexual conduct of the complainant.

In striking down the "rape shield" provision, the court said that the trial judge should decide—by means of a *voir dire* (trial within a trial)—whether evidence of a complainant's sexual activity with individuals other than the accused should be admitted. In their dissenting opinion, Justice Claire L'Heureux-Dubé and Justice Charles Gonthier said judges have shown they are not impartial concerning women, that section 246.6 was broad enough to allow some evidence of a victim's sexual conduct, and that any evidence excluded by the law is irrelevant.

As mentioned earlier, the 1983 sexual assault legislation has been subject to the criticism that it does not go far enough in protecting victims of sexual assault from what is perceived to be unfair and unequal treatment by the courts. The recent Supreme Court decision—and an anticipated response by Parliament (*Winnipeg Free Press* 6 September 1991)—will no doubt mean that legal reform in the area of sexual assault will continue to be a topic of discussion and debate

DOMESTIC VIOLENCE

With attention increasingly focused on the nature and extent of violence against women, the issue of violence in the home has come under increasing scrutiny. Traditionally, domestic violence was considered a "private dispute" between husbands and wives. Police were often reluctant to intervene or to define the situation as a criminal matter. In 1981, the CACSW released its report entitled *Wife Battering in Canada: The Vicious Circle*. Linda MacLeod, author of the report, noted that "[w]omen are kicked, punched, beaten, burned, threatened, knifed and shot, not by strangers who break into their houses or who accost them on dark streets, but by husbands and lovers they've spent many years with—years with good times as well as bad" (MacLeod, 1980:6). MacLeod also estimated that, every year, one in ten Canadian women who is married or in a relationship with a live-in lover is battered. In a subsequent report, MacLeod (1987:7) raised that estimate by suggesting that "almost 1 million women in Canada may be battered each year." When the issue was raised in the House of Commons (on May 12, 1982), it was met with laughter! Public outrage ensued, and there was an insistence by women's groups, front-line workers and members of the general public that policy makers take concerted action to deal with the problem of wife abuse. One result of this lobbying effort has been the redefinition of the problem from a "private trouble" to a "public issue."

In examining wife abuse as a public issue, connections have been drawn between the existence of wife abuse and the recognition that women as a group experience structured inequality in Canadian society (Comack, 1987). This structured inequality is manifested in a number of ways. Socially, women's structured inequality is reflected in and supported by a cultural belief system that prescribes very different gender roles and expectations for men and women. Despite the impact of the women's movement, females by and large continue to be socialized to expect that their primary role in life will be a familial one: as wife, mother, and homemaker. Yet 84 percent of Canadian women can expect to spend a significant portion of their adult lives in "husbandless" households (National Council of Welfare, 1990) and the majority of Canadian families now require two income earners to make ends meet. Many women are therefore ill prepared to take on an economic role. Even so, when they do, they encounter structured inequality in the economic sphere.

Although women's economic participation in the labour force has increased dramatically over the last two decades, Canadian women continue to encounter vertical and horizontal segregation in the job market. About 60 percent of all employed women are concentrated in clerical, sales, and service occupations. Only 8 percent of employed women occupy managerial and administrative positions (CACSW, 1985b). Women are concentrated in jobs where wages are lowest, and even when age and educational levels are taken into account, women's earnings are considerably less than men's. One result of this economic disparity is what some commentators have referred to as the "feminization of poverty." More than one out of five Canadian women live in poverty. Single mothers are especially at risk. As many as 85 percent of single-parent families are headed by women. In 1987, 57 percent of these families were living below the poverty line (National Council of Welfare, 1990).

The main implication to be derived from women's structured inequality is that, in Canadian society, women's choices are limited. As a result, the life experience of many Canadian women is one of social and economic dependency on a male provider. That is, women's dependency is supported and maintained, not just by a lack of economic choices, but by strong cultural prescriptions that place an emphasis on marriage and the family as the "proper" place for women.

Indeed, the law itself has historically played a key role in maintaining the subordinate position of women. Women were not considered "legal persons" in Canada until 1929, and then only after a Supreme Court ruling had been overturned by the Privy Council in London, England (Atcheson et al., 1984). The belief that women were the "property" of their husbands has been upheld by several legal enactments, including the old rape laws which gave immunity to husbands who sexually assaulted their wives. Under English common law, the husband was very much the "lord of his castle." Upon marriage, women surrendered their legal identity and their rights to own property, to personal credit, and to guardianship of their children. Husbands, on the other hand, were accorded the "right to consortium," which meant that wives had a legal obligation with respect to the "consummation of marriage, cohabitation, maintenance of conjugal rights, sexual fidelity, and general obedience and respect for his wishes" (Dobash and Dobash, 1979:60). A husband was granted the right to use force in order to ensure that his wife fulfilled her obligations. Under the "rule of thumb" doctrine, husbands could physically discipline their wives so long as the stick they used was no wider than the width of their thumb (Edwards, 1985).

Clearly, the ideal of the family as a "private domain" and a "resting place" or "sanctuary" has been shattered by the finding that violence in the home is a frequent occurrence in contemporary society, and that violence between adults is systematically and disproportionately directed against women. Indeed, the widespread incidence of wife battering in Canada can be taken as one of the most obvious and severe manifestations of women's dependency and subordination.

Given the structured inequality of women as a group, the options available to those who are caught up in an abusive relationship will be extremely restricted. MacLeod's (1987) research, for example, found that 87 percent of the women who sought shelter in 1985 had small children. Over half (56 percent) had lived with their partners for more than five years. Although 20 percent of the women were working outside the home, 41 percent of these women earned less than $7000 a year, 27 percent earned between $7000 and $10 000, and 27 percent earned between $10 000 and $20 000. Using Statistics Canada income-cutoffs, MacLeod estimated that at least 68 percent of the women who were working for pay would be living below the poverty line if they tried to support themselves and their children with their own earnings. As MacLeod states:

> These statistics add a practical dimension to the emotional bonds women feel for their husbands and their concern for their children's futures which keep so many battered women with their partners . . . . Even if their lives with their husbands are also uncertain and brutal, being on their own with small children undoubtedly and *realistically* looks equally terrifying for many of the women in the sample. (MacLeod, 1987:21)

Confronted with inadequate financial means to support herself and her children, limited social support networks that would facilitate leaving, the fear (often instilled by her partner) of losing custody of the children, and the threats made (against herself, her children, and her relatives) in the event she does leave, a battered woman will, more often than not, "choose" to remain in the relationship. Even if she does end the relationship, the violence may continue.

The lobbying efforts by women's groups have resulted in some significant policy changes within the criminal justice system. In 1983, a national directive was implemented to encourage police to lay charges in wife-battering cases (previously, the decision was left to the wishes of the complainant). In addition, police training has been upgraded to stress sensitive intervention in cases of wife assault, and several provinces have established specialized courts to deal with domestic violence. These various initiatives have resulted in increasing numbers of abusive men being dealt with by the courts. In the province of Manitoba alone, for example, the number of individuals (approximately 96 percent of whom were men) charged with spousal assault increased from 1136 in 1983 to 2035 in 1988/89 (Ursel, 1991).

The changes which have occurred within the criminal justice system have a symbolic value in that they carry a strong message of society's unwillingness to tolerate wife battering. Nevertheless, questions have been raised as to whether the traditionally punitive and adversarial nature of the system is the most effective means of combatting the problem. Advocates within the women's movement have also been concerned with the provision of adequate protection for battered women (restraining orders and peace bonds), counselling for male batterers, and support for battered women and their children in the form of shelters and secondary housing. With regard to the latter, the number of shelters in Canada increased from 85 in 1982 to 264 in 1987 (MacLeod, 1987:3). Since 1985, over 13 400 women and children in Manitoba have turned to abuse shelters for help (*Winnipeg Free Press*, 27 December 1989).

WIFE-BEATER'S SENTENCE ASSAILED

Manitoba's justice system fails when a man who punches a kitten receives a stiffer sentence than one man who beat his wife with a garden spade, spokesmen for domestic abuse shelters charge.

Lesley McCorrister was commenting on a decision last Thursday in which a Gladstone man with a history of wife abuse received a two-year suspended sentence for his latest attack on his common-law wife.

John Albert Richard, 24, pleaded guilty to assault with a weapon before provincial court Judge Bruce McDonald, who told him he had used his wife "for a punching bag for quite a number of years."

Court was told Richard broke the handle of a spade over his wife's hand while she attempted to defend herself during an alcohol-fuelled argument last June.

Police found her lying naked face-down on the bed with bruises on her side and right shoulder when they responded to a complaint about the assault.

A 10-year-old boy was also struck by an errant blow, court was told.

Crown attorney Ed Sloane told the court that there had been numerous reports of Richard assaulting his wife since 1982. He received a conditional discharge in 1984 for beating his wife and another woman.

'IT'S PRETTY IRONIC'

"It's pretty ironic that a 21-year-old Winnipeg man gets three months in jail for beating a kitten and a man gets no sentence for beating his wife," said McCorrister, a counsellor with the Evolve program at Klinic Community Health Centre in Winnipeg.

A Winnipeg man received a three-month sentence last Friday after he was found guilty of cruelty to animals Feb. 17 in provincial court. Witnesses said the man punched his kitten repeatedly and submerged it in water.

Judge Charles Newcombe called the crime "shocking cruelty" and said his sentence might tell the public people who abuse animals will be punished if they are caught.

But, citing the Gladstone case, McCorrister said the same message is not getting across to spouse-abusers.

"That says it all when we value a kitten more than we value human lives," she added.

"It's total ineptitude on the part of our court system."

McCorrister called the suspended sentence, which does not involve spending time in jail, "a slap on the wrist."

Portage Women's Shelter co-ordinator Ann Maxwell agreed that such sentences deliver the wrong message to men—that violence in the home is acceptable.

"The charges (for assault on spouses) are often lenient and the sentences are ridiculous," Maxwell said.

"Until the legal system starts holding the perpetrators accountable, it's just going to go on and on," McCorrister added, referring to domestic abuse.

"It's not OK to give out heavy sentences just to people who beat cats."

Source: Randy Turner. "Wife-beater's sentence assailed." *Winnipeg Free Press* 24 February 1988.

IMPLICATIONS FOR CRIMINOLOGY

The reality of violence against women was made most evident on December 6, 1989, when Marc Lépine entered a classroom at the École Polytéchnique in Montreal, separated the men from the women students, proclaimed "You're all a bunch of feminists," and proceeded to gun them down. Fourteen women were killed that day and thirteen others wounded. Lépine's suicide letter explicitly identified his action as politically motivated: he blamed "feminists" for the major disappointments in his life. Police also found a "hit list" containing the names of prominent women.

A TIME FOR GRIEF AND PAIN

MONTREAL

Fourteen women are dead for one reason: they are women. Their male classmates are still alive for one reason: they are men. While gender divides us in thousands of ways every day, rarely are the consequences of misogyny so tragic.

I found out about the murders early yesterday morning. I came home from dinner with friends about 1 a.m., and listened as usual to my answering machine. It was the last message that gave me a jolt. It was a good friend telling me there would be a vigil last night for the 14 women who had been killed at the University of Montreal.

Not believing my ears and desperate for news, I turned on the radio. I ended up listening to an open-line show. The talk was about relationships between young men and women these days.

Most of the callers were men. They blamed the murders on everything from drugs and condom distributors in high schools to women who have made men feel insecure. Many callers said they did not understand what had happened. It's all very well and fine to be misogynous, said one caller, but you can't lose your head.

I realized, as I was listening to this show, that I was trembling. So were the voices of the female callers. I felt something I had not experienced in a very long time: fear of being alone in my apartment. There were sounds at the window I would normally ignore. Now I could not. Immobilized, I was afraid to stay alone and afraid to go out.

It does not matter that the man who decided to kill 14 women—and he clearly did decide to do that—killed himself afterward; it is not of him I am afraid. I am afraid of what he represents, of all the unspoken hatred, the pent-up anger that he expressed. Hatred and anger that is shared by every husband who beats his wife, every man who rapes his date, every father who abuses his child, and by many more who would not dare.

It happened at the École Polytéchnique in Montreal but it could have been anywhere.

It would be a great mistake, I think, to see this incident as some kind of freak accident, the act of a madman that has nothing to do with the society in which we live. The killer was angry at women, at feminism, at his own loss of power. He yelled: "You're all a bunch of feminists" on his way to killing 14 women.

Now there is little that is comforting to say to women. It is a time for grief for all of us; grief for those who have died, and pain at being reminded of how deep misogyny still runs in our society.

Source: Diana Bronson. "A time for grief and pain." *The Globe and Mail*
8 December 1989:A7.

The Montreal Massacre has served to reinforce what women's groups across the country have been arguing for decades: that violence against women is a widespread and pervasive feature of our society. It takes the form of sexual harassment in the workplace, of date rape, of violent sexual assaults, of incest, and of wife abuse. While the murder of fourteen women in Montreal has understandably received the attention and publicity it deserves, it is also noteworthy that the violence that women encounter at the hands of men has become "routine." In August 1990 alone, eleven women in Montreal were killed by their male partners, many of them estranged. Yet, two of every three women going to a shelter in Montreal are turned away because of lack of space (*The Globe and Mail*, 26 September 1990).

Making violence against women a central issue has required a dramatic restructuring and reordering of criminological theory and practice. Much of traditional criminology has tended to mirror the cultural construction of rape, which essentially blames women for their own victimization. In his "classic" study of rape, for example, Menachem Amir (1971) introduced the notion of "victim precipitation." The concept suggests that some women are "rape prone" or invite rape, and his work essentially blames the victim for the violence she encounters. Criminology has also tended to take as a "given" the authority exercised by males in both the private and public spheres. However, by calling into question the traditional structures which reinforce the unequal position of women in society, attention is directed to questions such as: Why is it that many men in our society believe they have the right to abuse women? To what extent are such beliefs reflected in law and legal practice?

Making violence against women a central issue also has implications for criminal justice policy and practice. For example, it raises questions such as: Is incarceration of offenders the most effective means for breaking the cycle of violence? What supports are offered to victims of violence? In addition to the need to protect women from violence, what steps can be taken to end the social and economic dependency which women as a group encounter in our society? Clearly, the efforts of the women's movement to improve the conditions and quality of women's lives have had far-reaching effects on the nature of the criminological enterprise.

FEMINISM IN THE ACADEMY: EXPLAINING WOMEN'S CRIMINALITY

Coinciding with the social and political activities of the women's movement, the last two decades have witnessed the growing impact of feminist scholarship. One of the basic findings of feminist scholars has been that women have been rendered invisible by codified knowledge (Spender 1980, 1981). Historically, the producers of that knowledge have all been male. They have produced theories and analyses and have checked with one another as to their accuracy. Over time, each of the academic disciplines has developed its own canon, that is, a body of knowledge considered essential to a full understanding of the discipline, its claims, and its major findings. That canon, and the views of the world reflected by it, are both very much male-defined and male-centred.

Women have not only been excluded as producers of knowledge, they have also been missing as research subjects. One implication of this exclusion is that scientific studies have tended to generalize what they have learned from the study of men to the lives of women. When women are considered, they tend to be measured against male norms and standards (Gilligan, 1982). In response, one of the tasks of feminist scholarship has been to develop knowledge that is *women-centred:* knowledge that is about and for women.

MAINSTREAM THEORIES IN CRIMINOLOGY

Criminology is not exempt from this criticism. Since the 1970s, traditional approaches to explaining crime have come under increasing scrutiny. Writers like Carol Smart (1976), Eileen Leonard (1982), Frances Heidensohn (1985), Allison Morris (1987), and Ngaire Naffine (1987) have highlighted the general failure of the mainstream theories in criminology to adequately explain or account for the differential crime rates of men and women.

For example, in explaining crime in relation to the strain that results from the disjunction between culture goals (like monetary success) and institutionalized means (education, jobs), Robert Merton's anomie theory reflected a sensitivity to the class inequalities that exist in society. The same could not be said, however, with regard to an awareness of sexual inequalities. If, according to Merton, lower-class individuals were more likely to engage in crime because of a lack of access to the institutionalized means for achieving monetary success, then it follows that women—who as a group experience a similar lack of access—should also be found to commit crime as a consequence of this strain. This is not the case. In a reformulation of anomie theory, Leonard (1982) has suggested that females may be socialized to aspire to different culture goals than males—in particular, relational ones concerning marriage and having children. If this is the case, then women's low rate of criminality would be explained by the relatively easy manner in which females can realize their goals. As Allison Morris (1987) suggests, however, such a formulation relies upon an idealized and romanticized version of women's lives. Not only does it display an insensitivity to the strains and frustrations associated with women's familial role, it fails to acknowledge the economic concerns that women confront.

Like strain theory, Edwin Sutherland's differential association theory is presented as a general theory of crime. In focusing on the processes by which individuals learn definitions of the legal codes as either favourable or unfavourable, Sutherland posited the existence of a "cultural heterogeneity" in society with regard to pro- and anti-criminal associations. While this cultural heterogeneity accounted for men's involvement in crime, women were the anomaly or exception in that they displayed a "cultural homogeneity." In Sutherland's view, women were more altruistic and compliant than men. As Naffine (1987) has noted, Sutherland missed a great opportunity when he neglected to explore this apparent cultural homogeneity in females. Given his critical outlook on the individualism and competition which he felt characterized American society, an examination of women's conformity could have provided Sutherland with clues to better understand crime and its causes.

Travis Hirschi's work on social control theory is also characterized by a neglect of the female. While other criminologists focused their attention on explaining deviance, Hirschi set out to explain conformity. In this regard, since women appear to be more conformist than men, it would have made sense to treat women as central to his analysis. Nevertheless, despite having collected data on female subjects, Hirschi set them aside and—like his colleagues—concentrated on males. While subsequent efforts have been made to apply control theory to female delinquents (Jensen and Eve, 1976; Hagan et al., 1979; Shover et al. 1979), their results have been inconclusive. As Naffine (1987:74–75) has noted: "Although there is considerable evidence of the greater 'bonding' of females to society, this has yet to be linked consistently with either femininity, as conventionally conceived, or to conformity."

With the advent of the labelling and conflict theories during the 1960s and 1970s, the potential for a more inclusive approach to crime increased. Nevertheless, while Howard Becker's labelling perspective raised the question "whose side are we on?" and advocated an approach to deviance that gave a voice to those who were subject to the labelling process, it was never fully realized in the case of women. Similarly, Taylor, Walton, and Young's *The New Criminology* (1973), which offered up a devastating critique of the traditional criminological theories, failed to give any mention to women.

In general, when sex differentials in crime are considered by the mainstream theories, the tendency has been to rely on stereotypical constructions of masculinity and femininity: men are aggressive, independent, daring, and adventurous; women are submissive, dependent, and compliant. In the process, female offenders are cast as a rather "dull lot." Even in their deviance they are less interesting than men. Moreover, such stereotypical depictions of women have been considered "so obvious" that they require no further discussion (see, for example, Cohen, 1955:142)—let alone theoretical or empirical concern.

We have seen in Chapter 4 that females commit less serious offences, in smaller numbers, and with less frequency than males. Criminologists have typically responded to this by formulating their theories to account for only male crime and delinquency. The ramifications of this tendency have been spelled out by Gelsthorpe and Morris:

> Theories are weak if they do not apply to half of the potential criminal population; women, after all, experience the same deprivations, family structures and so on that men do. Theories of crime should be able to take account of both men's and women's behaviour and to highlight those factors which operate differently on men and women. Whether or not a particular theory helps us to understand women's crime is of *fundamental*, not marginal importance for criminology. (Gelsthorpe and Morris, 1988:103, emphasis added)

THEORIES OF WOMEN'S CRIME

While women have been relegated to the role of "other" in the mainstream theories in criminology, there have been other theories which have attempted to account for female criminality.

The Early Approaches

Historically, a particular pathway can be followed when tracing the initial attempts to explain women's criminality. It begins with the publication of Cesare Lombroso and William Ferrero's *The Female Offender* in 1895, and is followed by W.I. Thomas's *The Unadjusted Girl* in 1923, and Otto Pollak's *The Criminality of Women* in 1950. In each of these works, women are viewed as "naturally inferior" to men, and it is this inferiority which is used to explain women's criminality.

For example, in applying the concepts of atavism and social Darwinism, Lombroso and Ferrero suggested that women possessed limited intelligence. They were also less sensitive to pain than men, full of revenge and jealousy, and naturally passive and conservative. These "feminine traits" were seen as physiological in their origins. Women's natural passivity, for instance, was caused by the "immobility of the ovule compared to the zoosperm" (Lombroso and Ferrero, 1895:109). Atavistically, women were considered to display fewer signs of degeneration than men. The reason, according to Lombroso and Ferrero, was that women (and nonwhite males) had not advanced as far along the evolutionary continuum as (white) males, and so could not degenerate as far. Given that women were relatively "primitive," the criminals among them would not be highly visible. However, those women who were criminal were cast as excessively vile and cruel in their crimes. They combined the qualities of the criminal male with the worst characteristics of the female: cunning, spite, and deceitfulness. Lacking the "maternal instinct" and "ladylike qualities," criminal women were seen as genetically more male than female.

W.I. Thomas's work on female delinquency was premised on a similar kind of biological determinism. Thomas suggested that human behaviour was based on four "wishes": desires for adventure, security, response, and recognition. These wishes corresponded to features in the nervous system, which were expressed as biological instincts of anger, fear, love, and the will to gain status and power respectively. However, Thomas asserted that men's and women's instincts differed both in quantity and quality. Since women had more varieties of love in their nervous systems, their desire for response was greater than men's. According to Thomas, it was this need to feel love that accounted for women's criminality, and especially prostitution.

Thomas believed the behaviour of men and women to be governed by different moral codes: whereas men were controlled in the area of productive tasks, women were controlled in the area of sexual conduct. With the breakdown of traditional community ties, which allowed women to work outside the home and to marry outside of their community group, previous restraints were no longer effective. As a consequence, women, especially lower-class women, were more likely to become promiscuous.

Thomas essentially saw women as property: their value lay in the fact that they were objects to be "desired" and "adored." Accordingly, middle-class girls were socialized to sublimate their natural desires and to treat their chastity as an investment for marriage. Lower-class girls, lacking this socialization process, became amoral and engaged in promiscuity to fulfil their desire for adventure. In short, "good girls" were the ones who kept their bodies as capital to sell in matrimony for security; "bad girls" traded their bodies for excitement. Either way, women were scheming and vain: they manipulated male desires for sex to achieve their own ends.

Otto Pollak carried this tradition further in his attempt to account for the "masked" nature of women's crime. Sceptical of the official data on gender differences in crime, Pollak suggested that women's crime was vastly undercounted. To explain this, he put forward the view that female criminality was more likely to be hidden and undetected. Women were more often the instigators than perpetrators of crime. Like Eve in the Garden of Eden, they manipulated men into committing offences. Women were also inherently deceptive and vengeful: they engaged in prostitution, blackmailed their lovers, as domestics they stole from their employers, and as homemakers they carried out horrendous acts on their families, like poisoning the sick and abusing children. According to Pollak, woman's devious nature was rooted in her physiology. While a man must achieve erection in order to perform the sex act and, hence, will not be able to hide his failure, a woman can fake orgasm (Pollak, 1961:10). This ability to conceal orgasm gave women practice at deception. Pollak also suggested, in true Freudian fashion, that female crime was caused by the vengefulness, irritability, and depression women encountered as a result of their generative phases. Menstruation, for example, in reminding women of their inferior status (and their ultimate failure to become men), drove women to acts of revenge. The concealed nature of their crimes, the vulnerability of their victims, and their chivalrous treatment by men who cannot bear to prosecute or punish them, all combined to "mask" women's offences. When these factors are all taken into account, women's crimes are equal in severity and number to those of men. Indeed, Pollak even went so far as to suggest that male white-collar criminals—who go largely unprosecuted—employ female servants who steal, therefore equalizing the amount of criminal activity.

In the following passage, Otto Pollak offers us an illustration of a male-centred view of what has been traditionally referred to as the "woman problem" and its relationship to female criminality:

The student of female criminality cannot afford to overlook the generally known and recognized fact that [women's] generative phases are frequently accompanied by psychological disturbances which may upset the need satisfaction balance of the individual or weaken her internal inhibitions, and thus become causative factors in female crime. Particularly because of the social meaning attached to them in our culture, the generative phases of women are bound to present many stumbling blocks for the law-abiding behavior of women. Menstruation with its appearance of injury must confirm feelings of guilt which individuals may have about sex activities which they have learned to consider as forbidden. As a symbol of womanhood, it must also, because of its recurrent nature, aggravate any feeling of irritation and protest which women may have regarding their sex in a society in which women have had, and still have, to submit to social inequality with men. In both instances, it must lead to a disturbance of the emotional balance of the individual and thus become potentially crime-promoting. Pregnancy in a culture which frowns upon illegitimacy and fosters in large sectors of society limitation in the number of children or even childlessness must become a source of irritation, anxiety, and emotional upheaval in many instances. The menopause in a society which makes romance and emotional gratification the supreme value in a monogamous marriage system must be experienced, at least by married women, frequently as a threat to the basis of their emotional security if not to their general marital existence. In view of these cultural implications of the generative phases and their psychological consequences, it is difficult to understand why the existing literature contains so little discussion of their possible crime-promoting influence.

Source: Otto Pollak. (1961). *The Criminality of Women* (pp 157–58). New York: A.S. Barnes.

As Heidensohn (1985:122) notes, these early approaches to explaining women's crime lent an aura of intellectual respectability to many of the old folktales about women and their behaviours. They reflected the widely held assumptions about "women's nature," including the "good girl/bad girl" duality and a double standard that viewed sexual promiscuity as a sign of "amorality" in women but "normality" in men. Relying on "common sense," anecdotal evidence, and circular reasoning—that is, "things are as they are because they are natural, and they are natural because that is the way things are" (Smart, 1976:36)—the early theorists failed to call into question the structural features of their society and the gendered nature of the roles of men and women. Instead, sex (a biological difference) and gender (a cultural prescription) were equated as one and the same, with the "ladylike qualities" of the middle- and upper-class white woman used as the measuring rod for what is inherently female. In the process, the theories constructed were not only sexist, but classist and racist as well.

While we can look back on these early theories with some amusement, it bears noting that the kinds of assumptions and beliefs reflected in the works of Lombroso and Ferrero, Thomas, and Pollak have not disappeared. As Klein (1979:61) comments, "The road from Lombroso to the present is surprisingly straight." Throughout the 1960s, researchers continued to rely on the assumptions and premises of the earlier approaches. Cowie, Cowie, and Slater (1968), for example, in the tradition of Lombroso and Ferrero, looked for "constitutional predisposing factors" to explain female delinquency. Accordingly, delinquent girls were characterized as "oversized, lumpish, uncouth and graceless" (1968:167). Gisella Konopka (1966), in extending Thomas' analysis, equated sexual delinquency in girls with a desperate need for love. As recently as the 1980s, hormonal changes associated with women's menstrual cycles have been linked to crime (Nicholson and Barltrop, 1982), and prostitution continues to be viewed as a sign of individual psychopathology (McLeod, 1982). As Smart (1976) has noted, the early approaches have had a long-lasting and harmful effect, not only on the understanding of female crime, but also on the treatment of women offenders. To the extent that the policies and practices of the criminal justice system mirror and reinforce the stereotypes of women and girls found in the theories, they will also mirror and reinforce the inferior and unequal status of women in society.

Sex Role Socialization and the Women's Liberation Thesis

In the 1970s, theories of women's crime began to shift toward a more sociological orientation. One of the most prominent approaches during this time was role theory, which looked at female criminality in terms of the differing gender roles and socialization processes of males and females. Dale Hoffman-Bustamante (1973), for example, suggested that the lower rate of delinquency for girls can be accounted for by differential socialization and child-rearing practices. Whereas boys are encouraged to be aggressive, outgoing, and ambitious, and are allowed greater freedom, girls are taught to be passive and domesticated, and are more closely supervised. Since girls are taught to be nonviolent, they do not acquire the skills, technical ability, or physical strength to engage in violent acts like gang fighting. And when women do engage in violent behaviour, their actions reflect their greater domesticity. For example, women murderers are more likely to use kitchen knives than guns. The finding that women are more likely to be charged with shoplifting offences is similarly explained with reference to their gender roles and socialization. Women are traditionally the consumers in society and, when they steal, girls are more likely to take small items like make-up. Role theory, then, offers an explanation in terms of differential gender socialization for both the types and nature of offences that women commit.

Carol Smart (1976) has commented that role theory can only offer a partial explanation of crime. Because of a failure to situate the discussion of gender roles in broader structural terms, little attention is devoted to *why* socialization patterns are gender differentiated and *how* they have come to be that way. In the absence of a structural analysis, it is too easy to fall back on explanations that view such differences as biological, and not social, in their origins: "role is destiny" can therefore act as a ready substitute for "anatomy is destiny" (Morris, 1987:64).

The 1970s also saw the emergence of the women's liberation thesis. As reflected in the work of Rita Simon (1975) and especially Freda Adler (1975), the basic idea behind this thesis was that changes in women's gender roles will be reflected in their rates of criminal involvement. Simon suggested that the increased employment opportunities that accompanied the women's movement would also bring an increase in opportunities to commit crime (such as embezzlement from employers). Adler linked the apparent increase in women's crime statistics to the influence of the women's movement and suggested that a "new female criminal" was emerging: women were becoming more violent and aggressive, just like their male counterparts.

The women's liberation thesis received considerable attention from criminologists, and has already been discussed at some length in Chapter 4. Suffice it to say, however, that it is an approach that can be faulted on a number of grounds. In particular, in drawing connections between the women's movement and crime, it equates "being liberated" with "freedom to be male," as opposed to a resistance to and rejection of traditional gender stereotypes. Chesney-Lind (1980) has interpreted the women's liberation thesis and the attention it generated as part of a more general backlash to the women's movement. She likens it to the moral panic around witch hunts that sought to enforce appropriate female roles. This concern over women's emancipation and crime is certainly not new in criminology. Criminologists since Lombroso have issued warnings about the possible harmful effects of women's increased freedom. In this respect, the argument that improving women's position in society only brings increased crime adds fuel to the conservative fire in that it intimates: "See what happens when women are let out of their homes."

In a more recent attempt to place role theory in a structural context, John Hagan and his colleagues (Hagan, Simpson, and Gillis, 1979, 1987; Hagan, Gillis, and Simpson, 1985, 1990) have advanced a power-control theory of sex and delinquency. Power-control theory is designed to explain the sex difference in delinquency by drawing linkages between the variations in parental control and the delinquent behaviour of boys and girls. More specifically, Hagan and his colleagues suggest that parental control and adolescents' subsequent attitudes toward risk-taking behaviour will be affected by family class relations. They distinguish two ideal types of family: the *patriarchal family* where the husband is employed in an authority position in the workforce and the wife is not employed outside the home, and the *egalitarian family* in which both husband and wife are employed in authority positions outside the home. Hagan and his colleagues suggest that, in the former, a traditional gender division will exist, whereby fathers and especially mothers are expected to control their daughters more than their sons. Given the presence of a "cult of domesticity," girls will be socialized to focus their futures on domestic labour and consumption activities, while boys will be prepared for their participation in production activities. In the latter form, parents will redistribute their control efforts such that girls are subject to controls more like those imposed on boys. "In other words, in egalitarian families, as mothers gain power relative to husbands, daughters gain freedom relative to sons" (Hagan et al., 1987:792).

In terms of delinquent behaviour, Hagan and his colleagues rely on the control theory assertion that delinquency is a form of risk-taking behaviour. Given that risk taking is associated with the entrepreneurial activity associated with production, and that, in egalitarian families, both sons and daughters will be socialized to assume roles in the productive sphere, the authors predict that "patriarchal families will be characterized by large gender differences in common delinquent behaviours while egalitarian families will be characterized by smaller gender differences in delinquency" (Hagan et al., 1987:793).

In their efforts to draw the connections between class, gender divisions in the family, and female delinquency, Hagan, Simpson, and Gillis have done much to advance role theory by informing it with a more structural analysis. Throughout the 1980s, such a project became even more explicit in the work of the feminist criminologists.

Feminist Criminology

In its initial stages of development, feminist criminology consisted of a critique of both mainstream approaches and theories of women's crime. In and of itself, however, this critique does not constitute a "feminist criminology." As Smart noted in the conclusion to her book: "...it is not adequate to present a theory which is based solely on the negation of existing theories" (1976:183). Over the past two decades, what began as a critique soon moved toward the task of constructing explicitly feminist theories and frameworks to better understand and explain women's crime. In general terms, this work has been characterized by (1) an attempt to break away from the sexist assumptions that are both implicit and explicit in the existing approaches, and (2) an effort to locate women's crime in its broader structural context. As this task has unfolded, it has become evident that the development of a comprehensive theory of women's crime required stepping outside the traditional boundaries of criminology. As a result, much of the work in this area has drawn on the various feminist frameworks (Jaggar, 1983; Tong, 1989) that have been developed to understand the nature of the oppression which women as a group encounter in society.

For example, socialist feminism is a theoretical framework which represents a revision or reformulation of traditional Marxism in order to rectify its "sex-blindness" (Hartman, 1981). Marxism is a theoretical approach which gives primacy to the exploitative class relations in a capitalist society. In traditional Marxist thought, the emphasis is on the *sphere of production*, where the labour power of the worker is transformed to produce surplus value or profit for the capitalist. Socialist feminists, however, argue that an equally important labour process is that which takes place in the *sphere of reproduction.* This reproductive or domestic labour is theorized as a necessary complement of the wage labour/capital relation and involves four interrelated tasks: looking after adult members of the household (reproducing labour power on a daily basis); childbirth and child-rearing; housework (cooking, cleaning, and washing clothes); and the transformation of wages into goods and services for household use ("making ends meet" by shopping, sewing clothes, growing and preserving food) (Luxton, 1980:18–19). While reproductive labour is found in all societies, under capitalism the productive and reproductive spheres have been separated or divided into public and private spheres. In the process, "housework" has become synonymous with "women's work." More-over, while productive labour (working for wages) generally takes place outside the home, reproductive (or domestic) labour—previously integrated with the other labour of the household—has become "devalued." It is con-sidered "unproductive" labour because it does not directly contribute to the surplus value or profit of the capitalist class.

Socialist feminists focus on the interconnection between capitalism (class) and patriarchy (gender) and the manner in which class and gender relations are manifested in the productive and reproductive spheres of society. In this way, the socialist feminist framework puts forward an account of the specific nature of women's oppression in a patriarchal capitalist society. On the one hand, attention to class leads to analyses of women's work in both the productive and reproductive spheres. For example, although women have been entering the labour force in large numbers in recent decades, they have, by and large, been restricted to the lowest paid, most monotonous, and least secure jobs (Wilson, 1991). In addition, since domestic labour in the house-hold continues to be relegated to women, those who work for wages carry the burden of a double day's work (Armstrong and Armstrong, 1984).

Attention to gender, on the other hand, leads to analyses of the particular ways in which men exercise control over women and women's sexuality. This is done both overtly through such means as the medicalization of childbirth, the objectification of women's bodies in pornography, and violence against women in the forms of rape and wife abuse, and covertly, in the form of a "monogamous heterosexuality" which historically has legitimated male con-trol over children and property and reinforced the ideology that women are dependent on men for both their economic and sexual needs. Moreover, male dominance is maintained not only by the family and economic system, but also by the state, media, and religious and educational systems. Socialist feminists, therefore, maintain that, like the class relations under capitalism, gender relations under patriarchy have both material (economic) and ideo-logical (cultural) dimensions.

The adoption of frameworks such as socialist feminism has directed feminist criminologists to an investigation of a number of salient issues. For example, Francis Heidensohn (1985) suggests that the issue of women's criminality and conformity can best be approached from the perspective of social control, both in terms of the roles women play *in* social control (for example, in the domestic sphere as socialization agents) and in terms of the formal and informal controls which constrain and modify women's behaviour. While the former direct attention to the ways in which women themselves have played key parts in perpetuating the existing system, Heidensohn argues that they pale in comparison to the controlling forces operating *upon* women. For example, women's isolation in the home under the supervision of men is seen as very much akin to a prison; it acts as a powerful disciplining force. Women also confront a public sphere that is both controlled and defined by men.

With regard to women who come into conflict with the law, the available data reflect the class and gender inequalities of the larger society. Women offenders tend to be young, poor, undereducated, and unskilled. Many are addicted to alcohol and other drugs. Large numbers have been victims of physical and sexual abuse, and many are emotionally and financially dependent on abusive male partners (Johnson, 1987:26). In addition, while Native people in Canada are disproportionately represented in crime statistics, the over-representation of Native women in jail is even greater than that of Native men (LaPrairie, 1987), which suggests that the structure of inequality in Canadian society extends to not only class and gender, but race as well.

The types of offences committed by women can also be viewed in the context of their structural position in a patriarchal capitalist society. Women are typically involved in property crimes. For example, in 1985, of all women charged with criminal offences, 40.4 percent were charged with theft and 13.1 percent with fraud. This is more than twice the proportion of men charged with these offences (16.3 percent theft and 6.1 percent fraud). Johnson (1987:26, 29) suggests that "women's participation in property offences is consistent with their traditional roles as consumers and, increasingly, as low income, semi-skilled, sole support providers for their families. In keeping with the rapid increase in female-headed households and the stresses associated with poverty, greater numbers of women are being charged with shoplifting, cheque forging and welfare fraud." In contrast to the women's liberation thesis, feminist criminologists would suggest that increases in women's crime are more directly connected with the "feminization of poverty" than with women's emancipation. Moreover, according to Johnson, women's involvement in prostitution is also a reflection of their subordinate social and economic position in society:

> Prostitution thrives in a society which values women more for their sexuality than for their unskilled labour, and which puts women in a class of commodity to be bought and sold. Research has shown one of the major causes of prostitution to be the economic plight of women, particularly young, poorly educated women who are unable to find other employment. Entry into prostitution is also typically characterized by running away from home, often to escape physical and sexual abuse. Rather than providing a refuge from ill-treatment, however, street life puts women at greater risk of further violence and abuse, and

significantly increases their vulnerability to identification and arrest by police. (Johnson, 1987:29–30)

Another issue being investigated by feminist criminologists is the treatment of women offenders by the criminal justice system. In the tradition of writers like Otto Pollak, it has long been held that women offenders fare better than men in the criminal justice system because of the "chivalry" factor, whereby law enforcement and court officials are viewed as showing more leniency to females than males. Research which supports this hypothesis indicates that chivalry, when it does exist, benefits some women more than others—in particular, the few white middle- or upper-class women who come into conflict with the law. It also appears to apply only to those female suspects who behave in a stereotypical fashion, that is, "crying, pleading for release for the sake of their children, claiming men have led them astray" (Rafter and Natalazia, 1981:92). In this regard, Rafter and Natalazia have argued that chivalrous behaviour should be seen as a tool for the preservation of patriarchy rather than as a benign effort to treat women with some special kindness.

Feminist criminologists have also addressed the situation of women in prison. For those women in Canada who are incarcerated, the fact that they have been deemed "too few to count" (Adelberg and Currie, 1987) means that the facilities and programs made available to them pale in comparison to those available to male prisoners. While there are over 40 prisons in Canada for men serving sentences of two years or more, there is currently only one federal institution for women, the Prison for Women in Kingston, Ontario. This means that women are denied the same opportunities as men for transfer to facilities with a reduced security classification or special program options, or to a preferred geographical location (Johnson, 1987). Most of the programs for women prisoners reflect the gender stereotyping found in the wider society—cooking, cleaning, childcare, cosmetology, sewing, and typing—and prospects for release are more often than not tied to a woman's ability to live up to the expectations associated with traditional notions of femininity (Elliot and Morris, 1987). Moreover, given women's reproductive role in society, incarceration for long periods and at great distances from their homes and families places a special burden on women prisoners. In a report prepared for the Ministry of the Solicitor General, Linda MacLeod estimated that 4 percent of women admitted to correctional institutions are pregnant, 50 percent have borne children, and 30 percent had been living with their children prior to incarceration (cited in Johnson, 1987:39).

SUMMARY

As feminist criminology has developed, attention has increasingly been focused on the structural constraints which limit and constrain women's lives. In the process of formulating alternative approaches, there has been considerable discussion and debate as to the specific direction and form which a feminist criminology should take. Smart, for one, has cautioned against a "separatist" approach. She suggests that singling out women and crime as a separate area of study within the discipline could easily lead to a "ghettoization" of the subject matter. Similar arguments have been made with regard to women's studies as a separate area within the academy. Clearly, women and men do not act separately in society. Their lives interconnect in intricate and complex ways. At the same time, however, there is a need to redress the sex imbalance that has historically existed within academic scholarship. "Women only" spaces are needed for women's experiences to be named, captured, and validated.

What this suggests, therefore, is that the task of feminist criminology, and criminology in general, is twofold. First, there is a need to further explore and develop a women-centred analysis within criminology. This will involve a re-evaluation of the accumulated knowledge about female offenders, the nature of their offences, and the claims made about their "differences" from men. It will also require an examination of the practices and policies of the legal system as they apply to women. Such analyses must be situated within the broader economic, political, and social spheres that have an impact on women's status and position in society. As such, they will need to be sensitive to the ways in which gender, class, and race interconnect and intersect. Second, mainstream criminology must itself be redirected. Making women more visible in criminology will require not simply letting women in to the mainstream of the discipline, but developing alternative ways of conceptualizing and studying the social world so that the interests and concerns of both men and women are included. In this respect, it could be argued that criminological theories have tended to be sexist, not just in their treatment of women, but also in the stereotypical ways in which they have portrayed men and manhood. If these tasks are pursued, it is clear that, in the process, the criminological enterprise will itself be transformed.

BIBLIOGRAPHY

Adler, Freda. (1975). *Sisters in Crime.* New York: McGraw-Hill.
Amir, Menachem. (1971). *The Patterns of Forcible Rape.* Chicago: University of Chicago Press.
Armstrong, P., and H. Armstrong. (1984). *The Double Ghetto.* (rev. ed.). Toronto: McClelland and Stewart.
Atcheson, M. Elizabeth, Mary Eberts, and Beth Symes. (1984). *Women and Legal Action: Precedents, Resources and Strategies for the Future.* Ottawa: CACSW.
Boyd, Susan B., and Elizabeth A. Sheehy. (1989). "Overview." In T. Caputo et al. (eds.), *Law and Society: A Critical Perspective.* (pp. 255–70). Toronto: Harcourt Brace Jovanovich.
Boyle, Christine. (1984). *Sexual Assault.* Toronto: Carswell.

————. (1991). "Sexual Assault: A Case Study of Legal Policy Options." In Margaret Jackson and Curt Griffiths (eds.), *Canadian Criminology: Perspectives on Crime and Criminality* (pp. 99–109). Toronto: Harcourt Brace Jovanovich.

Brownmiller, Susan. (1975). *Against Our Will: Men, Women and Rape.* New York: Bantam Books.

Canadian Advisory Council on the Status of Women. (1985a). *Sexual Assault.* Ottawa: CACSW.

————. (1985b). *Women and Poverty.* Ottawa: CACSW.

Chesney-Lind, Meda. (1980). "Rediscovering Lilith: Misogyny and the 'New Female Criminality.' " In C. Taylor Griffiths and M. Nance (eds.), *The Female Offenders.* Vancouver: Simon Fraser University.

Clark, Lorenne, and Debra Lewis. (1977). *Rape: The Price of Coercive Sexuality.* Toronto: Women's Press.

Cohen, Albert. (1955). *Delinquent Boys.* Glencoe, IL: The Free Press.

Comack, Elizabeth. (1987, 1988). "Women Defendants and the 'Battered Wife Syndrome': A Plea for the Sociological Imagination." *Crown Counsel's Review* 5(11) (December) and 5(12) (February).

Cowie, John, Valerie Cowie, and Eliot Slater. (1968). *Delinquency in Girls.* London: Heinemann.

Dobash, R. Emerson, and Russell Dobash. (1979). *Violence Against Wives: A Case against Patriarchy.* New York: Free Press.

Edwards, Susan. (1985). "Gender 'Justice'? Defending Defendants and Mitigating Sentence" in S. Edwards (ed.), *Gender, Sex and the Law* (pp. 129–55). Kent: Croom Helm.

Elliot, Liz, and Ruth Morris. (1987). "Behind Prison Doors." In Adelberg and Currie (eds.), *Too Few to Count: Canadian Women in Conflict with the Law* (pp. 145–62). Vancouver: Press Gang.

Gelsthorpe, Loraine, and Allison Morris. (1988). "Feminism and Criminology in Britain." *British Journal of Criminology* 28:93–110.

Gilligan, Carol. (1982). *In a Different Voice: Psychological Theory and Women's Development.* Cambridge MA: Harvard University Press.

Gunn, Rita, and Candice Minch. (1988). *Sexual Assault: The Dilemma of Disclosure, the Question of Conviction.* Winnipeg: University of Manitoba Press.

Hagan, J., A.R. Gillis, and J. Simpson. (1985). "The Class Structure of Gender and Delinquency: Toward a Power-Control Theory of Common Delinquent Behaviour." *American Journal of Sociology* 90:1151–78.

————. (1990). "Clarifying and Extending Power-Control Theory." *American Journal of Sociology.* 95(4) (January):1024–37.

Hagan, J., J. Simpson, and A.R. Gillis. (1979). "The Sexual Stratification of Social Control: A Gender-Based Perspective on Crime and Delinquency." *British Journal of Sociology* 30:25.

————. (1987). "Class in the Household: A Power-Control Theory of Gender and Delinquency." *American Journal of Sociology* 92(4) (January):788–816.

Hartman, H. (1981). "The Unhappy Marriage of Marxism and Feminism: Towards a More Progressive Union." In L. Sargent (ed.), *Women and the Revolution: A Discussion of the Unhappy Marriage of Marxism and Feminism* (pp. 1–41). Boston: South End Press.

Heidensohn, Frances. (1985). *Women and Crime.* London: Macmillan.

Hinch, Ron. (1985). "Canada's New Sexual Assault Laws: A Step Forward for Women?" *Contemporary Crises* 9:33–44.

Hoffman-Bustamante, Dale. (1973). "The Nature of Female Criminality." *Issues in Criminology* 8:117–36.

Jaggar, Alison. (1983). *Feminist Politics and Human Nature*. Totowa, NJ: Rowman and Allanheld.

Jensen, Gary, and Raymond Eve. (1976). "Sex Differences in Delinquency: An Examination of Popular Sociological Explanations." *Criminology* 13 (February):427–48.

Johnson, Holly. (1987). "Getting the Facts Straight: A Statistical Overview." In Adelberg and Currie (eds.), *Too Few to Count: Canadian Women in Conflict with the Law* (pp. 23–46). Vancouver: Press Gang.

Johnson, Holly, and Peter Chisholm. (1989). "Family Homicide." *Canadian Social Trends* (Autumn):16–18.

Kinnon, Dianne. (1981). *Report on Sexual Assault in Canada*. Ottawa: CACSW.

Klein, Dorie. (1979). "The Etiology of Female Crime." In Adler and Simon (eds.), *The Criminology of Deviant Women* (pp. 58–81). Dallas: Houghton Mifflin.

Konopka, Gisella. (1966). *The Adolescent Girl in Conflict*. Englewood Cliffs, NJ: Prentice-Hall.

LaPrairie, Carol. (1987). "Native Women and Crime: A Theoretical Model." In Adelberg and Currie (eds.), *Too Few to Count: Canadian Women in Conflict with the Law* (pp. 103–12). Vancouver: Press Gang.

Leonard, Eileen. (1982). *Women, Crime and Society: A Critique of Theoretical Criminology*. New York: Longman.

Lombroso, C., and W. Ferrero. (1985). *The Female Offender*. London: Fischer Unwin.

Luxton, Meg. (1980). *More Than a Labour of Love*. Toronto: Women's Press.

MacLeod, Linda. (1980). *Wife Battering in Canada: The Vicious Circle*. Ottawa: CACSW.

———. (1987). *Battered but Not Beaten: Preventing Wife Battering in Canada*. Ottawa: CACSW.

Malamuth, Neil. (1981). "Rape Proclivity among Males." *Journal of Social Issues* (Fall).

McLeod, E. (1982). *Working Women: Prostitution Now*. London: Croom Helm.

Medea, A., and K. Thompson. (1974). *Against Rape*. New York: Farrar, Straus & Giroux.

Messerschmidt, James. (1986). *Capitalism, Patriarchy and Crime: Toward a Socialist Feminist Criminology*. Totowa, NJ: Rowman and Littlefield.

Metro Toronto Action Committee on Violence Against Women and Children. (1988). "Initial Response to the Report of the Ontario Court's by the Hon. T.G. Zuber." (January).

Morris, Allison. (1987). *Women, Crime and Criminal Justice*. Oxford: Basil Blackwell.

Naffine, Ngaire. (1987). *Female Crime: The Construction of Women in Criminology*. Sydney: Allen and Unwin.

National Council of Welfare. (1990). *Women and Poverty*. Ottawa.

Nicholson, J., and K. Barltrop. (1982). "Do Women Go Mad Every Month?" *New Society* 59:226.

Pollak, Otto. (1961). *The Criminality of Women*. New York: A.S. Barnes.

Rafter, N.H., and E.M. Natalazia. (1981). "Marxist Feminism: Implications for Criminal Justice." *Crime and Delinquency* 27 (January):81–98.

Ruebsaat, Gisela. (1985). "The New Sexual Assault Offenses: Emerging Legal Issues." Ottawa: Ministry of Supply and Services.

Scully, D., and J. Marolla. (1985). " 'Riding the Bull at Gilly's': Convicted Rapists Describe the Rewards of Rape." *Social Problems* 32:251–63.

Shover, N., N. Norland, J. James and W. Thorton. (1979). "Gender Roles and Delinquency." *Social Forces* 58:162.

Simon, Rita. (1975). *Women and Crime*. Lexington, MA: D.C. Heath.

Smart, Carol. (1976). *Women, Crime and Criminology: A Feminist Critique*. London: Routledge and Kegan Paul.

———. (1989). *Feminism and the Power of Law*. London: Routledge.

Spender, Dale. (1980). *Man Made Language*. London: Routledge and Kegan Paul.

Spender, Dale (ed.). (1981). *Men's Studies Modified: The Impact of Feminism on the Academic Disciplines.* Oxford: Pergamon Press.

Taylor, I., P. Walton, and J. Young. (1973). *The New Criminology.* London: Routledge and Kegan Paul.

Thomas, W.I. (1967). *The Unadjusted Girl.* New York: Harper and Row.

Tong, Rosemarie. (1989). *Feminist Thought: A Comprehensive Introduction.* San Francisco: Westview Press.

Ursel, Jane. (1991). "Considering the Impact of the Battered Women's Movement on the State: The Example of Manitoba." In E. Comack and S. Brickey (eds.), *The Social Basis of Law: Critical Readings in the Sociology of Law.* (2nd ed.). Toronto: Garamond.

Wilson, S.J. (1991). *Women, the Family and the Economy.* (3rd ed.). Toronto: McGraw-Hill Ryerson.

FURTHER READING

Adelberg, Ellen, and Claudia Currie (eds.). (1985). *Too Few to Count: Canadian Women in Conflict with the Law.* Vancouver: Press Gang.

Boyd, Susan B., and Elizabeth A. Sheehy. (1989). "Overview." In T. Caputo et al. (eds.), *Law and Society: A Critical Perspective.* Toronto: Harcourt Brace Jovanovich.

Boyle, Christine. (1991). "Sexual Assault: A Case Study of Legal Policy Options." In Margaret Jackson and Curt Griffiths (eds.), *Canadian Criminology: Perspectives on Crime and Criminality.* Toronto: Harcourt Brace Jovanovich.

MacLeod, Linda. (1987). *Battered but Not Beaten: Preventing Wife Battering in Canada.* Ottawa: CACSW.

Smart, Carol. (1976). *Women, Crime and Criminology: A Feminist Critique.* London: Routledge and Kegan Paul.

PART II

EXPLANATIONS OF CRIME

The field of criminology is multidisciplinary. Lawyers, sociologists, political scientists, psychologists, biologists, physicians, historians, and philosophers all may consider the study of crime as part of their discipline. Nowhere is this diversity more apparent than in the development of theories of crime causation. Why some people commit crime while others do not has been addressed from each of these perspectives.

Part II covers many of the most popular explanations of crime. While the debate over which of these explanations is "best" has often become heated, no attempt is made to resolve this issue here. It would be premature to impose such a judgement on a field that has been described as consisting of "a number of fitful leads from one partially examined thesis to another."* Instead, each theory is presented by an author who has had experience (and some sympathy) with it, and who presents the theory's strengths and weaknesses. A number of researchers are now trying to synthesize several of the different approaches, and some of the authors discuss this integrative work.

Part II illustrates how theories of crime causation have developed over time. In Chapter 6, several of the earliest approaches to the explanation of crime are discussed. The most important point made in this chapter is that explanations of crime arise from particular historical milieus and reflect the

---

* Paul Rock. (1980). "Has Deviance a Future?" In Hubert M. Blalock (ed.), *Sociological Theory and Research* (pp. 290–303). New York: Free Press.

social and intellectual fashions of the day. Chapters 7 and 8 present theories that focus on the traits of individuals. Both biological and psychological perspectives have been with us for many years, and are still popular today. Chapters 9 to 12 are concerned with sociological explanations of crime. They illustrate the diverse ways in which social structure and social processes may promote or restrain criminal behaviour.

CHAPTER 6

EARLY THEORIES OF CRIMINOLOGY

By Tullio Caputo and Rick Linden

INTRODUCTION

*P*rior to the 18th century, theories of crime causation were inspired by religious beliefs and superstitions. Crime was equated with sin. Its cause was attributed to evil spirits and other supernatural forces. Quite often, wrong-doers were suspected of being tempted or possessed by the devil. These unfortunate individuals were thought to have little hope of recovering and were treated quite harshly. Evidence of one's guilt was secured through a series of trials designed to differentiate between the righteous and the sinner. These included trial by battle, trial by ordeal, trial by fire, and trial by water. In most cases, the accused had little to look forward to, whether innocent or guilty, since the trial itself was extremely severe and often fatal. These practices reflected belief in supernatural forces which were thought to control both natural and social phenomena. However, these early views had little scientific merit. This chapter focuses on the theoretical explanations that have been developed to study crime in a scientific and systematic way.

Early theorizing about crime and the beginning of our modern system of criminal justice can be traced to 17th- and 18th-century Europe. During that time, feudalism was undergoing a dramatic transformation. "It was an era of racing industrial revolution, enclosure movements, growing capitalism and growing cities" (Sylvester, 1972). These developments were hastened by a rapidly expanding population and by the growth of trade and manufacturing.

The feudal economy was based on agricultural production with clearly established relations between the aristocracy who owned the land and the peasants who worked it. A system of mutual rights and obligations bound these two classes together and when this relationship was challenged, the entire system was threatened. Increasingly, feudalism was unable to meet the needs of the growing population. It is estimated that England's population soared from 2.8 million in 1500 to 8.9 million in 1800. Similar increases were reported for the rest of Europe (Pfohl, 1985). This surge in population fuelled a period of colonial expansion as European monarchs sought havens for their surplus population and access to the markets and raw materials which colonies could provide. Europe's merchant classes gained considerable power during this period, as their economic activities offset the mounting economic shortfall.

Changes in the economy were mirrored by changes throughout the society. Revolutionary developments were taking place in philosophy, art, music, literature, and other intellectual pursuits. Progressive thinkers of the day fought to usher Europe into a new era. They argued against fanaticism and religious superstition, advocating "naturalistic" explanations of the world based on people's ability to reason. The Enlightenment philosophers believed that people were free and rational beings. This belief led them to call for the establishment of individual rights and freedoms. In their view, society was based on a "social contract" under which people chose to relinquish a small portion of their individual autonomy in order to ensure their own safety and the well-being of the entire group. These ideas were clearly contrary to the collectivist orientation of feudalism and the notion of noble privilege held by its rulers. If realized, a system based upon rights and freedoms could seriously undermine the bonds of fealty which held feudalism together. At the same time, these bonds restricted the availability of labour and hampered the development of manufacturing and industry. Herein lies the essence of the conflict between the aristocracy and the merchants. What was useful for one was detrimental to the other. Each group fought to advance its own interests.

The merchant classes enjoyed little political influence despite their growing economic power. Participation in the legislatures of the day was restricted to landowners, and since the merchants owned little land, they were barred from political power. Land was not considered a commodity, that is, as something that could be bought and sold. It was held primarily for its immediate use in agricultural and other pursuits. Given the inaccessibility to political power, the merchants turned to the legal arena to have their interests served.

In an ironic twist, the merchant classes found an opportunity to strengthen their position in society by financing the costly wars being fought by European monarchs over new colonies. The European aristocracy was forced to turn to the merchants for funds as their own resources were depleted. In exchange for their financial assistance, the merchants were able to gain significant legal concessions. While many of these concessions were aimed specifically at enhancing mercantile activities, a number of important legal principles were established which reflected the ideals of the Enlightenment philosophers. It was within this milieu that the Classical School of criminology made its most significant contributions to the establishment of our modern criminal justice system.

THE CLASSICAL SCHOOL

In 1764, Cesare Beccaria published his major work, *An Essay on Crimes and Punishments.* While this work contained little that was novel, "it captivated the attention of Europe, much more than did the voluminous lucubrations of theologians and publicists ... for it summed up in a masterly, unanswerable manner the conceptions and aspirations of the progressive minds of the age" (Phillipson, 1970). Beccaria focused his attention on the cruelty and inhumanity that characterized the criminal justice system of his day. In so doing, he provided a focus for the growing dissatisfaction with the existing order, and gave impetus to the humanitarian reform movement which was gaining momentum throughout Europe.

WITCHCRAFT AND TORTURE

It is estimated that five hundred thousand people were convicted of witchcraft and burned to death in Europe between the fifteenth and seventeenth centuries. Their crimes: a pact with the Devil; journeys through the air over vast distances mounted on broomsticks; unlawful assembly at sabbats; worship of the Devil; kissing the Devil under the tail; copulation with incubi, male devils equipped with ice-cold penises; copulation with succubi, female devils.

Other more mundane charges were often added: killing the neighbor's cow; causing hailstorms; ruining the crops; stealing and eating babies. But many a witch was executed for no crime other than flying through the air to attend a sabbat....

Torture was routinely applied until the witch confessed to having made a pact with the Devil and having flown to a sabbat. It was continued until the witch named other people who were present at the sabbat. If a witch attempted to retract a confession, torture was applied even more intensely until the original confession was reconfirmed. This left the person accused of witchcraft with the choice between dying once and for all at the stake or being returned repeatedly to the torture chambers. Most people opted for the stake. As a reward for their cooperative attitude, penitent witches could look forward to being strangled before the fire was lit.

Source: Marvin Harris (1974). *Cows, Pigs, Wars and Witches*. New York: Vintage Books.

Abuses in the administration of justice were routine. Practices established in the notorious Court of Star Chamber and the institutionalized terror of the Inquisition had become commonplace. "The existence of criminal law of eighteenth-century Europe was, in general, repressive, uncertain, and barbaric. Its administration encouraged incredibly arbitrary and abusive practices" (Mannheim, 1972). Few safeguards existed for the accused, and judicial torture was a routine method of securing confessions and discovering the identities of accomplices (Langbein, 1976). "A great many crimes were punished by death not infrequently preceded by inhuman atrocities" (Mannheim, 1972). This was particularly evident in the fanatical attack against heresy and witchcraft that swept across Europe.

The more popular forms of torture for these crimes included the rack, the ducking stool, thumbscrews, and other mechanical devices designed to inflict severe pain. The death penalty was administered in a number of ways, including burning at the stake, hanging, decapitation, and drawing and quartering.

In 18th-century England, as many as 350 offences were punishable by death. About 70 percent of death sentences were given for robbery and burglary (Newman, 1978). Practices in the colonies were similar in the early 1800s. The first person executed in Toronto was hanged for passing a bad cheque.

Clamour for the reform of such practices had started long before Beccaria's book was published. Humanitarian appeals were heard from jurists, writers, and philosophers of the era, including Hobbes, Locke, Montesquieu, and Voltaire. The administration of the criminal law, in particular, embodied practices which were in direct contrast to many of the principles advocated by the Classical theorists. It vitiated the ideals of Rousseau's social contract, as it denied the average citizen fair and impartial treatment at the hands of the state. European society was ripe for the liberating ideas of the Classical theorists and their humanitarian reforms. Beccaria's book served as a catalyst for these sentiments. The reform of a barbaric system of justice provided an excellent vehicle through which the ideas of the Classical theorists could be focused.

THE CONTRIBUTIONS OF THE CLASSICAL SCHOOL

The major ideas of the Classical School were based on the social contract doctrine. In the opening chapter of his book, Beccaria writes:

> Laws are the conditions whereby free and independent men unite to form society. Weary of living in a state of war, and of enjoying a freedom rendered useless by the uncertainty of its perpetuation, men will willingly sacrifice a part of this freedom in order to enjoy that which is left in security and tranquility. (quoted in Monachesi, 1972)

Crime was understood to be rationally calculated activity and not the result of some supernatural force or demonic possession. Laws could be used to control people's behaviour if punishment was swift, certain, and graded to fit the crime. If these conditions are met, the rational actor will decide against committing a criminal offence.

Beccaria argued that "the right to punish is an essential consequence of the nature and scope of the contractual relations of men in society" (Monachesi, 1972). He warned, however, that any punishments which exceed the minimum necessary for preserving this bond are unjust. The brutality of torture and the practice of executing people for minor offences must be abolished, as they are abuses of state power.

Beccaria felt that criminal matters should be dealt with in public according to the dictates of the law. He wanted to restrict the power of judges which had been exercised in an arbitrary manner, in private, and generally without recourse for the defendant. Beccaria sought to restrict this power by separating the lawmaking power of the legislature from the activities of the judges. In his view, the law should be determined by the legislature; it should be accessible to all; trials should be public; and the role of the judiciary should be restricted to the determination of guilt and the administration of punishment set out in law.

The reforms suggested by Beccaria represented a call for equality and the establishment of due process safeguards. The creation of graded punishments effectively restricted the arbitrariness and inequality which characterized the existing system. By arguing that the punishment should "fit the crime," Beccaria shifted the focus away from the actor and onto the act. In this way, both noble and peasant would be judged on the basis of what they did and not who they were. Moreover, the judiciary was stripped of its discretion in sentencing, since judges were bound to give punishments that were fixed by law. This was a powerful directive for equality, since the preferential treatment formerly accorded to those of wealth and power could no longer be granted.

The ideals of the social contract theorists were being translated into progressive criminal justice policy in the reforms promoted by the Classical School. In the process, the excesses and injustices which existed were attacked and the foundations of our modern legal system established. The due process safeguards which are taken for granted today, as well as reforms such as the guarantee of individual rights, equality before the law, the separation of judicial and legislative functions, and the establishment of fixed penalties, remain as the legacy of the Classical School of criminology.

ASSESSING THE CONTRIBUTIONS OF THE CLASSICAL SCHOOL

One of the most serious shortcomings of the Classical School stems from its basic approach to reform. In seeking to limit the power of the judiciary, the Classical School advocated a system that was rigid and inflexible. Although punishments could be rationally decided upon on paper, their application in real life often resulted in gross injustices. The courts were bound to follow the letter of the law and could not use discretion to temper the justice being meted out. For example, the hardship which results from having to pay a $1000 fine varies dramatically depending on whether a person is wealthy or poor. The courts, however, could not take this into account. Further, they were unable to consider mitigating circumstances or situations which would alter the responsibility of the convicted person. In this way, the attempt to enforce equality resulted in a system that produced a great deal of injustice.

The rigidity produced by limiting the power of the judiciary led to a number of modifications to the justice systems of Western Europe. In France, the Penal Code of 1791, which reflected the views of the Classical School, was revised in 1810 and again in 1819. With each revision, the rigid nature of the Code was modified to include more discretion for judges as well as a consideration of extenuating circumstances. The result of these and subsequent changes is called the "neo-Classical" approach. This is the basis of many of today's criminal justice systems.

A second consideration regarding the impact of the Classical School is its emphasis on deterrence. The approach the Classical School advocated was based more on a theory of deterrence than on a theory of crime, and it can be assessed on these grounds. The issue of deterrence continues to be an important element of this approach as modern-day Classical theorists emphasize its message. The work of James Q. Wilson, for example, is a current example of Classical thinking. "He argues that penalties need not be long and severe as long as they are swift and certain" (Pfohl, 1985). However, for most offences, the likelihood of punishment is so small, and the time between the criminal event and any punishment that is given is so great, that the Classical theorists' hopes of reducing crime by changing the legal codes have not been met.

An additional problem with the Classical School is its overly simplified view of human nature and the theory of human behaviour which this supports (Thomas and Hepburn, 1983). The Classical theorists wholly accepted the image of the free and rational human being. This view completely ignores the objective reality faced by different individuals as they make their choices, the inequality they experience, the state of their knowledge at any given time, and a multitude of other factors which may influence their decisions.

Finally, the emphasis on the rational dimension of human behaviour did not stem from the collection of empirical evidence but was based mostly on philosophical speculation. The Classical School developed its stand on the basis of its own view of human nature and the social order. Little effort was made to examine these theoretical ideas in the real world. The notion of deterrence based on a rationally calculated set of punishments was assumed to work because it was felt that most reasonable people would follow the same logic.

In spite of the problems with the ideas of the Classical School, their contribution to our modern criminal justice system cannot be denied. Legal principles such as due process and equality before the law are the hallmark of our legal system. Many of the reforms brought about by the Classical School are visible in a piece of modern Canadian legislation governing young people, the Young Offenders Act. This legislation provides for a number of legal protections for young people, including clearly defined procedural rules and legal representation for all young people accused of a crime. Moreover, it prescribes the least amount of legal intervention possible, and no intervention unless the situation warrants. Young people are held accountable and may be punished for their misdeeds. It specifies penalties for various infractions, thus limiting the discretion of the judiciary.

The influence of the Classical School is also evident in the Canadian constitution. For example, in section 15, Canadians are guaranteed the right to equal treatment before and under the law. They are protected from cruel and unusual punishment by section 12. In sections 7 through 11, a whole array of procedural safeguards are outlined, guaranteeing Canadians the due process of law. Clearly, modern criminal justice owes a great debt to the Classical theorists and the reforms which they introduced.

THE STATISTICAL SCHOOL

The first half of the 19th century saw an approach to criminology emerge that differed markedly from that of the Classical School. This was evident in the work of André-Michel Guerry (1802–1866) in France, Adolphe Quetelet (1796–1874) in Belgium, and Henry Mayhew (1812–1887) in England. These researchers believed that crime, like other human behaviour, was the result of natural causes. Once discovered, these causes could be altered through the application of scientifically derived knowledge. Guerry, Quetelet, and Mayhew's reliance on objective empirical data, as opposed to philosophical conjecture or speculation, identified them as "positivists."

Members of the Statistical School did not share the image of the rational individual held by the Classical theorists. Instead, they saw behaviour as the product of a whole host of factors. They systematically analyzed the statistical information available to them and tried to find a relationship between this information and crime. They analyzed such things as population density, education, and poverty (Thomas and Hepburn, 1983). A great deal of their work was based on a geographical or cartographic analysis which involved the plotting of various crime rates onto maps.

These theorists went far beyond simply describing what they learned from their maps and graphs. Many of their ideas anticipated the work of modern theorists as they addressed issues related to criminal careers, delinquent subcultures, and social learning theory. They provided a critical and insightful perspective, as well as a thorough statistical analysis of criminal behaviour in their work.

Perhaps the most significant contribution of these theorists is their conceptualization of the group nature of human behaviour and the recurring social patterns demonstrated by group life. Quetelet, for example, argued that "rather than being the result of our individual free wills, [our behaviour] is the product of many forces that are external to us" (Thomas and Hepburn, 1983). The fact that these forces appeared in regular and recurring patterns prompted these theorists to believe that human behaviour was governed by certain laws akin to those found in the natural or physical sciences.

In a style which anticipated much modern thinking about crime, these theorists focused on inequalities and other structural features of their society. People in certain social circumstances were seen to have few options open to them. In Quetelet's words, "the society prepares the crime and the guilty are only the instruments by which it is executed" (Thomas and Hepburn, 1983).

The influence of the Statistical School was, unfortunately, limited. This was not the result of any shortcomings on their part, but reflected the wider appeal of the biological theories of Cesare Lombroso and his colleagues. Nevertheless, these early pioneers of statistical analysis in criminology provided a uniquely sociological contribution to this emerging field of inquiry and demonstrated the value of testing theoretical formulations with empirical observations.

LOMBROSO AND THE POSITIVE SCHOOL

The Positive School of criminology is also known as the Italian School, because its most influential members were the Italian criminal anthropologist Cesare Lombroso (1835–1909) and his students Enrico Ferri (1856–1929) and Raffaelo Garofolo (1852–1934). Lombroso was influenced by the evolutionary theories of Charles Darwin, by the positivist sociology of Auguste Comte, and by the work of the sociologist Herbert Spencer, who attempted to adapt Darwin's theory to the social world.

Like the members of the Statistical School, Lombroso brought the methods of controlled observation to the study of criminals, comparing them with noncriminals in order to isolate the factors which caused criminality. His own research was badly flawed, and his work is remembered because of his use of the scientific method rather than because of the specific findings he reported.

Lombroso had worked as an army doctor and as a prison physician. He was interested in psychology and at one stage of his career was a teacher of psychiatry. These diverse interests are reflected in his theory of criminality. Lombroso's interest in physiology led him to note certain distinct physical differences between the criminals and soldiers with whom he worked. His thoughts on the subject came together during an autopsy he was performing on the notorious thief Vilella. He noted that many of the characteristics of Vilella's skull were similar to those of lower animals. In a remarkable description of the moment of discovery, Lombroso recalled:

> This was not merely an idea, but a revelation. At the sight of that skull, I seemed to see all of a sudden, lighted up as a vast plain under a flaming sky, the problem of the nature of the criminal—an atavistic being who reproduces in his person the ferocious instincts of primitive humanity and the inferior animals. Thus were explained anatomically the enormous jaws, high cheek-bones, prominent superciliary arches, solitary lines in the palms, extreme size of the orbits, handle-shaped or sessile ears found in criminals, savages, and apes, insensibility to pain, extremely acute sight, tattooing, excessive idleness, love of orgies, and the irresistible craving for evil for its own sake, the desire not only to extinguish life in the victim, but to mutilate the corpse, tear its flesh, and drink its blood. (Wolfgang, 1972)

This discovery led Lombroso to believe that criminals were throwbacks to an earlier stage of evolution, or "atavisms." His theory has been succinctly described by Gould (1981):

> These people are innately driven to act as a normal ape or savage would, but such behaviour is deemed criminal in our civilized society. Fortunately, we may identify born criminals because they bear anatomical signs of their apishness. Their atavism is both physical and mental, but the physical signs, or stigmata as Lombroso called them, are decisive. Criminal *behaviour* can also arise in normal men, but we know the "born criminal" by his anatomy. Anatomy, indeed, is destiny, and born criminals cannot escape their inherited taint.

The contrast between the primitive nature of the criminal and the more completely evolved contemporary man is shown in Lombroso's explanation of the use of professional slang, or "argot," by criminals. Born criminals talk differently because they experience the world differently. "They talk like savages because they are veritable savages in the midst of this brilliant European civilization" (Parmelee, 1912).

To support his theory, Lombroso had to show that organisms lower on the evolutionary ladder were naturally criminal. Thus, primitive humans were described as "savages." Even when evidence of their savagery was absent, Lombroso was able to save his theory by speculating that among honourable primitives the conditions for criminality simply did not yet exist. For example, "it is not possible ... to steal when property does not exist or to swindle when there is no trade" (Lombroso, 1912). Once these supposed savages take on a little civilization, their criminality is inevitable. Lombroso went even further down the evolutionary ladder, finding evidence of criminality in the behaviour of animals, insects, and even insectivorous plants.

Lombroso tested his ideas by observing many imprisoned criminals. In one study, he compared the physical characteristics of a group of criminals with those of a group of soldiers and found that the criminals had many more of the atavistic stigmata than did the soldiers. In another piece of research, he found that stigmata were present in 30 to 40 percent of anarchists, but in less than 12 percent of members of other extremist movements (Taylor et al., 1973). He also concluded that different types of offenders were characterized by different physiological characteristics. For example, "robbers have ... small, shifting, quick-moving eyes; bushy connecting eyebrows; twisted or snub noses, thin beards ... and foreheads almost receding," while "habitual homicides have glassy, cold, motionless eyes, sometimes bloodshot and injected. The nose is often aquiline, or rather hawklike, and always voluminous" (Lombroso, 1972).

Lombroso initially postulated two types of offenders—born criminals and occasional criminals. However, in response to his critics he later added several more categories, including the following.

1. *Epileptics.* In addition to their disability, epileptics also had the atavistic characteristics of criminals.
2. *Criminal insane.* This is the category of those whose insanity has led to their involvement in crime.
3. *Criminals of passion.* These are criminals who contrast completely with born criminals in that they lack any of the criminal stigmata. They commit crimes because of "noble and powerful" motives such as love or politics.
4. *Criminaloids.* This is a grab-bag category which includes anyone who commits a crime but does not fall into one of the other classifications. Lombroso felt that precipitating factors other than biological ones caused criminality among this group.

Some have interpreted this expansion of categories as a softening of Lombroso's commitment to his biological theory. This view seems to be supported by his last major work, *Crime: Its Causes and Remedies*, in which he discusses social and environmental causes of crime along with biological causes. However, examination of these modifications suggests that this change was more apparent than real. While there were differences between atavistic criminals, the insane, and the epileptics, all three categories had elements of degeneration that stemmed from epilepsy, which he called the "kernel of crime" (Lombroso, 1912). Criminaloids may lack some of the stigmata, but he felt that they differ from born criminals only in degree, not in kind. After long periods in prison, criminaloids may even come to resemble born criminals. While those who commit crimes out of passion do not show any of the stigmata, Lombroso does suggest that they show some points of resemblance with epileptics. The only category which has no connection with atavism or epilepsy is that of the occasional criminals. Even these pose no threat to his theory, however, for he suggests they should not be called criminals at all.

THE CONTRIBUTION OF THE POSITIVE SCHOOL

In its day, Lombroso's work was influential and attracted a large following among those interested in studying the causes of criminality. The stigmata were used as indicators of criminality in many trials and Lombroso himself appeared as an expert witness on several occasions. In one case, the court had to decide which of two brothers had killed their stepmother. Lombroso's testimony that one of the men had the features of a born criminal helped secure the man's conviction.

Criminal anthropology reached the attention of novelists as well as theorists. Compare Bram Stoker's description of Count Dracula with Lombroso's description of the born criminal:

Dracula: "His [the Count's] face was ... aquiline, like the beak of a bird of prey."

> Lombroso: "[The criminal's] nose on the contrary is often aquiline like the beak of a bird of prey."
> *Dracula:* "His eyebrows were very massive, almost meeting over the nose ..."
> Lombroso: "The eyebrows are bushy and tend to meet across the nose."
> *Dracula:* "...his ears were pale and at the tops extremely pointed ..."
> Lombroso: "with a protuberance on the upper part of the posterior margin ... a relic of the pointed ear...."
>
> Source: Leonard Wolf. (1981). In *The Mismeasure of Man.* Stephen Jay Gould. New York: W.W. Norton.

However, Lombroso's theory of criminal anthropology has not stood up to empirical test. As mentioned, Lombroso's research was poorly done by today's standards. His comparison groups were chosen unsystematically, his statistical techniques were crude, his measurements were often sloppy, and he assumed that those in prison were criminals and those out of prison were noncriminals. Many of the stigmata he mentioned in his research, such as tattooing, were social factors which could not possibly have been inherited. Yet despite these weaknesses, his work did represent an attempt at providing a scientific explanation of the causes of criminality.

Perhaps the most lasting contribution of Lombroso was his discussion of the criminal justice system. The Classical theorists felt that crime could be controlled if society could design punishments to fit the crime. Positive theorists, on the other hand, felt that the punishment should fit the *criminal.* Radzinowicz and King (1977) have nicely outlined the difference between the two perspectives: "The Classical School exhorts men to study justice, the Positivist School exhorts justice to study men."

Because Lombroso believed that people became involved in criminality for different reasons, he felt that they should be treated differently by the criminal justice system. If a respectable man committed murder because of passion, honour, or political belief, no punishment was needed, as that man would never repeat the crime. For other offenders, indeterminate sentences would best ensure rehabilitation. Born criminals should not be held responsible for their actions, though they needed to be incarcerated for the protection of society. However, this was to be done in a humane way. He recommended that "sentences should show a decrease in infamy and ferocity proportionate to their increase in length and social safety" (Lombroso-Ferrero, 1972).

Some born criminals could be channelled in a socially useful direction. For example, banishment and transportation to one of the colonies might allow their tendencies to be redirected toward the difficult business of building settlements in a hostile environment. For others, more severe sanctions were required. "There exists, it is true, a group of criminals, born for evil, against whom all social cures break as against a rock—a fact which compels us to eliminate them completely, even by death" (Lombroso, 1912).

A number of features of our current criminal justice system stem from the concern of Lombroso and his followers with individualizing the treatment of offenders. Probation, parole, indeterminate sentences, and the consideration of mitigating circumstances by the court were all influenced by Lombroso's work. The rational man of Classical theory now had a past and a future.

BIOLOGICAL THEORIES IN THE EARLY TWENTIETH CENTURY

CRIME AND PHYSICAL CHARACTERISTICS

During his lifetime, Lombroso's theories came under frequent attack. In 1889 he responded to his critics by challenging them to compare 100 born criminals, 100 people with criminal tendencies, and 100 normal people. He promised to retract his theories if the criminals did not turn out to be different from the other groups. His challenge was ultimately taken up by an English prison medical officer, Dr. G.B. Griffiths, and completed by his successor, Dr. Charles Goring, who succeeded Griffiths in 1903 shortly after the project began.

Goring carefully measured and compared the physical and mental characteristics of 3000 English convicts with those of diverse samples of "normals," including British university students, schoolboys, university professors, insane Scots, German Army recruits, and British Army soldiers (Goring, 1972). Based on his comparison of these groups on 37 physical and 6 mental traits, Goring concluded that there was no evidence of a distinct physical type of criminal. Lombroso's "anthropological monster has no existence in fact" (Goring, 1913). Criminals were no more or less likely to possess stigmata than were members of the control groups. Goring did find that criminals were physically inferior to normals, but attributed this fact to social selection processes.

Goring's most important finding was the high correlation between criminality and low intelligence. This led to his own explanation that crime was inherited and that the most important constitutional mechanism through which crime was genetically transmitted was through mental inferiority. Unlike Lombroso, Goring did feel that hereditary predispositions could be modified by social factors such as education. However, he also supported eugenic measures which would restrict the reproduction of the constitutional factors leading to crime.

In some respects, Goring's research represented a major advance over the work of Lombroso. His measurement was far more precise and he had access to statistical tools which were not available to Lombroso. However, his work also contained a number of serious methodological flaws. Among them was the fact that he was comparing officially labelled criminals, who were not a representative sample of all criminals, with diverse groups of other people who did not represent the noncriminal population. While many of the other criticisms of Goring's research are quite technical, they are serious enough to cause doubt both about his own theories and about his refutation of Lombroso (Driver, 1972).

The search for individual differences as the cause of crime did not end with Goring. This theme was picked up again in the 1930s by Ernest A. Hooton, a Harvard anthropologist. He compared more than 13 000 criminals with a sample of noncriminals drawn from groups of college students, firemen, hospital out-patients, militiamen, mental hospital patients, people using the change-house at a public beach, and others. On the basis of this comparison, Hooton concluded that "criminals as a group represent an aggregate of sociologically and biologically inferior individuals" (1939). Among the new stigmata he attributed to criminals were such characteristics as "low foreheads, high pinched nasal roots, nasal bridges and tips varying to both extremes of breadth and narrowness" and "very small ears" (1939).

While Hooton was not as concerned as some of his predecessors with the policy implications of his research, he did not hesitate to draw the obvious conclusion. Since "crime is the resultant of the impact of environment upon low grade human organisms ... it follows that the elimination of crime can be effected only by the extirpation of the physically, mentally, and morally unfit, or by their complete segregation in a socially aseptic environment" (1939).

Hooton's work stirred up a great deal of controversy. His findings were challenged on a variety of grounds. He was accused of using poor scientific methods and circular reasoning. For example, he used conviction of a crime as a method of separating criminals from noncriminals; he then examined the convicted groups and concluded they were inferior; finally, he used this finding of inferiority to account for their criminality (Empey, 1982). Only in this way could a trait such as thin lips be turned into an indicator of criminality.

There are several other criticisms of Hooton's methods worth considering. His control group did not represent the general population. Students, firefighters, and mental patients have particular characteristics which distinguish them from the rest of the population. Furthermore, his findings show tremendous differences within the various control groups he used. In fact, the differences between his control groups drawn from Boston and Nashville were actually greater than between prisoners and controls (Pfohl, 1985). As in the case of Lombroso, Hooton's attempt to link criminal behaviour to physical types was thoroughly discredited.

This kind of research has made periodic appearances in a variety of forms since the days of Lombroso and Hooton. In the 1950s, William Sheldon attempted to re-establish the link between body type and criminality in his elaboration of a "somatotype" theory. He described three basic body types, which, he argued, were related to particular types of personalities and temperament. These consisted of endomorphs, with fat, round bodies and easy-going personalities; ectomorphs, who are tall and lean individuals with introverted personalities and nervous dispositions; and mesomorphs, who have well-built, muscular bodies with aggressive personalities, and are quick to act and insensitive to pain. Sheldon related each of these types to particular kinds of criminal behaviour. He found that the muscular mesomorphs were the type that were most likely to become involved in delinquent or criminal behaviour.

Sheldon fared no better than his predecessors, however, when his work was subjected to scrutiny. It was found that he had done an extremely poor job of measuring delinquency among the young people he had studied. He had used vague and inconsistent categories which have been described as being scientifically meaningless.

These criticisms could not be levelled at the Gluecks, who followed up on Sheldon's ideas. They applied his somatotype theory to a study of 500 juvenile delinquents. In their study, they compared the bodies of 500 adjudicated delinquents with a matched sample of nondelinquents. The Gluecks concluded from their work that delinquents were more likely to be mesomorphs. However, this finding may have raised more questions than it answered. Putting aside a whole host of methodological criticisms levelled at the Gluecks, it may be that mesomorphs actually look more like stereotypical delinquents than either endomorphs or ectomorphs. As a result, people may respond to mesomorphs differently and they may be more likely to be labelled delinquent than those who are nonmesomorphs. Also, other social selection factors may have been involved. Youths who are athletic, muscular, and active may be better candidates for Little League baseball, hockey, or delinquency than their less athletic peers.

CRIME AND INTELLIGENCE

Other examples of the biological approach have focused on a variety of factors which have been associated with individual differences. Goring proposed one such point of view when he suggested that instead of looking for defective body types, the focus should be on genetic weaknesses demonstrated by low intelligence.

One famous study of family and heredity involved tracing the legitimate and illegitimate offspring of an army lieutenant, Martin Kallikak. Young Martin fathered an illegitimate son with a feebleminded barmaid before he settled down and married a "respectable" woman. The study compared the family trees of the descendants of Kallikak's feebleminded mate to those of his "normal" wife. The offspring of the feebleminded barmaid produced a collection of deviants and feebleminded degenerates. By contrast, the family of his wife showed no such weakness. (Goddard, 1912).

Even if the enormous methodological weaknesses of Goddard's study are ignored (Gould [1981] has shown that even the photographs showing the "depraved" Kallikaks had been retouched to make them look like defectives), little is left of scientific consequence. It is hardly surprising that children raised under difficult and impoverished circumstances should be less than model citizens. In fact, a requirement for life under these conditions may be that an individual learns a great deal of undesirable behaviour simply to survive. The absence of any consideration of the social factors involved in this comparison clearly undermines the findings of Goddard's research.

Goddard continued his work using the Binet-Simon intelligence test which had recently been developed in France. This IQ test was based on the notion of "mental age." Goddard studied the residents of a New Jersey mental institution, and on the basis of this work established the mental age of twelve as the cutoff point for determining feeblemindedness. Goddard then applied this IQ test to the inmates of jails and prisons throughout the New Jersey area. He found that in approximately half of the institutions, 70 percent of the inmate population was at or below the mental age of twelve. From these findings he concluded that IQ was an important determinant of criminal behaviour. He also concluded that feeblemindedness was directly inherited and could only be eliminated by denying those he called "morons" the right to reproduce (1914).

The acceptance of Goddard's position was short-lived. In 1926, Murchinson published the results of a study in which he compared IQ data from World War I army recruits with that of a group of inmates (Pfohl, 1985). He found that 47 percent of the recruits, compared to only 30 percent of the prisoners, had IQ scores which fell below the mental age of twelve. This startling finding implied that almost half of a very large sample of normal American men could be considered mentally feeble. The absurdity of these findings forced Goddard to lower his cutoff point for feeblemindedness from twelve years to nine. This reduction resulted in the disappearance of any significant differences between inmates and soldiers, or anyone else for that matter (Pfohl, 1985).

The controversy over IQ tests has continued. A number of serious flaws in the assumptions behind this approach have been realized. For example, it has been suggested that high scores on these tests may have more to say about test-taking ability than they do about intelligence. Furthermore, the composition of these tests has been found to be biased in favour of the cultural groups of the designers of the tests. In a dramatic demonstration, Adrian Dove, a black sociologist, devised an IQ test based on the cultural referents and language of the black ghetto (Pfohl, 1985). While black respondents who were familiar with this culture did well on the tests, white middle-class respondents did poorly. The viability of IQ tests remains suspect and their use has often been linked with racist ideology and propaganda.

A number of other recent formulations have sought to reestablish a link between individual characteristics and criminal behaviour. These include a focus on such things as chromosomes, unusual EEG results, hypoglycemic disorders, and premenstrual tension. These theories, and others, will be considered in Chapter 7.

The results in many of these cases are similar. It would be foolhardy to deny the biological or psychological dimensions of human behaviour. The evidence supporting a link between pathology and criminal behaviour, however, is weak. Moreover, this approach ignores the essentially political nature of social control, for what one society praises and rewards, another may condemn. Given this variability in what we define as crime, an assessment of the underlying social and political context is indispensable.

The continued search for individual differences and the erroneous identification of a normal "us" and a criminal "them" carries with it distinct political overtones. The emergence of a positive science coincided with the rise of a powerful capitalist class and expanded colonial activity. Both of these developments welcomed the ideological justification contained within the Darwinian notion of "survival of the fittest." Social Darwinism and a positivist criminology flourished in this environment.

This approach offered a ready-made and "humane" way of dealing with the problems of social control. This was extremely important at a time when the population was being transformed into a disciplined industrial labour force. Rather than applying the harsh and barbaric punishments of the past, a scientifically designed technology of control could be used to "treat" troublesome individuals. This focus on the pathologies of individuals also serves to conveniently remove one's gaze from the social structure. If it is certain that problems like crime are the result of individual deficiencies, then it is not necessary to be concerned with the social structure. If, on the other hand, the structural sources of inequality, such as racism, sexism, and other social ills, are examined, the very nature of the society may be called into question.

SUMMARY

This chapter began with a discussion of the revolutionary ideas of the Social Contract theorists. Speaking for the rising merchant class, they articulated the ideals of a newly emerging social order. In so doing, they challenged the existing order and offered bold new alternatives. The application of these ideas to the criminal justice system formed the basis of the Classical School of criminology, which called for the immediate reform of the criminal justice system. These theorists argued that human beings were free and rational actors who willingly entered into a social contract. Given this approach, barbarous punishments and excessive cruelty were unnecessary for maintaining the social order. It was more important that punishments be swift, certain, and graded so that they "fit the crime." The eventual adoption of these ideas resulted in a criminal justice system that was rigid and inflexible. While many of the excesses of the old regime were remedied, many new injustices appeared. This led to a series of "neo-Classical" reforms which form the basis of the modern criminal justice system.

The emergence of the Positive School marked the beginning of the modern era of criminology. These theorists insisted on the use of scientific methods to replace the philosophical approach of the Classical School. The work of Lombroso and his colleagues had a significant impact on subsequent developments in the field. His efforts spawned a long and varied search for the pathological sources of criminal behaviour. His deterministic perspective overshadowed the simplistic notions of free will advanced by the Classical School and shifted the emphasis away from individual responsibility to a conception of the criminal as a defective person who needs to be treated more than punished. Enlightened treatment by trained specialists was, in fact, the suggested way of dealing with criminals.

Each of the theories considered in this chapter was located in its respective historical milieu. Each reflected the larger currents of the time. There is no magic involved in the development of social theory; rather, it reflects the dominant social, economic, and political currents of a given era. Each generation develops its own questions and seeks answers that best fit its particular situation. In order to critically assess the contributions of any theory, we must bear this in mind and examine both the types of questions that are asked and the kinds of answers that are accepted.

BIBLIOGRAPHY

Driver, Edwin D. (1972). "Charles Buckman Goring." In *Pioneers in Criminology*. Montclair, NJ: Patterson Smith.

Empey, LaMar T. (1982). *American Delinquency: Its Meaning and Construction*. Homewood, Il: The Dorsey Press.

Goddard, H.H. (1912). *The Kallikak Family: A Study in the Heredity of Feeble-Mindedness*. New York: Macmillan.

————. (1914). *Feeble-Mindedness: Its Causes and Consequences*. New York: Macmillan.

Goring, Charles. (1913). *The English Convict*. London: His Majesty's Stationery Office.

————. (1972). *The English Convict*. Montclair, NJ: Patterson Smith.

Gould, Stephen Jay. (1981). *The Mismeasure of Man*. New York: W.W. Norton.

Hooton, Ernest Albert. (1939). *The American Criminal: An Anthropological Study*. Cambridge, MA: Harvard University Press.

Langbein, John H. (1976). *Torture and the Law of Proof*. Chicago: University of Chicago Press.

Lombroso, Cesare. (1912). *Crime: Its Causes and Remedies*. Boston: Little, Brown and Company.

————. (1972). "Criminal Man." In *The Heritage of Modern Criminology*. Cambridge, MA: Schenkman.

Lombroso-Ferrero, Gina. (1972). *Criminal Man According to the Classification of Cesare Lombroso*. Montclair, NJ: Patterson Smith.

Mannheim, Hermann (ed.). (1972). *Pioneers in Criminology*. (2nd ed.). Montclair, NJ: Patterson Smith.

Monachesi, Elio. (1972). "Cesare Beccaria." In Hermann Mannheim (ed.), *Pioneers in Criminology*. Montclair, NJ: Patterson Smith.

Newman, Graeme. (1978). *The Punishment Response*. New York: J.B. Lippincott.

Newman, Katherine. (1983). *Law and Economic Organization: A Comparative Study of Preindustrial Societies*. London: Cambridge University Press.

Parmelee, Maurice. (1912). "Introduction to the English Version." In *Crime: Its Causes and Remedies*. Little, Brown and Company.

Pfohl, Stephen J. (1985). *Images of Deviance and Social Control*. New York: McGraw-Hill.

Phillipson, Coleman. (1970). *Three Criminal Law Reformers*. Montclair, NJ: Patterson Smith.

Radzinowicz, Sir Leon, and Joan King. (1977). *The Growth of Crime*. London: Pelican Books.

Sylvester, Sawyer F., Jr. (1972). *The Heritage of Modern Criminology*. Cambridge, MA: Schenkman.

Taylor, Ian, Paul Walton, and Jock Young. (1973). *The New Criminology: For a Social Theory of Deviance*. London: Routledge and Kegan Paul.

Thomas, Charles W., and John R. Hepburn. (1983). *Crime, Criminal Law and Criminology*. Dubuque, IA: Wm. C. Brown Company Publishers.

Wolfgang, Marvin E. (1972). "Cesare Lombroso." In *Pioneers in Criminology*. Montclair, NJ: Patterson Smith.

FURTHER READING

Beccaria, Cesare Bonesana, Marquis. (1819). *An Essay on Crimes and Punishments*. Philadelphia: Philip H. Nicklion Publishers. This is Beccaria's major work. It is important to read the original text since it contains the ideas that inspired many of the criminal justice reforms of the period.

Lombroso-Ferrero, Gina. (1972). *Criminal Man According to the Classification of Cesare Lombroso*. Montclair, NJ: Patterson Smith. Lombroso's daughter Gina complied this work which contains the major ideas developed by her father. First published in 1911, it provides a number of vivid examples of how Lombroso applied his theory to a whole range of offenders.

Maestro, Marcello T. (1942). *Voltaire and Beccaria as Reformers of Criminal Law*. New York: Columbia University Press. An excellent source for delineating the ideas of Beccaria in relation to the intellectual developments of the era. Maestro presents a clear and thorough treatment of Beccaria's work in light of both social contract and Classical theories.

Monachesi, Elio. (1972). "Cesare Beccaria." In Hermann Mannheim (ed.), *Pioneers in Criminology*. Montclair, NJ: Patterson Smith. A useful introduction to Beccaria and his ideas. This article is informative and concise and helps the reader to appreciate the conditions that existed when Beccaria was writing.

Phillipson, Coleman. (1970). *Three Criminal Law Reformers*. Montclair, NJ: Patterson Smith. An excellent source on the contributions of Beccaria. It presents a thorough discussion of his work and the conditions surrounding the rise of the Classical school.

Sylvester, Sawyer F., Jr. (1972). *The Heritage of Modern Criminology*. Cambridge, MA: Schenkman Publishing Company. This book contains short selections from the major works of such early criminologists as Beccaria, Lombroso, Quetelet, and Mayhew.

Vold, George B. (1979). *Theoretical Criminology*. New York: Oxford University Press. In this classic text in criminology, Vold presents a colourful description of Lombroso and the development of the Positive School of criminology.

CHAPTER 7

BIOLOGICAL FACTORS IMPLICATED IN THE DEVELOPMENT OF CRIMINAL BEHAVIOURS

By Sheilagh Hodgins

THE ROLE OF BIOLOGICAL FACTORS IN THE DEVELOPMENT OF BEHAVIOUR

*B*iological factors play a role in the development of all human behaviour. However, like all factors involved in determining behaviour, they do not act alone. Rather, each factor interacts with numerous other biological and nonbiological factors in a complex causal chain. Biological factors mediate nonbiological factors; incoming stimuli are modulated and responses are made based on an interaction between the individual and his or her environment. Thus, each of us perceives and reacts to the world in a unique way.

The importance of biological factors in determining behaviour varies enormously. In Down's syndrome, for example, a chromosomal abnormality is responsible for the multiple symptoms—limited intelligence, small stature, cardiovascular malformations—which characterize the disorder. Consider a second example, in which an endocrine disorder is partially responsible for the behaviour of a fifteen-year-old who develops a robot to clean the garage. Owing to low thyroid levels, the boy reacts slowly. As a small boy, he realized that he was a poor athlete, so he spent much of his time alone reading and playing with electrical equipment. In the first example, the biological variable is an important determinant, while in the second it has some, but not much importance. Even in the first example, however, other factors play a key role. Depending on the learning experiences of the individual with Down's syndrome, he or she could spend his or her life in an institution being cared for by others or living alone in an apartment. In the second example, other determinants of the boy's skills include the influence of his older brother who was studying electrical engineering and the presence of electronics magazines and old equipment that the brother left lying around.

To sum up, biological factors play a role in determining all human behaviours. In so doing, they interact among themselves and with nonbiological factors. Their importance varies depending on the behaviour in question.

OBSTACLES TO RESEARCH ON THE ROLE OF BIOLOGICAL FACTORS IMPLICATED IN CRIME

Three major obstacles hinder the study of the role of biological factors in determining criminality. First, the methods available to study biological factors are limited. There is often no way to observe biological factors as they interact with other factors to determine behaviour. Nor is it possible to conduct experiments to discover if a biological factor will produce a criminal. Only relations among variables can be investigated and inferences drawn about the importance of each factor in determining a behaviour.

The second obstacle is the definition of *criminal.* Crime is defined socially. Each society defines it somewhat differently. In addition, different societies have different rates of crime resolution, and some subjects are more likely to be arrested than others. For example, large numbers of men who regularly assault their female partners and their children never come to the attention of the criminal justice system. Yet they repeatedly commit violent crimes. Crime is a very heterogeneous category including very different behaviours. However, in order to discover the role played by biological factors it is important to study precisely defined behaviours, not a socially defined generic term which lumps together many very different behaviours.

The third obstacle in studying the role of biological factors implicated in criminal behaviour is a conceptual one. The assumption that there is *a cause* of crime is unreasonable. Given the very different behaviours which are defined as illegal, it is likely that there are many different causal pathways, each involving complex interactions of numerous factors.

To sum up, research designed to tease apart biological factors which determine criminal behaviour is limited to nonexperimental methods except in those rare instances where experimental situations exist in nature. Such investigations advance knowledge insofar as they examine specific behaviours rather than socially or legally defined categories of persons who exhibit very different kinds of behaviour. It is reasonable to propose that each of these kinds of behaviour is determined by different combinations of factors.

GENERALIZING RESULTS FROM ONE SOCIETY TO ANOTHER

Before beginning to look at the data, one final comment is necessary. Here in Canada, we are very attentive to research findings from the United States. Given the quantity and quality of much of this research, we learn a great deal from our neighbours. However, in terms of crime, and particularly violent crime, the United States is an aberration when compared to other industrialized Western countries. For example, looking at 1975 rates of murder per 100 000 inhabitants, in the United States it is 9.6, in Canada 2.7, in Holland 7.3, in Sweden 3.7, and in Denmark 1.8 (*Face à la Justice,* 1980). Such differences are very important to an understanding of the determinants of criminal behaviour. Biological factors interact with nonbiological factors to determine behaviour. One society may exaggerate the importance of a biological factor while another may limit it. The environments in which research, even biological research, is carried out are thus important in understanding the findings. In this light, it is surprising that longitudinal studies (where individuals are studied intensively from a young age to late adulthood) which have been conducted in many different countries have produced similar results. As will be discussed, these investigations have succeeded in identifying a group of young boys who become recidivistic adult criminals.

BIOLOGICAL STATES AND FACTORS DIRECTLY RELATED TO CRIMINAL BEHAVIOUR

DESTRUCTIVE BRAIN PROCESSES

Research with several non-human species and with humans (see, for example, Moyer, 1976) has shown that there are specific brain structures which elicit and terminate aggressive behaviour. Different forms of aggressive behaviour are associated with different structures. If these structures are impinged upon by tumours, inflammatory processes, or other brain diseases, aggressive behaviour, verbal and physical, will result. For example, several recent studies have identified some older women who show antisocial behaviour as a result of degenerative brain disease (Hodgins, Hébert, and Baraldi, 1986). However, such conditions are extremely rare (Shah and Roth, 1974).

BRAIN DAMAGE

Violent behaviour is one possible result of head traumas severe enough to cause loss of consciousness (Detre, Kupfer, and Taub, 1975). In one study, for example, it was found that 70 percent of patients who had brain injuries were aggressive and irritable (McKinlay et al., 1981). In a study of men who requested treatment for wife battering, 61 percent had suffered head traumas of sufficient severity as to cause brain injury (Rosenbaum and Hoge, 1989). Among serious delinquent offenders referred for psychiatric evaluation, an elevated rate of treatment for head trauma was documented (Lewis, Shanok, and Balla, 1979). It is unlikely, although possible, that such trauma is a direct cause of the aggressive behaviour. Head trauma at an early age, however, may very likely be the cause of the minor brain damage which characterizes children who become offenders. This research is reviewed in a subsequent section of the chapter.

EPILEPTIC DISORDERS

There is some evidence that if the brain structures which elicit and terminate aggressive behaviour are activated by abnormal electrical activity, aggressive behaviour will result (Monroe, 1970; Bach-Y-Rita et al., 1971). This condition, the dyscontrol syndrome, is very rare.

Epilepsy is a disorder in which a small number of brain cells have been damaged. As a result, they sometimes produce excessive electrical activity which provokes a seizure. In some cases, depending on the location of the damaged cells, the seizure may take the form of aggressive behaviour. When epilepsy is accompanied by diffuse brain damage there appears to be a relation with aggressive behaviour. However, even in these cases where brain damage is evident, it has been shown that other, nonbiological factors, such as social class, learning, and family functioning, contribute to the development of aggressive behaviour (Shah and Roth, 1974).

ENDOCRINE DISORDERS

Dalton (1961) and d'Orban and Dalton (1980) have reported that a disproportionate number of women convicted of crimes committed the illegal acts in the days preceding menstruation or on the first day of menstruation. Epps (1962), studying shoplifters, found no such relation. Dalton (1961) has argued that some women suffer from premenstrual syndrome and that treatment with progesterone eliminates their antisocial behaviour. Recent studies, using better control methods, have not found that progesterone is any more effective than placebos, however (Maddocks et al., 1986). In looking at all the findings in this area, it appears that only some female offenders are prone to aggressive behaviour during the premenstrual and menstrual periods. It is hypothesized (Asso, 1984) that the endocrine changes present during these periods act as triggers to exaggerate characteristics such as aggressivity.

To sum up, biological states and factors which are directly related to criminal behaviour are very rare. Tumours, inflammation, brain disease, certain forms of epilepsy (when accompanied by diffuse brain damage), and one endocrine disorder have all been associated with various types of criminal behaviour.

BIOLOGICAL FACTORS INDIRECTLY RELATED TO CRIMINAL BEHAVIOUR

Longitudinal studies conducted in several countries throughout the world— England (Farrington and West, 1990), Finland (Pulkkinen, 1988), Sweden

(Janson, 1989; Magnussen, 1988) and the United States (McCord, 1979; Robins, 1979)—have consistently shown that a small number of boys begin offending early and continue offending through early adulthood. While few in number, they are responsible for the majority of crimes committed. The results of these longitudinal studies and of numerous cross-sectional investigations agree that before they begin offending, these boys are different from their peers on a number of biological and behavioural measures. Their families behave differently toward them than families of boys who do not subsequently offend behave toward their sons. This constellation of factors, individual and familial, predicts adult criminality (for review see Loeber and Dishion, 1983; Loeber and Stouthamer-Loeber, 1987).

GENETIC FACTORS

Each human receives two sets of 23 chromosomes at conception, one from each parent. Each chromosome carries numerous genes, or proteins, which program the development of the individual. Except in some very rare disorders, such as Huntington's disease, this program of development is highly influenced by several other biological and nonbiological factors. For example, although an individual's height is largely determined by one's genes, the mother's eating habits during pregnancy as well as one's own nutritional history interact with the hereditary factor to determine the individual's height as an adult. The mother's nutritional habits in turn have been influenced by her social class origins as well as her social class at the time of the pregnancy, her attitudes toward the pregnancy, and so on. Even in this case, where the genetic factor is powerful, many other factors interact with it to determine an individual's height.

Chromosome Studies

The current knowledge about the role of genetic factors in the determination of complex adult behaviours has happily ended an era marked by the search for chromosomal abnormalities which might cause criminality. Such abnormalities, which involve many genes, lead to severe disorders, each characterized by a highly stable symptom pattern. The last vestige of this kind of research involved the study of men possessing an extra male, or Y chromosome. These men, known as XYY men, were said to be highly aggressive and disproportionately represented among prison inmates and security-hospital patients. What appears to be true, however, is simply that XYY males are taller than the average male, and less intelligent. The investigation which put to rest this line of research included all men who had been born in Copenhagen in 1944, 1945, 1946, and 1947 (Witkin et al., 1977). In 1975, the chromosomes of all the 4139 men who were over 184 cm tall were examined. Twelve were identified who had an XYY profile. While these twelve men had more criminal convictions than did XY men of their age, height, intelligence, and social class, there was no evidence of violent behaviour on their part.

Family Studies

It has been repeatedly noted that criminals have numerous close relatives who are also criminals. Several well known studies of juveniles (for example, Glueck and Glueck, 1968; Robins, 1966; West and Farrington, 1977) have all noted that a large proportion of those who became adult criminals had parents who were convicted offenders. Although such investigations suggest that the family is important in determining criminal behaviour, they do not help us to separate its specific determinants such as learning, social class, heredity, and so on.

Twin Studies

Studies of the similarities between twin pairs with respect to criminal behaviour have been carried out in an effort to discover if a genetic factor can be implicated as a determinant of adult criminality. Such investigations compare concordance rates (proportion of twin pairs where both twins manifest the characteristic under study) for monozygotic twins (twins who have the same genes) with those of dizygotic twins (twins who have, on average, half the same genes). If monozygotic pairs have higher concordance rates for criminal behaviour than dizygotic paris, it is reasonable to postulate that a genetic factor may partially determine the criminal behaviour. In all the published investigations of this kind (see reviews by Ellis, 1982; Mednick and Volavka, 1980; Rosenthal, 1975) concordance rates for monozygotic twins are greater than those for dizygotic twins, clearly suggesting that a genetic factor is involved in determining criminal behaviour. Such studies also provide information about the importance of the genetic factor. Concordance rates for the monozygotic pairs never reach 100 percent, thereby indicating that other factors play a causal role. This conclusion applies only to adult criminality: concordance rates for juvenile delinquency do not differ for monozygotic and dizygotic twins (Cloninger et al., 1978).

These data are not, however, conclusive proof that a genetic factor is implicated in the determination of criminal behaviour. All of the twin pairs in these studies had been reared together, thereby confounding possible causal factors. The monozygotic twins may have been treated more similarly than the dizygotic pairs because they look so much alike. Such an interpretation would suggest that psychosocial factors, not a genetic factor, explain the higher concordance rates for monozygotic twins.

Adoption Studies

Cross-fostering studies provide a naturally occurring experimental design which separates genetic factors from all the others. The most recent example of such an investigation was carried out by Mednick, Gabrielli, and Hutchings (1984). All 14 427 nonfamilial adoptions which took place in Denmark between 1927 and 1947 were examined. A small number of subjects were lost because their date and/or place of birth was unknown. Court records were obtained for 65 516 biological parents, adoptive parents, and adopted children. As can be seen in Table 7.1, the children of biological parents with criminal records were more likely than those whose parents had no such records to have been convicted of criminal offences themselves. (The female adoptees are excluded from these analyses because of their low conviction rates). This relation between biological parent convictions and adoptee convictions remains significant within each socio-economic level.

As Figure 7.1 indicates, the relation between the convictions of the male adoptees and the degree of recidivism of their biological parents is statistically significant for property crimes but not for violent offences.

For purposes of the analysis, chronic offenders were defined as those with three or more convictions. Although they represented 4.1 percent of the male adoptees, they were responsible for 69.4 percent of all the male adoptees' convictions. As can be seen in Figure 7.1, the proportion of chronic adoptee offenders increases as a function of recidivism in the biological parent. But this genetic influence is not sufficient to produce a criminal adoptee. Seventy-five percent of the adoptees whose biological parents have three or more convictions were never convicted of a crime. Of the other 25 percent, 16 percent had one or two convictions while 9 percent had three or more.

The importance of these results is increased when the following methodological issues are considered. The cohort studied is very large, and the follow-up period was lengthy. The country in which the data were collected

TABLE 7.1
"CROSS-FOSTERING" ANALYSIS: PERCENTAGE OF
ADOPTED SONS WHO HAVE BEEN CONVICTED OF
CRIMINAL LAW OFFENCES

ARE ADOPTIVE PARENTS CRIMINAL?	ARE BIOLOGICAL PARENTS CRIMINAL?	
	YES	NO
Yes	24.5 (143)	14.7 (204)
No	20.0 (1226)	13.5 (2492)

Note: The numbers in parentheses are the total Ns for each cell.

Source: W.F. Gabrielli and S.A. Mednick. (1983). "Genetic Correlates of Criminal Behavior." *American Behavioral Scientist,* p. 61.

FIGURE 7.1
PERCENTAGE OF ADOPTEES CONVICTED OF VIOLENT AND
PROPERTY OFFENCES AS A FUNCTION OF BIOLOGICAL PARENTS'
CONVICTIONS

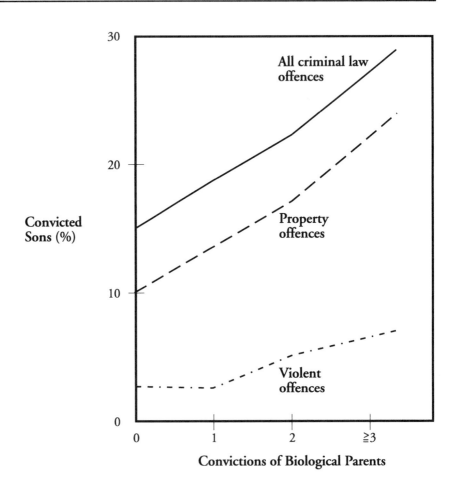

Source: S.A. Mednick, W.F. Gabrielli, and B. Hutchings. (1984). "Genetic Influences in
    Criminal Convictions: Evidence from an Adoption Cohort." *Science*, p. 893.
    Copyright 1984 by the AAAS

has very accurate criminal registers and a high rate of crime resolution. The
adoptees who were excluded do not appear to differ from those who were
included in the cohort: both had similar conviction rates and similar rearing
status. Age of transfer to the adoptive home did not interact with the genetic
influence. There was not an effect due to labelling the adopted child "criminal": the fact that the adoptive parents were informed of the biological

parents' criminality did not alter the likelihood that the adoptee would be convicted of a crime.

Using this same cohort, the relations between social class and crime were analyzed (Van Dusen et al., 1983). The rates of conviction of the adopted sons varied inversely with the social class of their biological parents and with that of their adoptive parents. These relations held for property offences but not for violent offences, where neither the social class of the biological parents nor that of the adopted parents was related to the adoptees' violent behaviour. The class/crime relation identified for overall conviction rates and for convictions for nonviolent offences is not specific to adoptees, but has been demonstrated for a cohort of 31 434 Danish men (Moffitt et al., 1981).

Social class of the biological parents and social class of the adoptive parents contribute independently to the criminal behaviour of the adoptees. However, the social class of the adoptive parents can exaggerate or mitigate the influence of the biological parents' social class. Similarly, it has been shown (Gabrielli and Mednick, 1984) that an urban environment can potentiate the genetic factor and a rural environment compensate for it. Again, in this latter investigation, no interaction was found between the genetic factor and the social one. Each contributed independently to the determination of criminal behaviour.

In a large adoption study (Sigvardsson et al., 1982) carried out in Sweden, it has been shown that the genetic factor related to adult criminality is the same for both sexes, but the nonbiological factors differ. While male criminality is more prevalent, female criminals have more relatives who are criminals than do male criminals. This finding indicates that the predisposition to criminality in a woman must be greater than that of a man in order for her to manifest criminal behaviour. It is suggested that because boys are encouraged to behave aggressively and independently while girls are taught the opposite, the adult women who do behave aggressively and independently have a greater genetic predisposition to these behaviours than their male counterparts.

While unstable preadoptive placement and low socio-economic status have been shown to relate to male criminality, no such relation exists for female criminality. However, prolonged early institutional care and being reared in an urban environment increase the risk of female criminality but not that of male criminality (Sigvardsson et al., 1982; Wolkind, 1974). While for males, the social class of the adoptive parents has more influence than that of the biological parents, the reverse is true for females. These findings correspond to others in the child development literature which suggest that little boys are more fragile and reactive to family functioning (and dysfunctioning) than are girls (Maccoby and Jacklin, 1974; Rutter, 1971).

These sex differences in the determination of adult criminal behaviour alert us to the probable complexity of the causal process. As noted at the beginning of the chapter, it is unlikely that all criminals have followed the same developmental path. In a study in Sweden (Bohman et al., 1982; Cloninger et al., 1982; Sigvardsson et al., 1982) of a cohort of adoptees, it was found that genetic as well as certain social antecedents of petty nonviolent criminal activity are different than those of alcohol-related criminality, which is more often violent and repetitive. Another adoption study (Crowe, 1974) carried out in the United States also distinguished these two kinds of criminality.

The studies discussed do not completely distinguish between genetic and perinatal (the period from conception through birth) factors. Although, theoretically, the biological factor that has been shown to be important in determining criminal behaviour could be genetic or perinatal, the latter appears unlikely. First, the relations established between biological fathers and adoptees are indicative of a genetic factor. Second, in a study of 9125 babies born during a two-year period in a large metropolitan hospital in Denmark, no relation between perinatal factors and adult criminality was found (Van Dusen et al., 1983).

To sum up, data from recent investigations point to the existence of a genetic factor in determining criminal behaviour. This factor, while consistently present, acts in concert with a multitude of other biological and nonbiological factors. Therefore, even if a genetic factor is present the individual does not necessarily become a criminal. The genetic factor appears to be neither necessary nor sufficient to determine adult criminality. Just as the genetic factor differs by type of criminality, the other etiological factors, too, appear to vary by gender and by type of criminality. Such results clearly indicate that there is not one causal pathway to adult criminality but several different ones.

These findings have important implications for social intervention programs. It appears that some individuals who have a constitutional predisposition to adult criminal behaviour never manifest this predisposition. This suggests that other, nongenetic, factors have protected them. If we could identify these factors we could attempt to create experiences and/or environments which would mitigate the influence of genetic factors.

MINIMAL BRAIN DAMAGE

Neuropsychological tests measure various cognitive functions and indicate brain dysfunction which may be general or limited to one specific brain area. A recent review (Moffit, 1990) found that in all but one of 32 studies, juvenile delinquents scored poorly on a substantial proportion of the tests administered. The more methodologically rigorous the study, the clearer the indication that boys and girls who become juvenile offenders evidence deficits in verbal functions (receptive and expressive language, oral, and written) and in executive functions (abstraction, planning, inhibition of inappropriate responses, mental flexibility, sequencing, attention, and concentration) before offending. In a study of an unselected birth cohort composed of more than a thousand fifteen-year-old New Zealand children, neuropsychological testing revealed that verbal, memory, and visual-motor integration deficits characterized those boys and girls who reported offending. Self-reports of offending correlated highly with parental reports. This relation between brain function and self-reported delinquency was independent of social class, family adversity (Moffitt and Silva, 1988) and IQ (Moffitt and Henry, 1989).

Intelligence tests (IQ), if used with subjects matched to those on whom the test was developed and standardized, reflect the quality of brain functioning. Many studies (for a review, see Wilson and Herrnstein 1985; Moffitt, 1990) have found that juvenile delinquents have lower IQs than nondelinquents. For example, in a longitudinal study of working-class boys in London (West and Farrington, 1973), Farrington found that low IQ characterized those convicted at the earliest ages (10–13 years) and those who offended repeatedly. This association between low IQ scores and delinquency was independent of family income and family size. Similarly, in two Swedish longitudinal studies of entire birth cohorts it was found that three different measures of global intelligence were negatively related to being an extreme multiple offender. The relationship between intelligence and official criminality is unaffected by differences in population size, density, and homogeneity of the community in which the subject is raised (Reichel, 1989).

The minor brain damage reflected by neuropsychological and IQ tests could be due to various kinds of insults to the brain during pregnancy or early life—for example, the mother's falling during pregnancy, the effects of instrument delivery, the young child's falling, or the child's being beaten. There are some studies showing that many aggressive offenders have suffered severe head injuries. As well, children who were physically abused are at increased risk for adult criminality, and particularly violence (Spatz Widom, 1989). This could be due to head injuries that they sustained.

In this regard, it is interesting to note that in all cultures, most offences are committed by boys and men. It is now known that the central nervous system of boys, from conception to puberty, is more fragile than that of girls (Jacklin, 1989). Thus, an event occurring either during or after pregnancy which damages a boy's brain does not always injure a girl's brain.

Another indication of minor brain damage in children is the presence of motor restlessness, impulsivity, and difficulty in paying attention. As can be seen in Figure 7.2, boys who at age thirteen were judged by their teachers to show these three characteristics and often to behave aggressively were significantly more likely than the others to be juvenile offenders. They were also more likely to become adult criminals (Magnussen, 1988).

In another longitudinal study in Finland, Pulkkinen (1983) has obtained similar results using teacher ratings made when boys were only eight years old. Similarly, in a U.S. study (Loeber and Bowers, 1985), it has been shown that teacher and parent ratings of motor activity, impulsivity, attention problems, and aggressive behaviour predict rates of juvenile offending. In addition, in the longitudinal study in London, England (Farrington, Loeber, and van Kammen, 1989) motor activity, impulsivity, and attention problems were found to be predictive of juvenile offending. Boys who show this

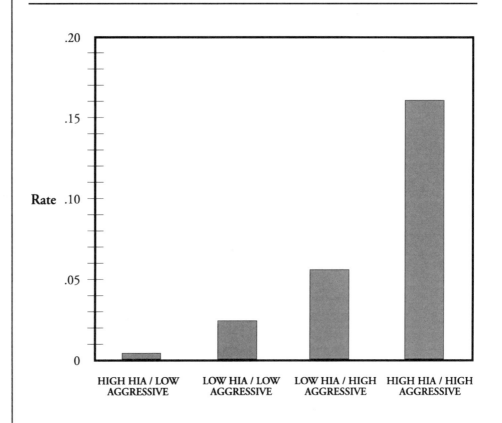

FIGURE 7.2
THE PREDICTIVE RELATIONSHIP BETWEEN HYPERACTIVITY,
IMPULSIVITY, AND ATTENTIONAL PROBLEMS (HIA),
AGGRESSIVENESS, AND THE RATE OF OFFENDING PER YEAR
IN JUVENILES

Source: R. Loeber. (1988). "Behavioral Precursors and Accelerators of Delinquency."
    In W. Buikhuisen and S.A. Mednick (eds.), *Explaining Criminal Behavior*
    (pp. 51–67). New York: E.J. Brill.

constellation of factors—motor hyperactivity, impulsivity, attention problems, and aggressive behaviour—and who offend as juveniles also show
significant impairment on neuropsychological tests (Moffitt, 1990).

Attention Deficit Disorder (sometimes called hyperactivity, hyperkinesis,
or minimal brain damage) is a syndrome involving severe difficulty in paying
attention and concentrating, impulsivity, fidgeting, restlessness, constant
activity, aggressive behaviour, and, in adolescence, low self-esteem. This
syndrome, which is ten times more prevalent among boys than girls (Al-Issa,
1982), is thought to result from minor damage to the central nervous system.

Follow-up studies (see for example, Hechtman, Weiss, and Periman, 1984; Hechtman and Weiss, 1983) indicate that a subgroup of these individuals become antisocial adults presenting many of the same symptoms that they did in childhood.

BRAIN NEUROCHEMISTRY

The brain is composed of several circuits, each of which functions with a different chemical. One of these circuits, which uses serotonin, appears to be the basis for impulsive, aggressive behaviour (Roy and Linnoila, 1988; Brown and Linnoila, 1990). Studies of impulsive homicide offenders (Linnoila et al., 1983), and impulsive male arsonists (Virkkunen et al., 1987) have shown that these offenders have low levels of brain serotonin, in comparison to those who planned their crimes. In other investigations, subjects with similarly low levels of brain serotonin have been shown to have a history of aggressive behaviour (Brown et al., 1979), to have more frequent police contacts than other subjects (van Praag, 1986a, 1986b), to be irritable (Brown and Goodwin, 1986), and to be hostile (Rydin, Schalling, and Asberg, 1982; van Praag 1986b; Roy, Adinoff, and Linnoila, 1988). Children diagnosed as having an Attention Deficit Disorder, Conduct Disorder, or Oppositional Defiant Disorder show low brain serotonin levels. The children's levels of brain serotonin were negatively related to self-reports of the total number of aggressive incidents toward others (Kruesi et al., 1990). Low serotonin levels do not directly lead to impulsive aggressive behaviour. Rather, low levels of this neurotransmitter appear to render an individual irritable, hyperreactive, and impulsive. In the presence of a noxious stimulus, then, aggressive behaviour may frequently occur (Coccaro, 1989).

PSYCHOPHYSIOLOGICAL FACTORS

Several recent studies demonstrate distinctive functioning of the autonomic nervous system in some adult male criminals. (The autonomic nervous system is composed of the parts of the peripheral and central nervous systems which regulate visceral functions.) Studies of the electrodermal responses (electrical activity of the sweat glands in the skin) show that slow recovery to baseline rates measured in young boys relates to delinquency (Loeb and Mednick, 1977) and to aggressiveness (Siddle et al., 1977; Clark, 1982), while among adult male criminals it predicts recidivism (Hare, 1978). However, in a longitudinal study of 1800 children on the island of Mauritius, while skin conductance measured at age 3 was related to parent and teacher ratings of antisocial behaviour at ages 9 to 11, the relationship differed from that identified in other studies. In children from high-social-class families, antiso-cial behaviour was related to high skin conductance levels. In children from low-social-class families, the reverse relationship was observed (Venables and Raine, 1984). Low pulse rate at age 11 has been related to severe delinquency at age 21 (Wadsworth, 1976). Those boys who subsequently committed violent crimes or sex offences had particularly low pulse rates at age 9. Similarly, low heart rate has been found to be predictive of juvenile offending (Raine and Venables, 1988). This relation appears to hold equally well for girls (Hume, 1986).

ENDOCRINE FACTORS

There is some evidence to suggest that boys who offend as juveniles and as adults have abnormally low levels of adrenalin. (This hormone is produced by the adrenal glands during states of general excitement or anxiety.) In a longitudinal study in Sweden (Magnussen, 1988), individuals who offended as juveniles and as adults showed lower levels of adrenalin at age thirteen than those who never offended. The children with low adrenalin levels were rated by teachers and peers as being aggressive and restless. Olweus (1985) has shown that low adrenalin levels characterize boys who behave aggressively when not provoked. In three separate studies carried out in England (Woodman and Hinton, 1978; Woodman, Hinton, and O'Neill, 1977a, 1977b), it has been found that men convicted of violent offences show low levels of adrenalin and high levels of noradrenalin. (Noradrenalin, the chemical precursor of adrenalin, is also produced by the adrenal glands.)

These findings are consistent with more general knowledge indicating that high adrenalin levels are associated with good social and personal adjustment (Bergman and Magnussen, 1979; Lambert et al., 1969).

Testosterone, a male sex hormone, has been related in animal studies to aggressive behaviour. The research with humans suggests that *some* violent offenders may have elevated plasma testosterone levels. In one study, for example, it was found that while prisoners with the lowest levels of testosterone had committed only nonviolent offences, those with the highest levels had all committed violent offences (Dabbs et al., 1987). In another investigation, a group of violent offenders had higher levels of testosterone than did nonviolent offenders, who in turn had higher levels than did nonoffenders (Schiavi et al., 1984). Elevated testosterone levels may be related only to certain forms of aggressive behaviour. Olweus (1983) found that plasma testosterone in adolescent boys related only to ratings of aggression "...involving a response to provocation, including threat or unfair treatment." Scaramella and Brown (1978) studied hockey players and obtained similar results. Given that different forms of aggression are associated with different neural structures, it is not surprising to find that other biological correlates differ as well.

Ever since the appearance of a report by Hill and Sargant in 1943, a link between hypoglycaemia (a low level of sugar in the blood) and aggressive behaviour has been suspected. More recently, a group of 60 habitually violent offenders and 47 percent of a sample of arsonists have been shown to react abnormally on a glucose tolerance test (Virkkunen and Huttunen, 1982; Virkkunen, 1982, 1984). It is proposed that low blood sugar levels, exacerbated by inadequate nutrition and high alcohol intake, lead to confusion, memory loss, and impulsive violent behaviour.

Our knowledge of the biological factors which are indirectly related to criminal behaviour is limited. A genetic factor has been implicated in the determination of adult criminal behaviour. Such a factor can, however, be present without the individual becoming a criminal. Its importance appears to be modified by the social class and type of environment in which the individual has been reared. Boys who have difficulty paying attention and who are overactive, impulsive, and aggressive are at high risk of becoming criminals in adulthood. This constellation of factors may well be indicative of minimal brain damage. Neuropsychological testing has consistently found that deficits in verbal and executive functions distinguish children who eventually offend. Methodologically sound investigations have shown that these deficits are present well before the appearance of criminal behaviour. Self-reports of offending, as opposed to official statistics, which identify those who get caught, demonstrate that there is real association between brain dysfunction and offending. Some individuals who behave aggressively in an impulsive manner have been shown to have abnormally low levels of brain serotonin. While generally the autonomic nervous system of criminals reacts like that of noncriminals, slow recovery rates of the electrodermal response and slow cardiovascular functioning in certain situations have been shown to distinguish the two groups. Low adrenalin levels distinguish children who subsequently offend. High testosterone levels have been associated with certain kinds of aggressive behaviour. Abnormal blood sugar reactions have been found to characterize habitually violent offenders and some arsonists.

TWO THEORIES OF THE ROLE OF BIOLOGICAL FACTORS IN DETERMINING CRIMINAL BEHAVIOUR

Mednick (Mednick and Finello, 1983; Mednick, 1977) has proposed a theory to account for the behaviour of chronic offenders which attempts to integrate much of the biological data presented here. Mednick hypothesizes that the genetic factor which has been identified programs the offender's autonomic nervous system, which generally reacts like that of nonoffenders, to return to the baseline level abnormally slowly after a response. It has been shown previously that such characteristics of the autonomic nervous system are heritable. Mednick proposes that low autonomic reactivity, as indicated by adrenalin levels and electrodermal, heart rate, and pulse rate measures, would prevent an individual from learning to inhibit responses and to react in anticipation of aversive stimuli.

Mednick states that in order to learn to behave in accordance with social norms a child requires (1) a censuring agent; (2) an adequate fear response; (3) the ability to learn the fear response in anticipation of an antisocial act;

and (4) fast dissipation of fear to provide a natural positive reinforcement for the inhibitory response. Mednick's hypothesis of the absence of a censuring agent has received experimental support. Longitudinal, observation-based studies have now demonstrated that the families of children who become delinquent do not track their behaviours and do not consistently indicate to the children what are acceptable and unacceptable behaviours (Patterson, 1986). Mednick has further theorized that the chronic offender does not inherit an autonomic nervous system which can react as in (2), (3), and (4). The results of many investigations suggest that this hypothesis may explain some criminal behaviour.

While the above theory may describe one possible way in which delinquency develops, another chain of causal factors is also evident. Children who begin life with limited verbal and executive abilities, who are impulsive, unable to sit still, frequently aggressive, and unable to pay attention are difficult to deal with both for parents and teachers. If such a child is raised in the type of family described above, he will not learn what is right and wrong. Aggressive behaviour is tolerated in these families. The child, with limited verbal skills, is not helped to learn how to resolve interpersonal disagreements verbally. The child's frustration at not being able to cope with the demands of a traditional classroom, because he can't sit still and pay attention, is not attended to. Low self-esteem, marginalization, lack of interest in school, and low academic achievement follow.

BIOLOGICAL FACTORS IMPLICATED IN PSYCHOPATHY

In recent years, a group of criminals fulfilling the criteria for psychopathy have been studied. Most of these investigations employed different methods for identifying psychopaths, thereby limiting the generalizations which can be made from the results. Hare, at the University of British Columbia, has developed a scale to select psychopaths which has proven to be both reliable and valid (Hare, 1980; Hare, 1985; Schroeder, Schroeder, and Hare, 1983). This scale, presented in Table 7.2, identifies subjects who would receive a diagnosis of Antisocial Personality Disorder (American Psychiatric Association, 1981; Hare, 1985).

Male criminals identified as psychopathic by this scale commit more crimes and more crimes of violence than those identified as nonpsychopathic (Hare and McPherson, 1984; Wong, 1984). Wong (1984) has found that psychopaths represent about 22 percent of the inmate population of eight federal penitentiaries.

There is evidence that a genetic factor contributes to the development of psychopathy (Schulsinger, 1977). Fifty-seven adult men who had been adopted away from their biological parents shortly after birth were clinically diagnosed as psychopaths. Their biological fathers, but neither the biological mothers nor the adopted parents, included a large number of psychopaths.

TABLE 7.2
THE 22 ITEMS OF THE PSYCHOPATHY CHECKLIST

1. Glibness/superficial charm
2. Previous diagnosis as psychopath (or similar)
3. Egocentricity/grandiose sense of self-worth
4. Proneness to boredom/low frustration tolerance
5. Pathological lying and deception
6. Conning/lack of sincerity
7. Lack of remorse or guilt
8. Lack of affect and emotional depth
9. Callousness/lack of empathy
10. Parasitic life-style
11. Short temper/poor behavioural controls
12. Promiscuous sexual relations
13. Early behaviour problems
14. Lack of realistic, long-term plans
15. Impulsivity
16. Irresponsible behaviour as parent
17. Frequent extra-marital relationships
18. Juvenile delinquency
19. Poor probation or parole risk
20. Failure to accept responsibility for own actions
21. Commission of many types of offence
22. Drug or alcohol abuse

Source: R.D. Hare. (1980). "A Research Scale for the Assessment of Psychopathy in
        Criminal Populations." *Personality and Individual Differences* 1:111–19. Oxford:
        Pergamon Press.

There is now considerable evidence to show that, overall, the autonomic
nervous system of psychopaths does not differ from that of nonpsychopaths.
However, three very specific differences have been discovered. First, psychopathic inmates show lower tonic electrodermal activity levels (Hare, 1978;
Hodgins, 1976). Second, some studies have indicated that psychopaths react
little or not at all in anticipation of positive and negative events (Hare, 1978).
However, the author's own study (Hodgins, 1976) failed to replicate this
finding. On the contrary, in one experiment (Schmauk, 1970), when psychopathic subjects were paid to play a game involving the avoidance of shock,
their electrodermal responses were similar to those of nonpsychopaths in
anticipating the aversive stimulus. Third, the psychopath's electrodermal
activity returns to baseline levels abnormally slowly after a response. In
addition to these differences in the psychopaths' electrodermal responses,
their heart rate responses in anticipation of a noxious stimulus appear to differ

from those of nonpsychopaths. Hare (1978) has proposed that these autonomic nervous system differences indicate that psychopaths tune out or attenuate incoming stimuli and thereby inhibit fear.

More corroborating evidence for Hare's proposition comes from work by a group of Swedish researchers (Lidberg et al., 1978). They measured levels of adrenalin and noradrenalin in the urine of psychopathic and nonpsychopathic men waiting to appear in criminal court. The psychopaths showed no elevation of the hormone levels. Again, the researchers interpreted this finding as suggesting that psychopaths do not experience fear in anticipation of noxious events.

Two other studies have shown that psychopaths with a history of violent crime react differently than nonpsychopaths with a similar history, on a glucose tolerance test (Virkkunen and Huttunen, 1982; Virkkunen, 1982). Many of the characteristics of the psychopath, it is proposed, are the result of insufficient blood sugar levels. In the studies, the offenders all reacted differently from a group of nonoffenders. All the offenders had been under the influence of alcohol at the time of their last violent crime. In the case of the psychopaths, it is hypothesized that alcohol exaggerates the abnormal tolerance of glucose.

Historically, there has been speculation that psychopathy is caused by inadequate functioning of the frontal lobes of the brain. Hare (1984), in a careful study, has shown that the performance of psychopathic inmates on cognitive tasks which are indicative of frontal lobe functioning does not differ from that of nonpsychopathic inmates or noncriminal control subjects.

However, other studies indicate that there may be differences in brain functioning of psychopaths and nonpsychopaths. One of these studies (Jutai and Hare, 1983, reported in Hare and McPherson, 1984) involved the recognition and categorization of words presented to either the right or left visual field. (Information presented to the right visual field is processed by the left hemisphere of the brain where the structures related to verbal abilities are found. Information presented to the left visual field is processed by the right hemisphere.) In another of these studies (Hare and McPherson, 1984), auditory tasks were employed and again the information going to one or the other of the brain hemispheres was controlled. Psychopathic inmates, like nonpsychopathic inmates and noncriminal subjects, showed left-hemisphere superiority for simple verbal tasks, but unlike the nonpsychopaths, they showed right-hemisphere superiority when carrying out a more complex verbal task. The results of the auditory tasks also suggest that the brain hemispheres of the psychopathic subjects are less specialized than those of most people.

These findings have been interpreted to suggest that psychopaths have an abnormal balance in arousal levels between the right and the left brain hemispheres. As Hare has noted, these two explanations are not exhaustive, nor are they incompatible with each other. If these hypotheses were true, it would mean that psychopaths' behaviour and cognitive strategies are not based on verbal, logical, or sequential operations. Similarly, language would exert little control over their behaviour. This line of thinking is intriguing not only because it has produced substantial findings, but because it relates to numerous clinical descriptions of the psychopath as a person whose eloquent verbal discourses in no way correspond to that person's behaviour.

Research has implicated a genetic factor in the determination of psychopathy. Psychopaths, when compared to nonpsychopaths, show differences in electrodermal response. They have lower baseline levels, no reaction in anticipation of negative events (except when rewarded for doing so), and slow recovery to baseline levels after a response. Their cardiovascular response and adrenalin and noradrenalin levels in anticipation of negative events are also different from those of nonpsychopaths. The psychopaths' tolerance of glucose has been shown to differ from that of nonpsychopathic offenders and from nonoffender control subjects. Recent neuropsychological studies suggest that the hemispheres of the psychopaths' brains are less specialized than those of nonpsychopaths.

Trasler (1978) has proposed a theory to account for psychopathy. He presumes initially that the prime characteristic of the psychopath is an "insusceptibility to social influences." The psychopath simply doesn't learn from negative experiences or punishment. Trasler suggests that law-abiding behaviour is learned principally by a procedure that is called passive avoidance learning—that is, learning not to make a response which would elicit punishment. Even though one may be tempted to make such a response (for example, to steal a handsome shirt), one inhibits the response after realizing the negative consequences (being arrested) which would ensue. The emotional reactions (fear, shame, and anxiety) accompanying the thoughts of the negative consequences are relieved when the response is inhibited so that one doesn't steal the shirt. Thus, the behaviour of not stealing is positively reinforced by the reduction of the feelings of fear, shame, and anxiety. This kind of learning is controlled by specific structures and pathways in the brain. Trasler theorizes that psychopaths are poor passive avoidance learners: they fail to learn not to commit illegal acts because they feel no or little fear. Trasler interprets the findings that the electrodermal and cardiovascular systems of psychopaths react abnormally in anticipation of a noxious stimulus as suggesting that they do not emotionally anticipate negative consequences.

MAJOR MENTAL DISORDER

Recent investigations of representative samples of U.S. jail inmates (Abram, 1989; Daniel et al., 1988) and prison inmates (Collins and Schlenger, 1983; Hyde and Seiter, 1987; Neighbors et al., 1987) and Canadian penitentiary inmates (Hodgins and Côté, 1990) have shown that the prevalence of major mental disorders (schizophrenia, major depression, bipolar disorder) within these populations exceeds that in the general population. In the Canadian study the prevalence rate of schizophrenia among inmates was seven times higher than among nonoffender males, the rate of bipolar illness was four times higher, while the rate of major depression was about three times higher.

These investigations have corrected the weaknesses which characterized previous studies. All employed the same diagnostic criteria (DSM-III, American Psychiatric Association, 1980), and so their results are comparable. All used standardized, reliable, and valid instruments to measure mental disorder. Consequently, comparisons between the prevalence of disorders in the general population and inmate populations can be made with some confidence. Finally, these recent studies, unlike earlier ones, examined random samples of inmates.

Thus, many convicted offenders suffer from severe, chronic mental disorders which devastate individuals throughout their lives, beginning in late adolescence. The causes of these disorders are primarily biological. Powerful genetic factors have been implicated in all three disorders. The relationship of the mental disorder to the criminality is at present unknown.

ALCOHOL AND DRUG ABUSE AND DEPENDENCE

In the study referred to previously (Hodgins and Côté, 1990) of a representative sample of Canadian penitentiary inmates, it was found that among those who had never suffered from a major mental disorder, 67 percent had met or did meet the medical criteria for alcohol abuse and/or dependence. Almost half (49 percent) of the inmates had, at least one time in their lives, met the medical criteria for drug abuse and/or dependence. This overrepresentation of substance abusers among criminals has often been documented (see, for example, Janson, 1989). Substance abuse is associated both with violent criminal offending (Janson, 1989; Toch and Adams, 1989) and with violent behaviour which does not lead to criminal charges (see, for example, Hodgins and Larouche, 1980). Genetic factors leading to abnormal brain processing of alcohol are a cause of alcoholism. Many of the same childhood factors which are associated with adult offending are also associated with drug abuse (Magnussen, 1988).

CONCLUSION

The role of biological factors in the development of human behaviour is still poorly understood. Consequently, our limited knowledge of those biological factors implicated in the development of criminal behaviour is not surprising. Biological factors interact with each other and with other nonbiological factors in complex causal chains to determine behaviour. The more precisely the behaviour in question is defined, the more likely it is that the determinants can be identified. Many different behaviours are defined as criminal; each has a distinct combination of determinants. Investigations of the biological factors involved in determining such behaviours often fail to take into account characteristics of the society which may alter the importance of the biological factor.

As has been discussed, biological states and factors are in some rare cases directly implicated as causes of behaviours labelled criminal. However, in most instances, biological factors act indirectly in determining such behaviours. In all cases they interact with numerous other factors. Longitudinal studies of unselected birth cohorts from early age until late adulthood are beginning to provide invaluable documentation on these various pathways to crime. The findings from these studies are powerful: factors are measured before offending begins; and factors both internal and external to the subject are examined simultaneously. These investigations are providing an understanding of the complex interactions of factors which determine criminal behaviours. Such information is necessary for the development of successful prevention programs.

SUMMARY

Biological factors play a role in determining behaviour. They interact among themselves and with other nonbiological factors in complex causal chains. The importance of any biological factor in determining a behaviour varies from very little to a great deal, depending on the factor and the behaviour in question. The role played by biological factors in determining criminal behaviour cannot often be directly observed. Appropriate research designs are limited. Investigations succeed in identifying the causal factors insofar as they examine specific behaviours. Each of these behaviours, it is proposed, has a specific set of determinants.

Biological states and factors directly related to criminal behaviours exist but are very rare. Tumors, inflammation, brain disease, certain forms of epilepsy when accompanied by diffuse brain damage, and the premenstrual syndrome have been associated with certain kinds of criminal behaviour. Most biological factors, however, are related only indirectly to criminal behaviour.

The evidence to date indicates that a genetic factor is involved in the determination of adult criminal behaviour. This factor acts in concert with a multitude of other factors. It is the combination of factors which determines the criminal behaviour. The importance of this factor is modified by other factors such as social class, rearing, and type of environment. This factor is specific to sex and to type of criminal behaviour.

Young children who have difficulty sitting still and paying attention, who are impulsive and aggressive are at great risk for antisocial behaviour as adults. These children's endocrine systems react differently from those of other children. As well, it is now clear that children who become juvenile delinquents have fewer verbal and executive abilities than other children. These deficits are indicative of minor brain damage, as is the lower verbal intelligence of children who subsequently become delinquents. Not only do the children who become criminals have fewer skills to cope with life than others, their families don't teach them acceptable behaviours, such as how to resolve an interpersonal conflict without resorting to a physical fight. Some studies have shown that the electrodermal system, the cardiovascular system, and the adrenal glands of criminals react differently in some situations from those of noncriminals. These findings have been interpreted by Mednick as the manifestations of the genetic factor which has been implicated in criminal behaviour, and as an indication of an inability to learn to anticipate negative events. When a child with these biological characteristics is raised in an unstable family environment where there is no consistent censuring agent, criminal behaviour results. In addition, abnormal brain neurochemistry, specifically low serotonin levels, characterize impulsive, aggressive children and adults.

Investigations of male inmates fulfilling the criteria for psychopathy have uncovered several biological characteristics specific to them. In comparison to nonpsychopathic males, these subjects show lower baseline levels and slower recovery times to baseline in the electrodermal system. There appears to be little or no response of the electrodermal system, cardiovascular system, and adrenal glands in anticipation of a noxious event. Evidence suggests that there may be a genetic base to these differences. As well, some recent investigations show less specialization of the brain hemispheres of psychopathic subjects. Trasler has proposed that these results indicate an inability on the part of psychopaths to learn to passively avoid making a response which will lead to negative consequences. This inability, he hypothesizes, results from the psychopaths' failure to experience fear in anticipation of noxious events. As a result, psychopaths are not positively reinforced by the relief of that fear when they inhibit the response and thereby avoid the negative consequences.

Almost one-quarter of incarcerated offenders have been found to suffer from major mental disorders. The relation of these disorders to offending is unknown. Large numbers of incarcerated offenders are or have been dependent on alcohol and/or drugs. There are many causal chains which lead to the development of substance abuse. Both biological and nonbiological factors are involved.

Our knowledge of the role of biological factors in determining behaviour in general, and criminal behaviours in particular, is advancing. Many pitfalls confront researchers attempting to uncover the complex causal chains which determine the various behaviours that are defined as criminal. Longitudinal studies of children from an early age throughout adulthood are providing invaluable data on the factors which compose these causal chains. Such data are essential for the development of successful programs to prevent these behaviours.

BIBLIOGRAPHY

Abram, K.M. (1989). "The Effect of Co-occurring Disorders on Criminal Careers: Interaction of Antisocial Personality, Alcoholism, and Drug Disorders." *International Journal of Law and Psychiatry* 12:133–48.

Al-Issa, I. (1982). "Gender and Child Psychopathology." In I. Al-Issa (ed.), *Gender and Psychopathology* (pp. 54–83). Toronto: Academic Press.

American Psychiatric Association. (1980). *Diagnostic and Statistical Manual of Mental Disorders* (3rd ed.). Washington, DC: American Psychiatric Association.

———. (1981). *Diagnostic and Statistical Manual* (3rd ed.). Washington, DC: American Psychiatric Association.

Asso, D. (1984). *The Real Menstrual Cycle*. Toronto: Wiley.

Bach-Y-Rita, C., J.R. Lion, C.E. Climent, and I.R. Ervin. (1971). "Episodic Dyscontrol: A Study of 130 Violent Patients." *American Journal of Psychiatry* 127:49–59.

Bergman, L.R., and D. Magnussen. (1979). "Overachievement and Catecholamine Excretion in an Achievement-Demanding Situation." *Psychosomatic Medicine* 41, 181–88.

Bohman, M., R. Cloninger, S. Sigvardsson, and A.-L. Von Knorring. (1982). "Predisposition to Petty Criminality in Swedish Adoptees: I. Genetic and Environmental Heterogeneity." *Archives of General Psychiatry* 39:1233–41.

Brown, G.L., J.C. Ballanger, M.D. Minichiello, and F.K. Goodwin. (1979). "Human Aggression and Its Relationship to Cerebrospinal Fluid 5-Hydroxyindoleacetic Acid, 3-Methoxy, 4-Hydroxyphenylglycol, and Homovanillic Acid." In M. Sandler (ed.), *Psychopharmacology of Aggression* (pp. 131–48). New York: Raven Press.

Brown, G.L., and F.K. Goodwin. (1986). "Cerebrospinal Fluid Correlates of Suicide Attempts and Aggression." In J.J. Mann and M. Stanley (eds.), *Psychobiology of Suicide. Annals of the New York Academy of Sciences* 487:175–88.

Brown, G.L., and M.I. Linnoila. (1990). "CSF Serotonin Metabolite (5-HIAA) Studies in Depression, Impulsivity, and Violence." *Journal of Clinical Psychiatry* 51(4):31–41.

Clark, F. (1982). "Relationship of Electrodermal Activity at Age 3 to Aggression at Age 9: A Study of Physiologic Sellstrate of Temperament." Unpublished doctoral dissertation, University of Southern California.

Cloninger, C.R., K.O. Christiansen, T. Reich, and I. Gottesman. (1978). "Implications of Sex Differences in the Prevalences of Antisocial Personality, Alcoholism and Criminality for Familial Transmission." *Archives of General Psychiatry* 35:941–51.

Cloninger, C.R., S. Sigvardsson, M. Bohman, and A.-L. Von Knorring. (1982). "Predisposition to Petty Criminality in Swiedish Adoptees: II. Cross-Fostering Analysis of Gene-Environment Interaction." *Archives of General Psychiatry* 39:1242–47.

Coccaro, E.F. (1989). "Central Serotonin and Impulsive Aggression." *British Journal of Psychiatry* 155(8):52–62.

Collins, J.J., and W.E. Schlenger, (1983). "The Prevalence of Psychiatric Disorder among Admissions to Prison." Paper presented at the 35th annual meeting of the American Society of Criminology, Denver, CO.

Crowe, R.R. (1974). "An Adoption Study of Antisocial Personality." *Archives of General Psychiatry* 31:785–91.

Dabbs, J.M., R.L. Frady, T.S. Carr, and N.F. Besch. (1987). "Saliva Testosterone and Criminal Violence in Young Adult Prison Inmates." *Psychosomatic Medicine* 49:174–82.

Dalton, K. (1961). "Menstruation and Crime." *British Medical Journal* 2:1752–53.

Daniel, A.E., A.J. Robins, J.C. Reid, and D.E. Wilfley. (1988). "Lifetime and Six-Month Prevalence of Psychiatric Disorders among Sentenced Female Offenders." *Bulletin of American Academy of Psychiatry and the Law* 16:333–42.

Detre, T., D.J. Kupfer, and J.D. Taub. (1975). "The Nosology of Violence." In W.S. Fields and W.H. Sweet (eds.), *Neural Bases of Violence and Aggression.* St. Louis, MO: Warren H. Green.

D'Orban, P.T., and J. Dalton. (1980). "Violent Crime and the Menstrual Cycle." *Psychological Medicine* 10:353–59.

Ellis, L. (1982). "Genetics and Criminal Behavior." *Criminology* 20:43–66.

Epps. P. (1962). "Women Shoplifters in Holloway Prison." In T.C.N. Gibbens and J. Prince (eds.), *Shoplifting* (pp. 132–45). London: Institute for the Study of the Treatment of Delinquency.

Face à la Justice. (1980). "Les données empiriques: Sentences et taux de criminalité." 3:3–7.

Farrington, D.P., R. Loeber, and W.B. van Kammen. (1989). "Long-Term Criminal Outcomes of Hyperactivity-Impulsivity-Attention Deficit and Conduct Problems in Childhood." In L.N. Robins and M. Rutter (eds.), *Straight and Devious Pathways from Childhood to Adulthood* (pp. 62–81). Cambridge: Cambridge University Press.

Farrington, D.P., and D.J. West. (1990). "The Cambridge Study in Delinquent Development: A Long-Term Follow-up of 411 London Males." In H.-J. Kerner and G. Kaiser (eds.), *Criminality: Personality, Behavior, Life History* (pp. 115–38). Berlin: Springer Verlag.

Gabrielli, W.F., Jr., and S.A. Mednick. (1983). "Genetic Correlates of Criminal Behavior." *American Behavioral Scientist* 27:59–74.

———. (1984). "Urban Environment, Genetics, and Crime." *Criminology* 22:645–52.

Glueck, S., and E. Glueck. (1968). *Delinquents and Non-delinquents in Perspective.* Cambridge, MA: Harvard University Press.

Hare, R.D. (1978). "Electrodermal and Cardiovascular Correlates of Psychopathy." In R.D. Hare and D. Schalling (eds.), *Psychopathic Behaviour: Approaches to Research* (pp. 107–44). Toronto: Wiley.

———. (1980). "A Research Scale for the Assessment of Psychopathy in Criminal Populations." *Personality and Individual Differences* 1:111–19.

———. (1984). "Performance of Psychopaths on Cognitive Tasks Related to Frontal Lobe Function." *Journal of Abnormal Psychology* 93:133–40.

———. (1985). "A Comparison of Procedures for the Assessment of Psychopathy." *Journal of Consulting and Clinical Psychology* 53:7–16.

Hare, R.D., and L. McPherson. (1984). "Violent and Aggressive Behaviour by Criminal Psychopaths." *International Journal of Law and Psychiatry* 7:35–50.

Hechtman, L., and G. Weiss. (1983). "Long-Term Outcome of Hyperactive Children." *American Journal of Orthopsychiatry* 53:532–41.

Hechtman, L., G. Weiss, and T. Periman. (1984). "Hyperactives as Young Adults: Past and Current Substance Abuse and Antisocial Behavior." *American Journal of Orthopsychiatry* 54:415–25.

Hill, D., and W. Sargant. (1943). "Homicide in Hypoglycaemia." *Lancet* i:526–27.

Hodgins, S. (1976). "Psychopathy: A Critical Examination." Unpublished doctoral dissertation, McGill University, Montreal.

Hodgins, S., and G. Côté. (1990). "The Prevalence of Mental Disorders among Penitentiary Inmates." *Canada's Mental Health* 38:1–5.

Hodgins, S., J. Hébert, and R. Baraldi. (1986). "Women Declared Incompetent to Stand Trial and/or Not Guilty by Reason of Insanity: A Follow-up Study." *International Journal of Law and Psychiatry* 8:203–16.

Hodgins, S., and G. Larouche. (1980). *Violence conjugale: Antécédents et conséquences.* Rapport de recherche soumis au Solliciteur général du Canada.

Hume, W.I. (1986). "Heart Rate Levels in Female Subjects and Their Association with Antisocial Behaviour and Eysenck's Three Personality Dimensions." Unpublished manuscript, University College, London, Department of Psychology.

Hyde, P.S., and R.P. Seiter. (1987). *The Prevalence of Mental Illness among Inmates in the Ohio Prison System.* The Department of Mental Health and the Ohio Department of Rehabilitation and Correction Interdepartmental Planning and Oversight Committee for Psychiatric Services to Corrections.

Jacklin, C.N. (1989). "Female and Male: Issue of Gender." *American Psychologist* 44(2):127–33.

Janson, C.G. (1989). "Psychiatric Diagnoses and Recorded Crimes." In C.G. Janson and A.M. Janson (eds.), *Crime and Delinquency in a Metropolitan Cohort* (pp. 31–55). Stockholm: University of Stockholm.

Jutai, J.M., and R.D. Hare. (1983). "Psychopathy and Selective Attention during Performance of a Complex Perceptual-Motor Task." *Psychomyology* 20(2):146–51.

Kruesi, M.J.P., J.L. Rapoport, S. Hamburger, E. Hibbs, W.Z. Potter, M. Lenane, and G.L. Brown. (1990). "Cerebrospinal Fluid Monoamine Metabolites, Aggression, and Impulsivity in Disruptive Behavior Disorders of Children and Adolescents." *Archives of General Psychiatry* 47:419–26.

Lambert, W.W., G. Johansson, M. Frankenhaeuser, and I. Klackenberg-Larsson. (1969). "Cathecholamine Excretion in Young Children and Their Parents as Related to Behavior." *Scandinavian Journal of Psychology* 10:306–18.

Lewis, D.O., S.A. Shanok, and D.A. Balla. (1979). "Perinatal Difficulties, Head and Face Trauma, and Child Abuse in the Medical Histories of Seriously Delinquent Children." *American Journal of Psychiatry* 136:419–23.

Lidberg, L., S. Levander, D. Schalling, and Y. Lidberg. (1978). "Urinary Catecholamines, Stress, and Psychopathy: A Study of Arrested Men Awaiting Trial." *Psychosomatic Medicine* 40:116–25.

Linnoila, M., M. Virkkunen, M. Scheinin, A. Nuutila, R. Rimon, and F.K. Goodwin. (1983). "Low Cerebrospinal Fluid 5-Hydroxyindoleacetic Acid Concentration Differentiates Impulsive from Nonimpulsive Violent Behavior." *Life Science* 33:2609–14.

Loeb, J., and S.A. Mednick. (1977). "A Prospective Study of Predictors of Criminality. 3. Electrodermal Response Patterns." In S.A. Mednick and K.O. Christiansen (eds.), *Biosocial Bases of Criminal Behavior* (pp. 245–54). New York: Gardner Press.

Loeber, R. (1988). "Behavioral Precursors and Accelerators of Delinquency." In W. Buikhuisen and S.A. Mednick (eds.), *Explaining Criminal Behavior* (pp. 51–67). New York: E.J. Brill.

Loeber, R., and B. Bowers. (1985). "A Five Year Follow-up Evaluation of the Multiple Gating Procedure." Unpublished manuscript, Western Psychiatric Institute and Clinic, Pittsburgh, PA.

Loeber, R., and T. Dishion. (1983). "Early Predictors of Male Delinquency: A Review." *Psychological Bulletin* 94:68–99.

Loeber, R., and M. Stouthamer-Loeber. (1987). "Prediction of Delinquency." In H.C. Quay (ed.), *Handbook of Juvenile Delinquency* (pp. 325–82). New York: Wiley.

Maccoby, E., and C.N. Jacklin. (1974). *The Psychology of Sex Differences.* Stanford, CA: Stanford University Press.

Magnussen, D. (ed.). (1988). *Individual Development from an Interactional Perspective.* Hillsdale, NJ: Lawrence Erlbaum Associates.

McCord, J. (1979). "Some Child-rearing Antecedents of Criminal Behavior in Adult Men." *Journal of Personality and Social Psychology* 37:1477–86.

McKinlay, W.W., D.N. Brooks, J.D. Bond, et al. (1981). "The Short-Term Outcome of Severe Blunt Head Injury, as Reported by the Relatives of the Injured Persons." *Journal of Neurology, Neurosurgery and Psychiatry* 44:285–93.

Mednick, S.A. (1977). "A Biosocial Theory of Learning of Law-Abiding Behavior." In S.A. Mednick and K.O. Christiansen (eds.), *Biosocial Bases of Criminal Behavior* (pp. 1–8). New York: Gardner Press.

Mednick, S.A., and K.M. Finello. (1983). "Biological Factors and Crime: Implications for Forensic Psychiatry." *International Journal of Law and Psychiatry* 6, 1–15.

Mednick, S.A., W.F. Gabrielli, Jr., and B. Hutchings. (1984). "Genetic Influences in Criminal Convictions: Evidence from an Adoption Cohort." *Science* 224:891–94.

Mednick, S.A., and J. Volovka. (1980). "Biology and Crime." *Crime and Justice: An Annual Review of Research* 2:85–158.

Moffitt, T.E. (1990). "The Neuropsychology of Juvenile Delinquency: A Critical Review." In M. Tonry and N. Morris (eds.), *Crime and Justice—A Review of Research* (pp. 99–169). Chicago: University of Chicago Press.

Moffitt, T.E., W.F. Gabrielli, S.A. Mednick, and F. Schulsinger. (1981). "Socioeconomic Status, IQ and Delinquency." *Journal of Abnormal Psychology* 90:152–56.

Moffitt, T.E., and B. Henry. (1989). "Neuropsychological Deficits in Executive Function in Self-reported Delinquents." *Development and Psychopathology* 1:105–18.

Moffitt, T.E., and P.A. Silva. (1988). "Neuropsychological Deficit and Self-reported Delinquency in an Unselected Birth Cohort." *Journal of the American Academy of Child and Adolescent Psychiatry* 27:233–40.

Monroe, R.R. (1970). *Episodic Behavioural Disorders: A Psychodynamic and Neurophysiologic Analysis.* Cambridge, MA: Harvard University Press.

Moyer, K.E. (1976). *The Psychobiology of Aggression.* New York: Harper and Row.

Neighbors, H.W., D.H. Williams, T.S. Gunnings, W.D. Lipscomb, C. Broman, and J. Lepkowski. (1987). *The Prevalence of Mental Disorder in Michigan Prisons.* Final report submitted to the Michigan Department of Corrections, MI.

Olweus, D. (1983). "Tertosterone in the Development of Aggressive Antisocial Behavior in Adolescents." In K.T. Van Dusen and S.A. Mednick (eds.), *Prospective Studies of Crime and Delinquency* (pp. 237–47). Boston: Kluwer-Nijhoff.

———. (1985). "Aggression and Hormones. Behavioral Relationships with Testosterone and Adrenaline." In D. Olweus, J. Block, and M. Radke-Yarrow (eds.), *The Development of Antisocial and Prosocial Behavior: Research, Theories, and Issues.* New York: Academic Press.

Patterson, G.R. (1986). "Performance Models for Antisocial Boys." *American Psychologist* 41(4):432–44.

Pulkkinen, L. (1983). "Search for Alternatives to Aggression in Finland." In A.P. Goldstein and M. Segall (eds.), *Aggression in Global Perspective.* New York: Pergamon Press.

———. (1988). "Delinquent Development: Theoretical and Empirical Considerations." In M. Rutter (ed.), *Studies of Psychosocial Risk* (pp. 184–99). Cambridge: Cambridge University Press.

Raine A., and P.H. Venables. (1984). "Tonic Heart Rate Level, Social Class, and Antisocial Behaviour in Adolescents." *Biological Psychology* 18:123–32.

Reichel, H. (1989). "The Intelligence-Criminality Relationship. A Comparative Study." *Crime and Delinquency in a Metropolitan Cohort.* (Research Rep. no. 26). Stockholm, Sweden.

Robins, L. (1966). *Deviant Children Grown Up.* Baltimore: Williams and Wilkins.

Robins, L.N. (1979). "Study Childhood Predictors of Adult Outcomes: Replications from Longitudinal Studies. In J.E. Barrett et al. (eds.), *Stress and Mental Disorder* (pp. 219–35). New York: Raven Press.

Rosenbaum, A., and S.K. Hoge. (1989). "Head Injury and Marital Aggression." *American Journal of Psychiatry* 146(8):1048–51.

Rosenthal, D. (1975). "Heredity in Criminality." *Criminal Justice and Behavior* 2:3–21.

Roy, A., B. Adinoff, and M. Linnoila. (1988). "Acting Out Hostility in Normal Volunteers: Negative Correlation with Levels of 5-HIAA in Cerebrospinal Fluid." *Psychiatry Research* 24:187–94.

Roy, A., and M. Linnoila. (1988). "Suicidal Behavior, Impulsiveness and Serotonin." *Acta Psychiatrica Scandinavica* 78:529–35.

Rutter, M. (1971). "Parent-Child Separation: Psychological Effects on the Children." *Journal of Child Psychology and Psychiatry and Allied Disciplines* 12:233–60.

Rydin, E., D. Schalling, and M. Asberg. (1982). "Rorschach Ratings in Depressed and Suicidal Patients with Low CSF 5-HIAA." *Psychiatry Research* 7:229–43.

Scaramella, T.J., and W.A. Brown. (1978). "Serum Testosterone and Aggressiveness in Hockey Players." *Psychosomatic Medicine* 40:262–65.

Schiavi, R.C., . Theilgaard, D.R. Owen, and D. White. (1984). "Sex Chromosome Anomalies, Hormones, and Aggressivity." *Archives of General Psychiatry* 41:93–99.

Schmauk, F.J. (1970). "Punishment, Arousal and Avoidance Learning in Sociopaths." *Journal of Abnormal Psychology* 76: 325–35.

Schroeder, M.L., K.G. Schroeder, and R.D. Hare. (1983). "Generalizability of a Checklist for the Assessment of Psychopathy." *Journal of Consulting and Clinical Psychology* 51:511–16.

Schulsinger, F. (1977). "Psychopathy: Heredity and Environment." In S.A. Mednick and K.O. Christiansen (eds.), *Biosocial Bases of Criminal Behavior* (pp. 109–25). New York: Gardner Press.

Shah, S., and L. Roth. (1974). "Biological and Psychophysiological Factors in Criminality." In D. Glaser (ed.), *Handbook of Criminology* (pp. 101–71). Chicago: Rand McNally and Company.

Siddle, D.A.T., S.A. Mednick, A.R. Nicol, and R.H. Foggitt. (1977). "Skin Conductance Recovery in Antisocial Adolescents." In S.A. Mednick and K.O. Christiansen (eds.), *The Biosocial Bases of Criminal Behavior* (pp. 213–16). New York: Gardner Press.

Sigvardsson, S., C.R. Cloninger, M. Bohman, and A.-L. Von Knorring. (1982). "Predisposition to Petty Criminality in Swedish Adoptees: III. Sex Differences and Validation of the Male Typology." *Archives of General Psychiatry* 39:1248–53.

Spatz Widom, C. (1989). "The Cycle of Violence." *Science* 244:160–66.

Toch, H., and K. Adams. (1989). *The Disturbed Violent Offender*. London: Yale University Press.

Trasler, G. (1978). "Relations between Psychopathy and Persistent Criminality—Methodological and Theoretical Issues." In R.D. Hare and D. Schalling (eds.), *Psychopathic Behaviour: approaches to Research* (pp. 273–98). Toronto: Wiley.

Van Dusen, T., S.A. Mednick, W.F. Gabrielli, Jr., and B. Hutchings. (1983). "Social Class and Crime in an Adoption Cohort." *The Journal of Criminal Law and Criminology* 74:249–69.

van Praag, H. (1986a). "Affective Disorders and Aggression Disorders: Evidence for a Common Biological Mechanism." *Suicide and Life-Threatening Behavior* 16:21–50.

———— . (1986b). "Aggression and CSF 5-HIAA in Depression and Schizophrenia." *Psychopharmacology Bulletin* 22:669–73.

Venables, P.H., and A. Raine. (1988). "Biological Theory." In B. McGurk, D. Thornton, and M. Williams (eds.), *Applying Psychology to Imprisonment: Theory and Practice* (pp. 3–28). London: HMSO.

Virkkunen, M. (1982). "Reactive Hypoglycemic Tendency among Habitually Violent Offenders." *Neuropsychobiology* 8:35–40.

———. (1984). "Reactive Hypoglycemic Tendency among Arsonists." *Acta Psychiatrica Scandinavica* 69:445–52.

Virkkunen, M., and M.O. Huttunen. (1982). "Evidence for Abnormal Glucose Tolerance Test among Violent Offenders." *Neuropsychobiology* 8:30–34.

Virkkunen, M., A. Nuutila, F.K. Goodwin, and M. Linnoila. (1987). "Cerebrospinal Fluid Metabolite Levels in Male Arsonists." *Archives of General Psychiatry* 44:241–47.

Wadsworth, M. (1976). "Delinquency, Pulse Rates and Early Emotional Deprivation." *British Journal of Criminology* 16:245–56.

West, D.J., and D.P. Farrington. (1973). *Who Becomes Delinquent?* London: Heinemann.

———. (1977). *The Delinquent Way of Life.* London: Heinemann.

Wilson, J.Q., and R.J. Herrnstein. (1985). *Crime and Human Nature.* New York: Simon & Schuster.

Witkin, H.A., S.A. Mednick, R. Schulsinger, E. Bakkestrom, K.O. Christiansen, D. Goodenough, K. Hirschhorn, C. Lundsteen, D.R. Owen, J. Phillips, D.B. Rubin, and M. Stocking. (1977). "Criminality, Aggression and Intelligence among XYY and XXY Men." In S.A. Mednick and K.O. Christiansen (eds.), *Biosocial Bases of Criminal Behavior* (pp. 165–88). New York: Gardner Press.

Wolkind, S.N. (1974). "Sex Differences in the Aetiology of Antisocial Disorders in Children in Long-Term Residential Care." *British Journal of Psychiatry* 125:125–30.

Wong, S. (1984). *The Criminal and Institutional Behaviours of Psychopaths.* (Programs Branch User Report). Ottawa: Ministry of the Solicitor General Canada.

Woodman, D., and J. Hinton. (1978). "Catecholamine Balance during Stress Anticipation: An Abnormality in Maximum Security Hospital Patients." *Journal of Psychosomatic Research* 22:447–83.

Woodman, D.D., J.W. Hinton, and M.T. O'Neill. (1977a). "Abnormality of Catecholamine Balance Relating to Social Deviance." *Perceptual and Motor Skills* 45:593–94.

———. (1977b). "Relationship between Violence and Catecholamines." *Perceptual and Motor Skills* 45:702.

FURTHER READING

Hare, R.D., S.E. Williamson, and T.J. Harpur. (1988). "Psychopathy and Language." In T.E. Moffitt and S.A. Mednick (eds.), *Biological Contributions to Crime Causation* (pp. 68–92). Boston: Martinus Nijhoff Publishers.

Janson, C.G. (ed.). (1989). "Crime and Delinquency in a Metropolitan Cohort." *Project Metropolitan Research Report* No. 26. Stockholm.

Magnussen, D. (ed.). (1988). *Individual Development from an Interactional Perspective.* Hillsdale, NJ: Lawrence Erblaum Associates.

Moffit, T.E. (1990). "The Neuropsychology of Juvenile Delinquency: A Critical Review." In M. Tonry and N. Morris (eds.), *Crime and Justice—A Review of Research* (pp. 99–169). Chicago: University of Chicago Press.

Olweus, D. (1988). "Environmental and Biological Factors in the Development of Aggressive Behavior." In W. Buikhuisen and S.A. Mednick (eds.), *Explaining Criminal Behaviour* (pp. 90–120). Leiden: E.J. Brill.

CHAPTER 8

PSYCHOLOGICAL PERSPECTIVES ON CRIMINALITY

By David N. Cox and Ronald Roesch

Psychological theory is primarily concerned with explanations of behaviour at the level of the individual. Theories of personality or learning are generated to account for a given individual's behaviour in a specific situation. Psychologists have generally used this model when they have attempted to understand, explain, and predict criminal behaviour, although there is considerable controversy regarding the utility of this approach. For example, Reppucci and Clingempeel (1978) reviewed published research dealing with offenders for over ten years. Nearly all of the research could be characterized as reflecting one of two value assumptions. The first is the "assumption of offender deficit," which asserts that theories and interventions are premised on the notion that there is something psychologically wrong with offenders. The second is the "assumption of discriminating traits," which holds that criminals differ from noncriminals, particularly in such traits as impulsivity and aggression. Research based on this assumption would involve studies of offender and nonoffender populations, and would utilize a number of personality tests in an attempt to find traits that differentiate the two groups.

Reppucci and Clingempeel (1978) are critical of psychology's primary reliance on these two assumptions. They point to two major omissions in psychological research. One is that there is typically very little emphasis placed on studies of the strengths of offenders. Most of the research and interventions focus on the deficits rather than on the positive characteristics of individuals. Secondly, the psychological research tends to ignore the potential importance of situational and environmental factors which affect individual behaviour.

Sarbin (1979) has also been critical of the approach taken in developing psychological theories of crime, which is essentially based on the expectation that it is possible to classify individuals as criminals and noncriminals. Sarbin argues that this cannot be done reliably. He points to studies of self-reported delinquency, white-collar crime, and corporate crime as examples of the pervasiveness of criminal behaviour.

Conversely, the work of David Farrington (1978, 1979) illustrates the importance of understanding individual differences. While he has found that inconsistent discipline and poor parental supervision were associated with future deviance, he also reports that in broken homes in which the parent-child relationship was a positive one, the incidence of delinquent behaviour was lower. Conversely, in homes where the relationship was strained, the risk for delinquent behaviour was high. Farrington views criminal behaviour as the consequence of a chain of processes that incorporates several of the theories which are presented in this text. According to Farrington, motivation to commit delinquent acts arises primarily out of a desire for material goods or a need for excitement. If these desires cannot be satisfied in a socially approved manner, then an illegal act may be chosen. The motivation to commit delinquent acts will be influenced by psychological variables, including the individual's learning history and the beliefs he or she may have internalized regarding criminal behaviour.

Eysenck and Gudjonsson (1989) support this position suggesting that "psychological factors and individual differences related to the personality are of central importance in relation to both the causes of crime and its control." They contend that psychology, with its focus on individual differences, is the central discipline in the study of criminal behaviour and that "no system of criminology has any meaning that disregards this central feature of all criminology: the individual person whom we are trying to influence."

Hollin (1989), while acknowledging that psychology's most important contribution to understanding criminal behaviour is its focus on individual-level concerns such as motivation, psychopathology, and personality, also expresses concern about the failure to unify the various aspects of psychological inquiry into criminal behaviour. He states, "Psychological theories of criminal behavior can be similarly criticized for concentrating too much on the individual, to the neglect of the context of the crime. In short, psychology has in the main been *about* crime: what is lacking is a psychology of and for crime, in other words, a *criminological psychology*." If achieved, a criminological psychology would be expected to integrate the methodology of psychology with the theoretical base of criminology.

While the individual perspective is clearly the dominant one in psychology, there are other psychological perspectives, such as those of community psychology (Roesch, 1988), that are quite closely akin to sociological perspectives. Commonly, such psychologists view social problems from what Rappaport (1977) has termed a "levels of analysis" perspective. Briefly, the four levels are (1) *individual level*, in which social problems are defined in terms of individual deficit; (2) *small-group level*, which suggests that social problems are created by problems in group functioning, essentially problems in interpersonal communication and understanding; (3) *organizational level*, in which the organizations of society have not accomplished what they have been designed to accomplish; and (4) *institutional or community level*, in which it is suggested that social problems are created by institutions rather than by persons, groups, or organizations. At this level the emphasis is on the values and policies underlying institutional functioning.

An example that cuts across these four levels would be the way in which "victimless" crimes, such as drug addiction and prostitution, are defined. If the problem is defined at the individual level, individuals would be examined to determine what psychological problems they have. Once this has been determined, direct interventions could be employed in changing these individuals so that they might fit into society better and conform to the existing laws. At the small group-level, the influence of peers, such as drug-addicted friends, could be viewed as influencing the individual's behaviour. At the next level, organizations such as law enforcement agencies would be seen as having insufficient resources to prevent or deter individuals from engaging in criminal behaviour. Finally, if this problem is defined at the institutional level, it might be said that the problems that individuals face are caused by the laws their society has created. Therefore, the focus would be on changing the laws so that they do not affect people negatively. This would certainly follow from a labelling theory approach, which would hold that the individual-level problems are caused by the labels that society attaches to certain individuals. If the problem is defined at the institutional level, therapy for an individual would be inappropriate if the cause of the problem was, for example, related to socio-economic factors (Seidman and Rabkin, 1983). Community psychologists tend to define social problems at the organizational and institutional levels and have a theoretical perspective that has much in common with sociologists.

These concerns and alternative perspectives should be kept in mind as different psychological theories of criminal behaviour are considered, since these theories focus, for the most part, on individual-level variables and explanations. The remainder of this chapter will review psychological theories that can be directly related to understanding criminal behaviour.

PSYCHOANALYTIC THEORY

Sigmund Freud is the figure most associated with psychoanalytic theory, but he did not make any significant attempts to relate his theory specifically to criminal behaviour. Other psychoanalysts have, however, attempted to explain criminal behaviour with psychoanalytic concepts (Alexander and Healey, 1935; Bowlby, 1953; Friedlander, 1947; Polansky, Lippitt, and Redl, 1950; Redl, 1966).

A basic premise of psychoanalytic theory is that people progress through five overlapping stages of development. These are the oral, anal, phallic, latency, and genital stages. Freud believed that personality is composed of three forces: the id (biological drives); the ego (which screens, controls, and directs the impulses of the id and acts as a reality tester); and the superego (conscience). Psychoanalytic theory holds that the ego and superego are developed through the successful resolution of conflicts presented at each stage of development. It is believed that both biological and social factors are involved in the resolution of each stage.

Psychoanalytic theory presents an elaborate, comprehensive view of the psychological functioning of individuals. It deals with all aspects of human behaviour, but the discussion here will be limited to its impact on the study of criminal behaviour. Briefly, this theory suggests that criminal behaviour occurs when "internal (ego and superego) controls are unable to restrain the primitive, aggressive, antisocial instincts of the id" (Nietzel, 1979). It is suggested that criminal behaviour is the consequence of an individual's failure to progress through the early stages of development, which leaves the superego inadequately developed or deficient. The individual, as a result, is left suscep-tible to antisocial behaviour (Martin, Sechrest, and Redner, 1981).

Warren and Hindelang (1979) have summarized five other interpreta-tions of criminal behaviour that can be derived from psychoanalytic theory:

> (1) criminal behavior is a form of neurosis which does not differ in any fundamental way from other forms of neuroses (e.g., while some neurotics work too hard, others set fires); (2) the criminal often suffers from a compulsive need for punishment in order to alleviate guilt feelings and anxiety stemming from unconscious strivings; (3) criminal activity may be a means of obtaining substitute gratification of needs and desires not met inside the family; (4) delinquent behavior is often due to traumatic events whose memory has been repressed; and (5) delinquent behavior may be an expression of displaced hostility.

Schoenfeld (1971) offered a theory of juvenile delinquency that illustrates psychoanalytic theory. Schoenfeld proposes that delinquent behaviour re-flects a weak, defective, or incomplete superego that is unable to control the oral, anal, and phallic impulses that are resurrected at puberty. Schoenfeld believes that parental deprivation and lack of affection, especially during the first few years of a child's life, is the cause of a weak superego. Boys raised in a fatherless home, he adds, will be especially prone to deviant behaviour as an attempt to establish their male identity. Perhaps even more important is the role of the mother. Psychoanalytic theory places a great emphasis on the establishment of a biological and emotional bond with the mother, which is necessary for the child to become socialized (Bowlby, 1953).

There are a number of studies which support the view that family life is important in determining levels of socialization (see Feldman, 1977, for a review). Bowlby stressed that a stable attachment to a mother in the first few years of life allows the child to show affection toward others and to care for them. If this attachment does not occur, the child will be unable to show affection and, thus, may damage others without remorse (through various forms of victimization). Again, however, individual differences seem to play an important role. While some studies have provided data which appear to confirm the importance of parental bonding, others report no relationship (Feldman, 1977).

One of the difficulties in assessing psychoanalytic theory is that many aspects of the theory are untestable because they rely on unobservable under-lying constructs. As Cohen (1966) points out, "Aggressive or acquisitive acts are often explained by underlying aggressive or acquisitive impulses."

The tautological nature of this explanation makes scientific verification impossible. For example, studies have failed to demonstrate that criminals desire to be punished or suffer from guilt or anxiety, as one psychoanalyst

(Abrahamsen, 1944) suggested. In fact, as Nietzel (1979) asserts, "criminals are very successful in their efforts to prevent detection or if detected, elude official prosecution and conviction. Most offenders do not appear unduly frustrated or further guilt-ridden by the fact that their 'crime pays' at least some of the time." Nevertheless, psychoanalytic theory is regarded by some as a useful conceptual framework for understanding the importance of early development on later behaviour of all types, including criminal behaviour.

THEORIES OF MORAL DEVELOPMENT

A central issue in understanding criminal and delinquent behaviour is the manner in which individuals develop a sense of morality and responsibility. There are many theories of moral development, including the elegant work of Jean Piaget. Kohlberg, expanding on Piaget's (1932) theory of moral development, has hypothesized that there are six stages of moral development. The stages are age related and progression through the stages occurs as "the developing child becomes better able to understand and integrate diverse points of view on a moral-conflict situation and to take more of the relevant situational factors into account" (Jennings, Kilkenny, and Kohlberg, 1983). Kohlberg believes that all individuals go through the same sequence of stages, although the pace may vary and some individuals may never progress beyond the first few stages.

Kohlberg categorizes the six stages into three levels of moral judgement development, each with two stages of moral reasoning.

The first is the *pre-conventional* level, characteristic of children under age eleven and of many adolescent and adult offenders. At this level, the morals and values of society are understood as "do's" and "don'ts" and are associated with punishment. The pre-conventional person is one for whom roles and social expectations are something external to the self.

The *conventional* level reflects the average adolescent and adult in our society and others. He or she understands, accepts, and attempts to uphold the values and rules of society. For a conventional person, the self is identified with or has internalized the rules and expectations of others, especially those of authorities.

The *post-conventional* level is the level at which customs are critically examined in terms of universal rights, duties, and moral principles. It is characteristic of a minority of adults after the age of twenty. The post-conventional person has differentiated his or her self from the rules and expectations of others and defined his or her value in terms of self-chosen principles (Jennings, Kilkenny, and Kohlberg, 1983).

Considerable research has been done on the relationship between Kohlberg's theory of moral development and delinquency. Kohlberg believes that people with high moral development are more likely to make individual choices and be less influenced by friends or by consequences of actions. Thus, an inverse relationship between moral development and delinquency would be predicted. Jennings et al. (1983) reviewed a large number of studies on this relationship and concluded that "the overwhelming weight of the empirical data reviewed here supports the notion that juvenile delinquents' moral judgement is at a less advanced level than that of non-delinquent controls matched on a variety of variables." But they are careful to point out that a cause-effect relationship has not been established. Individuals at the same level of moral development may or may not become delinquent. They add that

> these studies lend support to the more modest claims that moral reasoning of increased maturity has an insulating effect against delinquency. Advanced stages of moral judgment cause one's moral orientation to be more integrated, stable and consistent. Higher reasoning makes one a more reliable moral agent and thus better able to withstand some incentives to illegal conduct postulated by a variety of sociological and psychological theories of the etiology of delinquency.

This last statement suggests that moral development theory has considerable relevance for a sociological explanation of criminal behaviour. Indeed, Morash (1983) has discussed at length the possible integration of moral development and sociological theories, suggesting that it may be more fruitful to study the interaction of personal and situational variables. She concludes:

> Most serious delinquency would result from social conditions, primarily those that are enduring, that impinge on youths who possess the personality factors and the pre-conventional reasoning conducive to serious delinquent behavior. An advantage of this explanation is that it allows for the many pre-conventional individuals who do not break the law regularly or not at all, and it accounts for different patterns in delinquency—that is, the repeated serious delinquency and sporadic and/or less serious delinquency.

In conclusion, there is evidence to suggest that level of moral reasoning is related to behaviour (see also Hogan, 1973). However, the correlations reported in many studies are often quite low. Moral development is likely an important characteristic that affects how an individual behaves in a given context, but it is clear that other characteristics of the individual, as well as the situation, will also be important determinants of behaviour.

EYSENCK'S THEORY OF CRIME AND PERSONALITY

Hans Eysenck, a noted British psychologist, has developed an elaborate theory of how personality characteristics are related to criminal behaviour (Eysenck, 1977). This theory has generated considerable research, in large part because it lends itself quite readily to the identification of groups of offenders and to predictions about their behaviour.

Eysenck believes that illegal, selfish, or immoral behaviour is simple to explain. These behaviours are inherently reinforcing and, hence, it is more fruitful to try to explain why people do *not* commit crimes. Eysenck claims that children will naturally engage in such acts and only refrain from doing so if they are punished. Eysenck's theory is based on *classical conditioning*. Each time a child is punished, he or she may experience pain and fear. This pain and fear may be associated with the act itself. Thus, whenever the child contemplates the act, he or she will experience fear, which will tend to inhibit the response. Eysenck equates this conditioned fear with conscience. Delinquents and criminals do not readily develop this conditioned response, either because of lack of exposure to effective conditioning practices by parents and others, or because they are less susceptible to conditioning. Eysenck (1984) states:

> Depending on the frequency of pairings between the conditioned and unconditioned stimulus in the field of social behavior, and on the precise content of the conditioning program, children will grow up to develop appropriate types of behavior. Conditionability is a crucial factor on the social or environmental side. In a permissive society where parents, teachers, and magistrates do not take seriously the task of imposing a "conscience" which would lead them to behave in a socialized manner, a large number of individuals with poor or average conditionability will acquire a "conscience" too weak to prevent them from indulging in criminal activities, although had they been subjected to a stricter regime of conditioning, they might have grown up to be perfectly respectable and law-abiding citizens.

As Eysenck points out, the concept of "strictness" is not a function of excessive strength of the conditioning process, but a result of the certainty and frequency of pairings of the conditioned and unconditioned stimulus.

There are three dimensions of personality, according to Eysenck. *Extraversion* is a personality characteristic with highly sociable, impulsive, and aggressive people at one extreme of the continuum. Highly introverted, introspective, and inhibited people are the other extreme. *Neuroticism* is linked to the psychiatric concept of neurosis. People who are high on this dimension are characterized by such symptoms as anxiety, restlessness, and other emotional responses. The opposite extreme of neuroticism is referred to as stability. The third dimension, *psychoticism*, is a recent addition. According to Eysenck and Eysenck (1976), a person who is high on this dimension is "cold, impersonal, hostile, lacking in sympathy, unfriendly, untrustful, odd, unemotional, unhelpful, antisocial, lacking in human feelings, inhumane, generally bloodyminded, lacking in insight, strange, with paranoid ideas that people are against him."

A number of hypotheses have been generated about the relationship of these dimensions to criminal behaviour. Extraverts, because of their high need for excitement, their impulsivity, and relatively weak conscience, are believed to be more prone to criminal behaviour. In addition, persons high on both neuroticism and extraversion would be predicted to be delinquents or criminals. Persons high on psychoticism would tend to be more serious offenders, with a propensity for violence. Hare (1982) investigated the relationship between these three dimensions and psychopathy. While neuroticism and extraversion did not correlate with measures of psychopathy, psychoticism did. It is concluded that this may be because each taps a common element of psychopathy (criminal and antisocial tendencies), rather than those psychological features which are assumed in the diagnosis of psychopathy (for example, lack of remorse, lack of empathy).

Eysenck and others have developed psychological measures of each of these dimensions. Research in testing predictions about offenders has produced mixed results. In their extensive and excellent review of Eysenck's theory, Farrington, Biron, and LeBlanc (1982) summarized data from sixteen studies, most of which were conducted in Great Britain, and found that while some studies support the predictions of Eysenck's theory, other studies found that the predictions do not hold. Bartol (1980) comes to a similar conclusion. Nevertheless, Eysenck's theory is important because it offers a comprehensive model of criminal behaviour. While the evaluation of his theory has been mixed, it is likely that the theory will benefit from modifications resulting from ongoing empirical work. Eysenck (1984) himself states that what he has proposed is indeed a theory, which requires more empirical evidence to address the concerns raised about it. It should be noted that although Eysenck argues strongly for the importance of individual differences, he does recognize the importance of societal influences: "Crime ... is essentially a function of the ethos of the society in which we live; it reflects the practices of positive and negative reinforcement, of reward and punishment, of teaching and conditioning, which are prevalent, and these in turn are mirrored and reflected by the types of films we see, television programs we watch, books and newspapers we read, and teaching and examples we receive at school." In the next section, it will be seen that social learning theory reflects this perspective more explicitly.

SOCIAL LEARNING THEORY

A good example of a theory that lends itself to an integration of sociology and psychology is social learning theory. Although this theory focuses on individual behaviour, it takes into account the influence of the environment and the influence of social conditions on the individual. Cognitive functioning, the ability to think and make choices, is central to social learning theory.

An important element of social learning theory is the role of modelling. Individuals can learn new behaviours through direct experience or by observing the behaviour of others. The latter, also referred to as vicarious learning, can be a most effective and efficient way to acquire new behaviours. Albert Bandura, a Stanford University professor of psychology, is a leading social learning theorist. He suggests that "virtually all learning phenomena resulting from direct experiences can occur on a vicarious basis through observation of other persons' behavior and its consequences for them" (Bandura, 1979).

Social learning theory has been used to explain how aggression is learned. Since this is of great concern to criminology theory, aggression will be used as an example of an application of social learning theory.

Bandura (1979) suggests that aggressive behaviour can be learned from three sources. The *family* is one source, with a number of studies showing that children of parents who respond aggressively to problems will tend to use similar tactics. Bandura also points to research on child abuse, which shows that many children who have been abused will later become abusers themselves. Another source of aggressive behaviour can be referred to as *subcultural influences*, or the influence of social models and peers. Bandura suggests that "the highest incidence of aggression is found in communities in which aggressive models abound and fighting prowess is regarded as a valued attribute." The third source of learned aggressive behaviour is through *symbolic modelling*. An example of this is violence on television, which provides models of aggressive behaviour.

Bandura's research on the role of film models reinforced existing concerns about the effects of television on aggressive behaviour. Geen (1983) reviewed the research on the relationship between viewing television violence and aggression. He first looked at the vast number of correlational studies, the majority of which support the conclusion that there is a positive relationship between viewing violence and aggressive behaviour. A typical study is the one by Teevan and Hartnagel (1976), which showed that high school students who described their favourite television shows as violent also reported committing more aggressive acts than students whose favourite shows were nonviolent.

The problem with correlational research, as Geen points out, is that the direction of causation is unknown. It is possible that people who are more likely to behave aggressively simply prefer more violent television shows. Thus, it cannot be concluded through correlational studies alone that viewing violence is the cause of aggressive behaviour. Cook, Kendzierski, and Thomas (1983) reanalyzed data from several large-scale studies of the effects of television violence. They concluded that an association between television viewing and aggression by children can be found regularly, but the level of association is typically quite small, and often not statistically significant. Nevertheless, they conclude that the association is most probably a causal one, that watching violence on television does have an effect on children's aggressive behaviour.

In addition to the direct effect on aggressive behaviour that observing television violence has, it is also possible that exposure increases one's tolerance toward violence and decreases one's sensitivity to acts of violence. Thomas et al. (1979) found that both adult and child subjects showed less autonomic reactivity to a scene of real life interpersonal aggression if they had first watched a violent scene from a television show. Malamuth and Check (1981) reported similar results in their study of the effects of film violence on attitudes toward violence. Male and female university students were randomly assigned to view either a violent-sexual or a control feature-length film. The films were shown as part of the regular campus film program and subjects believed they were viewing the films as a film-rating task. Several days later, they were asked to respond to a number of attitude measures, but were unaware of any relationship between the film and the questionnaire. Malamuth and Check found that exposure to the film portraying violent sexuality was associated with a greater acceptance of interpersonal violence against women. This finding was true only for male subjects. Female subjects had a nonsignificant tendency in the opposite direction, as women exposed to violence tended to be less accepting of interpersonal violence than control females. It is important to realize, however, that this study does not provide any data on whether males exposed to violence would actually behave differently toward women. But the study does demonstrate that such exposure may have a significant effect on attitudes.

In his analysis of antisocial behaviour, Bandura (1986) suggests that the best deterrent to such activity is the provision of more attractive prosocial alternatives. However, he acknowledges that "when inducements to criminal acts are strong, when personal sanctions against such conduct are weak, and when people lack socially acceptable means of getting what they want, fear of punishment serves as a major deterrent to transgressive conduct." Deterrence may take two forms — direct or vicarious. In the former, punishment is used to discourage current transgressors of such activity in the future. In the latter, punishment serves as a general deterrent to others. Bandura identifies three major sources of deterrence against criminal activity: legal sanction, social sanction, and self-sanction. Legal sanctions derive from the belief that there are legal consequences to transgressions, despite the reality that most crime goes unpunished. Bandura cites research by Clastner (1967) in stating that "people who are not in the habit of breaking the law share a distorted perception of legal threats, in which they greatly overestimate the risks of getting caught and punished for unlawful acts. In contrast, offenders judge personal risks to be lower and more in line with the actual probabilities." Social sanctions reflect the negative social consequences criminal stigmatization can have for an individual and the powerful deterrent effect this risk has. Self-sanctions are self-imposed moral standards; they are seen as the most effective deterrent, as they are operative even when there is no risk of detection involved. Bandura (1986) states "In the absence of self-sanctions rooted in societal standards, whenever personal desires conflict with societal codes, external threats in the form of legal and social sanctions, and extensive social surveillance are needed to insure that the rights and welfare of others are not completely disregarded."

OPERANT CONDITIONING

Another learning theory is based on the principle of operant conditioning. This involves the use of rewards to increase the probability or frequency of a given response. B.F. Skinner is the psychologist most identified with this theory and, indeed, his research forms the basis for both the theoretical and applied applications of operant conditioning.

One way a response can be learned is through a process referred to as shaping. This involves rewarding approximations of a target behaviour until the behaviour gradually progresses to the desired response. Behaviour can also be learned through punishment, which can either be a withdrawal of a positive reinforcer or the introduction of a negative stimulus, such as the use of aversive stimuli (for example, an electric shock).

There have been a number of attempts to use operant conditioning theory to account for the acquisition of criminal behaviour. Notable among this work is that of Jeffery (1965) and that of Burgess and Akers (1966). Considerable research has been conducted on the application of learning theory to the treatment of delinquents. The "teaching-family" group-home model begun in the late 1960s has been at the centre of group-home development. The approach

> rests on the view that an adolescent's behavior patterns, behavior discriminations, and skills are functions of past behavior-environment interactions (learning history), currently ongoing behavior-environment interactions, and genetic organismic variables (Braukman, Kirigin, and Wolf, 1980). In this conceptualization, inherited characteristics and environmental features in childhood, particularly parenting practices (relationship development, teaching, supervision, and discipline) affect later development. In adolescence, earlier developed antisocial patterns tend to persevere (indeed, are self-perpetuating) and can be maintained further by ongoing behavior-environment interactions associated with inappropriate parenting, deviant peers, and school failure. (Braukman and Wolf, 1987)

The group home provides the reinforcing environment designed to change existing behavioural interactions in the direction of functional and prosocial skills. The emphasis is on learning social and family life skills. The best known of these programs is Achievement Place, a cottage-style treatment facility for delinquents (Phillips, 1968). Youth in this program live in residence with trained "house-parents." The heart of the program is a token economy system in which points can be earned (or lost). For example, residents can earn points for being at class on time, cleaning their bedroom, and engaging in other positive behaviours. Disruptive behaviour in the classroom, making aggressive statements or fighting, and being late for class can result in a loss of points. The points can be used to purchase privileges and material goods. Research on Achievement Place has demonstrated that "contingent token consequences could both establish behaviors basic to participation in lawful, productive intra- and extra-treatment activities, and eliminate behaviors likely to get the participants in further trouble" (Braukman and Wolf, 1987). A comprehensive outcome study on the teaching-family program (Braukman, Wolf, and Ramp, 1985) indicates that this approach has considerable short-term positive effects; however, the long-term implications are less positive. To this end, increased emphasis has been placed on systematic aftercare to help maintain treatment effects.

ANTISOCIAL PERSONALITY

The antisocial personality provides a good example of how psychological theory can be applied to criminal populations. Some confusion has resulted from the variety of terms used to describe basically the same set of behaviours: sociopathy, psychopathy, moral insanity, antisocial personality, and Antisocial Personality Disorder. There has also been a tendency for some to use the term very loosely as a "wastebasket" category for antisocial individuals generally. There is, however, strong empirical evidence that the traits underlying this disorder form a valid and clinically meaningful cluster (Hare and Cox, 1978). For many, this term is associated with images of violent and sadistic murderers as portrayed countless times on television or, all too often, demonstrated in real life. The brutal murders committed by Theodore Bundy, or Charles Manson and his followers in California, are frequently cited examples of psychopathy. Indeed, while there is some debate over the most appropriate diagnosis for Manson, many would argue that his behaviour best fits the clinical picture of psychopathy. As Nathan and Harris (1975) point out:

> Charles Manson acted upon society in an unbelievable variety of antisocial ways. At one time or another he robbed, deceived, assaulted, exploited, seduced—and murdered. But despite the extraordinary range of antisocial acts for which he had been responsible, perhaps his most surprising characteristic was that at no time did he show guilt or remorse about anything he had done. During his trial for the Tate murders, he said, "I've considered innocence and guilt and I know the difference between them and I have no guilt" (quoted from the *New York Times*, Dec. 25, 1969). A man who could be charming and captivating, brutal and ruthless, Manson could not be guilty, at least in his own eyes. What kind of human being feels no remorse over murder? Why would a person keep committing crimes despite repeated punishment? How can a man charm so many people and yet never relate with genuine feeling to anyone?

These questions are difficult to answer because the crimes Manson or Bundy committed seem so senseless to society. However disturbing they may be, murders motivated by greed or passion are possible for most people to understand. But the murder of Sharon Tate and others by Manson cannot be explained by either of these motivations.

TED BUNDY—WHY?

Born in 1946, Theodore Robert Bundy seemed destined for a charmed life; he was intelligent, attractive, and articulate (Holmes and DeBurger, 1988). A Boy Scout as a youth and then an honor student and a psychology major at the University of Washington, he was at one time a work-study student at the Seattle Crisis Clinic. Later he became assistant to the chairman of the Washington State Republican Party. It is likely that about this time he claimed his first victim; a college-age woman was viciously attacked while sleeping, left alive but brain-damaged. During the years from 1974 through 1978, Bundy stalked, attacked, killed, and then sexually assaulted as many as 36 victims in Washington, Oregon, Utah, Colorado, and Florida. Apparently some of the women were distracted when the good-looking casual Bundy approached, seeming helpless because of being on crutches or with an apparent broken arm. He usually choked them to death and then sexually abused and mutilated them before disposing of their bodies in remote areas (Nordheimer, 1989).

It is characteristic of the psychopathic personality or sociopath to maintain a facade of charm, so that acquaintances will describe him (as they did Bundy) as "fascinating," "charismatic," and "compassionate." At his trial for the murder of two Chi Omega sorority sisters in their bedrooms at Florida State University, he served as his own attorney (Bundy had attended two law schools). But he was convicted; he was also found guilty of the kidnapping, murder, and mutilation of a Lake City, Florida, girl who was 12 years old.

Bundy was sentenced to death. Shortly before he was executed on January 24, 1989, Bundy gave a television interview to California evangelist James Dobson in which he attributed the cause of his problems to pornography. He said: "Those of us who are ... so much influenced by violence in the media, in particular pornographic violence, are not some kind of inherent monsters. We are your husbands, and we grew up in regular families" (quoted by Lamar, 1989, p. 34). Bundy claimed that he spent his formative ages with a grandfather who had an insatiable craving for pornography.

He told Dr. Dobson, "People will accuse me of being self-serving but I am just telling you how I feel. Through God's help, I have been able to come to the point where I much too late, but better late than never, feel the hurt and the pain that I am responsible for" (quoted by Kleinberg, 1989, p. 5A).

The tape of Bundy's last interview, produced by Dobson and titled "Fatal Addiction," has been widely disseminated, especially by those who seek to eliminate all pornography. (Dr. Dobson served on a federal pornography commission during the Reagan administration.) But Bundy's claim that pornography was the "fuel for his fantasies" has been received skeptically by others, who saw it as one last manipulative ploy to gain further time. Even his mother stated that no evidence existed in her son's first 28 years (before he became a murder suspect for the first time) that hinted at any aberrant behavior (Nordheimer, 1989). In none of his previous interviews, including extensive conversations in 1986 with Dorothy Lewis, a psychiatrist he had come to trust, did he ever cite "a pornographic preamble to his grotesqueries" (Nobile, 1989, p. 41). Bundy had decided at that time that he needed psychiatric testimony in order to escape the electric chair—that is, by being diagnosed as not competent to stand trial because he was supposedly too confused and irrational to assist in his own murder defense. Despite Dr. Lewis's testimony in 1986, the judge would not declare Bundy incompetent. Thus, perhaps at that time he decided to portray himself as a normal youth who had been corrupted by pornography (Nobile, 1989).

According to psychiatrist Park Dietz, most serial sexual killers have two distinct qualities: sexual sadism and psychopathy, or the lack of normal inhibitions about acting on that desire (quoted by Nobile, 1989). This classification seems a succinct summary of Ted Bundy.

Source: Lawrence S. Wrightsman. (1990). *Psychology and the Legal System* (pp. 108–109). Pacific Grove, CA: Brooks/Cole Publishing Company.

This section began with a discussion of Charles Manson because it is this image that best fits the common conception of persons with an antisocial personality. It is a misleading picture, however, because many individuals with diagnoses of antisocial personality do not have a history of violence and, even among those who do, very few would exhibit the extreme forms that Manson did. The term *sociopath* was later used instead of the term *psychopath* to convey this less violent picture. More recently, the use of the term *Antisocial Personality Disorder* has become common (see Chapter 7).

The current edition of the American Psychiatric Association's *Diagnostic and Statistical Manual of Mental Disorder* (DSM-III-R) defines Antisocial Personality Disorder in the following manner:

> The essential feature of this disorder is a pattern of irresponsible and antisocial behavior beginning in childhood or early adolescence and continuing into adulthood. For this diagnosis to be given, the person must be at least 18 years of age and have a history of Conduct Disorder before the age of 15.

Lying, stealing, fighting, truancy, and resisting authority are typical early childhood signs. In adolescence, unusually early or aggressive sexual behaviour, excessive drinking, and use of illicit drugs are frequent. In adulthood, those kinds of behaviour continue, with the addition of inability to sustain consistent work performance or to function as a responsible parent, and failure to accept social norms with respect to lawful behaviour. After age 30 the more flagrant aspects may diminish, particularly sexual promiscuity, fighting, criminality, and vagrancy. It is estimated that between 15 percent and 30 percent of the inmate population in Canadian prisons could be considered psychopathic (Ogloff, Wong, and Greenwood, 1990).

In his book *The Mask of Sanity*, Cleckley (1976) provided a clinical description of the antisocial personality and described the psychopath in terms of the following criteria: unreliability, insincerity, pathological lying and deception, egocentricity, poor judgement, impulsivity, a lack of remorse, guilt, or shame, an inability to experience empathy or concern for others and to maintain warm, affectionate attachments, an impersonal and poorly integrated sex life, and an unstable life plan with no long-term commitments.

Since the 1960s, Hare and his colleagues have devoted considerable attention to the development of a reliable and valid procedure for the assessment of psychopathy. This program has culminated in the Revised Psychopathy Checklist (PCL-R) (Hare, 1990), a twenty-item checklist of traits and behaviours associated with psychopathy (see Table 7.2). Research has continued to support the use of this scale in male prison populations. Hare and others have found in numerous studies that the checklist can be used reliably and is able to discriminate between inmates with high and low ratings of psychopathy. For example, Hare and McPherson (1984) report that the crimes and behaviour of psychopaths, compared with those of other criminals, are more violent and aggressive.

DSM-III-R estimates that the prevalence of Antisocial Personality Disorder is 3 percent for men and less than 1 percent for women. However, estimates of this diagnostic classification in prison populations are, not surprisingly, considerably higher. Indeed, depending on how one interprets the diagnostic criteria, virtually all inmates could be so classified. The differences in interpretation may partly account for the large disparity in prison studies of this disorder, reflecting, in part, changes in diagnostic procedures and criteria. In a Canadian study of the prevalence of Antisocial Personality Disorder, Hare (1983) had two clinicians examine a provincial and a federal prison inmate sample. The clinicians found approximately one-third of the provincial sample, and 42 percent of the federal sample, to meet the criteria for Antisocial Personality Disorder. Overall, 39 percent of the total prison sample received this diagnosis. However, in a previous study described in the same paper, Hare, using the initial criteria proposed in a draft of DSM-III-R, found that 76 percent of a sample of 145 white male criminals met the criteria for Antisocial Personality Disorder. The reason for the difference is that the published version of DSM-III-R required that more stringent criteria be met before a diagnosis of Antisocial Personality Disorder could be made. Hare's work was influential in the decision to change the criteria. The two studies provide a clear illustration of how changes in diagnostic criteria and procedures can influence the perceived prevalence of antisocial personality. It is interesting to note that the DSM-IV Task Force's Axis II Work Group has identified Antisocial Personality Disorder as the personality disorder whose classification is most likely to undergo major revisions. The concern is that the current criteria be simplified and focus more on the personality traits central to the traditional diagnosis of psychopathy (Hare, Hart, and Harpur, 1991).

A leading theory about antisocial personality is that these individuals do not learn from negative experiences because they do not become anxious in circumstances which should elicit anxiety. Also, they do not have sufficient fear of the consequences of their behaviour (Brodsky, 1977; Hare, 1970). Applying Eysenck's model, reviewed earlier in this chapter, the psychopath can be viewed as an extravert who does not easily acquire conditioned responses or, if he or she acquires them, extinguishes them very rapidly. Given these characteristics, particularly the inability to learn from punishment or to experience fear or anxiety, it is understandable that Brodsky (1977) concludes that imprisonment is unlikely to have much effect on the post-release behaviour of such individuals.

Heilbrun (1979) conducted an interesting study of the influence of intelligence on the relationships between psychopathy, violence, and impulsiveness. His sample of 76 white male prisoners was divided into psychopathic and nonpsychopathic groups ($N=38$). Two personality measures were used (one of which, incidentally, was validated in a study by Craddick [1962] using a Canadian prison sample). He further divided the groups into high-intelligence and low-intelligence subgroups. Heilbrun found that intelligence level does indeed have an influence on violence and impulsiveness. The more intelligent psychopaths were neither violent nor impulsive, and were more likely to have attained educational goals. This study points to the importance of viewing persons with the label of psychopath, or antisocial personality, in multidimensional ways. Not all such individuals should be expected to be violent or impulsive.

The Heilbrun study should also serve as a reminder that studies of prison populations may present a misleading picture of antisocial personality. Most of the research on antisocial personality has used samples obtained from institutional populations. This may give a distorted view because the impressions one has about people with antisocial personalities are, thus, based on people who committed criminal acts but were not able to avoid apprehension. Furthermore, it is certainly true that not all persons with this label are criminals (Cleckley, 1976). An exception to the focus on institutionalized populations is the work of Cathy Spatz Widom (Spatz Widom, 1977; Spatz Widom and Newman, 1985). In one study, Spatz Widom placed an advertisement in a local newspaper asking for "charming, aggressive, carefree people who are impulsively irresponsible but are good at handling people and at looking after number one." Twenty-nine applicants were interviewed. The demographic and personality test data applied to these people revealed some interesting information about this noninstitutionalized population. Only two subjects had not finished high school, and most had some college. Nearly two-thirds had at least one arrest, but the conviction rate was quite low (18 percent), even though many of the charges were felonies. While 50 percent had been incarcerated, most had been in jail less than two weeks. The subjects scored high on the extraversion and neuroticism scale of the Eysenck Personality Inventory, consistent with Eysenck's (1977) notions of psychopathy. Scores on the Minnesota Multiphasic Personality Inventory (MMPI), an objective personality test, fit the classic profile of psychopathy (high scores on the psychopathic deviate and manic scales). Subjects had low scores on the measure of socialization, and most also had low scores on the empathy scale.

While many of the results of Spatz Widom's study were similar to those found in institutional populations, Spatz Widom's study presents a picture of somewhat more successful antisocial persons. That is, they are better educated and more successful at avoiding conviction and lengthy incarceration. These results support the conclusion of Spatz Widom and Newman (1985) that research on the antisocial personality must avoid a primary focus on the incarcerated criminal. Her methodology appears successful in drawing a sample of noninstitutionalized persons who meet the antisocial personality criteria.

CRIME AND MENTAL ILLNESS

Let this section begin a discussion of crime and mental illness with a most extreme statement: all crime is symptomatic of mental illness. While this may seem a preposterous statement to some, many mental health professionals have held this belief. Hakeem (1958) has summarized these views:

> So powerful is the conviction of some psychiatrists that crime stems from mental disease, that they have held that the commission of crime in itself constitutes evidence of the presence of mental disease. Again, this aspect of the ideology usually draws on the medical analogy. The thesis runs as follows: just as fever is a symptom of physical disease, so crime is a symptom of mental disease.

Today, most would disagree with this position. Indeed, the current view is that while some criminals exhibit symptoms of mental illness, the majority do not (Freeman and Roesch, 1989). In the remainder of this section, some of the current theories of crime and mental illness will be reviewed. In particular, the extent to which persons charged with crimes are in need of mental health intervention will be examined.

Studies of the prevalence of mental illness in jail or prison populations are difficult to assess because of the diversity of findings. Teplin (1983) reported rates of mental illness ranging from 3 percent to 50 percent in jail populations. Silber (1974) argues that the rate of severe mental illness is quite low, as do Brodsky (1972) and Guze (1976). Monahan and Steadman (1983) reviewed a number of studies addressing the issue of prevalence and concluded that the rates of mental illness in jails or prisons are no higher than the rates in the general population, controlling for social class.

The above studies are based on U.S. prison samples. There have been only a few studies in Canada on the extent of mental health problems in jail populations. Allodi, Kedward, and Robertson (1977) reported that increases in referrals of jail inmates to a jail psychiatric unit were associated with decreases in mental hospital populations in the Toronto area. Statistics Canada data on the number of admissions to psychiatric units within correctional facilities also support the view that the referral rate has increased (see Borzecki and Wormith, 1985, for a review of this issue). A study by Hodgins and Côté (1990) of 650 inmates in Quebec prisons revealed a high rate of mental disorder. Indeed, these researchers report that "the prevalence of schizophrenic disorders ... is about seven times that observed in samples of non-incarcerated adult males." Hodgins and Côté also comment on the fact that most of the inmates diagnosed with a major mental disorder did not receive any mental health treatment during their confinement in prison (see Steadman, McCarty, and Morrissey, 1988, for similar conclusions based on a national survey of U.S. jails).

There is little question that individuals with mental health problems are increasingly involved with the legal system. The first contact is usually by police officers. These officers have considerable discretion in responding to the mentally ill, although changes in the civil commitment laws have placed some limits on them. Jacobsen, Craven, and Kushner (1973) found that police rarely arrested persons they suspected of being mentally ill, indicating that they believed that hospitalization was more helpful than jail. The police officers frequently looked for alternatives to jail, such as contacting a responsible person, family counselling, or not taking any action at all.

There is some evidence, however, that the discretionary powers of the police in dealing with the mentally ill have been affected by the deinstitutionalization movement. This movement resulted in the release of large numbers of mental patients from mental hospitals. At the same time, the civil commitment laws were changed so that commitment had to be based on findings of mental illness and dangerousness. As a consequence, police could no longer use the mental hospital as an alternative disposition to jail, and were often forced to arrest a mentally ill person.

If this is true, does it suggest that there is a significant relationship between crime and mental disorder? In his study of the rates of mental disorder in prisons, Gunn (1977) answers this question with a note of caution. Gunn suggested that, as other alternatives for the placement of mentally ill persons were blocked off, it would be expected that a greater number of persons previously detained in mental hospitals would now end up in prisons. But as Roesch and Golding (1985) point out, the increased rate of mental disorder in prisons is the result of "institutional and public policy practices that have nothing to do with individual deviance *per se*. In fact, the individual behaviour may not have changed at all. What has changed, however, is the manner in which institutions of our society react to that individual behaviour."

With these cautions in mind, it will be instructive to review some recent studies on the extent to which persons considered to be mentally ill are arrested for criminal offences.

Most of the research on arrest rates of the mentally ill has relied on police or court records. Such research is limited by the availability of information in the files, which are often incomplete and inaccurate. One of the few researchers to actually observe how the police dealt with the mentally ill was Linda Teplin (1984). She was interested in examining the probability of arrest for mentally ill persons as compared to persons who were not mentally ill.

Teplin's sample was 1382 police-citizen encounters involving 2555 citizens. Overall, the probability of arrest was low, occurring in only 12 percent of 884 encounters (traffic-offence and public-service incidents were deleted from the total). In individual terms, 506 of the 1798 citizens involved were considered suspect, but only 29 percent were arrested.

Does the presence of symptoms of mental illness affect the probability of arrest? Teplin's data suggest that it does. Of 506 suspects, 30 were considered by observers to be mentally ill. Nearly one-half (14) were arrested, compared to an arrest percentage of 27.9 percent for those not mentally ill. Furthermore, this difference was not accounted for by differences in type of charge. In other words, mentally ill suspects were not arrested more often because they were suspected of committing more serious crimes. The difference held up across type of crime.

Lamb (1982) also examined police arrests of mentally ill persons. The sample was 102 inmates who had been referred to a forensic unit within a county jail. Ninety percent had a history of prior hospitalization and 92 percent had prior arrests. Lamb was interested in why the police chose to arrest rather than hospitalize these individuals. About one-half were arrested for felonies, so police had little choice but arrest, since persons who have allegedly committed serious crimes are almost uniformly arrested, regardless of mental condition. Lamb argues that police have become reluctant to take persons charged with less serious crimes to mental health treatment centres because they have learned through experience that the centres frequently release such people because of bed shortages, or because they do not meet the criteria for civil commitment. Lamb concluded that "the police may well book the person into jail—which is less time-consuming and ensures the person's removal from the community pending further evaluation—rather than take him to the hospital."

In a most comprehensive review of studies of arrest rates of mental patients, Rabkin (1979) did find a consistent pattern of higher arrest rates of mental patients after discharge (compared to the general population) but this finding was largely accounted for by the increase in the number of mental patients with prior criminal records. She found that mental patients as a group are not more likely to engage in criminal activity than people with similar demographic backgrounds who do not have a history of mental illness. She concludes that the inappropriate use of mental hospitals as an alternative to the criminal justice system is responsible for the finding that arrest rates of mental patients are increasing over time.

In conclusion, it is likely that theories of criminal behaviour which rely on models of mental illness will not account for the behaviour of most criminals. It is certainly true that some people who commit crimes can be considered to be mentally ill, but these individuals make up only a small percentage of the total criminal population. In a legal sense, most criminals are responsible for their actions in that they are aware of their behaviour and can distinguish between right and wrong.

SUMMARY

Each of the psychological theories reviewed in this chapter makes a contribution to the understanding of criminal behaviour. However, there is a need for greater integration of sociological and psychological perspectives, so that both situational determinants and individual differences can be taken into account in attempts to explain criminal behaviour (Monahan and Splane, 1980). A study by Conger (1976) provides an excellent example of an attempt to integrate the two approaches. Conger examined the relationship between two models of delinquent behaviour, the social control model (which is discussed in Chapter 12) and a social learning model. Based on data collected from a sample of grade seven boys, Conger demonstrated how social learning theory, particularly the effects of differential reinforcement and punishment, can be used to explain how an individual's bonds to society can be strengthened or weakened. Conger argued that the combination of the two theories can provide a more comprehensive theory of delinquent behaviour than can either theory by itself. It is likely that the same arguments can be made for any of the theories reviewed in this chapter.

BIBLIOGRAPHY

Abrahamsen, D. (1944). *Crime and the Human Mind.* New York: Columbia University Press.
Alexander, F., and M. Healey. (1935). *Roots of Crime.* New York: Knopf.
Allodi, F., H. Kedward, and M. Robertson. (1977). "Insane but guilty: Psychiatric Patients in Jail." *Canada's Mental Health* 25:3–7.
American Psychiatric Association. (1987). *Diagnostic and Statistical Manual of Mental Disorders.* (3rd ed., rev.) Washington, DC: American Psychiatric Association.

Bandura A. (1979). "The Social Learning Perspective: Mechanisms of Aggression." In H. Toch (ed.), *Psychology of Crime and Criminal Justice*. New York: Holt, Rinehart and Winston.

———. (1986). *Social Foundations of Thought and Action: A Social Cognitive Theory.* Englewood Cliffs, NJ: Prentice-Hall.

Bartol, C.R. (1980). *Criminal Behavior: A Psychosocial Approach.* Englewood Cliffs, NJ: Prentice-Hall.

Borzecki, M., and J.S. Wormith. (1985). "The Criminalization of Psychiatrically Ill People: A Review with a Canadian Perspective." *Psychiatric Journal of the University of Ottawa* 10:241–47.

Bowlby, J. (1953). *Child Care and the Growth of Love.* Baltimore: Penguin Books.

Braukman, C.J., K.A. Kirigin, and M.M. Wolf. (1980). "Group Homes Treatment Research: Social Learning and Social Control Perspectives." In T. Hirschi and M. Gottfredson (eds.), *Understanding Crime: Current Theory and Research.* Beverly Hills: Sage.

Braukman, C.J., and M.M. Wolf. (1987). "Behaviorally Based Group Homes for Juvenile Offenders." In C.J. Braukman and M.M. Wolf (eds.). *Behavioral Approaches to Crime and Delinquency.* New York: Plenum Press.

Braukman, C.J., M.M. Wolf, and K.K. Ramp. (1985). "Follow-up of Group Home Youths into Young Adulthood." (Progress Report, Grant MA 20030). Achievement Place research project. The University of Kansas, Lawrence, KA.

Brodsky, S.L. (1972). *Psychologists in the Criminal Justice System.* Urbana, IL: University of Illinois Press.

Burgess, R.L., and R.L. Akers. (1966). "A Differential Association Reinforcement Theory of Criminal Behavior." *Social Problems* 14:128–47.

Clastner, D.S. (1967). "Comparison of Risk Perception Between Delinquents and Nondelinquents." *The Journal of Criminal Law, Criminology and Police Science* 58:80–86.

Cleckley, H. (1976). *The Mask of Sanity.* St. Louis: Mosby.

Cohen, A.K. (1966). *Deviance and Control.* Englewood Cliffs, NJ: Prentice-Hall.

Conger, R.D. (1976). "Social Control and Social Learning Models of Delinquent Behavior: A Synthesis." *Criminology* 14:17–40.

Cook, T.D., D.A. Kendzierski, and S.V. Thomas. (1983). "The Implicit Assumptions of Television Research: An Analysis of the 1982 NIMH Report on Television and Behavior." *Public Opinion Quarterly* 47:161–201.

Craddick, R. (1962). "Selection of Psychopathic from Non-Psychopathic Prisoners Within a Canadian Prison." *Psychological Reports* 10:495–99.

De Vita, E.L., A.E. Forth, and R.D. Hare. (1990). "Family Background of Male Criminal Psychopaths." Paper presented at the meeting of the Canadian Psychological Association, Ottawa, ON.

Eysenck, H.J. (1977). *Crime and Personality.* London: Routledge and Kegan Paul.

Eysenck, H.J., and S.B.G. Eysenck. (1976). *Psychoticism as a Dimension of Personality.* London: Hodder and Stoughton.

Eysenck, H.J., and G.H. Gudjonsson. (1989). *The Causes and Cures of Criminality.* New York and London: Plenum Press.

Farrington, D.P. (1978). "The Family Background of Aggressive Youths." In L.A. Hersov, M. Berger, and D. Shaffer (eds.), *Aggression and Antisocial Behavior in Childhood and Adolescence.* Oxford: Pergamon.

———. (1979). "Environmental Stress, Delinquent Behavior, and Conviction." In I.G. Sarason and C.D. Spielberger, (eds.), *Stress and Anxiety*, vol. 6. Washington, DC: Hemisphere.

Farrington, D.P., L. Biron, and M. LeBlanc. (1982). "Personality and Delinquency in London and Montreal." In J. Gunn and D.P. Farrington (eds.), *Abnormal Offenders, Delinquency, and the Criminal Justice System*. Chichester, England: Wiley.

Freeman, R.J., and R. Roesch. (1989). "Mental Disorder and the Criminal Justice System: A Review." *International Journal of Law and Psychiatry* 12:105–15.

Friedlander, K. (1947). *The Psychoanalytic Approach to Juvenile Delinquency*. New York: International Universities Press.

Geen, R.G. (1983). "Aggression and Television Violence." In R.G. Geen and E.I. Donnerstein (eds.), *Aggression: Theoretical and Empirical Reviews*. New York: Academic Press.

Gunn, J. (1977). "Criminal Behaviour and Mental Disorder." *British Journal of Psychiatry* 130:317–29.

Guze, S. (1976). *Criminality and Psychiatric Disorders*. New York: Oxford University Press.

Hakeem, M. (1958). "A Critique of the Psychiatric Approach to Crime and Correction." *Law and Contemporary Problems* 23:650–82.

Hare, R.D. (1970). *Psychopathy: Theory and Research*. New York: Wiley.

———. (1977). "Criminal and Dangerous Behavior." In D.C. Rimm and J.W. Somervill (eds.), *Abnormal Psychology*. New York: Academic Press.

———. (1982). "Psychopathy and the Personality Dimensions of Psychoticism, Extraversion and Neuroticism." *Personality and Individual Differences* 3:35–42.

———. (1983). "Diagnosis of Antisocial Personality Disorder in Two Prison Populations." *American Journal of Psychiatry* 140:887–90.

———. (1984). "Crime and Personality." In D.J. Muller, D.E. Blackman, and A.J. Chapman (eds.), *Psychology and Law*. Chichester, England: Wiley.

———. (1990). "Manual for the Revised Psychopathy Checklist." Unpublished manuscript, University of British Columbia, Vancouver, Canada.

Hare, R.D., and D.N. Cox. (1978). "Clinical and Empirical Conceptions of Psychopathy, and the Selection of Subjects for Research." In R.D. Hare and D. Schalling (eds.), *Psychopathic Behavior: Approaches to Research*. Chichester, England: Wiley.

Hare, R.D., S.D. Hart, and T.J. Harpur. (in press). "Psychopathy and the DSM-IV Criteria for Antisocial Personality Disorder." *Journal of Abnormal Psychology* 100(3) (August):391–98.

Hare, R.D., and L. McPherson. (1984). "Violent and Aggressive Behaviour by Criminal Psychopaths." *International Journal of Law and Psychiatry* 7:35–50.

Heilbrun, A.B., Jr. (1979). "Psychopathy and Violent Crime." *Journal of Consulting and Clinical Psychology* 47:509–16.

Hodgins, S., and G. Côté. (1990). "Prevalence of Mental Disorders among Penitentiary Inmates in Quebec." *Canada's Mental Health* (March):1–4.

Hogan, R. (1973). "Moral Conduct and Moral Character: A Psychological Perspective." *Psychological Bulletin* 79:217–32.

Hollin, C.R. (1989). *Psychology and Crime*. London and New York: Routledge.

Jacobsen, D., W. Craven, and S. Kushner. (1973). "A Study of Police Referral of Allegedly Mentally-Ill Persons to a Psychiatric Unit." In J.R. Snibbe and H.M. Snibbe (eds.), *The Urban Policeman in Transition: A Psychological and Sociological Review*. Springfield, IL: C.C. Thomas.

Jeffery, C.R. (1965). "Criminal Behavior and Learning Theory." *Journal of Criminal Law and Criminology*. 56:294–300.

Jennings, W.S., R. Kilkenny, and L. Kohlberg. (1983). "Moral-Development Theory and Practice for Youthful and Adult Offenders." In W.S. Laufer and S.M. Day (eds.), *Personality Theory, Moral Development, and Criminal Behavior*. Lexington, MA: Lexington Books.

Lamb, H.R. (1982). *Treating the Long-Term Mentally Ill.* San Francisco: Jossey-Bass.

Malamuth, N.M., and J.V.P. Check. (1981). "The Effects of Mass Media Exposure on Acceptance of Violence Against Women: A Field Experiment." *Journal of Research in Personality* 15:436–46.

Martin, S.E., L.E. Sechrest, and R. Redner (eds.). (1981). *New Directions in the Rehabilitation of Criminal Offenders.* Washington, DC: National Press Academy.

Monahan, J., and S. Splane. (1980). "Psychological Approaches to Criminal Behavior." In E. Bittner and S. Messinger (eds.), *Criminology Review Yearbook.* Beverly Hills, CA: Sage.

Monahan, J., and H.J. Steadman. (1983). "Crime and Mental Disorder: An Epidemiological Approach." In M. Tonry and N. Morris (eds.), *Crime and Justice: An Annual Review of Research.* Chicago: University of Chicago Press.

Morash, M. (1983). "An Explanation of Juvenile Delinquency: The Integration of Moral-Reasoning, Theory and Social Knowledge." In W.S. Laufer and J.M. Day (eds.), *Personality Theory, Moral Development, and Criminal Behavior.* Lexington, MA: Lexington Books.

Nathan, P.E., and S.L. Harris. (1975). *Psychopathology and Society.* New York: McGraw-Hill.

Nietzel, M.T. (1979). *Crime and Its Modification: A Social Learning Perspective.* New York: Pergamon.

Ogloff, J.R.P., S. Wong, and A. Greenwood. (1990). "Treating Criminal Psychopaths in a Therapeutic Community Program." *Behavioral Sciences and the Law* 8:181–90.

Phillips, E.L. (1968). "Achievement Place: Token Reinforcement Procedures in a Home Style Rehabilitation Setting for 'Pre-Delinquent' Boys." *Journal of Applied Behavior Analysis* 1:213.

Piaget, J. (1932). *The Moral Judgment of the Child.* New York: Free Press.

Polansky, N., R. Lippitt, and F. Redl. (1950). "An Investigation of Behavioral Contagion in Groups." *Human Relations* 3:319–48.

Rabkin, J. (1979). "Criminal Behavior of Discharged Mental Patients: A Critical Appraisal of the Research." *Psychological Bulletin* 86:1–27.

Rappaport, J. (1977). *Community Psychology: Values, Research, and Action.* New York: Holt, Rinehart and Winston.

Redl, F. (ed.). (1966). *When We Deal With Children: Selected Writings.* New York: Free Press.

Reppucci, N.D., and W.G. Clingempeel. (1978). "Methodological Issues in Research with Correctional Populations." *Journal of Consulting and Clinical Psychology* 46:727–46.

Roesch, R. (1982). "Community Psychology and the Criminal Justice System: Alternative Directions for Psychologists." *Canadian Journal of Community Mental Health* 1:67–74.

———. (1988). "Community Psychology and the Law." *American Journal of Community Psychology* 16:451–63.

Roesch R., and S.L. Golding. (1985). "The Impact of Deinstitutionalization." In D.P. Farrington and J. Gunn (eds.), *Aggression and Dangerousness.* New York: Wiley.

Sarbin, T.R. (ed.). (1979). "The Myth of the Criminal Type." In *Challenges to the Criminal Justice System: The Perspectives of Community Psychology.* New York: Human Sciences Press.

Schoenfeld, C.G. (1971). "A Psychoanalytic Theory of Juvenile Delinquency." *Crime and Delinquency* 19:469–80.

Seidman, E., and B. Rabkin. (1983). "Economics and Psychosocial Dysfunction: Toward a Conceptual Framework and Prevention Strategies." In R.D. Felner, et al. (eds.), *Preventive Psychology.* Elmsford, NY: Pergamon.

Silber, D.E. (1974). "Controversy Concerning the Criminal Justice System and Its Implications for the Role of Mental Health Workers." *American Psychologist* 29:239–44.

Spatz Widom, C. (1977). "A Methodology for Studying Non-Institutionalized Psychopaths." *Clinical Psychology* 45:674–83.

Spatz Widom, C., and J.P. Newman. (1985). "Characteristics of Non-Institutionalized Psychopaths." In D.P. Farrington and J. Gunn (eds.), *Aggression and Dangerousness.* New York: Wiley.

Steadman, H.J., D.W. McCarty, and J.P. Morrissey. (1988). *The Mentally Ill in Jail: Planning for Essential Services.* New York: Guilford.

Teevan, J.J., and T.F. Hartnagel. (1976). "The Effects of Television Violence on the Perceptions of Crime by Adolescents." *Sociology and Social Research* 60:337–48.

Teplin, L.A. (1983). "The Criminalization of the Mentally Ill: Speculation in Search of Data." *Psychological Bulletin* 94:54–67.

———. (1984). "Criminalizing Mental Disorder: The Comparative Arrest Rate of the Mentally Ill." *American Psychologist* 7:794–803.

Warren, M.Q., and M.J. Hindelang. (1979). "Current Explanations of Offender Behavior." In H. Toch (ed.), *Psychology of Crime and Criminal Justice.* New York: Holt, Rinehart and Winston.

FURTHER READING

Bartol, C.R., and A.M. Bartol. (1986). *Criminal Behavior: A Psychological Approach.* (2nd ed.) Englewood Cliffs, NJ: Prentice-Hall. An overview of the contributions of psychology to the field of criminology. The emphasis is on the interactionist approach in which criminal behaviour is viewed as the interaction of dispositional and learning factors with social and environmental factors.

Feldman, M.P. (1977). *Criminal Behaviour: A Psychological Analysis.* London: Wiley. This book provides a good analysis of the application of learning theories in explaining criminal behaviour. Both psychological and sociological approaches are reviewed, and there is a chapter on treatment approaches.

Hilton, N.Z., M.A. Jackson, and C.D. Webster (eds.). (1990). *Clinical Criminology: Theory, Research and Practice.* Toronto: Canadian Scholar's Press. This is an edited text which brings together papers and articles representing a decade (the 1980s) of work by influential theorists in the field of forensic psychiatry and psychology. The exception is a 1953 paper by the late B.F. Skinner that outlines the basic principles of operant conditioning.

Hollin, C.R. (1989). *Psychology and Crime.* London and New York: Routledge. Topics include reviews of psychological approaches to criminal behaviour, mental disorder and crime, psychology in the courtroom, psychology and the police, and crime prevention.

Jacks, I., and S.G. Cox (eds.). (1984). *Psychological Approaches to Crime and Its Correction: Theory, Research, Practice.* Chicago: Nelson-Hall. This is an edited volume with contributions by well-known theorists (Eysenck, Rosenthal, Eron, Quay, and Rosenhan, among others) on aggression, heredity, and television and violence, as well as sections on treatment approaches.

Laufer, W.S., and J.M. Day. (1983). *Personality Theory, Moral Development, and Criminal Behavior*. Lexington, MA: Lexington Books. This is an edited volume with a chapter on interpersonal maturity theory, one by Eysenck on antisocial personality, and several chapters on moral development theory.

CHAPTER 9

STRAIN THEORIES
By James C. Hackler

THE STRUCTURAL-FUNCTIONALIST FOUNDATIONS

DURKHEIM: THE FUNCTIONS OF CRIME AND ANOMIE

*T*he term *strain theory* is more fashionable today than it was 30 years ago. Criminologists of an earlier generation would have referred instead to *structural functionalism*. In his book *The Division of Labor in Society* (1933), Durkheim argued that crime was necessary for the creation of laws which would identify certain behaviour as criminal. How does this happen?

> Crime brings together upright consciences and concentrates them. We have only to notice what happens, particularly in a small town, when some moral scandal has just been committed. They stop each other on the street, they visit each other, they seek to come together to talk of the event and to wax indignant in common.... That is the public temper.

While it is true that crime might be dysfunctional in some respects to society, in terms of cost, injury, or disruption, Durkheim argues that it is also functional in that it tends to remind members of a community about the interests and the values they share. Community bonds are strengthened. The deviant act inspires indignation. And, even more important, deviance reassures the "good" members of a community that their morality is the acceptable one. Since crime is functional to society, society actually encourages, or at least permits, a certain amount of deviance.

There must be a balance between the functional and dysfunctional aspects of deviance. Excessive crime and deviance would destroy a society, but if there were none at all, society would almost be compelled to create some. Even in a society of saints someone would have to be defined as pushing the limits of proper behaviour. Although behaviour is restrained, there will be someone who will violate that code. For Durkheim, every society needs its quota of deviants.

In a study of the early Puritan colonies in the United States, Kai Erikson (1966) described three "crime waves" during the first 60 years of settlement in Massachusetts. Each of these occurred at a time when unity in the colonies was waning. Erikson argued that the crime rates actually remained fairly stable during that period but that crime in the colonies served certain boundary definition and maintenance functions. By creating or exaggerating a crime, such as accusing someone of being a witch, and by reacting to it in a vigorous way, the new and fragile society was able to identify the boundaries of acceptable behaviour and offer a sense of stability.

One must be careful about this functionalist approach to crime. Punitive reactions to deviance can lead to repressive societal conditions that stifle the creativity that deviance often represents (Mead, 1918). By repressing deviant behaviour, a society may be less able to examine itself and make changes to face new situations. And although a modest amount of crime might be functional for a simple homogeneous society, for a modern heterogeneous society that values diversity in customs and norms, certain situations will create dilemmas. In some societies it has been considered appropriate for a father to surgically remove the clitoris of his daughter so that she would grow up to be a moral woman. If an immigrant from such a society decides to perform the same operation on his daughter who has been attending school in Canada for the last ten years, the daughter might view the act as a crime and appeal to the authorities in her adopted country. This illustration is simply one of many which suggests that heterogeneous societies experience a clash of customs from time to time.

Durkheim popularized the concept of anomie to explain crime in more advanced and differentiated urban societies. Heterogeneity and increased division of labour weakened traditional societal norms. The resultant changes loosened the social controls upon people, allowing greater materialism and individualism. When social cohesion breaks down in society and social isolation is great, society loses its traditional social control mechanisms and eventually suffers from a high rate of crime.

DURKHEIM'S GENERAL MODEL OF DEVIANCE
Community Characteristics Influence Both Suicide and Crime

In his classic work on suicide, Durkheim argues that similarity in some characteristics which society considers important leads to social cohesiveness (1951). Suicide, crime, and general deviance is inhibited in cohesive communities. Durkheim noted that some communities in France were homogeneous with regard to religion—that is, 100 percent Catholic or 100 percent Protestant. Other communities were heterogeneous, perhaps 50 percent Catholic and 50 percent Protestant.

Those communities with great similarity in religion tended to have low suicide rates, while those which were heterogeneous tended to have higher suicide rates. Although one could certainly measure homogeneity and heterogeneity using other variables besides religion, for example, race, language spoken, and so on, it is interesting to see that similarity in religion alone had a powerful explanatory value. One can generalize the argument from the specific act of suicide to the larger category of crimes, as illustrated in the sequence below:

AN OVERSIMPLIFIED MODEL OF DURKHEIM'S EXPLANATION OF SUICIDE AS A GENERAL EXPLANATION OF CRIME

Lack of Similarity ⟶ Lack of Social Cohesion ⟶ Suicide and Crime

The structural-functional approach argues that if a society is made up of many different elements it will be difficult to create a high degree of social cohesion. There will be less consensus on what is good and this will result in a higher rate of crime. This simple explanation has been generally supported in many different situations. It also presents us with something of a dilemma. If we believe in the value of a heterogeneous and diversified society where people with different cultures, languages, and tastes can mix, it is said, we should accept that there will be problems of social cohesion and crime. Some of us, however, are not happy with the implications of such an explanation, and prefer to think that the diversity that makes for interesting societies also helps us to be tolerant. For example, the Canadian prejudices against the Chinese and the Japanese during the first 50 years of the 20th century have gradually given way to tolerance, acceptance, and finally the appreciation of valuable cultural traits which enrich our nation.

Explaining society is the primary task of social science, but like any other socialized human beings, criminologists may "like" a theory because it provides policy direction in ways that are compatible with other values. For some, Durkheim's theory may have merit, but criminologists also want a theory which tells us how we may attain a diverse, multiracial, multilingual society which still has a reasonable degree of social cohesion and a low rate of crime.

MERTON: THE GAP BETWEEN ASPIRATIONS AND MEANS

In the 1950s and '60s, the most-cited article in criminology was a paper in which Robert K. Merton (1938) discussed social structure and anomie. For

Merton, crime is a symptom of the dissociation or gap between culturally prescribed aspirations and the socially structured avenues for realizing those aspirations. The culturally prescribed aspirations are the goals which are held up for all members of society. Merton argues that in America the accumulation of money, and the status which results from material wealth, is a universal goal. Socially structured avenues such as schooling are the accepted institutionalized means of reaching such goals. The socially structured avenues to achieve these goals may not be a problem for certain members of the society. If one comes from a family where the father is a medical doctor, it may be realistic for the son or daughter to aspire to the same occupation and social status. The family may live in a nice neighbourhood, the children may attend schools that condition students toward thinking about a college education, and there may be a home environment that encourages reading and getting good grades. Although certain individual characteristics, such as a certain level of intelligence, may be required, the means to achieve culturally prescribed aspirations may be available to many middle-class youths.

By contrast, the child of an immigrant family, especially a racial minority family, could find things a bit more difficult. If the father has abandoned the family, if an older sibling has already been in trouble with the law, and if the mother has been on welfare, the means available to achieve success may not be readily available. A youth coming from such an environment may not respect the school system, and may have poor grades and minimal likelihood of entering college. Or on the other hand, he or she might like to be a doctor and have both the material and social rewards that accrue to that occupation.

The gap between goals and means is small for certain portions of the society but large for others. The strain resulting from the gap between goals and means to achieve those goals could result in some sort of innovation, usually deviant in nature. In simpler terms, when society encourages people to want things but makes it difficult for certain groups to get them, members of these groups are more likely to steal or go into prostitution.

Merton's argument seems to fit many forms of lower-class crime. It may also fit certain upper-class crimes, where the criminal aspires to great wealth. The legitimate avenues to success may not be sufficient because of severe competition, and other businesspeople may be "cutting corners" in a variety of ways. Thus, if there is a gap between the desired goals and the means, innovation or illegimate tactics may be used.

THE SHIFT FROM CONTROL TO OPPORTUNITY STRUCTURES

Durkheim argued that human aspirations had to be regulated and channelled. Since human aspirations were boundless, and people could not always have what they want, they had to be persuaded to accept what they received. When people were not persuaded, the society became anomic. The moral guidelines were unclear. Social control broke down and some people violated the norms established by those in power.

Merton began his argument in a similar manner and suggested that American society had an overriding dominant goal, material success, but the guidelines for achieving that success were not always clear. If this type of anomie was so widespread, however, why wasn't crime distributed evenly throughout society? Merton accepted the argument that crime was distributed unevenly—that it was higher in the urban slums, for instance. To explain this social-class-specific crime by anomie, he redefined anomie as the disjuncture between the cultural goal of success and the opportunity structures by which this goal might be achieved (Box, 1971:103–6). Anomie was shifted from normlessness to relative deprivation, whereby it was not the entire community that was anomic but rather specific individuals who were committed to the goal of wealth while being barred from the means that would lead to the realization of that goal.

INTERPRETING MERTON

The most frequent application of Merton's work has been in the area of juvenile delinquency. Many scholars have worked to translate these ideas into measures that could be tested empirically. Debates have arisen over what Merton meant. Were his ideas intended to explain the behaviour of individuals, or, as Thomas Bernard argued, the behaviour of aggregates or groups (1987a)? Bernard argued that it is not correct to interpret strain or anomie in psychological or social psychological terms; rather, these are properties of social structures. Merton uses the word *anomia* as the sociological counterpart of the psychological concept *anomie*. According to Bernard, Merton's theory would predict that societies whose cultures overemphasize the goal of monetary success and underemphasize adherence to legitimate means will have high rates of instrumental crime. If legitimate opportunities to achieve those monetary goals are unevenly distributed then instrumental crime will be unevenly distributed.

One must note the distinction between *cultural* factors and *structural* factors in a society. In societies where structural features create an uneven distribution of legitimate opportunities, that is, where there are many blocked opportunities, there will be pockets of instrumental crime, regardless of cultural values. In a culture that emphasizes the ruthless pursuit of wealth, even if everyone has an equal opportunity, crime will be widespread, and such a society will have a high rate of crime.

Perhaps Bernard is correct in his interpretation, but many of us find it useful to apply Merton's ideas to individuals (Agnew, 1987). For example, Merton describes one type of adaptation to strain as innovation, where there is an acceptance of cultural goals but rejection of institutionalized means. It is easier to visualize *persons* who are frustrated in their striving for monetary gains than aggregates. Whether or not Merton meant to restrict his analysis to groups, it is also legitimate to develop a hypothesis that can be applied to individuals. When we later review some of the evidence, we will be less concerned with faithfulness to Merton's original intention than with the

244 EXPLANATIONS OF CRIME

validity of the various interpretations and extensions of these influential ideas.

Gwynne Nettler (1984) is critical of the clarity of Merton's concepts. Is what people say they want out of life an adequate measure of their aspirations? When asked what we'd like, it is easy for us to answer: "money and status." But Nettler questions the uniformity of wants or values in society, at least insofar as we are prepared to act on those wants. The serious offender may have a philosophy that is different from that of the majority in that it is cynical, hedonistic, hostile, and distrustful. Herman and Julia Schwendinger (1967) present the philosophy of serious offenders as: "Do unto others as they would do unto you ... only do it first"; "If I don't cop it ... somebody else will."

Nettler also feels that the concept of "opportunity" is vague. Is there a difference between perceived opportunities and real ones? *"Opportunities are by their nature much easier to see after they have passed than before they are grasped"* (1984:209). If people do not end up equally happy and rich, is this due to differences in opportunity? We must avoid the circular argument of explaining the cause by using the outcome. Problems with the meaning of these concepts have led to considerable debate, as scholars have tried to develop operational definitions to test these ideas.

No theory of crime has engendered so much reworking by criminologists as this one. For several decades, sociologists with a similar orientation were finding support for these ideas. Later, the theory's critics joined the debate. By the 1980s there was renewed interest in strain theory. We will sample some of these developments later in the chapter.

OPPORTUNITY STRUCTURES

KOBRIN: OPPORTUNITIES IN THE COMMUNITY

Although there may be strains which create a pressure toward criminal behaviour, there are also different opportunity structures which may facilitate breaking the law. Some communities, or some situations, may not provide opportunities for crime even though individuals are discontented. In one of the most seminal articles in criminology, Sol Kobrin (1951) argues that opportunities differ in various types of communities. Although the typology offered in Table 9.1 does not appear explicitly in that article, Kobrin does agree with the typology.

Kobrin points out that we live in communities which sometimes offer a variety of opportunities, both legitimate and illegitimate. No community entirely lacks legitimate opportunities for its inhabitants to attain their aspirations, or entirely lacks illegitimate opportunities. All communities offer a mixture of possibilities. Table 9.1 oversimplifies those possibilities to make its point. If communities have legitimate opportunities and/or illegitimate opportunities, four types of communities are possible. Although communities

TABLE 9.1
TYPOLOGY OF COMMUNITY OPPORTUNITY STRUCTURES
IMPLICIT IN KOBRIN (1951)

TYPE OF COMMUNITY	I "STABLE SLUM"	II "TRANSITORY SLUM"	III "SUBURBIA"	IV UNLIKELY
Legitimate Opportunities	Yes	No	Yes	No
Illegitimate Opportunities	Yes	No	No	Yes

Source: Adapted from Sol Kobrin. (1951). "The Conflict of Values in Delinquency Areas." *American Sociological Review* 16:653–61.

exist which approximate these four types, this typology oversimplifies reality, in which there will always be gradation in opportunities. Nonetheless, it is useful to think in terms of ideal types.

In Type I communities, there are illegitimate opportunities as well as legitimate ones. One might call this type of community a "stable slum," where prostitution, gambling, and a variety of other illegal activities are well organized. The organized criminal element may concentrate on certain activities and avoid, or even discourage, violence and other types of crime that would upset the community and the forces of control. In such stable lower-class neighbourhoods, one would expect to find a number of legitimate opportunities which reflect the normal ongoing activities of a city. They would include restaurants, stores, repair shops, and all the other normal economic activities that arise to meet the needs of any urban society.

The Type II community might be called a "transitory slum," as typified by a decaying housing project. In such a disorganized community there is extensive unemployment. No business dares to establish a store in the neighbourhood because of the fear of robbery. Paperboys do not deliver in the area because customers would probably lose their papers, the paperboys might be attacked, and the newspaper would find it unprofitable. Restaurants are not established; thus, there are few opportunities for waitresses, dishwashers, or cooks. In other words, it is an area with very few legitimate opportunities for earning money. Even the illegitimate opportunities are minimal, because the neighbourhood is poorly organized. Prostitutes find it dangerous to work there, those who wish to gamble go to the more stable slum areas, and although the residents may occasionally attack each other, the pickings are rather slim. In these disorganized areas, there is little sense of community life and families tend to be poorly integrated. Minimal opportunities exist for either legitimate or illegitimate enterprise.

The Type III community has legitimate opportunities but practically no illegitimate opportunities. Perhaps "suburbia" fits this description. A teenager can find work mowing lawns, especially if the neighbours know that the teenager comes from a good, solid family. Paper routes are available, and through their contacts in the community, juveniles may learn of opportunities for summer work and other part-time jobs. Adults and adolescents are involved in economic activities which create opportunities for work and the anticipation of future work. Illegitimate opportunities are rare. A would-be suburban prostitute might find difficulty in approaching customers out peacefully walking their dogs. A college student may not find much success trying to sell an armful of stolen hubcaps door-to-door in his or her suburban neighbourhood. Such a community can be expected to be lacking in illegitimate opportunities.

What about the Type IV community? Although such a combination is theoretically possible, it is probably unlikely that any neighbourhood could develop a wide range of illegitimate opportunities without also spawning some legitimate ones. If the illegitimate opportunities were well organized, we would expect restaurants, stores, laundries, and other facilities to develop to provide those stable lower-class communities with normal services. If either organized crime or the citizenry had things fairly well under control, the community could become viable. While the control mechanisms may differ in such neighbourhoods, the suggestion is that it would be very unlikely to find a community with well-organized illegitimate opportunities alone.

Kobrin (1951) calls our attention to the dual characteristics of lower-class communities. Both legitimate and illegitimate opportunities exist together in greater or lesser degree. How these two structures interact, and what draws people to one or the other, have interested a number of sociologically oriented criminologists.

RICHARD CLOWARD: ILLEGITIMATE OPPORTUNITY STRUCTURES

Just as there are differences between legitimate and illegitimate opportunities, there are different types of illegitimate opportunities. Cullen (1984) points out the importance of "structuring variables." Cloward asserts that simply being subjected to socially generated strain does not enable a person to deviate in any way he or she chooses. People can only participate in a given adaptation if they have access to the means to do so (Cullen 1984:40). Even though members of the lower class may be under a great deal of strain, they are unlikely to engage in violations of financial trust, political corruption, and other white-collar crimes in order to achieve their goals. In an article (1959) and then in a book with Lloyd Ohlin entitled *Delinquency and Opportunity* (1960), Cloward extended the ideas of Merton by combining them with themes found in Sutherland's "differential association" (see Chapter 11).

Sutherland argued that criminal behaviour is learned through associations with others who define criminal activity favourably. While Merton emphasized legitimate means, Sutherland concentrated on illegitimate means (Cullen, 1988). People under strain cannot become any kind of criminal they choose; they are limited by the opportunities available to them. Dealing in drugs is not automatically available to a "square" college professor as a means of supplementing her income; she probably lacks the skills and contacts to obtain a source of illegal drugs. In other words, illegitimate means are not readily available to people simply because they lack legitimate means. While Durkheim and Merton developed plausible theories of structurally induced pressures, it remained to Cloward to try to explain the resulting adaptive behaviour.

Merton appreciated Cloward's insights and extension of his ideas, as was apparent in the commentary Merton wrote in the *American Sociological Review*, which appeared immediately after Cloward's article. Merton noted that some earlier research showed there were five times as many fraud convictions in Texas as in Massachusetts. Perhaps, he went on, it was more difficult to sell someone a dry oil well in Massachusetts than in Texas. Illegal opportunities for certain types of fraud are more available in some areas than others.

Opportunity theory fits many different types of deviance, but Cloward and Ohlin are best known for the application of these ideas to juvenile delinquency. Although undergoing strain, juveniles face different barriers to resolving that strain than adults do. The way they respond to social barriers for achieving goals could lead to three different types of gangs or subcultures: *criminal, conflict,* and *retreatist* gangs. Herbert Costner, in lectures at the University of Washington, used the diagram illustrated in Figure 9.1 to explain how these gangs are formed.

There are pressures toward conventional goals and there are pressures toward achieving middle-class values, such as respectability and conventional success. When juveniles overcome those barriers, as most middle-class juveniles do, they commit little crime. However, lower-class males may actually have different goals. Instead of respectability, they may be more interested in money, a car, and showing off for their girlfriends. Under certain economic conditions, this might be achieved by working in areas where their skills are scarce, working in a hazardous occupation, or possibly being fortunate as an athlete. In other words, it is possible to be successful in a working-class style of life. These ideas differ somewhat from Merton in that aspirations are not universal, as Merton had argued. Striving for success can mean different things to different people.

However, Cloward emphasizes the barriers to lower-class goals as well as middle-class goals. Not only is there an opportunity structure for the goals of the lower-class, but crime also has an opportunity structure of its own. If legitimate opportunities are blocked, the next step may be to search for illegal

FIGURE 9.1
BARRIERS TO LEGAL AND ILLEGAL OPPORTUNITIES
IMPLICIT IN THE WORK OF CLOWARD AND OHLIN (1960)

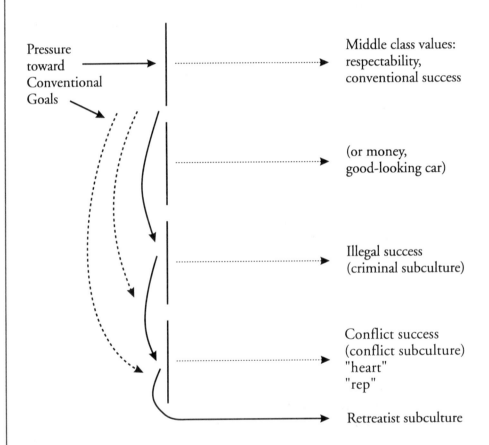

Social Barriers
to Achieving Goals

Pressure
toward
Conventional
Goals

Middle class values:
respectability,
conventional success

(or money,
good-looking car)

Illegal success
(criminal subculture)

Conflict success
(conflict subculture)
"heart"
"rep"

Retreatist subculture

success, but even here there are barriers. Without certain contacts it may be difficult to get into illegal gambling or learn the skills of a successful safe-cracker. Many juveniles will have difficulty learning the skills necessary to succeed in these areas. However, if there are barriers to profitable property crime, juveniles can still turn to conflict as a means of attaining status, at least among their peers.

Juveniles who are unskilled as thieves can show their bravery by fighting for their "turf." This will show others that they have "heart"; their courageous behaviour will give them a "rep." But even conflict success has barriers. Not every juvenile is keen on wielding a bicycle chain in a gang war. Some may lack strength or courage, or both. These juveniles may employ a third delinquent alternative: the use of drugs. In the drug or retreatist subculture there are practically no barriers.

MARGINAL OPPORTUNITY STRUCTURES

Francis Cullen (1988) believes that many scholars have not fully appreciated the contributions made by Cloward because they are focused primarily on the gap between aspirations and perceived opportunity. In fact, other deviant styles of adaptation to illegitimate opportunities become apparent when one looks beyond traditional types of crime.

Cloward's work may also offer an explanation of certain marginal activities, such as being an oil company spy. In Alberta, where many oil companies drill wells in the wilderness and try to keep their findings secret, spies from rival companies sometimes pose as hunters or wilderness trekkers to observe drilling operations without being detected. This often hazardous activity highlights the presence of particular opportunities and particular barriers to potentially profitable tasks. Kobrin and Cloward have applied these ideas to conventional crime, but there may be a much wider range of marginal behaviours that would fit these models.

In Figure 9.1, one can see that there are a number of barriers or structuring variables which influence the choice of activities. If all opportunities are blocked, skid row may be the alternative. P.J. Giffen (1966) describes the "revolving door" in Toronto where skid-row alcoholics go in and out of jail on a regular basis.

The question of opportunity structures, including illegitimate ones, poses an interesting policy question for society. Which is more desirable: having skid-row alcoholics with no opportunities, or having prostitutes and gamblers engaging in activities that are seen as deviant by society? While legitimate opportunities are clearly preferable to illegitimate ones, is it possible that the integration of some borderline, or even obvious, deviance would be better than the total breakdown represented by some of society's rejects? In a society that must sometimes choose between levels of evils, would policy makers be wise to consider the nature of different opportunity structures and assess the impact of selected illegimate opportunities on society?

EMPIRICAL EVIDENCE FOR THE THEORY OF ILLEGITIMATE OPPORTUNITY STRUCTURES

One of the logical conclusions of the theory of illegitimate opportunity structures is that it would lead to the selection and evolution of deviant adaptations; that is, specific types of subcultures would develop. According to Figure 9.1, we would expect to see three distinct types of gangs corresponding to the criminal, conflict, and retreatist subcultures. However, there has been little empirical evidence for three distinct types of gangs corresponding to these adaptations (Short and Strodtbeck, 1965). It seems that stealing, fighting, and drug use are more likely to be found in combination than in distinct subcultural forms. Even though the specialized subcultures are not readily apparent, the one idea that persists is that there can be barriers to illegitimate success as well. In other words, there is an opportunity structure in crime just as there is in the legitimate world. It is likely that individual characteristics, such as race, are related to some of these barriers. Thus, black youth in the United States may be more represented in drug subcultures because they find it more difficult to overcome barriers to both legitimate and certain illegitimate success. Violence and drugs may be the only things left. In Canada, abuse of alcohol by many Natives may also be the product of barriers to both legitimate and illegitimate opportunities.

Another question that has been raised about both Merton's and Cloward's ideas is the relevance of long-term occupational goals for many individuals, especially those with a lower-class orientation. John Quicker (1974) argues that frustrated occupational goals do not seem to be particularly influential in producing delinquency. However, goal frustration other than occupational goal frustration may be quite relevant. For lower-class youth there are other goals—more immediate than occupational goals—which could produce delinquency. Quicker argues that educational goals, when frustrated, will lead to delinquency. Doing poorly in school is a humbling experience in itself. Even without long-term plans, one's self-esteem is connected to success in the classroom. In general, the concerns of the present may be more important than the longer-range goals postulated by Cloward and Merton. As one young person told Quicker, "Man, I can't worry about what kind of job I'm going to have when I grow up, I may never get there. The world may not be here that long" (1974:85).

While barriers to achieving immediate goals may be important, other studies indicate an awareness of the lack of longer-range opportunities available to certain lower-class groups. Young black males in Chicago seemed quite aware that they would face financial problems if they got married and raised children (Short and Strodtbeck, 1965). The debate over the awareness of barriers to short-term and long-term goals is by no means a fatal flaw in Cloward's work on opportunity structures. Both seem to exist even if it is not certain which ones are the most relevant.

EDUCATIONAL VERSUS FINANCIAL GOALS

Some critics, such as Hirschi (1969), have argued that the gap between aspirations and expectations is not as meaningful as the aspirations themselves. Strain is redundant as an explanation of delinquency; goal commitment is enough (Kornhauser, 1978). Margaret Farnworth and Michael Leiber (1989) provide evidence of the potency of educational aspirations, but in addition they found that the disjunction between economic goals and educational means was an even better predictor of delinquency. That is, those who want lots of money but don't anticipate attending college were more likely to be delinquent.

ALBERT K. COHEN: THE MIDDLE-CLASS MEASURING ROD

Strain theories focus on a given situation without paying much attention to the way the situation develops. A more dynamic approach to barriers to success is presented in the very influential book by Albert K. Cohen entitled *Delinquent Boys: The Culture of the Gang* (1955). Cohen differs from Cloward in that he feels that lower-class boys aspire to middle-class goals when they enter the educational system. Cloward's work tends to neglect the opportunity structure of schools and the ways in which schools block opportunity. According to Cohen, schools are dominated by the "middle-class measuring rod," which sets up a certain set of standards: sophistication, good appearance, selling oneself, controlling aggression, respect for authority, deferred gratification, and those general characteristics that make young boys and girls a success in a middle-class world. If a student follows these standards, he or she is likely to have success in school. The clear implication is that this will lead to success in the larger society. This process begins early. The lower-class child begins school with desires and goals that are similar to those of other young children. The difference is that the lower-class child may have difficulty meeting the standards set by the middle-class measuring rod. While middle-class children are taught to respect books and be polite, the lower-class child may have been taught to stand up for her rights and not let people push her around. The middle-class child has been taught to "save for a rainy day," but the lower-class child has learned that men who win money gambling spend it quickly and treat their friends.

Other strain theorists have attempted to identify sources of stress but have spent less time explaining the dynamics of how an individual adapts to that stress. A lower-class student could make an effort to change his or her behaviour to please the teacher, but there may be little support from home and from peers. A second alternative is to withdraw from the contest and lead an isolated existence. Cohen argues that male juveniles who fail in the educational system when they cannot meet middle-class standards can gain status by reversing those standards. In this third alternative, juveniles try to modify the goals and begin looking for others who are in the same predicament. If the goals have been turned upside down, "good" boys become "squares," and teachers' pets. Instead of respecting authority, one challenges it. "Tough" guys gain prestige. Fighting becomes important; "rep" and "heart" are important to show that a boy is capable of participating in a gang rumble. The juvenile strives for higher prestige among the gang. Instead of saving money and developing economical habits, one shares with fellow gang members. Destroying property shows contempt for those whose goals one has rejected. Instead of being courteous, the gang member emphasizes discourtesy and dresses in a manner to provoke middle-class teachers.

Reaction formation is a psychological mechanism for redefining goals when the individual cannot meet the standards expected of him or her. However, reversing middle-class standards cannot be done by one individual alone. This is a collective process brought about through *mutual conversion.* In relations with others, people typically explore the nature of the response from others before they commit themselves too far. The juvenile who is doing poorly in school notices that there are others who are not succeeding in school. While walking home together, two boys might explore their feelings about school. "What do you think about the teacher?" The other responds cautiously, "I dunno, do you like him?" Response: "Not much, how about you?" "I don't like him at all."

The mutual conversion continues. Each boy commits himself a bit more until they have mutually agreed that the teacher is unfair, the teacher's pet is a creep, and so is the boy who gets good grades. As the process continues they can rebuild a new set of values and different standards, which they can meet more easily than middle-class standards.

It is important to note that as these boys achieve new status among gang members, such status is limited to the inner group. Outside of the gang their status is low and becomes even lower. As a result, they turn more to the gang for gratification and become even more separated from the middle-class orientation of the school.

THE STATIC STATE OF STRAIN THEORIES

With the exception of Cohen, most strain theorists offer rather static explanations which do not take into account the dynamic nature of social interaction. Most strain theories ignore group dynamics, which makes them inadequate for explaining certain types of crime. An excerpt from a book by Robertson Davies, *The Manticore* (1972), begins with the description of the book's protagonist joining some other boys in breaking into a cabin in the woods of Ontario.

> We got in after a few minutes. The house was even more fussy inside than the outside had promised. It was a holiday place, but everything about it suggested elderly people.
>
> "The first move in a job like this," Bill said, "is to see if they've got any booze."
>
> They had none, and this made them enemies, in Bill's eyes. They must have hidden it, which was sneaky and deserved punishment. He began to turn out cupboards and storage places, pulling everything onto the floor. We others didn't want to seem poor-spirited, so we kicked it around a little. Our lack of zeal angered the leader.
>
> "You make me puke!" he shouted and grabbed a mirror from the wall.... He lifted it high above his head, and smashed it down on the back of a chair. Shattered glass flew everywhere.

"Hey, look out!" shouted Jerry. "You'll kill somebody."

"I'll kill you all," yelled Bill, and swore for three or four minutes, calling us every dirty name he could think of for being so chicken-hearted.... He could make you do things you didn't want to do by a kind of cunning urgency. We were ashamed before him. Here he was, a bold adventurer, who had put himself out to include us—lily-livered wretches—in a daring, dangerous, highly illegal exploit, and all we could do was worry about being hurt! We plucked up our spirits and swore and shouted filthy words, and set to work to wreck the house.

Our appetite for destruction grew with feeding. I started gingerly, pulling some books out of a case, but soon I was tearing out pages by handfuls and throwing them around. Jerry got a knife and ripped the stuffing out of the mattresses. He threw feathers from sofa cushions. McQuilly, driven by some dark Scottish urge, found a crowbar and reduced wooden things to splinters. And Bill was like a fury, smashing, overturning, and tearing. But I noticed that he kept back some things and put them in a neat heap on the dining-room table, which he forbade us to break. They were photographs.

The old people must have had a large family, and there were pictures of young people and wedding groups and what were clearly grandchildren everywhere. When at last we had done as much damage as we could, the pile on the table was a large one.

"Now for the finishing touch," said Bill. "And this is going to be all mine."

He jumped up on the table, stripped down his trousers, and squatted over the photographs. Clearly he meant to defecate on them, but such things cannot always be commanded, and so for several minutes we stood and stared at him as he grunted and swore and strained and at last managed what he wanted, right on the family photographs.

How long it took I cannot tell, but they were critical moments in my life. For as he struggled, red-faced and pop-eyed, and as he appeared at last with a great stool dangling from his apelike rump, I regained my sense and said to myself, not "What am I doing here?" but "Why is he doing that? The destruction was simply a prelude to this. It is a dirty, animal act of defiance and protest against—well, against what? He doesn't even know who these people are."

Strain theory is clearly lacking in its power to explain this behaviour. While some of the static variables may have been relevant at the beginning of the incident, the inter-stimulation and the dynamics of the events themselves seem to play a much more powerful role. What are the conditions that lead a potential participant to refuse to take part right from the beginning and possibly change the entire direction of the process? These elements are lacking in the structural-functional explanations of crime. This may be their greatest weakness. Explanations that do consider these elements are presented in Chapter 11, which discusses interactionist theories.

ASSESSING FUNCTIONALIST AND OPPORTUNITY THEORIES

Despite the criticisms of strain theory, there has recently been renewed interest in it. While these recent discussions dispute a variety of issues, there is considerable agreement that Merton, Kobrin, and Cloward still offer some of the more useful ideas for explaining crime (Bernard, 1987a, 1987b; Agnew, 1987; Cullen, 1988; Farnworth and Leiber, 1989). It is not really necessary to treat different theoretical perspectives as distinct and competing explanations. Clearly, there has been a convergence of ideas that permits strain theory, differential association, and control theory to complement one another. Nevertheless, few criminology studies bring these ideas together. An interesting attempt in this direction, using strain theory as a base, is offered by Robert Agnew (1985). He argues that adolescents located in unpleasant environments from which they cannot escape, such as school, are more likely to be delinquent. Although strain has usually been defined in the past in terms of blocked opportunities in education and jobs, Agnew reminds us that there are other stresses that lead to the search for illegitimate alternatives.

It is important to note that when Durkheim introduced his ideas, scholars were still explaining crime primarily by genetics and inner psychological forces. Durkheim focused attention on social forces, a radical idea at the time, but now the dominant methodology for explaining crime. His attempts to explain the link between crime and modernization may or may not be accurate, but it seems that the basic patterns of crime that have evolved in Western Europe have also occurred in Eastern European countries and in the emerging nations of Asia, Africa, and Latin America as they moved toward modernization (Shelley, 1981).

Durkheim was less accurate in his description of premodern nations as stable, crime-free societies. In fact, many had high levels of violence. Furthermore, Western countries seem to have experienced a long-term decline in crime over the last few centuries (Gurr, 1981). Despite the continual complaints we hear today, during the 17th century the average citizen in most cities in Western Europe would rarely leave the security of a locked home after dark.

Merton's discussion of anomie also presents some difficulties. One problem is the distinction between means and ends. Why did the Reichmann family buy Gulf Canada? Did they want more money? Or is it more realistic to see a blurring of means and ends? The process of achieving may be as important as the achievement itself. It would be difficult to explain the behaviour of the Reichmann family or the Thomson family of press barons in terms of striving for wealth. Doing the job well becomes both the means and the end.

Some sociologists have criticized strain models for incorrectly assuming that there is a gap between aspirations and expectations. Kornhauser (1978) argues that delinquents have both low aspirations and low expectations. She holds that such youths are not strained because although they don't expect to get much, they don't want much either. Elliot Liebow's work among street-corner men illustrates these ideas. Among these black, lower-class men, he argues, values were not passed from father to son as part of a valued cultural heritage, but both father and son experienced the same failures and maintained certain fictions to protect themselves against these failures. These fictions have been interpreted as "lower-class culture," but Liebow concludes that "what appears as a dynamic, self-sustaining cultural process is, in part at least, a relatively simple piece of social machinery which turns out, in a rather mechanical fashion, independently produced look-alikes" (1967:223). It is the structure of a society that guarantees blocked economic opportunities that leads to their behaviour, not culturally induced values that create unrealistic aspirations.

Liebow argues that these men are driven by social forces to do things they would rather not do, not by cultural values, but by socially structured situations that guide behaviour. Liebow's strain theory does not reject Merton, Cohen, and Cloward and Ohlin. However, it argues that the behaviour of these lower-class males is "independently produced" by similar socially structured situations.

The strongest criticisms of strain theories come from radical scholars such as Herman and Julia Schwendinger (1985). They argue that these ideas depend on official statistics that distort reality. For some radicals, strain theory cannot be salvaged with minor modifications and interpretations—they see it as basically wrong. David Greenberg (1977) is an exception in that he sees areas of compatiblity between radical and strain theories. The radical position is covered more thoroughly in Chapter 10, on conflict theories.

Another long-standing deficiency of most strain theories is their neglect of the gender issue. The differential rates of crime for men and women have frequently been discussed by criminologists, but a strain theory explanation might argue that women are less concerned about educational and economic opportunities or that the female role is not as subject to stress as the male role. Such assumptions are not tenable today. The material reviewed in this chapter illustrates the male bias which underlies the debates over strain theory. In general, the scholarship takes for granted certain sexist distortions of female roles; for example, it ignores the stresses and frustrations which women face in both public and private spheres. In actuality these stresses might be greater than those faced by men, and what needs to be explained is why the female response to stress is not as likely to include criminal behaviour.

In Chapter 5, "Women and Crime," Elizabeth Comack raises some of these issues. It remains to be seen whether the neglect of the gender discrepancy will reflect on the inadequacy of strain theories or whether these theories can be recast in such a way as to explain the differences in crime rates between men and women.

Other evidence that questions strain theory comes from a study showing that blocked opportunities were more associated with delinquency among whites than among blacks (Cernkovich and Giordano, 1979). Blacks may develop an attitude of resignation toward future occupational goals. It is also possible that strain and delinquency are the result of degradation and loss of status that occurs when juveniles fail in school. Even though they may not view school as a means to an end, failure in itself is demeaning and frustrating. In a broader sense, the whole notion of opportunity structures may not take into account the fact that people find satisfying roles in life that do not emphasize material success. The skilled craftsperson may take pride in his or her work, the academic may be comfortable in his or her role, but material success may be modest. Merton's work overlooks the broader notion of simply having a niche, even a modest one, as part of being a conforming member of society. Thus, while strain theory calls attention to some characteristics of society that might create situations which increase the likelihood of deviance, it might be wiser to view these ideas as heuristic rather than as complete explanations. They call our attention to settings that might produce crime.

HEURISTIC USES OF STRAIN THEORY

CORPORATE CRIME AND THE PETROCHEMICAL INDUSTRY

Despite the inadequacy of strain theory in explaining some situations, it is quite plausible in others. Alan Block and Thomas Bernard (1988) have described the way in which some refiners of waste oil moved into the illegal but profitable activity of adding a variety of toxic chemicals, which they had agreed to dispose of, to their waste oil. They then proceeded to sell the contaminated materials as regular fuel oil. Hospitals, universities, and others could buy the contaminated oil, and by burning it, send the toxic elements up their chimneys to settle on the surrounding neighbourhood. Recently, authorities in Ontario revealed that some of these companies had been exporting this contaminated fuel into Canada.

While one could explain this behaviour in terms of the lucrative business of getting rid of highly undesirable waste products, Block and Bernard point out that many refiners of waste oil operated profitably and legitimately until the shortage of oils modified the price structure of petroleum products, which led to the decline in legitimate opportunities just as the illegitimate opportunities began to increase. Thus, shrinking legitimate opportunities, and the availability of illegitimate ones, maximized the likelihood that these companies would commit their crimes. Sutherland (1949) argued that influential groups are able to influence legislation so that their own self-interested actions are defined as legal. When laws criminalize their activities, unscrupulous individuals already working together have little trouble convincing themselves that such activities are worth continuing.

Since not all reprehensible behaviour is a crime, it may be argued that despicable behaviour by the powerful might also be explained by questionable, if not necessarily illegitimate, opportunities. Is it possible that Alberta offered increased opportunities for gains of a questionable nature during the oil boom? The Principal Group companies were able to sell financial certificates by misleading the public into thinking they were guaranteed by the government. The Alberta government showed itself unwilling to take action even when it became aware of irregularities. Don Cormie, who was the head of the Principal Group, has now been indicted on criminal charges, but in the past it has been very difficult to obtain convictions in these types of situations.

Was it easier to exploit people in Alberta than in other provinces where longer experience with stock exchanges and financial institutions may have exposed shady practices earlier? Did the watchdog role of the Alberta Securities Commission fall short of that performed by similar commissions elsewhere? In other words, were illegitimate, or at least questionable, opportunities created by the booming economy in Alberta in the 1960s and 1970s?

THE DISPOSAL OF TOXIC WASTES: A NEW ILLEGITIMATE OPPORTUNITY STRUCTURE FOR CANADA?

Russell Mahler owned a number of companies which handled 6 percent of the waste oil in the U.S. In the summer of 1978, the U.S. Coast Guard discovered an oil spill on Newtown Creek in Queens, N.Y. The oil was traced to a corporation owned by Mahler. He paid a fine of $1000, while the government spent $5000 cleaning up the spill (Block and Bernard 1988). The pattern of industrial polluters paying occasional small fines which have little impact on profits, while taxpayers pay for the damage, is a typical scenario in Canada and the U.S.

Mahler continued his practices, which included having truck drivers pour toxic wastes down a bore hole behind a gas station that led to the Susquehanna River. Three million gallons of toxic wastes were dumped down this bore hole over a two-year period (Rebovich, 1986). The company and people involved were fined $750 000, and Mahler served a one-year prison sentence, becoming one of few who served time for such offences. The clean-up cost to the public was approximately $10 million. Mahler worked out a "consent order" with the government, acknowledging at least sixteen different violations, paid a fine of $50 000, and posted bond of $250 000 against future violations. He also reorganized his operations into a new company called Quanta Resources, which was allowed to operate in New York without a licence. Despite the fact that Mahler owned the company, he was no longer liable for previous illegal operations (Block and Bernard, 1988).

Can governments increase illegitimate opportunities? The Reagan government deliberately relaxed requirements and decommissioned regulatory controls. As the new head of the Environmental Protection

Agency, Anne Gorsuch abolished the E.P.A.'s Office of Enforcement. The E.P.A. appeared to be a "captured" agency, whose aim was to ensure industry profitability rather than to elicit compliance with the law (Block and Bernard, 1988). Cuts in regulatory agencies also contributed to the Savings and Loan débâcle, which will eventually cost U.S. taxpayers hundreds of billions of dollars.

Would the Scientific Research Tax Credit scheme in Canada be a parallel example? Companies could get tax relief if they did scientific research, but this led to the creation of pseudo-research operations. Those companies engaged in this type of activity might understandably pressure the various governmental bodies involved to continue the scheme even though it became apparent that it was being abused.

Let us now turn to situations where there is a different combination of opportunities, such as those which might result when there is a greater mix of social classes.

JOHN BRAITHWAITE: GREATER CLASS MIX AND THE REDUCTION OF CRIME

Braithwaite (1979) argues that one must look at the interaction between the social class of individuals and the social class of the neighbourhood in order to answer the question whether or not an increase in class heterogeneity in neighbourhoods would reduce crime. He offers two propositions. The first is that crime is most likely when both exposure to illegitimate opportunities is high and exposure to legitimate opportunities is low. The second states that crime is unlikely either when legitimate opportunities are high, or when illegitimate opportunities are low. In other words, in three out of the four possible combinations, there would be factors that would inhibit crime. Only when both illegitimate opportunities and a lack of legitimate opportunities exist would there be a marked increase in crime.

Braithwaite also argues that belonging to the lower class has more effect on delinquency for youth in lower-class areas than for youth in middle-class areas. Consequently, cities with relatively large numbers of lower-class people living in predominantly middle-class areas, and relatively large numbers of middle-class people living in predominantly lower-class areas, have relatively low crime rates. That is, greater class mix results in less crime.

This implies that if the middle classes could keep together, they would be better off; while if the lower classes stay together, they would be even worse off. Hence, it may be to the advantage of those with power and influence to keep themselves segregated. The quality of life for the society as a whole, however, would be improved if residential heterogeneity characterized the society.

Braithwaite's ideas seem most applicable to property crime, but another study shows that if there is a culture of violence, its roots are to be found in racial and economic inequalities (Blau and Blau, 1982). Spatial mixing in neighbourhoods would be more easily achieved with a reduction of racial and economic inequalities. Some observers have suggested that part of the reason Canada has a lower crime rate than the United States is that our housing policies have been less likely to "ghettoize" the poor in areas that could develop very high crime rates.

REDUCING UPPER-CLASS CRIME

Braithwaite also offers an interesting idea about crime among the upper classes. He argues that "too little power and wealth creates problems of living, and this produces crime of one type; too much power corrupts, and this produces crime of another type" (1979:200). This does not mean that upper-class people are more criminal than lower-class people. If lower-class people were exposed to the same vast opportunities as white-collar criminals, they, too, would engage in large-scale "power" crimes. Powerful people abuse their occupational power. Lawyers, business owners, pharmacists, and medical doctors all have unique opportunities to commit crimes with very little risk. It makes little sense to ask which social class commits more crime. Rather, opportunities differ by social class. However, the class-mix logic described above applies to the upper class as well. By reducing the power of these people, that is, reducing their opportunities for crime, white-collar crime would also be reduced. If lower-class people commit crimes because of a lack of power and wealth, increasing their influence and well-being might help. Braithwaite (who admits a socialistic bias) argues that greater economic equality and a greater distribution of influence among people would modify to some extent those factors that lead to crime.

Lower-class crime may be caused by the failure to achieve success goals. By contrast, upper-class crimes arise from an unprincipled overcommitment to success goals. One study of college students found that those most dedicated to monetary success were those most likely to argue that they "can't afford to be squeamish about the means." Similarly, certain occupational structures can increase commitment to illegitimate success. Richard Quinney (1963) found that retail pharmacists tended to fall into two divergent categories with different role expectations: professional and business. Those who were oriented toward the professional role were bound by guidelines for compounding and dispensing prescriptions. Those oriented toward the business role subscribed to the popular belief that self-employment carries with it independence and freedom from control. For them, professional norms exercised less control. Prescription violations occurred more frequently among the business-oriented pharmacists. As both Quinney and Braithwaite would argue, the mutual support of like-minded individuals insulated from the broader society, and from their professional colleagues, increased the likelihood of crime.

An anecdote describing the way John D. Rockefeller helped to educate his sons fits this line of reasoning. "I cheat my boys every chance I get; I want them sharp. I trade with the boys and skin them and just beat them every time I can. I want to make them sharp" (Braithwaite, 1979:191).

There is a potential link here with control theory, which will be discussed in Chapter 12. If contact with a broader base in society is achieved, one has a stronger social bond with others and a stronger belief in the rules that guide the larger society. However, if one's only social bond is with others who condone or rationalize criminal behaviour, criminal behaviour is likely. In this situation, control theory and strain theory complement each other.

It is interesting to note that Braithwaite applies opportunity structure as developed by other scholars in a way they do not. While some radical criminologists have criticized the "conservative" theories offered by Merton and by Cloward and Ohlin, they might find the way these theories have been applied by Braithwaite more congenial to their thinking.

POLICY IMPLICATIONS

THE APPLICATION OF STRAIN THEORY: EMPLOYMENT FOR EX-FELONS

Strain theories suggest that having a job would help individuals to avoid crime. Thus, helping ex-felons find and hold a job should also reduce crime. While such an idea seems obvious, only recently has the evidence become convincing. The Transitional Aid Research Project (TARP) provided unemployment benefits to released prisoners in Georgia and Texas. The findings from a study of this project suggest that unemployment benefits can be helpful, but that programs of this nature should be careful not to reward ex-inmates for not working (Berk, Lenihan, and Rossi, 1980). Successful work experiences also help to break a vicious cycle of self-defeating behaviours and attitudes that interfere with future employment (Liker, 1982).

While these social-structural consensus models may have their limitations, they do provide the occasional hint for modest but potentially meaningful contributions for improving society. Some would argue that this "fine tuning" of social programs is an appropriate role for social scientists (Rossi, 1980). Strain theories suggest some useful tools to accomplish this.

OPPORTUNITY STRUCTURE AND THE WAR ON POVERTY

In the 1960s, the Mobilization for Youth Project was launched in New York City following the principles outlined by Cloward and Ohlin. This project attempted to improve education, create work opportunities, organize lower-class communities, and provide a variety of social services. There is little evidence to suggest that the project was successful in an overall sense (Marris and Rein, 1973; Short, 1975; Helfgot, 1981). It is not likely that the program could ever have been able to alter the social-structural arrangements that create barriers to opportunity. Moreover, the programs were later taken over by traditional social service bureaucracies that normally act to protect and enhance their own interests. Under their jurisdiction, actual implementation involved attempts to change individuals instead of making basic changes in the structure of society. In his book *Betrayal of the Poor*, Rose (1972) argues that the War on Poverty in the United States failed because it was transformed to serve the interests of poverty-serving agencies.

Opportunities for Youth (OFY) in Seattle was another attempt to use work opportunities to reduce delinquency that met with little success (Hackler, 1966). One might argue that temporary job programs do not have a meaningful impact on the larger community. However, this same project had an impact on the attitudes of the adults living in the four communities where the project was conducted (Hackler and Linden, 1970). Furthermore, parents of black children seemed particularly responsive to the idea of job opportunities for their children. Like so many programs launched during the 1960s, OFY attempted to utilize strain theories. Lower-class populations did respond and became involved. Although evidence of crime reduction in the short term is lacking, the opportunity structure was altered for some lower-class families.

Unfortunately, opportunities for the lower classes may have decreased in North America in the past decade. While there has been a dramatic increase in the wealth of the upper classes, the frequent display of a luxurious lifestyle, especially on television, creates all the more strain for those who aspire to a share of that material wealth.

It may appear that an inordinate amount of effort is put into assessing the merits and demerits of criminological theories. Attacking traditional theories is part of the academic game. Finding support for them or using them in new ways is also a time-honoured strategy. We should not treat these dynamics cynically, because this process usually leads to a better understanding of our society. Moreover, scholars do not have to be in complete agreement regarding strain theory before applying many of its principles to public policy in the important pursuit of reducing the gap between rich and poor. Nor should we ignore the warning Merton voiced in his 1938 article: *The ruthless pursuit of profit creates a criminogenic society.* Increasing opportunities for the less privileged members of society makes a great deal more sense than rewarding the wealthy to encourage them to invest (for a profit, of course) so that some of the wealth will trickle down to the poor. The self-serving policies advocated by many powerful people in North America in recent years should, according to any version of strain theory, lead to more crime.

CONCLUSION AND SUMMARY

There seems to be a need to put labels on criminologists, even when their ideas do not fit comfortably into neat categories. Some of the debates about and among the various theorists can be productive. However, greater progress will probably be made in the future as scholars move more comfortably from one perspective to another. David Greenberg (1977), for example, points to the structural sources of adolescent crime which can be found in the exclusion of juveniles from the world of adult work. This exclusion exaggerates teenagers' dependence on peers for approval and eliminates the possibility of their obtaining funds to support their social activities. Juveniles fear, with good reason, that this lack of employment will persist into adulthood. They become anxious over the achievement of traditional role expectations. This anxiety can lead to a high level of violence. Greenberg points out that the links between Marxist criminology and strain theory are no cause for concern for theorists who lean toward either perspective. Those who wish to use criminological theory effectively must remember that the arbitrary categories that provide the chapter headings for this book offer a convenient way of reviewing different explanations of crime. These distinctions are artificial. The real world does not necessarily recognize these boundaries. If elements of strain theory emerge in some of the other chapters, the reader should not fear contamination. It can be like the beef stock which forms the basis of the soup. By itself it may not be exciting, but it makes a worthwhile contribution.

To summarize, this chapter began with a review of the structural-functionalist perspective and then applied it to several situations. Durkheim argued that crime was more frequent when social cohesion was less, when there was anomie or normlessness. Merton modified the idea of anomie to that of relative deprivation caused by the gap between goals and means. The focus on opportunity structures grew out of these ideas. Kobrin showed that communities offer different types of opportunities, and Cloward suggested that juvenile gangs performed similar functions.

Use of the concept of opportunity structures also makes sense when explaining certain types of white-collar crime, as illustrated by the study of the fuel oil business and the disposal of toxic wastes. It is important to note that governments can influence these opportunity structures. Some of the financial disasters in Canada, such as the failure of the Principal Group in Alberta, make more sense when we make use of Braithwaite's application of opportunity structures.

Despite the criticisms, strain theory has been applied with some utility to a number of issues relevant to public policy. Criticisms of this orientation are included in a general assessment of strain theories, but this chapter concludes that these traditional ideas are still very useful and, at times, compatible with more radical perspectives.

BIBLIOGRAPHY

Agnew, Robert. (1985). "A Revised Strain Theory of Delinquency." *Social Forces* 64: 151–67.

———. (1987). "On Testing Structural Gain Theories." *Journal of Research in Crime and Delinquency* 24:281–86.

Berk, Richard, Kenneth Lenihan, and Peter Rossi. (1980). "Crime and Poverty." *American Sociological Review* 45 (October): 766–801.

Bernard, Thomas. (1987a). "Testing Structural Strain Theories." *Journal of Research in Crime and Delinquency* 24:262–80.

———. (1987b). "Reply to Agnew." *Journal of Research in Crime and Delinquency* 24:287–90.

Blau, Judith, and Peter Blau. (1982). "Metropolitan Structure and Violent Crime." *American Sociological Review* 47 (February):114–29.

Block, Alan, and Thomas Bernard. (1988). "Crime in the Waste Oil Industry." *Deviant Behaviour* 9:113–29.

Block, Alan, and Frank Scarpitti. (1985). *Poisoning for Profit.* New York: William Morrow.

Box, Steven. (1981). *Deviance, Reality, and Society.* (2nd ed.). London: Holt, Rinehart and Winston.

Braithwaite, John. (1979). *Inequality, Crime and Public Policy.* London: Routledge and Kegan Paul.

Cavan, Ruth, and Jordan Cavan. (1968). *Delinquency and Crime: Cross-Cultural Perspectives.* Philadelphia: Lippincott.

Cloward, Richard. (1959). "Illegitimate Means, Anomie, and Deviant Behavior." *American Sociological Review* 24 (April):164–76.

Cloward, Richard, and Lloyd Ohlin. (1960). *Delinquency and Opportunity.* Glencoe, IL: Free Press.

Cohen, Albert. (1955). *Delinquent Boys: The Culture of the Gang.* Glencoe, IL: Free Press.

Cullen, Francis. (1984). *Rethinking Crime and Deviance Theory: The Emergence of a Structuring Tradition.* Totowa, NJ: Rowman and Allanheld.

———. (1988). "Were Cloward and Ohlin Strain Theorists? Delinquency and Opportunity Revisited." *Journal of Research in Crime and Delinquency* 25:214–41.

Davies, Robertson. (1972). *The Manticore.* Toronto: Macmillan.

Durkheim, Émile. (1933). *The Division of Labor in Society.* New York: Free Press.

———. (1951). *Suicide.* New York: Free Press.

Elliott, Delbert, Suzanne Ageton, and Rachelle Canter. (1979). "An Integrated Theoretical Perspective on Delinquent Behavior." *Journal of Research in Crime and Delinquency* (January):3–27.

Elliott, Delbert and Harwin Voss. (1974). *Delinquency and Dropout.* Lexington, MA: Lexington Press.

Erikson, Kai. (1966). *Wayward Puritans.* New York: Wiley.

Farnworth, Margaret, and Michael Leiber. (1989). "Strain Theory Revisited." *American Sociological Review* 54:263–74.

Giffen, P.J. (1966). "The Revolving Door: A Functional Interpretation." *Canadian Review of Sociology and Anthropology* 3 (August):154–66.

Greenberg, David. (1977). "Delinquency and the Age Structure of Society." *Contemporary Crises* 1:189–223.

Gurr, Ted. (1981). "Historical Forces in Violent Crime." In Michael Tonry and Norval Morris (eds.), *Crime and Justice,* Vol. 3. Chicago: University of Chicago Press.

Hackler, James C. (1966). "Boys, Blisters, and Behavior." *Journal of Research in Crime and Delinquency* 3 (July):155–64.

Hackler, James C., and Eric Linden. (1970). "The Response of Adults to Delinquency Prevention Programs: The Race Factor." *Journal of Research in Crime and Delinquency* 7 (January):31–45.

Helfgot, Joseph. (1981). *Professional Reforming: Mobilization for Youth and the Failure of Social Science.* Lexington, MA: Heath.

Hirschi, Travis. (1969). *Causes of Delinquency.* Berkeley: University of California Press.

Kobrin, Sol. (1951). "The Conflict of Values in Delinquency Areas." *American Sociological Review* 16 (October):653–61.

Kornhauser, Ruth. (1978). *Social Sources of Delinquency.* Chicago: University of Chicago Press.

Krahn, Harvey, Timothy Hartnagel, and John W. Gartrell. (1986). "Income Inequality and Homicide Rates: Cross-National Data and Criminological Theories." *Criminology* 24 (May):269–95.

Liebow, Elliot. (1967). *Tally's Corner.* Boston: Little, Brown.

Liker, Jeffrey. (1982). "Effects of Employment on Affective Well-being of Ex-felons." *American Sociological Review* 47 (April):264–83.

Macnaughten-Smith, Peter. (1976). *Permission to Be Slightly Free.* Ottawa: Law Reform Commission of Canada.

Marris, Peter, and Martin Rein. (1973). *Dilemmas of Social Reform.* (2nd ed.). Chicago: Aldine Press.

Mead, George Herbert. (1918). "The Psychology of Punitive Justice." *American Journal of Sociology* 23 (March):577–602.

Merton, Robert. (1938). "Social Structure and Anomie." *American Sociological Review* 3 (October):672–82.

———. (1957). *Social Theory and Social Structure.* (rev. ed.). New York: Free Press.

———. (1968). *Social Theory and Social Structure.* (2nd. ed.). New York: Free Press.

Nettler, Gwynne. (1984). *Explaining Crime.* New York: McGraw-Hill.

Newman, Graeme. (1976). *Comparative Deviance: Perception and Law in Six Cultures.* New York: Elsevier.

Owram, Douglas. (1978). "The Morals of Patronage in Nineteenth Century Canada." Unpublished paper, Department of History, University of Alberta.

Quicker, John. (1974). "The Effect of Goal Discrepancy on Delinquency." *Social Problems* 22 (October):76–86.

Quinney, Richard. (1963). "Occupational Structure and Criminal Behavior: Prescription Violation by Retail Pharmacists." *Social Problems* 11 (Fall):179–95.

Rebovich, David. (1986). *Understanding Hazardous Waste Crime.* Trenton, NJ: Northeast Hazardous Waste Project.

Reckless, Walter. (1961). "A New Theory of Delinquency and Crime." *Federal Probation* 34 (December):1–5.

Rose, Stephen. (1972). *The Betrayal of the Poor: The Transformation of Community Action.* Cambridge, MA: Schenkmann.

Rossi, Peter. (1980). "The Challenge and Opportunities of Applied Social Research." *American Sociological Review* 45 (December):889–904.

Schwendinger, Herman, and Julia Schwendinger. (1985). *Adolescent Subcultures and Delinquency.* New York: Praeger.

Sellin, Thorsten. (1938). *Culture Conflict and Crime.* New York: Social Science Research Council.

Shelley, Louise. (1981). *Crime and Modernization.* Carbondale, IL: Southern Illinois Press.

Short, James, Jr. (1975). "The Natural History of an Applied Theory: Differential Opportunity and Mobilization for Youth." In N.J. Demerath (ed.), *Social Policy and Sociology*. New York: Academic Press.

Short, James, Jr., and Fred Strodtbeck. (1965). *Group Process and Gang Delinquency*. Chicago: University of Chicago Press.

Sutherland, Edwin. (1949). *White Collar Crime*. New York: Dryden.

Tappan, Paul. (1947). "Who Is the Criminal?" *American Sociological Review* 12 (February):96–102.

Vaz, Edmund, and John Casparis. (1971). "A Comparative Study of Youth Culture and Delinquency: Upper Middle-Class Canadian and Swiss Boys." *International Journal of Comparative Sociology* 12 (March):1–23.

FURTHER READING

Agnew, Robert. (1985). "A Revised Strain Theory of Delinquency." *Social Forces* 64:151–67. An innovative way of using strain theory to show that the unpleasant experiences juveniles have at home and in school can lead to delinquency.

Bernard, Thomas. (1987). "Testing Structural Strain Theories." *Journal of Research in Crime and Delinquency* 24: 262–80. This article and the two that follow debate the application of strain theory to individuals or groups.

Block, Alan, and Frank Scarpitti. (1985). *Poisoning for Profit*. New York: William Morrow. A discussion of the new illegitimate opportunities which have opened up for those in the waste-disposal industry. The authors believe that strain theory explains these new crimes.

Braithwaite, John. (1979). *Inequality, Crime and Public Policy*. London: Routledge and Kegan Paul. Focusing on opportunity structure, Braithwaite makes a number of cross-cultural comparisons.

Cullen, Francis. (1984). *Rethinking Crime and Deviance Theory: The Emergence of a Structuring Tradition*. Totowa, NJ: Rowman and Allanheld. An elaboration and interpretation of strain theories.

Cohen, Albert. (1955). *Delinquent Boys: The Culture of the Gang*. Glencoe, IL: Free Press. One of the classic studies of delinquency which linked ideas of opportunity structure to the subculture of gang delinquency. Influenced later studies of delinquency extensively.

Greenberg, David. (1977). "Delinquency and the Age Structure of Society." *Contemporary Crises* 1:189–223. One of the few radical scholars who integrates opportunity structures and conflict theory.

Kornhauser, Ruth. (1978). *Social Sources of Delinquency*. Chicago: University of Chicago Press. A review of delinquency theories with several criticisms of strain theory.

Merton, Robert. (1968). *Social Theory and Social Structure.* (2nd ed.) New York: Free Press. The third revision of Merton's classic anomie theory of crime.

CHAPTER 10

CONFLICT AND MARXIST THEORIES

By Ronald Hinch

*C*onflict and Marxist theories have been controversial from the beginning. They are controversial because of their critique of other perspectives, especially consensus theories, and because they pose challenges to dominant assumptions about how the social order is maintained. Whereas consensus theory (see Chapter 9) assumes a societal-wide consensus concerning the protection and preservation of values, the theories presented in this chapter argue that no such consensus exists. They argue that contemporary societies are characterized by conflict and dissension. The extent to which the theories discussed in this chapter challenge the notion of consensus vary according to their assumptions regarding the source and nature of conflict. As a result, some of them offer a greater challenge to assumptions about social order than do others. To highlight their differences and similarities, they have been grouped under the following headings: *cultural conflict theories, group conflict theories, Weberian conflict theories*, and *Marxist theories*. The chapter on women and crime also summarizes several feminist theories of crime and criminality which could be considered variations of either conflict or Marxist theories.

CULTURAL CONFLICT THEORIES

Cultural conflict theory developed from the Chicago School. The Chicago School was one of the most influential forces shaping both sociology and criminology prior to 1940. It incorporated several approaches to the study of society. One approach, symbolic interactionism (see Chapter 11), focused on the analysis of the way people learn to be members of their societies by interpreting and using symbolic communications. Another approach, social disorganization theory (see Chapter 12), focused on the lack of organization within and between segments of society. Each of these approaches may be found in Sellin's (1938) theory of *conduct norms*, as well as Sutherland's (1939) theory of *career criminality*.

According to Sellin (1938), all cultures establish their own behaviour codes, or conduct norms. Bringing divergent cultures into direct contact within the same society results in conflict. This conflict is heightened whenever one culture is able to have its beliefs and practices protected by inclusion in the criminal code. Where this happens, other cultures, whose beliefs and practices differ, must either alter their culture and behaviour, or risk conflict with the dominant culture. Sellin's theory has been used to explain the crime pattern among the Italian population in Montreal.

CULTURE CONFLICT AND CRIME AMONG ITALIAN IMMIGRANTS

The research we have conducted in Montreal with the Italian population utilizes the traditional definition which sees culture conflict as arising from the migration of conduct norms from one culture to another.... The crime rate is lowest at the centre of the [Italian] immigrant colony and rises proportionally as one approaches the periphery. In the centre of the colony, the conflicts are minimal, but as one gradually approaches the periphery, the conflicts increase proportionally so that many kinds of antagonism are produced which influence the development and growth of criminality. The distance of the protective group affects the nature of criminality which is initially cultural, but then eventually becomes transformed, taking on a character similar to that of the indigenous culture.

The study bearing on the cultural distance of the migrant finds the migrant criminalizing process results from cultural mutation related especially to place of birth and to age at the time of immigration but is entirely independent of the length of time spent in the host country. The immigrant Italian living in Montreal commits specific cultural offences in the first phase of acculturation; when he becomes marginally or culturally ambivalent, this cultural vacuum replaces the traditional values. When the process of acculturation is nearly complete, individuals now detached from their birth culture commit acts common to the indigenous population of the host country.

The criminalizing process of the serious recidivist does not seem to be related to acculturation, but more specifically to alienation from the familial milieu, and to stigmatization implicit in his "black sheep" role. The rejected individual finds himself alone, with no frame of reference and having crime as his only means of existence. His separation from family, from the outset, represents an impossible obstacle to overcome, which results in his becoming a known recidivist.

Source: François Ribordy. (1980). "Culture Conflict and Crime among Italian Immigrants." In Robert A. Silverman and James J. Teevan (eds.), *Crime in Canadian Society* (2nd ed.) (pp. 190, 202). Toronto: Butterworths and Company (Canada) Ltd.

In addition to Sellin's theory of conduct norms, Sutherland's (1939) theory of *career criminality* incorporated elements of social disorganization theory and symbolic interactionist theory. The key elements of this theory were that behaviour is learned in association with others (a notion he borrowed from symbolic interactionism), that the various cultural groups in society establish their own conduct norms (borrowed from Sellin), and that the proliferation of cultural groups leaves both society and some of these cultural groups disorganized (see Chapter 12). Career criminality, he said, is more common in some subcultures because members of these groups are exposed to social and cultural forces which encourage behaviour patterns that place them in conflict with better organized, more powerful cultures. In this context, each culture attempts to use the law to control other cultures.

For both Sellin and Sutherland, the objective was to propose an alternative to those theories of crime which said that criminality was a product of individual pathology. They argued that culture was more important than individual pathology. Sellin explicitly rejected the notion that culture was important only when individuals perceived its influence. It was not necessary, he said, for individuals to perceive the influence of culture in order for culture to have an influence on human behaviour.

A second objective for both Sellin and Sutherland was to expand criminological investigation beyond explanation of violations of the criminal code. Sellin argued that because criminal definitions varied from country to country, and over time, it was unreasonable to study only violations of criminal codes. To restrict criminological theory to explanations of criminal law would mean that a different theory would be needed to explain each type of rule breaking. Violations of civil law and other norms would each require a different theory. Sellin argued that rule-breaking behaviour of all types could be explained by a single theory, his theory of *conduct norms.*

CRITIQUE OF CULTURAL CONFLICT THEORY

Culture conflict theory may be criticized for failure to appreciate how noncultural factors, such as economic disparity and inequalities of power, affect the power to define and enforce social norms of all kinds. While cultural conflict theorists recognize group differences on these dimensions, these differences are said to be less important than cultural differences.

Sellin has been criticized for assuming that universal laws of behaviour govern rule-violating behaviour. Tappan (1947) has argued that Sellin could not establish what these universal laws of behaviour—the conduct norms—were. In Tappan's assessment, Sellin's advocacy of conduct norms resulted in a circular argument. Sellin had argued that legal norms are too varied and variable to provide a universal standard by which to assess and judge behaviour, but then suggested that the category *conduct norms* be used as the universal standard. He could not, however, establish it as a universal standard. Taylor, Walton, and Young (1973) have suggested that Sellin and other cultural deviance theorists create the impression that people simply receive culture passively and that culture exists beyond human control: it influences, but is not influenced by, people.

Sutherland's theory was not well received. Critics were dissatisfied with the theory because of its poor linkage of symbolic interactionism, cultural conflict theory (Sellin), and social disorganization theory. Even Sutherland (1947) later rejected the concept of social disorganization because when combined with the concept of culture conflict it implies that some cultural groups are disorganized. Rather than saying that these groups are disorganized, his later version of the theory (see Chapter 11) proposed that these groups are organized in different ways for different purposes.

GROUP CONFLICT THEORY

Group conflict theory emerged primarily as a response to the failure of cultural conflict theorists to offer a full account of societal conflict and the role that conflict plays in the creation and enforcement of social rules. The most prominent group conflict theorist was George Vold (1958). Vold, like the cultural conflict theorists, sought to direct criminological theory away from theories of individual pathology toward explanations based on the analysis of conflicts between social groups. He argued that the number and diversity of social groups produced conflict. In order to secure its own place in society, each group forms alliances with other groups. It may even be necessary to alter alliances whenever an existing alliance is no longer useful.

Vold applied this analysis of group interaction to the specific problem of understanding how criminal laws were made and enforced. According to Vold, the ability to influence the creation and enforcement of criminal law represents the triumph of an alliance of one set of groups over other groups. Without the ability to influence law creation through forming alliances, the probability that any group could maintain or enhance its place in society is reduced. Those who managed to have a law passed would be the ones most likely to conform to the new law, and to put pressure on law enforcement agents to enforce it. Those who opposed the law, or whose actions were the target of the new law, would be the ones least likely to obey the law, and would attempt to mount pressure on law enforcers to ensure that the law would not be enforced. This implies that conflict is most likely whenever groups which are organized for the purpose of promoting opposed values come into direct contact.

Criminalization is most likely when those groups Vold refers to as "minority groups" (his examples included juvenile gangs and conscientious objectors during the Second World War) come in contact with law enforcement agents who enforce the law according to the wishes of those who sought its passage. Conversely, so long as groups do not come into contact with groups with opposed viewpoints or behaviour patterns, they are not likely to find themselves in conflict, and are not likely to become criminalized.

To illustrate the political nature of criminal behaviour, Vold offered brief descriptions of four patterns of conflict. In the first, he said, definitions of behaviour as criminal may result from expressions of political dissent or protest. This may include violent revolutionary action, burglary, bribery, perjury, and fraud undertaken to win an election. While some or all of these actions may be condemned publicly, they may still form an important part of day-to-day activity in many democratic societies, and are to be considered as part of the struggle between groups. For example, members of the Quebec-based protest group, the FLQ, believed themselves to be engaging in political protest when they kidnapped a Quebec government official and a foreign government representative in October 1970 (these incidents are discussed in Chapter 15). The reaction of the governments of Canada and Quebec to these incidents in implementing the War Measures Act, and the subsequent criminal convictions of the kidnappers, clearly resulted in these protests being labelled as criminal actions. The FLQ's acts of protest were stripped of any claim to legitimacy in the eyes of many Canadians.

A second pattern of conflict emerges out of the efforts of managers to manage their organizations as they see fit, and the efforts of employees to obtain better wages and working conditions. It is not uncommon for both sides in labour disputes to violate the law, and to offer as a defence the explanation that they were protecting their rights. Both sides may see the law which condemns their lawbreaking as less important than their conformity with the norms of their group.

A third conflict pattern emanates from the effort to unionize. When opposing labour unions attempt to organize the same group of workers, one union or the other, or both, may resort to violence to gain support. Those who use violence to gain group ends are generally given the support of the group. They are seen as engaging in behaviour which is consistent with group values and objectives.

A fourth conflict pattern arises from race relations. In various parts of the world, different racial groups attempt to maintain their positions of dominance via creation and enforcement of laws restricting the behaviour of other races. This was evident in the old segregation laws in many states of the United States, and is still evident in South African laws which deny black Africans the right to vote. It is also evident in struggles to outlaw racial discrimination. In such disputes, both sides may attempt to use the law to promote their own viewpoint and behaviour pattern.

CRITIQUE OF GROUP CONFLICT THEORY

Group conflict theory has been criticized for being unable to explain irrational or impulsive criminal behaviour. For example, it is unable to account for the "non-utilitarian, malicious and negativistic" acts, such as vandalism, fighting, bullying, and shoplifting then throwing away the stolen item, which Cohen (1955) says lower-class gang delinquents engage in "for the hell of it."

However, it should be noted that Vold had not intended his theory to explain such behaviour.

Group conflict theory has also been criticized for having a simplistic conception of power relations between and within groups. The theory does not recognize the possibility that relatively small, elite groups might control the law-making process, and that some members of a group might engage in behaviour condemned by the group, or might otherwise refuse to do as the group expects.

WEBERIAN CONFLICT THEORY

While it is possible to trace the origins of Weberian conflict theory to the philosophers of ancient Greece, most contemporary adherents of this perspective look directly to the work of Max Weber himself. Like many of his contemporaries, Weber sought an alternative to Marxist theory. Whereas Marx believed that class is the most powerful force shaping human societies, Weber thought that class was simply one of several forces shaping human societies. He suggested that the effects of class were moderated by status and power. Class was defined by Weber in terms which emphasized material wealth and the control of economic enterprise, while status was defined in terms of prestige or esteem, and power as the ability to control the actions of others.

According to Weber, societies do not distribute the rewards of class, status, and power evenly. Some people will occupy high class positions, others will not. Some will be held in high esteem, others will not. Some will have power, but not others. Some may occupy a high class position, but may not be either as esteemed, or as powerful as others. Some may possess power, but may not be held in high esteem or occupy a high class position. Furthermore, some people may be powerful only in certain contexts. For example, a police officer has the power to arrest, but has considerably less power and prestige than the solicitor general or minister of justice when it comes to creating criminal law. The result of these differences is conflict. Those who are among the upper classes, who are held in high esteem, and who occupy positions of power are better able to control their life chances and the life chances of others than are those among the lower classes who lack status and power.

CONTEMPORARY WEBERIAN THEORIES

Weberian conflict theorists do not necessarily argue that all previous theory must be set aside. For example, Dahrendorf (1959) argued that conflict theory should supplement, not replace, consensus theory. Some situations, said Dahrendorf, could best be understood by the use of consensus theory, while other situations could best be analyzed using conflict theory. Dahrendorf departed from consensus theory, however, in arguing that conflict, not consensus, was the normal condition operative in any society. Any society displaying a high degree of consensus should be considered abnormal.

Nonetheless, contemporary Weberian conflict theories received their greatest impetus from a sense of dissatisfaction with other theories. Consensus theories and the early conflict theories seemed unable to account for the types of conflicts present in contemporary societies. For example, it seemed obvious to some that the emergence of various reform movements during the 1950s and 1960s, including the civil rights movement, the anti-war movement, the student movement, and the women's movement could not be explained by either consensus theory or the early conflict theories. Some Weberians were also concerned that the influence of some of these social movements was creating a partisan criminology which would not be able to offer an impartial analysis of the conflicts plaguing society. Therefore, some Weberians focused their attention on those aspects of Weber's work which suggested the possibility of a nonpartisan conflict theory.

Some of the best known Weberian conflict theorists include Austin Turk (1969, 1977, 1979), William J. Chambliss and Robert Seidman (1971), and Richard Quinney (1970). While each argues a slightly different version of the theory, they are in general agreement that the different segments of society, including both economic and cultural interests, compete to create and enforce definitions of crime. The competition is not a competition between equals. Some interests have a greater capacity to influence both law creation and law enforcement than do others. According to Quinney (1970), those with the greatest power in society are able to manipulate public images of crime and criminality. Through their control of the mass media these powerful people help create an image of crime in the streets as the most threatening form of crime. This helps deflect attention away from their own socially injurious behaviour, such as environmental pollution and other forms of corporate crime.

Because it is arguably the most prominent of the contemporary Weberian theories, Turk's *nonpartisan conflict theory* will be explained here in greater detail.

"NONPARTISAN" CONFLICT THEORY

Turk (1977, 1979) argues that nonpartisan analysis is essential in order to avoid substituting dogma for truth. He criticizes Marxists for transforming criminology into a partisan enterprise by implying that their perspective has an absolute standard of what is right and what is wrong, what is deviant and what is not. According to Turk, no such standard exists. Deviance, and by implication criminality, is always assessed in relative terms. Like Dahrendorf, Turk argues that any situation in which there appears to be universal agreement is a situation that should be scrutinized to discover how such agreement was achieved.

Turk (1969, 1977) argues that conflict is inherent in social interaction, and is most evident in hierarchical societies, within which some people have much more power than others. Those who have greater capacity to define, interpret, and enforce their views through the law are known as *authorities*, while those who are the "... acceptors or resistors, but not the makers of such law creating, interpreting, and enforcing decisions" are *subjects*. Both authorities and subjects must constantly learn and relearn their roles in order to minimize conflict between the two groups. This constant learning process leads to endless revision of criminal law and to inevitable conflicts, as authorities try to ascertain the most effective control structure and subjects try to achieve relative freedom from control.

In outlining the conditions which are likely to result in legal conflicts, Weberians such as Turk place strong emphasis on the interplay between the levels of agreement among (1) the espoused norms and actual behaviour of both groups, (2) their degree of organization, and (3) their level of sophistication. First, with respect to agreement between the espoused social and cultural norms and actual behaviour, it should be noted that there may be disagreements not only between authorities and subjects, but within each group. Both groups might advocate a certain norm while habitually breaking it. Where the actual behaviour of the authorities conforms to a high degree to the norms they espouse, and where the subjects' behaviour pattern conforms to a high degree to an opposed norm that the subjects espouse, the prospect for conflict is high. Conversely, in situations where authorities and subjects espouse different norms, conflict is less likely to occur if there is a low level of agreement between the espoused norms and actual behaviour of both groups. Conflict is also unlikely when both authorities and subjects have high levels of agreement on the same norms and behaviours.

Second, the probability of conflict is also dependent on the extent and type of organization within both groups. When subjects are highly organized to promote social and cultural norms which are opposed to those of authorities who are similarly highly organized to defend their own social and cultural norms, the potential for conflict is high. Conflict is least likely if subjects and authorities are poorly organized and indifferent about the defence of their respective norms.

Finally, Turk addresses the problem of sophistication, or the "... knowledge of patterns in the behaviour of others which is used in attempts to manipulate them." Unsophisticated subjects (subjects who lack awareness of how to avoid the rule-creating and rule-enforcing patterns of authorities) organized in defence of their norms are likely to encounter more conflict with highly sophisticated, well-organized authorities than are more sophisticated, highly organized subjects. For example, Hagan (1974) notes that Canadian aboriginal peoples encounter more legal conflicts resulting from their drinking patterns than do other groups in Canada. This is the consequence of their less sophisticated pattern of drinking in public places. Because they are more likely to drink on the street, they are more likely to encounter public and police hostility than are those who drink in their own homes or who can drink in bars. (Some bars refused to serve aboriginal customers.)

While it is one thing to be in a state of conflict, it is quite another to become criminalized. Therefore, Turk specifies the conditions which are likely to result in criminalization. In addition to the level of agreement between cultural and social norms of subjects and authorities, Turk notes, there are also differences in *power* and *realism*. In this case, power is defined as the ability or capacity to control others. Different authorities have more or less power to enforce rules, while different subjects have more or less power to resist. For example, "first-line authorities," such as the police, have more power to criminalize than do other authorities. Highly resistant subjects with little power, who encounter those authorities who have the most power to criminalize, run the greatest risk of criminalization. Further, the risk of criminalization is even greater if the behaviour engaged in by the subject is a flagrant violation of highly valued authority norms. If the subject behaves in an unrealistic fashion—for example, criticizing the police by punching a police officer in the nose—the probability of criminalization is much greater than if the subject were to write a letter to the editor of a local newspaper.

POLITICAL CRIMINALITY:
THE DEFIANCE AND DEFENCE OF AUTHORITY

Political organization inevitably favours the parties with the greater initial power, who predictably will try to use their advantage to consolidate their disproportionate control of the resources. Because there is never total certainty that security has been achieved, there is a very strong ... tendency for the aim of absolute, rather than relative, control of violence, economic, political, ideological, and diversionary resources. Of course, people may neither know nor care about the power aspect of a particular relationship; and both very intimate and very distant relationships are most secure when relative power is of no concern.

The key to understanding the process of political organization at the societal level is to analyze the relationship between criminality and political policing. A polity is characterized by the emerging hierarchical differentiation of authorities and subjects. Intrinsic to that differentiation is the transformation of power into authority, a problematic and reversible movement toward the establishment of military dominance, jurisdictional boundaries, institutionalized policing, demographic continuity, and ideological hegemony. To the degree that people learn to live with one another in terms of the complementary social norms of dominance and of deference, and to believe the charismatic, rational, and/or traditional justifications legitimating their unequal life chances, the power structure that is the polity is also an authority structure. Insofar as the complete and final authority is not and cannot be realized, political policy is relied upon to define and control intolerable resistance to political socialization. Political criminality becomes understandable as a socially defined reality, produced by conflict between people who claim to be authorities and people who resist or may resist being their subjects.

Source: Austin Turk. (1982). *Political Criminality* (p. 36). Beverly Hills: Sage
  Publications.

Turk also suggests that some authorities may not have a strong commitment to certain norms. While some authorities display strong congruence between legal and other norms, others do not. In some cases, this may mean that the police may place more emphasis on sanctioning a violated norm than on recognizing those legal norms which grant rights to the accused. For example, Henshel (1983) reports that some Toronto police officers were guilty of systematic torture during questioning of suspects. When complaints were made by suspects, the police altered evidence to favour themselves. They also covered up misconduct by fellow officers. This pattern of police misconduct is especially evident when the suspect is perceived to have little power to resist the lawbreaking authority.

CRITIQUE OF CONTEMPORARY WEBERIAN THEORIES

One of the most significant criticisms of Weberian conflict theory is that it gives an overly simplistic analysis of power. For example, Sykes (1974) argues that Weberian conflict theories fail to distinguish between the intended (manifest) and unintended (latent) functions of criminal law. These functions are twisted so that the unintended result—that the poor and disadvantaged are negatively affected by law creation and enforcement—is presented as if it were the intended result. Sykes believes that this hypothesis is in need of a great deal more empirical support.

Working from a Marxist perspective, Taylor, Walton, and Young (1975) criticize Turk for saying that it is not necessary to know how authority-subject relations become established, and for suggesting that capitalist social relations are inevitable. They argue that these relations may be powerful, but they are not necessarily here to stay. It is possible, even desirable, to alter these relations and to bring an end to capitalism. Taylor, Walton, and Young (1973) have also argued that Turk's analysis of factors influencing the negotiation of criminal status is incomplete. It does not offer an assessment in the same way that interactionist theory (see Chapter 11) does of the impact of criminalization upon the individual. They point to Turk's (1969) statement that subjects are conditioned to accept social reality as defined by authorities as evidence that he simply fails to understand the active role subjects play in creating their consciousness of the world.

Finally, Liska (1981) criticizes Turk for not offering a clear definition of *conflict*. Liska questions whether or not Turk refers to "... fighting in the streets, struggling in the legislative halls and courts, or [to] refusal on the part of subject to obey authorities...." when he refers to conflict. Because it is not clear from Turk's presentation what type of conflict is being specified, it is difficult to determine the exact nature of the link between conflict and criminalization. In this regard, Liska questions whether it is necessary for conflict to exist in order for criminalization to occur. Liska implies that Turk does not supply a clear answer. It could be argued that this critique applies to all forms of conflict theory.

MARXIST THEORIES

It has been argued that all conflict and Marxist theories should be grouped together under the general heading of conflict theory. However, some analysts argue that there are fundamental differences between the two perspectives, which should not be ignored (see Wood, 1983; Hinch, 1989a, 1989b). To ignore the differences is to assume that superficial similarities are more important than core propositions.

It should be noted, in this context, that Marx never offered a systematic analysis of crime. When Marx did venture to comment on crime or criminals his comments were frequently made with tongue in cheek, or stated as pure sarcasm. For example, he once said that crime served the useful purpose of providing jobs for policemen and other criminal justice workers (Marx, 1979:191). This sarcastic remark was really intended as a critique of the notion that crime does indeed serve a useful purpose. In some of his other comments on criminals, he made it very clear that criminals were essentially parasites whose behaviour left them open to becoming the "bribed tool of reactionary intrigue" (Marx and Engels, 1971:43). Because Marx did not offer a systematic analysis of crime, some Marxists have said that crime is an inappropriate object of study for Marxists (Bankowski, Mungham, and Young, 1977; Hirst, 1975). Other Marxists disagree (Hinch, 1983; Taylor and Walton, 1975). They argue that just because Marx did not offer a systematic analysis of crime and criminality, that is no reason for Marxists not to do so.

The place of Marxist criminology within contemporary criminology as a whole is also controversial: it poses the most direct challenge to the major assumptions and practices of the other theoretical perspectives, and of Western, capitalist society itself. Marxist theories of crime are also the least understood theories. There is a strong tendency among non-Marxist scholars to assume that there is only one Marxist theory of crime and criminality, whereas in reality there are several. Furthermore, it is assumed that this one Marxist theory is an extreme example of a style of argument known as *economic determinism* when, in fact, this type of argument is a highly contentious issue within Marxism. If there is one element common to the four examples of Marxist analysis to be presented in this chapter, it is that they all begin with the assumption that class relations are the most significant factor affecting the definition of crime and the process of criminalization. It should become clear, however, that they assess the issue of class relations differently, and give varying levels of significance to noneconomic factors.

INSTRUMENTALISM

Simply stated, instrumentalist Marxism holds that the criminal laws are created and enforced for the protection of the capitalist class. The list of instrumentalist Marxists includes Richard Quinney (1974), Mark Kennedy (1974), David Gordon (1971, 1975), John Hepburn (1977), John Casey (1985), and many others. Instrumentalists argue that class is the most important factor affecting the definition of crime and the enforcement of criminal law. Marxists see capitalist society as divided between two great classes: the capitalists, defined as the owners of the means of production, and the proletariat, defined as those who sell their labour power for a wage to capitalists. Instrumentalist Marxists argue that the greater economic power of the capitalist class allows it to control the lawmaking, interpreting, and enforcement apparatus of the state. Those members of the state charged with the day-to-day tasks of making, interpreting, and enforcing the law favour the capitalists in order to enhance or protect their own privileged positions as servants of capitalism.

For example, Goff and Reasons (1978) argue that Canada's anti-combines legislation was not only shaped to minimize government interference in corporate affairs, but that it has been enforced in a political fashion. Even the director of investigations under the Combines Act, they say, has used his office to allow corporations to evade prosecution. According to Goff and Reasons, only 0.003 percent of corporate mergers from 1960 to 1972 resulted in charges being laid, and only 0.0005 percent were successfully prosecuted. Thus, the misdeeds of the ruling class are made to seem less significant than those of other groups.

Even the act of defining crimes such as murder, rape, assault, and theft of personal property, as well as the act of protecting human rights, serves the interests of capital. This is accomplished by making it appear that the state has a general interest in defining these acts and in defending the rights of those who are victimized by violations of the protective statutes governing these acts. In actual fact, the state creates a smokescreen around the activities of the ruling class that renders them invisible while it focuses attention on the misdeeds of other classes. Deaths caused by deliberate violation by employers of workplace health and safety laws are treated much less seriously than deaths caused by other deliberate means.

STRUCTURALIST MARXISM

One of the more interesting debates in contemporary Marxism is found in the dialogue of Miliband (1972), who presents the instrumentalist perspective, and Poulantzas (1972), who presents the structuralist. Their debate sets out the most important differences between the two positions. In essence, structuralists reject the notion that the capitalist class acts as if it had one mind and body, as well as the notion that the state serves the interests of the capitalist class directly. Structuralists argue that capitalist societies are composed of a variety of classes. The capitalists and the proletariat may be the most important classes, but there are other, minor classes, such as the petty bourgeoisie, which also play a role in shaping legal relations. Furthermore, all classes are divided into various fractions, many of which are in direct competition not only with other classes but with others in their own class. Thus, structuralists argue, it is impossible for any one class, or class fraction, to dominate the state.

The state must maintain an image of itself as autonomous from specific interests if it is to serve capital. It must be seen to be independent of the interests of specific capitalists, and even capital itself. If the state appears to give, or does give, the interests of a particular class or fraction more consideration, or unfair consideration over other interests, then these other interests are more likely to resist efforts by the state to control them.

For example, with respect to law creation, Smandych (1985) argues that the creation of the Canadian anti-combines legislation was a symbolic gesture intended to avert a clash between capital and labour. During the late 1800s and early 1900s, labour felt itself increasingly vulnerable to what it considered the excesses of monopoly capitalism. These included poor working conditions, low wages, and failure to recognize the legitimacy of trade unions and collective bargaining. As labour's efforts to resist these excesses became increasingly better organized, the government of the day took a keen interest in the voting power of the emerging labour movement. In order to maintain an image of itself as an honest broker between the two antagonists, and also to maintain capitalist interests in capital accumulation, the state created a weak law. This law gave labour the impression that its voice was being heard, but offered no significant impediment to the accumulation of capital and the continuation of the capitalist system in Canada.

Further, with respect to law enforcement, Balbus (1973) argues that state agents must satisfy the demands of formal legal rationality. State agents cannot violate the law as they see fit because of the checks and balances established in law to prevent such violations. The state must follow prescribed legal procedures and apply, without prejudice, universally applicable legal standards. In this way, the law acts as a significant restraint upon the actions of state agents and the state. Balbus is not saying that legal authorities always conform to legal demands. What he is saying is that even when some state agents, especially the police and prosecutors, abandon normal procedure, the people they process are given their day in court. Their appearance in court is subject to formal legal rules which are difficult, if not impossible, to abandon in such a public forum. State agents can be, and often are, held accountable for their criminal actions and their failure to observe the legal rights of other people. When state agents behave in an unacceptable way, the people whose rights they abuse may be seen as the victims of state power. Thus, the phrase "equality before the law" has a double meaning. On the one hand, the law must treat all who come before it without obvious prejudice with respect to judgements of social or economic background, thereby protecting the disadvantaged from arbitrary decision making. On the other hand, by refusing to consider inequalities in living conditions as legitimate reasons for committing crime, the law protects the state, and thereby reinforces the capitalist system.

In essence, structuralists contend that not only does the structure of the society with its various competing parts, or classes and class fractions, prevent one class or fraction of a class from gaining total control of the society, but the structure of the law and law enforcement apparatus itself prevents similar single-interest domination. Nonetheless, the complex structure of the society and the apparent autonomy of the law mask the underlying conflict between capital and labour. This makes the conflict appear to be either nonexistent or irrelevant as a factor contributing to the definition and enforcement of criminal law.

A THEORY OF CONTRADICTIONS

A somewhat different approach to Marxist analysis has been adopted by William Chambliss (1986) and others. According to Chambliss, societies are composed of a number of competing interests, and "… every society, nation, economic system, and historical period contain within them certain contradictory elements which are the moving force behind social changes—including the creation of law" (Chambliss and Seidman, 1982). From this viewpoint, all societies are characterized by a pattern of conflict resolution and creation, in which resolutions of existing contradictions produce new contradictions in need of solution. It should be noted that Chambliss and Seidman (1982) take special care to indicate that people, not systems (as in structuralist approaches), create law, and that it is people who are faced with the task of finding solutions to ever-emerging contradictions.

For example, Hinch (1988a, 1988b, 1991) argues that passage of Canada's sexual assault legislation in 1983 resulted from an attempt to resolve conflicts between men and women over the definition and enforcement of the rape law as it existed prior to 1983. Critics of the old rape law claimed it was openly sexist. Married men could not be charged with raping their wives, and the sexual history of rape victims was subject to scrutiny during a trial, while the sexual history of the offender was not. Law enforcement practices also ensured that women were often treated by the criminal justice system as if they, not the rapists, were the wrongdoers. In order to address these and other problems with the law, law reformers sought to amend the law (see Hinch, 1985). Some reformers, those benefiting from patriarchal and capitalist relations, sought either greater protection from false accusations of rape or increased police powers. Other reformers, primarily feminists opposed to patriarchy, claimed that men's concerns over false accusations of rape were unfounded. Feminists sought law reforms, such as lower penalties for sexual assault offences and removal of the marital privilege, which would make it easier for police to make arrests and for the courts to convict.

The reforms introduced in 1983 did little to alter the basic contradictions in the social and economic positions of men and women (Hinch, 1991). While some sources of conflict between men and women were removed, others remained. The state removed the marital privilege and gave victims of sexual assault greater protection from character assassination in court, but women's sexual histories can still be examined in court as a means of challenging the victim's credibility, and the social pressures on women which prevent them from reporting victimization at the hands of their husbands were unaffected by the reforms. Hinch argues that these social pressures are frequently a more significant influence than the law on women's decisions to report the abuse they receive from their husbands. In the end, the contradictions of patriarchy and capitalism remain, while men and women remain enmeshed in conflicts; and although these conflicts may lead to further legal reform, it will still not deal with the contradictions which cause the conflicts. It is impossible, then, to change the contradictions by changing the law. A much more profound change in the social order would be required.

A similar situation exists with regard to labour relations. Concern that the workplace can be dangerous for the worker has been expressed for at least two centuries. Chambliss and Seidman (1982) cite research which indicates that work-related injuries and illnesses cause five times as many Americans to be killed on the job as are murdered in the "conventional" sense. Comparable Canadian data (Reasons et al., 1981) indicate that Canadians are eighteen times more likely to die from work-related illness or injury than they are to be murdered. A significant amount of the death and injury rate is the direct result of employers' failure to comply with existing health and safety laws, and of putting profits ahead of safety. Yet the problem does not receive as much attention as conventionally defined murder.

IT'S A CRIME

We have been taught to think of crime as involving an easily identifiable victim and offender. For example, if our spouse poisons us and we subsequently die then we have been murdered by our spouse, who is liable to prosecution for murder. However, if our company causes us to be exposed to toxic substances and we subsequently die from this exposure, the company is not criminally liable for our deaths and will at the most be cited for violations of health and safety regulations. For example, ... [a petroleum company] was found guilty of violating job-site safety regulations, resulting in the death of three men. The law provided for a maximum $5000 fine and/or imprisonment of up to six months. [The company] was fined $5000 for killing the three men, who were single and in their early twenties.... The company did not provide respiratory equipment and an external gauge on an enclosed tank, thus, the men had to go inside the tank without protective equipment and subsequently were overcome with toxic fumes. Furthermore, the company had not trained the workers concerning the hazards of the job and the need for such equipment.

Isn't this just an unfortunate accident? No, the deaths of these three young men could have been avoided if the proper training and equipment had been provided. While the company undoubtedly did not mean to kill these specific three men, it established the conditions for their death by violating the law. By analogy, we could view murder during an armed robbery as an accident. Most armed robbers do not intend to kill the robbery victim but merely want to make some money. However, their act of robbery with a dangerous weapon sets the conditions for such violence. Likewise, a company saving money by not purchasing safety equipment may be merely pursuing profit, but its action establishes the conditions for an "accident" or "disaster."

Source: Charles E. Reasons, Lois L. Ross, and Craig Paterson. (1981). *Assault on the Worker: Occupational Health and Safety in Canada* (pp. 6–7). Toronto: Butterworths and Company (Canada) Ltd.

Nonetheless, in the face of organized opposition from labour, governments have taken some steps toward reclassifying work-related health hazards as illegal, and occasionally criminal. Reasons et al. note that Canadian workers, through their unions and through both legal and illegal strikes, have a long history of fighting dangerous working conditions and have had some success in having legislative changes made to promote greater job safety. Despite opposition by capital, lawmakers have created legislation reducing the amount of freedom employers have in setting conditions of work.

It is also clear that this legislation created new conflicts. The new problems centre on the enforcement process and on deciding whether violations of health and safety legislation are to be labelled as simply illegal or as criminal. Further, while Chambliss and Seidman (1982), Reasons et al. (1981), and DeKeseredy and Hinch (1991) recognize that, in certain circumstances, workers have been able to obtain better enforcement of health and safety legislation, they also observe that enforcement practices require further improvement. Indeed, Chambliss and Seidman claim that in some cases law reforms have actually resulted in more, not less, job-related illness and injury. In such cases, legal bureaucracies with intimate connections to capital fail to take the problem as seriously as they do other forms of crime. Further, the law does not always provide sufficient penalties to force compliance. In some cases, this means that endangering worker safety or health may be termed illegal but not criminal. It may also mean that potential penalties, such as fines, may be interpreted as simply "another cost of doing business."

The more general point is that criminal law should not be regarded as simply the product of the interests of specific capitalists or of the system as a whole. Nor can it be seen as simply the product of struggles between capital and labour or between feminism and patriarchy. Criminal law is a product of the ongoing struggles within capital and patriarchy to control the state for the purpose of creating legislation which resolves conflicts but does not resolve basic contradictions. Given that capitalist and patriarchal forces are stronger and generally better organized than either labour or anti-patriarchal forces, it is to be expected that they will have a greater (even if not absolute) influence on law creation and enforcement.

LEFT REALISM

Left realism is the most recent development in Marxist criminology. It emerged during the early 1970s in Britain (see Lea, 1987; Lea and Young, 1984; Matthews, 1987; Young, 1979, 1987), but has also found advocates in Canada (see MacLean, 1989; Currie, et al., 1990), the United States (Gross, 1982; Michalowski, 1983) and elsewhere (see Hogg and Brown, 1988). Left realism emerged as a response to a perceived shift to the political right, and specifically to the politics of law and order. Left realists argued that other Marxists were not responding to the concerns of working-class people that something be done about the crime problem. As a result, they said, the political right was able to assume control of law and order issues, leaving the working class in the precarious position of having to accept crime-control solutions which resulted in greater repression of the working class itself. They argued that if Marxism is to play a significant role in reshaping society, it has to take the problem of crime, as experienced by working-class people, more seriously. Marxism has to be involved in reshaping crime-control policies in a way that allows the working class to assume greater control of the police and the process of constructing crime-control strategies.

According to Matthews, there are four central elements to realist criminology:

1. a commitment to detailed empirical investigation
2. a recognition of the independence and objectivity of criminal activity
3. an emphasis on the disorganizing effect of crime
4. a statement of the possibility and desirability of developing measures to reduce crime (1987:371)

Left realists argue that the notoriously problematic nature of crime statistics generated by the police and other sources is no reason to cease doing empirical work. Careful, critical analysis of official crime statistics is needed in order to illustrate the biased functioning of the criminal justice system and to understand the crime process itself; such an analysis reveals that crime is an intra-class, not inter-class activity, that there is universal opposition to street crime, and that lower-class criminals are those most likely to be criminalized by the state (see MacLean, 1986; Young, 1979). Left realists call for greater effort to be devoted to the empirical investigation of the crimes of the powerful. Although the data are not complete, they point out, the economic costs of corporate crime far exceed the economic costs of street crime. For example, it has been estimated that a single case of corporate fraud involved higher monetary losses than all street crime combined for one year in the United States (Simon and Eitzen, 1986). More recently, criminal activity associated with the Scientific Research Tax Credit program in Canada and the Savings and Loan scandal in the United States has cost taxpayers and investors many billions of dollars. The exact toll of the Bank of Credit and Commerce International fraud is not yet known. It has been estimated that "between 5.8 billion and 17 billion [dollars] remains unaccounted for" in "the most massive fraud in history" (MacDonald, 1991:24–25).

THE EQUITY FUNDING FRAUD

The Equity Funding Corporation of America began in 1960 as a legitimate insurance business with $10 000. In the mid-sixties, it became the fastest-growing life insurance company in the United States. From 1967 to 1972, sales increased from $54 million to $1.32 billion, and insurance in force from $109 million to $6.5 billion. The stock in the company went public in 1964 at $6 a share and during the company's phenomenal growth period sold as high as $80. In April 1973, this growth was found to be the result of fraud. The corporation filed for bankruptcy and the stock was declared of no value. At a representative price of $40 a share, shareholders lost $300 million. Since 1967, it had *never* made any money. All earnings reported during those years had been false. What appeared to be growth was the result of issuing 64 000 phony policies with a face value of $2 billion. These bogus policies were then sold to other insurance companies for cash. In addition, Equity Funding routinely faked assets and earnings in its annual reports, sold counterfeit bonds, and forged death certificates. The result was that policy holders, stockholders, and other insurance firms lost between $2 and $3 billion. Other money was also indirectly lost because of the resulting scandal. For example, in the week that the *Wall Street Journal* published the story of the scandal, the value of all shares on the New York Stock Exchange dropped by $15 billion.

Source: David R. Simon and D. Stanley Eitzen. (1986). *Elite Deviance* (2nd ed.) (p. 91). Boston: Allyn and Bacon, Inc.

Left realists focus on demonstrating the independence and objectivity of criminal activity—that even though the concept of crime itself is problematic, crime is independent of the will of particular interests, and has a definite ("objective") impact on social behaviour. Crimes are "conflicts or disputes which cannot be resolved within 'normal' social relations" (Matthews, 1987). Legal crimes are part of the larger process of social control, and are an indication that informal control mechanisms are ineffective in controlling some types of conflicts. The objective of criminology is to understand which conflicts require informal as opposed to formal control strategies. The definition of crime categories, expressed as (among others) the so-called index crimes of murder, theft, assault, robbery, and rape, is part of the collective process of learning how to live in social groups and of learning how to control those elements of society who elect antisocial behaviour patterns.

It is no secret that crime has a negative impact on the quality of human life, and on the cohesiveness of society. Crime and disorder go together. Crime is an indicator of individualistic values: the criminal places his or her needs above those of others. In some cases, for example where women fear rape and people avoid urban areas believed to be frequented by muggers, thieves, and other criminals, crime also restricts people's freedom of movement and their activities to areas and situations which reduce the risk of victimization. In urban centres, high-crime areas suggest that no one cares, and so their existence incites still more crime. Ultimately, crime among the working class is a response to the brutalization of working class life, and crime itself adds to that brutalization.

Realists argue that the potential to reduce crime by implementation of effective policies is enormous. The task of the left realist is to ensure that crime reduction is achieved through the creation and implementation of policies formulated by the left, and not by the right. This means finding ways to allow those most affected by crime to become involved in the crime control process. Working-class involvement in the crime-control apparatus of the state risks making that apparatus a more efficient agent of repression of the working class; at the same time, however, it also creates an opportunity for the working class to take part in the creation of crime-control policies which more genuinely reflect its needs. By becoming involved in the creation of crime-control strategies and the crime control apparatus, the working class has the opportunity to create crime-control measures that, instead of increasing the penalties for crime or increasing the coercive character of the state, *minimize* the "intervention necessary to protect the population against predatory criminal forces—and unallayed market forces" (Young, 1987:353). Crime control, then, becomes part of the struggle to expand the ability of the working class to control its own living conditions. If it does not become involved, it abdicates this potential and must therefore live under crime-control policies which reflect the concerns of the upper classes.

For example, aboriginal peoples have argued that granting them greater control over their lives, and especially control over the criminal justice system as it affects them, would help reduce their crime rate. With this in mind, an Alberta task force report recommended that aboriginal peoples have some involvement in all levels of the criminal justice system. Left realists and many aboriginal groups would go even further than the Alberta task force. They recommend giving aboriginals more control over the administration of justice in aboriginal communities.

CRITIQUES OF MARXIST CRIMINOLOGY

Marxist criminology has been criticized for its heavy reliance on economic factors as the primary force behind the creation of criminal law. However, it has had difficulty in demonstrating the exact economic utility of much of the criminal law for the ruling classes. In this regard, Turk (1977) says that Marxists rely more on assertion than on the verifiability of their claims (see also Downes and Rock, 1982).

Sykes's (1975) critique of conflict theory also applies to both instrumentalist and structuralist Marxists. Their conceptions of the relation between power and interests are extremely simplistic. Indeed, Hinch (1983) and Matthews (1987) have argued that the instrumentalist argument that crime is defined solely in the interest of capital leads to the absurdly romantic assumption that all criminal acts are acts of resistance against capitalism. If we accept the left realist argument, however, we find that most criminal acts victimize working-class people, and result in increased surveillance and control of the working class. Hinch is also critical of the instrumentalist assumption that socialist societies will be "crime-free" and otherwise free of conflict.

As for the structuralist argument, it is said to lack a full understanding of how real people create and sustain social systems. By placing so much emphasis upon "the system," structuralist argument loses contact with the real people engaged in the struggle.

The theory of contradictions—that criminal definitions emerge out of a continual process of finding solutions to conflicts embedded in the contradictions of patriarchy and capitalism—fails to specify how the cycle of "contradiction, resolution, contradiction" can be brought to a conclusion. A central part of this thesis is that the resolution of contradictions always leaves the forces of capital in secure control, even if they must encounter new difficulties in maintaining that control. Yet Marxist thought has always insisted that it can be applied in practice to the revolutionary transformation of contradictions. Thus, this orientation does not resolve the problems of the structuralist argument, and specifically its assumption of a relatively independent and immobile "system."

Left realist criminologists have been severely criticized by other Marxists who argue that any effort to utilize the state to achieve socialist aims is doomed. The state, they argue, serves the interests of those forces which created it, the interests of capital. Thus, co-operation with the state as recommended by left realists will only help the state control the working class. It will force the working class to "play the game" according to rules established by the state in the interests of capital.

CONCLUSION

The theoretical models summarized in this chapter offer profoundly differing conceptions of contemporary social life. In each case, the theorists present data which they believe demonstrate the validity of their own theory or undermine the credibility of opposed theories. But the extent to which any one theory is accepted as an accurate statement describing the nature and origins of criminal behaviour is dependent on factors other than the accuracy of its propositions and observations. As Kuhn (1962) explains, theories may gain acceptance, or be rejected, for reasons other than their scientific validity. Their reception may also be based on their ability to conform to prevailing social attitudes and beliefs. Theories which conform most to prevailing beliefs, or ideologies, are likely to gain more acceptance than are theories which resist or criticize dominant ideologies.

Thus, Turk (1977) is probably correct in saying that Weberian conflict theory is likely to gain greater social acceptance than Marxist theories in academia and in society in general. Nonetheless, the mere popularity of a theory is not an accurate test of its validity. Criminologists judge the credibility of a theory by assessing the methods by which it gathers data and by assessing the data itself and its interpretation of the data. The disagreements that persist even after these assessments are made reflect the commitment of the assessors to their theoretical orientation, as well as the ongoing debates within criminology over appropriate research methods. For example, significant differences exist among criminologists regarding the use of official crime data as an indicator of the crime rate and of who commits crimes (see chapters 3 and 4). So long as these kinds of differences exist, there will continue to be differences of opinion regarding theories and their acceptability.

SUMMARY

Culture-conflict theorists, such as Sellin and Sutherland, argue that conflicts in cultural expectation produce differential potentials for criminalization. Cultures with greater potential to influence societal legal norms are more likely to have their interests protected in law and are less likely to be criminalized. These theories were criticized, however, for failing to consider the influence of noncultural factors on law creation and enforcement. This failure helped provide the impetus for the development of the conflict theories of Vold and the Weberians. While these theorists were indebted to the work of Sellin, they went beyond his theory to specify that political and economic interests must be considered. In turn, these theorists have been criticized for having an overly simplistic conception of power and interests, making it appear that the less powerful segments of society have no interest in or ability to influence law creation and enforcement. Marxist criminology emerged as a direct challenge to dominant social beliefs and practices. As a group, Marxists are concerned that capitalist social relations and interests are given greater legal protection than other types of social relations and interests. The four approaches to Marxist criminology presented in this chapter have been criticized for specific weaknesses. Instrumentalists are said to have an overly romantic image of criminality, while structuralists have been criticized for failing to explain how people change the structures which they create and under which they live if, as they assume, the state inevitably acts in the interests of capital. Marxists who argue that criminal law is the product of an ongoing process of finding solutions to conflicts without resolving the contradictions inherent in capitalism or patriarchy have been criticized for failing to offer an explanation of how this process could be or would be terminated. Finally, left realists have been criticized for naïvely believing that the capitalist state can promote working-class interests.

BIBLIOGRAPHY

Balbus, Isaac. (1973). *The Dialectics of Legal Repression: Black Rebels before the American Criminal Courts.* New York: Russell Sage Foundation.

Bankowski, Zenon, Geoff Mungham, and Peter Young. (1977). "Radical Criminology or Radical Criminologist." *Contemporary Crises* 1(21) (January):37–54.

Casey, John. (1985). "Corporate Crime and the State: Canada in the 1980s." In Thomas Fleming (ed.), *The New Criminologies in Canada: State, Crime, and Control.* Toronto: Oxford University Press.

Chambliss, William J. (1986). "On Lawmaking." In Steven Brickey and Elizabeth Comack (eds.), *The Social Basis of Law.* Toronto: Garamond Press.

Chambliss, William J., and Robert Seidman. (1971). *Law, Order and Power.* Reading, MA: Addison-Wesley.

———. (1982). *Law, Order and Power.* (2nd ed.). Reading, MA: Addison-Wesley.

Cohen, Albert K. (1955). *Delinquent Boys: The Culture of the Gang.* New York: The Free Press of Glencoe.

Currie, Dawn, Walter S. DeKeseredy, and Brian D. MacLean. (1990). "Reconstructing Social Order and Social Control: Police Accountability in Canada." *The Journal of Human Justice* 2(1):29–53.

Dahrendorf, Ralf. (1959). *Class and Class Conflict in Industrial Society.* Stanford, CA: Stanford University Press.

DeKeseredy, Walter, and Ronald Hinch. (in press). *Woman Abuse: Sociological Perspectives.* Toronto: Thomson Educational Publishers.

Downes, David, and Paul Rock. (1982). *Understanding Deviance: A Guide to the Sociology of Crime and Rule Breaking.* Oxford: Claredon Press/Oxford University Press.

Goff, Colin, and Charles E. Reasons. (1978). *Corporate Crime in Canada.* Toronto: Prentice-Hall, Canada.

Gordon, David M. (1971). "Class and the Economics of Crime." *The Review of Radical Economics* 3(3):51–72.

———. (1975). "Capitalism, Class and Crime in America." In William J. Chambliss (ed.), *Criminal Law in Action*. Santa Barbara, CA: Wiley.

Gross, Bertram. (1982). "Some Anti-Crime Strategies for Progressives." *Crime and Social Justice* 19:51–54.

Hagan, John. (1974). "Criminal Justice and Native People." *Canadian Review of Sociology and Anthropology* Special Issue (August):220–36.

Henshel, Richard L. (1983). *Police Misconduct in Metropolitan Toronto: A Study of Formal Complaints*. Report no. 8. The LaMarsh Research Programme on Violence. Toronto: York University.

Hepburn, John R. (1977). "Social Control and the Legal Order: Legitimate Repression in a Capitalist State." *Contemporary Crises* 1(1):77–90.

Hinch, Ronald. (1983). "Marxist Criminology in the 1970s: Clarifying the Clutter." *Crime and Social Justice* (Summer):65–74.

———. (1985). "Canada's New Sexual Assault Laws: A Step Forward for Women?" *Contemporary Crises* 9(1):33–44.

———. (1988a). "Enforcing Canada's Sexual Assault Laws: An Exploratory Study." *Atlantis* 14(1):109–15.

———. (1988b). "Inconsistencies and Contradictions in Canada's Sexual Assault Law." *Canadian Public Policy* 14(3):282–94.

———. (1989a). "It's Marxism, Not Conflict Theory." *Canadian Critical Criminology* 2(3 & 4):2–8.

———. (1989b). "Teaching Critical Criminology and Critical Justice Studies in Canada." *Journal of Human Justice* 1(1):63–76.

———. (1991). "Contradictions, Conflicts and Dilemmas in Canada's Sexual Assault Law." In Gregg Barak (ed.), *Crimes by the State: The Politics of Governmental Control*. Albany, NY: State University of New York Press.

Hirst, Paul Q. (1975). "Marx and Engels on Law, Crime and Morality." In Ian Taylor, Paul Walton, and Jock Young (eds.), *Critical Criminology*. London: Routledge and Kegan Paul.

Hogg, Russell, and David Brown. (1988). "Law and Order Politics, Left Realism and Criminology: An Overview." Paper presented at the Annual Conference of the American Society of Criminology, Chicago, November 9–12.

Kennedy, Mark. (1974). "Beyond Incrimination." *Catalyst* 1(1):1–37.

Kuhn, Thomas. (1962). *The Structure of Scientific Revolutions*. Chicago: University of Chicago Press.

LaFree, Gary D. (1989). *Rape Crime and Criminal Justice: The Social Construction of Sexual Assault*. Belmont, CA: Wadsworth Publishing.

Lea, John. (1987). "Left Realism: A Defence." *Contemporary Crises* 11(4):357–70.

Lea, John, and Jock Young. (1984). *What Is to Be Done about Law and Order?* London: Penguin Books.

Liska, Allen E. (1981). *Perspectives on Deviance*. Englewood Cliffs, NJ: Prentice-Hall.

MacDonald, Marci. (1991). "A Bank Scandal." *Maclean's* 104(31) (August 5):24–28.

MacLean, Brian D. (1986). "Introduction: Critical Criminology and Some Limitations of Traditional Inquiry." In Brian D. MacLean (ed.), *The Political Economy of Crime: Readings for a Critical Criminology*. Scarborough: Prentice-Hall, Canada.

———. (1989). "Left Realism and Police Accountability in Canada." Paper presented at the Annual Conference of the Canadian Sociology and Anthropology Association, Quebec, June 4.

Marx, Karl. (1979). "Apologist Conception of the Productivity of all Professions." In Maureen Cain and Alan Hunt (eds.), *Marx and Engels on Law*. London: Academic Press.

Marx, Karl, and Friedrich Engels. (1971). *Manifesto of the Communist Party*. Moscow: Progress Publishers.

Matthews, Roger. (1987). "Taking Realist Criminology Seriously." *Contemporary Crises* 11(4):371–98.

McCleod, Linda. (1987) *Battered but Not Beaten: Preventing Wife Battering in Canada*. Ottawa: Canadian Advisory Council on the Status of Women.

Michalowski, Ray. (1983). "Crime Control in the 1980s: A Progressive Agenda." *Crime and Social Justice* 19:13–22.

Miliband, Ralph. (1972). "Reply to Poulantzas." In Robin Blackburn (ed.), *Ideology in the Social Sciences*. New York: Pantheon Books.

Poulantzas, Nicos. (1972). "The Problem of the Capitalist State." In Robin Blackburn (ed.), *Ideology in the Social Sciences*. New York: Pantheon Books.

Quinney, Richard. (1970). *The Social Reality of Crime*. Boston: Little, Brown and Company.

———. (1974). *Critique of Legal Order*. Boston: Little, Brown and Company.

Reasons, Charles E., Lois L. Ross, and Craig Paterson. (1981). *Assault on the Worker: Occupational Health and Safety in Canada*. Toronto: Butterworths.

Ribordy, Francois. (1980). "Culture Conflict among Italian Immigrants." In Robert A. Silverman and James J. Teevan (eds.), *Crime in Canadian Society*. Toronto: Butterworths.

Sellin, Thorsten. (1938). *Culture Conflict and Crime*. New York: Social Science Research Council.

Simon, David R., and D. Stanley Eitzen. (1986). *Elite Deviance*. (2nd ed.). Boston: Allyn and Bacon.

Smandych, Russell. (1985). "Marxism and the Creation of Law: Re-Examining the Origins of Canadian Anti-Combines Legislation." In Thomas Fleming (ed.), *The New Criminologies in Canada: State, Crime, and Control*. Toronto: Oxford University Press.

Sutherland, Edwin H. (1939). *The Principles of Criminology*. (3rd ed.). Philadelphia: Lippincott.

———. (1947). *The Principles of Criminology*. (4th ed.). Philadelphia: Lippincott.

Sykes, Gresham M. (1974). "The Rise of Critical Criminology." *Journal of Criminal Law and Criminology* 65:206–14.

Tappan, Paul. (1947). "Who Is the Criminal?" *American Sociological Review* 12:96–102.

Taylor, Ian, and Paul Walton. (1975). "Radical Deviancy Theory and Marxism: A Reply to Paul Q. Hirst's "Marx and Engels on Law, Crime and Morality." In Ian Taylor, Paul Walton, and Jock Young (eds.), *Critical Criminology*. London: Routledge and Kegan Paul.

Taylor, Ian, Paul Walton, and Jock Young. (1973). *The New Criminology: For a Social Theory of Deviance*. London: Routledge and Kegan Paul.

——— (eds.). (1975). *Critical Criminology*. London: Routledge and Kegan Paul.

Turk, Austin. (1969). *Criminality and Legal Order*. Chicago: Rand McNally.

———. (1977). "Class, Conflict and Criminalization." *Sociological Focus* 10:209–20.

———. (1979). "Analyzing Official Deviance: For Nonpartisan Conflict Analysis." *Criminology* 16(4):459–76.

———. (1982). *Political Criminality*. Beverly Hills: Sage.

Vold, George. (1958). *Theoretical Criminology*. New York: Oxford University Press.

Vold, George B., and Thomas J. Bernard. (1986). *Theoretical Criminology*. (3rd ed.). New York: Oxford University Press.

Wood, Robert E. (1983). "Conflict Theory as Pedagogy: A Critique from the Left." *Teaching Sociology* 10(4):463–85.

Young, Jock. (1979). "Left Idealism, Reformism, and Beyond: From New Criminology to Marxism." In Bob Fine, Richard Kinsey, John Lea, Sol Picciotto, and Jock Young (eds.), *Capitalism and the Rule of Law: From Deviancy Theory to Marxism.* London: Hutchinson and Company.
———. (1987). "The Tasks Facing a Realist Criminology." *Contemporary Crises* 11(4):337–56.

FURTHER READING

Caputo, T.C., M. Kennedy, C.E. Reasons, and A. Brannigan (eds.). (1989). *Law and Society: A Critical Perspective.* Toronto: Harcourt Brace Jovanovich, Canada. A collection of articles employing various conflict, Marxist, and feminist theories in the analysis of socio-legal problems in Canada and elsewhere.

Contemporary Crises 11(4). (1987). A collection of essays by the leading advocates of left realist criminology in Britain.

The Journal of Human Justice 1(1) (Autumn). (1989). This inaugural issue of the journal offers a state of the art review of the development of critical (conflict and Marxist) criminology in Canada.

MacLean, Brian D. (1986). *The Political Economy of Crime: Readings for a Critical Criminology.* Scarborough: Prentice-Hall, Canada. This is still one of the best collections of "critical"—mostly Marxist—readings on crime and crime control in Canada and elsewhere.

Ratner, R.S., and John L. McMullan (eds.). (1987). *State Control: Criminal Justice Politics in Canada.* Vancouver: University of British Columbia Press. A thoughtful collection of essays by various conflict and Marxist criminologists working in Canada. This is essential reading for anyone wishing to take a more advanced look at these theories.

Turk, Austin. (1982). *Political Criminality.* Beverly Hills: Sage. An assessment of the context and extent of political crime by the leading advocate of nonpartisan conflict theory.

Vold, George B., and Thomas J. Bernard. (1986). *Theoretical Criminology.* (3rd ed.). New York: Oxford University Press. This revision by Bernard of the classic text by Vold contains an updated version of Vold's theory, augmented by reference to contemporary conflict theorists and learning theorists.

CHAPTER 11

INTERACTIONIST THEORIES
By Robert A. Stebbins

*I*nteractionist theory in criminology, as elsewhere, centres on the interchanges people have with one another and on the meanings of these interchanges in the past, present, and future. Herbert Blumer (1986) notes that symbolic interactionism, the broader theory from which the interactionist theories of crime are derived, rests on three premises. First, people act toward the human and nonhuman objects in their lives according to the meanings that those objects have for them. Second, the meaning of those objects for each individual emerges from interactions between him or her and other people. Third, the meanings of objects learned in this manner are applied and occasionally modified as individuals interpret how the objects and their meanings fit particular social situations with reference to them and their reasons for being there.

Much of this chapter is about criminal interactions, meanings, interpretations, and situations. Before turning to these processes, however, let us set the stage for discussion with a brief illustration of the three premises operating in the sphere of crime. The following interview with Allen, about twenty years old, shows how the meaning of a situation changed through social interaction with other people on the scene in an all-night drugstore:

> From what I understand from them, they didn't go in there with the intent to rob or beat anybody up or anything. I think they only really wanted to buy some gum and cigarettes, but by being drunk, they was talking pretty tough, and so the lady behind the counter automatically get scared.... The druggist ... got a little pushy or ordered them out of the store, and by them being all fired up, naturally the next thing they did was jump on him.
>
> So now what do you have? You've got a drugstore. You've got a scared lady in the corner somewhere with her hands over her face. You've got a beat-up druggist laying on the floor. You've got three dudes that came in for chewing gum and cigarettes, but now they got two cash registers. So what do they do? They take the cash. Wasn't nothing to stop them, and it was there. Why would they leave it? They're thieves anyway and supposed to be hustlers.... There wasn't nothing to stop them, so they just took the money. (Katz, 1988)

THE DEVIANT CAREER

Interactionism centres chiefly on what happens to criminals once their deviant activities commence. Interactionists have observed, for example, that some groups or individuals have enough power to force the label of deviant on other less powerful groups or individuals. The labelling process, however, is by no means accurate. It is not even always fair. Some people who have deviated escape public detection of their behaviour. Some who have not deviated are nonetheless labelled as having done so, despite their protests to the contrary. The application of the deviant label is sometimes subject to considerable negotiation between possibly deviant people and those in a position to apply the label of deviant to them.

Thus, interactionist theory in criminology helps explain the establishment of moral rules, their application through labelling, and the long-term consequences of these two processes for deviants and society. In interactionist theory, labelling and its consequences are viewed as unfolding within the deviant career.

A *career*, whether in deviance or a legitimate occupation, is the passage of an individual through recognized stages in one or more related identities. Careers are further composed of the adjustment to, and interpretations of, the contingencies and turning points encountered at each stage. For example, Short (1990), in summarizing the research on juvenile delinquents, notes that careers in this form of deviance are likely to be prolonged after certain turning points are reached. One turning point is the early onset of delinquent activities, another is the development of an interest in drugs. The inability to find legitimate employment, a career contingency, also contributes to continued criminality. The type of offence, however, has been found to be unrelated to the length of careers in youth crime and even to the rate at which it is perpetrated. During the careers of juvenile delinquents and other deviants, there is a sense of continuity. This sense is fostered by the perception of increasing opportunities, sophistication, and perhaps recognition among one's associates for skill in, or at least commitment to, the special endeavour.

PRIMARY DEVIANCE

Edwin Lemert (1972) has contributed two important concepts to the study of deviant careers, namely, those of *primary deviation* and *secondary deviation*. Primary deviation occurs with little change in the individual's everyday routine or lifestyle. In general, this will be the case when the individual engages in the deviance infrequently, has few compunctions about it, and encounters few practical problems when doing it. A person who occasionally smokes marijuana supplied by someone else exemplifies primary deviation.

Primary deviation occurs in the early stages of the deviant career, between the first deviant act and some indefinite point where deviance becomes a way of life and secondary deviation (discussed later) sets in. According to Matza

(1969), one precondition of deviance is the willingness to engage in it. That is, the individual must have an affinity, innate or acquired, for the intended act (for example, theft, homicide, drug use). The affinity helps him or her choose among existing options. By way of illustration, imagine an individual who believes that the rich cheat others to get their money. This individual has an affinity for stealing from the rich. That affinity could lead the individual into crimes against the rich when faced with such unpleasant alternatives as poverty, unemployment, or tedious manual labour.

Behind the willingness to engage in deviance is a weak commitment to conventional norms and identities. At the same time, few young people have a strong value commitment to deviant norms and identities. Instead, they drift between the world of respectability and the world of deviance. They are "neither compelled to deeds nor freely choosing them; neither different in any simple or fundamental sense from the law abiding, nor the same; conforming to certain traditions in ... life while partially unreceptive to other more conventional traditions" (Matza, 1990).

Matza was writing about American males who were juvenile delinquents. He found these youths firmly attached to certain marginal, masculine, *subterranean traditions,* or ways of life. They found satisfaction in drinking, smoking, renouncing work, being tough, and pursuing the hedonistic pleasures of "real" men. Matza's subjects looked upon themselves as grown and mature, but their behaviour was hardly a true picture of adult life in general in the United States.

Lemert explains how this peculiar orientation can set one adrift toward deviance:

> While some fortunate individuals by insightful endowment or by virtue of the stabilizing nature of their situations can foresee more distant social consequences of their actions and behave accordingly, not so for most people. Much human behaviour is situationally oriented and geared to meeting the many and shifting claims which others make upon them. The loose structuring and swiftly changing facade and content of modern social situations frequently make it difficult to decide which means will insure the ends sought. Often choice is a compromise between what is sought and what can be sought.... All this makes me believe that most people drift into deviance by specific actions rather than by informed choices of social roles and statuses. (Lemert, 1972)

Social control has failed for the groups of delinquent adolescents and young adults. This failure occurs because it is important for each delinquent individual to be in good standing with his or her friends in the group. He or she attains good standing by honouring and practising the marginal, or subterranean, traditions that Matza describes. The quest for honour among peers helps explain how entire groups of juveniles can drift toward deviance (Hirschi, 1969).

It appears that much, if not all, of this is applicable to Canada. For instance, a comparative study conducted in California and Alberta indicates that ties to peers are important considerations among the sample of delinquent youth, while being in touch with home and school are valued much less (Linden and Fillmore, 1981).

The juvenile delinquent subculture (see Chapter 9) is composed of many elements, some of the most important being the "moral rhetorics" (Schwendinger and Schwendinger, 1985) that are used to justify deviant behaviour. Each rhetoric consists of a set of guiding principles that is largely taken for granted, sometimes logically inconsistent, and always selectively applied according to the social situations in which delinquents find themselves. The rhetoric of *egoism* is most often used by those who still feel guilty about their deviant acts. These are typically early delinquents, who have learned various ways to neutralize the stigma that comes with their behaviour, such as the claim that they steal in response to the greed and immorality of shopkeepers whose prices are unfair. Later delinquents are more likely to use the *instrumental* rhetoric to justify their acts. Here they stress the cunning and power that they can bring to bear against people who are otherwise more powerful and uncontrollable. Fraud, deceit, and violence are used in the pursuit of deviant aims whenever they appear to pay off, whenever they can take advantage of a weak moment in the lives of such people.

During the primary deviation stages of the deviant career, delinquents and young adults drift, in part, because they lack a value commitment to either conventional or deviant values. Value commitment is an attitude toward an identity, an attitude that develops when a person gains exceptional rewards from taking on that identity (Stebbins, 1970). Young men and women drifting between criminal and respectable pursuits have found few, if any, enduring benefits in either type of activity. Nonetheless, this pattern begins to change as they begin to have more contact with the agents of social control.

AGENTS OF SOCIAL CONTROL

The members of society who help check deviant behaviour are known as *agents of social control.* They include the police, judges, lawmakers, prison personnel, probation and parole officers, and ordinary citizens who take an active interest in maintaining law and order as they define it. Groups of ordinary citizens and lawmakers sometimes join hands in the capacity of moral entrepreneurs:

> Rules are the products of someone's initiative, and we can think of the people who exhibit such enterprise as *moral entrepreneurs.* Two related species—rule creators and rule enforcers—will occupy our attention. (Becker, 1963)

The prototype of the rule creator, Becker observes, is the "crusading reformer," whose dissatisfaction with existing rules is acute and who, therefore, campaigns for legal change (adding new laws or procedures, rescinding old laws or procedures) and, sometimes, for a change in attitude designed to produce what he or she considers proper behaviour. Canadian society is replete with crusades, both past and present. Different groups have sought to eliminate drug abuse, discourage the overuse of alcohol, reduce the availability of pornography, and stop the exploitation of women in the workplace. Organizations have been formed to stress the need for such things as protection against break and entry. Moral enterprise is currently at work in an attempt to curb electronic crime.

To conduct an effective crusade, moral entrepreneurs must construct an argument that is capable of convincing the community that it has a deep and genuine threat in its midst. This process of collective definition (Spector and Kitsuse, 1987; Hewitt and Hall, 1973) centres on, among other things, the "claims-making activities" of the entrepreneurs themselves. They:

1. assert the existence of a particular condition, situation, or state of affairs in which human action is implicated as a cause;
2. define the asserted conditions as offensive, harmful, undesirable, or otherwise problematic to the society but nonetheless amenable to correction by human beings;
3. stimulate public scrutiny of the condition from the point of view advanced by the claims-makers.

The claims are explained by "quasi-theories." Unlike scientific theories, quasi-theories are selectively constructed to square with the point of view of the claims-makers, are seldom responsive to empirical evidence, and contain simple explanations of complex and ill-defined problems.

Moral entrepreneurs also enforce rules. The rules make it possible to apply norms to those who misbehave or step out of line. The entrepreneurs' legislated rules provide the enforcers (police, security personnel) with jobs and justifications for them. Since the enforcers want to keep these jobs, they are eager to demonstrate that enforcement is being carried out properly. Yet they also realize that there are more infractions than they can possibly prevent and guard against. Therefore, they must establish priorities. Thus,

> whether a person who commits a deviant act is in fact labelled a deviant depends on many things extraneous to his actual behaviour: whether the enforcement official feels that at this time he must make some show of doing his job in order to justify his position, whether the misbehaver shows proper deference to the enforcer, whether the "fix" has been put in, and where the kind of act he has committed stands on the enforcer's list of priorities. (Becker, 1963)

It is no accident, then, that the least influential members of society (for example, the poor or certain ethnic groups) are often caught in the web of social control and labelled deviant out of proportion to their numbers.

THE MORAL ENTREPRENEUR AGAINST
DRUGS AND ALCOHOL

Prior to World War I, despite their long and persistent efforts, temperance supporters had been unable to implement plans for the national prohibition of alcohol. But war, with its simultaneous concerns for patriotism and efficiency (Thompson, 1972) proved a boon for the temperance cause. Temperance advocates were able to muster new and powerful arguments in favour of a "dry" Canada and to tap the emotional fervor of wartime (Hallowell, 1972:60).

Temperance proponents, due to their years of experience, had become skilful publicists (Hallowell, 1972:19) and those skills were put into use with great effect during World War I. Temperance rhetoric increasingly used warlike metaphors that emotionally aroused one's sense of patriotic duty. For instance, it was stated that, just as Canadians should "despise the army of the Kaiser for dropping bombs on defence-less people, and shooting down women and children," they should also despise the liquor traffic since it had "waged war on women and children all down the centuries" (McClung, 1915:163). A Reverend Hughson of Winnipeg counselled Westerners to "use ballots for bullets and shoot straight and strong in order that the demon of drink might be driven from the haunts of men" (*Manitoba Free Press*, 6 March 1916, p. 4). Even after the war it was declared that prohibition was a fight against "an enemy more mighty, more merciless, more beastly, more fiend-like, more diabolical than the Teuton" (*The Globe and Mail*, 29 Sept. 1919, p. 8).

Likewise, current descriptions of anti-drug efforts continue to use war metaphors and to identify drugs with political enemies. The former Canadian Ambassador to the United Nations, Stephen Lewis, recently used the term "narco-terrorism" to link drug trafficking and international terrorism (*Vancouver Sun*, 9 Dec. 1985). The Americans have gone beyond metaphors. Rather than "ballots for bullets," real bullets and soldiers are used in authentic wars on the production and distribution of narcotics, cocaine and other illicit drugs. The recent involvement of American military troops in Bolivia illustrates this fact (McDonald, 1986:20). Although Canadians have not been involved in acts of such magnitude, it appears that they are also engaged in an escalating program that could lead drug enforcement policies to the excesses of a war that had originally served as only a metaphor (Ward, 1988).

The emphasis placed on patriotism was an important plank in the prohibition platform. The contention that liquor was the antithesis of patriotism was clearly embodied in such statements as: "anyone who will vote in favor of liquor might as well enlist under the Kaiser as far as patriotism goes" (Thompson, 1972:294).

The call to patriotism was especially potent since it enabled the temperance movement to enlist in its ranks those who otherwise would not have supported it, especially recent immigrants eager to prove their loyalty (Thompson, 1972:294). Furthermore, linking patriotism and support for prohibition served as a strong weapon to intimidate and denounce those who might speak against prohibition.

Groups such as the Liberty League, opponents of prohibition, attempted to defend themselves by stating: "We are not booze-fighters, nor are we bought by the liquor interests; we are just British subjects asking to live our lives under the laws of God and the reasonable laws of man" (*The Globe and Mail,* 30 July 1919, p. 8)....

Today, those who hold "liberal" drug views, those who suggest less restrictive measures for dealing with drug problems or those who suggest the "drug problem" has been exaggerated continually face the threat of being labelled soft on drugs, soft-headed, or even that their views may deserve legal censure (Bakalar and Grinspoon, 1984:111; Graham, 1987). If a person suggests that certain aspects of drug policies are incorrect he or she may even be suspected of being a "druggie" attempting to advance his or her own self-interest. Students in my own university debate whether the professor who lectures on drug issues is himself involved with marijuana or some other illicit drug. In contrast, other professors, who lecture on topics such as terrorism or fascism, do not risk the suspicion of harbouring motives other than curiosity and the quest for knowledge and explanations....

The temperance supporter's ability to "destroy most of their opponents' arguments by mere charges of selfishness or of collaboration with the liquor interest" (Hallowell, 1972:28–29) is a tactic that endures. It would appear that prohibitionists of the past and present use similar means to quiet and discredit those who should suggest alternative methods and ideas for dealing with drug issues.

Source: A.R.F. Schweighofer. (1988). "The Canadian Temperance Movement: Contemporary Parallels." *Canadian Journal of Law and Society* 3:175–93. (The references cited in this excerpt are available in the original source.)

In other words, deviance is, in part, created by people in society. Moral entrepreneurs make certain laws. The infraction of these laws constitutes deviance. Moral entrepreneurs also apply these laws to particular people, thereby labelling them as deviants of some sort. As Becker (1963) points out: "Deviance is not a quality of the act.... The deviant is one to whom that label has successfully been applied; deviant behaviour is behaviour that people so label."

But the rules are applied to some people and not to others; the application process is sometimes biased. Hence, some people remain at large as secret, or potentially identifiable, deviants. Others go through life falsely accused of antisocial acts. To discover why only certain groups of people are labelled deviant by dint of their actions, labelling theorists also study those who make the laws that deviants violate and the ways those laws are applied.

Those publicly labelled as deviant typically meet with some sort of community or societal reaction to their misdeeds (Lemert, 1951). Depending on the nature of the deviance, one or more of the following may be the deviant's fate: imprisonment, ostracism, fines, torture, surveillance, and ridicule. All labelled deviants soon discover that they must cope with a stigma.

A *stigma* is the black mark, or disgrace, associated with a deviant identity. It is part of the societal reaction, inasmuch as it is a collective construction by the agents of social control and ordinary members of the community of the supposed nature of the unlawful act and the people who perpetrate it. As Goffman (1963) notes, the collective image of stigma is constructed from physical and psychological attributes the deviant is believed to possess. In this connection, imputed possession of the attributes is far more important than actual possession.

Jock Young (1975) describes the public image of the stigmatized marijuana user. The user is held to be an isolated person living in a socially disorganized area. He or she is possibly a drifter. According to the public image, such individuals are asocial and lack any substantial values, except a craving for drugs. Those who push marijuana are seen to be part of the criminal underworld. Users are believed to be immature, psychologically unstable people who resort to increasingly more powerful drugs (for example, heroin) in search of "kicks." The kicks are said to include extreme sexuality, aggressive criminality, and, perhaps, wildly psychotic episodes. Although Young's research refuted these notions, the public image of the marijuana user continues to influence legislation and social control.

Mark Watson (1984) found, after three years of participation observation with an outlaw motorcycle gang, that its members had a mentality and background noticeably different from that imputed to them by the general public. They were not especially hostile to most social institutions, including government, education, and the family. Most members had finished high school and had held jobs from time to time. Some had gone to college, some were military veterans. Nearly every member had been married at least once. They were, to be sure, not particularly successful in these areas of life—which helped account for their tendency to live for the moment, to be impulsive. And although they were basically not violent men, it was important to them to be seen as "manly" in the most traditional sense of the term.

SECONDARY DEVIATION

The existence of moral rules, and the societal reaction and stigma that occur when these rules are believed to have been violated, set the stage for secondary deviation. Deviation becomes secondary when deviants see that their behaviour substantially modifies their ways of living. A strong desire to deviate, or a feeling of extreme guilt, can foster this redefinition of one's deviant activities. But being accused of deviance is typically the most influential factor behind the redefinition. Being labelled by the authorities as a murderer, rapist, prostitute, or cheque forger and being sanctioned for such behaviour forces the deviant to change his or her lifestyle drastically. As Lemert (1972) puts it, "this secondary deviant … is a person whose life and identity are organized around the facts of deviance."

Among the factors leading to secondary deviation is the tendency of society to treat someone's criminality as a *master status* (Becker, 1963). This status overrides all other statuses in perceived importance. Whatever laudable achievements the deviant might have, such as a good job or a successful marriage, he or she is primarily judged in the community by the fact of deviance. The statuses of work and family are treated as subordinate to the master status of deviance.

Lack of success, or a perceived low probability of success, in attaining respectability among nondeviants may lead to interaction with other deviants. Here we shall consider a special aspect of this sort of interaction, interaction which takes place between the labelled deviant and the organized deviant group. There are several characteristics of this type of group life that stimulate or maintain such behaviour. These characteristics are effective partly because the wider community has rejected the deviant.

As Becker (1963) pointed out, the individual who gains entrance to a deviant group often learns from the group how to cope with the various problems associated with deviance. This makes being a deviant easier. Furthermore, the deviant acquires rationalizations for his or her values, attitudes, and behaviour, which come to full bloom in the organized group. While these rationalizations are highly varied, it is important to note that the very existence of rationalizations seems to point to the fact that some deviants feel a need to deal with certain conventional attitudes and values that they have also internalized.

Prus and Sharper (1977) quote one of their respondents, who was explaining how he developed the callous attitude prized by professional card hustlers:

> When I first got involved in hustling, my attitudes were less calloused [sic]. I might be at a stag of some sort and say some fellow is losing a little money. Through the course of the evening, talking back and forth, you find out that maybe he just got married, or that he has some kids and here he's writing cheques and I would slow down. If you pull something like this with a crew [of hustlers], the other guys will want to know what the hell you are doing! They're waiting for you to take him, and you're saying, "Well gee, the guy doesn't have much money." You would get the worst tongue lashing! The position they take is that "You can't have feelings on the road." And it's true, if you start saying to yourself, "Well, maybe I better not beat this guy or that guy," you would soon be out of business or at least you would really cut down on your profits.
>   When a crew is on the road, they have no feelings for the other

players. They say, "Well, if the sucker doesn't blow it to you, he's going to blow it to somebody else, so you might as well take him for his money. He's going to lose it one way or the other."

Because group forces operate to maintain and even promote deviance, it should not be assumed, as Goffman (1963) apparently does, that full-fledged deviants are always members of groups. There are some who reject the label of deviant during certain phases of their career, although they may be forced into that status. Some of these individuals spend part of their career trying to re-enter conventional life, often without success. Yet, the fact that they refuse to identify themselves as deviant leads them to avoid others who are so labelled (for example, shoplifters and embezzlers). There are, moreover, some forms of deviant behaviour that, whatever the reason, are typically enacted alone. Rape is an example of this behaviour, as is some cheque forging. It is probably true, nevertheless, that deviance has collective support in most instances.

The amount and kinds of interaction that take place between the individual who is suspected of deviant behaviour and the agents of social control are extremely important for the future course of that person's deviant career. In fact, the interaction that takes place here makes up a major set of deviant career contingencies. A *career contingency* is an unintended event, process, or situation that occurs by chance; that is, it lies beyond the control of the individual pursuing the career. Career contingencies emanate from changes in the deviant's environment, his or her personal circumstances, or both. Movement through the career is affected by the contingencies the deviant meets along the way.

Cohen (1965) has presented this process most clearly: alter (the agents of social control) responds to the action of ego (the deviant); ego in turn responds to alter's reaction; alter then responds to his perception of ego's reaction to him; and so forth. The final result is that ego's opportunity structure is in some way modified, permitting either more or fewer legitimate or illegitimate opportunities.

Where the opportunities for a deviant career are expanding, the steady growing apart of the deviant and the control agents leads to open conflict. Some proportion of these encounters lead in the opposite direction, however, resulting in some form of accommodation and a decrease in the opportunities for a deviant career (West, 1980).

This process of agent-deviant interaction is illustrated in the circumstances encountered by one of the respondents in Stebbins' study of nonprofessional criminals.

The respondent arrived in Toronto shortly after being released from prison in New Brunswick, only to be stopped while walking on a main street by two policemen in a prowl car. He was apparently immediately recognized and advised to return to his home province without further delay. But since he had just come from there, the respondent politely informed the police that he had important business in Toronto that would take a few days to accomplish, and after that he would consider leaving the city. This was not the sort of reaction the police were after, so they pressed their request again in a firmer manner. The respondent's reply was likewise more adamant, and the police left without success. That evening he was called from his rented room by his landlady only to be confronted by two different but "enormous" policemen who had just arrived in an ominous-looking police van. They again questioned him about his intentions to stay in Toronto, but the respondent, who could now see that he would probably remain in that city only in jail, replied that he had decided to return to New Brunswick after all. (Stebbins, 1971)

Another prominent contingency in secondary deviation is continuance commitment. *Continuance commitment* is "the awareness of the impossibility of choosing a different social identity ... because of the imminence of penalties involved in making the switch" (Stebbins, 1971). Like the value commitment mentioned earlier in this chapter, continuance commitment helps explain a person's involvement in a deviant identity. Unlike value commitment, which explains this involvement by stressing the rewards of the identity, continuance commitment explains involvement by describing the penalties that accrue from renouncing the deviant identity and trying to adopt a conventional identity.

Stebbins's study of male, nonprofessional property offenders in New-foundland reveals a number of commitment-related penalties. As ex-offenders with prison records, the men in the study had difficulty finding jobs within their range of personally acceptable alternatives. The work they found was onerous, low in pay, and low in prestige. Many of the men had accrued sizeable debts before they went to prison, which tended to discourage their return to a conventional livelihood upon release. Also penalizing were the questions from casual acquaintances about the nature of criminal life and the insulting remarks these people occasionally made about those who have been in jail. Even where their records were unknown, these nonprofessional offenders often heard people express unflattering opinions about men like them.

For these reasons and others, the man with a criminal record was often inclined to seek the company of those who understood him best, namely, other criminals, and to seek the way of life that afforded him at least some money and excitement, namely, crime. The police knew all this. Their knowledge of ex-offenders in the community helped them solve certain crimes there. They would question local ex-offenders to determine if they were possibly guilty of these crimes. The ex-offenders who were trying to "go straight" saw this as an additional penalty.

What is experienced as a string of penalties to the ex-offender is, from another perspective, a set of expressions of the societal reaction. In the everyday lives of ex-offenders, these expressions, when defined by the ex-offenders as penalizing, affect their deviant careers. The expressions force many of them into the company of other deviants. Here they find greater understanding for their circumstances. Here, also, is at least the possibility of a better living than they believe they can get in the conventional world.

What import does the process of continuance of commitment have for that of drift? Those teenagers and young adults who fail to drift out of crime into a more or less conventional way of life drift into a more or less solid commitment to crime. With a prison record and several years of secondary deviation, continuance commitment develops. Most deviants in this stage of their moral careers appear to be trapped in a self-degrading form of continuance commitment. The image they have of themselves is unflattering. It is one they wish they could abandon, if only they could find a palatable way of leaving the world of crime (see also Schwendinger and Schwendinger, 1985).

But some criminals, including professional offenders, are quite attached to their deviant activities. Since the professionals find leaving crime for a conventional way of life no easier than the nonprofessional offender, they are also committed to deviance. Nonetheless, theirs is a self-enhancing commitment. For the professionals, continuance commitment is of minor consequence, for they enjoy what they do and are disinclined to give it up.

REACTIONS TO COMMITMENT

Generally speaking, self-enhancing commitment presents no problem for deviants, in spite of the fact that they are more or less forced to retain their social role. There is little motivation to leave this role for reasons of self-conception. Self-degrading commitment, however, presents a dramatically different situation. A number of alternatives are open to an individual committed to an identity in this manner.

First of all, a person motivated by self-degrading commitment has the objective alternative of redefining the values and penalties associated with the committed identity in such a way that he or she becomes attached to them. Basically, this alters the individual's perception of the balance of penalties. Such a psychological leap from self-degrading to self-enhancing commitment in the same deviant identity is exemplified by some in Shover's (1983) sample of repeat offenders. These offenders wrestled with the frustrating gap between their legitimate aspirations and what they could actually achieve in life. Since conventional work offered them little, they turned to living from day to day, with crime being one of their more enjoyable activities.

Without really switching to a form of self-enhancing commitment, it is occasionally possible for the deviant to adjust psychologically to self-degrading commitment. This depends, of course, upon how strong a motivating force the current state of self-degrading commitment actually is for the deviant. Some types of mildly rejected deviants seem to manage this form of adaptation. Lemert (1972) refers to them as "adjusted pathological deviants." The subsequent development of character disorders is another possibility under these circumstances (Cormier et al., 1959). Successful adjustment at this point apparently depends, in part, on the availability of a role for them to play in the community.

Lemert also considers "self-defeating and self-perpetuating deviance." Among other forms, he cites alcoholism, drug addiction, and systematic cheque forgery as examples of this sort of vicious circle of cause and effect, characterized by an almost complete absence of durable pleasure for those involved. Finally, if the desire to escape self-degrading commitment is exceptionally high, and none of the alternatives mentioned so far appeals to the committed individual, suicide becomes a prominent alternative. Perhaps this was the motive behind some or all of the 109 prison suicides reported by the Correctional Service of Canada (National Task Force on Suicide in Canada, 1987) for the period 1973 to 1983.

Undoubtedly, there are many other alternatives to self-degrading commitment besides the ones discussed here. Much, it seems, depends upon the nature of the identity to which the deviant is committed. There are different ways in which commitment can manifest itself. Extensive research is still needed to isolate the kinds and circumstances of commitment, and the various reactions to it.

For many deviants, however, commitment is not a lasting contingency in their careers once they become aware of their entrapment in that identity. In fact, this is one of the reasons for stating the case for commitment in subjective terms. The deviant feels this way, but this does not always correspond to the objective state of affairs. Criminological theory and research support this notion. For instance, Matza (1990) contends that delinquents generally end their deviant career at maturation, with very few continuing on to adult crime (for supporting evidence, see Shannon, 1988). West (1980) and Wolfgang, Thornberry, and Figlio (1987) found that many adult criminals also mature out of their antisocial ways. This occurs when they take up a serious romantic relationship, find a legitimate job they like better than crime, or simply decide "to settle down." Thus, even deviants attached to their way of life often undergo disillusionment and shifts of interest (Shover, 1983). There is always the possibility of therapy for alcoholics, gamblers, and drug addicts. And, of course, some deviance requires youthful vigour, a quality lost with increasing years (Inciardi, 1974).

Undoubtedly, the same can be said for many other committed identities. The worker committed to his or her job by a pension plan and seniority arrangements is often relieved of this condition, if in no other way than by retirement. Divorce and remarriage are always possibilities for those in an unhappy union.

It is possible that the self-enhancing commitment lasts longer than the self-degrading variety. Underlying this suggestion is the assumption that self-degrading commitment, while preferable to certain alternatives in the conventional world, is still undesirable in itself. A mortifying self-conception acts as a special penalty. It furnishes a significant part of the pressure to deal with an unpleasant state of affairs. Commitment to an identity or expectation that creates a negative self-image is viewed as a lesser-evil choice when initially compared with certain alternatives, and as a greater-evil choice when subsequently compared with certain others. The strength of the individual's desire to abandon an unpleasant status is an important consideration in determining whether the transition will be made.

SOCIALIZATION INTO CRIME

The theories of criminality discussed in previous chapters help explain why people start a life of crime. By contrast, interactionism has been interested chiefly in what happens to criminals once their deviant activities commence. Still, two areas of interactionist theory, though not causal, can be properly seen as contributions to the study of socialization into crime. They are the processes of differential association and acquisition of a criminal identity.

DIFFERENTIAL ASSOCIATION

Edwin H. Sutherland first set out his theory of differential association in the 1939 edition of *Principles of Criminology*. The statement he made in that edition differs little from the most recent version written by Sutherland and Cressey (1978). The theory consists of nine propositions, which describe the complicated pattern of interaction Sutherland called *differential association*: (1) people learn how to engage in crime; (2) this learning comes about through interaction with others who have already learned criminal ways; (3) the learning occurs in small, face-to-face groups; (4) what is learned is criminal technique (for example, how to open a safe), motives, attitudes, and rationalizations; (5) among criminals one important learned attitude is a disregard for the community's legal code; (6) one acquires this attitude by differentially associating with those who hold it and failing to associate with those who do not; (7) differential associations with criminals and noncriminals vary in frequency, duration, priority, and intensity; (8) learning criminal behaviour through differential association rests on the same principles as learning any other kind of behaviour; and (9) criminal behaviour is a response to the same cultural needs and values as noncriminal behaviour. For instance, one individual steals to acquire money for a new suit of clothes, while another works as a carpenter to reach the same goal. Consequently, tying societal needs and values to crime fails to explain it.

Based on what is known about the antecedents of crime, Sutherland's theory offers a valuable, albeit partial, explanation of theft, burglary, prostitution, and marijuana use. Also, differential association is often a major antecedent in the use of addictive drugs, pursuit of homosexual relations, and dependence on alcohol. It may even play an explanatory role in some mental disorders.

However, many other factors, which dilute the importance of differential associations, must be considered when explaining these kinds of behaviour. For example, two processes discussed earlier in this chapter, drift and primary and secondary deviation, indicate that deviant motives and meanings are often gradually learned and tentatively applied and modified over time in interaction with both deviants and nondeviants. The motives and meanings are not mere causal antecedents of criminal acts and memberships in criminal groups (Davis, 1980). Although various tests of the theory of differential association have been carried out, convincing support for it has always been blocked by the difficulty of operationalizing for empirical study some of Sutherland's key concepts (for example, frequency, intensity, and duration of criminal and noncriminal associations). Nonetheless, in Nanette Davis's (1980) words, differential association theory was "a giant step forward" and "Sutherland's multidimensional view of association helped eradicate the notion of simple predispositional factors in human behaviour, eliminated an individualistic model of crime causation, and ended the, heretofore, almost exclusive attention given to lower-class crime."

CRIMINAL IDENTITIES

A *criminal identity* is a commonly recognized social category in which deviants are placed by others in the community and in which, eventually, they may place themselves. That is, the process of identification of an individual as deviant is a two-sided coin. Based on a variety of criteria (for example, appearance, actions, associates, and location), members of the community come to view someone as a particular kind of criminal. The woman wearing garish, suggestive clothing, who frequents a street corner in the red-light district, is identified as a prostitute. The man with long, unkempt hair, dirty jeans, and a black leather jacket who rides off on a Harley-Davidson motorcycle is identified, as we saw earlier, as a member of a gang bent on rape, violence, and drunkenness.

Moreover—and this is the other side of the coin—community identification of people tends to be very persuasive, even for the deviant. That is, with officials, neighbours, relatives, and others asserting that an individual is some sort of social outlaw, it becomes increasingly difficult for him or her to deny the charge. At the very least, the alleged prostitute must accommodate her everyday life to such opinion, whether or not she is selling sex. The motorcyclist has the same problem (Watson, 1984).

Acquiring a community reputation, or identity, for unsavoury behaviour often helps to further individual criminality. This is especially likely to happen when the reputed criminal is forced into association with others of similar reputation and away from those who are "respectable." Once deviant ties are forged and nondeviant ties sufficiently weakened, the socializing potential of differential association begins to take effect. Interactionists see social interaction and definitions of situation as underlying the processes of identification and differential association.

LIMITATIONS

Like all theories of crime and deviance, interactionist theory has its limitations. That is to say, it is not in itself a complete explanation of crime. It falls well short of explaining all crime under all the conditions in which it is committed. The foregoing pages have indicated where the theory is applicable. Drawing on Barry Glassner's (1982) review of the various critiques of this theory, its limitations will now be examined. These are discussed with reference to three categories: neo-Marxist, empiricist, and ethnomethodologi-cal. Each critique is also the nucleus of still another approach to the study of crime.

The principal *neo-Marxist* objection to interactionist theory is its failure to relate crime and other forms of deviance to the larger society. It fails to account for historical and contemporary political and economic interests. After all, deviant acts and careers do take place within such a context.

It is further charged that labelling theorists overlook the division between the powerful and the powerless in explaining deviance. Powerful members of society also violate laws and other norms, even while making some of them in their role as moral entrepreneurs. Consider the case of Henri Marchessault, former head of the Montreal Police Drug Squad. In November 1983, he was convicted of stealing and selling hashish and cocaine, which were available to him from a police vault. He was a detective captain at the time (*Calgary Herald* 26 November 1983).

The concept of moral entrepreneur and the categories of secret and falsely accused deviants suggest, however, that interactionists have some under-standing of the power differences in society. Perhaps the fairest criticism is that they have failed to go as far as they might in linking power to such ideas as labelling, deviant career, and agent of social control. Still, the observation that labelling theory overlooks the larger social context of deviance is apt. It exposes the predominantly social-psychological character of the perspective.

The *empiricists* find several research weaknesses in labelling theory and its empirical support. Glassner (1982) discusses three of these weaknesses. First, interactionists are said by the empiricists to examine only, or chiefly, labelled deviants—those who have been *officially* identified as having deviated (charged and convicted, or examined and hospitalized). It is true that labelling theorists have frequently followed this narrow conception of the labelling process. Some deviants, for example, religious fanatics or occultists, are deviant and labelled by the community as such, even though they rarely, if ever, gain official recognition. This exposes interactionists to the criticism that community labelling makes no practical difference to the individual.

Second, the empiricists argue that labelling as a cause of deviance is inadequately conceptualized. This is a misunderstanding. As this chapter points out, labels are seen by interactionists as interpretations, not causes. The label of deviant is a career contingency, an event, a process, or a situation interpreted by the deviant as having a significant impact on his or her moral career.

Third, the empiricists claim that labelling theory lacks testable proposi-tions. Consequently, data in this area can be explained in many different ways. Glassner notes that the empiricists hold that tests by quantitative, statistical means are the only definitive way of confirming propositions. Interactionists defend their approach by pointing out that qualitative methods, particularly participant observation, are more appropriate for the study of interaction, labelling, career, and self-conception. These phenomena rest on definitions of the situation, images of self and others, negotiations of reality, and similar processes that are difficult to measure and, therefore, largely unquantifiable. Nevertheless, qualitative research often proceeds from the intense examination of individual groups and cases. Such studies are difficult and time-consuming. As a result, there are relatively few of them. There is only suggestive, and still unconfirmed, evidence for many interactionist propositions.

The *ethnomethodologists* and conversational analysts are the modern-day inheritors of the phenomenology of Alfred Schutz. (In fact, Glassner refers to them as "phenomenologists" in his review of interactionist theory). The chief concern of the ethnomethodologists with labelling theory is its tendency to neglect the question: How do people make sense of their social world?

Kenneth Leiter (1980) defines ethnomethodology as the study of common-sense knowledge. Three phenomena are encompassed by this definition: Ethnomethodologists study the stock of knowledge that people have of the social and physical world around them; with this stock of knowledge, people engage in common-sense reasoning about the events, processes, things, and characteristics experienced in everyday life; when people reason together on common-sense basis, their thoughts often combine to form a suprahuman reality, a social reality. This social reality transcends the thoughts of those in the situation who are doing the reasoning.

Ethnomethodologists do not seek to confirm the validity of common sense. Rather, they note that, whether common sense is scientifically right or wrong, it is the way in which "we experience the social world as a factual object" (Leiter, 1980). By studying these three phenomena, we find answers to the question of how people make sense of their social world.

The people of interest to the ethnomethodologist are not always deviant, however. Rather, ethnomethodologists are interested in how agents of social control and ordinary citizens make sense of deviants and deviant acts. Interactionists are accused of ignoring the ways in which the conventional world identifies and classifies morally offensive individuals and their behaviour. The important data for ethnomethodologists are the clues people use to identify kinds of deviants and deviant acts. People use this knowledge to reach such conclusions as "guilty" or "innocent." Studying these two processes demonstrates how we all construct special social realities—the realities of who did what to whom, at what time, and at what place.

To some extent, interactionists are guilty as charged. Although there are occasional hints of ethnomethodological thinking in the interactionist literature on deviance, there has been until recently a tendency to rely heavily on official definitions, or labels, of what and who is deviant. But even official definitions and their applications are informed by common sense. They, too, warrant ethnomethodological analysis.

IMPLICATIONS

The most profound implication of interactionist theory is practical only in a general sense. The theory offers a unique perspective on deviance, which enhances understanding of this phenomenon. For instance, observations on moral enterprise underscore the arbitrariness of criminal law and call attention to patterns of local and national power (though rarely to the extent neo-Marxists would like). Practically speaking, there is little that can be done to counteract most moral enterprise. But interactionist research, at least, exposes its existence.

On a more practical level, interactionist theory stresses the pernicious effects of the deviant label. These effects are of at least two types. One, the label (to the extent that the wider community is aware of it) makes re-entry into that community problematic after sanctioning. Nondeviants are inclined to avoid known deviants. They do so because their own reputations could be damaged from being seen with deviants and, possibly, because they are revolted by the deviant's lifestyle and moral behaviour. Deviants are more than rule violators. They are also outcasts.

Two, labels colour the judgements many people make of those who are labelled. Labels are names for stereotyped images. Both the images and the labels help nondeviants, including practitioners, define situations involving deviants. These two effects of the deviant label have led Empey (1982), among others, to argue that the juvenile court should be used as a last resort for only the most serious cases. Juvenile diversion and decriminalization programs are a practical response to this implication of interactionist theory.

Interactionist theory calls attention to the deviant career as a set of factors that helps explain deviance beyond its initial causes. One practical implication stemming from this part of the theory is that, over time, people often become committed to certain lifestyles. To the extent that they have made substantial "side bets" (Becker, 1963) in one or more conventional identities, they are unlikely to deviate. Their possible deviance, if discovered and labelled, could ruin their reputations in the conventional world (for example, the politician exposed in the press for patronizing a prostitute). One antidote to initial or continued deviance, then, is to give people every possible opportunity to build a strong side bet in a "respectable" pursuit. By this reasoning, the juvenile should be encouraged to drift toward conventional interests. The adult ex-offender should also be encouraged to find noncriminal employment in new surroundings, away from his or her former deviant associates.

SUMMARY

Interactionist theory centres on the deviant interchanges people have with one another and the meanings of these interchanges in the present, past, and future. A deviant career is the passage of an individual through recognized stages in one or more related deviant identities. Primary deviation occurs in the early stages of the deviant career. Here, deviance is enacted with little change in the individual's everyday routine or lifestyle. One important precondition of primary deviation is that he or she is willing to try a particular kind of deviance. The attitude of being willing includes a weak value commitment to both conventional norms and deviant norms. That is, the deviant drifts between two moral worlds. Drift is facilitated by certain moral rhetorics and by other aspects of the subterranean tradition in delinquent subcultures.

Agents of social control play a role in checking deviant behaviour. Moral entrepreneurs create and enforce rules, the violation of which constitutes deviance. The result is that some people are labelled deviant, whereas others are not. There may be secret or falsely accused deviants. The labels applied to deviants and deviance generate a societal reaction, which includes stigma.

When the deviant sees his or her life as substantially modified by deviance, then he or she has progressed to secondary deviation. This sometimes means initial or deeper involvement in a deviant group. Interaction with agents of social control is a career contingency that may push the deviant either into or away from stigmatizing activities. Continuance commitment, or forcing a person to remain in an identity, is sometimes the outcome of these encounters. When self-degrading continuance commitment sets in, it motivates those so affected to redefine commitment penalties or adjust in some other way to this unsettling frame of mind.

Although the theory of criminal socialization has not been a central concern of the interactionist perspective, interactionists have contributed to the theory in two major ways. People learn crime through differential association with others who are already criminal. They are further socialized into it by acquiring a criminal identity, by being placed in such a category by other people, and by coming to accept (often grudgingly) this placement.

Like other theories of crime, interactionist theory has its limitations. These limitations have been noted by the neo-Marxists, empiricists, and ethnomethodologists, who are presently fashioning their own approaches to the study of crime. At the moment, however, none of these approaches has progressed beyond the concern with finding weaknesses in the interactionist perspective such that it could become a distinct orientation itself (Scull, 1988). Interactionist theory also has certain theoretical and practical implications. One of these is that, wherever possible, continuance commitment to deviance should be avoided for juveniles by deferring the official label of criminal.

BIBLIOGRAPHY

Becker, Howard S. (1963). *Outsiders: Studies in the Sociology of Deviance.* New York: Free Press.
Blumer, Herbert. (1986). *Symbolic Interactionism.* Berkeley: University of California Press.
Cohen, Albert K. (1965). "The Sociology of the Deviant Act." *American Sociological Review* 30:5–14.

Cormier, Bruno M., Miriam Kennedy, Jadwiga Sangowicz, and Michel Trottier. (1959). "The Natural History of Criminality: Hypotheses on Its Abatement." *Canadian Journal of Corrections* 1:35–49.

Davis, Nanette J. (1980). *Sociological Constructions of Deviance.* (2nd ed.). Dubuque, IA: Wm. C. Brown.

Empey, Lamar T. (1982). *American Delinquency.* Homewood, IL: Dorsey.

Glassner, Barry. (1982). "Labeling Theory." In M. Michael Rosenberg, Robert A. Stebbins, and Allan Turowetz, (eds.), *The Sociology of Deviance.* New York: St. Martin's Press.

Goffman, Erving. (1963). *Stigma: Notes on the Management of Spoiled Identity.* Englewood Cliffs, NJ: Prentice-Hall.

Hewitt, John P., and Peter M. Hall. (1973). "Social Problems, Problematic Situations, and Quasi-Theories." *American Sociological Review* 38:367–74.

Hirschi, Travis. (1969). *Causes of Delinquency.* Berkeley: University of California Press.

Inciardi, James A. (1974). "Vocational Crime." In *Handbook of Criminology.* Chicago: Rand McNally.

Katz, Jack. (1988). *Seductions of Crime: Moral and Sensual Attractions in Doing Evil.* New York: Basic Books.

Leiter, Kenneth. (1980). *A Primer on Ethnomethodology.* New York: Oxford University Press.

Lemert, Edwin. (1951). *Social Pathology.* New York: McGraw-Hill.

———. (1972). *Human Deviance, Social Problems, and Social Control.* (2nd ed.). Englewood Cliffs, NJ: Prentice-Hall.

Linden, Rick, and Cathy Fillmore. (1981). "A Comparative Study of Delinquency Involvement." *Canadian Review of Sociology and Anthropology* 18:343–61.

Matza, David. (1969). *Becoming Deviant.* Englewood Cliffs, NJ: Prentice-Hall.

———. (1990). *Delinquency and Drift.* New Brunswick, NJ: Transaction.

National Task Force on Suicide in Canada. (1987). "Suicide in Canada." Ottawa: Minister of National Health and Welfare, Government of Canada.

Prus, Robert C., and C.R.D. Sharper. (1977). *Road Hustler.* Lexington, MA: D.C. Heath.

Schwendinger, Herman, and Julia S. Schwendinger. (1985). *Adolescent Subcultures and Delinquency.* New York: Praeger.

Scull, Andrew T. (1988). "Deviance and Social Control." In Neil J. Smelser (ed.), *Handbook of Sociology.* Newbury Park, CA: Sage.

Shannon, Lyle W. (1988). *Criminal Career Continuity.* New York: Human Sciences Press.

Short, James F. (1990). *Delinquency and Society.* Englewood Cliffs, NJ: Prentice-Hall.

Shover, Neal. (1983). "The Later Stages of Ordinary Property Offender Careers." *Social Problems* 31:208–18.

Spector, Malcolm, and John I. Kitsuse. (1987). *Constructing Social Problems.* Hawthorne, NY: Aldine de Gruyter.

Stebbins, Robert A. (1970). "On Misunderstanding the Concept of Commitment: A Theoretical Clarification." *Social Forces* 48:526–29.

———. (1971). *Commitment to Deviance.* Westport, CT: Greenwood.

Sutherland, Edwin H., and David R. Cressey. (1978). *Principles of Criminology.* (10th ed.). Philadelphia: Lippincott.

Watson, J. Mark. (1984). "Outlaw Motorcyclists: An Outgrowth of Lower Class Cultural Concerns." In Delos H. Kelly, (ed.), *Deviant Behavior.* (2nd ed.). New York: St. Martin's Press.

West, W. Gordon. (1980). "The Short Term Careers of Serious Thieves." In Robert A. Silverman and James J. Teevan, Jr. (eds.), *Crime in Canadian Society.* (2nd ed.). Toronto: Butterworths.

Wolfgang, Marvin E., Terence P. Thornberry, and Robert M. Figlio. (1987). *From Boy to Man, from Delinquency to Crime.* Chicago: University of Chicago Press.

Young, Jock. (1975). "Police as Amplifiers of Deviancy." In Richard L. Henshel and Robert A. Silverman (eds.), *Perception in Criminology.* New York: Columbia University Press.

FURTHER READING

Becker, Howard S. (1963). *Outsiders.* New York: Free Press. A collection of key articles written by Becker, several of which contain original statements on labelling, the deviant career, moral entrepreneurs, and types of deviants.

Goffman, Erving. (1963). *Stigma.* Englewood Cliffs, NJ: Prentice-Hall. An essay on the nature and consequences of stigma for deviants, the handicapped, and those with physical blemishes.

Lemert, Edwin M. (1972). *Human Deviance, Social Problems, and Social Control* (2nd ed.). Englewood Cliffs, NJ: Prentice-Hall. A collection of key articles written by Lemert on such subjects as the deviant career, cheque forgery, social control, and primary and secondary deviation.

Matza, David. (1990). *Delinquency and Drift.* New Brunswick, NJ: Transaction. This book contains Matza's fullest development of the concepts of drift and subterranean tradition, as well as an introduction that links it with the 1964 edition.

Rubington, Earl, and Martin G. Weinberg (eds.). (1987). *Deviance: The Interactionist Perspective.* (5th ed.). New York: Macmillan. An anthology of theoretical and empirical articles written from the interactionist perspective.

Schur, Edwin M. (1984). *Labeling Women Deviant.* New York: Random House. An extensive examination of women and their deviance from a labelling perspective.

CHAPTER 12

SOCIAL CONTROL THEORY

By Rick Linden

*T*he origins of social control theory can be traced back at least as far as the work of the social contract theorists. These philosophers were concerned with the question of how social order is possible, given their assumption that individuals are chiefly motivated by self-preference (Stark, 1976). The answer provided by Hobbes and others was that men agreed to give up their freedom to a sovereign in exchange for protection from the predations of others. A life which would be "solitary, poor, nasty, brutish, and short" (Hobbes, 1958:107) could be avoided only if a system of law was established and enforced.

Social control theory assumes that by nature human beings are neither good nor evil. Rather, we are born morally neutral. Unlike most of the theories which have been discussed in previous chapters, control theory requires no special motivation to impel people to deviate. Since our natural propensity is to gratify ourselves with no concern for right and wrong, and since the "wrong" way may be the quickest and most efficient way of achieving our goals, it is conformity rather than deviance which is problematic. Other theorists ask, "Why do they do it?"; the control theorist is concerned with the question "Why don't we *all* do it?" The answer given by control theory is: "We all would, if only we dared, but many of us dare not because we have loved ones we fear to hurt and physical possessions and social reputations we fear to lose" (Box, 1971:140). All societies have developed ways of making people conform. The control theorist is concerned with these processes which bind people to the social order.

THEORIES OF SOCIAL DISORGANIZATION—DURKHEIM, THRASHER, AND SHAW AND McKAY

DURKHEIM AND SOCIAL INTEGRATION

In his monograph *Suicide* (1951), Durkheim pointed out the importance of social bonds in the understanding of deviant behaviour. Both egoistic suicide and anomic suicide, he said, were due to a lack of social integration. Egoistic suicide results from a situation in which a person's social ties are weakened to the extent that the person is freed from social constraints and acts only on the basis of private interests. Anomic suicide occurs when a lack of social integration, caused by factors such as rapid economic change, leaves a society without a clear system of moral beliefs and sentiments. Without socially regulated goals, deviance is more likely, as people either pursue their aspirations without check or succumb to the mindlessness of pursuing unattainable goals and end their lives.

We have seen in Chapter 9 that in Merton's reformulation of anomie theory he shifted from Durkheim's emphasis on a society's failure to define appropriate goals to an emphasis on the failure to define the appropriate means of reaching common culture goals, and on the unequal distribution of legitimate means of reaching these goals. More faithful to Durkheim's view of the effect of the social bond on deviance were the social disorganization theorists—among them Thrasher, and Shaw and McKay.

THRASHER AND *THE GANG*

Thrasher, and Shaw and McKay, focused their attention on ecological studies of the city. Thrasher's classic study *The Gang* is still the most extensive study of juvenile gangs ever done. Thrasher located gangs both geographically and socially where there are breaks in the structure of social organization. They occur "in city slums characterized by physical deterioration, rapid succession of inhabitants, mobility, and disorganization; along economic and ecological boundaries; along political frontiers; ... and during adolescence, an interstitial period between childhood and maturity" (Kornhauser, 1978:51). Gangs arise spontaneously in areas where social controls are weak. They may become more integrated through conflict with adults and other groups of juveniles. Gangs are not necessarily delinquent, though delinquency will often be the natural result of the activities of groups of adolescents in communities where social institutions are not able to direct and control their behaviour (Thrasher, 1963). In the slum setting, delinquency was often the most exciting and interesting thing for these youths to do.

SHAW AND McKAY—ECOLOGICAL ANALYSIS

Thrasher's ethnographic study of lower-class Chicago neighbourhoods was followed by more quantitative research by Shaw and McKay. In their ecological analyses of the city of Chicago, Shaw and McKay found that certain areas had disproportionately high rates of officially recorded crime and delinquency. Rates were highest in slum areas near the city centre and generally declined as one moved outward. The exceptions to this gradient were business and industrial areas located away from the city centre. Roughly similar findings have been reported for a number of other cities. (See Jarvis and Messinger [1974] for an ecological analysis of London, Ontario.) Areas with high crime and delinquency rates were characterized by "physical deterioration, decreasing population, high rates of dependency, [and a] high percentage of foreign-born and Negro population" (cited in Thrasher, 1963:361). In many of these neighbourhoods, crime rates remained high over a long period of time, even though the racial and ethnic characteristics of the residents changed as new waves of immigrants moved into the city. Shaw and McKay attributed these high rates of crime to the failure of neighbourhood institutions and organizations such as families, schools, and churches to provide adequate social controls.

Shaw and McKay went on to develop a mixed model of crime and delinquency causation which involved elements of subcultural transmission theory, but they saw the origins of crime and delinquency in the failure of the community to "supply a structure through which common values can be realized and common problems solved" (Kornhauser, 1978:63). One of the earliest sociological explanations of crime and delinquency, "the implications of this kind of theory were profound. Rather than some racial or biological defect in children, delinquency was attributable to the way society was organized. Indeed, Shaw and McKay stressed the idea that poverty, deteriorating neighborhoods, and ethnic conflict were important in producing delinquency only if they result in social disorganization. It is the absence of social control, more than poverty per se, that is the source of delinquent gangs and illegal conduct" (Empey, 1982:192).

While control theory was not fully developed in the work of Thrasher and Shaw and McKay, from the 1930s to the 1960s subcultural and strain theories so dominated the field that there were very few additions to the social disorganization model (Kornhauser, 1978). There are a number of reasons why control theory all but disappeared from the scene following this rather promising beginning. The most important of these was that the early research was methodologically flawed. The relationship between independent variables such as social class, mobility, and heterogeneity was consistent with social control theory, but it also was consistent with other perspectives such as strain theory, and Shaw and McKay never directly measured the degree of social control which existed in a particular community. They inferred, but did not demonstrate, that higher-income communities were better organized than were lower-class slums. The type of research done by Shaw and McKay was also subject to the problem of the ecological fallacy. For example, consider the finding that official crime rates are higher in lower-class areas than in middle-class areas. The conclusion usually drawn from this finding is that being a member of the lower class makes one more likely to become involved with crime. However, this inference cannot be made logically. Perhaps crimes in lower-class areas are committed by middle-class residents of those census tracts. Perhaps the resident population is not responsible for crime at all. In his study of the impact of licensed hotels, bars, and shopping centres on Edmonton crime rates, Engstad (1975) showed that certain facilities provide opportunities for crime which may be attractive to people from other areas. Chambliss (1973) found that middle-class adolescents migrated to other parts of the city to commit their delinquencies.

Shaw and McKay utilized only officially recorded crime and delinquency. The development of self-report measures and the discovery that crime was also commonly committed by the middle and upper classes made their claim that crime was primarily a lower-class slum phenomenon questionable. At least part of the overrepresentation of these areas in official statistics may be due to the behaviour of law enforcement agencies. For example, Hagan, Gillis, and Chan (1978) have shown that an official police response was made to a higher proportion of complaints in areas Shaw and McKay might have called disorganized than in other areas. Finally, the vague and often value-laden term "social disorganization" fell into disrepute among sociologists.

Despite these problems, Thrasher and Shaw and McKay did lay the foundations for a control theory of crime and delinquency. Delinquents come from communities which are poorly organized and whose institutions are not well integrated. Delinquents' families aren't able to socialize them adequately, and their schools are inadequate. These elements all reappear in the work of later theorists.

EARLY SOCIAL CONTROL THEORIES— REISS, NYE, AND RECKLESS

ALBERT REISS

While the social disorganization theorists had been concerned with controls, Reiss (1951) was the first to distinguish between *social* controls, which include ties to primary groups such as the family and to the community and its institutions, and *personal* controls, which have been internalized by an individual. If these controls are absent, if they break down, if they are in conflict, or if they cannot be enforced, delinquency will result. Using information collected in the court files of a group of male juvenile probationers, Reiss found that success or failure on probation was associated with the absence of both social and personal controls.

IVAN NYE

Theoretically, the work of Nye (1958) simply expanded upon that of Reiss. However, methodologically, it represented a great advance. While Reiss had relied on court records of youth who were officially defined as delinquent, Nye developed a technique for measuring self-reported delinquency and gathered his data from a random sample of high school students in three small American cities. His book represented one of the first attempts at unravelling the causes of delinquency using this approach.

While Reiss did not elaborate on the theory underlying personal and social controls, Nye was quite explicit in stating his theoretical perspective. To Nye, "control theory assumes delinquency is not caused in a positive sense (motivated by the gains to be derived from it) but prevented (determined by the relative costs of alternative benefits).... Weak controls free the person to commit delinquent acts by lowering their cost relative to available alternatives" (Kornhauser, 1978:140–41). Individuals are motivated to achieve certain goals as quickly as possible, but are prevented from doing so by the laws and customs which societies establish to protect their members.

In expanding upon Reiss's distinction between personal and social controls, Nye outlined four types of controls:

1. Direct control from outside, such as that imposed by the police and parents.
2. Internalized control, which is self-enforcing and is exercised through one's conscience. Violations of internalized values will cause a child to feel guilt.
3. Indirect control, which is a function of the degree to which a child has affective ties with parents and other conforming individuals. Fear of embarrassing or hurting the person to whom the child has ties encourages conformity.
4. Availability of alternative ways of reaching one's goals.

Nye considered the family to be the most significant group in the development of social controls. The extent to which the family enforced external controls and the degree to which family members got along with one another determined the extent to which a child would develop internal controls. While some of Nye's specific findings will be discussed later in this chapter, it should be mentioned here that the results of his research did support his hypotheses concerning the relationship between the family and delinquency. Children who came from families which were close and in which there was agreement on basic values were unlikely to be delinquent.

WALTER RECKLESS

Reckless began with some interesting questions: Why is it that some boys who live in high delinquency areas do not become delinquent? What makes them different from their peers who are chronically in trouble? In his search for the answers to these questions, Reckless and several colleagues used teacher ratings and police records to find 125 "good" boys who were attending the sixth grade in Columbus, Ohio. On the basis of a survey given to the boys and interviews with their mothers, they concluded that the boys were unreceptive to delinquency because they had non-delinquent self-images which insulated them against the misbehaviour prevalent in their communities (Reckless, Dinitz, and Murray, 1956). In a follow-up study done four years later, the researchers found that little had changed. Nearly all the boys were still "good" and they still defined themselves as non-delinquents (Scarpitti et al., 1960). A cohort of "bad" boys followed by the researchers also showed stability, though in their case this involved continued delinquency (Dinitz et al., 1962).

While the findings are interesting, they don't suggest much of a theory. However, over a period of several years, Reckless refined his original ideas into *containment theory*. This theory was similar to those of Reiss and Nye in that Reckless hypothesized that external and internal controls acted as a defence against the pressures and pulls that might otherwise lead to criminal behaviour. The sources of outer containment (or external controls) were to be found in primary groups, most notably the family. Inner containment was developed through socialization and was a function of several components of self, including a favourable self-concept, strong goal orientation, frustration tolerance, internalized morals and ethics, and a well-developed ego and superego (Reckless, 1962). Reckless felt that internal controls were more important than external, because in our society individuals are away from their primary groups so frequently.

The research carried out by Reckless and his colleagues did provide support for the view that self-concept was an important predictor of delinquency. However, their work has a number of serious methodological problems which make it impossible to have much confidence in their findings. The most important criticism is that their measure of self-concept is ambiguous and that it includes a number of items that may be a result of involvement in delinquency rather than its cause. Two critics, Tangri and Schwartz (1967), sum up this concern as follows: "If everything is self, then self becomes another word for everything and its value is destroyed! A general hodgepodge of items from the [California Personality Inventory], questions asked to mother, son, and teacher all thrown into the pot of self seems to destroy the meaning of self for research usage." Later work by Jensen (1973) has shown that better measures of self-concept are related to delinquency. Nettler (1984) has cited research which has supported other dimensions of internal containment. While this has provided at least partial vindication for Reckless, little subsequent research has been done on self-concept and criminality.

The work of Reiss, Nye, and Reckless provided a promising beginning for contemporary control theory. The work of other researchers such as the Gluecks (1950), the McCords (1959), and Gold (1963) provided evidence which was for the most part consistent with the theory. In fact, control theory received much more empirical support than did the theories of Merton, Cohen, Cloward and Ohlin, Miller, and Sutherland, which dominated the field. However, it was not for two decades after the work of Nye and Reckless that control theory became widely accepted by criminologists as one of the major paradigms in explaining crime and delinquency. One reason for this was the difficulty in measuring personal controls, internalized control, and inner containment, which formed part of these theories. Explaining conformity by internal controls is often tautologous, in that researchers have had difficulty separating measures of internal states from measures of the deviant behaviour they are trying to explain. Such explanations also have difficulty in accounting for changes in levels of criminal activity at different points in the life cycle. Control theory also suffered because it did not fit in with prevailing intellectual fashions, and from the fact that those concerned with social policy did not feel that the theory provided much guidance for reducing crime and delinquency.

HIRSCHI AND THE SOCIAL BOND

It was not until the publication of Travis Hirschi's *Causes of Delinquency* in 1969 that control theory began to receive wider attention. Hirschi developed a clear and concise version of control theory, and presented an empirical examination of his theory which showed that it explained delinquency better than did competing theories. Like earlier control theorists, Hirschi postulates that individuals are more likely to turn to illegitimate means if their bond to society is weak or broken. For Hirschi, there are four interrelated aspects of the social bond which constrain our behaviour: attachment, commitment, involvement, and belief.

ATTACHMENT

Attachment refers to the degree to which the individual has affective ties to other persons, particularly those who belong to their primary groups. If an individual is sensitive to the feelings of others and close to those others, this attachment will constrain his or her behaviour because that individual will not want to hurt or embarrass the people he or she likes. Those lacking such ties will not have to consider the feelings of others and will be free to deviate. Thus, the person who dislikes his or her spouse will be more likely to have an affair than the person whose marriage is close. Youths who do not get along with their parents will be more free to commit acts of delinquency than those who are close to their families.

We have noted the problem faced by the early control theorists in measuring the degree to which norms have been internalized. If we say that conformity is caused by internal controls, and if our evidence of the presence of internal controls is a person's conformity, then we have explained nothing. Hirschi suggests that the concept of attachment can replace that of internalization, since the "essence of internalization of norms, conscience, or superego ... lies in the attachment of the individual to others" (1969:18). By removing the psychological element from the theory it becomes more easily tested, since attachment can be measured independently of deviant behaviour. Attachment is also able to explain the transitory nature of most deviance. The strength of one's relationships with others varies from time to time. Individuals may have a temporary falling out with their parents, leave home, and get married, all of which might alter their susceptibility to deviance. This is a more satisfactory explanation of misconduct than the hypothesis that a person gains, loses, and regains his or her conscience at various stages of the life cycle.

COMMITMENT

The essence of commitment lies in the pursuit of conventional goals. "The idea, then, is that the person invests time, energy, himself, in a certain line of activity— say, getting an education, building up a business, acquiring a reputation for virtue" (Hirschi, 1969:20). If a person decides to engage in deviance, that person will be putting his or her investment at risk. Thus, the student who has worked hard in school and who aspires to become a professional may avoid the temptations of delinquency for fear of jeopardizing this future career. On the other hand, the youth who is failing in school and who has no career aspirations may not feel as constrained. For the second youth, the immediate rewards of delinquency might outweigh the potential costs. Just as attachments can change over time, so can commitments. For example, the phenomenon of maturational reform—as we get older, we get better—can be explained by the fact that adults typically have a greater investment in conventional lines of activity than do adolescents.

Box has noted the importance of looking at commitment from the point of view of the actor rather than trying to define it objectively. To an outsider, a lower-class person may not seem to have as much to lose as someone from the higher classes, but it may not be perceived that way by that person. "Many people with apparently high levels of commitment, such as a university or college education coupled with good occupational prospects, may still deviate, simply because these achievements are defined as attributes whose loss would not be mourned" (1981:129).

INVOLVEMENT

If people are busy with conventional activities, they will not have time to engage in deviant behaviour. For example, if a student is busy at school and is involved in extracurricular activities, that student will not have as much opportunity to commit delinquencies as will peers who are not as involved.

BELIEF

Our belief in conventional values, morality, and the legitimacy of the law will constrain our behaviour. Unlike cultural deviance theorists, who believe that deviants are tied to value systems different from those of the rest of the population, Hirschi claims that society does have a common value system. However, individuals vary in the degree to which they believe they should obey the rules. While cultural deviance theorists tell us that acts which are deviant from the perspective of those who have the power to make and enforce the rules are *required* by the beliefs of members of certain subcultures, the control theorist says that deviant acts are made possible by the *absence* of beliefs forbidding them.

For the most part, research has supported Hirschi's theory, particularly for the variables of attachment and commitment. Belief in the law has also been found to be related to delinquency (Jensen, 1973; Gomme, 1985). The evidence concerning involvement is mixed, in that involvement in school activities is related to delinquency, while participation in sports, hobbies, and part-time jobs is not (Hirschi, 1969). In the remainder of this chapter, we shall look in detail at some of the research evidence bearing on control theory, discuss the weaknesses of the theory, suggest ways in which the theory might be revised, and consider its social policy implications.

FAMILY RELATIONSHIPS

Social control theory places a major emphasis on family relationships, since these provide children with the attachments necessary to restrain their involvement in delinquency. A number of aspects of family relationships are related to delinquency. This section will consider several of these dimensions. It should be noted that they may only be analytically distinct and are likely to be highly interrelated within a given family context.

STRENGTH OF FAMILY TIES

To the control theorist, strong ties within the family are important in the development of the social bond. If parents are close to their children and provide a congenial atmosphere in the home, family relationships should act as a deterrent to delinquency. Children in such families should be concerned about what their parents think of them, and should be less likely to become involved in delinquency.

A number of studies confirm this view. Warm, affectionate family relationships are associated with low rates of delinquency, while mutual rejection and hostility are typical of the families of delinquents (Glueck and Glueck, 1950; Nye, 1958; Gold, 1963; McCord, 1979; Gove and Crutchfield, 1982). Several of these researchers have also found that conflict between the parents also characterizes the families of delinquents. A study of Edmonton youth found that boys who found their families attractive and who were concerned with pleasing their parents were less likely to be delinquent than boys who did not have such close ties to their parents (Kupfer, 1966).

PARENTAL SUPERVISION AND DISCIPLINE

Children who are adequately supervised by their parents and whose parents discipline them in an appropriate fashion will have lower delinquency rates than will their peers who do not share these advantages. It is clear that the children of indifferent parents do not benefit from the freedom from supervision that these parents provide. A large number of studies have demonstrated the importance of parents' knowing what their children are doing and ensuring that they play with friends whom the parents consider suitable (Glueck and Glueck, 1950; Nye, 1958; Hirschi, 1969; West and Farrington, 1973; Wilson, 1980). Studies of delinquency in Montreal and Edmonton have found that supervision was more strongly related to delinquency than any other family variable (Caplan, 1977; Biron and LeBlanc, n.d.; Kupfer, 1966).

Closely related to supervision is parental discipline. Studies have consistently found the disciplinary practices of delinquent families to be different from those of nondelinquent families. Those families in which discipline was inconsistent or lax were much more likely to have delinquent children (Glueck and Glueck, 1950; Nye, 1958; West and Farrington, 1973). Children do not appear to learn from punishment unless it is administered in a clear, consistent manner.

There is also some evidence that very strict discipline is also associated with delinquency, particularly if it is associated with harsh physical punishment (Fischer, 1980). Very strict discipline is likely seen as unfair and may lead to feelings of frustration and resentment on the part of the child. Harsh punishment may be effective in gaining immediate compliance, but more moderate punishment is more effective in encouraging children to internalize a set of values which will ensure long-term compliance (Aronson, 1984).

PARENTAL ROLE MODEL

The final dimension of family relationships to be considered here is the role model provided by the parents. In his initial formulation of control theory, Hirschi argued that ties to parents will act as a deterrent to delinquency involvement regardless of the criminality of the parents. However, there does appear to be a relationship between the criminality of the parent and that of the child. For example, West and Farrington (1973) found that boys with at least one parent convicted of a criminal offence were more than twice as likely to become delinquent as those whose parents had no convictions. "Youthful crime often seems to be part of a family tradition" (West, 1982:44). West does not attribute these findings to the parents' deliberately transmitting criminal values to their offspring, as few of the children were involved in their parents' criminality and the parents expressed disapproval of their childrens' involvement in delinquency. The relationship is at least partially explained by the fact that parents with criminal records were lax in applying rules and did not supervise their children effectively. In light of West's findings that criminal fathers were likely to be on social assistance and unemployment benefits and that this dependency was repeated among their sons, it would appear that families with criminal parents may have a variety of problems which are manifested in both parental criminality and poor family relationships. West and Farrington (1977) also suggest that part of the relationship between parental criminality and delinquency may be due to labelling, as an act of delinquency leading to arrest was more likely to result in a conviction if a boy came from a criminal family.

While there is little to suggest that direct modelling of parental behaviour is a major cause of delinquency, it may be a factor in some types of offences. Rutter and Giller (1984) suggest that "criminal parents may provide a model of aggression and antisocial attitudes, if not of criminal activities as such" (1984:183). The fact that a high proportion of abusive parents were themselves abused as children provides support for the view that family violence is learned in childhood in the home (Steinmetz and Straus, 1980).

FAMILY RELATIONSHIPS AND ADULT CRIMINALITY

While most juvenile delinquents do not become adult career criminals, those who do preponderantly begin as juveniles. Further, the earlier the age at which serious delinquency begins, the more likely it is to continue in adult life (Petersilia, 1980). While very few longitudinal studies have been done by criminologists, these confirm the relationship between childhood family relationships and adult criminality. McCord (1979) followed up a group of men who had been part of the Cambridge-Somerville study 30 years earlier. She found that variables describing family atmosphere (parental aggression, paternal deviance, maternal self-confidence, supervision, mother's affection, and parental conflict) were related to criminal behaviour. In their longitudinal study of British adolescents, West and Farrington (1973) found that pre-adolescent boys who were aggressive typically became aggressive teenagers. Thus, poor family relationships have an impact on adult criminality as well as on delinquency.

SCHOOLING

Like the family, the school is of primary importance in socializing young people and is an important determinant of delinquency. The school is a pervasive influence in a child's life. For most of the year, children spend all day in classes and return to school after hours for other activities such as sports and dances. More important, the school is an arena in which an adolescent's performance is constantly being judged. Those who are successful enjoy the prestige conferred by teachers, parents, and other adults as well as by many of their classmates. Those who fail may feel that they have been rejected by the adult world as well as by their peers (Hargreaves, 1967; Polk and Richmond, 1972). For those who are successful in school and who enjoy their educational experience, the school provides a stake in conformity. However, those who fail do not have this stake in conformity and hence are more likely to become involved in delinquency. The correlation between school failure and delinquency is relatively strong and has been replicated in Canada (Kupfer, 1966; Gomme, 1985), Britain (Hargreaves, 1967) and the United States (Hirschi, 1969; Polk and Schafer, 1972).

The school has an impact on delinquency in two distinct, but interrelated, ways. First, the school is "one of the fundamental determinants of an individual's economic and social position" (Polk and Schafer, 1972:10). The school has taken over many of the occupational socialization functions which in earlier times were filled by the family. Over the past hundred years, formal educational qualifications have become the basis for entry into most occupations. Thus, a child's experiences in school will have a profound impact on that child's future life chances. The second way the school is related to delinquency is through its effects on the daily life of the child. For some, the experience is interesting, pleasant, and enriching. For others it is irrelevant, degrading, and humiliating.

Both types of impact have an effect on a student's stake in conformity. Those whose school experiences will clearly not qualify them for meaningful occupations may not have the same degree of commitment as do their peers whose expectations are higher. The daily consequences of failure and the resulting lack of attachment to the school also affect the child. In fact, research suggests that the daily problems of coping with school failure may be more strongly related to delinquency than is concern about the future. Linden (1974) found that measures reflecting present school status (whether the child liked school, finished homework, skipped school, thought good grades were important, and got along with teachers) were more highly correlated with delinquency than were measures of educational aspirations and expectations. This supports the view that present school status is a more important factor in delinquency causation than is the anticipated effect that school failure will have on one's eventual career. This was at least in part due to the fact that most of the youth surveyed felt they would complete high school and go to college despite the difficulties many were having in school.

Some criminologists see a broader relationship between the school system and delinquency. From a structural perspective, the school "cuts adolescents off from participating in the social and economic life of the community: it reduces their commitments and attachments" (West, 1984:169). Even within the school, the educational process involves the student in only a passive way. Polk and Schafer (1972) illustrate the irrelevance of the student role by asking what happens when a student dies. The student disappears without leaving a social ripple aside from family bereavement. The student's role is not one which has to be filled by someone else. This marginality may contribute to delinquency by leaving the adolescent relatively free of the commitments which constrain deviance.

RELIGIOSITY

Conventional wisdom has long held that people with strong religious commitment are not likely to become criminals. In the early American penitentiaries which were the predecessors of our current prison system, Bible study was a major rehabilitative tool (Rothman, 1971). The first educational programs run in prisons were implemented in order to provide inmates with the basic literacy skills needed to read the Bible and other religious literature, which was expected to motivate the offender to mend his ways.

Support for this common-sense view was provided by several early studies which showed a modest negative relationship between religious involvement and criminal behaviour. However, in 1969, Hirschi and Stark reported the results of a study which found that religious commitment was not related to delinquency. Neither church attendance nor the belief in supernatural sanctions for those who broke the rules nor the religiosity of parents was associated with delinquency. Because the work of Hirschi and Stark was methodologically superior to that of earlier researchers (and perhaps because of a secular bias among criminologists) the results of this study were commonly accepted as definitive. Most contemporary theories of crime causation do not consider religion to be an important explanatory factor.

However, subsequent studies found strong negative correlations between church attendance and delinquency (Higgins and Albrecht, 1977; Albrecht et al., 1977). How are we to reconcile these conflicting findings? One plausible answer has been given by Stark, Kent, and Doyle (1982) who concluded that the key to resolving the contradiction was to look at differences in the communities in which the research was carried out. The studies which found no relationship between religiosity and delinquency were done in areas where religious participation was low, while those communities in which a relationship was found had high religious participation.

Using data collected by other researchers, Stark and his colleagues provided additional evidence to support this view. They compared samples of boys from Provo, Utah, where the church membership rate is very high, with boys from Seattle, where church membership rates are among the lowest in the United States at 280 per 1000 inhabitants. In Provo, the correlation (gamma) between church attendance and delinquency was $-.45$, while in Seattle it was only $-.13$. The relationship also holds for adult crime. In another paper (1980), they found a relationship between church membership and crime rates for 193 U.S. cities. Stark et al. conclude that religiosity is related to crime and delinquency in communities where religion is important, but not in highly secularized communities.

Their explanation of why this should be the case is worth considering, as it has broader implications for social control theory. Stark, Kent, and Doyle believe that an individualistic, psychological view of the manner in which religion constrains behaviour has led researchers astray. Rather than looking at religion as affecting deviance through an individual's fear of religious sanctions, they suggest that "religion only serves to bind people to the moral order if religious influences permeate the culture and the social interactions of the individuals in question" (1982). Religion will have its greatest impact where it serves to bind its adherents into a moral community. In such a community, religious teachings will be salient and are likely to be consistently reinforced. Under these circumstances, an individual is less likely to consider deviant behaviour. The costs to someone who does decide to violate community norms may be high and the likelihood of finding reference groups which support such a violation will be relatively low. Religion will have a greater impact if it is part of the community's institutional order than if it is a private matter.

It seems clear that religiosity does constrain involvement in delinquent and criminal behaviour. However, this relationship is complex—it is greatest where there is a strong religious community; to some extent it is mediated by one's relationships with family and friends (Elifson et al., 1983); and it has the most impact on behaviour which may not be universally condemned by other segments of society (Linden and Currie, 1977).

FEMALE CRIMINALITY

Since control theory views conformity rather than deviance as its central question, the fact that women have higher levels of conformity than men should have played an important part in the development of the theory. However, this has not been the case. While some control theorists have looked at female crime and delinquency, most have not looked explicitly at sex differences in the degree of adherence to social bonds. In fact, Hirschi excluded females from his analysis, even though he had collected data from them.

A number of studies have been done which have compared male and female delinquency using a control framework. Typical of the results was Linden's (1974) finding, using Hirschi's California data, that social bond variables were correlated with the delinquency of both boys and girls, though the magnitude of the correlations was typically lower for girls. Part of the sex difference in delinquency involvement was related to higher levels of parental supervision and a lower level of attachment to delinquent peers reported by the girls than the boys. However, there were still differences between the sexes which could not be accounted for by control variables.

This type of research has been extended by Hagan, Gillis, and Simpson. Since their work has been discussed at length in chapters 4 and 5, it will be sufficient here to recall that the theory dealt with socially structured differences in sex roles, and that parents were more likely to place controls on the activities of daughters than of sons.

Naffine (1987) has suggested an interesting new line of inquiry which may shed more light on the causes of female criminality. She is critical of the view of control theorists that "it is the stereotypically female qualities (passivity, compliance, dependence) which bond women to the conventional order" (1987:131). Citing the finding that, contrary to Freda Adler's liberation hypothesis, the presence of "masculine" expectations was not a good predictor of female delinquency—masculine females were found to have strong conventional attachments (Shover et al., 1989; Thornton and James, 1979)—Naffine proposes that

> the new idea for feminism is that law-abiding women are not vapid, biddable creatures, clinging helplessly to conventional society. Instead, they are, to use Hirschi's description of conforming men, responsible, hardworking, engrossed in conventional activities and people and perfectly rational in their calculation not to place all this at risk by engaging in crime. (1987)

She observes that women are heavily involved in conventional activities, including both work and child-rearing, and hypothesizes that their intense involvement in nurturing children provides women with more powerful attachments to the conventional order. This bonding explains why the female crime wave postulated by Adler has not taken place. Those increases which have occurred have been in petty crimes such as shoplifting, which can be seen as a response to the increased economic marginalization of women rather than as a result of their liberation from traditional roles. While Naffine's thesis is only speculative, it should generate research which will have an important impact on future versions of social control theory as well as on our understanding of female criminality.

CRITICISMS OF SOCIAL CONTROL THEORY

The evidence we have reviewed in this chapter is generally supportive of control theory—in fact, many observers believe that empirical research provides more support for control theory than for any of its competitors. However, a number of questions have been raised about the theory which will be addressed in this section. While we can fairly take issue with specific versions of control theory—for example, Thomas and Hepburn (1983) raise questions about some aspects of Hirschi's theory—we will limit discussion to more general criticisms of the control perspective. Among these criticisms are that the theory does not explain upperworld crime; it does not adequately account for the motivation to deviate; it ignores the deterrent effects of law; its emphasis is too individualistic; and it is too conservative.

CONTROL THEORY DOES NOT EXPLAIN UPPERWORLD CRIME

The focus of control theory has been on street crime and juvenile delinquency, not on occupational crime committed by high-status adults. In fact, upperworld crime would appear to contradict control theory's emphasis on the role of commitment in preventing crime. However, control theory can be used to understand such crime.

In his analysis of the Watergate cover-up in the United States, John Hagan (1985:171–73) has provided us with a control theory of upperworld crime. The Watergate affair took place over a two-year period from 1972 to 1974. It involved the attempt by high U.S. government officials to conceal their involvement in an unsuccessful plot to break into the offices of the Democratic National Committee. Ultimately, these events led to the resignation of President Richard Nixon and to the imprisonment of a number of his senior advisors.

From a control perspective, such illegal events could have been prevented by beliefs that such acts were wrong. However, North American society has not clearly defined upperworld morality. Politicians and business leaders rarely receive more than token punishments for illegal activities and are more likely to see their behaviour as being only technically wrong than to consider themselves criminals. Transcripts of tapes made by Nixon reveal no concern with morality or ethics. In the absence of moral constraints, "the occurrence of such behaviors will depend largely on the risks and rewards ... associated with violating public and financial trust" (Hagan, 1985:173). As will be seen in Chapter 16, the rewards of upperworld crime are often very great. What, then, about the risks?

> The situational controls operative at the time of the initial Watergate offenses were inadequate. White House aides were able to manipulate funds and personnel for criminal political reasons with little expectation of detection. One reason why there was so little expectation of detection, of course, was that the criminals in this case were people who controlled the institutions of legal control (who could have been better positioned to deviate than those who controlled the FBI, the Justice Department, etc?). Furthermore, once "caught," punishment became problematic in an atmosphere confused by promiscuous discussions of pardons. The uncertainties surrounding these events emphasize, then, the porous nature of the controls operative in one upperworld setting. (Hagan, 1985:173).

In the discussion of the policy implications of social control theory in the next section of this chapter, it will be seen that the theory does have a message for those who wish to control deviant behaviour—Monitor behaviour, recognize deviance, and punish deviant behaviour. While these principles are intended as advice for parents raising children, they seem applicable in the control of upperworld crime as well. As Hagan tells us: "If there is a message to the policy-minded in the Watergate experience ... it is that checks and balances on power are crucial. Upperworld vocations, particularly politics and business, often carry with them a freedom to deviate unparalleled in the underworld. As control theory reminds us, unchecked freedom is a criminogenic condition" (1985:173).

CONTROL THEORY DOES NOT ACCOUNT FOR THE MOTIVATION TO DEVIATE

While there has been strong research support for control theory, critics have noted that a theory should also account for the motivation to deviate. To the control theorist, we would *all* be criminal or delinquent but for the restraints provided by various types of social controls. However, it does appear that this is only a partial explanation. Several factors can be postulated to increase the likelihood of deviance among those who lack ties to the conventional order

(Box, 1981). We shall consider just one of these here—ties to deviant peers, which have been found to be one of the strongest correlates of delinquency.

This can be accomplished if we integrate differential association and control theories. These two theories present conflicting notions about the causation of crime and delinquency. For the differential association theorist, the crucial concept is ties to others who provide a source of definitions favourable to violation of the law, while the control theorist claims that it is those individuals with no ties to others—not even deviant others—who are most likely to become deviant.

Control theory conceives of an individual's social bond as having only a single dimension, weak to strong. In incorporating differential association's emphasis on the importance of ties to deviant peers into the control theory analysis, however, the social bond should be seen as multidimensional: conventional—weak to strong; unconventional—weak to strong. In bringing the two perspectives together, it is proposed that the first step in delinquency involvement is a weakness in the controls that bind an individual to the conventional system. An individual without these ties does not have to consider the consequences his or her actions will have on institutional and personal relationships. With the person "adrift" in this way (Matza, 1964), delinquency is a possible alternative. We are then faced with the problem of accounting for the motivation to commit acts of crime and delinquency (if we wish to go beyond the control theorists' reliance on natural motivation) and with explaining how one learns the techniques and rationalizations that facilitate deviance.

At least part of the answer to these questions can be found in differential association theory. It is postulated that the adolescent's lack of ties to the conventional order will increase the likelihood of association with deviant peers, since the adolescent no longer has anything to lose by such affiliation. These ties will in turn increase the probability that the adolescent will be involved in deviance. The relationship between the variables is shown in Figure 12.1.

This extension of control theory has been found to explain more of the variation in delinquency than can either of its parent theories alone (Linden and Hackler, 1973; Linden and Fillmore, 1981). However, both of these studies utilized cross-sectional data rather than the longitudinal data which are more appropriate to the sequential theory we have proposed.

The sequential model proposed here is more consistent with control theory than with Sutherland's differential association. The control-differential association model does not necessarily entail the strong element of normative approval required by Sutherland's cultural deviance perspective. Even if this normative approval is not a factor (and it probably isn't for most criminal offences—see Kornhauser, 1978), delinquency may be fun and profitable and is not disapproved of by the delinquent's peer group. The internal dynamics of the group are such that it would be difficult for a recalcitrant member not to go along. Several researchers, including Short and

FIGURE 12.1
RELATIONSHIP BETWEEN CONTROL AND DIFFERENTIAL ASSOCIATION VARIABLES

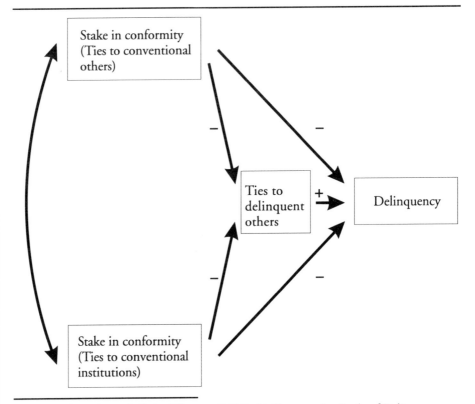

Source: Rick Linden and Cathy Fillmore. (1981). "A Comparative Study of Delinquency Involvement." *Canadian Review of Sociology and Anthropology* 18.

Strodtbeck (1965) and Velarde (1978), have found that delinquent boys may try to look "bad" or "tough" in front of the group even though they may express different views privately, as each believes the others are committed to such values. "An individual delinquent may wonder if or even think that his/her friends are not committed to delinquencies, but he/she can never confront the others to be sure of the degree of commitment they have" (Velarde, 1978).

Other sociologists have also attempted to integrate control theory with competing perspectives. Glaser (1978) has also tried to link control and differential association theories, and Akers (1977) and Conger (1980) have linked control theory and social learning theory. The most comprehensive extension of control theory has been carried out by Marc LeBlanc and several colleagues at the University of Montreal (LeBlanc and Tremblay, 1985; Caplan and LeBlanc, 1985; Fréchette and LeBlanc, 1985). In addition to control and differential association variables, these researchers have also included the variables of external social control, personality traits, and the structural conditions of sex and social status. Because none of the existing theories provides a complete explanation of crime and delinquency, it is likely that this integrative work will continue.

CONTROL THEORY IGNORES THE DETERRENT EFFECTS OF LAW

With their emphasis on the informal sanctioning system that is part of the process of socialization, most social control theorists pay little attention to formal legal sanctions. In fact, some have gone so far as to almost deny their effectiveness altogether. "For the great mass of infractions of the law ... the fear of consequences or the fear of punishment probably enters very little into causation" (Reckless, 1967). A more realistic view can be found in the work of Werner Stark, who has written extensively on the nature of the social bond:

> The assertion that a well-functioning and perfected legal system is the best safeguard of sociality and culture may at the first blush appear extravagant, but a short consideration will unavoidably prove it to be correct. The law, it is true, depends on social life, but social life in its turn depends for its continued existence on the law which it has created. If, in a thought experiment, we think away the law, and especially the executive organs of the law, we come face to face with the fact that in this case chaos would replace order, and universal insecurity, security. (1980:225–26).

To provide a more concrete example, the results of a police strike can be introduced. In Canada there have been several, the most notable occurring in 1969 in Montreal, during which thousands of apparently "law-abiding" citizens went on a rampage of theft and destruction (Clark, 1971). While it is true that most of the time most of the people obey the law without consciously thinking of the formal consequences, such sanctions are necessary in reinforcing the social controls which are operative most of the time.

Some control theorists have dealt with notions of deterrence. They have asked whether there is a relationship between an individual's perception of the likelihood of being caught and punished and deviant behaviour. Jensen (1969) found that boys whose attachments and commitments were low were less likely to be delinquent if they perceived that offenders faced a strong likelihood of being caught. While the work of Jensen and others has shown that perception of the likelihood of formal sanctions must be considered, it is a variable that has been largely ignored by control theorists.

CONTROL THEORY IS TOO INDIVIDUALISTIC

Recent work in control theory has focused on the social processes which tie individuals to the social order and has emphasized relationships with family, school, peer group, and church. Some have been critical of the theory for not examining larger structural factors which effect crime and delinquency (Box, 1981).

While this is a fair criticism of recent work, it is certainly not one which necessarily applies to a theory which has its roots in the work of Durkheim and the social disorganization theorists, who were quite concerned with the relationship between social structure and crime. What has been lacking since the 1930s is research on the linkage between structural factors and the individual. This would enable the question of why different groups vary in their rates of deviance to be addressed. Some work has been done in this area. For example, Linden, Currie, and Driedger (1985) have studied the structural characteristics of Mennonite society which contribute to its low rate of problem drinking. The work by Hagan, Gillis, and Simpson (1979) discussed in Chapter 4 suggests that the informal social controls provided by the family are greater for females than for males and at least partly account for their lower rates of involvement in delinquency. This conclusion has also been supported by Gomme (1985).

More work of this type must be done if control theory is to provide the beginnings of a comparative sociology of crime. For example, we might ask if control theory can account for differences in crime rates between different countries. Are the differences in crime rates between Japan and the United States due to differences in family structure or to the relevance of the school experience? Does the greater homogeneity of Japanese society make it easier to control deviance? Is there a stronger belief among Japanese in the morality of law, and does the type of loyalty shown by the Japanese corporation to its employees create stronger bonds to society?

CONTROL THEORY IS TOO CONSERVATIVE

The preceding chapters have shown that there is no simple explanation of crime. Research on the causes of crime is far from conclusive, and there are many different perspectives which can teach us something about these causes. In the absence of any consensus, some criminologists have taken an ideological approach in which theories are accepted or rejected on the basis of whether they are sufficiently conservative or radical. Robert Bohm has observed that "political and value preferences, ideology, empiricism, and positivism ... stand in the way of any unity between traditional and radical criminologists" (1987:327). For example, some radical criminologists have been very critical of theories of crime, such as control theory, which do not focus on the political and economic structures which produce crime.

To some degree, this critique is a fair one and is related to the criticism that control theory is too individualistic. Control theorists have emphasized people's immediate environment, and since the work of Shaw and McKay have not considered the political and economic structures of their communities. However, the mistake these critics make is to reject the theory, rather than recognize the fact that there is ample scope for incorporating control variables within a structural perspective. For example, Shaw and McKay pointed out the importance of community variables in the development of social bonds. The way in which control theory explains individual differences in criminal involvement is compatible with any number of structural theories, including radical theories, and provides the link between society and individual which these structural theories lack.

While the focus of control theory is on an individual's relationships with social institutions, it is obvious that there are structural factors which condition these relationships. Thus, while crime involves the behaviour of individuals, it has its origins in the social structure in which these individuals live. Lynch and Groves (1989) point out that "persons are more likely to conform when they stand to gain by doing so. But to make conformity attractive society must do something for the individual; it must provide minimal satisfaction for both human and culturally defined needs. Social structures which provide for these needs are more likely to encourage conformity" (1989:78).

In a society with low rates of deviance, social institutions will work together to encourage and to support conforming behaviour. If these institutions do not work together, and if individuals and groups are alienated from their society's institutions, rates of deviance will be high. Consider, for example, the problems faced by Canada's aboriginal people. They have far less power and fewer resources than other Canadians. They must cope with systems of education and religion imposed from outside which are not compatible with aboriginal customs and traditions. Forced attendance at residential schools and forced adoption outside of the community have destroyed family ties among them; crippling rates of unemployment mean no job ties. School curricula which are irrelevant to aboriginal students mean that children do not become attached to their schools. Many aboriginal Canadians must face daily encounters with racism. They must submit to government policies which do not allow aboriginal communities to achieve effective institutional integration. Under these conditions, strong social bonds are very difficult to develop and the high rates of crime described in Chapter 4 can be expected. As Manitoba's Aboriginal Justice Inquiry has concluded: "From our review of the information available to us, including the nature of the crimes committed by Aboriginal people, and after hearing the hundreds of submissions presented to us in the course of our hearings, we believe that the relatively high rates of crime among Aboriginal people are a result of the despair, dependency, anger, frustration and sense of injustice prevalent in Aboriginal communities, stemming from the cultural and community breakdown that has occurred over the past century" (1991:91). The impact of structural conditions on social bonds and on rates of crime and other deviant behaviour is illustrated in the following discussion of life on the Grassy Narrows reserve. In incorporating control elements within a structural perspective, it demonstrates the complementarity of the control and radical approaches.

The Grassy Narrows Reserve as Case Study

On July 25, 1991, Ontario Provincial Police Sergeant Tom Cooper was shot to death on the Grassy Narrows reserve near Kenora in northern Ontario. Arrested for the murder was a resident of the reserve who other residents have said was addicted to gas-sniffing. Behind this shooting lies a tragic story which illustrates the problems which have faced aboriginal people in Canada. The two excerpts which follow are from a book by Anastasia Shkilnyk, *A Poison Stronger Than Love: The Destruction of an Ojibwa Community.* The first is by the author, the second from the book's foreword by Kai Erikson, a sociologist who has spent many years studying the impact of natural disasters on people's lives. First, Shkilnyk describes some of the symptoms of the problems in Grassy Narrows:

> People who have never lived under such conditions may find it difficult to comprehend that there could be a human settlement in which odds of dying a natural death from sickness, old age, or misadventure hover around 25 percent. Yet, at Grassy Narrows, if the trend continues, three out of every four persons will die from an act of violence. This extraordinary probability of violent death spares no one, regardless of age. For people under nineteen, the odds of dying violently are even greater, and their deaths still more disturbing, because they will probably die by their own hand.
>
> There are other indications that Grassy Narrows is a deeply disturbed community. Cases of acute child neglect, for example, are in general extremely rare among Indian peoples, who are known for their indulgent devotion to their young. At Grassy Narrows, however, in just one year, the Children's Aid Society had to take away over a third of all children between the ages of five and fourteen because they had been physically abused, severely neglected, or simply abandoned. When this evidence of a discontinuity in the ability of a people to care for and protect their offspring is viewed alongside data on the extent of alcoholism and alcohol-related illness among adults, the inescapable conclusion emerges that aberrant and self-destructive behaviour has become the collective norm for this community. Social pathology, usually confined to a minority of the population, becomes represented by the majority. The data speak for themselves. The social conditions at Grassy Narrows are very serious, far worse than those found among other Indian bands in the region, and comparable to those documented for indigenous populations that have been through a major upheaval or disaster. (1985:10)

Erikson describes his perception of some of the reasons for the problems at Grassy Narrows:

> I had been asked to visit Grassy Narrows originally because thousands of pounds of methyl mercury had been dumped into the network of lakes and rivers surrounding the reserve, polluting the whole area. There were good reasons to suppose that the mercury had already found its

way into living human tissues, which meant that the people of Grassy Narrows were already suffering from the effects of the poison or were doomed to wait for months, years—even generations—to learn whether harm would yet be done to them or their offspring. And if that did not seem peril enough, the contamination of the waterways had created wrenching problems of an economic and a spiritual sort as well. The Ojibwa of Northwest Ontario have always seen the waterways as a source of life itself, and this had become doubly the case in recent years among the people of Grassy Narrows because virtually all the men of the band had been employed in one or another aspect of commercial fishing. The closing of the waters simply spelled the end of meaningful employment at the reserve, and by the time I visited Grassy Narrows, that proud band of hunters and trappers and fishermen had begun a slide into dependency and humiliation that is the main subject of this book.

It turns out, however, that the susceptibility of the people of Grassy Narrows to the effects of mercury poisoning was all the greater because of an event that had occurred some years earlier, one that seemed quite routine at the time but looks now, with the sharper vision that time sometimes confers, as even more traumatic. This was the relocation of the Grassy Narrows band from its old reserve along the edges of the English and Wabigoon river system to the narrow strip of land it now occupies.

In the sixty or so years that had preceded the relocation, the people of Grassy Narrows had experienced several shocks that served to weaken the fibre of Ojibwa society. Each of these shocks can be traced directly or indirectly to white contact, and each of them can be justly described as a disaster from the point of view of the people exposed to it. There was an awful influenza epidemic in 1919, for example, that not only killed off more than half the population but placed an enormous strain on the Ojibwa belief system because traditional ways of controlling the rages of nature proved powerless. At the same time, Indian children were being taken to residential schools many miles from the reserve and, as a matter of deliberate policy, were being stripped of their language, their native skills, and their very identity as Indians. And, meanwhile, a combined force of missionaries and Royal Canadian Mounted Police—not such good guys as the movies of my youth taught me—did everything it could to discourage the practice of Ojibwa religion, raiding sacred ceremonies and harassing other religious activities until the old faith had been driven underground. In the end, then, native religion became a private preoccupation of the aging rather than an integrative force for the young, and the people of Grassy Narrows, like their Indian neighbours elsewhere, lost much of the spiritual insulation that had been their ancestors' major protection against the effects of disaster and disruption.

This roster of troubles could go on at greater length, of course, but the relocation that took place in 1963 belongs at its head. The reasons for the move, Shkilnyk points out, seemed wholly sensible at the time, not only to white authority but to Indian leadership. But the costs turned out to be enormous. For one thing, dwellings in the new reserve were tightly bunched together in the manner of an agricultural village, violating the sense of space that is natural to hunting and gathering people everywhere. Moreover, an Ojibwa band is, first, a gathering of clans, and the way land is parcelled and arranged in the new reserve mixes up clan alignments to the point that frictions increase and factions multiply. Most important of all, perhaps, the new reserve is laid out in such a way as to disturb the ancient relationship between the Ojibwa and the rest of nature, for people now feel separated from the land and the water and the creatures of the forest, with which they have always felt a special kinship. They are, in a very real sense, removed from their natural habitat.

As a result of all this, Shkilnyk shows movingly, the Ojibwa of Grassy Narrows are truly a broken people. They neglect themselves out of an inability to believe that they matter, and though it may be difficult for those of us who live in secure comfort to understand, they not only neglect but abuse their own children. They live a life of sullen pain, blurred for days at a time by joyless bouts of drinking. And they die suddenly. Among these deaths are some that any coroner would feel compelled to call suicide, but there are others, impossible to document accurately, that come as a result of people destroying themselves out of simple failure to care. Grassy Narrows is a place of rape and murder and incest and thoughtless vandalism. It is a place of tremendous rage and frustration. It is, as one of the older men said to us, "a diseased place to live." (1985:xii–xv)

In looking for the causes of aboriginal crime, we can see the complementarity of the control and radical approaches. At one level, members of groups with high crime rates typically lack the social bonds that tie the rest of us to the social order. However, if we ask why the strength of social bonds is less among those who, like aboriginal people, are forced to live on the margins of society, we must turn to the work of radical theorists and their analysis of the political and economic forces which have created the poverty, powerlessness, and inequality which shape their lives.

POLICY IMPLICATIONS OF CONTROL THEORY

One additional criticism which has been made of social control theory is that it has few implications for social policy. Critics question the usefulness of a theory of the causes of delinquency if that theory implies no recommendations concerning what can be done about it (West, 1984). While not necessarily agreeing that this is a fair criticism (many sociologists argue that knowledge is of value in its own right and that even apparently useless knowledge may be of practical value in the future), control theory is not as bereft of policy implications as its critics believe. In fact, early control theorists were very aware of the policy implications of their work. For example, Shaw established and worked for many years with the Chicago Area Project, which was set up to strengthen community ties in a slum community. To illustrate some of the possible uses to which the findings of research done from a social control perspective might be put, we can consider the role of the family and the school in delinquency prevention.

POLICY IMPLICATIONS—THE FAMILY

Research has shown the importance of family relationships in the causation of delinquency. However, we are a long way from knowing what to do about this problem. How can we strengthen the family and make sure that parents love and care for their children? If anything, we are living in an era in which the family is becoming less stable as an institution.

While many of the problems in the family relationships of delinquents may require structural solutions, some small beginnings have been made in the task of trying to re-establish a bond between parent and child. One of the best examples of this is the work of Gerald Patterson and his colleagues at the Oregon Social Learning Center.

"When I met him, he was six and a half years of age. There was nothing about his appearance that identified him as the boy who had set the record." The words are those of Gerald R. Patterson, a family therapist at the Oregon Social Learning Center, in Eugene. The "record" to which he referred was the frequency—measured with painstaking care by the Learning Center's staff—with which Don, a small boy, displayed rotten behaviour. Nearly four times a *minute* while in his home, Don would whine, yell, disobey, hit, or shove. When he was not at home, telephone calls from teachers and merchants would mark his progress through the neighborhood: "He left school two hours early, stole candy from a store, and appropriated a toy from a neighborhood child."

Don had "a sleazy look about him," Patterson wrote, "like a postcard carried too long in a hip pocket." His violent outbursts were frightening; any simple request or minor provocation would trigger obscene shouts, attacks on other children, or assaults on the furniture. His mother was tired, depressed, and nearly desperate as a result of coping unaided with this monster—no babysitter would take on the job of minding Don, whatever the pay. She nevertheless persevered, changing his wet sheets, bathing and dressing him, even feeding him, all the while talking to him in tones that vacillated between cajolery and scolding, murmurs and shouts. When her seemingly bottomless patience was at last at an end, she would threaten or hit him with a stick. That produced only temporary compliance. When the father was home, things were not much different. The shouting and fighting between Don and his younger brother continued, occasionally punctuated by the father slapping both children.

Children like Don are the youthful precursors not only of difficult teenagers but sometimes of delinquents and adult criminals. The progression from violent, dishonest youngster to violent, dishonest teenager is not automatic, but it is common.

Source: James Q. Wilson. (1983). "Raising Kids." *The Atlantic* (October):45.

Based on his experiences treating several hundred families of antisocial children and on very detailed observation of interaction patterns within these families, Patterson (1980:89) concluded that since "antisocial acts that are not punished tend to persist," the key to changing the behaviour of these troublesome children was to punish their misdeeds. Hirschi observed that "this conclusion may come as no surprise to those millions of parents who have spent years talking firmly to their children, yelling and screaming at them, spanking them, grounding them, cutting off their allowances, and in general doing whatever they could think of to get the little bastards to behave; but it is exceedingly rare among social scientists, especially those who deal with crime and delinquency" (1983:53).

While this approach might seem disturbingly authoritarian to some, in fact Patterson is merely advocating techniques used by families which are successful in avoiding delinquency. You will recall that parental supervision and disciplinary practices were strongly related to delinquent behaviour. Patterson has determined that the key aspects of this process involve several steps which have been summarized as "(1) monitor the child's behavior; (2) recognize deviant behavior when it occurs; and (3) punish such behavior" (Hirschi, 1983:55). In a properly functioning family, the parents understand this process and the system is activated by the bonds of affection and caring which exist between parent and child. The key is not just punishment—many parents of problem children were found to punish them more often and more harshly than did the parents of normal children. However, the parents of problem children did not know how to punish their children, and punishment actually made things worse. Discipline was used, but it was erratic and unpredictable and not directed specifically at the child's misbehaviour. "The failure of parents to use reasonable reinforcements contingent on steadily monitored behaviour places the child in a situation in which he comes to understand that he cannot control by his own actions what happens to him" (Wilson, 1983:53). As a result, the children in effect train their parents (and others, such as teachers) to accept their misbehaviour.

Working with the families of pre-adolescent problem children, Patterson has developed a program in which parents are taught how to shape their children's behaviour by using nonphysical punishments (such as time-outs), by rewarding good conduct, and by interacting more positively as a family. This training process is often long and difficult. Many of the parents did not like their children, did not identify with the role of parent, and refused to recognize that their children were deviant (Patterson, 1980). Many were trying to cope with difficult economic and family situations as well as with the problems created by their antisocial children and resisted help.

The results suggest this program has potential. One evaluation showed that stealing was reduced from an average of 0.83 incidents per week to 0.07 incidents per week after the parent training program. The treatment effects persisted for six months, but by one year stealing rates had gone back to pre-treatment levels (Moore, 1979). This suggests that parental retraining may be necessary. Longer-term results were obtained with children diagnosed as aggressive, with whom program effects lasted longer than twelve months. The program also had a positive impact on siblings, indicating that the parenting skills of the parents had improved.

Programs like Patterson's are probably too expensive to be implemented on a broad scale. However, given the high concentration of criminality in a relatively small proportion of families shown by West and others, they do have some potential for reducing overall crime rates. The demonstration that improved parenting can have an impact on misbehaviour should provide encouragement to those advocating structural changes such as reduced un-employment, which are at least partly aimed at providing more family stability, and programs like day care, which provide substitute parents for children who might otherwise be left on their own. The results also suggest that research should be done on other methods of increasing parenting skills, such as providing training in high schools and for the parents of newborn children.

THE SCHOOLS AND SOCIAL POLICY

In their assessment of the role of the school in delinquency, Schafer and Polk suggest that the school fails in two ways: "The school not only fails to offset initial handicaps of lower income and minority group children, but actively contributes to education failure and deterioration. If this is true, the school itself becomes an important active force in the generation of delinquency insofar as it is linked to failure" (1967:236).

Research suggests that some schools and some teachers are better than others in helping children to function both educationally and behaviourally. Rutter and Giller (1984) have suggested a number of factors differentiating good and bad schools. These include the standards and values set and maintained by the school; the degree to which the students are allowed to participate in decision making; school and class size; staff turnover; and the degree of concentration of intellectually and socially disadvantaged pupils. Each of these factors has rather obvious policy implications.

A number of studies have looked at the impact of the teacher-student relationship on students' behaviour. Several British researchers (Reynolds and Sullivan, 1979; Hargreaves et al., 1975) have found that some teachers provoked deviance, while others were able to get students to co-operate more easily. Failure to get along with teachers may weaken an adolescent's commitment to school. It may also affect grades, by leading teachers to make negative judgements about a youth's abilities and character. Thus, the classroom process may help to weaken an adolescent's attachment and commitment to the school.

Others have proposed changes in the type of curriculum and in the manner in which this curriculum is taught. Weis and Hawkins (1978) have recommended that schools make greater use of programs like performance-based education, which involves establishing learning goals for each student and developing individually paced programs with rewards for improvement. They also suggest the use of cross-age tutoring and other ways of involving students in the operation of the school, thus enhancing their level of commitment.

Other research (Elliott, 1966; LeBlanc, 1983) suggests the importance of mechanisms for ensuring a transition from school to work, especially among those students who are not going on to university.

Schools must also ensure that their curriculum is relevant to the lives of their students. An example of irrelevancy can be found in the system of residential schools which serve Natives in the Canadian North. A child who grows up in a small settlement on the Arctic coast will be flown south to Yellowknife or another southern point for high school. Besides being cut off from family and community, the student is educated into a way of life which is very different from that which exists in the home village. As a result, students may no longer fit into their home communities. However, they are also not completely acculturated into southern ways (Brody, 1975). Increasing rates of crime and other deviance among people who lack strong community ties are one consequence of this system.

We should not conclude that it will be easy to make changes in the schools to reduce the likelihood that students will get involved in delinquency and subsequent adult criminality. It is difficult to make significant changes in large institutions which reflect an uneasy balance between a number of different interest groups. Even if we could make changes quickly, we could not be certain that they would have the desired effect. For example, research on the role of the schools would suggest that eliminating the system of placing students in tracks reflecting different capabilities would reduce delinquency. This may indeed be the case. However, Jensen and Rojek have pointed out that doing away with tracking may not reduce overall delinquency rates if we may assume that "youth in the more prestigious track have lower delinquency rates because they are in that track, and [we] suppose the prestigious track's insulating quality stems from the fact that it is limited to certain students." In that case, they argue, abolishing tracking could increase rather than decrease delinquency (1980:85). This is a rather speculative conclusion, but it makes the point that social intervention may not always have the desired result. Programs which separate misbehaving students may also have unintended consequences. Schafer and Polk (1967) discuss a program in which students with academic and behaviour problems were put into special classes and provided with individual instruction by specially selected teachers. The outcome of the program was negative—placement in a class with other poorly motivated students compounded their problems and further alienated them from the mainstream of school life.

Despite these potential problems, there is merit in trying to work within the school system. The research which has been done represents a promising beginning, but what is needed is a program in which the lessons learned are systematically applied to the schools on an experimental basis. The types of reforms which would be most likely to succeed would be beneficial to all students and possibly reduce delinquency as well. They would be relatively inexpensive (Rutter and Giller, 1984).

THE NEED FOR SOCIAL CHANGE

We constantly hear people advocating simple solutions to crime. If we can just lock more people up, or make sentences longer, or bring back capital punishment, they argue, crime rates will quickly go down. The discussions in this book of the causes of crime should make readers very sceptical about such quick and easy answers. Even the important steps of working with families and schools advocated in this section will not be enough to address the structural problems which produce crime.

If the linkages between control theory and radical theories of criminology are taken seriously, a realization of the importance of reforming social institutions in order to strengthen social bonds quickly follows. Both the need for this change and its magnitude were illustrated by the description of the problems facing the residents of Grassy Narrows. The consequences of not making changes are implied in the statement of Ovide Mercredi to Manitoba's Aboriginal Justice Inquiry: "If you accept our assertion that much of the root cause of Indian peoples' disproportionate conflict with the justice system lies in their poverty and marginal position in Canadian society, then what do you think is going to happen in the next 10 to 20 years, if radical changes are not made?" (Hamilton and Sinclair, 1991:90).

The inquiry recommended massive reforms in the way aboriginal peoples are dealt with. Among them are the resolution of land claims and the establishment of aboriginal self-government. The legacy of mistreatment of aboriginal peoples makes addressing their problems a very critical priority. But it is important that issues such as inequality and racism be addressed in all parts of Canada, if crime is to be reduced.

SUMMARY

The social control theorist assumes that individuals are more likely to become involved in crime and delinquency if their bonds to conventional society are weak or broken. Those who are not attached to others, who are not committed to school or occupational goals, and who lack strong belief in the legitimacy of the law will have the least to lose as a consequence of deviance.

Research has provided stronger support for social control theory than for any of its competitors. Family, school, and religious bonds have all been found to be related to delinquency involvement. Family relationships are the most important. The evidence shows that parents who do not get along with their children, who do not care about their children, and who do not supervise their children's activities are the most likely to be the parents of delinquents.

Now that the relationship between social bonding variables and delinquency has been well established, research from the social control perspective will be likely to follow three directions. First, more work will be done which integrates social control variables with those of other theories. Second, structural aspects of social control theory will be explored. Comparative research will look at the way structural differences between societies (or between different groups within a society) are reflected in different rates of crime and delinquency. Finally, more policy-related work based on the social control perspective will be done. Our knowledge of the factors that lead to deviance may enable us to reduce it.

BIBLIOGRAPHY

Akers, Ronald L. (1977). *Deviant Behaviour: A Social Learning Approach.* Belmont: Wadsworth.

Albrecht, Stan I., Bruce A. Chadwick, and David S. Alcorn. (1977). "Religiosity and Deviance: Application of an Attitude-Behavior Contingent Consistency Model." *Journal for the Scientific Study of Religion* 16:263–74.

Aronson, Elliot. (1984). *The Social Animal.* New York: W.H. Freeman.

Biron, Louise, and Marc LeBlanc. "Family and Delinquency." Unpublished paper, Université de Montréal.

Bohm, Robert. (1987). "Comment on 'Traditional contributions to radical criminology' by Groves and Sampson." *Journal of Research in Crime and Delinquency* 24 (November):324–31.

Box, Steven. (1971). *Deviance, Reality and Society.* London: Holt, Rinehart and Winston.

———. (1981). *Deviance, Reality and Society.* (2nd ed.). London: Holt, Rinehart and Winston.

Brody, Hugh. (1975). *The People's Land.* Markham, ON: Penguin Books.

Caplan, Aaron. (1977). "Attachment to Parents and Delinquency." Paper presented at the annual meeting of the Canadian Sociology and Anthropology Association, Fredricton, NB.

Caplan, Aaron, and Marc LeBlanc. (1985). "A Cross-Cultural Verification of a Social Control Theory." *International Journal of Comparative and Applied Criminal Justice* 9(2):123–38.

Chambliss, William. (1973). "The Saints and the Roughnecks." *Society* 11:24–31.

Clark, Gerald. (1971). "What Happens When the Police Strike." In Donald R. Cressey (ed.), *Crime and Criminal Justice.* Chicago: Quadrangle Books.

Conger, Rand. (1980). "Juvenile Delinquency: Behavior Restraint or Behavior Facilitation." In Travis Hirschi and Michael Gottfredson (eds.), *Understanding Crime: Current Theory and Research.* Beverly Hills: Sage.

Dinitz, Simon, Frank R. Scarpitti, and Walter C. Reckless. (1962). "Delinquency Vulnerability: A Cross Group and Longitudinal Analysis." *American Sociological Review* 27:515–17.

Durkheim, Émile. (1951). *Suicide.* Translated by John A. Spaulding and George Simpson. New York: Free Press.

Elifson, Kirk W., David M. Petersen, and C. Kirk Hadaway. (1983). "Religiosity and Delinquency: A Contextual Analysis." *Criminology* 21:505–27.

Elliott, Delbert S. (1966). "Delinquency, School Attendance and Dropout." *Social Problems* 13 (Winter):307–14.

Empey, LaMar T. (1982). *American Delinquency: Its Meaning and Construction.* Homewood, IL: The Dorsey Press.

Engstad, Peter A. (1975). "Environmental Opportunities and the Ecology of Crime." In Robert A. Silverman and James J. Teevan (eds.), *Crime in Canadian Society.* Toronto: Butterworths.

Fischer, Donald G. (1980). *Family Relationship Variables and Programs Influencing Juvenile Delinquency.* Ottawa: Ministry of the Solicitor General.

Fréchette, M., and Marc LeBlanc. (1985). Des Délinquantes: Émergence et Développement. Chicoutimi: Gaëtan Morin.

Glaser, Daniel. (1978). *Crime in Our Changing Society.* New York: Holt, Rinehart and Winston.

Glueck, Sheldon, and Eleanor Glueck. (1968). *Delinquents and Non-Delinquents in Perspective.* Cambridge, MA: Harvard University Press.

Gold, Martin. (1963). *Status Forces in Delinquent Boys.* Ann Arbor: University of Michigan Press.

Gomme, Ian. (1985). "Predictors of Status and Criminal Offences Among Male and Female Delinquency in an Ontario Community." *Canadian Journal of Criminology* 26:313–23.

Gove, Walter R., and Robert D. Crutchfield. (1982). "The Family and Juvenile Delinquency." *The Sociological Quarterly* 23:301–19.

Hagan, John, A.R. Gillis, and Janet Chan. (1978). "Explaining Official Delinquency: A Spatial Study of Class, Conflict and Control." *The Sociological Quarterly* 19:386–98.

Hagan, John, A.R. Gillis, and John Simpson. (1985). "The Class Structure of Gender and Delinquency: Toward a Power-Control Theory of Common Delinquent Behavior." *American Journal of Sociology* 90:1151–78.

Hamilton, A.C., and C.M. Sinclair. (1991). *Report of the Aboriginal Justice Inquiry of Manitoba.* Vol. 1. Winnipeg: Queen's Printer.

Hargreaves, David H. (1967). *Social Relations in a Secondary School.* London: Routledge and Kegan Paul.

Higgins, Paul C., and Gary L. Albrecht. (1977). "Hellfire and Delinquency Revisited." *Social Forces* 55:952–58.

Hirschi, Travis. (1969). *Causes of Delinquency.* Berkeley: University of California Press.

Hobbes, Thomas. (1958). *Leviathan.* Parts I and II. Indianapolis: Bobbs-Merrill.

Jensen, Gary F. (1973). "Inner Containment and Delinquency." *Journal of Criminal Law and Criminology* 64:464–70.

Jensen, Gary F., and Dean G. Rojek. (1980). *Delinquency: A Sociological View.* Lexington, MA: D.C. Heath.

Kornhauser, Ruth Rosner. (1978). *Social Sources of Delinquency.* Chicago: University of Chicago Press.

Kupfer, George. (1966). "Middle Class Delinquency in a Canadian City." Unpublished Ph.D. dissertation, Department of Sociology, University of Washington.

LeBlanc, Marc. (1983). "Delinquency as an Epiphenomenon of Adolescence." In Raymond R. Corrado, Marc LeBlanc, and Jean Trepanier (eds.), *Current Issues in Juvenile Justice.* Toronto: Butterworths.

LeBlanc, Marc, and Richard Tremblay. (1985) "An Integrative Control Theory of Delinquent Behavior: A Validation 1976–1985." Paper presented at the annual meeting of the American Society of Criminology, San Diego.

Linden, Eric. (1974). "Interpersonal Ties and Delinquent Behavior." Unpublished Ph.D. dissertation, University of Washington.

Linden, Rick, and Raymond Currie. (1977). "Religiosity and Drug Use: A Test of Social Control Theory." *Canadian Journal of Criminology and Corrections* 19:346–55.

Linden, Rick, Raymond F. Currie, and Leo Driedger. (1985). "Interpersonal Ties and Alcohol Use Among Mennonites." *The Canadian Review of Sociology and Anthropology* 22:559–73.

Linden, Rick, and Cathy Fillmore. (1981). "A Comparative Study of Delinquency Involvement." *Canadian Review of Sociology and Anthropology* 18:343–61.

Linden, Rick, and James C. Hackler. (1973). "Affective Ties and Delinquency." *Pacific Sociological Review* 16:27–46.

Lynch, Michael, and W. Byron Groves. (1989). *A Primer in Radical Criminology.* (2nd ed.). Albany: Harrow and Heston.

McCord, Joan. (1979). "Some Child-Rearing Antecedents of Criminal Behavior in Adult Men." *Journal of Personality and Social Psychology,* pp. 1477–86.

McCord, William, and Joan McCord. (1959). *Origins of Crime: A New Evaluation of the Cambridge-Somerville Youth Study.* New York: Columbia University Press.

Moore, D.R., B.P. Chamberlain, and L. Mukai. (1979). "Children at Risk for Delinquency: A Follow-up Comparison of Aggressive Children and Children Who Steal." *Journal of Abnormal Child Psychology* 7:345–55.

Naffine, Ngaire. (1987). *Female Crime: the Construction of Women in Criminology.* Sydney: Allen and Unwin.

Nettler, G. (1984). *Explaining Crime.* (4th ed.). New York: McGraw-Hill.

Nye, F. Ivan. (1958). *Family Relationships and Delinquent Behavior.* New York: Wiley.

Patterson, G.R. (1980). "Children Who Steal." In Travis Hirschi and Michael Gottfredson (eds.), *Understanding Crime: Current Theory and Research.* Beverly Hills: Sage.

Petersilia, Joan. (1980). "Career Criminal Research: A Review of Recent Evidence." In Norval Morris and Michael Tonry (eds.), *Crime and Justice: An Annual Review of Research.* Chicago: University of Chicago Press.

Polk, Kenneth, and F. Lynn Richmond. (1972). "Those Who Fail." In Kenneth Polk and Walter E. Schafer (eds.), *Schools and Delinquency.* Englewood Cliffs, NJ: Prentice-Hall.

Polk, Kenneth, and Walter E. Schafer. (1972). *Schools and Delinquency.* Englewood Cliffs, NJ: Prentice-Hall.

Reckless, Walter C. (1962). "A Non-Causal Explanation: Containment Theory." *Excerpta Criminologica* 1:131–34.

———. (1967). *The Crime Problem.* (4th ed.). New York: Appleton-Century-Crofts.

Reckless, Walter C., Simon Dinitz, and Ellen Murray. (1956). "Self-Concept as an Insulator Against Delinquency." *American Sociological Review* 21:744–46.

Reiss, Albert J., Jr. (1951). "Delinquency as the Failure of Personal and Social Controls." *American Sociological Review* 16:196–207.

Rothman, David J. (1971). *The Discovery of the Asylum.* Boston: Little, Brown and Company.

Rutter, Michael, and Henri Giller. (1984). *Juvenile Delinquency: Trends and Prespectives.* New York: The Guilford Press.

Scarpitti, Frank R., Ellen Murray, Simon Dinitz, and Walter C. Reckless. (1960). "The 'Good' Boy in a High Delinquency Area: Four Years Later." *American Sociological Review* 25:555–58.

Schafer, Walter E., and Kenneth Polk. (1967). "Delinquency and the Schools." In *The President's Commission on Law Enforcement and Administration of Justice, Task Force Report: Juvenile Delinquency and Crime.* Washington: U.S. Government Printing Office.

Shkilnyk, Anastasia M. (1985). *A Poison Stronger Than Love.* New Haven: Yale University Press.

Short, James, Jr., and Fred Strodtbeck. (1965). *Group Process and Gang Delinquency.* Chicago: University of Chicago Press.

Shover, N.S., J. Norland, J. James, and W. Thornton. (1979) "Gender roles and delinquency." *Social Forces* 58.

Stark, Rodney, Daniel P. Doyle, and Lori Kent. (1980). "Rediscovering Moral Communities: Church Membership and Crime." In Travis Hirschi and Michael Gottfredson (eds.), *Understanding Crime: Current Theory and Research.* Beverly Hills: Sage.

———. (1982). "Religion and Delinquency: The Ecology of a 'Lost' Relationship." *Journal of Research in Crime and Delinquency* 19:4–24.

Steinmetz, Suzanne K., and Murray A. Straus. (1980). "The Family as a Cradle of Violence." In Delos H. Kelly (ed.), *Criminal Behavior.* New York: St. Martin's Press.

Tangri, Sandra S., and Michael Schwartz. (1967). "Delinquency Research and Self-Concept Variable." *Journal of Criminal Law, Criminology and Police Science* 58:182–90.

Thomas, Charles W., and John R. Hepburn. (1983). *Crime, Criminal Law and Criminology.* Dubuque, IA: Wm. C. Brown.

Thornton, W.E., and J. James. (1979). "Masculinity and Delinquency Revisited." *British Journal of Criminology* 19.

Thrasher, Frederic M. (1963). *The Gang.* Chicago: University of Chicago Press.

Velarde, Albert J. (1978). "Do Delinquents Really Drift?" *British Journal of Criminology* 18.

Weis, Joseph G., and J. David Hawkins. (1979). *Preventing Delinquency: The Social Development Approach.* Seattle: Center for Law and Justice, University of Washington.

West, D.J. (1982). *Delinquency: Its Roots, Careers, and Prospects.* London: Heinemann.

West, D.J., and D.P. Farrington. (1973). *Who Becomes Delinquent?* London: Heinemann.

———. (1977). *The Delinquent Way of Life.* London: Heinemann.

West, W. Gordon. (1984). *Young Offenders and the State: A Canadian Perspective on Delinquency.* Toronto: Butterworths.

Wilson, Harriet. (1980). "Parental Supervision: A Neglected Aspect of Delinquency." *British Journal of Criminology* 20:203–35.

Wilson, James Q. (1983). "Raising Kids." *The Atlantic Monthly*, pp. 45–56.

FURTHER READING

Box, Steven. (1981). *Deviance, Reality and Society.* (2nd ed.). London: Holt, Rinehart and Winston. A readable book presenting an explanation of deviance based on several of the theories studied.

Gold, Martin. (1970). *Delinquent Behavior in an American City.* Belmont, CA: Brooks/Cole. A good example of how delinquency causation can be studied empirically.

Hirschi, Travis. (1969). *Causes of Delinquency.* Berkeley: University of California Press. The classic statement of contemporary social control theory. Hirschi explains the theory and tests it against its major competitors.

Kornhauser, Ruth. (1978). *Social Sources of Delinquency.* Chicago: University of Chicago Press. One of the best theoretical discussions of delinquency causation.

Polk, Kenneth, and Walter E. Schafer. (1972). *Schools and Delinquency.* Englewood Cliffs, NJ: Prentice-Hall. Good examples of the way in which the school can be involved in causing and preventing delinquency.

Stark, Werner. (1976). *The Social Bond: An Investigation into the Social Bases of Law-Abidingness,* Vol. 1. New York: Fordham University Press. This book is recommended for those interested in the philosophical basis of social control theory.

Thrasher, Frederic M. (1963). *The Gang.* Chicago: University of Chicago Press. First published in 1927, this book remains the classic study of urban gang delinquency.

P A R T

III

PATTERNS OF CRIMINAL BEHAVIOUR

Many different types of behaviour are illegal but vary in seriousness. Murder, for instance, is in a different category than not putting enough change in a parking meter. In Part III, we look at some of the kinds of misconduct that frequently occur in Canada.

When the average citizen thinks of crime, the images that most commonly come to mind are the so-called street crimes—robbery, assault, break and enter, and so on. These are also the kinds of offences that occupy most of the time and attention of the criminal justice system. In Chapter 13, many of these crimes are discussed. The routine activities theory, an attempt to account for patterns of criminal victimization, is also discussed using data collected on these conventional crimes.

Chapter 14 looks at the "organized" criminals who are in the business of providing access to illegal goods and services. Chapter 15 examines one of the most difficult types of crime to define—political crime. To illustrate the complex nature of political crime, several different examples are analyzed from three competing theoretical perspectives.

The final chapter in this text looks at crimes committed by "respectable" people: many of our leading citizens are white-collar criminals and many of our largest businesses are corporate offenders. This chapter makes the important point that the power we give to those in positions of authority and ownership in modern corporations may encourage them to become involved in illegal activities that cause a great deal of social harm.

It has been noted that the classification of theories into different types is somewhat artificial. However, some classification system is useful in organizing the work of many different theorists. In Part III, different patterns of crime are described, and they too are classified into types. Here as well there may be overlap between the different categories. A recently revealed fraud case involving the Bank of Commerce and Credit International (BCCI) is an interesting illustration, as it involves elements of all four types of crime which will be discussed in this section.

The BCCI case is extremely complex, and a brief description of the bank's activities will show the difficulty in placing it in any category. BCCI was chartered in Luxembourg, but had branches in 69 different countries. The easiest of BCCI's activities to identify is massive bank fraud. Financial investigators estimate that between $5.8 billion and $17 billion cannot be accounted for (*Maclean's* 5 August 1991: 24–28). While this money disappeared in many different ways, one of the simplest was fictitious loans made to individuals who apparently do not exist.

While this alone may be the largest bank fraud in history, it does not exhaust the criminal activity of those running BCCI. A number of terrorists, including Abu Nidal, used the bank's services to run their operations. The bank was also heavily involved in money laundering for both organized criminals and dictators such as Panama's Manuel Noriega and Iraq's Saddam Hussein, who wished to loot their countries' treasuries and move the money to a safe place. The bank's Canadian branch may have been used for laundering money. According to *The Globe and Mail*, a single customer may have deposited over $65 million in cash over a seven-year period. The deposits, which ranged from $600 000 to $1 million, were never properly recorded as cash deposits by the bank, and were not detected by bank inspectors. The money was not credited to anyone's account, but was put into the bank's own transit account, converted into U.S. currency, and transferred to a BCCI bank in Switzerland (*The Globe and Mail*, 15 August 1991:A1–2).

What's more, within BCCI there was apparently a division called the "black network" which operated its own arms dealing business and smuggled drugs and gold. According to *Time*, this network was involved in bribery, extortion, kidnapping, and possibly murder. Many security and intelligence agencies, including the CIA, maintained accounts at BCCI and used them to finance covert operations. For example, the U.S. National Security Council used BCCI to fund arms shipments for Iran at a time when there were no official dealings between the two countries (*Time* 29 July 1991). There has been speculation that these contacts with governments have led some governments to interfere with the investigation into BCCI activities.

BCCI has therefore engaged in white-collar crime (bank fraud), organized crime (laundering drug money), political crime (financing terrorist activities), and conventional crime (murder and extortion). There is every likelihood that BCCI is a prototype for criminal enterprises of the future.

CHAPTER 13

CONVENTIONAL CRIME
By Daniel J. Koenig

*C*onventional crime generally refers to individual or small group violations of traditional criminal laws in which there is some proximate contact between the offender and the victim or the victim's possessions. Such violations are only a subset of crime and do not necessarily include crimes or other behaviours which cause the most financial loss, physical harm, or deaths.

Police statistics for homicide, and victimization survey data for other crimes, will be presented in this chapter to discover patterns of conventional crimes. Offences which will be examined include homicide, sexual assault, nonsexual assault, robbery, break and enter, motor vehicle theft, personal theft, and household theft. Each of these offences constitutes a violation of the Criminal Code. Each involves an immediate and clearly identifiable victim, and is customarily of concern to public police departments.

There are, as earlier chapters of this book have indicated, many competing and sometimes contradictory explanations of why crimes occur. Most of these explanations have been concerned with offender motivation. Since the 1970s, however, criminologists have been asking different types of questions and coming up with new insights. In addition to asking why a person commits a crime, criminologists also have been asking why one person rather than another is victimized by a crime. Offender motivation is seen as only one aspect of the answer to this question.

THE LIFESTYLE/EXPOSURE, ROUTINE ACTIVITIES APPROACH

The best known of these new insights is probably the lifestyle/exposure theory developed by Hindelang et al. (1978). This theory accounts for personal victimization. The theory states that the probability of crime varies by time, space, and social setting. The lifestyle and routine activities of people place them in social settings with higher or lower probabilities of crime. Lifestyles, in other words, expose people to higher or lower risks of being victimized. Hindelang and his associates found support for this theory using data from the National Crime Surveys in the United States.

A LIFESTYLE/EXPOSURE THEORY OF CRIME

Hindelang and his associates developed a "lifestyle/exposure" theory of personal crime. They cite a wide range of data about crime which are consistent with, and supportive of, the eight propositions in their theory. The propositions are as follows:

1. The probability of suffering a personal victimization is directly related to the amount of time that a person spends in public places (for example, on the street, in parks, etc.), and particularly in public places at night.
2. The probability of being in public places, particularly at night, varies as a function of lifestyle.
3. Social contacts and interactions occur disproportionately among individuals who share similar lifestyles.
4. An individual's chances of personal victimization are dependent upon the extent to which the individual shares demographic characteristics with offenders.
5. The proportion of time that an individual spends among nonfamily members varies as a function of lifestyle.
6. The probability of personal victimization, particularly personal theft, increases as a function of the proportion of time that an individual spends among nonfamily members.
7. Variations in lifestyle are associated with variations in the ability of individuals to isolate themselves from persons with offender characteristics.
8. Variations in lifestyle are associated with variations in the convenience, the desirability, and vincibility of the person as a target for personal victimization.

Source: Michael J. Hindelang et al. (1978). *Victims of Personal Crime: An Empirical Foundation for a Theory of Personal Victimization* (pp. 251–64). Cambridge, MA: Ballinger Publishing Company, a subsidiary of J.B. Lippincott Company.

Cohen and Felson (1979) refined the lifestyle exposure theory into a "routine activities approach." This approach begins with the observation that three factors must be present simultaneously for a crime to occur: a motivated offender, a suitable target, and a lack of effective guardianship of that target. Effective guardianship refers to actions such as removing ignition keys from a car and locking the door (by motorists), drawing a steel mesh curtain overnight across glass display windows of jewellery (by shopkeepers), or taking evening walks on streets where there are many people rather than walking alone in an isolated park or down a dark alley (by pedestrians).

SOCIAL CHANGE AND CRIME TRENDS:
THE COHEN-FELSON ROUTINE ACTIVITIES APPROACH

As it was originally stated, the lifestyle/exposure theory was somewhat static in orientation. Cohen and Felson added a more dynamic aspect to the general approach by showing that crime trends have been consistent with longer-term social changes in routine activities. In the following passage, they ask a number of questions. In the article, itself, they provide persuasive data to answer these questions affirmatively.

Routine activities may occur (1) at home, (2) in jobs away from home, and (3) in other activities away from home. The latter may involve primarily household members or others. We shall argue that, since World War II, the United States has experienced a major shift away from the first category into the remaining ones, especially those nonhousehold activities involving nonhousehold members. In particular, we shall argue that this shift in the structure of routine activities increases the probability that motivated offenders will converge in space and time with suitable targets in the absence of capable guardians, hence contributing to significant increases in the direct-contact predatory crime rates over these years.

   If the routine activity approach is valid, then we should expect to find evidence for a number of empirical relationships regarding the nature and distribution of predatory violations. For example, we would expect routine activities performed within or near the home and among family or other primary groups to entail lower risk of criminal victimization because they enhance guardianship capabilities. We should also expect that routine daily activities affect the location of property and personal targets in visible and accessible places at particular times, thereby influencing their risk of victimization. Furthermore, by determining their size and weight and in some cases their value, routine production activities should affect the suitability of consumer goods for illegal removal. Finally, if the routine activity approach is useful for explaining the paradox presented earlier, we should find that the circulation of people and property, the size and weight of consumer items, etc., will parallel changes in crime rate trends for the post–World War II United States.

Source: Lawrence E. Cohen and Marcus Felson. (1979). "Social Change and Crime Rate Trends: A Routine Activity Approach." *American Sociological Review* 44 (August):588–608.

   The Cohen-Felson routine activities approach is very similar to the lifestyle/exposure theory of Hindelang et al. Crime trends are seen to be expected outcomes of routine activities and reflect changes in patterns throughout society. Cohen and Felson take offender motivation as a given. Their objective is to demonstrate the relationship of crime trends with changes in target suitability and effective guardianship.

The research findings to be reported in this chapter are consistent with a lifestyle/exposure or routine activities approach. Before looking at specific types of crimes in detail, a brief overview of some of these findings will be provided.

WHO

For crimes of violence, such as nonsexual assault and homicide, rates of both victimization and offending are highest among younger people, males, and those who spend a large number of evenings in activities away from the home. It is also the case that offenders overwhelmingly select lone victims rather than multiple victims. In other words, a young man spending his evenings on the streets or in bars is exposed to a greater risk of victimization than is an older man spending evenings at home with his family.

If people with certain lifestyles are going to be more exposed to crime victimization as they go about their routine activities, then the probability of becoming a victim of crime is not randomly distributed. People who have been victimized once, therefore, should have a higher probability of being victimized a second time than people who have not been victimized at all would have of being victimized a first time. These probabilities will change, of course, if the typical lifestyle and exposure of the already victimized person is changed to reduce the risk of subsequent victimization. Repeated victimization of the same victim (or victim's household), by both the same type of crime and different crimes, has been observed frequently in surveys both in the United States (U.S. Dept. of Justice, 1974a, 1974b; Hindelang et al., 1978; Sparks, 1981) and in Canada (Koenig, 1977; Sacco and Johnson, 1990). For example, the General Social Survey conducted in 1988 indicated that fewer than one out of four Canadians fifteen years of age or older had been victimized in the preceding year. However, of those who were victimized, more than one out of three were victimized more than once. Such a pattern provides support for the lifestyle/exposure theory.

WHERE

Crimes involving personal contact are more likely to occur in less guarded surroundings than they are in the home or neighbourhood, or at work. At first glance, the theory appears to be contradicted because the home is so often a locus for personal crime. However, if one were able to calculate the risk of being victimized in each setting per thousand hours of exposure within that setting, the safety of the home would become much more apparent. Cohen and Felson (1979) did make those calculations with data from the U.S. crime victimization surveys. The results supported their general theory.

WHEN

Crimes of personal violence generally peak during the summer months. With the longer days and warmer weather, people are more likely to place themselves at risk as suitable targets by being outdoors more, or to have windows and doors open if they are at home. It is probable that an individual's actual risk of victimization at these times is lower because there are so many other people about. However, people expose themselves to these lower risks for much longer periods of time. Hence, their total risk and the actual amount of personal victimization both increase. Another peak for some crimes occurs in December, when people are likely to increase their interpersonal contacts during Christmas by shopping, visiting, or going to parties.

The *incidence* per hour of most crimes is highest in the evening, particularly from 6 P.M. to midnight. These are the hours when effective guardianship is minimized, as darkness reduces visibility and fewer people go about their routine activities in public places. It may, however, be the case that the *rates* at which most crimes are committed would be highest between midnight and 6 A.M., if crimes were calculated on the basis of the number of people awake at various hours of the day (and night) rather than on the basis of the number of crimes committed per total population asleep or awake.

An exception to the above is the crime of break and enter, which has a higher per-hour incidence 6 A.M. and 6 P.M. than during night-time hours. But this, too, is consistent with the theory. Because break and enter is a crime of stealth, it is most likely to be attempted when people are not present. This occurs most often during the daytime, when most people's routine activities and lifestyle make it most probable that their home will be unoccupied and not effectively guarded.

PATTERNS OF SPECIFIC CRIMES

To what extent is the lifestyle/exposure approach to understanding crime consistent with known facts about patterns of specific types of crime? To answer that question, types of conventional crime which are commonplace and/or which are a source of considerable concern to the public will be examined.

MURDER AND OTHER CRIMINAL HOMICIDES

LEGAL MEANINGS OF TYPES OF HOMICIDE

Homicide is a legal term which has somewhat different meanings in different countries and at different times. In Canada, it is a general category which refers to an act in which the life of one person is lost at the hands of another.

Some homicides are legally justifiable. In Canada, criminal homicide refers to first and second degree murder, manslaughter, and infanticide.

Criminal homicide is classified as murder when the person who causes death means to cause death or means to cause bodily harm which is likely to result in death. Murder is said to be in the first degree when the killing is planned and deliberate; when the victim is employed in certain occupations concerned with the preservation and maintenance of public order (for example, police officer, correctional worker) and acting in that capacity; or when the killing occurs in connection with certain specific offences such as sexual assault, kidnapping, or hijacking. Other murders are second degree murders. Manslaughter is a type of criminal homicide in which one person kills another in the heat of passion caused by a sudden provocation. Infanticide is an archaic category of criminal homicide applying to women who cause the death of their newborn children in a disturbed state of mind as a consequence of giving birth.

Police statistics probably underestimate the true number of criminal homicides. Some missing persons, particularly young women and children, are likely to have been murdered. If neither a body nor other evidence of a murder is discovered, however, one cannot conclude that a specific missing person has been murdered. Homicides also may be disguised as accidental deaths or suicides, although the police are skilful at detecting the differences. Despite these problems, and despite the limitations inherent in all official police crime statistics, heavy reliance must be placed on police statistics.

Incidence

What do police statistics tell us about homicide? In 1989, there were 657 criminal homicides reported for Canada. Almost half of these were first degree murders. Forty-three percent were second degree murders, 7 percent were manslaughters, and a total of three were infanticides. There were an additional 829 attempted murders. In contrast to these 657 criminal homicides, there were approximately 3500 deaths by suicide and 4000 traffic fatalities. Homicides accounted for less than one-half of one percent of violent crimes.

In 1989, the number of criminal homicides per 100 000 population for Canada was 2.51. This was typical of the rate for the 1980s, and below the highest recorded rate of 3.09 in 1975. The Canadian rate of criminal homicides was almost exactly twice the rate for England and Wales, where there were 627 criminal homicides in 1989. In contrast, in the United States during 1989 the FBI (1990) recorded 8.7 murders (including "non-negligent manslaughters") for every 100 000 people, a 4 percent increase in the murder rate from the previous year. This was down from the recent peak of 10.2 per 100 000 in 1980, when more than 23 000 murders were tallied.

Provincially, Statistics Canada (1990b) reported that Manitoba had the highest homicide rate (3.96) in 1989, as it had over the ten-year period from 1979 to 1988. Prince Edward Island had the lowest rate in 1989, with 0.77

homicides per 100 000 residents, as well as the lowest average rate of all provinces throughout the preceding ten-year period. Generally, the western provinces and Quebec have homicide rates higher than the Canadian norm, while Ontario and the Atlantic provinces have homicide rates lower than the Canadian norm. Montreal's rate of 4.14 homicides per 100 000 residents was the highest rate for any of Canada's 25 census metropolitan areas in 1989. In order, the other census metropolitan areas with homicide rates above the Canadian norm in 1989 were Edmonton (3.86), Winnipeg (3.12), and Vancouver (2.99).

Pattern

Contrary to impressions conveyed by news media and entertainment programs, only about one-sixth of the murders which took place in Canada in 1989 were committed in connection with another crime, most often robbery. Most Canadian victims of homicide knew their assailants. For homicides solved in 1989, Statistics Canada (1990b) disclosed that a large proportion of victims (41 percent) were acquainted with their slayer as a lover, as part of a love triangle, as a business associate, as a close friend, or as a casual acquaintance. A similarly large proportion of homicide victims (37 percent) were related to their slayers through an immediate, extended, or common law family relationship.

About five out of six of these family relationships involved victims and offenders who were immediate family members. The most common pattern was for men to kill their legal or common law spouses (76 cases), after which slightly more than one-third then took their own lives. Only 2 of the 22 women who killed their spouses also took their own lives. There were also 16 parents killed by their children, 43 children killed by their parents, and 10 victims slain by a sibling.

This general pattern is similar for England and Wales, as well as for the United States. In the United States, however, the incidence of homicides involving victims and offenders known to one another is somewhat lower, and the incidence of homicides committed in connection with another crime is somewhat higher than in Canada.

Other than this and the vast differences in the murder rates among the countries, the other major difference among Canada, the United States, and England and Wales is the method of homicide most often used. For 1989, Statistics Canada (1990b) counted shootings (33 percent) as the most common method of homicide, followed by stabbings (26 percent) and beatings (19 percent). The proportion of U.S. homicides involving a firearm was almost twice the Canadian proportion. The FBI (1990) recorded 62 percent of murders in the United States during 1989 as being committed by a firearm, usually a handgun. By contrast, in England and Wales, shootings were the fifth most common method of homicide and accounted for only 7 percent of homicide deaths during 1989. There, the Home Office (1990) reported that during 1989 the most common methods of homicide were the use of a sharp instrument (32 percent), hitting or beating (18 percent), strangulation (15 percent), and the use of a blunt instrument (12 percent).

For 1989, Statistics Canada (1990b) reported that one-half of all homicides occurred in the residence of the victim, and another one-tenth in the residence of the accused. An additional 16 percent occurred in another private place or in the workplace. Only 14 percent were known to have taken place in a public place. Ten percent of victims were slain in an unknown location. The location of Canadian homicides is consistent with the findings that homicide victims and their assailants are usually known to one another, and that homicide is frequently the culmination of an argument engaged in by people as they go about their routine daily activities.

THE LAST DANCE

Many criminal homicides entail husbands killing their wives when their wives start to run their own lives. The following is an example.

"What's this about divorce?" he said.

"Oh, when did you get back in town?"

"I've been back in town for a day or two. I guess we should get this divorce thing finished."

" Well, I've got the thing all ready. You just have to go up to this guy and sign the papers."

As Stella Morrison went to get the address, her husband of 24 years pulled out his gun ... and shot her....

"Maybe I possessed my wife," he explains. "Maybe I never did love my wife. Maybe my wife was one of my possessions, maybe, maybe, I don't know what love is. Maybe, like the doctor claims I'm a narcissist, that I don't love anybody but myself."

"But I was certainly a good husband to my wife...."

Source: Neil Boyd. (1988). *The Last Dance: Murder in Canada* (p. 91). Scarborough: Prentice-Hall of Canada, Ltd.

Victims

During 1989, approximately five out of every eight homicide victims in Canada were male. The percentage of female victims was somewhat higher than normal and represented the highest proportion of female victims since 1981. Typically, about one out of four victims is between 20 and 29 years of age, and almost as many are between 30 and 39 years of age. Statistics Canada (1990b) reported that during 1989 almost half of the victims were single and about a quarter were married. Most of the rest were separated or divorced, although about one out of twenty was widowed. Proportionately, female victims were more likely than male victims to be married, while male victims were more likely than female victims to be single.

Suspects

Information about suspects is based on police records. In 1989, police in Canada cleared 89 percent of the homicides committed (Statistics Canada, 1990a). About five-sixths of these were cleared by charge, and one-sixth cleared otherwise. The most common reason for clearing a homicide other than by charge was that a suspect committed suicide, often immediately after committing the homicide.

In 1989, almost 10 percent of suspects were under 18 years of age, and approximately half ranged from age 18 to age 29. In general, another 20 to 25 percent are in their thirties, with sharply decreasing percentages at higher ages. Extrapolating from data reported for 1989 by Statistics Canada (1990b), it appears that almost half of all suspects were single, and more than 35 percent were married (a category which includes common law marriage).

However, this pattern varies by gender. At the time they were accused, 61 percent of men but only 29 percent of women were single. Female accused were more likely than male accused to be married (46 percent compared to 29 percent). As was typical throughout the 1980s, almost nine out of ten suspected killers were males. Women as well as men are much more likely to be killed by men than by women.

The overall pattern to homicide is consistent with a lifestyle/exposure, routine activities orientation. Homicide is typically the final word in an argument arising among people known to one another as they engage in their normal daily activities. Even the locale of homicide, most often the victim's own home, is where most people spend the greatest proportion of their time.

Methods of homicide also reflect lifestyle. Firearms, particularly handguns, account for the majority of homicides in the United States, where they are widely owned. The percentages of homicides attributed to firearms drops sharply in Canada, and especially in England and Wales, as do the percentages of the population in these countries who own handguns. In Canada, and particularly in England and Wales, methods of homicide tend to reflect the routine availability of potential weapons—knives, fists and feet, blunt instruments, and so on. Finally, both homicide suspects and victims are disproportionately young, male, and unmarried—characteristics that are associated with less structured lifestyles and higher levels of physical aggression.

ASSAULTIVE BEHAVIOURS

People may experience assaults of both a sexual and a nonsexual nature. Most assaults are not reported to the police. Consequently, police statistics about these offences may reveal more about the operations of the police and the criminal justice system than about the characteristics of the crimes themselves (Ericson 1981, 1982; Ericson and Beranek, 1982).

DOES VIOLENCE BREED VIOLENCE?

Gwynn Nettler has undertaken an exhaustive and painstaking review of research related to homicide. A variety of evidence, some of it included below, has led him to conclude that research data indicate that violence does breed violence.

Another aspect of continuity is noted in the contagion of violence. The contagion has been measured in many ways. It has been recorded, for example, in short-term modelling. Watching violence induces it.... This common observation has been authenticated by laboratory studies.... Publicity given to bizarre crimes stimulates their imitation....

Another repeatedly noted aspect of the contagion of violence is that children who have been brutally treated tend to become brutal....

Contagion is demonstrated by the fact that violent times produce violent acts. This is not a tautology; it is a statement of the continuity of homicide across dimensions of magnitudes of violence. For example, the causal web in which behavior is generated may be described as a "moral atmosphere." One part of that atmosphere is indicated by living in countries that go to war. Archer and Gartner (1976) have compiled a Comparative Crime Data File that includes time-series rates of homicide during this century for more than 100 governments. From these data Archer and Gartner tallied changes in domestic homicide rates experienced by 50 states that engaged in what the investigators call "nation-wars" against changes in "internal" homicide rates experienced by 30 control countries that had not engaged in such wars. Substantial postwar increases in domestic homicide rates are found among those countries that had gone to war. Archer and Gartner report that "these increases were pervasive ... [they] occurred after large wars and smaller wars, with several types of homicide rate indicators, in victorious as well as defeated nations, in nations with both improved and worsened postwar economies, among both men and women ... and among offenders of several age groups" (p.937).

Source: Gwynn Nettler. (1982). *Killing One Another* (pp. 220–21, 267). Cincinnati, OH: Anderson Publishing Company.

To learn more about these crimes, criminologists and public officials have surveyed samples of the population, asking them directly about their experiences as victims of specific types of crimes. Large-scale surveys of this nature have been undertaken annually in the United States since 1973 and intermittently in England and Wales since 1981 (1972 for burglary of dwellings). These surveys produce results which are claimed to be generalizable to the entire populations of those countries, notwithstanding the inherent problems of such surveys as noted by Nettler (1984).

The closest Canadian approximations to these are the General Social Survey (GSS) conducted in 1988 and scheduled to be repeated in 1993, and the Canadian Urban Victimization Survey (CUVS) conducted in 1982. The remainder of this chapter will have heavy reliance on these surveys.

The Canadian studies also have some limitations. The Canadian Urban Victimization Survey was administered only in seven urban areas and it is now becoming somewhat dated. It was administered only to people at least sixteen years of age (as against fifteen years of age for the General Social Survey), and both studies surveyed only people with telephones—which effectively excluded transients. Transients, in particular, are thought to have high rates of both victimization and offending.

SEXUAL ASSAULT

Long-term comparisons of the Canadian incidence of various types of sexual assault are difficult because the Criminal Code of Canada was changed in 1983. Under the new law, a variety of sex-related offences were reclassified as sexual assaults, of which there are three types. These are sexual assault (not involving a weapon or serious injury), sexual assault with a weapon (including threats to a third person or causing bodily harm), and aggravated sexual assault (which entails wounding, maiming, disfiguring, or endangering the life of the victim).

While there may be a gender-related physiological base to aggression, it also appears that the power (domination) component of coercive sexual assault is linked to learned gender roles. In the case of forcible rape, for example, it is almost invariably the male (or role-playing male) who is the assailant and the female (or role-playing female) who is the victim. This is as true of heterosexual rapes as it is of homosexual rapes within prisons, a vast number of which appear to go unreported.

HOMOSEXUAL RAPE WITHIN PRISON

Homosexual rape is a severe problem in prisons. In the following passage, an ex-convict alludes to convicts' fears of being gang raped during a prison riot (a "bingo").

Two notorious drag queens wasted no time in setting up business on the first floor of B-block by closing off the front of their drums [cells] with blankets. They even went so far as to knock down the brick wall partition that separated their cells to enlarge their sleeping quarters, dragging in mattresses from nearby empty cells and then painting their light bulbs red! A sign hanging out in front of their drums declared that this was a "Liberated Zone"! Contrary to vicious rumours later circulated by the frustrated guards, no youthful offender was muscled or forced to submit to sexual activities. That's not to say that a lot of the younger prisoners weren't scared about being raped. To be on the safe side a lot of the weaker cons asked some of the tougher ones if they could cling to them for protection, thinking that it would be better to submit to one guy rather than to an imaginary wolfpack.

Source: Roger Caron. (1985). *Bingo* (p. 128). Toronto: Methuen. Reproduced with permission from Stoddart Publishing Co. Limited.

Feminists, criminologists, and others have long contended that police statistics grossly underreport the true incidence of both rape and the sexual abuse of children. One reason for this is that many victims never report their victimization to the police. Another is that when they do so, the police do not necessarily believe their account of the incident. Clark and Lewis (1977) conducted an early study into the correlates of rapes reported to a Canadian police department. They discovered that the police did not consider the majority of the reported rapes to have been actual rapes. They also ascertained that the majority of the rape victims in their study were young (under 25) and single, a conclusion consistent with the findings of most victimization surveys.

For 1989, Statistics Canada (1990a) data indicate that five-sixths of sexual assaults reported to the police were considered by the police to be actual cases of sexual assault. Almost nine out of ten cases of aggravated sexual assault and of sexual assault with a weapon were considered by the police to be actual crimes.

Incidence

The rate of police-reported sexual assaults in 1989 was 102 known incidents per 100 000 population. More than 95 percent of these were common sexual assaults. Somewhat more than 3 percent were sexual assaults with a weapon, and the remainder were aggravated sexual assaults.

The 1988 GSS sample was too small to generate enough cases of sexual assault to reliably generalize the findings. However, the 1982 seven-city Canadian victimization survey reported a rate of victimization by sexual assault of 3.5 per 1000 persons at least sixteen years old. About half of these were cases of molestation, with the remainder split about evenly between rape and attempted rape. Only 38 percent of these incidents were reported to the police. Of those victims who did not report incidents of sexual assault to the police, 33 percent were fearful of revenge and 43 percent were deterred by the attitudes of the criminal justice system. (Respondents could give more than one reason.) As a CUVS bulletin (1984:10) noted: "For sexual assault victims, then, the ability of the police to mitigate the dangerousness of the situation or to prevent recurrence may be in question, and for many there seems to be concern that police intervention would compound rather than alleviate the problem."

Victims

The CUVS bulletins also provide information about victims of sexual offences. Canadians most at risk were women, young people (under 25 years of age), those with lower family incomes, and those who are most likely to engage in evening activities outside of the home. The U.S. Bureau of Justice Statistics (1990) report similar correlates for rape (or attempted rape) from the annual American victimization surveys. The rate of rape was higher for young American women between the ages of 16 and 19 than at any other age. Although the rate of rape declined with age, it remained substantial through age 34.

Offenders

Of those charged by Canadian police with some type of sexual assault during 1989, more than 98 percent of adults charged were men. About one in four was a young offender. Victim surveys provide additional information about the characteristics of offenders. De Verteuil and Johnson (1986) have provided some CUVS data that, together with other data from CUVS bulletins, permits a calculation that most incidents (85 percent) involved a single offender and three-fourths of assailants were over 25 years of age. They also reported that in 1982 almost two-thirds of the assailants of young Canadian women (aged 16 through 24) were strangers.

This differs from more recent data on one type of sexual assault reported by Flanagan and Maguire (1990) from the National Crime Survey of 1988 for the United States. These data indicate that victims of rape and attempted rape in the United States were somewhat more likely to be victimized by nonstrangers than by strangers. In about one out of five attacks the offender was a relative, usually a spouse or ex-spouse. An additional 45 percent of these nonstranger assailants were well known to their victims, and 35 percent were casual acquaintances. These variations may result from cultural differences, differing methodologies, the more inclusive "sexual assault" category in the Canadian data, or a greater tendency in 1988 than in 1982 to consider as a crime what has come to be called date rape or acquaintance rape.

Patterns

CUVS found that 30 percent of all attacks occurred within the victims' own homes, 19 percent in the neighbourhood, 7 percent at work, and 44 percent elsewhere. About one-quarter of the sexual assaults involved the use of a weapon, particularly when younger offenders were involved. An injury was suffered by the victim in 65 percent of sexual assaults; 32 percent of these involved a financial loss through property damage or theft, with the average loss being $266 among those who did suffer such a loss.

The phenomenon of date or acquaintance rape probably accounts for Flanagan and Maguire's (1990) finding of the high proportion of American rape incidents reported to have taken place at or in the victim's home (25 percent) or at, in, or near the home of a friend, neighbour, or relative (15 percent). Including both stranger and nonstranger assailants, Flanagan and Maguire report that one out of five U.S. victims of rape or attempted rape were attacked on the street, not near their own or a friend's home. Most of the remaining victims were attacked in other public places which were not near their own or an acquaintance's home.

The American victims were most likely to be attacked between 6 P.M. and midnight. Gibson et al. (1980) reported a similar pattern in Winnipeg, where more than four out of five rapes known to police occurred between 8 P.M. and 8 A.M. Gibson et al. also reported that a considerable number, a quarter of the total, involved female victims who accepted rides from strangers, were hitchhiking, or were followed home from a late night out. They used their findings in developing a "situational theory of rape," in which rape was seen as the outcome of a number of situational facilitants such as time, place, the presence or absence of others, and so forth.

Such a view is broadly similar to the lifestyle/exposure approach and the routine activities approach of Cohen and Felson. A pool of motivated offenders (emotionally immature potential assailants) can be assumed to exist. Females, or children (in the case of various types of child molestation), are seen as suitable targets by such motivated offenders. To the degree that the lifestyles or routine activities of potential victims bring them into contact with motivated offenders under situations where they are ineffectively guarded (being young, being out alone at night, being intoxicated, hitchhiking, going to the home of strangers, inviting potential offenders—nonstrangers as well as strangers—into their own home, and so on), then the essential components for the commission of the crime are all present. As was the case with homicide, lifestyle is related to victimization.

CHILD MOLESTATION

Sexual assaults against children generally do not come to the attention of the authorities, nor do the standard victimization surveys provide information about child molestation. Nevertheless, the 1984 Parliamentary Report of the Committee on Sexual Offences against Children and Youth (the Badgley Report) demonstrated that this is a significant problem in Canada, as Garbarino's (1989) survey of the research indicates that it is in the United States.

The Badgley report estimated that about one-half of females and one-third of males have been victimized by unwanted sexual acts, such as being exposed to, being sexually threatened, being touched on sexual parts of the body, or being sexually assaulted (including attempts). Most of these incidents initially happened when the victims were children or youths. About one-half of the assailants were friends or acquaintances, approximately one-quarter were family members or persons in a position of trust, and only about one-sixth were strangers. Thus, it is not surprising that a majority of sexual assaults against Canadian children occurred in the homes of victims or suspects. Almost all assailants of children and youth were males.

NONSEXUAL ASSAULT

As with sexual assault, amendments to the Criminal Code of Canada in 1983 created three levels of nonsexual assault parallel to sexual assaults. Level 1 common assaults accounted for 80 percent of all nonsexual assaults in 1989. Fewer than 10 percent were level 2 assaults (with a weapon or causing bodily harm), and fewer than 2 percent were level 3 aggravated assaults. There are additional special categories of assaults. These include unlawfully causing bodily harm; discharging a firearm with intent to kill, maim, or disfigure, to threaten life, or prevent an arrest; assaults on police; assaults on other public peace officers; and other assaults. These special categories made up less than 10 percent of all police-reported nonsexual assaults in 1989.

Incidence

Statistics Canada (1990a) tallied 726 nonsexual assaults per 100 000 Canadian population (or about 7 per 1000) for 1989. This compares with 68 assaults per 1000 Canadians at least 15 years of age that were reported for 1987 in the General Social Survey. Statistics Canada (1990c) notes that police-reported assaults per capita increased by about one-half during the 1980s, and that the police-reported assault rate per 1000 Canadians in 1989 was about five times what it had been in 1962.

Some of this increase may be attributable to a slightly increased probability of reporting assaults to the police when they occur. Most of it, however, is likely attributable to the fact that many behaviours which are now reported to the police and treated as crimes were considered to be private or noncriminal matters in the past. Domestic assaults, child abuse, sibling violence, and elder abuse are examples (as are date rape, child molesting, and sexual touching, in the case of sexual assaults). Support for this interpretation is provided by the annual National Crime Surveys in the United States. These surveys show that self-reported victimization by violent crime decreased by more than 10 percent between 1973 and 1989. Generally, survey-reported rates of violent victimization were lower in the 1980s than in the 1970s, though the reverse tended to be true for police-reported rates of violent crime.

Pattern

The 1987 General Social Survey defined assault as involving the presence of a weapon, an actual attack, or a threatened attack. Sacco and Johnson (1990) have assembled various tabulations to indicate that a weapon was present in almost one out of five assaults reported in the GSS. Five out of eight assaults involved a physical attack, most commonly involving the victim's being hit, kicked, slapped, or knocked down. Frequently, as well, the victim was grabbed, held, tripped, jumped, or pushed.

One-half of these assaults occurred in a private residence, usually the victim's own home. About one in ten took place in a bar or restaurant. The location of the remainder was likely to be some other public place or, somewhat less likely, at the workplace or in another commercial building. Assaults were most likely to take place in the months of September, October, and November; the three subsequent winter months had the lowest incidence of assaults.

Nine percent of the GSS assault victims required outpatient medical care, and an additional 4 percent received some type of medical attention away from a hospital. About one out of five victims reported some difficulty carrying out their main activities after the assault, usually for only one day. A somewhat smaller proportion reported an economic loss as the result of the assault. Only about one victim in nine sought the help of an agency to help them deal with their victimization. Most victims did not know whether any agency existed to help them, and almost one out of four victims did not feel that they needed any help from an agency.

Victims

People most likely to be nonsexually assaulted were males, younger people, those who engaged in the largest number of evening activities outside of the home, those whose principal activity was being a student, and the separated or divorced. Generally, these characteristics appear to have independent effects in increasing the risk of victimization. For example, males between the ages of 15 and 24 who engaged in 30 or more evening activities outside the home monthly were between three and four times as likely to be nonsexually assaulted as were other Canadians. However, women engaging in frequent evening activities outside of the home were more likely to be nonsexually assaulted if they were between 25 and 44 than if they were 15 to 24 years of age. There was also a tendency for the risk of victimization to increase among those who consumed alcoholic beverages, particularly among males who averaged two or more drinks per day.

Men were most likely to be victims of assault if they were single; women if they were separated or divorced. Both men and women were most likely to report that they had experienced a recent assault if they had some postsecondary education. This may be the consequence of such respondents defining as assaults behaviours which others might not perceive to be an assault. Rates were also higher in urban areas than in rural areas, and British Columbians were twice as likely to report that they had been assaulted than were other Canadians. Assault rates were also higher in the Prairies and the Atlantic provinces than the Canadian norm, but in Quebec the self-reported rate was substantially less than half the Canadian norm.

Offenders

The GSS indicated that most victims knew their assailants. About twice as many offenders were acquaintances as were relatives. In only 27 percent of the cases was the assailant said to be a stranger. In almost three-quarters of the attacks a sole offender was involved. Of those who were charged by Canadian police in 1989 for one of the three levels of nonsexual assault, one out of six was under 18 years of age; of the adults charged, almost 90 percent were males. In the earlier CUVS survey, De Verteuil and Johnson (1986) reported that about half of all assailants were estimated by victims to be less than 25 years old, most commonly between 18 and 25. They also noted that young female offenders disproportionately assaulted females (80 percent), and young male offenders typically assaulted males (two-thirds). Because of the greater frequency of male assailants, however, female victims were about as likely to be assaulted by a male as a female, and more so in the American victimization surveys.

DOMESTIC ASSAULTS

Domestic assaults, particularly "series assaults" (those carried out on a repeated basis), have long been of concern to women's groups and others. MacLeod (1980:21) estimated that "every year, 1 in 10 Canadian women who are married or in a relationship with a live-in lover are battered." She argues, as do others (Gates, 1978), that mate-battering is a socially learned aspect of the male role, rather than an inherent biological aspect of maleness. Those who advance such an explanation point to violence by an individual playing the male role in homosexual relationships as an example of this learned role. Whatever the explanation, one fact is clear. When domestic violence occurs, it is overwhelmingly the woman who is the victim of domestic assault. For example, the CUVS revealed that three-fourths of the victims of family-related assaults were women. This rate increased even more when the assaults were between current or former spouses. Women who were assaulted by a spouse or former spouse were about twice as likely to be injured and about four times as likely to receive medical treatment as were women who were assaulted by other males.

IS BATTERY TIED TO GENDER ROLES?

In the following passage, a lesbian discusses her experience as a battered mate. The larger context of her report makes it clear that she was the subordinate and dependent partner, characteristics commonly learned in our society to be associated with feminine gender roles.

Lesbian battery is much more than physical violence between two lesbians. Leading up to the physical violence is the psychological preparation of the battered by the batterer. The daily psychological dose of criticism and lack of respect for me as a whole woman eroded my sense of myself. When the physical violence started, I felt dependent upon her and stayed whereas just six months earlier I had vowed I would leave if she ever hit me (she battered her two previous lesbian lovers). But deeper than the physical ties were the psychological ones that had been created; my "love" for her made me feel that she would change; she "promised" she would change; I felt I was "giving up too easy" if I left, etc.

Source: Susan Marie. (1984). "Lesbian Battery: An Inside View." *Victimology* 9(1):16–20.

In recent years, other types of family violence have been recognized as problems for intervention. These include parental assaults on adolescents and violence by children directed against one another and against parents. As with spousal assaults, many criminal assaults are not perceived to be crimes when committed against other family members.

Historically, little attention has been paid to these assaults, and so we know little about them. Even when they have been studied, they have been typically studied more from a child-welfare than a criminal perspective. Consequently, past studies have tended to lump together both criminal and noncriminal types of behaviour under the rubric of "child abuse and neglect." Family assaults on or by adolescents are only now emerging into public consciousness as criminal matters.

Based upon Pagelow's (1989) review of the largely U.S. literature, it appears that adolescents twelve through seventeen years of age represent from about one-third to one-half of the cases of child mistreatment. The severity of abuse tends to increase after the child has reached fifteen years of age. Victims are disproportionately girls, from lower income groups, and from families with either one child only or with four or more children. There is a suspicion that abuse may be higher than reported among boys and families at other income levels, but that such abuse might be concealed by victims, either because of learned male gender roles (toughness, "taking it like a man," and so forth) or a tendency on the part of middle-income groups to treat such assaults as private matters because of a concern about "respectability."

Of course, violence involving adolescent children is a two-edged sword. Adolescent children can also be quite violent both outside and within the family. However, as Pagelow has noted, parents may deny all but the most serious abuse by their children because of shame or a desire to keep the matter private, and sibling violence may be underreported either because the victims may not be believed or because adolescent violence is viewed as normal. As well, parents may wish to protect their children from involvement with the criminal justice system. For reasons such as these, we know almost nothing about the incidence and patterns of such a problem, though Wiehe (1990) provides some limited data on the basis of questionnaires returned from a self-selected sample of 150 U.S. respondents, mostly female. One thing we do know is that one-sixth of those charged by Canadian police with assault in 1989 were below the age of eighteen. It is probable that those who engage in violence outside of the family are also more likely to engage in violence within the family.

ELDER ABUSE

The abuse of elderly people can take place in both domestic and institutional living situations. Moreover, like child abuse, there are numerous types of abuse which are not necessarily violations of any criminal law. Some types of neglect, psychological abuse, and even material abuse are examples of antisocial behaviours which may not be criminal matters. But most authorities agree that physical violence toward elders constitutes a criminal assault.

In Canada, Podnieks (1989) notes that the 1986 Census indicated that 91 percent of Canada's nearly two and a half million seniors lived in private dwellings (not necessarily their own). Based on a national random sample in that year, Podnieks reported a (cumulative) prevalence of about 5 per 1000 elderly persons, or approximately 12 000 in total, who had been subjected to physical violence. A mere one of four victims had reported the incident to the police. In only one case were criminal charges laid. The most common reasons for not reporting the incident were that it was either a family matter or not serious enough to report to the police.

The majority of the victims suffered physical injuries; more than one-fourth required medical attention. Podnieks reported that the victim's spouse was the abuser in a significant majority of these cases. Almost two-thirds of the victims were men, despite the far greater number of women among the elderly population. Finally, victims were more likely than nonvictims to report that they lived with a person with serious health, emotional, or alcohol abuse problems.

This pattern of elder abuse is quite different from the pattern reported by Wolf and Pillemer (1989) Massachusetts, New York State, and Rhode Island.

Elder abuse in the latter study, however, was not limited to physical violence but included a wide range of additional phenomena, lawful as well as unlawful. The differences in results between the two studies merely highlight the fact that our awareness and knowledge of elder abuse is probably as limited now as was our knowledge about spousal assaults and child abuse two or three decades ago.

It is significant to note that neither of these studies explored the issue of elder abuse within institutions. It appears to be assumed that because very few elders live in institutions, most elder abuse will take place outside of institutions. While that assumption may be true, there is no reason to believe that elder abuse does not exist in institutions, where it might even be proportionately more prevalent and more severe than in private dwellings. Very simply, we do not have a sufficient base of reliable data upon which to base *any* firm conclusions about the incidence, severity, or characteristics of elder abuse.

LIFESTYLE FACTORS IN ASSAULTS

Lifestyle factors, obviously, are involved in assaults. Victimization is particularly high among the young, males, those who are not married (other than widowed), students, and the unemployed. These are people who are most likely to be out in public places and engaging in evening activities outside of the home. These are precisely the circumstances strongly associated with the probability of experiencing an assault.

Effective guardianship also plays a role in the probability of experiencing an assault. Not only are most assaults perpetrated upon a lone victim, but the risk of assault increases, especially on the basis of risk per hour of exposure, as one moves away from the watchful eyes of family, neighbours, and work associates. An exception to this generalization is the phenomenon of spousal assaults and assaults on the elderly. The home is not a place of effective guardianship for these victims. This is because so many of these assaults are of a domestic nature, perpetrated by a current or former spouse, or a current or former dependent child, who may have easy access both to the home and to the victim. Such assaults also tend to be inordinately brutal, possibly because of the nonrational, emotional affect which motivates them.

ROBBERY

Like assault, robbery is considered a violent crime. It occurs when there is threatened or actual use of force or of a weapon in conjunction with taking, or attempting to take, something from another person. But robbery is a much rarer crime than assault. Police statistics for 1989 showed that of all violent crimes, more than 75 percent were nonsexual assaults, while little more than 10 percent were robberies, almost the same percentage as sexual assaults.

Incidence

Statistics Canada (1990a) reported that 25 percent of robberies known to the police involved a firearm in 1989, while an additional 29 percent involved some other offensive weapon. The police-reported rate of robberies was just under 10 per 100 000 Canadians in 1989. This contrasts with a GSS rate of 13 per 1000 Canadians at least fifteen years of age in 1987. Police statistics typically report robbery rates well in excess of the national norm in Quebec. However, the GSS indicates that Quebec's victim-reported robbery rate was not only substantially below the Canadian norm, it even included too few cases to make reliable estimates about the circumstances involving robbery in that province.

Pattern

Sacco and Johnson's (1990) compilation of results from the 1987 GSS shows that while a weapon was present in only 28 percent of robberies, victims were attacked in almost three out of four attempted and actual robberies. In almost two out of three of these attacks the victim was hit, kicked, slapped, or knocked down, and in over half the victim was grabbed, held, tripped, jumped, or pushed. About one-quarter of the robbery victims had some difficulty carrying out their main activities after the incident. Fewer than one victim in ten sought assistance from any victim assistance agency after the incident. Most victims did not know if any agency existed to help them.

Just over one out of three victims reported something stolen as a result of the incident. About another 15 percent reported they had suffered an economic loss from something damaged, though nothing was stolen.

As would be predicted by the lifestyle/exposure theory, there is a direct relationship between the risk of robbery and the number of evening activities engaged in outside of the home. Those who were involved in 30 or more evening activities outside of the home in an average month were more than twice as likely to be robbed as were others (Sacco and Johnson, 1990). A total of 42 percent of the robberies studied by Sacco and Johnson occurred in a public place, where the victim usually would be less protected by familiar surroundings and acquaintances; 36 percent took place in a private residence, usually the victim's own home.

ROBBERY: WHEN DOES ONE GET INJURED?

There is a tendency for victims to be hurt more often in attempted crimes than in completed crimes. Perhaps this occurs because the victim is less inclined to resist the offender when the offender has a more lethal weapon than when the offender is without a weapon or has a less lethal weapon. The victim, of course, is more likely to foil the completion of a crime if he or she resists, but is also more likely to be hurt than if he or she acquiesces to the completion of the crime. The following case studies illustrate the difference.

When the offender has lethal resources, he/she will warn or prod the victim in order to demonstrate capacity and determination and thereby intimidate the victim:

> Offender #7: I wouldn't kill anybody. But sometimes I'd hit them. Like this one guy, you know, was stalling around, saying he didn't know the combination of the safe. So I just smacked him on the side of the head with the gun and said "Open it." So he suddenly remembers the combination. I guess he figured I'd waste him if he kept stalling.

But when the offender has nonlethal resources, he/she will use additional force to exact compliance:

> Offender #10: So we hit him on the head, you know, to knock him out.... But I guess we didn't hit him hard enough because he started fighting back. He fought pretty good. I guess he thought he was fighting for his life. So we just hit him harder, you know, to take him out.

Source: David F. Luckenbill. (1981). "Generating Compliance: The Case of Robbery." *Urban Life* 10(1) (April):25–46.

Victims

People most likely to be robbed (Sacco and Johnson, 1990) were males, younger people, those who engaged in the largest number of evening activities outside of the home, those whose principal activity during the preceding year was being a student, and those who had not completed secondary school. Single people were proportionately more than twice as likely as others to be robbed; there were too few separated and divorced robbery victims to calculate a reliable probability of their likelihood of being robbed. The risk of robbery was marginally higher among urban than rural residents, and was substantially above the national norm among residents of the Prairies.

Offenders

In one-third of the cases, Sacco and Johnson's (1990) tallies of GSS victim data indicate that the offender was an acquaintance, and in only 45 percent was the offender a stranger. The remainder were relatives or an unspecified individual or individuals. Robberies were more than twice as likely to be committed by a lone offender than by multiple offenders. Statistics Canada (1990a) reported that one out of four robbers charged by Canadian police in 1989 was a young offender and more than nine out of ten adults charged were men. Studies by Gabor and Normandeau (1989) in Quebec and the FBI in the United States suggest that robbery offenders are not particularly sophisticated. The U.S. Bureau of Justice Statistics (1988) noted that in more than three-fourths of bank robberies investigated by the FBI, offenders used no disguise, despite the widespread use of surveillance equipment. Indeed, 86 percent never even inspected the bank prior to the offence and only 5 percent had a long-range scheme to avoid capture and to spend the money without being noticed.

THE ARMED ROBBER'S PERSPECTIVE

A group of criminologists have studied armed robberies in Montreal. Gabor and Normandeau have summarized some of their findings, which dispel the media stereotype of the meticulous professional.

The targets in Quebec are usually convenience stores and other small businesses. The most common type of weapon, by far, was a firearm of some sort....

The age of suspects ... usually was under 22 years. No disguises were worn in three-quarters of the incidents studied. Almost two-thirds of the robberies brought the offenders less than $500. The most typical amount stolen was $100. Even these very modest amounts often had to be divided up. The most frequent scenarios ... were either one or two offenders....

The actual deployment of weapons occurred in only about eight percent [of the incidents].... If one also includes jostling, punching, and the tying up of victims, then about 30 percent of the robberies involved physical force....

Close to half the subjects either did no planning whatsoever or at most undertook about an hour of preparation....

Many indicated that armed robbery constitutes the fastest and most direct way of getting money. Burglary and fraud were seen as more complicated and less lucrative. The younger robbers, in particular, like the thrills, status, and feelings of power afforded by the crime.

Source: Thomas Gabor and André Normandeau. (1989). "Armed Robbery: Highlights of a Canadian Study." *Canadian Police College Journal* 13(4):273–82.

BREAK AND ENTER

Because both crimes involve theft, people sometimes confuse robbery with break and enter (or burglary, as it is also called). The difference between the two is simple. Robbery involves face-to-face contact with the threat of force. Break and enter involves stealth. The burglar seeks to avoid all contact with anybody in the residence or building which is being illegally entered.

Incidence and Patterns

For 1989, Statistics Canada's (1990a) tally of police statistics yielded about thirteen break and enters for every 1000 Canadians. There were almost twice as many residences as business premises broken into. Almost half of those charged with break and enter were under the age of eighteen. Of adults charged, fewer than 5 percent were women.

Statistics Canada (1990d) reported that 54 out of every 1000 households in the GSS experienced a break and enter in 1987. Seventy percent of victims said that they reported the offence to the police. The offence rate was particularly high for semi-detached residences, row houses, and duplexes, and it was very slightly above the average for rental households. The rate of break and enters was extremely low for one-person households and highest for two-person households. Thereafter, as household size increased, the probability of break and enter decreased.

Residential break and enters were particularly likely to take place in the summer months of June, July, and August, when school is out. They then declined regularly until they reached their low point in the spring months of March, April, and May (Sacco and Johnson, 1990).

Sacco and Johnson's (1990) data show that nothing was stolen in almost one-half of these incidents. There was not even any loss from damage in one out of five of these residential break and enters. When a loss was suffered, in almost one out of five cases the economic loss was under $100, but the loss exceeded $1000 in slightly more than one out of four cases. When something was stolen, almost nine times out of ten nothing was recovered by police or the owner.

Few respondents sought help from an agency in coping with their victimization. The majority of victims were not aware of any agency that could help them, and most of the remainder did not think that assistance was necessary. Nevertheless, about one victim in five reported that the break and enter subsequently created some difficulty for them in carrying out their main activities.

Such findings are broadly consistent with the results of earlier, local Canadian studies. Waller and Okihiro (1978) intensively studied break and enters in Toronto. They found that almost half of the break and enters involved no forced entry. Entry was gained through open or unlocked doors and windows. Often nothing was taken. A similar pattern was reported by Wall (1981) for Saanich, B.C. Experienced burglars generally steal for income rather than for excitement. Consequently, they are interested in expensive, portable, compact items which can be sold or disposed of easily: cash, auto parts, jewellery, and electronic goods such as portable computers, VCRs, tape decks, stereos, and so on. If items such as these are not available in a burgled house, often nothing will be taken.

A Crime of Opportunity

Research findings suggest that break and enter is largely a crime of opportunity in which the perceived risk of being caught is low. Moreover, the perceived risk is heavily influenced by the potential victim's lifestyle: whether entrance accesses are secured, whether a dwelling is occupied or appears to be occupied; and by a variety of environmental factors, such as "surveillability." Support for the hypothesis that the prospect of a large gain is not a substantial factor in the selection of a target is the very marginal relationship between household income and the probability of household burglary revealed by the GSS.

Additional evidence of the opportunistic nature of break and enter is the fact that frequently nothing is stolen. Such a pattern would suggest that ease of entry rather than pursuit of any particular valuable object is a major factor in the selection of the target. Moreover, the high frequency of attempted rather than completed break and enters would again suggest that potential targets are selected haphazardly rather than as the consequence of careful planning. As Mayhew (1984) has suggested, such unsuccessful burglaries may tell us a great deal about the value of security and target hardening. While burglars may not be deterred from attempting a break-in by improved hardware (locks, etc.) and security (alarms, etc.), they may be defeated by such measures from succeeding in their efforts. The frequency of unsuccessful attempts also reinforces the opportunistic nature of burglary. Clearly, many attempted break-ins are unsuccessful, presumably because of inopportune circumstances.

Bennett and Wright (1984a, 1984b) directly asked older, experienced burglars which factors influenced their choices of targets. They found that the prospect of a large gain was less often a consideration than the certainty that there was something present worth taking. Ease of entry was not reported to be a major consideration (though it will be recalled that many attempts at break-in apparently are foiled once begun). The majority of these older, experienced burglars also stated that they would be deterred, either conditionally or unconditionally, by the presence of dogs. Bennett and Wright (1984a) concluded that the major consideration in target selection is factors affecting risk, such as the belief that nobody is present in the home and the apparent "surveillability," or visibility, of entrance accesses from nearby overlooking buildings or by passers-by and neighbours. In other words, a major factor in the risk of break and enter is the degree to which one's lifestyle decreases the exposure of the household through effective guardianship.

OTHER OFFENCES

MOTOR VEHICLE THEFT

In a *Juristat* bulletin prepared by Morrison, Statistics Canada (1991) notes that police statistics indicate that 1 of every 183 registered motor vehicles was stolen in 1989, a total of more than 100 000 vehicles. To this must be added a further 300 000 thefts (usually of radios/stereos) from motor vehicles. Over a quarter of the stolen vehicles were not recovered. Fewer than one-fifth of motor vehicle–related thefts were cleared. The GSS produced an estimate that thefts of and from motor vehicles, as well as vandalism to them, cost Canadians more than $700 million in 1987. (By contrast, the Insurance Bureau of Canada reports a typical loss of little more than $3 million per year from bank robberies.)

Based upon a partial study, Morrison estimates that approximately three of five thefts of and from motor vehicles take place in parking lots, with the next largest proportion taking place in residential areas. The thefts are most likely to take place between midnight and 6 A.M. Morrison also notes that the 1989 provincial rate (per 1000 registrations) of motor vehicle theft was highest in Quebec, followed by Manitoba. Otherwise, the rate of motor vehicle theft increased across the country from east to west. For Canada as a whole, the theft rate *from* motor vehicles was more than three times as high as the theft rate *of* motor vehicles. The Northwest Territories are a special case. The rate of motor vehicle theft there was more than seven times the Canadian average. In the Northwest Territories thieves are more than three times as likely to take the entire motor vehicle than merely to steal something from it.

Drawing upon the GSS, Statistics Canada (1990d) relates that motor vehicle offences occur disproportionately among rental households and residents of apartment buildings. The likelihood of victimization by motor vehicle theft was also directly related to household size. This may be because households with more members might have a larger average number of motor vehicles. As is true of break and enter, motor vehicle–related thefts are at their peak in the summer months and then decline until they reach their low point in early spring.

As with break and enter, the GSS cannot reveal much about the characteristics of motor vehicle thieves. Because this is a crime of stealth, the victim usually does not have any knowledge about the offender. However, Statistics Canada (1990a) reports that young offenders made up 48 percent of those believed by the police to have stolen motor vehicles, 45 percent of those suspected of theft over $1000 from a motor vehicle, and 52 percent of those suspected of theft under $1000 from a motor vehicle. Of adults, men accounted for approximately 95 percent of those charged within each of the above categories.

LARCENY

There are a variety of other types of theft. A term frequently used to describe many of these offences is *larceny*. Larceny is theft (without force or threat of force) from a person or location where one has a legal right to be. Thus, unauthorized entry into a residence or a store (when it is closed) is break and enter. However, stealing from a store during business hours is larceny, as would be a household theft by a repairperson invited into a home by the owner.

There are numerous types of larceny: shoplifting; stealing watches, wallets, or blankets at the beach; stealing unattended gifts from an unlocked car; stealing bicycles; stealing from vending machines; and so forth. Only a minority of larceny incidents are reported to the police. And only a minority of those are cleared by the police.

Who are the larcenous offenders? Unlike the situation with some other crimes, victims of larceny-theft can't provide much information about the offender because the crime usually involves stealth. It is only some time after the offence that the victim realizes that something has been stolen, and so the victim frequently will not know who stole it. Nor can police and correctional statistics tell us much about offenders. Suspects are identified for only a small number of these offences. Such suspects may not be at all representative of actual offenders, but rather representative of people more likely to come to police attention for reasons other than their offences.

Personal Larceny

Data tabulated by Sacco and Johnson (1990) from the GSS in 1987 provide an estimate that one of seventeen Canadians over the age of 25 experienced an attempted or actual personal theft in 1987. Those who reported their principal activity in the past year as being a student had more than twice the normal probability of reporting that they were victimized by personal theft. For both sexes and among almost all age groups, the probability of being victimized by personal theft increased along with the total monthly evening activities in which the respondents engaged. Those whose principal activity had been keeping house had a rate less than half the norm. The rate was also somewhat elevated among women who were working at a job or business. Overall, women were slightly more likely than men to be victimized by personal theft.

Proportionately, personal theft was also more likely in urban than in rural areas, and it increased from east to west, except for Quebec, where the rate was lower than for any of Canada's five regions. As expected, rates of victimization were highest among younger people and those who were single, regardless of gender. Both men and women who had gone beyond secondary school had the highest rates of personal theft victimization, particularly among those who had not completed their postsecondary education.

These personal larcenies were most likely to occur in the summer and autumn months. Forty percent occurred at a factory, commercial, or office building, 28 percent at the victim's own home, and 23 percent in some public place (other than a restaurant or bar where an additional 6 percent occurred). A majority of these victimizations involved a loss of less than $100, though in about one of seven cases some or all of the stolen property was recovered. While about one of nine experienced some difficulty—usually lasting only a day—as a result of their victimization, it was rare for victims to seek assistance from a victim support agency. In fact, the majority did not even know whether any such agency existed to assist them.

WHAT CAN BE DONE?

Koenig et al. (1983) and Koenig and DeBeck (1983) have applied the Cohen-Felson routine activities approach to develop a forecast for Canadian crime trends and to suggest approaches to minimize crime. It will be recalled that Cohen and Felson believe that the three components of target suitability, ineffective guardianship, and a motivated offender must converge in space and time if a crime is to occur. We are unlikely to see a reduction in target suitability. We live in a society that values consumer goods. We also prefer our goods, electronic and otherwise, to be as compact, lightweight, and portable as possible. The focus, therefore, must be on effective guardianship and motivated offenders; specifically, how a particular person (or household) can avoid victimization and how crime itself can be reduced.

EFFECTIVE GUARDIANSHIP

It does not appear that the Canadian GSS asked whether victims took self-protective measures against offenders. The U.S. National Crime Survey for 1988, however, suggests that such self-protection can be a two-edged sword. Flanagan and Maguire's (1990) tabulations indicate that self-protective measures were more likely to be used against nonstrangers than against strangers. They generally appear to have been effective in thwarting some offenders. However, the risk of injury to the victim also tended to increase when self-protective measures were used, particularly if the assailant was a nonstranger.

Truly effective guardianship should attempt to prevent an offence rather than to counter it once initiated. As has been pointed out repeatedly in this chapter, a person's chance of being victimized by crime is influenced by his or her lifestyle. For the most part, people will be unwilling to alter their lifestyles (evening activities outside of the home, style of dress, and so on) in order to reduce their probability of being victimized. Nevertheless, they can take sensible precautions to reduce the risk of being victimized without fundamentally altering their lifestyles.

An example would be planning ahead and parking in a location where one need not walk down a dark and deserted street alone at night to return to the car. Such planning would also reduce the probability of theft of the car or car parts, if the car is locked and parked in a location visible to frequent passers-by. In the case of a person's home, planning ahead would involve locking doors and windows, particularly when nobody is home, and making the home appear to be occupied by leaving lights and a radio on. Seeking to enhance a house's visibility to neighbours and passers-by (for example, pruning shrubs or high hedges which obstruct surveillability and provide hiding places for burglars to force windows or doors) could also deter break-ins.

Defensive measures of this nature can be expected to produce an overall reduction in crime, for the reason that some crime is opportunistic. For many or most crimes, however, such measures will simply displace crime from one victim or location to another. For while some offenders are opportunistic— that is, they do not seek out potential targets but will take advantage of a target that presents itself—others are highly motivated. Offender motivation or motivated offenders must be the focus if any vast reduction of crime is to occur.

MOTIVATED OFFENDERS

Prevention

Many criminologists see society as resembling a faulty assembly line that continuously produces defective "products," such as criminals. Rather than constantly "repairing" (or "rehabilitating") these defective products, such criminologists would rather overhaul the assembly line so that it would produce sound products, that is, noncriminals. Orientations often are derived from a strain theory of the causes of crime. Criminals are seen as fundamentally good people who for one reason or another are "driven" to crime and develop offender motivation. As Waller (1985:v) puts it: "Persistent and serious criminals tend to be males brought up in socially disadvantaged situations." This approach to crime prevention has been described as "social development."

Recently, the Canadian Criminal Justice Association (1989) produced 27 recommendations for preventing crime through social development in the areas of parenting/family, schools, social housing and neighbourhoods, employment, substance abuse, the media, and health. While the list is too long to reproduce here, its recommendations are targeted at the known correlates of those who get caught up in the criminal justice system (youth, males, born into poverty or Native), at inadequate parenting skills or practices, at the cycle of delinquent friends, trouble in school, employment difficulties, and so forth.

Incapacitation

A somewhat different approach, often influenced by control theory, sees the criminal as one for whom the usual internal and external controls against becoming a criminal have been neutralized. It follows that until such time as those controls have redeveloped, the most chronic of the motivated offenders must be incapacitated in order to prevent them from committing further offences. In this way, it is argued, crime will be reduced.

The challenge then becomes one of identifying the most highly motivated offenders—that is, the career criminals who offend at very high rates. In turn, this implies predicting which offenders are likely to be casual offenders and which will make crime a way of life.

Over the last several decades, various criminologists have attempted to profile diverse types of criminals, such as "the professional thief," "the bank robber," "the class cannon" (sophisticated pickpocket), "the embezzler," and so on. In the 1960s, criminologists such as Gibbons, Roebuck, and Clinard and Quinney were attempting to develop criminal typologies for which the behaviour systems of criminal types could be elucidated. The problem with these typologies was that they attempted to abstract types which do not exist. With the notable exception of Roebuck (1967), who had practical experience working as a prison classification officer as well as an academic, most of these typologies assumed an unrealistic degree of offender specialization. Roebuck analyzed the records of 400 offenders. The most common pattern which he found was what he called a "mixed pattern (Jack-of-all-trades) offender," followed by a double pattern of burglary and larceny. Together, these accounted for more than one-third of all of the cases. Roebuck was on the right track, but typological analyses seemed to be going nowhere and interest in them faded. In the real world, criminal careers seemed to be far more complex than a typology was capable of capturing.

Interest in criminal typologies was reawakened during the 1980s with a Rand Corporation study which claimed that the U.S. crime rate could be significantly reduced if the small proportion of highly active criminals were incapacitated through incarceration. As Petersilia (1980) has noted, recent research has corrected many myths about the professionalism of career criminals. In fact, we now know that a large proportion of criminals do not specialize or plan their crimes. They work alone rather than as part of a group, especially as they age. Most of them realize a small amount of income, averaging a few thousand dollars a year, from crime—and this income does not increase substantially as their criminal career progresses. How, therefore, can highly active criminals be identified?

DO JUVENILE DELINQUENTS BECOME ADULT CRIMINALS?

Joan Petersilia has reviewed recent research on criminal careers. The following has been extracted from her summary of conclusions.

The following propositions recapitulate some of the major findings on criminal careers that were presented above. They are tentative....

Less than 15 percent of the general population will be arrested for the commission of a felony and, of these, perhaps 50 percent will never be arrested for another. Very roughly, only 5 percent of the population will demonstrate the beginnings of a criminal career. But once three contacts with the police have been recorded, the probability that still another contact will be made is high.

Criminal careers predominantly begin early in life, commonly between the ages of fourteen and seventeen years. The earlier criminal activities begin, the more likely it is that sustained serious criminal conduct will ensue in the adult years. Nevertheless, relatively few juvenile delinquents become career criminals.

Criminal careers sometimes begin as youthful adventures, for thrills and excitement and to achieve peer status....

Drugs and alcohol play significant roles in a majority of criminal careers....

At every stage of his career, the offender will commit a variety of offence types rather than specialize. The mixture may shift from one stage to the next, often increasing in seriousness, but not as a consistent rule. Crime targets are more likely to be opportunistic than the results of methodical planning.

Source: Joan Petersilia. (1980). "Criminal Career Research: A Review of Recent Evidence." In Norval Morris and Michael Tonry (eds.), *Crime and Justice: An Annual Review of Research* (pp. 321–79). Chicago: University of Chicago Press.

Violent Predators

The Chaikens (1984) extended both the earlier efforts at constructing criminal typologies and the Rand Corporation study by classifying male offenders on the basis of the combinations of crimes which they committed. What they found was a very high volume of crime committed by that 15 percent of their sample who reported committing a combination of robberies, assaults, and drug deals. These prisoners were labelled "violent predators." They were extremely young, averaging less than 23 years of age when first incarcerated, but they had been committing serious crimes, especially violent crimes, for at least six years. They had considerably more total arrests than other offenders, including those much older than themselves. Moreover, they had spent considerable time in juvenile facilities and were more likely than other offenders to have been granted parole and to have had it revoked. Finally, they were also more socially unstable than other offenders and were unlikely to be regularly employed, married, or to have other family obligations. There is also a strong suggestion that drug use, particularly multiple drug use involving heroin or barbiturates, is often characteristic of violent predators.

ARE THERE DIFFERENCES AMONG CONVICTED CRIMINALS?

The Chaikens gathered self-report and official record data about more than 2000 male prison and jail inmates in three states. From their data they identified a subset of offenders they called "violent predators." These violent predators indiscriminately commit robberies, assaults, and drug deals at high rates. They also commit break and enter, theft, and other crimes at high rates, often at far higher rates than those who specialize in those crimes. While all who commit robberies would not be classified as violent predators, some of the Chaikens' analyses indicate the extent to which a small proportion of the total incarcerated population may be responsible for a very large portion of the total amount of crimes which are committed.

Offenders in the survey sample whose characteristics indicated their robbery rate "should," according to the regression analysis, be in the highest 20 percent actually had, on the average:
- Robbery rates 65 times as high as those predicted to be in the lowest 20 percent;
- Burglary rates 66 times as high;
- Auto theft rates 346 times as high;
- Other theft rates 10 times as high; and
- Drug dealing rates 5 times as high.

Source: Marcia R. Chaiken and Jan M. Chaiken. (1984). "Offender Types and Public Policy." *Crime and Delinquency* 30(2) (April):213.

Psychopaths

The profile of violent predators very closely resembles the profile of psychopathic male criminals as outlined by Jutai and Hare (1983) in terms of both psychological characteristics and criminal patterns (more offences, more violence, earlier age at first contact, and so on). Almost certainly there is considerable overlap among the populations of psychopaths and violent predators. As Nettler (1982) has observed, it is generally believed that psychopaths are inadequately motivated and do not learn from either positive or negative reinforcement. Unlike run-of-the-mill offenders, it is doubtful that psychopaths would be prevented from committing crimes through "social development." Psychopathic crime will be prevented only if the psychopath is institutionalized or otherwise unable to commit crime. Some, therefore, advocate longer prison sentences for that minority of convicted criminals who fit the profiles of "violent predators" or of psychopaths.

Ethical Concerns

Some criminologists, such as von Hirsch (1984), however, strenuously object to such proposals for selective incapacitation. They argue that it is unjust to sentence a person to a long term in prison not for something that person has done, but for what that person might do if he or she were not imprisoned. This is particularly true considering the fact that there tends to be a high rate of "false positives" (50 to 60 percent of the total) in most predictive studies, including the original Rand Corporation study on which the Chaikens' study was modelled. As von Hirsch (1984:177) expressed it: "The 'false positive'— that is, the person erroneously designated to be a future recidivist—loses his liberty on account of an injury that he will not in fact commit."

SUMMARY

Conventional crime refers to those traditional, illegal behaviours that most people think of as crime. People may threaten our physical and material well-being by doing other legal or illegal actions, or by failing to act, far more than by committing conventional crime. Some conventional crime is called violent crime because it threatens or causes actual physical harm to the victim. Included are homicide, sexual and nonsexual assaultive behaviours, and robbery. These are also called crimes against the person or personal crimes. When the term *personal crime* is used, it sometimes includes thefts from a person, such as pickpocketing and other unobtrusive thefts of personal property.

Thefts of personal or household property traditionally have been described as property crimes or crimes against property. These include break and enter (burglary), automobile theft, and a variety of larcenies, such as shoplifting and other thefts of goods left unguarded by their owners.

Hindelang and his associates developed the influential lifestyle/exposure theory to explain correlates of crimes against the person. Cohen and Felson extended such reasoning to crimes against property, as well as long-range crime trends, by documenting how ongoing social changes have altered people's routine daily activities. These changed routine activities, in turn, have had extensive implications for increasing target suitability and reducing effective guardianship.

The pattern and correlates of crime discussed in this chapter are consistent with such a routine activities approach. Crimes against property tend to be committed disproportionately against those whose lifestyles leave their possessions least effectively guarded. These relationships become particularly acute if one calculates, as Cohen and Felson have, the rates for risk of victimization per hour of potential victimization (exposure) in certain locales or social settings.

Crimes against the person have some different correlates than do crimes against property, but most of these differences are consistent with the lifestyle/exposure theory. Although a burglary or an auto theft is most likely to occur when nobody is present, an assault or a robbery requires the presence of a victim. Thus, crimes against the person may be far more likely to occur in the home or among nonstrangers than would property crimes.

The home and nonstrangers, nevertheless, provide more effective guardianship against crime for people than do public places and strangers. This reality is overlooked if one analyzes correlates of violent crime strictly by the percentages of the crimes occurring in various settings. What is overlooked is the victimization incidence in a given setting per hour of risk (exposure) in that setting. For instance, a higher percentage of assaults may occur in the home than at work, but even a person who worked full time would probably spend only about 20 percent of the hours of a year at work (sick days, holidays, vacation, and so on included). If we consider people who don't work for pay outside of the home at all, or only part time, perhaps the population sixteen years of age and over spends about 10 percent of their life at work versus 60 percent or more at home. On the basis of per-hour risk, therefore, the assault rate should be at least six times higher at home than at work, but it is much less than this. Hence, the risk of assault, on a per-hour basis, is less at home than at work. This is consistent with the theory.

This observation is not intended to negate the trauma and the serious nature of domestic violence. However, domestic violence represents neither the typical domestic relationship nor the typical crime. For the "typical" crimes, the victims (as well as the offenders) are most likely to be the young, males, and those who are most likely to engage in evening activities away from home—that is to say, people whose lifestyle places them in social settings with well-known higher risks of being victimized by crime.

Consistent with the theoretical explanation of crime, possible approaches to its reduction would include increased effective guardianship and strategies to reduce the presence of motivated offenders. Two such strategies would be deflecting the motivation of potential offenders through social development, and selectively incapacitating those most likely to become hard-core, motivated offenders at a very early stage of their criminal career.

BIBLIOGRAPHY

Badgley, R. (Report). See Canada, Parliamentary Committee on Sexual Offences Against Children and Youth.

Bennett, Trevor, and Richard Wright. (1984a). *Burglars on Burglary*. Brookfield, VT: Gower Publishing.

Bennett, Trevor, and Richard Wright. (1984b). "Constraints to Burglary: The Offender's Perspective," In Ronald Clarke and Tim Hope (eds.), *Coping with Burglary* (pp. 181–200). Boston: Kluwer-Nijhoff Publishing.

Boyd, Neil. (1988). *The Last Dance: Murder in Canada.* Scarborough: Prentice-Hall, Canada.

Canada, Parliamentary Committee on Sexual Offences Against Children and Youth. (1984). *Sexual Offences Against Children: Report of the Committee on Sexual Offences Against Children and Youth.* Ottawa: Minister of Supply and Services Canada.

Canadian Criminal Justice Association. (1989). "Safer Communities: a Social Strategy for Crime Prevention in Canada." *Canadian Journal of Criminology* (October).

Canadian Urban Victimization Survey Bulletin. (1984). *Crime Prevention: Awareness and Practice.* Ottawa: Solicitor General Canada.

Caron, Roger. (1985). *Bingo.* Toronto: Methuen.

Chaiken, Marcia R., and Jan M. Chaiken. (1984). "Offender Types and Public Policy," *Crime and Delinquency* 30(2) (April):195–226.

Clark, Lorenne M.G., and Debra J. Lewis. (1977). *Rape: The Price of Coercive Sexuality.* Toronto: Women's Educational Press.

Cohen, Lawrence E., and Marcus Felson. (1979). "Social Change and Crime Rate Trends." *American Sociological Review* 44 (August):588–607.

Committee on Sexual Offences Against Children and Youth (Canada). See Canada, Parliamentary Committee on Sexual Offences Against Children and Youth.

CUVS. See Canadian Urban Victimization Survey Bulletin.

de Verteuil, Jacques, and Holly Johnson. (1986). *Young People and Crime: Findings of the Canadian Urban Victimization Survey.* Ottawa: Solicitor General Canada.

Ericson, Richard V. (1981). *Making Crime: A Study of Police Detective Work.* Toronto: Butterworths.

Ericson, Richard V. (1982). *Reproducing Order: A Study of Police Patrol Work.* Toronto: University of Toronto Press.

Ericson, Richard V., and Patricia M. Beranek. (1982). *The Ordering of Justice.* Toronto: University of Toronto Press.

FBI. See U.S. Dept. of Justice, FBI.

Flanagan, Timothy J., and Kathleen Maguire (1990). *Sourcebook of Criminal Justice Statistics—1989.* U.S. Dept. of Justice, Bureau of Justice Statistics. Washington, DC: U.S. Dept. of Justice, 1990.

Gabor, Thomas, and André Normandeau. (1989). "Armed Robbery: Highlights of a Canadian Study." *Canadian Police College Journal.* 13(4):273–82.

Garbarino, James. (1989). "The Incidence and Prevalence of Child Maltreatment." In Lloyd Ohlin and Michael Tonry (eds.), *Crime and Justice: A Review of Research,* (pp. 219–61) Vol. 11. Chicago: University of Chicago Press.

Gates, Margaret. (1978). "Introduction." In Jane Roberts Chapman and Margaret Gates (eds.), *The Victimization of Women.* Beverly Hills: Sage.

Gibson, Lorne, Rick Linden, and Stuart Johnson. (1980). "A Situational Theory of Rape." *Canadian Journal of Corrections* 22(1) (January):51–65.

Heal, Kevin, and Gloria Laycock. (1986). *Situational Crime Prevention: From Theory into Practice.* London: Her Majesty's Stationery Office.

Hindelang, Michael J., Michael R. Gottfredson, and James Garofalo. (1978). *Victims of Personal Crime: An Empirical Foundation for a Theory of Personal Victimization.* Cambridge, MA: Ballinger Publishing.

Home Office. See U.K. Home Office.

Jutai, Jeffrey W., and Robert D. Hare. (1983). "Psychopathy and Selective Attention during Performances of a Complex Perceptual Motor Task." *Psychophysiology* 20(2):146–51.

Koenig, Daniel J. (1977). "Correlates of Self-reported Victimization and Perceptions of Neighbourhood Safety." In Lynn Hewitt and David Brusegard (eds.), *Selected Papers from the Social Indicators Conference, 1975* (pp. 77–90). Edmonton: Alberta Bureau of Statistics.

Koenig, Daniel J., and E. Paula DeBeck. (1983). "Proactive Police Intervention and Imminent Social Change." *Canadian Police College Journal* 7(4):310–328.

Koenig, Daniel J., E. Paula DeBeck, and Janet Laxton. (1983). "Routine Activities, Impending Social Change, and Policing." *Canadian Police College Journal* 7(2):96–136.

Luckenbill, David F. (1981) "Generating Compliance: The Case of Robbery." *Urban Life* 10(1) (April):25–46.

MacLeod, Linda. (1980). *Wife Battering in Canada: The Vicious Circle* (prepared for the Canadian Advisory Council on the Status of Women). Ottawa: Canadian Government Publishing Centre.

Mayhew, Pat. (1984). "Target-Hardening: How Much of an Answer?" In Ronald Clark and Tim Hope (eds), *Coping with Burglary.* (pp. 29–44). Boston: Kluwer-Nijhoff Publishing.

Nettler, Gwynn. (1982). *Killing One Another.* Vol. 2 of *Criminal Careers.* Cincinnati: Anderson Publishing.

———.(1984). *Explaining Crime.* (4th ed.) New York: McGraw-Hill.

———. (1988). *Criminology Lessons: Arguments about Crime, Punishment and the Interpretation of Conduct, with Advice for Individuals and Prescriptions for Public Policy.* Cincinnati: Anderson Publishing.

Pagelow, Mildred Daley. (1989). "The Incidence and Prevalence of Criminal Abuse of Other Family Members." In Lloyd Ohlin and Michael Tonry (eds.), *Crime and Justice: A Review of Research,* Vol. 11 (pp. 263–313). Chicago: University of Chicago Press.

Petersilia, Joan. (1980). "Criminal Career Research: A Review of Recent Evidence." In Norval Morris and Michael Tonry (eds.), *Crime and Justice: An Annual Review of Research,* Vol. 2 (pp. 321–79). Chicago: University of Chicago Press.

Podnieks, Elizabeth. (1989) (October). *A National Survey on Abuse of the Elderly in Canada: Preliminary Findings.* Toronto: Ryerson Polytechnic Institute.

Roebuck, Julian B. (1967). *Criminal Typology.* Springfield, IL: Charles C. Thomas Publisher.

Sacco, Vincent F., and Holly Johnson. (1990). *Patterns of Criminal Victimization in Canada.* Ottawa: Statistics Canada (Housing, Family and Social Statistics Division), Minister of Supply and Services Canada.

Sparks, Richard F. (1981). "Multiple Victimization: Evidence, Theory and Future Research." In National Institute of Justice, *Victims of Crime: A Review of Research Issues and Methods.* Washington DC: U.S. Dept. of Justice.

Statistics Canada. Canadian Centre for Justice Statistics. (1990a) (September). *Canadian Crime Statistics, 1989.* Ottawa: Minister of Supply and Services Canada.

———. Canadian Centre for Justice Statistics. (1990b) (October). *Juristat* 10(14), *Homicide in Canada, 1989.* Ottawa: Minister of Supply and Services Canada.

———. Canadian Centre for Justice Statistics. (1990c) (October). *Juristat* 10(15), *Violent Crime in Canada.* Ottawa: Minister of Supply and Services Canada.

———. Canadian Centre for Justice Statistics. (1990d) (October). *Juristat* 10(16), *Criminal Victimization in Canada: The Findings of a Survey.* Ottawa: Minister of Supply and Services Canada.

———. Canadian Centre for Justice Statistics. (1991) (February). *Juristat* 11(2), *Motor Vehicle Theft and Vehicle Vandalism* (prepared by Peter Morrison). Ottawa: Minister of Supply and Services Canada.

Susan Marie. (1984). "Lesbian Battery: An Inside View." *Victimology* 9(1):16–20.

U.K. Home Office. (1990) (November). *Criminal Statistics: England and Wales, 1989.* London: Her Majesty's Stationery Office.

The U.S. Bureau of Justice Statistics. (1988) (April). *BJS Data Report, 1987.* Washington, DC: U.S. Dept of Justice.

The U.S. Bureau of Justice Statistics. (1990) (December). *Criminal Victimization in the United States, 1988.* Washington, DC: U.S. Dept of Justice.

U.S. Dept. of Justice. (1974a) (July). *Crime in Eight American Cities.* Advance Report. Washington, DC: U.S. Dept. of Justice.

———. (1974b) (June). *Crimes and Victims: A Report on the Dayton-San Jose Pilot Study of Victimization.* Washington, DC: U.S. Dept. of Justice.

U.S. Dept. of Justice, FBI. 1990 (August). *Uniform Crime Reports for the United States, 1989.* Washington, DC: U.S. Government Printing Office.

von Hirsch, Andrew. (1984). "The Ethics of Selective Incapacitation: Observations on the Contemporary Debate." *Crime and Delinquency* 30(2) (April):175–94.

Wall, Dale. (1981). *Saanich Crime Analysis.* Municipality of Saanich, BC: Saanich Police Department.

Waller, Irvin. (1985). *Crime Prevention through Social Development.* Ottawa: Canadian Council on Social Development and Canadian Criminal Justice Association.

Waller, Irvin, and Norm Okihiro. (1978). *The Victim and the Public.* Toronto: University of Toronto Press.

Wiehe, Vernon R. (1990). *Sibling Abuse: Hidden Physical, Emotional, and Sexual Trauma.* Toronto: Lexington.

Wolf, Rosalie S., and Karl A. Pillemer. (1989). *Helping Elderly Victims: The Reality of Elder Abuse.* New York: Columbia University Press.

FURTHER READING

Canadian Criminal Justice Association. (1989). "Safer communities: a social strategy for crime prevention in Canada." *Canadian Journal of Criminology* (October). A state of the art review about factors suspected to predispose individuals to crime and how these factors, and offender motivation generally, can be combatted through social development.

Heal, Kevin, and Gloria Laycock. (1986). *Situational Crime Prevention: From Theory Into Practice.* London: Her Majesty's Stationery Office. A slim book discussing case studies and the arguments for and against target hardening and effective guardianship.

Nettler, Gwynn. (1988). *Criminology Lessons: Arguments about Crime, Punishment and the Interpretation of Conduct, with Advice for Individuals and Prescriptions for Public Policy.* Cincinnati: Anderson Publishing Co. A *tour de force* of multifaceted quantitative research systematized and interpreted from the perspective of classic liberalism.

Ohlin, Lloyd, and Michael Tonry (eds.). (1989). *Crime and Justice: A Review of Research,* Vol. 11, *Family Violence.* Chicago: University of Chicago Press. A state of the art review of what is known about assaultive behaviours against spouses, siblings, children, adolescents, parents, and seniors, and mechanisms by which such violence may be dissipated.

Sacco, Vincent F., and Holly Johnson. (1990). *Patterns of Criminal Victimization in Canada*. Ottawa: Statistics Canada (Housing, Family and Social Statistics Division), Minister of Supply and Services Canada. Catalogue 11-612E, No. 2; March 1990. This report provides a plethora of tabulations from the 1987 General Social Survey in Canada, together with some interpretive and contextual narrative.

Statistics Canada. *Juristat*. A serial, containing approximately twenty issues per year, which reports the latest available information about various facets of the Canadian criminal justice system.

CHAPTER 14

ORGANIZED CRIME

By Rodney T. Stamler

*O*ver the past century, governments and their enforcement agencies in North America have become increasingly involved with problems associated with organized crime. The public demand for illegal goods and services has produced illicit supply systems which have significantly influenced the presence, size, structure, and power of organized crime groups in Canada, as in other regions of the world. These activities are extremely profitable, since groups that are able to obtain a monopoly over goods and services which the public strongly desires can set their own price. Legitimate competitors are excluded because of the illegality; illegitimate competitors are controlled by force.

WHAT IS ORGANIZED CRIME?

The term *organized crime* has not been defined in Canadian criminal law and there is no offence in Canada that makes it a crime to be a member of an organized crime group.

Authors, criminologists, and drafters of legislation have had difficulty in defining organized crime. Many of these people have tried to develop an all-encompassing definition which would include every type of organized crime group. In doing so, the definitions that have been created have become broad and general. Some of the definitions have clearly distinguished organized crime groups from petty thieves, disorderly persons, and other individuals who are involved in criminal activity. Other definitions of organized crime have used the partnership or business entity approach, which outlines organizational effort, planning, leadership, division of work, and co-operation. Other definitions have identified the social elements involved in organized crime, and have tended to utilize a more fraternal atmosphere in their definitions, emphasizing family-type co-operation where members pledge lifelong loyalty, trust, and obedience (Pennsylvania Crime Commission, 1980).

Some definitions of organized crime clearly delineate one organized crime network, while others confine themselves to one element of organized crime. Several authors, after studying or examining street gang activity, have described these groups as though they operate autonomously from any other group or level of authority. These authors tend to come to the mistaken conclusion that organized crime is not organized at all, but is a collection of uncontrolled bandits, outlaws, and crooks who work together at times in order to coexist in the unfriendly street environment. This conclusion will undoubtedly be reached when one fails to carefully examine all crime groups that operate in a given territory from the top of the hierarchy to the street-level active group. Street groups tend to be the most visible part of an organized crime network, but, like the greater part of an iceberg, the highly organized elements remain hidden from public view. Only a careful examination of the cash flow involved in street crimes will identify the hierarchy of the network.

Jean-Pierre Charbonneau, in his book *The Canadian Connection* (1976), states that the underworld is not an organization but an environment. This environment consists of crooks, bandits, dealers, and outlaws of every description. Within this milieu a multitude of gangs, clans, or organizations exist or coexist. Some are powerful, well organized, and stable; others are loose and haphazard, and may include temporary coalitions of odd-job criminals and journeyman crooks.

In his book entitled *Mob Rule: Inside the Canadian Mafia* (1985), James Dubro says, "Organized crime is easy to define." It is, as the official Canadian police definition of organized crime goes, "two or more persons consorting together on a continuing basis to participate in illegal activities, either directly or indirectly for gain...." Ralph Salerno, an American organized crime expert who frequently advises Canadian enforcement authorities on the subject, sharpens the focus a bit in his definition of organized crime.

> We say that organized crime will constitute a self-perpetuating group that will go on in a continuing conspiracy for many years, even if the original members of the conspiracy die, go to prison or elect to retire. There will be a continuum of the organization over a long period of time with the use of force or fear as part of the ongoing methodology.

It becomes clear that an all-encompassing definition of organized crime must be very general if it is to include all crime groups from the street-level operators to the top-level financiers. These definitions do not adequately describe or express the complexities of major regional, national, or international crime organizations, such as the Mafia, the Triads, or the North American outlaw motorcycle gangs. These organizations, with their binding ethnic ties, or their binding common interests, have developed rituals, codes of conduct, and secrecy that provide them with the protection and security to continue as distinctive criminal societies.

A Pennsylvania State Task Force on Organized Crime never came to grips with the problem of defining organized crime. Instead, the task force proposed a description that explained the nature of organized crime activity and then explained what is *not* organized crime. One United States law enforcement agency has supplemented their simple definition of the characteristics of a crime organization. In defining organized crime one could do no better than to use the Canadian police definition (Dubro, 1985), supplemented with the description developed by the U.S. Federal Bureau of Alcohol, Tobacco and Firearms (Pennsylvania Crime Commission, 1980):

> "Organized Crime" refers to those self-perpetuating, structured, and disciplined associations of individuals, or groups, combined together for the purpose of obtaining monetary or commercial gains or profits, wholly or in part of illegal means, while protecting their activities through a pattern of graft and corruption.
>
> Organized crime groups possess certain characteristics which include but are not limited to the following:
>
> 1) Their illegal activities are conspiratorial;
> 2) In at least part of their activities, they commit or threaten to commit acts of violence or other acts which are likely to intimidate;
> 3) They conduct their activities in a methodical, systematic, or highly disciplined and secret fashion;
> 4) They insulate their leadership from direct involvement in illegal activities by their intricate organizational structure;
> 5) They attempt to gain influence in Government, politics, and commerce through corruption, graft, and illegitimate means;
> 6) They have economic gain as their primary goal, not only from patently illegal enterprises such as drugs, gambling and loan sharking, but also from such activities as laundering illegal money through and investment in legitimate business.

THE ROOTS OF ORGANIZED CRIME

Many of the activities of organized crime are a result of the demand for illegal goods and services such as drugs and gambling by the "law-abiding" citizenry. In many respects, the need to serve these illicit markets has determined the structure and scope of organized criminal activities. Consider drug trafficking, which is now the most lucrative of organized criminal activities. The basis of this activity is a public demand for a product, in this case a drug such as cocaine, marijuana, or heroin. Since governments in many countries have decided to make these drugs illegal, this demand for the product is relatively inelastic. That is, those using the drug, many of whom are addicts, have a very strong desire for it which cannot be met by any other product. Those who are prepared to run the risk of supplying the product illicitly can charge a premium for it because competition has been restricted by the laws forbidding the normal distribution of the drug.

The nature of the illicit marketplace also determines the structure of organized crime. If one intends to break into homes and to steal and sell stereos and television sets, the largest criminal network required is the thief and a "fence" who will pay for and distribute the stolen articles. However, much more is required to move a drug from the fields of Colombia or Thailand to the streets of Vancouver and Toronto. For this, fairly elaborate organizations must be established, including financiers, buyers, sellers, and people to transport the drug over several international borders. While the structure of the organization might not be nearly as bureaucratic as our image of the traditional Mafia "family," and while membership in the organization might be rather fluid, especially at the street level, a well-organized network must be in place for drug trafficking to be successful on a large scale.

Other types of criminal activity also flow out of the illicit market structure. In order to maintain or increase their share of the market, organized criminals may use violence to discourage competition. Recent gang-related shootings in any number of American cities as well as in Toronto's Asian community are the result of competition for markets by rival groups. Violence is also used to ensure that debts are paid and other obligations met, as the normal channels for enforcing these transactions cannot be used because of the need to conceal illegal activities. The enormous profits which can be earned from the illicit market lead to activities such as laundering money to conceal its source, to loansharking, and to investment in legitimate businesses which then come under the control of criminal syndicates. Finally, in order to prevent the legal system from interfering with its activities, officials may be bribed to ignore them. In fact, by selectively enforcing the law, the police and courts may assist organized criminals by shutting down any competition which might arise.

Many of us are not surprised to hear of corruption in cities such as New York and Chicago which have had long traditions of dishonest police, court officials, and politicians. However, it is much more widespread throughout the United States than commonly thought. In the following passage, William Chambliss describes some dimensions of corruption associated with organized crime in Seattle, a city which has a reputation as being one of the most progressive in the United States. The crime network he describes involved all levels of the Seattle police department, the King County sheriff, the county prosecutor, members of City Council, and many people in Seattle's legitimate and illegitimate business communities. At the heart of the conspiracy was a policy of selectively enforcing state anti-gambling laws in exchange for payoffs.

Whatever the particulars, the ultimate result is the same: a crime network emerges—composed of politicians, law enforcers and citizens—capable of supplying and controlling the vices in the city. The most efficient network is invariably one that contains representatives of all the leading centers of power. Businessmen and bankers must be involved because of their political influence, their ability to control the mass media, and their capital. The importance of cooperating businesses was demonstrated in Seattle by the case of a fledgling magazine that published an article intimating that several leading politicians, in particular the county prosecutor, were corrupt. Immediately, major advertisers cancelled their advertisements in the magazine. One large chain store refused to sell that issue of the magazine in any of its stores....

The networks must also have the cooperation of lawyers and businessmen in procuring the loans which enable them individually and collectively to purchase legitimate businesses as well as to expand the vice enterprises. One member not only served along with others in the network on the board of directors of a loan agency, but he also helped wash money and advise associates on how to keep their earnings a secret. He served as a go-between, passing investment tips from associates to other businessmen in the community....

The political influence of the network is more directly obtained. Huge tax-free profits make it possible to generously support political candidates. Often the network members assist both candidates in an election, thus assuring influence no matter who wins.

Source: William J. Chambliss. (1978). *On the Take: From Petty Crooks to Presidents.* Bloomington: Indiana University Press.

While this type of corruption is widespread in the United States, it is not common in Canada. You will see in Chapter 15 that our politicians have not always been honest. However, there have been relatively few instances of systematic corruption involving organized criminals, police, court officials, and politicians, as occurred in Seattle. Sacco (1986) has given a number of reasons for this: political power in the United States is highly decentralized, which makes it easier to corrupt people holding certain key offices; there are a large number of elected political, law enforcement, and court officials, many of whom are associated with political "machines" financed by organized crime; and Canadians have been less inclined to try to control moral behaviour through laws than Americans, so there are fewer opportunities to establish illicit markets. To these we might also add the fact that our law enforcement agencies and court officials have worked very hard to maintain their reputations for honesty and have seldom been involved with organized corruption.

One recent development shows the operation of the illicit market structure in Canada. Over the past few years, taxes on cigarettes have driven the price so high that it can now cost over $5000 a year to support a two-pack-per-day habit. In the United States, cigarettes are readily available for a fraction of this price. Thus Canadian tax policy has made it very profitable to sell American-bought cigarettes in Canada. The structure of this illicit market does not need to be nearly as complex as it is for cocaine or heroin, since the product can be obtained legally just over the border. Thus individuals can smuggle cigarettes for their own use and people such as cross-border truckers can easily bring in a few extra cartons on each trip for resale. However, there are indications that larger groups are organizing to sell cigarettes in greater quantities than can be managed by individual entrepreneurs.

WHO IS INVOLVED IN ORGANIZED CRIME?

James Dubro states that organized crime in Canada, as in the United States, is not the territory of just one or two ethnic groups. There are many more ethnic groups involved in organized crime than the criminal association known as the "Mafia," the "Cosa Nostra," or the "Honoured Society." In North America, just about every major ethnic group has participated in organized crime over the years—Irish, English, Italians, Jews, French Canadians, blacks, Chinese, Gypsies, chicanos, and many others (Dubro, 1985).

The Italian-based Mafia groups are perhaps the most widely known and publicized crime organizations in the Western world. The term *Mafia*, which was originally used to identify a specific Sicilian crime group, is now commonly used to identify any ethnic or regionally based crime organization. The Colombian Mafia, the Turkish Mafia, and the Asian Mafia are all major international crime groups, but have no direct connection with the membership of the Italian-based Mafia.

Today's major internationally connected crime organizations started at the family or local level. It was the strong family or cultural connection that permitted these organizations to enforce their code of conduct and secrecy to counter any intrusive action from law enforcement. As the crime groups grew in size, their members moved to other regions. This migration served to broaden the base of the crime groups by adding new territories which, in turn, resulted in the expansion of their illegal operations. Ethnic-based crime groups, which are now situated in different regions of the world, use their ties in these expanded territories to develop their international connections and penetrate the illicit markets of the world. In this way, crime groups have the advantage of developing efficient international illegal distribution systems for illicit goods and services. At the same time, they are able to set up international money laundering schemes which are used to hide and distribute their illegal profits.

Besides facilitating international networks, ethnic ties may benefit organized crime groups in other ways. For example, members of some ethnic groups have interpersonal ties which make it difficult for strangers to infiltrate their organizations. Racial and language differences also make law enforcement much more difficult. Finally, members of ethnic groups may be systematically excluded from other means of social mobility, so that crime becomes an attractive alternative (Sacco, 1986).

MAJOR CRIME GROUPS IN CANADA

Major international organized crime groups have found it profitable, over the years, to establish a base of operations in Canada. In addition, crime groups that originated in Canada have grown and established ties with related groups in other parts of the world. At the present time, there are at least seven major types of crime groups operating in Canada. The history and development of these groups can be largely attributed to the fact that Canada has a long and open border with the United States. This allows easy access for criminals and illicit goods to move from one country to the other. Also, Canada, like the United States, enjoys a multicultural society which extends ethnic ties to all regions of the world.

The most prominent internationally connected crime organizations with established crime bases in Canada include the Italian Mafia, Chinese Triads and other Asian groups, the Colombian Mafia, motorcycle gangs, and other Canadian ethnic-based drug trafficking groups.

THE ITALIAN-BASED MAFIA

The present Mafia organizations of Italy are major criminal societies that are permanent, secret, and powerful. Members of the organizations engage in criminal activity for profit (Arlacchi, 1985).

The first Mafia-style organization in Italy was the Camorra. This group was established in Sicily in the 19th century and was a direct offshoot of the 15th-century hill bandits who formed a guerrilla force known as the Garduna. The Camorra based itself on a hierarchical system of control, with the godfather at the top of the hierarchy and soldiers at the bottom. Income was derived from protection rackets, robbery, murder for hire, blackmail, kidnapping, and loansharking. Their members were recruited from prisons. New members to the Camorra were required to serve probationary periods before entering the ranks of the society. Eventually, the Camorra gave way to the Sicilian Mafia, which had a family-based recruitment system. This organization became a powerful crime syndicate (Maclean, 1974).

In the late 19th century, members of the Sicilian Mafia found their way to the United States, Canada, and Australia. As they became established in their new homelands, they began to carry out their traditional patterns of criminal activity. Mafia members sent letters threatening serious injury or death to the recipients. The letters were signed with the outline of a black hand. This was the earliest report of organized crime activity in North America, and the "black hand" became synonymous with the Mafia (Glaser, 1978).

The first city in the United States where a Mafia group became established as a criminal society was New Orleans. New York City became the second area and from there Mafia groups were quickly formed in other parts of the eastern United States (Glaser, 1978).

The Mafia groups controlled gambling, narcotics, and other rackets. They became deeply involved in political patronage in Harlem and Brooklyn. By 1917, they dominated the illegal activities that took place throughout New York.

Mafia groups first surfaced in Ontario as early as 1906. In this era, Toronto, Hamilton, and the Niagara Peninsula became the centres of Canadian Mafia activity. In 1909, the arrest of five so-called Black-Handers in Hamilton was a major event (Dubro, 1985).

By 1920, the Mafia gangs in southwestern Ontario increased in number and size. By 1921, murders, bombings, and extortion were common occurrences.

Prohibition in the United States caught the Mafia by surprise. They could not adjust their illegal operations to supply illicit alcohol to the public. This resulted in other organized crime groups forming in the United States. In Chicago, New York, and other major cities, it was those groups involved in the manufacture, importation, and sale of illicit alcohol who began to reap huge profits. These new organized crime groups quickly took over power and control.

Street wars between gangs trying to acquire or maintain control of valuable territorial rights continued for a decade. Organized crime groups with a variety of ethnic backgrounds emerged. There were Irish gangs in bootlegging, Jewish groups in money laundering, and the original Mafia families trying to regain control. In the 1930s, Lucky Luciano brought together a federation of North American Mafia families which covered every major city in the United States and Canada. He made alliances with other major ethnic groups, which resulted in a unified crime syndicate. In the United States this syndicate has been termed La Cosa Nostra (LCN). They invested their illegal profits into legitimate business, which included legal gambling casinos in Nevada and Cuba. Meyer Lansky became the chief money launderer and banker for the syndicates. He perfected money laundering systems through secret-numbered bank accounts in tax havens. (Maclean, 1974).

By the 1930s, LCN was firmly based in Montreal, Toronto, and Vancouver. The Italian Mafia, as one of its main ethnic components, operates very much like a corporate entity. The godfather, capo, or family boss takes the position of the chief executive officer. The under-bosses, or lieutenants, act as vice-presidents and head the various branches of the organization. These branches may be engaged in different types of criminal activity. Soldiers are given licences to operate in specific territories and are authorized to carry out specified types of criminal activity. They are required, in return, to pay a percentage of their profits to the management level of the organization. The upper levels of this criminal organization invest their laundered proceeds into legitimate business entities. They prefer to appear as legitimate business executives within their respective communities.

The Quebec Crime Probe report of 1977 concluded that the Italian Mafia exists in Montreal and that this organization is a significant factor in organized crime. The report goes on to state:

> This secret society was reserved for criminals of Sicilian and Italian ancestry ... and is a direct descendant of similar secret societies which did and do exist in southern Italy. This statement is supported by many meetings between mafiosi leaders from all over America and elsewhere, particularly Italy....

The report describes the background and scope of the Cotroni-Violi Mafia family of Montreal, and describes how members of this group are recruited and selected. The report points out that there were a number of employees or independent partners of this crime family, which provided the infrastructure of an association of criminals from different ethnic backgrounds. Some of these associates were French Canadians, Jews, Anglo-Saxons, Slavics, and blacks, and were under the authority and control of this one Mafia family. (Quebec, 1977b).

CHINESE TRIADS

Just as the Mafia was founded as a guerrilla movement in Sicily, so the earliest Triad societies came into existence in Fukien Province in China in the latter part of the 17th century. They began as resistance fighters against the Manchu invaders. While the societies' original purpose was self-protection and opposition to various Chinese dynasties, they eventually developed into crime groups (Bresler, 1980).

As the membership of the Triad societies grew, they dispersed throughout southeast Asia. Their members were bound together by an intricate system of rituals, oaths, passwords, and a ceremonial intermingling of their blood. During the politically turbulent years of China's history, with the rise and fall of various governments, the Triads entrenched themselves in criminal activity for profit. This move provided them with the power to ensure their continued existence as a society. Like the Mafia, the Triads engaged in criminal activities such as gambling, narcotics trafficking, prostitution, loan sharking, and extortion.

With Chinese migration to North America, it was not long before the Triads began to develop within North American communities. In Canada and the United States, the gangs followed the basic Triad principles they had followed in China. They formed cellular groups, which were controlled by certain members operating within the group. They retained a secretive system by not disclosing details of criminal activity to other cells.

The various cells often join together for specific purposes such as opposing other groups in their attempt to acquire or maintain control over territory. Behind each cell, which is directly involved in crime activity, is a second group or cell which provides support but is not directly involved in the criminal activity. The members of these types of cells are, however, former members of the crime cells. They are the advisers to the crime group whose approval must be solicited before any major criminal enterprise is carried out by the crime cells. The Triad groups remain almost exclusively within the Chinese communities and very little of their criminal activity except their illicit drug distribution activities directly affects members of the wider public.

In Hong Kong alone, there are an estimated 80 000 Triad members in over 30 known Triad syndicates. At least 10 percent of these members are directly involved in criminal enterprises. The 30 syndicates are, in turn, broken down into approximately 200 gangs or cells, each seldom exceeding 20 persons (Bresler, 1980).

CHINESE GANGS EYE TORONTO

SAINTJOHN,N.B.—Could Toronto become the next power base for the worldwide operations of the Chinese mafia?

Canada's top cops think the threat grows stronger as 1997 draws nearer.

That's when the British colony of Hong Kong is due to be handed back to the Chinese government.

The communists will exterminate crime gangs like the Kung Lok, the 14K and Ghost Shadows without mercy. And like rats leaving a sinking ship, the triad leaders are planning for the future.

Police in Canada and other nations are already tracking moves by the triad gangs to liquidate their assets and move them to "safer" territories.

Huge investments have been made in real estate in the four North American cities where the tongs have established firm footholds.

Toronto on the list
In Toronto, Vancouver, San Francisco and New York, these tongs control criminal activities in the same way outlaw bike gangs and the mafia control their operations—through fear.

It's already established that former Hong Kong policemen, known as the Five Dragons and directly tied to triads, have made substantial investments in Toronto. Other triad investments—made with the profits from heroin, which is refined, imported and distributed by the tongs—include a luxury condominium-office-retail complex in downtown Toronto.

And like their Sicilian and Calabrian rivals, the triads keep things humming along with the age-old art of extortion while raking in huge profits from gambling dens and prostitution.

But unlike the mafia, the North American triads are still orchestrated—to some extent—by the triad generals in the mother country.

And what the Canadian Association of Chiefs of Police are worried about is that as 1997 approaches, some 3 million people currently living in Hong Kong are part of a readymade smoke screen to conceal the escape of the gangs' generals.

Criminals among refugees
In the late 1970s and early '80s the flood of immigration by ethnic Chinese escaping the purges of Vietnam similarly concealed young

criminals. This handful of gang members came to Canada as "Boat People" and almost immediately turned to crime.

The Vietnamese gangs have racked up a deadly track record in a short period: Murder, beatings, extortion and robberies.

They even took on the Kung Lok in Toronto by staging armed holdups of that gang's fan-tan gaming clubs.

The threat of Toronto or Vancouver becoming the triads' new international power base is real and it has dangerous connotations. Nothing sparks an underworld war faster than a territorial dispute.

A report on organized crime, tabled at the CACP conference here yesterday, levels a warning: "The major investment in real estate in Canada and the huge anticipated influx of immigrants mean we must work now to ensure the triads do not simply pick up their business and bring their assets and operations here."

Let's hope police are successful. Immigrants come to Canada hoping for a new life. It would be tragic if they arrived to find they have jumped from the frying pan into the fire.

Source: *Toronto Sun* 30 August 1985.

The southeast Asian region involving the tri-border area of Burma, Laos, and Thailand, commonly known as the Golden Triangle, is currently a major supplier of heroin to the Western world (Buruma and McBeth, 1984/85). The Triad organizations acquired control of this illegal operation and developed major illicit drug distribution systems throughout the world. They made direct connections with Triad groups in Canada, the United States, and Europe. Major drug shipments are made regularly between Bangkok, Hong Kong, and Vancouver or from Hong Kong via Amsterdam to Montreal and Toronto.

Hong Kong is the centre for Triad groups throughout the world. Drug trafficking activities have made them wealthy and powerful. Many have invested their funds in legitimate enterprises. The expectation is that the colony of Hong Kong will come under some form of control by the Chinese mainland government in 1997. This factor will give rise to further migration by many who are not anxious to reside under the rule of the People's Republic of China. Organized crime groups, or those who have profited from this activity, will likely seek refuge in other parts of the world. This will in all likelihood further broaden the base of these organized crime syndicates.

Organized crime groups originating in Vietnam and Japan pattern themselves along the lines of Chinese Triads. The Japanese Yakuza (gangsters) are professional racketeers in Japan specializing in blackmail, extortion, and the sale of illicit drugs and guns. The Vietnamese crime groups originated during the war in Vietnam. They specialized in the sale of black-market goods and illicit drugs. When the war ended many gang members immigrated to North America. Both crime groups, attracted by the lucrative profits derived from extortion, and from drug trafficking and other consensual crime, are beginning to emerge in Canada and the United States (Buruma and McBeth, 1984/85; *Time*, 1983).

THE COLOMBIAN MAFIA

The Colombian organized crime syndicates are situated in most cities in Colombia, but are centred in Bogota, Medellin, and Cali. They are divided into 20 organized crime families, 4 of which are the most prominent and influential. Although all are involved in traditional organized crime activity in Colombia, their Canadian base of illegal operation is centred on illicit drug trafficking. Their cocaine and marijuana crime families are organized along the same pattern as the Italian Mafia—a corporate organizational style. These syndicates each have related groups that act as investors, bankers, and lawyers. In addition, most have logistics experts, exporters, chemists, and specialists in wholesaling, retailing, and market development. They have separate groups that provide support services in the areas of manufacturing, transportation, distribution, finance, and security. Few of the group members are aware of the others that are involved. The loss of one member or even a whole group does not threaten the stability or security of the remaining parts.

These Colombian crime organizations provide at least 75 percent of the cocaine that is consumed in Canada and the United States, which amounts to a multi-billion dollar annual profit. The managers or top end of each crime organization are completely removed from physical trafficking activities. They have related groups operating in the Caribbean and in major cities in the United States as well as in Canada. In addition, they have established a strong presence in Spain to facilitate cocaine distribution throughout Europe.

Members of these crime families are assigned to foreign illicit distribution networks on a rotational basis. Members, who are Colombian citizens, will move into a Canadian city for a period of six months and then return to Colombia and be replaced by other members. This system of constantly changing membership makes it more difficult for law enforcement to identify the size and specific drug trafficking activities of the group.

These crime families effectively control illicit cocaine distribution in South America, the Caribbean, Europe, the United States, and Canada. They are continually expanding to develop distribution networks in other parts of the world. Their propensity to be highly organized and, at the same time, commit violent crimes such as serious assaults and homicide in an effort to acquire new territory has made them potentially the most dangerous crime groups in the world. With their current wealth in the billions of dollars range and the potential to earn billions more, these crime organizations could eventually dominate crime activity in the Americas and Europe for decades.

OUTLAW MOTORCYCLE GANGS

Motorcycle gangs began to form in North America during the late 1940s. These motorcycle enthusiasts were, for the most part, ordinary individuals who enjoyed cycling for part-time recreation. They formed the American Motorcycle Association (AMA) which, in turn, sponsored tours, races, and rallies. On July 4, 1947, the AMA sponsored one such event. It was a tour through California called the Gypsy Tour. On the same day the town of Hollister, California, situated 60 miles south of Oakland, held its annual motorcycle "dirt hill climb races." In previous years, small groups of motorcycle enthusiasts from the surrounding area attended these annual races. On this occasion, however, more than 3000 AMA riders invaded the small town. The AMA participants included a number of different motorcycle clubs, including a group known as Booze Fighters and another called Hell's Angels. A number of violent clashes broke out and caused the police to arrest many of the bikers involved. Both police officers and bikers were seriously injured. Broken beer bottles and damaged property left the main street of the small town in a shambles.

In the days following this event, the AMA publicly drew a distinction between the legitimate members of the AMA and the now newly classified renegades. The association characterized 99 percent of its members as clean-living folks enjoying pure sport. It condemned the other 1 percent as antisocial barbarians.

The renegade groups exploited this event by publishing this condemnation with bold defiance. They developed a motorcyclist patch called the "one-percenter." This patch is still worn in addition to regular "colours" and identifies the member as a so-called "outlaw biker." This single incident clearly served to unify and develop a unique type of major organized crime society in North America. Hollywood, with the film version of the Hollister riots entitled *The Wild One* and such movies as *Easy Rider* and *Hell's Angels on Wheels*, gave the motorcycle gang a distinctive image by romanticizing the outlaw biker. New chapters of outlaw groups subsequently formed in almost every part of the United States and Canada (Canada, 1980).

Canadian chapters of the Outlaws, Satan's Choice, Chosen Few, Grim Reapers, Hell's Angels, and Los Bravos are present in one or more major centres. While Ontario is largely dominated by the Outlaws chapter, Quebec has 30 different groups that can be termed "one-percenters." They number over 900 members (Quebec, 1980). The most powerful group in British Columbia is the Hell's Angels. In Manitoba Los Bravos is the dominant group. Other lesser-known groups have chapters in Saskatchewan and the Maritimes (Canada, 1980).

All groups function in the same general manner. They are tightly organized and their hierarchical system maintains a highly exclusive control over a particular territory alone or through alliances with other clubs. Smaller gangs often find it more expedient to support a larger, better-organized gang.

DEADLY WORLD OF HELL'S ANGELS IN SPOTLIGHT

By Chrys Goyens
Special to The Star
MONTREAL—Imagine the surprise of musicians in the Quebec Symphony Orchestra who recently discovered one of their number was a member of the Hell's Angels motorcycle gang.

"We almost fell over backwards when we read the story," said symphony spokesman Micheline Goulet, when the musicians learned that trumpeter Claude Berger "wears the colors" when he isn't performing Bach and Beethoven.

Other exploits of the notorious motorcycle gang known in Quebec as "Les Hells" have not been as classical.

Ontario warning

The Canadian Association of Chiefs of Police meeting in Saint John, N.B. this week received a report that says motorcycle gangs are the largest organized crime threat in Canada, surpassing even the Mafia.

Prepared by the recently organized Criminal Intelligence Service of Canada, the report also predicts a possible gang war in Ontario as the Montreal-based Hell's Angels move on their sworn enemies, The Outlaws, whose turf is Ontario.

Quebecers have had a steady diet of "Les Hells" in their daily news reports all year and the exploits of the bikers bode ill for Ontario if their brand of violence and mayhem crosses the provincial border.

The intelligence service report linked 22 Canadian murders to motorcycle gangs, mostly in clashes over the drug trade.

Those statistics will have to be revised upward after revelations this week at a special coroner's inquest in Joliette, northeast of Montreal.

This week it was learned that the bombing of a downtown Montreal highrise in November, which killed four men in Montreal's drug underworld, was the work of a Hell's Angel, now turned Crown informer.

The inquest was also told this week that club leaders of various chapters arranged the deaths of at least 12 fellow Hell's Angels for "poor behavior."

Yves (Apache) Trudeau told coroner Jean B. Falardeau he packed 35 pounds of plastic explosives inside a television set and delivered it to an apartment belonging to Paul April, 42.

When he knew April was in the apartment with three other men, Trudeau detonated the bomb by radio signal from outside the building. All four men were killed and another eight residents of the building were injured.

Trudeau told the inquest he killed April because the latter had bragged of murdering a west-end cocaine dealer who regularly did business with Les Hells.

Trudeau, 39, was serving a one-year sentence for possession of an illegal weapon when he volunteered to testify at the inquest into the murders last March of six Hell's Angels.

Their bloated bodies, wrapped in sleeping bags and weighted down by chains and cement blocks, were fished from the St. Lawrence River in April and May.

Trudeau's testimony cannot be used against him. He told the inquest he got no special promises from police other than a guarantee of protection for his wife and child.

Trudeau has been in special protective custody since Aug. 5.

He decided to testify because he was one of seven Hell's Angels from Laval who were sentenced to die at a Lennoxville chapter meeting on March 24.

Six killed

Other gang chapters decided to disband the Laval club and kill its members because they had personally used more than $200 000 worth of drugs earmarked for sale and were no longer considered "reliable."

Trudeau was spared because he was enrolled in a drug detoxification program and could not attend the meeting. He later learned a $50 000 contract had been taken out against his life.

Laurent (L'Anglais) Viau, Jean-Pierre (Matt le Crosseur) Mathieu, Guy-Louis (Chop) Adam, Jean-Guy Geoffrion and Michel (Willie) Mayrand were killed at the Lennoxville meeting. And another biker, Claude (Coco) Roy, was murdered a week later, the inquest was told.

The meeting ostensibly was called to discuss outstanding problems with The Outlaws gang and was attended by Hell's Angels from Lennoxville, Laval, Sorel and Halifax.

After detaining most of the 10 Hells suspected of murder, provincial police raided five club hangouts, netting an estimated $8 million worth of illicit drugs, in addition to automatic weapons, baseball bats, machetes, sleeping bags and a cement block attached to chains, like those found on the biker corpses found in the river.

Six of 10 Hell's Angels jailed in June and July were granted conditional release earlier this week when the coroner decided no hard evidence linked them with the murders. Still detained are Luc Michaud, Yvon Rodrigue, Charles Filteau and Yvon Bilodeau.

Lawyers for the Hell's Angels have fought ferociously against the powers of the coroner's office unique to Quebec in Canadian jurisprudence.

They succeeded in having one coroner, Judge John D'arcy Asselin, disqualified but attempts to have the inquest dismissed were defeated in Quebec Superior Court.

Quebec coroners now run inquests like regular court proceedings. The inquest is expected to continue well into September.

Source: *Toronto Star* 31 August 1985.

A gang member can never fully retire from the group. New members are recruited with care to ensure that agents or informants of law enforcement or rival gangs do not easily penetrate the group. A "striker," in bike parlance, is a would-be member aspiring to join the group. Strikers are recruited from "hangers-on" who generally ride with the gang on their tours or runs but at the back of the pack. Strikers may occasionally enter the club headquarters, but only to carry out minimal tasks. This period of membership may last as long as six months. Several criminal acts will likely have to be committed by the striker to the satisfaction of the peers. In addition, he may be required to attack or embarrass a rival gang member.

Crimes of violence are committed by gang members to establish territory, expand their membership through mergers, intimidate the public, or for "entertainment purposes." Most groups are, however, involved in major traditional organized-enterprise crime activity such as extortion, prostitution, and drug trafficking. They are mainly responsible for the manufacture and sale of illicit chemical drugs such as LSD, methamphetamine (speed), and PCP (angel dust). They traffic in all types of illicit drugs including marijuana, hashish, cocaine, and chemical drugs. The street value from the sale in Canada of these illicit drugs alone amounts to millions of dollars (Canada, 1985).

The Canadian groups connect with their United States and European counterparts to facilitate their drug trafficking operations. Unlike other crime organizations, the outlaw biker is visibly identifiable as a member of a particular group. Yet evidence of their illegal activities is difficult for law enforcement to obtain. The very structure of outlaw motorcycle groups, their internal discipline, their intimidating behaviour and other violent actions are the tools used to protect themselves from prosecution. Potential witnesses and informants become the special targets of the gangs. Their intimidating approach and their barbaric behaviour make the public cautious in confronting the groups, even when they are committing crimes.

A number of groups involved in highly successful crime enterprises have found it even more profitable to take on the public appearance of successful businessmen rather than the image of outlaw bikers. From their disguised position they find it useful and more effective to use corruption rather than brute force to expand their enterprises' crime interests. Perhaps what is evolving is a second-level crime group in the fashion of the Triad society.

THE CANADIAN ETHNIC-BASED DRUG TRAFFICKING GROUPS

In Canada, as in the United States, there is a large number of citizens or residents who, because of their individual cultural backgrounds, have strong family or ethnic ties to other regions of the world. When certain organized crime enterprises emerge in those other regions it becomes profitable for crime groups to establish a base in Canada, and Canadian citizens or residents become members of the illegal enterprise.

Major illicit drug distribution systems controlled by strong organized crime groups currently exist in the southwest Asian area of Pakistan, Iran and Afghanistan, in Lebanon, and in India. These networks have now established connections with groups in Canada, the United States, South America, and Europe. Illicit drugs are supplied to Canadian-based groups, who then sell the illicit product to any other organized crime groups who subsequently distribute the drugs in their own established territory.

Some drug trafficking groups in drug source countries are involved in national political violence. When this situation occurs there is the merging of organized crime and terrorism through the common interest of trafficking illicit drugs. Thus, the drug-terrorism link not only increases revenue for political purposes but intensifies the political effect of the terrorist group by connecting with a group, usually along ethnic lines, that has traditionally been involved only in enterprise crime activity.

THE NATURE OF ORGANIZED CRIME ACTIVITY

Businessmen and other investors are attracted to the commercial activity and investment that produce the highest profit with the lowest risk. Criminals who engage in crime for financial gain are also attracted by high income and seek out criminal activities that produce the highest profit with the least amount of risk. Although organized crime groups derive profits from a wide range of criminal activity including kidnapping, robbery, theft, and fraud, in North America their most sought-after criminal ventures involve consensual-type crimes. Crimes related to drug trafficking, gambling, prostitution, and pornography produce massive profits yet leave no victim behind to complain to law enforcement authorities that a financial loss has been incurred. When the criminal act has been committed, the crime group members are relatively free to use the proceeds for their own benefit. Without a victim to bring a complaint to the attention of the police and no legitimate legal owner to bring an action of recovery for loss of property, the consensual crime will occur without creating an incident or a visible social problem in the community.

EXTORTION

Crimes of violence such as serious assaults, property damage, and homicides are also included in the lexicon of organized crime activities. These violent acts are generally committed to intimidate the public or individuals, eliminate witnesses or informants, acquire or secure territory, or enforce directives or rules on customers and group members. Special organized crime groups also function for profit as enforcers for other crime groups. Since these contracts for murder or violent acts are often carried out on a national or international basis, there will be no previous contact or connection between the victim and his assailant. With no visible evidence of motive and no witnesses to establish any contact between the victim and the criminal, the crime falls into a low-risk category for criminal groups engaged in this type of activity.

FORMER DRUG WITNESS SHOT TO DEATH

TORONTO (CP)—A key Crown witness in a marijuana-importing trial in Metropolitan Toronto last year has been found shot to death in Maine.

Michael Sanborn, 34, of Sanford, Me., was found Monday with a gunshot wound to his head. His body was beside a car parked a few metres from where he was working as a painter.

Nick Gess, the state's assistant attorney general, said Wednesday that police have no suspect.

Sanborn testified last year against Robert (Rosie) Rowbotham, 35, of Toronto, who was eventually sentenced to 20 years for importing hashish and marijuana with a street value of about $60 million.

Sanborn had been paroled after serving 30 months of a five-year jail sentence for his part in a marijuana-importing operation.

Source: *Ottawa Citizen* 19 September 1985.

In Toronto during the 1970s and early 1980s the enforcers for organized crime were the Commisso family. Remo Commisso had arrived in Canada from Calabria at the age of 15 in 1961 with his two brothers and his mother. His older brother, Cosimo, was 23 and his younger brother, Michele, was 13 at the time. Their father, Girolamo Commisso, had been a don in the Siderno area in Italy until he was gunned down in a Mafia feud in the late 1940s (no one was ever arrested for his murder). The Commissos quickly became part of organized crime in Ontario. They became involved in drug trafficking, counterfeit money, and extortion contracts. Their mainstay activity, however, became heavy-duty extortions and collections in the process of enforcing rules for other crime groups. Bombings, arson, brutal conspiracies to kill, and cold-blooded murder were the crimes that became a matter of public record. One of their top hit men, Cecil Kirby, defected from the Commisso ranks and offered his services to the RCMP as an informant and an agent. Kirby later testified against the Commissos and they were subsequently convicted and sentenced to lengthy prison terms in 1984 (Dubro, 1985).

CORRUPTION

Although extortion has become an accepted tool of organized crime to enforce its rules, corruption is also an effective means of obtaining co-operation. This is particularly true when public or corporate officials are needed to support a particular measure useful to an organized crime group. When organized crime remains unchecked in its illegal activity, its corrupting influences usually penetrate all levels of law enforcement agencies, even national governmental, judicial, and political officials. Benefits are paid in such subtle ways that it becomes almost impossible to uncover a well-designed bribery payment scheme. In addition to payments made to foreign secret bank accounts and trust schemes, they can take the form of staged winnings at a gambling casino where the official is either allowed to win at some game or given chips which would represent winnings. The sale or transfer of shares of corporations, real estate, or other investments at an undervalued price which will subsequently appear as a capital gain is also popular, as is allowing officials to participate in fraudulent schemes where investment will increase dramatically over a short period of time. Providing well-paid employment to family members or friends is also a common practice (Quebec, 1977a).

INVESTMENTS IN LEGITIMATE BUSINESS

The activities of organized crime are not limited to the collection of illegal proceeds that flow directly from criminal operations. When organized crime groups derive profits from illegal activity and then conceal those profits through a laundering scheme, they invest such profits in legitimate business ventures. Their infiltration into otherwise legitimate business will again result in a secondary type of business crime. This follows when illegal methods such as extortion and corruption are used to eliminate or control lawful competition. Judge Jean L. Dutil, quoting the late Senator Robert Kennedy, wrote:

> When racketeers bore their way into business the cost is borne by the public. When the infiltration is into business or labour relations, the racketeer's cut is paid by higher wages and higher prices, in other words, by the public. (Charbonneau, 1976)

The Quebec Crime Commission found that the accumulation of proceeds directly derived from crime by organized criminals tends to result in significant wealth and power coming into their hands. Their ability to infiltrate and take over legitimate enterprises follows logically (Quebec, 1977a).

The combined effect of the high profitability of consensual criminal activity, together with the use of laundering systems and the investments in legitimate business institutions, has given crime organizations a dimension where they are capable of undermining the institutions involved in legitimate trade and commerce; in some cases, they are threatening the integrity of governments.

THE NATURE OF CONSENSUAL CRIME ACTIVITY

When governments use the law to curtail the distribution and supply of goods or services that are reasonably high in public demand, a so-called black market results. In this market the traders or businesspeople become the criminals and their business entities become the crime organizations. They will operate without regard to territorial boundaries, taxation systems, or regulations that control legitimate trade and commerce. The cost of corruption for bribes and payoffs, and contracts for intimidation and extortion, will be the only price crime organizations will pay directly to maintain their base of control. In this environment the consumer will pay the highest price for the lowest-quality product that the market will bear, and the crime organization will achieve its prime objective, which is to accumulate profit and power.

Consensual crime produces more income for crime organizations than any other type of criminal activity. Drug trafficking alone accounts for over 85 percent of the proceeds obtained from consensual-type crime such as prostitution, gambling, pornography, and loansharking. (See Figure 14.1.)

The profitability of drug trafficking may be demonstrated by examining the increase in value of illicit drugs as they progress from the producer or manufacturer to the consumer. (See Table 14.1.) An illicit opium producer may receive from $1350 to $1500 for 10 kilograms of opium. This, in turn, produces one kilogram of pure heroin that sells in the production areas for up to $11 500. When that one kilogram is delivered to Canada, it will sell for as much as $225 000. The final product that emerges after being cut and diluted is a capsule dosage unit containing 5 to 6 percent pure heroin which sells for between $35 and $60. This means that the one kilogram of pure heroin can generate retail sales that could total in excess of $12 to $15 million.

The Royal Canadian Mounted Police *National Drug Intelligence Estimate* for 1983 estimates that the retail value of the illicit drugs supplied to the Canadian market in 1983 was approximately $9.6 billion, while the United States authorities estimate that the retail sales in the United States for the year 1983 were in excess of U.S. $80 billion. The United Nations Fund for Drug Abuse Control (UNFDAC) states in a 1980 publication that "the profits from

FIGURE 14.1
CONSENSUAL CRIME KNOWN 1981

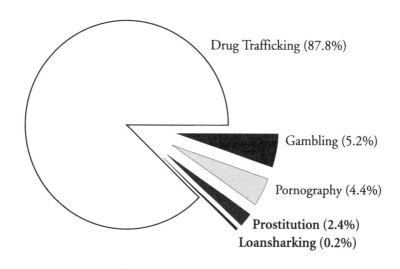

Source: Canadian Association of Chiefs of Police—Canada-Wide Survey, 1981.

street sales worldwide are now estimated at around U.S. $200 billion a year" (United Nations, 1980).

While the illicit opium producer may make several thousands of dollars from his annual harvest, the organized criminals who sell heroin in the illicit markets of the world will make billions of tax-free dollars annually. Judge Jean L. Dutil stated that the trade in narcotics pours tens of millions of dollars into the coffers of traffickers in Canada, financing their operations in other fields, and permitting them to spread their criminal activity over a much larger area (Charbonneau, 1976; Dubro, 1985).

MONEY LAUNDERING SCHEMES

One of the few ways that a street gang's illegal activities can be connected to a national or international organized crime group is by tracing the money flow from the "street crimes." In most organized crime groups the transfer of the profits or proceeds is the only tangible link that exists between the unlawful acts and the top-level organizers and planners of the group. Therefore, movements of funds are carefully concealed through the use of specially devised transfer systems. These systems are usually called "money laundering schemes."

TABLE 14.1
REPRESENTATIVE PRICES FOR SOUTHEAST ASIAN (SEA)
AND SOUTHWEST ASIAN (SWA)
HEROIN AT SUCCESSIVE STAGES OF TRAFFICKING, 1984

Southeast Asian (SEA) Heroin

Farmer—10 kg of opium—$1350–$1500
Laboratory (Golden Triangle)—1 kg of No. 4 heroin (pure)—
$4200–$5800

Distribution Centre (Bangkok)—1 kg of No. 4 heroin (pure)—
$7400–$11 500

Canada—1 kg of No. 4 heroin (pure)—$225 000
—1 ounce (28 grams) of No. 4 heroin (pure)—$6000–$13 000
—1 gram of No. 4 heroin (pure)—$600–$1000
—1 capsule of No. 4 heroin (5%–6% pure)—$35–$60

Southwest Asian (SWA) Heroin

Farmer—10 kg of opium—$900–$1000
Laboratory (Golden Crescent)—1 kg of No. 4 heroin (pure)—
$5200–$7150

Distribution Centre (Europe)—1 kg of heroin (pure)—
$50 000–$85 000

Canada—1 kg of heroin (pure)—$225 000
—1 ounce (28 grams) of heroin (pure)—$6000–$13 000
—1 gram of heroin (pure)—$600–$1000
—1 capsule of heroin (5%–6% pure)—$35–$60

Note: Prices for heroin in Canada at each level of the distribution system do not
fluctuate greatly regardless of country of origin.

Source: RCMP. *National Drug Intelligence Estimate 1984/85.*

**MAFIA INFORMER DESCRIBES LINK BETWEEN BANKS,
DIRTY MONEY**

By William Marsden of The Gazette
NEW YORK—On Nov. 11, 1980, Salvatore Amendolito, 52, a
well-dressed, distinguished-looking Italian with salt-and-pepper hair,

walked into the Bank of Nova Scotia in Nassau, Bahamas, and deposited $233,387.20 cash in small bills.

The next day he deposited another $329,983.12, this time in money orders, travellers' cheques and cashiers' cheques all under $10,000.

Those deposits, Amendolito told a U.S. federal court recently, were a small fraction of the millions of dollars of "dirty money" the Mafia gave him to launder through Canadian banks in the Bahamas.

Amendolito, who turned informer when police agreed to drop charges against him, is a key witness in a trial here of 22 people charged in a heroin ring and money-laundering operation known as the Pizza Connection.

The trial began six months ago and is expected to continue for several more months.

Court records show that the Mafia used the Bank of Nova Scotia and the Royal Bank in Nassau and other international financial institutions to launder money—give it a clean history—and send about $10 million U.S. to Switzerland in 1980–81.

The New York Mafia also funnelled $20.5 million U.S. to Switzerland from March to September 1982 through currency-trading accounts at the New York offices of brokerage companies E.F. Hutton and Merrill Lynch, records show.

The banks and brokerage firms have not been charged with any crime.

Defendants in the case—labelled the Pizza Connection because pizzerias were used to hide drug trafficking and money laundering—also attempted in 1983 to launder unspecified amounts of cash through unnamed Montreal boutiques, controlled by somebody they called "Anna Maria of Montreal," FBI wiretaps indicate.

According to court documents and a 130-page indictment, Anna Maria of Montreal flew from Montreal to La Guardia airport in Queens, where she met Gaetano Mazzara and Francesco Castronovo, two restaurant-business partners from New Jersey, who are among the Pizza Connection defendants. Police said they cannot reveal more information on this connection.

Banks and similar institutions are the first step in giving dirty money a clean history, and Canadian banks—which handle 80 per cent of the banking business in the Bahamas—have been key instruments in laundering money.

Laws that forbid Bahamian bankers to disclose records ensure protection from investigation by foreign narcotics and tax agents.

And once a drug trafficker has deposited his cash into a Bahamian bank, he can wire it anywhere in the world, no questions asked.

Source: *The Gazette*, Montreal, 24 April 1986.

Although there is a wide variety of money laundering schemes, the most difficult to penetrate and, therefore, the most popular, are those which utilize secret banking and corporate facilities in tax haven countries.

It is now recognized by international law enforcement organizations that the only successful way to identify and prosecute organized crime figures is to trace the proceeds of crime from the source to the ultimate beneficiaries. James Dubro found that

> when the Commissos got involved in land deals they concentrated on hidden titles, a money laundering operation to hide the sources of profits made from drugs and contract murders. In one documented case, Remo and Cosimo were in secret partnership with Alberto Bentivogli in owning a Toronto restaurant, as well as 23 acres in Richmond Hill and land in Burlington. (Dubro, 1985)

In another case, law enforcement officers from the United States, Canada, Hong Kong, Singapore, and Thailand attempted to identify and seize money being transferred from North America to Thailand via the Netherlands, Hong Kong, and Singapore. They followed the transfer of $2 million, derived from heroin sales in the western United States and Canada, and transported in cash lots, first to the Netherlands and then to Hong Kong, where it was deposited in a bank. From this bank it was transferred to a Chinese Hong Kong import-export company which operated primarily as an underground money laundering service for the Southeast Asian Chinese community.

When the funds were received by the import-export company in Hong Kong, a corresponding credit appeared with another related import-export company in Singapore. Instructions from the company in Singapore caused a further paper transfer to occur in Thailand where the last transaction in the chain occurred. Cash was then paid to an unidentified individual and it was believed that the funds were moved to northern Thailand to the benefit of a major drug trafficking organized crime group. No assets were seized as a result of this investigation, but is was established that over $52 million had been moved through this one laundering system. Similar laundering systems also exist for other ethnically based organized crime groups (Stamler, 1984a).

Although Europeans have been using protected banking facilities in Switzerland since the early 19th century, in North America tax havens have grown in popularity in recent times as one of the few means of placing funds beyond the reach of government authorities or tax collectors. This guarantee of financial privacy became attractive to a wide variety of persons, including those whose primary interest was not necessarily to avoid taxes. It was not long before crime organizations found the sanctuary of tax havens too inviting to ignore. With the development of multinational banking systems and international business and commerce it became easy to develop sophisticated laundering schemes designed to move money obtained directly from criminal activity into the foreign banks protected from intrusion by law enforcement officials. For the organized criminal, this financial privacy is an indispensable aid in concealing the proceeds of crime. Many countries and territories, at times unwittingly, provide this type of protection.

These countries and territories not only allow easy access to banking institutions with secret numbered accounts, but have also extended corporate and secrecy laws to allow the establishment of an unlimited number of beneficially owned corporations. These so-called offshore corporations are operated by local agents or lawyers, but manipulated by the beneficial owners. When these corporate entities are combined with several numbered bank accounts, a maze of financial transactions can be structured in a way that makes the tracing of assets a very complex task. If questionable funds are then moved from one tax haven jurisdiction to another, using the combination of beneficially owned corporations with secret numbered bank accounts, the complexities are significantly increased.

Laundering schemes used to move illegally obtained funds vary as widely and are as complex as legitimate business and commercial transactions. Through a variety of transactions, cash can be secretly transferred anywhere in the world. This includes the use of corporations, business entities, or phony business transactions, all done under the guise of a legitimate commercial enterprise (United States Government, 1983).

CONTROLLING ORGANIZED CRIME

LEGALIZATION OF ILLICIT GOODS AND SERVICES

Legalizing the products and services supplied to meet a public demand is one of the most effective means of curbing the profits and income of crime groups. This factor has, in turn, a direct effect on development, growth, and continuation of organized crime within a society.

There is no doubt that when the United States Congress passed the country-wide Volstead Act on October 28, 1919, prohibiting the manufacture and sale of alcohol, organized crime moved into the business and became the major supplier of what became then an illegal product. From 1920 to 1933 organized crime groups in the United States grew and flourished from the profits derived from the sale of illicit alcohol, only because it was a product prohibited by the government.

The United States stayed dry (at least legally) until 1933. In the thirteen years that the sale of alcohol was prohibited in the United States, profits from the sale of illicit alcohol topped all other income from unlawful activity. When prohibition ended, crime groups turned to gambling, illicit drugs, and prostitution as the high-income enterprises.

In more recent times, gambling laws in North America have been liberalized. Organized crime is now focusing on illicit drugs, pornography, and prostitution as its primary sources of income.

While the liberalization of liquor and gambling laws in both Canada and the United States had an effect on reducing the income for organized crime from those illegal activities, the dramatic increase in the demand for illicit drugs since the 1960s has more than filled the gap. Beginning in the early 1980s, drug trafficking clearly became one of the most profitable enterprises for organized crime (Canada, 1983, 1984/5).

Legalizing this product may, however, prove more difficult than with alcohol or gambling, as Canada, along with 130 countries of the world, has ratified a United Nations Convention agreeing to prohibit the manufacture, distribution, and sale of narcotic drugs except for medical, scientific, or research purposes. At this time, the trend at the international level is toward greater control. In this international environment it would be difficult for one country to move against this established trend (United Nations, 1961, 1971).

LAWS, ENFORCEMENT TECHNIQUES, AND INTERNATIONAL ACTION TO CURB THE ACTIVITIES OF ORGANIZED CRIME

Canadian criminal laws, like the laws of most countries in the world, are generally preoccupied with the detection, apprehension, and conviction of those individuals involved in specific criminal acts which have occurred within a particular territorial jurisdiction. The process relies on victims and witnesses to report the occurrences of such criminal acts and participate in the proceedings that are instituted.

Organized criminals who are involved in supplying illegal goods and services to a co-operating public, and who utilize corruption, extortion, and other intimidating techniques, accumulate their profits through the commission of a series of criminal acts carried out by a number of different individuals over a substantial period of time, and involve many different territorial jurisdictions.

POLICE INVESTIGATIONS

An effective police investigation must be proactive in nature, especially when it is directed against an organized crime group involved in consensual crime. It must include a number of lawful covert law enforcement techniques. The covert techniques should include the use of paid informants, trained undercover police officers, electronic surveillance equipment to surreptitiously record the private conversations of organized crime members, and covert physical surveillance techniques. The police and enforcement authorities must have an adequate witness protection program available, so that potential witnesses will be protected from any acts of intimidation or violence by the organized crime groups. The use of financial investigations to trace, freeze, seize, and forfeit the proceeds of crime will serve to remove the profits of the criminal enterprise. This type of investigation will also assist in gathering evidence to implicate top levels of organized crime with the criminal activity carried out by the group.

NATIONAL CRIMINAL LAWS AND PROCEDURES

National criminal laws and procedures must be adequate to ensure that organized crime is not able to profit from the proceeds generated by criminal activity, no matter where a crime has occurred. Canada has enacted a criminal law which makes it an offence to possess the proceeds of crime in Canada. Section 312 of the Criminal Code of Canada makes it an offence to possess anything that was obtained or derived directly or indirectly from the commission of an indictable offence or from any act committed anywhere which, if committed in Canada, would be classified as an indictable offence. This provision, combined with the laws of conspiracy, makes it possible to prosecute in Canada anyone who conspires to possess proceeds of crime within Canada, even if all the conspirators are outside of Canada. The law was designed to prosecute organized crime figures in the United States who possess the proceeds of crime in this country or to prosecute them for using financial institutions in Canada to move their money inside or through Canada. While the law will serve to prosecute those that possess the proceeds of crime, it was not designed to remove the proceeds from the possession of the criminals. There are, in fact, few provisions in the law that can be used to dismantle financial empires that are in the possession of Canadian organized crime groups.

INTERNATIONAL CO-OPERATION

Effective action at the international level to prevent organized crime from profiting from its criminal activities requires the establishment of international standards. Standards for national criminal laws must ensure that no country or territory can be used as a haven for organized crime figures or their profits.

Initiatives taken by the United Nations will be extremely useful to combat the spread of organized crime; but treaties, standards, and enforcement programs will take years to develop, implement, and co-ordinate before any positive results are achieved.

In the meantime, organized crime will likely grow as a criminal subculture in the world. Canada, through its institutions, may alter its laws and ability to react more quickly to problems associated with organized crime. It may develop laws or enforcement programs that make it undesirable or unprofitable for organized crime groups to establish a base of operations in Canada. Establishing programs designed to reduce the demand for any illicit product is one certain way to achieve results. Public-awareness programs that are designed to prevent organized crime groups from becoming established is another. Finally, effectively prosecuting individual members of organized crime groups and seizing and removing the accumulated profits of crime will result in dismantling crime organizations before they become more firmly entrenched in our society.

SUMMARY

The demand for illegal goods and services influences the presence, size, and structure of organized crime in our society. The phenomenon of organized crime is best described as the operation of illegal business entities whose members are bound together because of their group interest and their desire to profit from illegal activity. More than seven major organized crime groups exist in Canada and connect with other groups in other regions of the world to distribute their illicit goods and services. As well, these groups launder their illicit profits through countries whose laws are designed to protect bank and investment records.

Crime organizations establish territorial distribution areas and utilize extortion and corruption to develop regions under their control and enforce their rules.

Laundered profits are invested in legitimate business, which provides the members in the upper levels with a cover and, in turn, respectability in the community.

While the size, structure, and presence of organized crime is determined by the public demand for illegal goods and services, government control is exercised through police enforcement and prosecution before the courts. Since it is no offence in Canada to be a member of a crime group, enforcement must be based on specific crimes committed by individual members of organized crime groups.

International action and co-operation is necessary to control organized crime. In this regard, the United Nations and other international agencies are increasingly developing systems to help identify and investigate organized crime groups at the international level.

BIBLIOGRAPHY

Arlacchi, Pino. (1984). Italian Parliamentary Committee for Mafia Phenomenon. *Effects of the New Anti-Mafia Law on the Proceeds of Crime and on the Italian Economy.* Rome: Government of Italy.

————. (1985). Italian Parliamentary Committee for Mafia Phenomenon. *International Society of Social Defence.* Rome: Government of Italy.

Bresler, Fenton. (1980). *The Trial of the TRIADS: An Investigation into International Crime.* London: Weidenfeld and Nicolson.

Buruma, Ian, and John McBeth. (1984/85). "An East-Side Story." *Far Eastern Economic Review* Dec. 27–Jan. 3.

Canada. (1980). "No Biker Problems in Canada?" *Royal Canadian Mounted Police—Gazette.* Ottawa: RCMP:42:10.

————. (1983). RCMP *National Drug Intelligence Estimate 1982.* Ottawa: Queen's Printer.

————. (1984). RCMP *National Drug Intelligence Estimate 1983.* Ottawa: Queen's Printer.

———. (1985). *RCMP National Drug Intelligence Estimate 1984/5.* Ottawa: Queen's Printer.

Chambliss, William J. (1978). *On the Take: From Petty Crooks to Presidents.* Bloomington: Indiana University Press.

Charbonneau, Jean-Pierre. (1976). *The Canadian Connection.* Ottawa: Optimum Publishing Company.

Dubro, James. (1985). *Mob Rule: Inside the Canadian Mafia.* Toronto: Macmillan.

Glaser, Daniel. (1978). *Crime in Our Changing Society.* New York: Holt, Rinehart and Winston.

Maclean, Don. (1974). *Pictorial History of the Mafia.* New York: Pyramid Books.

Pennsylvania Crime Commission. (1980). *A Decade of Organized Crime.* Pennsylvania State Printer.

Quebec. (1977a). Police Commission of Inquiry on Organized Crime. *Organized Crime and the World of Business.* Quebec: Éditeur Officiel.

———. (1977b). *The Fight Against Organized Crime in Quebec.* Quebec: Éditeur Officiel.

———. (1980). Commission de Police du Québec, Enquête sur le Crime Organisé. *Les Bandes de Motards au Québec.* Quebec: Éditeur Officiel.

Sacco, Vincent F. (1986). "An Approach to the Study of Organized Crime." In Robert A. Silverman and James J. Teevan (eds.), *Crime in Canadian Society.* (3rd ed.) (pp. 214–26). Toronto: Butterworths.

Stamler, Rodney T. (1984a). *Background Document—Proceeds of Drug Trafficking.* Vienna: United Nations Division of Narcotic Drugs Report. DND/Wp 1984/9.

———. (1984b). "Forfeiture of the Profits and Proceeds of Drug Crimes." *United Nations Bulletin on Narcotics.* Vienna. 36(4):3–19.

Stamler, Rodney T., and Robert C. Fahlman. (1983). "The Profits of Organized Crime: The Illicit Drug Trade in Canada." *United Nations Bulletin on Narcotics.* Vienna. 35(2):61–70.

Time Magazine. (1983). "The New Ellis Island." (June 13):18–25.

United Nations. (1961). *Single Convention on Narcotic Drugs.*

———. (1971). *Convention on Psychotropic Substances.*

———. (1980). *Opium Poppy—Fight Drugs through Development.* Vienna: United Nations Division of Narcotic Drugs.

United States Government. (1983) (February). Permanent Subcommittee on Investigations. *Crime and Secrecy: The Use of Offshore Banks and Companies.* Washington, DC: U.S. Government Printing Office.

———. (1984) (March). The President's Commission on Organized Crime. Record of Hearing 11: March 14, 1984, New York, NY. *Organized Crime and Money Laundering.* Government Printing Office.

———. (1984)(October). The President's Commission on Organized Crime. Interim Report to the President and the Attorney General. *The Cash Connection: Organized Crime, Financial Institutions and Money Laundering.* Washington, DC: U.S. Government Printing Office.

FURTHER READING

Abadinsky, Howard. (1981). *Organized Crime.* Boston: Allyn and Bacon.

Albini, J. (1971). *The American Mafia—Genesis of a Legend.* New York: Appleton-Century-Crofts.

Anderson, A.J. (1979). *The Business of Organized Crime*. Palo Alto, CA: Stanford University, Hoover Institute Press.

Bers, M.K. (1970). *The Penetration of Legitimate Business by Organized Crime—An Analysis*. Washington, DC: Law Enforcement Assistance Administration, U.S. Department of Justice.

Blakey, G.R. (ed.) (1980). *Techniques in the Investigation and Prosecution of Organized Crime* (3 Vols.). Ithaca, NY: Cornell Institute on Organized Crime.

Burchfiel, K.J. (1977–1980). "The Economic Organization of Crime: A Study of the Development of Criminal Enterprise." *Criminal Law Quarterly* 20:478–512.

Clinard, Marshall B. (1952). *The Black Market: A Study of White Collar Crime*. New York: Holt, Rinehart and Winston.

Cook, James. (1980). "The Invisible Enterprise." *Forbes* (September 29):1980, 60–77.

———. (1980). "The Invisible Enterprise, Part 2: Money Makes the Mob Go Round." *Forbes* (October 13):120–28.

Glaser, Daniel. (1978). *Crimes in Our Changing Society*. New York: Holt, Rinehart and Winston.

Hess, Henner. (1973). *Mafia and Mafiosi: The Structure of Power*. Translated by Ewald Oser. Lexington, MA: D.C. Heath.

Horner, F. (1979). *Guns and Garlic*. Indiana: Purdue University Press.

Schultz. (1974). "Investing Dirty Money: Section 1962(a) of the Organized Crime Control Act of 1970." *Yale Law Journal* 83:1441–1515.

Smith, D.C. (1978). "Organized Crime and Entrepreneurship." *International Journal of Criminology and Penology* 6:161–77.

Smith, Dwight. (1975). *The Mafia Mystique*. New York: Basic Books.

Teresa, Vincent, and Thomas C. Renner. (1973). *My Life in the Mafia*. Garden City, NY: Doubleday.

United States. (1977). Comptroller General. Report to the Congress. *War on Organized Crime Faltering: Federal Strike Forces not Getting the Job Done*. Washington, DC: General Accounting Office.

———. (1979). National Association of Attorneys General, Committee on the Office of Attorney General. Organized Crime Control Special Report. *Recent Developments in Organized Crime Control*. Raleigh, NC.

———. (1975). National Association of Attorneys General, Committee on the Office of Attorney General. Organized Crime Special Report. *The Use of Civil Remedies in Organized Crime Control*. Raleigh, NC.

———. (1977). National Association of Attorneys General, Committee on the Office of Attorney General. *The Use of Civil Remedies in Organized Crime Control*. Raleigh, North Carolina.

Wilson, W. (1970). "The Threat of Organized Crime: Highlighting the Challenging New Frontiers in Criminal Law." *Notre Dame Lawyer* 46: 41–54.

CHAPTER 15

POLITICAL CRIME IN CANADA

By Raymond R. Corrado

MULTIPLE PERSPECTIVES ON POLITICAL CRIME IN CANADA

*B*rutality, fear of terrorism, and the abuse of public trust by corrupt officials elicit emotional responses. Political crime involves issues of power and authority. Threats to the status quo can be undesirable, affecting self-interest, ideology, lifestyle, and life opportunities. Perceptions of political crime in Canada are, therefore, influenced by a complex interaction of emotional, practical, and ideological considerations. Ideology, in particular, is important in analyzing political crime. How one views Canadian society and politics is essential to the conceptualization and explanation of political crime. The purpose of this chapter is to conceptualize and examine political crime in Canada through various competing theoretical perspectives. In this way, a comprehensive analysis of this complex phenomenon may be offered.

THE CONCEPTUALIZATION OF POLITICAL CRIME

The concept of political crime in its modern sense was first employed during the French Revolution at the end of the 18th century (Ingraham, 1979). Before this period, terms such as *treason* in common law and *crimen laesae majestatis* in Roman law were employed to refer to what is now identified as political crime. Roman law defined such acts as betrayal to a foreign enemy, challenges to political authority, hindrance of official functions, and usurpation of granted powers. By the 12th century, laws were created specifically to address crimes involving sovereign powers such as treason, conspiracy, and felonies against heads of state. The official response to these crimes was far more severe than to crimes involving individuals or property. The primary goal was not simply to regulate or deter, but rather to destroy any threat to the state (Schafer, 1974).

Machiavelli was among the first political theorists to discuss the complex concept of political crime and delineate its numerous manifestations. Not only did he include threats against the state in the category of political crime, but also crimes committed by governments for the sake of expedience and political advantage. In fact, machiavellianism is a concept which is used to denote treacherous and deceitful authorities involved in questionable political practices. By the end of the 19th century, other European scholars such as Cesare Lombroso (who published his work in 1872) and Louis Proal (who published in 1898) articulated the concept of political crime. Lombroso viewed political crime broadly as any unlawful attack on societal structures or traditions. Proal expanded Lombroso's definition of political crime to include "crimes perpetrated by government for alleged reasons of state and by politicians for alleged reasons of expediency or political advantage" (Proal, 1973). Proal, therefore, conceived political crime as being corruptive behaviour designed either to alter or to preserve the institutions and structure of power in society. He maintained that political crime could involve ordinary as well as extraordinary crime. His definition considered the fact that ordinary crimes such as robbery, kidnapping, and homicide could also have political implications along with the more explicit politically motivated crimes such as treason and espionage.

The absence of a legal definition of political crime has hampered scholars in conceptualizing the term. Conventional crimes such as homicide and robbery are explicitly or operationally defined in criminal codes or statutes. By contrast, political crime is not legally defined, but rather is alluded to by Criminal Code offences such as treason, espionage, assassination, sabotage, and rebellion. Although criminal codes do not usually refer to these offences as political crimes, there is general agreement among scholars that such crimes should be conceptualized and operationalized as political crimes. The disagreement in recent literature focuses on whether political crime should include the deceitful and sometimes violent behaviour of governments and their representatives, and whether political crime should include all conventional crimes as well as specific, extraordinary crimes such as treason.

CRIMES BY AND AGAINST GOVERNMENT

Some scholars define political crime in terms of actual or perceived threats to the social order (Minor, 1975; Schafer, 1974; Turk, 1982). Austin Turk, in particular, argues that political crime should not include the illegal behaviour of governments or their authorities. He argues that even illegal acts of political repression should be excluded, so as not to confuse political criminality with political policing and conventional politics. Political criminality should be limited to events that "have any direct significance for the basic struggle over authority itself" (Turk, 1982). Since it is the authorities who legally have power, challenges to the existing structured relationship between authorities and their subjects should be conceived of as political crimes. In this light, the purpose of the police, whether through legal or illegal means, is to maintain this status quo authority structure. Turk's conceptualization of political crime is embedded in a theoretical framework which focuses on the inherent conflict over power in all social relationships and the inevitable evolution of political crime and political policing as social order and societal structures emerge (Turk, 1982). Most importantly, Turk's definition avoids defining conventional crime and crimes committed by state officials as political crime.

Illegal government behaviour, however, can also be politically threatening. Clinard and Quinney (1973) restrict their definition of political crime to office holders and government agents "who in the attempt to preserve a particular social order violate a higher law, as seen, for example, in police brutality, the denial of free speech, and the restriction of free assembly." Proal (1973) believes that corrupt officials, whatever their personal motives, are also political criminals. The betrayal of public trust and the abuse of official functions provide the political dimension to consider corrupt and violent police conduct as political crimes. Studies of the police in the United States (Barker and Roebuck, 1973; Chambliss, 1971; Stoddard, 1968; Westley, 1970) and more recent studies in Canada (Ericson, 1982; Sawatsky, 1980) provide considerable evidence about police misconduct across a wide range of official and unofficial functions.

THE DISTINCTION BETWEEN POLITICAL AND CONVENTIONAL CRIME

Conceptual distinctions and typologies have been developed to discriminate between political and conventional crime. Most of these distinctions can be traced to Robert Merton's differentiation between nonconforming and aberrant behaviours.

> The nonconformer, in contrast to the aberrant, (1) announces his dissent publicly, (2) challenges the legitimacy of the norms and laws he violates, (3) aims to change the norms he is denying in practice, (4) is acknowledged by conventional members of the society to depart from prevailing norms for disinterested purposes and not for what he personally can get out of it, and (5) lays claim to a higher morality and to ultimate values rather than to the particular norms of the society. (Clinard and Quinney, 1973)

This conceptualization underlies the view that "legalistic criminals" (Horton and Leslie, 1965), "ideological criminals" (Schafer, 1974), and "social movement criminals" (Hancock and Gibbons, 1975; Sykes, 1974) do not engage in full-time criminal activity, do not consider themselves as criminals, and do not engage in personal or private acts. Unlike conventional criminals, political criminals "carry out their illegal activities in pursuit of an ideal" (Clinard and Quinney, 1973). These types and characteristics reflect the more narrow conception of political crime.

The broadest conceptualization of political crime emphasizes fundamental societal processes including power, conflict, and interest group politics (Reasons, 1974) as well as the structure of social, economic, and political institutions (Quinney and Wildeman, 1977). The process of defining and enforcing criminal laws is political. Criminal codes are legislative acts which reflect the dominant ideological values of society. In this light, any criminal act is, by definition, a challenge to the political status quo and therefore a political crime.

In narrowing this broad conceptualization of political crime, Roebuck and Weeber (1978) developed a definition of political crime that includes

> violations of international law, violations of regulatory agency rules and statutes, pollution of the environment, manufacture of evidence, repression of legal dissent, entrapment, illegal domestic intelligence operations, illegal awards of state and federal contracts and leases, bribery to influence the political process, unlawful police acts, military war crimes, illegal arms sales and illegal abuse of prisoners.

Their list excludes only those conventional crimes which do not have direct implications for the political process. Although murder, robbery, sexual assault, or even environmental pollution obviously involve a political dimension, political crimes are generally distinguished by more salient threats to the political system. Crimes threatening the state, such as rebellions, insurrections, or insurgent terrorism, as well as crimes committed by state officials, such as political corruption or state terrorism, constitute such direct threats to the existing socio-political system and are, therefore, considered to constitute political crime.

In this chapter, *political crime* will include both crimes threatening the state and crimes committed by state officials. The perspective involving conventional crime as political crime will only be mentioned in relation to theoretical viewpoints which provide for such rationalizations.

EXAMINING POLITICAL CRIME IN CANADA

There are three theoretical perspectives that can be used to explain political deviance. The *representative democratic* perspective is premised primarily on the structural imperatives (electoral majority and the supremacy of Parliament) that characterize Canadian government. The *pluralist democratic* perspective goes beyond these institutions and proposes that the essence of the Canadian political system involves a process of bargaining and accommodation between interest group elites. Finally, the *capitalist democratic* perspective is a conflict theory derivation which refines pluralist conceptions of amorphous "interest groups" into a notion of corporate elite dominance through the control of government elites. Together, these three perspectives provide a comprehensive analysis of specific instances of political deviance where individual theoretical constructs may be inadequate. By making explicit the philosophical assumptions which underlie various case-specific interpretations, these perspectives serve as the bases for informed comparisons between often-competing explanations. All three perspectives provide for interpretations of Canadian history. The dominant perspective, however, appears to be a pluralist democratic one. Nonetheless, there are numerous characteristics of the Canadian political system that suggest it can be viewed as a representative democracy or a capitalist democracy. Before applying these theoretical perspectives, a brief description of each is necessary.

THEORETICAL PERSPECTIVES ON POLITICAL CRIME

REPRESENTATIVE DEMOCRACY

The two essential criteria of representative democracy are citizen participation in politics and government responsiveness to public problems (Mill, 1951; Pitkin, 1967). Structurally, the Canadian political system has the attributes of a representative democracy. The franchise is universal and elections are held every five years. Members of the federal and provincial parliaments are elected by a simple majority vote. Governments are usually formed and maintained according to the majority principle, as well. In effect, the executive, consisting of the prime minister or premier and the cabinet, must either be supported by the majority of elected parliamentary members or resign. Because of this, government has to represent the values of the majority of citizens or it will be defeated and replaced by politicians who will reflect these values. Assuming, then, that representative democracy exists in this form in Canada, it is necessary to examine it in its relationship to political crime.

From this perspective, behaviour that is threatening to the legitimacy of the established authority is manifestly criminal because it strives to undermine the institutions and processes created to reflect the majority values. Political crimes, therefore, are seen to be committed by persons who are unwilling to abide by the will of the majority as expressed in democratically determined criminal laws. Depending upon the severity of the political crime, the majority would support escalating police measures and criminal justice sanctions to deal with it.

The most significant criticism of the representative democratic perspective is that it does not place sufficient emphasis on the position of interest groups in the political process. This criticism holds that, instead of reflecting an inherently legitimate imposition of state interests, the legislative enactment of criminal law represents the triumph of one group (and its specific interests) at the expense of another. Inevitably, conflict rather than consensus characterizes social interaction. In this light, then, the main focus of Canadian politics would appear to be competition and bargaining among interest groups, rather than concern for the desires of the majority of the electorate. This is the pluralist democratic perspective.

PLURALIST DEMOCRACY

Perhaps the most influential proponent of the pluralist democratic theory was Robert Dahl (1961). His theory was based on his research indicating that voters exercised only an indirect influence on leaders' decisions, and that no monopoly of power was exercised by either elites or leaders of political associations. Interest group leaders bargained among themselves and attempted to reach a consensus decision that was acceptable to most of the electorate.

According to the Canadian political scientist H.G. Thorburn (1978), the influence of the United States resulted in the transplanting of democratic pluralism to the Canadian context. He describes it as

> an open system which perceives the political process as one of bargaining between organized groups, with the government participating in this process and giving its authority to the accommodation achieved.... Parliament and cabinet are merely a smallish part of the greater process of group interaction, better called elite accommodation.

At the federal level, the Liberal and Conservative parties have been dominant. These parties have been strictly controlled by a closed elite made up of certain members of Parliament, senators, party officials, and fundraisers. Most fundraisers are professionals, usually lawyers and senior-level executives. Senior-level civil service officials are another elite component. Intricate and long-standing connections exist among these elite components within the federal system (Porter, 1965; Presthus, 1973; Stevenson, 1979).

In exercising political power, the Canadian elite recognize the importance of the values of the majority of Canadians. Popular policies such as welfare and unemployment insurance have been implemented even though they were not favoured by key Canadian elite factions. Compromises with the electorate, therefore, represent the price elites are willing to pay to remain in power.

According to the pluralist perspective, then, the occurrence of political crimes threatens the process of accommodating elites. This threat was exemplified when the ultimate demands of the Quebec nationalist elite were too radical to accommodate. Occasional minor incidents of corruption, or isolated incidents of major and systematic corruption or coercion, are seen to reflect the breakdown of the pluralist process of accommodating recognized elite objectives. Extreme forms of corruption are considered unacceptable because they entail the risk of alienating the majority of the electorate who might then challenge the legitimacy of the entire pluralist political process. Where structural rather than individual cases of serious corruption are identified, elites are likely to effect changes in the pluralist process in accordance with the perceived values of the electoral majority.

The ability of elites to retain blatantly self-serving economic and political power in Canada, despite the electoral process which theoretically should give ultimate political control to the majority of citizens, suggests to certain theorists that the pluralist democratic perspective is an incomplete explanation of Canadian politics and, consequently, an invalid explanation of political crime. From the capitalist democratic perspective, a valid explanation of Canadian politics and political crime requires an examination of the impact of economic structures and processes on the evolution of political power, authority, and legitimacy.

CAPITALIST DEMOCRACY

The assertion that fundamental economic forces involving the struggle of social groups over the control of land, labour, and capital determine the political and social structures of any society is the central tenet of Marxism. This perspective provides the basis for the contemporary conflict perspective. The analysis of political crime from this viewpoint focuses on two essential aspects of power in an advanced industrial pluralist society and their relationship—capitalist economic structures and processes, and democratic political structures and processes.

Capitalist democracies emerged during the advanced stages of the development of capitalism. Economic changes brought about mass production and distribution units controlled by complex, impersonalized national and multinational corporations. The corporate elite became the dominant faction within the capitalist ruling class.

Capitalism has led to economic crises in the form of depressions and recessions. To maintain the legitimacy of the capitalist democratic process, the ruling class has allowed adjustments to take place, even though these adjustments were ideologically distasteful. Such adjustments included welfare programs, graduated personal income taxes, corporate taxes, and regulatory agencies. Anti-elite measures such as occupational safety laws were often ignored. The effect of these adjustments ultimately strengthened the state's dominance. The basic structural inequalities in wealth and political power remained and the masses were appeased by minor reforms. Turk (1982) maintains that the state is able to manipulate its citizens in the following manner:

> Whatever teaches people that order is always better than disorder, that consensus is always better than dissensus, that governance is the prerogative of some and obedience the duty of others, that authority goes with power, helps to deaden concern about inequalities in the distribution of life chances and about the institutions that maintain those inequalities.

Wallace Clement (1977) portrays Canada as a capitalist democracy. He details the elaborate connections between the corporate elite and every significant political institution. These connections consist mainly of personal ties, political party financing, and domination of state decision-making bodies. Clement concludes that the Canadian state ensures the conditions for capital accumulation by the capitalist class. The state, paradoxically, has to moderate the inequalities of capitalism in order to maintain its legitimacy, "but it draws the line at the greatest inequality: that of the private power of property" (Clement, 1977). It is this structural inequality that is most responsible for political crime.

In capitalist democracies, the massive process of rationalizing control through hegemonic values creates contradictions. The state expediently identifies responses to these contradictions as political crime. Spitzer (1983) identifies five of the most obvious contradictions. First, state-regulated formal social control agencies such as public and private police forces incur enormous costs. The state, therefore, imposes taxes to finance them. However, political problems arise because often these social control agencies are considered to be either ineffective or abusive of their powers. Second, automation in manufacturing and in extracting natural resources, along with the importation of less costly manufactured products from countries where labour costs and the standard of living are considerably lower, have caused massive unemployment. The social costs of unemployment are alcoholism, suicide, and domestic violence. These problems become potentially threatening political issues. Third, democratization results in minority group demands which are often threatening to ruling class interests and, consequently, are ignored or met with hostility. Fourth, different administrative occupations created by the state have developed interests of their own that resist the state's attempt to impose measures such as wage controls or job redundancies. Because of their strategic and service functions in the state authority apparatus, these interests pose a direct threat to basic state operations. The fifth contradiction is that the major areas of capital investment leading to job creation are human services such as education and crime control—the same areas where many states are, through budget constraints, reducing services. The fiscal crisis of most contemporary advanced industrial economies is, therefore, exacerbated by the growing structural unemployment created by contradictory government policies.

The standard state response of making adjustments to address these contradictions would involve major social and economic concessions that are unacceptable to the national and international capitalist classes. The other option for state reaction is to expand its social control forces. It has the ability to do this: police powers have been enhanced dramatically with recent technological advances; virtually every behaviour can be monitored. In reacting this way, the state will make available as needed criminal sanctions to deal with political threats. Furthermore, state domination of the mass media allows the state to portray any threats to its authority and legitimacy simply as criminal acts or to designate such threats as mentally disordered behaviour. The state will go to any lengths to discredit serious political threats, even by dominating legitimate and nonviolent expression (Turk, 1982).

An examination of political crime in Canada from the capitalist democratic perspective is, therefore, based on the central proposition that political crime occurs because of the need of the corporate-dominated ruling class to cope with the inevitable contradictions that result from enhancing capital accumulation in advanced industrial democracies. The focus, then, is on the dominant role of the corporate elite in Canada.

EXAMPLES OF POLITICAL CRIME IN CANADA AND THEORETICAL INTERPRETATIONS

In this section, some examples of political crime in Canada will be described and then discussed in terms of the three theoretical perspectives. These examples include the October Crisis of 1970, the Winnipeg General Strike of 1919, the Pacific Railway scandal, the Sky Shops affair, the Gouzenko affair, and recent corrupt practices by provincial politicians.

THE FRONT DE LIBÉRATION DU QUÉBEC AND THE OCTOBER CRISIS OF 1970

The FLQ was an indigenous ethnic national terrorist group which operated almost exclusively within Canada. Its purpose was to bring about an independent Quebec. Its anti-state, terrorist tactics were often violent.

During the 1960s, three successive waves of bombings occurred in Quebec, mainly in Montreal. Canadian national symbols, such as post boxes, were targets. Several police officers were casualties of this violence. Each wave of bombings was more sophisticated and violent than the last. This escalation appeared to be associated with the growing frustration and anger felt by certain radical Québécois nationalists identified as FLQ members, or "*feliquistes*." Pierre Vallières (1971) discussed the reasons for this anger in his book *White Niggers of America*. Until the election of the Parti Québécois government in 1976, it appeared to Vallières that the political process in Quebec and, ultimately, in Canada, would not allow for the nonviolent creation of an independent Québécois state. It was felt that without the creation of this state, francophones would continue to be culturally discriminated against by the English-Canadian majority and would be economically dominated by both Canadian anglophones and by the American business community. Ultimately, the Québécois culture would be anglicized and disappear. The election of Pierre Trudeau in 1968 was interpreted by many Québécois nationalists as another example of the long-standing ability of the Canadian political system to co-opt the French-Canadian elite. While Trudeau might have succeeded in effecting cosmetic changes in favour of Québécois culture, the structural basis for the destruction of the culture remained intact.

The October Crisis of 1970 began when the FLQ kidnapped James Cross, a British trade official in Montreal, and Pierre Laporte, the labour minister in the province's Liberal government. The kidnappings, and subsequent murder threats, were part of the dramatic escalation of violence promised by the FLQ if their political demands were not met. They further warned government and police officials that other public targets would be attacked if the federal and provincial governments refused to negotiate with the FLQ over their demands. One of those demands was the public broadcast of an FLQ communiqué outlining their political views. The communiqué consisted of a vitriolic Marxist critique of Canadian society focusing on English-Canadian and American imperialism in Quebec and the repression of the working class. In response to these events, the provincial government of Robert Bourassa requested, along with Mayor Drapeau of Montreal, that federal troops be sent to Quebec to relieve provincial and municipal police from protecting public officials and buildings in order to pursue the FLQ cells. In the process, the Trudeau government invoked the War Measures Act and Parliament passed subsequent public-order measures which suspended certain civil liberties in order to deal with a state of apprehended insurrection. The murder of Laporte and the discovery of his body in the trunk of an automobile added to the fear that was growing in Ottawa, as well as in Montreal and Quebec City. The immediate crisis ended with the negotiated release of Cross and the safe exile of his "Libération cell" kidnappers to Cuba. Members of the "Chénier cell" involved in the Laporte murder were subsequently arrested, convicted, and imprisoned.

About the same time, 467 other persons were arrested under the provisions of the War Measures Act and related public orders. Only 61 of these were eventually charged, of whom 13 were convicted. Only 1 of these 13 was found to have been associated with the Laporte case.

There is no disagreement that members of the FLQ engaged in terrorism. Public statements by those involved with the Laporte kidnapping confirmed their intention to commit crimes, including murder, to subvert Canadian political institutions in order to achieve their long-term goal of an independent Quebec state (Simard, 1982).

The major unresolved issue is whether the Trudeau government used the October Crisis to rationalize and facilitate its own state terrorist effort to discredit and defeat the legitimate Quebec nationalist movement embodied in the Parti Québécois and its dynamic leader, René Lévesque. Were the two FLQ kidnappings and the murder of Laporte in effect exploited by the Trudeau government? Pierre Vallières (1971) and other nationalists, as well as certain proponents of the conflict perspective (see Fidler, 1978), argue that the Trudeau government was simply waiting for the FLQ terrorism, and possibly encouraging it through *agents provocateurs*. The Trudeau government then used the spectre of insurrection as a rationale for bold criminal sanctions against Quebec nationalism. Trudeau had substituted his own controversial bilingual and bicultural policies for virulent Quebec nationalism. It has been argued that Trudeau needed the October Crisis to overcome both English-Canadian opposition to his view of Canada and the scepticism of French Canadians that his policies would never be accepted by English Canadians.

This alternative explanation of the October Crisis of 1970 was partly suggested by the draconian nature of the government's response to the two kidnappings—imposition of the War Measures Act—although René

Lévesque and civil libertarians were cautioning federal and provincial governments not to overreact. It was not until the crisis had ended that alternative explanations were seen to be plausible.

In assessing the FLQ threat, Vallières (1972), who had been described by the mass media as the FLQ's chief theoretician, maintained that "there has never been an FLQ organization as such, but only cellules or little groups few in number, supplies, and means, without intergroup structural connections, without a guiding core, and without a true strategy." Vallières (1977) suggested that the RCMP and even the United States Central Intelligence Agency (CIA) paid *agents provocateurs* who were involved in FLQ activities.

Academics and civil libertarians such as Herbert Marx, J. Noel Lyon, and Brian Grosman presented elaborate and convincing arguments that there was no need whatsoever to suspend civil liberties to deal with the FLQ. The Criminal Code of Canada contained numerous provisions to investigate, charge, and prosecute violent political acts. Certain sanctions were even more severe than those available under the War Measures Act. The question, then, is why did Trudeau, a noted civil libertarian, impose the War Measures Act and charge that his civil libertarian critics were "bleeding hearts"?

The Representative Democratic Perspective

Judy Torrance (1977) puts forth a cultural explanation that, in dealing with the October Crisis, Trudeau acted in the same manner as other prime ministers who were faced with the political crimes of rebellion and insurrection (for example, the Red River Uprising of 1869–70, the Northwest Rebellion of 1885, the Quebec City Riots of 1918, the Winnipeg General Strike of 1919, and the Regina Riot of 1935). The patterns were similar for each of these incidents: keeping key crisis decision making in the cabinet, ensuring geographical containment of the insurrection, labelling the political acts as criminal, isolating and exiling the leaders, and influencing public opinion. The governments used diplomacy and, in extreme cases, violence to gain popular support. Pierre Berton (1976) apparently concurs with the cultural interpretation of Trudeau's imposition of the War Measures Act:

> This trampling of civil rights would be quite impossible in the United States. First, the American Bill of Rights—a far more powerful document than our own—would make it impossible. But I think it's fair to say that even if it were possible the American people would not stand for it. They have seen far more violence and far more political assassinations than we have. Nine of their presidents have been shot or shot at. But it has never occurred to any responsible American official to suspend the right of habeas corpus or to jail people for weeks on end—on mere suspicion without a charge against or access to a lawyer.

It should be recognized that Berton is correct insofar as the Canadian Bill of Rights (at the time the major piece of legislation protecting civil rights) was not nearly as powerful as the American Bill of Rights; however, contrary to his assertion, there are numerous historical incidents of infringements of civil rights in the United States. For example, from 1870 to 1935 the labour movement was treated as an outlaw organization. Repressive government measures in the form of draconian laws and excessive police violence were on many occasions used to restrict the right to assemble peacefully, organize, strike, boycott, and picket (Goldstein, 1978). In addition, many First Amendment rights, such as freedom of expression and freedom of assembly, were violated during the "red scare" of the 1950s.

Available to partisans of the representative democratic perspective is the argument that the actions and justifications of the governments of Canada and Quebec represented the wishes of the Canadian majority. The overwhelming support in Parliament for the War Measures Act, and public support expressed in opinion surveys and subsequent Liberal Party electoral victories in Quebec and Montreal, appear to add support to the representative democratic perspective on the October Crisis of 1970.

The Pluralist Democratic Perspective

Thorburn (1978) maintains that both the FLQ terrorism and the government's response to it reflect the breakdown of the pluralist political process over the issue of Québécois nationalism. Historically, the anglophone and francophone elites have always reached accommodation on divisive political issues. The Québécois nationalists appear to have broken the pluralist pattern, since their bargaining position left little room for accommodation. They were unwilling to accept anything less than independence. The radical Québécois nationalists were even more uncompromising because they were willing to employ terrorism to achieve their political goal. Thus, for Trudeau, the War Measures Act was justified by his desire to demonstrate that no political group would be allowed to alter the political rules that had kept the anglophone and francophone societies linked in a federal pluralist system.

The Capitalist Democratic Perspective

The conspiracy explanation of the October Crisis of 1970 is consistent with a conflict perspective, since state repression is a fundamental part of the Canadian political structure. According to Richard Fidler (1978), a member of the Revolutionary Workers League and author of *RCMP: The Real Subversives:*

> The use of repression as an instrument of government policy is rooted in the very nature of Canada. Like the Czarist empire, the Canadian state is a veritable "prison house of nations." It was built on the oppression of the Québécois, the near annihilation of native peoples and the degradation of the Acadians and Francophones outside Quebec.... Moreover, extreme differences of wealth and privilege within

Canadian society as a whole have created a history of deep-going class struggles.

It seems obvious from this perspective that the government's activities during the October Crisis are characteristic of its inherent repressive nature. Fidler argues further that the provincial Keable Commission and the federal Mac-Donald Commission investigations simply reflected the respective political biases of the Parti Québécois and the Liberal Party. These biases inhibited the uncovering of what actually went on during the October Crisis of 1970. Conflict perspective interpretations such as those of Fidler and Vallières are, however, based on conjecture.

The conspiracy view is rejected by former cabinet minister and close Trudeau advisor Gérard Pelletier (1971), who reiterates the representative democratic view that Trudeau and his cabinet, the provincial Bourassa government, and Mayor Drapeau may have all misjudged the actual threat posed by the FLQ in the 1970 crisis. These governments had to assume the worst in the face of incomplete information and growing public fear of political anarchy. The imposition of the War Measures Act, therefore, was a legal and democratically approved reaction of a government to an insurrection. No similar justification, however, can be made for the RCMP Security Service activities that occurred in the aftermath of the October Crisis.

STATE TERRORISM: ILLEGAL RCMP SECURITY SERVICE ACTIVITIES

The Keable and MacDonald commissions and criminal trials confirmed the following unlawful activities conducted by the ultra-secret subsection of the RCMP Security Service:

> They have burned a barn, stolen dynamite, engaged in surreptitious entries for investigative purposes, harassed suspected extremists, arranged questionable access to government records never intended for police purposes, falsified documents, engaged in prima facie illegal search and seizure, opened mail in direct contravention of postal legislation and copied the records of a legitimate political party. (French and Belieau, 1979)

The essential policy goal here consisted of gathering detailed information about the FLQ and any other potential terrorist group, as well as their financial and logistical support structure. As Gérard Pelletier (1971) claimed, insufficient information made it difficult to assess the extent of the FLQ threat. Another major policy goal involved an aggressive preventative strategy against terrorism. This strategy was considered to be another reason for the escalation of the FLQ kidnappings into a crisis. Additionally, a policy change initiated in the late 1960s consisted of restructuring the RCMP Security Service to allow it more autonomy from the traditional RCMP command, recruitment, and policy structures. The outcome of these policies resulted in a more aggressive national security agency than the one that had failed to anticipate the October Crisis.

Two incidents revealed the aggressive and autonomous strategy of the Security Service in the first half of the 1970s. Operation BRICOLE involved surreptitiously entering the premises of an obscure radical news agency, l'Agence de Presse Libre du Québec, and a related group, le Mouvement pour la Défense des Prisonniers Politiques du Québec. Essential records and membership lists were removed for intelligence analysis of potential terrorist threats. As well, with the loss of these records, it was hoped, fundraising would become difficult and the members of the two groups would be demoralized. The operation was conducted without the approval of senior Security Service officials.

Operation HAM also involved entering and removing documents from an organization, this time the Parti Québécois. Computer membership tapes were copied and returned without being missed. The operation was authorized by the director general of the Security Service to assess whether the Parti Québécois had illegitimately established the subversive "Parizeau" network, consisting of federal bureaucrats passing on government documents. It also intended to check membership lists for financial information about foreign money possibly sent from Cuba, and to investigate whether or not the radical nationalist members of the Parti Québécois were conspiring to subvert the Security Service. Apparently, no significant information about these security concerns emerged from Operation HAM (French and Beliveau, 1979).

Although there were disquieting rumours and accusations made by radical groups such as the Workers Revolutionary League about RCMP state terrorist tactics, there was no evidence for them until a Security Service officer on trial for planting a bomb for personal reasons blurted out a statement suggesting that he had engaged in even more serious criminal activity for the RCMP. The next critical revelation came when two Security Service officers exposed the details of their illegal activities (Sawatsky, 1980). Various police officers subsequently were charged with criminal offences and convicted. They received lenient sentences, despite the gravity of their acts and their political implications. Many of the police officers who were alleged to have participated in the illegal activities were not charged at all, and some of the officers brought to trial were acquitted.

The Representative Democratic Perspective

The apparent reluctance to charge more police officers in the RCMP trials, especially those in senior positions, coupled with the difficulty of obtaining convictions and the lenient sentences imposed, may be seen to reflect the representative democratic view of the Canadian political system. In passing sentences in these cases, certain judges remarked that overzealousness in protecting Canada from anti-state terrorism was the motive for the criminal acts. In effect, while the police tactics were illegal, their goals were laudable, since most Canadians would vehemently oppose any violent threats to their government. The intricate arguments of civil libertarians about due process and state terrorism, while significant in terms of legal philosophy, did not negate the majority's desire to confront anti-state terrorism. And, it was believed, if mistakes were made by officials in the process of protecting Canadians, these should not be automatically held against them. Excesses committed by those in authority would be dealt with by royal commissions and appropriate legislation. This procedure was evident in the creation of a civilian security agency designed to inhibit future illegal anti-terrorist behaviour. Thus, the symbolic condemnation of this illegal, but patriotic, behaviour and the new security service legislation reflect the representative democratic perspective that the RCMP's state terrorist acts were, in fact, acts of misguided idealism within an inappropriate organizational structure. This interpretation is further supported by the fact that state terrorism, despite the extensive media coverage, did not become a decisive political issue for the major political parties in the following federal elections.

The Pluralist Democratic Perspective

A different interpretation of the Security Service's illegal activities considers their state terrorist acts to have been a result of organizational problems within the Security Service, incomplete cabinet and ministerial control of police agencies, and the machinations of interest-group politics (French and Beliveau, 1979; Mann and Lee, 1979; Sawatsky, 1980). In staffing their security division, the RCMP relied primarily on their own police officers, whose main education in security matters was six months of depot training and regular police duties. Senior RCMP officials avoided close relationships with the senior-level policy makers in the Ministry of the Solicitor General. Attempts to recruit more civilians into intelligence functions, as recommended by the MacKenzie Commission Report of 1968, were ignored. In light of all this, the security division was accused of ineptitude in conducting its intelligence functions primarily because its personnel were not adequately trained and specifically directed. Senior RCMP officials wanted to maintain their traditional prerogatives, thereby blocking the establishment of a civilian security agency and other MacKenzie Commission recommendations.

The October Crisis of 1970 confirmed the inability of the RCMP Security Service to handle intelligence needs, especially with reference to counter-terrorism. The determination of the Security Service to overcome this inept image led to their adoption of aggressive and illegal activities. According to Sawatsky (1980), "In the aftermath of the FLQ failure, the mood turned ugly and the Security Service, especially the Quebec Division, committed scoundrelly acts and engaged in roguish attempts to recruit informers. The acts were strategically unsound as well as illegal."

A study by French and Beliveau (1979) on the RCMP Security Service argues that the abuses committed in the course of the Service's counter-subversion efforts ... indicate that the policies of active prevention and decentralization of authority required a considerably tighter and more sophisticated management philosophy. In the case of the Security Service activities in Montreal during 1971–1973, the disintegration of the channels of communication between various levels of authority resulted in a complete breakdown in the capacity of management to direct, to control, to hold subordinates accountable, to advise its political masters, and to be held accountable by them.

It would appear that senior bureaucrats and cabinet ministers were reluctant to force the RCMP senior command into making effective changes in the organization of the Security Service. Political confrontation with RCMP supporters in Parliament on this issue was viewed as messy, complex, and politically unrewarding. The RCMP senior command, in turn, strenuously opposed any significant attempts to diminish their monopoly of national police functions, including their intelligence and counter-subversion roles. However, senior RCMP officials were not in an organizational position to inquire into the affairs of the autonomous Security Service. Its autonomy was, after all, designed to facilitate an aggressive counter-terrorist strategy. Consequently, political in-fighting among interest-group elites, not "the odd irresponsible soul" or "an organized and nefarious conspiracy," led to the organizational breakdown that was directly responsible for the RCMP political crimes.

The Capitalist Democratic Perspective

The "nefarious conspiracy" view of the RCMP political crimes is central to the capitalist democratic perspective. Proponents of this explanation maintain that the RCMP, along with other police forces, have always been employed to serve ruling-class interests. Brown and Brown (1973), for example, contend that their predecessors, the North West Mounted Police, were created to facilitate the transfer of Indian territories to the federal government "with a minimum of expense and bloodshed." Further, these authors argue that the NWMP collaborated with business interests such as the Canadian Pacific Railway at the expense of the rights and interests of the indigenous populations. It was therefore predictable that state terrorism would be directed against the most serious potential threat to the Canadian capitalist democracy—Quebec nationalism. English-Canadian and American capitalists controlled the Quebec economy and profited (accumulated capital) at the expense of working-class francophones who suffered discrimination and oppression. The threat of Québécois nationalism (including the Parti Québécois position that key sections of the capitalist economy should be nationalized) was enough to send English Canadians and capital out of Quebec. The FLQ and Marxist organizations such as the Revolutionary Workers League went much further and advocated abolishing capitalism. In order to destroy this threat, the capitalist ruling class criminalized Quebec nationalism and resorted to state terrorism. Having criminalized this legitimate political movement, the ruling class could then justify to the majority of Canadians the necessity of employing coercion against Quebec nationalism. In addition, much of the violent coercion was simply hidden from most Canadians, since attempts to inform the public were inhibited by the capitalist-controlled mass media.

CONTEMPORARY POLITICAL TERRORISM

The political crimes of the FLQ and the Security Service can be considered the most serious in Canadian history. These terrorist acts posed fundamental threats to the Canadian political system. Other terrorist groups in Canada, such as the Squamish Five, also employed violent means to draw attention to their cause. The bombings of the Litton Industries plant in Toronto, a hydroelectric transmission station in British Columbia, and the firebombing of a Red Hot Video Store were all directed toward specific issues: the production and testing of cruise missiles in Canada, the destruction of the environment, and the public sale and availability of pornography. Armenian, Croatian, and Sikh nationalists also have employed terrorist tactics in Canada; sometimes this has involved bombings and assassinations of foreign diplomats and other opponents. The violent actions have been carried out by international, ethnic, nationalist terrorist groups seeking publicity and support for their cause within Canada. On the other hand, ideological terrorist groups such as the Red Brigades in Italy, whose main goal is the precipitation of an ideological revolution, have not been evident in Canada. Ideological rationales and goals, however, can be integrated with nationalist goals, as was the case with the FLQ. A discussion of the different types of terrorist groups can be found in Stohl (1988); Ross (1988) discusses the attributes of Canadian terrorism.

THE WINNIPEG GENERAL STRIKE OF 1919

Another serious type of political crime, with a long history of violence, involves industrial disputes. One of the most important examples is the Winnipeg General Strike of 1919.

The early history of the Canadian labour movement was characterized by the co-optation of the leaders and members of skilled trade unions by the Conservative and Liberal party organizations. Legislation legitimizing these types of unions was gradually allowed in exchange for electoral support (Robin, 1968). By the First World War, the labour movement had evolved considerably with the enormous expansion of the industrial economy fuelled by the massive influx of immigrants, mainly coming from Europe. These immigrants brought with them their cultural values pertaining to the economic and political organization of the working class. Unlike the situation in Europe, revolutionary ideologies such as communism, socialism, and anarchism were not influential in Canada. When certain union members began resorting to coercive tactics to obtain economic demands and legal rights considered by business and political leaders to be ideologically revolutionary, the basis for violent confrontation was set. One such confrontation broke out in 1919, when trade unions in Winnipeg overwhelmingly endorsed a general strike as a bargaining tactic to force management to accept their wage demands and to recognize their right to collective bargaining. The tactic had worked in previous bitter negotiations over the right of civic employees to strike, and had not then precipitated any violence.

In the interval, however, radical trade unionists, mainly from western provinces, had been striving to organize the "one big union." It was intended to be "a radical Marxist labour union, industrial or syndicalist in nature and sympathetic to the aims and aspirations of the Bolsheviks" (Bercuson, 1975). This union was in complete conflict with the principles of North American trade unionism, which eschewed the direct entry of unions into politics and believed that it was necessary to restrict unions to the few highly skilled workers. North American trade unions limited their political activities to supporting candidates or parties sympathetic to labour. The Winnipeg General Strike was already in progress when the "one big union" was created. This constituted a crucial factor in the harsh response of the federal government of Robert Borden, and especially of the minister of the interior and acting minister of justice, Arthur Meighen.

Meighen co-ordinated the government response with the Citizens' Committee of 1000 in Winnipeg, composed mainly of anti-Bolshevik, anti-union citizens attempting to co-ordinate services disrupted by strikers. A special police force was created, because local police officers joined the strike. Both the military and the Royal Northwest Mounted Police were sent to Winnipeg with a secret shipment of arms from Ottawa.

There were conflicting views over who precipitated the violent confrontation between marching strikers and the police force. However, the result was that one person was killed and many were wounded. The ten principal leaders of the strike were arrested and tried in criminal court on charges that were primarily political, such as sedition. Five of the charged were acquitted; the others were found guilty and received sentences of six months to two years. Additional repressive measures were introduced by Meighen, such as amendments to the Immigration Act which allowed for the deportation without trial of subversives, both foreign and native. During the strike, Meighen used these hurriedly enacted amendments to arrest six strike leaders and to have them deported immediately (Penner, 1975).

The Representative Democratic Perspective

From the representative democratic perspective, a key question is whether a general strike, such as the Winnipeg General Strike, constitutes an attempt to force both the government and the majority to accede to the demands of unions. In other words, does a general strike constitute a subversion of the basic premises of the supremacy of Parliament and majority rule—the basis of the Canadian political system of representative democracy? Obviously,

Meighen and Borden viewed the Winnipeg General Strike as a direct political crime of subversion. The Borden cabinet revealed part of their reasoning through Meighen's rhetorical question:

> If unions were going to be allowed to combine into larger unions [he asked], where was the logical end to the process going to be? Eventually there would be one union capable of calling one tremendous strike which would bring anarchy to the country. This, he warned, could not and would not be allowed to happen. (Bercuson, 1975)

Meighen claimed that revolutionary anarchy and Bolshevism were the only goals of the "one big union." Government fear of Bolshevism bordered on hysteria, primarily because of the revolution in Russia. Meighen feared the Bolsheviks and their socialist sympathizers in the western provinces. Consequently, he requested that a British cruiser be sent to Vancouver to provide a steadying influence (Penner, 1975).

The Pluralist Democratic Perspective

According to the pluralist democratic perspective, the Winnipeg General Strike of 1919 occurred because of the competition between the conservative business and government elites on the one hand, and the emerging militant trade union interest groups on the other. The demands of the latter groups did not follow the traditional rules of the pluralist competition among governments, management, and unions. Union tactics and goals, therefore, were considered sufficiently threatening to government and business elites to be identified as political crimes.

While the momentum of the union movement suffered a definite setback from which it recovered only after the Second World War, the Winnipeg General Strike of 1919 set in motion interest-group changes that eventually paved the way for the unions' future success. In 1921, the Conservative Party, now led by Meighen, lost the federal election to the Mackenzie King Liberals as a result of the strike's impact and its aftermath. Mackenzie King showed open sympathy to the labour movement in order to gain the leadership of his party. As prime minister, he sought to avoid the creation of a Canadian labour party which would draw votes away from the Liberals (Penner, 1975). In effect, the Liberal Party elite attempted to accommodate the labour movement elite, albeit gradually, in order not to alienate the business community.

The Capitalist Democratic Perspective

Meighen's uncompromising and violent reaction to the Winnipeg General Strike of 1919 was predictable in the evolving capitalist democracy. Militant unions were attempting to interfere directly with the fundamental process of capital formation by reducing profits and efficiency. The city of Winnipeg was organized along class lines, with the business elite controlling its political

TABLE 15.1
THEORETICAL PERSPECTIVES

EVENT	Representative Democratic	Pluralist Democratic	Capitalist Democratic
October Crisis	Suppression of FLQ activities reflected the wishes of the majority	Government actions intended to demonstrate that no single group would be allowed to threaten the status quo	Government actions reflected the repressive nature of state social control agencies
Illegal RCMP-Security Service Activities	Although some officers may have been overzealous, the majority of the public felt that the actions were necessary to preserve law and order	The events can be attributed to an organizational breakdown within the system; in particular, conflict between the RCMP senior command and the Security Service	The RCMP-Security Service was used to eliminate a potential threat to the interests of business elites (primarily English-Canadian and American) who controlled the economy of Quebec
Winnipeg General Strike	The strike represented a threat to the interests of the majority; the supremacy of Parliament and majority rule were in danger of being usurped by a powerful union.	The incident was a result of competition between business elites and militant trade unions; precipitating factor was the union's failure to adhere to traditional rules of pluralist competition	Capitalist elites manipulated the legal and political system in order to destroy the militant labour movement

institutions. According to this perspective, the Citizens' Committee of 1000 simply represented capitalism, as did the "Special Police." The capitalists sought a confrontation in order to destroy the militant labour movement by labelling it Bolshevik and anti-Canadian, and did not shrink from deceiving the Canadian public by using conspiratorial methods such as the federal government's secret shipment of arms via the military and the Royal Northwest Mounted Police. The brutal attacks by the police on the peacefully marching strikers were designed to intimidate workers and break their spirit. They were successful, as the strike ended immediately.

The government's use of violence in the Canadian capitalist democracy may be seen in the long list of strikes terminated by the state. Labour-management conflicts were more likely to lead to violence in Canada than in European countries, in spite of the latter's class-based unions and political parties, which appeared to have had a history of turmoil and violence (Jamieson, 1968). Changes in the Immigration Act were a blatant manifestation of the capitalists' ability to criminalize the legitimate political and economic interests of the working class.

CORRUPTION IN THE POLITICAL PROCESS

Not all political crimes involve violence. Corruption of the political process for personal motives or political advantage is not usually as dramatic a threat to the authority or legitimacy of the state as is terrorism. However, any discussion of political crime in Canada would be incomplete without examining political corruption. This section will briefly describe a number of incidents of corruption—the Pacific Railway scandal, the Duplessis regime, the Sky Shops affair, political party kickback schemes in the Maritime provinces, and the scandal-ridden administration of the Mulroney government. Then the phenomenon of corruption in the political process will be examined from the three political perspectives.

THE PACIFIC RAILWAY SCANDAL

The Pacific Railway scandal was the first in a steady stream of incidents where elected politicians or appointed officials have engaged in illegal or unethical behaviour. In order to build and operate the Canadian Pacific Railway, which was needed to ensure the entry of British Columbia into Confederation, Macdonald's finance minister approached financier Sir Hugh Allen to devise a business enterprise that could raise the capital. Two other competitors submitted rival plans. Allen, however, had negotiated secret agreements with the Macdonald government that appeared to give him an advantage. Allen attempted to bribe a rival financier into joining his corporation, but failed. He donated over a third of a million dollars to the election funds of Conservative ministers. In 1873, after the press and the opposition Liberals discovered this and persisted in their allegations of corruption, the Macdonald government resigned. Macdonald was defeated in the subsequent election (McDougall, 1968).

The Pacific Railway scandal is an important example of corruption in the political process because it demonstrates the early interdependency between business and government in Canada. Business can reap substantial profits from government contracts and favourable regulations. Politicians can gain financial resources for election campaigns as well as for personal use.

THE DUPLESSIS REGIME

One of the most notable historical examples of political corruption involved the Duplessis regime which dominated Quebec politics by forming five consecutive governments, ending in 1960. Through his conservative, rural-based Union Nationale party, Duplessis established a formidable party machine which he dominated as "brazenly as any Latin-American dictator." According to one biographer, Leslie Roberts (1963), no politician could have "excelled him in ruthlessness and contempt for the political rule book." Duplessis ran this party machine primarily to ensure his re-election. Moreover, although he demanded total loyalty from his supporters, including having them engage in corrupt electoral practices, he contemptuously dismissed accusations of taking a dictatorial approach. He had little use for opposition politicians and media criticism emanating from "Montreal sophisticates." Duplessis shamelessly violated basic civil rights such as freedom of religion, political expression, and economic association. But to his rural, conservative Catholic supporters, he was viewed as a champion of French-Canadian autonomy and traditional values.

Like his predecessors, Duplessis engaged in profit-producing schemes for the sake of political advantage. For example, in 1958, six of his cabinet ministers were accused of engineering a $20-million market scheme based on inside information about the sale of Hydro-Québec. The ministers purchased shares at low prices and then sold them at enormous profits once the shares went public. These types of business transactions were commonplace. A Commission of Inquiry instituted in 1960 confirmed what most observers, including journalists, already knew, but were afraid to reveal—that financial kickback schemes were a routine requirement for conducting business in Quebec. Executives of major corporations accepted the political payoffs they made as just another cost factor (Roberts, 1963).

THE SKY SHOPS AFFAIR

The Sky Shops affair revealed a process of corruption, similar to that of the Duplessis scandals, at work in the federal government. Liberal Senator Louis Giguère was given $95 000 to assist Sky Shops Export Limited in reversing the federal transport ministry decision not to extend the company's lease to operate a duty-free shop at government-owned Dorval Airport in Montreal,

POLITICAL CRIME IN CANADA   441

but rather to open the lease to competitive bidding. Although Senator Giguère unexpectedly was found not guilty of conspiring to accept a benefit in the affair, two prominent businessmen, former National Hockey League president Clarence Campbell and Gordon Brown, were found guilty on two counts of conspiring to give Giguère the $95 000 in return for his political influence.

The Sky Shops scandal, involving senior party figures, leading cabinet ministers, and prominent businessmen, provides an example of political corruption from recent Canadian history. According to the three theoretical perspectives outlined in this chapter, such an incident may be explicated in reference to inadequate laws allowing for the self-interest of politicians and businessmen to dominate, the illegal advantages of one interest group threatening the process of accommodating elites, and, of course, profit motives.

SKY SHOPS PROBE LINKS CABINET AIDES

OTTAWA(CP)—Assistants to two federal cabinet ministers are implicated in an investigation into the involvement of senior Liberal party figures in the so-called Sky Shops affairs, Ottawa broadcast reports said Thursday night.

Jean Rivard, Ottawa correspondent for Telemedia, the Quebec radio network, quoted letters showing that former aides of Jean Marchand and Don Jamieson are involved in the case.

The Sky Shops affair has been under police investigation since last fall, when RCMP raided the offices of Senator Louis Giguère, a Liberal party fund-raiser, after parliamentary allegations about his dealings in shares of Sky Shops Export Ltd. of Montreal.

The case involves the 1972 cabinet extension, without competitive bids, of a Sky Shops license to operate a duty-free store at Montreal's Dorval airport.

As reported Thursday by Rivard and also by Dan Turner on the Ottawa TV station CBOT, documents obtained in the investigation show the following sequence of events.

In October, 1971, a senior political figure visited the office of Jean Marchand, at that time minister of regional economic expansion and head of the Quebec caucus of the federal Liberal party.

On Oct. 26, 1971, Marchand aide Carmel Carrière sent a handwritten note on ministerial stationery to Andrew Chatwood, executive assistant to Don Jamieson, then transport minister. The Oct. 26 note said Mr. Marchand insisted on reversal of transport ministry advice to call for competitive bids for the duty-free license at Dorval, rather than simply renewing the Sky Shops licence. On Nov. 12, 1971, a Carrière note in the same vein went to Mr. Chatwood.

On Nov. 23, 1971, Mr. Chatwood wrote to William Huck in the air transport division of the transport ministry, with a copy of the letter going to O.G. Stoner, deputy transport minister, saying Mr. Marchand was insisting that no competitive bids be called.

On May 1, 1972, a typewritten letter from Mr. Chatwood informs Mr. Carrière in Mr. Marchand's office that the decision on putting the Dorval duty-free license up for competitive bid had been reversed.

On June 9, 1972, Senator Giguère obtained Sky Shops shares for $5,000, he has said. On Aug. 24, 1972, Senator Giguère sold his shares for $100,000, a fact he has stated publicly in the Senate while saying at the same time he is innocent of any wrongdoing in the dealings.

Mr. Marchand, currently environment minister, and Mr. Jamieson, minister of industry and trade, each have turned over files to the RCMP, the Commons was told Thursday.

A senior federal authority said Thursday night that the exchange of correspondence between the ministerial aides had been turned up in the investigation, but were considered a minor element in the case. In the Commons, opposition members urged the government to speed legal action and quizzed the ministers about involvement of their aides in the case. Mr. Jamieson was transport minister and Mr. Marchand regional expansion minister in the period referred to by the minister, said Mr. Bothwell. He said he understood the correspondence referred to was routine and unimportant to the case.

Source: *Winnipeg Free Press* 9 April 1976.

The RCMP investigated whether any ministers, and in particular Jean Marchand, were responsible for making recommendations on government contracts for Quebec. While Marchand was not charged, it was understood that the government contracts were linked to electoral finances: "The Sky Shops affair can be situated then in the days when electoral finances were traditionally secret. Contributions were paid to middlemen who then concerned themselves with refreshing the memory of the elected when it was time for granting contracts" (Pelletier, 1980).

CORRUPTION IN THE ATLANTIC PROVINCES

Some of the most recent incidents of political corruption have involved provincial politics in the Atlantic provinces.

The most controversial events involved the Hatfield regime in New Brunswick, where corruption included not only traditional kickback schemes, but also allegations that Premier Hatfield received special considerations during a police investigation and during his trial on a drug charge. Richard Hatfield was elected in 1970 on a pledge of clean government. He worked assiduously to establish a reputation as an incorruptible provincial leader in a region not noted for such an image: "It has been an open secret for generations that patronage and other forms of questionable political behaviour are probably more dominant in New Brunswick than anywhere else in Canada" (Folster, 1977). Instead of cleaning up corruption, Hatfield was alleged to have allowed a kickback scheme where successful bidders for government contracts had to make a flat payment and/or pay 4 percent of gross monthly income to the Conservative Party finance committee. It was further alleged that Hatfield and other cabinet ministers attended a meeting where the collection of this money was discussed.

To complicate matters, in 1985 Hatfield was charged with possession of marijuana. He was tried in a bizarre trial where the judge, who had been appointed to the bench by Hatfield, accused a journalist of planting the drug in the premier's luggage. The journalist was immediately exonerated by the police. Hatfield then implied that the RCMP had conspired to embarrass him for political reasons. Hatfield was publicly accused by two university students of giving them drugs, including cocaine, and of paying their expenses to accompany him on an unofficial trip to Montreal. Hatfield denied the drug allegations. Prior to his trial, Hatfield had met with the federal solicitor general, a fellow Maritimer, who had ultimate responsibility for the RCMP investigation. He had also phoned the minister of justice, who had ultimate responsibility for final prosecutorial decisions. Hatfield was acquitted.

The government of Newfoundland has also been implicated in political corruption. There, the government of Conservative premier Frank Moores became embattled in allegations of kickback schemes in the public works department and attempts to cover up criminal acts such as arson (Plaskin, 1978).

In June 1990, allegations of corruption were made against the government of Nova Scotia premier John Buchanan. The allegations charged that the premier's cottage had been painted by government workers being paid on government time, that multimillion-dollar contracts had been given to friends of the premier, and that on some occasions he had received kickbacks. Although Buchanan vociferously denied any involvement in such incidents, he provided few details to refute the accusations. After a period of intense media attention, Premier Buchanan resigned his seat in the provincial legislature and was immediately appointed to the Senate by Prime Minister Mulroney. Subsequent to Buchanan's appointment came revelations that he had been paid large amounts of money by the Conservative Party to pay his debts and prevent his banktuptcy.

CORRUPTION AND THE MULRONEY CONSERVATIVES

Since sweeping to power in September 1984, the Progressive Conservative government of Brian Mulroney has firmly established itself as one of the most ethically bankrupt administrations in Canadian history. The seemingly end-less list of scandalous affairs is as varied as it is numerous. The most notable Tory indiscretions include objectionable spending habits, blatant patronage, and a variety of serious, massive scandals categorized purely in terms of the unethical behaviour involved.

Throughout their regime, the Tories have been less than exemplary in so far as financial restraint is concerned. In October 1985, it was revealed that Robert Coates's personal expenses (largely for travel and hospitality) exceeded $70 000 during five months as defence minister, and that Secretary of State Walter McLean spent between $100 000 and $150 000 on a trip to Africa with his wife and one aide. This was indicative of a recurrent pattern of irresponsibility. Perhaps the most distressing example of Mulroney's personal disregard for public funds surfaced on April 1, 1987, with news of a loan he had secured from the PC Canada fund for $300 000 for custom renovations to 24 Sussex Drive.

Despite Prime Minister Mulroney's rising to power on the strength of a platform which promised reform of patronage, blatant patronage appoint-ments to government positions remained manifest throughout the Progressive Conservative government's tenure. The first four months of Mulroney's term saw 150 Order-in-Council appointments. On February 16, 1986, Tory organizer and fundraiser William Hawkins was appointed to the department of regional economic expansion's Textile and Clothing Board, despite a self-admitted complete lack of knowledge of either clothing or textiles. Less than a month later, Supply and Services Minister Stewart McInnes ordered the hiring of Conservative Party members as census commissioners, despite the fact that several had failed the examination administered to potential candidates. Conspicuous patronage appointments have in no way been con-fined to political positions and offices: governmental contractual awards have similarly been corrupted. It was disclosed on February 14, 1986, that at least 80 percent of all advertising contracts of over $5000 awarded in the preceding year had gone to agencies with Tory connections. Figures showed that 90 percent of all Quebec public works contracts since the 1985 federal election had gone untendered. During the same period, more than 45 percent of contracts worth over $5000 had also gone untendered. To date, the largest of these injustices surfaced in the *The Ottawa Citizen* on May 14, 1988, when it was reported that the $1.4 billion CF-18 maintenance contract was awarded to a Montreal-based consortium in 1986 as a result of the Tory political agenda. In fact, the proposal of Bristol Aerospace Ltd. of Winnipeg was better on price as well as technical competency.

As disturbing as these awards are, however, they seem to pale in the face of evidence of serious public trust abuses. On May 15, 1986, MP Marcel Gravel was charged with 50 counts of bribery, influence peddling, and abuse of public trust in connection with seeking $100 000 from companies wishing to do business with the government. February 13, 1987, saw the resignation of Minister of State Roch LaSalle over identical allegations.

There have been other major incidents of corruption in Canada under other governments, such as the Harbour Dredging scandal of the 1970s, where businessmen and politicians from Quebec and Ontario and a federal minister were implicated, and some were charged with criminal offences. It appears that political corruption is not limited to any one historical period, political party, province, or level of government. The theoretical explanations for this type of political crime are similarly varied.

The Representative Democratic Perspective

From the representative democratic perspective, corruption occurs because of the greed of politicians and businessmen. Persistent corruption is seen to reflect inadequate laws. The Rivard and Sky Shops scandals, for example, rocked the Liberal governments of Pearson and Trudeau, and eventually led to the reform of political party financing according to representative democratic values. As a result, the 1974 Election Expenses Act provided tax advantages to encourage individual citizens, rather than interest groups such as corporations and unions, to make donations to political parties. Public donations are limited annually to $25 000 in nonelection years and $50 000 in an election year.

There are critical political repercussions if corrupt politicians do not resign and if reforms are not forthcoming or perceived as inadequate: politicians and governments risk defeat at the polls. In virtually every major corruption scandal, there have been immediate or eventual political repercussions. For example, corruption can be seen as a factor in the defeat of the Macdonald government in 1873, the demise of the Union Nationale party in the 1960s, and the more recent defeat of the Hatfield government in New Brunswick and the resignation of Nova Scotia's John Buchanan.

The Pluralist Democratic Perspective

According to the pluralist democratic perspective, political corruption results when one interest group takes illegal advantage of its dominant position. In nearly every case, members of opposing interest groups play a significant role in exposing it. Members of Parliament are quick to make allegations of corruption against members of opposing political parties in order to gain advantage in the intense competition for government office. This competitive process involves the mass media in the attempt to influence public opinion and to gain electoral support. Politicians and government officials accused of corruption, in turn, typically attempt to distract media and public attention, hoping that their interest will dissipate, or that other more salient issues or events will capture the spotlight.

Political corruption occurs partly because many of the political interactions among interest groups are routinely kept from the attention of the media and the public. Political financing, for example, is a routine part of the interaction between politicians and businessmen, yet is usually done discreetly. The Duplessis regime and others have demonstrated the willingness of businesspeople to participate in kickback schemes in order to obtain government contracts and leases. The enormous power of the pluralist political process was illustrated in the unwillingness of the media and many opposition politicians to expose the corruption during the Duplessis regime, although it was common knowledge among interest group elites. Not only is there fear of confronting powerful political regimes, there is a self-serving motive: opposition interest groups expect to employ similar corrupt tactics once they achieve political power. However, it is ultimately necessary in the Canadian pluralist democracy to avoid any systematic political corruption that would alienate the majority of Canadians. When corruption does occur, most interest groups support reforms which restrict their own power in order to preserve the essential pluralist process.

The Capitalist Democratic Perspective

The persistence of the political crime of corruption in Canada since the Pacific Railway scandal can be interpreted from the capitalist democratic perspective as follows. Every example of corruption has implicated both political and business elites (including, on occasion, organized crime). Profit motives, therefore, are always a key factor, as is the desire to retain or obtain political power. Political party financing is structurally integrated into the business process, as a normal and critical part of accumulating profits and capital. This interdependency has been further confirmed by the constant interchange of personnel; politicians and senior bureaucrats routinely retire to lucrative business positions, while businessmen are recruited for key government and political party positions.

Political and business elites protect their mutual interests and, consequently, when corruption is exposed, criminal justice sanctions are minimal and symbolic. No matter how many political scandals are exposed and reforms are made, the fundamental interdependency remains. Again, it is this interdependency which reflects the dominant position of the ruling class in Canadian politics. The ruling class engages in political crimes as another opportunity to accumulate capital and, in turn, to ensure their political power.

SUMMARY

While the actual concept of political crime was first employed at the end of the 18th century, theorists since Machiavelli have endeavoured to discuss and explicate this complex phenomenon. Three basic conceptualizations have emerged over the years: the definition of political crimes as threats to the established political and social order; the inclusion of crimes by government officials in the definition of political crime; and the definition of political crime as any criminal act, excluding certain crimes such as murder, armed robbery, or sexual assault that are not directed against the authorities.

In addition to the varying conceptualizations of political crime, varying theoretical perspectives are applied in its study in attempts to explicate political crimes in any given system or historical era. In this chapter, political crime is examined in the Canadian context. Three major competing theoretical perspectives—the democratic, pluralist, and conflict perspectives—provide the theoretical basis for the analysis of political crimes in Canada.

Briefly, the democratic perspective maintains that political crimes are committed by persons who are unwilling to abide by the will of the majority as expressed in democratically determined criminal laws. In this light, criminal justice sanctions and police measures are widely supported. The pluralist perspective emphasizes the notion of competing elites. Consequently, the illegal use of elite positions or systematic corruption within government or public offices is seen as threatening the process of pluralism and accommodating elite objectives. The conflict perspective is based on the proposition that political crime occurs because of the need of the corporate-dominated ruling class to cope with the inevitable contradictions that result from capital accumulation in advanced industrial societies.

The range of Canadian political crimes discussed includes the Winnipeg General Strike of 1919, the FLQ crisis, illegal behaviour by government officials (as in the Pacific Railway scandal and the Sky Shops affair), unethical behaviour in the Mulroney administration, and various occupational crimes. Each theoretical perspective emphasizes different components and implications for each of the incidents of political crime discussed. This examination of political crime in Canada further provides evidence for the multifaceted and complex nature of the concept, both in its varying theoretical definitions and related practical manifestations.

BIBLIOGRAPHY

Barker, Thomas, and Julian B. Roebuck. (1973). *An Empirical Typology of Police Corruption.* Springfield, IL: Charles C. Thomas.

Bercuson, David. (1975). "The Winnipeg General Strike." In Irving M. Abella (ed.), *On Strike.* Toronto: James Lorimer and Company.

Berton, Pierre. (1976). "It's the Cops." *Quest* 5:2.

Chambliss, William J. (1971). "Vice, Corruption, Bureaucracy and Power." *Wisconsin Law Review* (December):1150–73.

Clement, Wallace J. (1971). "The Corporate Elite, the Capitalist Class, and the Canadian State." In Leo Panitch (ed.), *The Canadian State: Political Economy and Political Power.* Toronto: University of Toronto Press.

Clinard, Marshall B., and Richard Quinney. (1973). *Criminal Behavior Systems: A Typology.* New York: Holt, Rinehart and Winston.

Dahl, Robert. (1961). *Who Governs? Democracy and Power in an American City.* New Haven: Yale University Press.

Ericson, Richard. (1982). *The Ordering of Justice.* Toronto/Buffalo: Centre of Criminology, University of Toronto Press.

Fidler, Richard. (1978). RCMP: *The Real Subversives.* Canada: Vanguard Publications.

Folster, D. (1977). "Fredericton: Somebody's Got to Go." *Maclean's* 90:23–24.

French, Richard D., and André Béliveau. (1979). *The RCMP and the Management of National Security.* Montreal: Butterworths.

Goldstein, Robert J. (1978). *Political Repression in Modern America: 1870 to the Present.* New York: Schenkman.

Hancock, Kelley, and Don G. Gibbons. (1975). "The Future of Crime in American Society." Unpublished manuscript, Department of Sociology, Portland State University.

Horton, Paul B., and Gerald R. Leslie. (1965). "The Sociology of Social Problems." In Joseph S. Roucek (ed.), *Sociology of Crime.* (3rd ed.). New York: Appleton-Century Crofts.

Ingraham, Barton L. (1979). *Political Crime in Europe.* Berkeley: University of California Press.

Jamieson, Stuart. (1968). *Times of Trouble: Labour Unrest and Industrial Conflict in Canada, 1900–1966.* Privy Council Task Force on Labour Relations. Study No. 22. Ottawa.

Lombroso, Cesare. (1972). "Criminal Man." In Sawyer F. Sylvester, Jr. (ed.), *The Heritage of Modern Criminology.* Cambridge, MA: Schenkman.

Mann, Edward, and John A. Lee. (1979). *The RCMP vs. the People: Inside Canada's Security Service.* Don Mills, ON: General Publishing.

McDougall, J. Lorne. (1968). *Canadian Pacific: A Brief History.* Montreal: McGill University Press.

Mill, J.S. (1951). *Utilitarianism, Liberty and Representative Government.* New York: Dutton.

Minor, W. William. (1975). "Political Crime, Political Justice, and Political Prisoners." *Criminology* 12:385–98.

Pelletier, Gérard. (1971). *The October Crisis.* Toronto/Montreal: McClelland and Stewart.

Pelletier, Jean. (1980). "Impure Grits." *Toronto Sun* (May 22).

Penner, Norman. (1975). *Winnipeg 1919: The Strikers' Own History of the Winnipeg General Strike.* Toronto: James Lorimer and Company.

Pitkin, Hanna F. (1967). *The Concept of Representation.* Berkeley: University of California Press.

Plaskin, Robert. (1978). "Newfoundland: Letting the Fire out of the Bag." *Maclean's* 91:26.

Porter, John. (1965). *The Vertical Mosaic.* Toronto: University of Toronto Press.

Presthus, R. (1973). *Elite Accomodation in Canadian Politics.* Toronto: Macmillan.

Proal, Louis. (1973). *Political Crime.* Montclair, NJ: Patterson Smith.

Quinney, Richard, and John Wildeman. (1977). *The Problem of Crime.* New York: Harper and Row.

Reasons, Charles E. (1974). *The Criminologist: Crime and the Criminal.* Pacific Palisades, CA: Goodyear.

Roberts, Leslie. (1963). *The Chief.* Toronto: Clarke, Irwin and Company.

Robin, Martin. (1968). *Radical Politics and Canadian Labour.* Kingston, ON: Industrial Relations Centre, Queen's University.

Roebuck, Julian, and Stanley C. Weeber. (1978). *Political Crime in the United States.* New York: Praeger.

Ross, E.A. (1907). *Sin and Society.* Boston: Houghton Mifflin.

Ross, Jeffrey. (1988). "Attributes of Domestic Political Terrorism in Canada, 1960–1985." *Terrorism: An International Journal* 11(3):213–33.

Sawatsky, John. (1980). *Men in the Shadows.* Toronto: Doubleday.

Schafer, Stephen. (1974). *The Political Criminal.* New York: Free Press, Macmillan Publishing.

Simard, Francis. (1982). *Pour en finir avec octobre.* Montreal: Stanké.

Spitzer, Steven. (1983). "The Rationalization of Crime Control in the Capitalist Society." In Stanley Cohen and Andrew Scull (eds.), *Social Control and the State.* Oxford: Martin Robinson.

Stevenson, Garth. (1979). *Unfilled Union.* Toronto: Macmillan.

Stoddard, Ellwyn. (1968). "The Informal Code of Police Deviancy: A Group Approach to 'Blue Coat' Crime." *Journal of Criminal Law, Criminology, and Police Science* 59: 201–13.

Stohl, Michael (ed.). (1988). *The Politics of Terrorism.* Marcel Dekker.

Sykes, Gresham, M. (1975). "The Rise of Critical Criminology." *Journal of Criminal Law and Criminology* 65:206–14.

Thorburn, H.G. (1978). "Canadian Pluralist Democracy in Crisis." *Canadian Journal of Political Science* 11:4.

Torrance, Judy. (1977). "The Response of the Canadian Government to Violence." *Canadian Journal of Political Science* 10:473–96.

Turk, Austin T. (1982). *Political Criminality: The Defiance and Defense of Authority.* Beverley Hills: Sage.

Vallières, Pierre. (1971). *White Niggers of America.* Toronto: McClelland and Stewart.

Westley, William A. (1970). *Violence and the Police: A Sociological Study of Law, Custom and Morality.* Cambridge, MA: MIT Press.

FURTHER READING

Bercuson, David. (1974). "The Winnipeg General Strike." In Irving M. Abella (ed.), *On Strike.* Toronto: James Lorimer and Company. As a comprehensive and concise chronology and discussion of the Winnipeg General Strike, Bercuson's chapter is extremely useful.

Mann, Edward, and John Alan Lee. (1979). *The RCMP vs. the People: Inside Canada's Security Service.* Don Mills, ON: General Publishing. This is a thoroughly researched, highly readable account of the security police in Canada.

Porter, John. (1965). *The Vertical Mosaic.* Toronto: University of Toronto Press. This book examines the intricate relationship between elites and power in Canada. Porter discusses the apparent connection between class position, social mobility, positions of power, and ethnicity.

Sawatsky, John. (1980). *Men in the Shadows.* Toronto: Doubleday. Journalist John Sawatsky provides detailed information about the operations of the RCMP and their role in the anti-FLQ campaign.

Simpson, Jeffrey. (1988). *The Spoils of Power: The Politics of Patronage.* Toronto: W. Collins. This book provides an excellent analysis of the long Canadian tradition of political patronage.

Thorburn, Hugh G. (1979). *Party Politics in Canada.* Scarborough: Prentice-Hall. This book is a collection of essays on the development of the Canadian political party system. Written from varying perspectives, the essays deal with subjects ranging from the historical background of Canadian political parties to regional and third-party politics.

Turk, Austin T. (1982). *Political Criminality: The Defiance and Defense of Authority.* Beverly Hills: Sage. Turk discusses the concepts of political criminality and policing. He defines political crime as acts which threaten the socio-political order. The police are responsible for preserving the status quo and, therefore, may employ whatever sanctions are necessary, including illegal acts.

CHAPTER 16

WHITE-COLLAR AND CORPORATE CRIME

By John Hagan

*T*he topic of white-collar crime raises some important issues in the field of criminology. The term itself, introduced by Edwin Sutherland (1940) more than a half century ago, is probably one of the most popularly used criminological concepts in everyday life. However, despite its popularity, there is uncertainty about the precise meaning of the term. The fundamental point is that the topic of white-collar crime has forced a reconsideration of some very basic criminological assumptions.

No longer is it possible to take for granted the way in which crime itself is defined. No longer can the official data collected on crime by agencies of crime control be accepted uncritically. No longer can it be assumed that the poor are more criminal than the rich. The criminological enterprise takes on new form and substance when the topic of white-collar crime is made a central part of our thinking. These points are made by considering separately issues of class, crime, and the corporations; the social organization of work; and legal sanctions. Each is connected to the topic of white-collar crime.

CLASS, CRIME, AND THE CORPORATIONS

White-collar crimes are often committed through, and on behalf of, corporations. The involvement of corporations in crime has been recognized at least since the early part of this century when E.A. Ross (1907) wrote of a new type of criminal "who picks pockets with a 'rake-off' instead of a jimmy, cheats with a company prospectus instead of a deck of cards, or scuttles his town instead of his ship." Particular actions of corporations have been criminal offences in Canada since 1889 (Casey, 1985). However, it was not until after the Great Depression that Edwin Sutherland (1940) finally attached a lasting label to these offenders in his influential paper, "White-Collar Crime." Sutherland proposed in this paper that white-collar crime be defined "as a crime committed by a person of respectability and high social status in the course of his occupation."

From this point (Geis and Meier, 1977; Shapiro, 1980; Wheeler and Rothman, 1982), there has been confusion about the role of *occupation* and *organization* in the study of white-collar crime. For example, Wheeler and Rothman (1982) note that two influential works, Clinard's (1952) and Hartung's (1950) studies of black-market activities during the Second World War, defined white-collar crime in two rather different ways. Clinard defined white-collar crime occupationally, as "illegal activities among business and professional men," while Hartung included an organizational component, defining such crimes as "a violation of law regulating business, which is committed for a firm by the firm or its agents in the conduct of its business." A distinction is still often drawn today (see, for example, Coleman, 1985:8) between "occupational crime—that is, white collar crime committed by an individual or a group of individuals exclusively for personal gain," and "organizational crime—white collar crimes committed with the support and encouragement of a formal organization and intended at least in part to advance the goals of that organization."

The problem is that the occupational and organizational components of many white-collar crimes cannot be easily separated. Clinard and Yeager (1980) make this point with the example of a Firestone tire official who aided his corporation in securing and administering illegal political contributions benefiting the corporation, but then embezzled much of the funds for himself. The illegal activities of lawyers (Reasons and Chappell, 1985) are another common form of white-collar crime where it is often difficult to separate the individual component from what is done for and through the law firm. Nonetheless, it is important to note that locating white-collar offenders in terms of their ownership and authority positions in occupational and organizational structures is a key part of the class analysis of white-collar crime (Geis, 1984; Hagan and Parker, 1985; Weisburd et al., 1990). Sutherland's emphasis on "respect" and "status" in defining white-collar crime only begins to open up the issue of class position and its role in the understanding of white-collar crime. A key element of class is the power to commit major white-collar crimes that ownership and authority positions in occupational and organizational structures make possible.

However, as Sutherland recognized, the problem is not only one of our conception of white-collar offenders and their class positions, but also one of our conception of white-collar crime itself (cf. Shapiro, 1990). Sometimes our confused conceptions can seem mundane, so mundane that they pass unnoticed. For example, the *New York Times* recently published two stories in the same edition, one that warned and possibly discouraged its readers from "pirating" computer software (Lewis, 1989), and another which informed and likely encouraged its readers to acquire newly designed devices to copy audiotapes (Fantel, 1989). The contradiction probably was unnoticed, but the latter story nonetheless began with the mildly apologetic and perhaps not entirely facetious suggestion that:

> among the higher animals and human beings, larceny seems to be an
> innate trait held in check by social conditioning. But inhibitions fail,
> and the primal impulse asserts itself when it comes to tape recording.

Even decent folk, who refrain from pocketing silver spoons, think nothing of taping copyrighted music. (27)

Sutherland (1945) insisted that insofar as there exists a "legal description of acts as socially injurious and legal provision of a penalty for the act," such acts are, for the purposes of our research and understanding, crime (cf., Tappan, 1947). This is the case even though many such acts go undetected and unprosecuted. For example, many stock and securities frauds can be prosecuted under provincial securities legislation or under the Criminal Code of Canada. The former are considered "quasi-criminal" statutes. Yet the behaviours prosecuted under either body of law may be identical. It is an act of prosecutorial discretion that determines whether these behaviours are defined clearly and officially as crimes. Sutherland insisted that such acts of official discretion were not relevant to the categorization of these behaviours for the purposes of research. In either case, the behaviours were to be regarded as criminal. Such a position can make a major difference in terms of the relationship observed between class and crime.

Consider the issue of deaths and accidents that result from events in the workplace. Occupational deaths far outnumber deaths resulting from murder (Geis, 1975). In Canada (Reasons et al., 1981), occupational deaths rank third after heart disease and cancer as a source of mortality, accounting for more than ten times as many deaths as murder. While it cannot be assumed that all or most such deaths result from the intentions of employers to see employees die, there nonetheless is good reason to believe that the majority of such deaths are not the result of employee carelessness.

One estimate (Reasons et al., 1981) holds that more than one-third of all on-the-job injuries are due to illegal working conditions, and that about another quarter are due to legal but unsafe conditions. At most, a third of all such accidents are attributed to unsafe acts on the part of employees. Meanwhile, there are numerous well-documented examples of employers intentionally, knowingly, or negligently creating hazards. These include failing to follow administrative orders to alter dangerous situations and covering up the creation and existence of such hazards. For example, Reasons et al., discuss the case of Quasar Petroleum of Calgary, who were fined $15 000 for violating safety regulations when three men died while cleaning out a tank containing toxic fumes. The men were not provided with protective equipment nor were they trained to recognize the need for such equipment.

The case of asbestos poisoning involving administrative decisions within the Johns-Manville Corporation is but one of the best-known examples. Swartz (1978) notes that asbestos has been recognized as a serious health hazard since the turn of the century. Nonetheless, people working with it were not informed, and the government bureaucracy and the medical community ignored the hazard. At the Johns-Manville plant in Manville, New Jersey, company doctors regularly diagnosed lung diseases among the asbestos workers, but never told the workers that their lung problems were related to asbestos. The Johns-Manville case is not a problem unique to the United

States. As the accompanying excerpt from an Ontario royal commission indicates, the problems of asbestos poisoning are well documented in Ontario as well. The asbestos industry is not unique in this respect. Ermann and Lundman (1982) argue that many similar deaths occur in other industries as well. Swartz (1978) concludes that these deaths should be recognized as a form of murder, or what is sometimes called "corporate homicide."

HEALTH EFFECTS OF ASBESTOS IN ONTARIO

Residents of Ontario have more than the normal run of reasons to share the international feelings of apprehension that asbestos has aroused. This province is the scene of what we document in this Report to be a world-class occupational health disaster: the Johns-Manville plant in Scarborough, in the Municipality of Metropolitan Toronto. This plant, between 1948 and 1980, manufactured asbestos-cement pipe, using a mixture of two kinds of asbestos: chrysotile and crocidolite. At various times during its existence, this plant also manufactured asbestos-cement board, using only chrysotile, and asbestos insulation materials, using chrysotile and a third kind of asbestos called amosite.

As of 1983, the death toll from asbestos exposure in this plant, as measured by the number of claims awarded by the Ontario Workers' Compensation Board, was 68. This lone plant, whose annual employment never exceeded 714 workers, has already occasioned more deaths from industrial disease than the entire Ontario mining industry, which annually employs over 30,000 workers, occasions from industrial accidents in an average four-year period.

The death toll at this plant, which closed in 1980, offers harsh testimony to the nature of long-latency disease. It has mounted gradually and inexorably because individual deaths are separated from the beginning of the exposures that caused them by some 10 to 30 or more years. The dimensions of the disaster have therefore been growing over time; for example, between August 1981 and August 1982, the middle year in the existence of this Commission, 5 more ex-employees died of mesothelioma, a rare cancer that is specifically associated with asbestos exposure. It is a tragically safe assumption that, among those who worked in this plant, asbestos-related deaths will continue to occur, and that hence the disaster has yet to run its course....

The asbestos-induced disaster at this plant ranks with the worst that have been recorded in the international epidemiological literature on asbestos. It places the name Scarborough on an unenviable list with Charleston, South Carolina; Rochdale, England; and a handful of other places. The Scarborough plant accounts for half of all the asbestos deaths and disabilities that have been compensated by the Ontario Workers' Compensation Board. The remainder have been occasioned by exposure in a wide variety of work situations and industrial processes, for example, wartime gas mask manufacturing, brake manufacturing, and ship-building. The Ontario employers whose workers suffered asbestos disease and death are spread throughout the province; excluding Johns-Manville, only two have given rise to more than 5 awarded claims.

There is indeed reason to be apprehensive about asbestos in Ontario.

Source: Report of the Royal Commission on Matters of Health and Safety Arising from the Use of Asbestos in Ontario. Province of Ontario, 1984.
© Reproduced with permission from the Queen's Printer for Ontario.

This chapter does not attempt to debate the fine points in the definition of corporate homicide or to establish with any precision how many such homicides occur. It is enough to note summarily that such deaths occur in considerable numbers and that while the consequences of these deaths have only been (briefly) considered for employees, corporate homicides also involve many additional numbers of consumers and the general public. Corporate homicides seem likely to rival in number or even exceed those deaths resulting from homicide conceived in more traditional terms. Of immediate interest here is the meaning of corporate homicide, and crimes like it, for the relationship between class and crime.

To pursue this interest, a fundamental point must first be made about more conventional forms of crime and delinquency. There is increasing evidence that it is a relatively small number of offenders who account for a rather large proportion of serious street crimes (Greenwood, 1982; Wolfgang, 1972). The difficulty of including such persons in conventional research designs has probably obscured the relationship that exists between class position and this type of criminality.

A parallel point may be true of many kinds of white-collar crime. For example, crimes such as corporate homicide may occur with high incidence, but low prevalence, among highly selected sub-populations—that is, among particular employers in particular kinds of industries. The Johns-Manville Corporation and the asbestos industry in general is an example that has already been noted. Again, it may be difficult to pinpoint such employers in conventional research designs, and this may obscure the relationship between class position and this type of criminality.

Implicit in the preceding references to street crimes and corporate homicides is the high likelihood that crime is not a unidimensional concept. That is, these are different kinds of crime that likely have different connections to the concept of class. Among adults, class probably is related negatively to making the direct physical attacks involved in street crimes of violence (Nettler, 1978), and class probably is positively related to causing harms less directly through criminal acts involving the use of corporate resources. Similarly, among juveniles it may be that some common acts of delinquency (for example, forms of theft that include the illegal copying of computer software and the unauthorized use of credit and bank cards) are related positively to class (Cullen et al., 1985; Hagan et al., 1985; Hagan and Kay, 1990), while less frequent and more serious forms of delinquency are negatively related to class (Braithwaite, 1981; Colvin and Pauley, 1984; Elliot and Ageton, 1980; Hindelang et al., 1981; Kleck, 1982; Thornberry and Farnsworth, 1982). It has sometimes appeared that measures of status are not related to crime and delinquency at all (Tittle et al., 1978). However, the study of white-collar crime and delinquency provides increasing reason to believe that measures of class are connected to crime and delinquency in interesting, albeit complicated, ways.

WHITE-COLLAR CRIME AND THE SOCIAL ORGANIZATION OF WORK

Not all white-collar crimes are committed by white-collar persons. For example, much embezzlement is committed by relatively low-status bank tellers (Daly, 1989). However, if it is true that white-collar crime is positively related to class position, it is also reasonable to ask why it should be so. The answer may lie in the power derived from ownership and authority positions in the occupational and organizational structures of modern corporations. These positions of power carry with them a freedom from control that may be criminogenic. That is, to have power is to be free from the kinds of constraints that may normally inhibit crime. As will be seen, the modern corporation facilitates this kind of freedom with the presumed goal of enhancing free enterprise and the unintended consequence of encouraging crime.

It is recognized that the organizational form of the corporation is crucial to understanding most white-collar crime (Ermann and Lundman, 1978; Hagan, 1982; Reiss, 1980; Schrager and Short, 1978; Wheeler, 1976). As Wheeler and Rothman (1982) succinctly note, the corporation "is for white-collar criminals what the gun or knife is for the common criminal—a tool to obtain money from victims." Of course, the importance of the corporation is not restricted to the world of crime. From the industrial revolution on, it has become increasingly apparent that "among the variety of interests that men have, those interests that have been successfully collected to create corporate actors are the interests that dominate the society" (Coleman, 1974). This reference to men in particular is not accidental, for corporate entities are disproportionately male in employment, ownership, and control. Our interest is in developing an understanding of the link between the power of the corporate form and the criminogenic freedom that this powerful structure generates.

The corporation itself is a "legal fiction," with, as H.L. Mencken aptly observed, "no pants to kick or soul to damn." That is, the law chooses to treat corporations as "juristic persons," making them formally liable to the same laws as "natural persons." Some of the most obvious faults in this legal analogy become clear when the impossibility of imprisoning or executing corporations is considered. However, there are more subtle differences between corporate and individual actors with equally significant consequences.

For example, the old legal saw tells us that the corporation has no conscience or soul. Stone (1975) describes the problem well:

> When individuals are placed in an organizational structure, some of the ordinary internalized restraints seem to lose their hold. And if we decide to look beyond the individual employees and find an organizational "mind" to work with, a "corporate conscience" distinct from the consciences of particular individuals, it is not readily apparent where we would begin—much less what we would be talking about.

Stone goes on to suggest some interesting ways in which the corporate conscience and corporate responsibility could be increased (see also Nagorski, 1989). However, the point is that these mechanisms, or others, have not been put in place. Corporate power in this sense remains unchecked, and it is in this sense criminogenic.

The problem is in part the absence of cultural beliefs to discourage corporate criminality (Geis, 1962). C. Wright Mills (1956) captured part of the problem in his observation that "it is better, so the image runs, to take one dime from each of ten million people at the point of a corporation than $100,000 from each of ten banks at the point of a gun." Nonetheless, there is some evidence that cultural climates vary across time and regimes. For example, Sally Simpson (1986), who studied anti-trust violations in the United States between 1927 and 1981, found that such violations were more common during Republican than Democratic administrations. However, even when condemnatory beliefs about corporate crime have been strong, there have been too few controlling mechanisms in place to impose their controlling influence effectively.

Consider, for a moment, the internal structure of a typical modern corporation, as illustrated by Woodmansee's description of the General Electric Corporation (cited in Clinard and Yeager, 1980; see also Shearing et al., 1985). Note the complexity of this enterprise and its gender stratification.

> We begin by describing the way GE's employees are officially organized into separate layers of authority. The corporation is like a pyramid. The great majority of the company's workers form the base of the pyramid; they take orders coming down from above but do not give orders to

anyone else. If you were hired by GE for one of these lowest level positions, you might find yourself working on an assembly line, installing a motor in a certain type of refrigerator. You would be in a group of five to 50 workers who all take orders from one supervisor, or foreman, or manager. Your supervisor is on the second step of the pyramid; she or he, and the other supervisors who specialize in this type of refrigerator, all take orders from a General Manager.

There are about 180 of these General Managers at GE; each one heads a Department with one or two thousand employees. The General Manager of your Department, and the General Managers of the one or two other Departments which produce GE's other types of refrigerators, are in turn supervised by the Vice President/General Manager of the Refrigerator Division. This man (there are only men at this level and above) is one of the 50 men at GE responsible for heading GE's Divisions. He, and the heads of several other Divisions which produce major appliances, look up to the next step of the pyramid and see, towering above, the Vice President/Group Executive who heads the entire Major Appliance Group. While there are over 300,000 workers at the base of the pyramid, there are only 10 men on this Group Executive level. Responsibility for overseeing all of GE's product lines is divided between the ten. At about the same level of authority in the company are the executives of GE's Corporate Staff; these men are concerned not with particular products but with general corporate matters such as accounting, planning, legal affairs, and relations with employees, with the public and with government.

And now the four men at the top of the pyramid come into view; the three Vice Chairmen of the Board of Directors, and standing above them, GE's Chief Executive....Usually, these four men confer alone, but once a month, 15 other men join them for a meeting. The 15 other members of the Board of Directors are not called up from the lower levels of the GE pyramid; they drift in sideways from the heights of neighboring pyramids. Thirteen of them are chairmen or presidents of other corporations, the fourteenth is a former corporate chairman, and the fifteenth is a university president.

Could the board of directors of the above corporation exercise the kind of control over its employees that individual actors are expected by law to exercise, for example, over their dependants? Stone (1975) points out that top officers and directors, theoretically, are liable to suit by the corporation itself (via a shareholders' action) if they allow a law violation to occur through negligence. However, Stone then cites a frequently noted antitrust case to make the point that, legally, little is expected from corporations in the way of control over their individual actors. In dismissing the claim made in a case against the Allis-Chalmers Corporation, the judgement (Graham v. Allis-Chalmers Mfg. Co., 188 A.2d 125, 130 [Del. 1963]) indicates that "...absent cause for suspicion there is no duty upon the directors to install and operate a corporate system ... to ferret out wrongdoing which they have no reason to suspect exists." The effect of this kind of decision is to reinforce the power of top management to keep itself uninformed about the very details of illegal activities that the public interest may require they know.

Why would corporate executives feel pressure to commit illegal activities? There are likely many answers to this question, but one of the most basic is that corporations expect their managers to increase profits. This may help explain why some of our most respectable companies continue to victimize their customers despite prosecution for previous violations. Consider the case of the following corporate recidivist.

CROWN SEEKS MILLION-DOLLAR FINE IN SIMPSONS-SEARS RING "RIPOFF"

TORONTO(CP)—The federal Justice Department has asked a Toronto judge to levy a $1-million fine against Simpsons-Sears Ltd. after the retailer was found guilty of false advertising.

Crown counsel Rod Flaherty characterized the conduct of the company as "reprehensible" when it knowingly continued its "ripoff" of diamond-ring purchasers long after the federal combines branch informed the company it was breaking the law.

Simpsons-Sears and H. Forth and Co. Ltd., a small jewellery appraiser, were found guilty of 12 counts of misleading advertising. Simpsons-Sears had eight previous false-advertising convictions.

Flaherty said he asked Judge George Ferguson for the stiff fine because it would be the only sort of punishment which will make an impression on the company. Ferguson is to sentence the companies June 30.

Defence lawyer R.G. Carter suggested a fine of $80,000 to $100,000. The previous record fine for the offence was $85,000.

The charges stemmed from a highly successful advertising campaign which offered diamond rings at price reductions ranging from 33 to 50 percent below "appraised values." Each customer received a free appraisal certificate showing carat weight, color and retail value.

The company sold $7-million worth of the rings in the mid-1970s, all of which were improperly appraised by H. Forth with the knowledge of Simpsons-Sears officials.

Some rings were mismatched with certificates as to size, clarity and color, the judge found. In fact, one ring sold as two diamonds sandwiching an emerald was in fact two diamonds sandwiching a piece of green glass.

Ferguson said evidence indicated the "appraisal value" prices were fictitious ones agreed on by the companies.

> Flaherty said the company continued to sell the rings in this fashion despite its previous convictions and despite the fact that the combines branch was actively and visibly investigating the sales.
>
> Source: *Winnipeg Free Press* 10 June 1983.

An example of executive disengagement from crimes is hinted at in the well-known E.F. Hutton cheque-kiting scheme. In this case, the Hutton brokerage firm admitted operating a scheme that obtained billions of dollars in interest-free loans from dozens of banks from 1980 to 1982, by systematically overdrawing its bank accounts and purposely delaying the clearing of its cheques. Hutton paid a $2-million fine and agreed to make restitution to the banks that lost money. However, a central question that remains is, How high up in the executive structure of Hutton did knowledge of this improper overdrafting scheme go? The chairman of a U.S. congressional subcommittee that investigated the matter noted that "there is no tape of somebody confessing, but a look at the circumstantial evidence indicates that people at Hutton headquarters were encouraging this activity" (*The Toronto Star* 22 September 1985:B1). It is, of course, possible that such schemes were encouraged without the need for top officials to know the exact ways and means by which they were accomplished.

How widespread is this use of "executive influence from afar" and "executive distancing and disengagement" in corporate criminality? Two intriguing studies (Baumhart, 1961; Brenner and Molander, 1977) suggest that the problem is large and growing. The latter of these studies reports that the percentage of executives who indicate an inability to be honest in providing information to top management has nearly doubled since the earlier research, done in the 1950s. About half of those surveyed thought that their superiors frequently did not wish to know how results were obtained, as long as the desired outcome was accomplished. Furthermore, the executives surveyed "frequently complained of superiors' pressure to support incorrect viewpoints, sign false documents, overlook superiors' wrongdoing, and do business with superiors' friends" (Brenner and Molander, 1977).

The last set of findings suggest not only a growing freedom at the top of organizations from the need to know and accept responsibility for criminal activity below, but also a growing pressure from the top down that is itself criminogenic. Farberman (1975) has referred to such pressures in the automotive industry, and in other highly concentrated corporate sectors, as constituting a "criminogenic market structure." The crime-generating feature of these markets is their domination by a relatively small number of manufacturers who insist that their dealers sell in high volume at a small per unit profit. Dealerships that fail to perform risk the loss of their franchises in an industry where the alternatives are few. A result is high pressure to maximize sales and minimize service. More specifically, Farberman suggests that dealers in the car industry may be induced by the small profit margins on new cars to compensate through fraudulent warranty work and repair rackets. The connection between these findings is that the executives of the automotive industry can distance themselves from the criminal consequences of the "forcing model" (high volume/low per-unit profit) they impose. The result is an absence of control over repair and warranty frauds at the dealership level.

Farberman also points out that corporate concentration can be criminogenic in that it diminishes the corrective role competition can play in restraining criminal practices that increase the costs of production. Asch and Seneca (1969) conclude from their research that high concentration is in particular related to higher rates of crime in consumer-goods industries. This receives further support from Clinard and Yeager's (1980) finding that the oil, auto, and pharmaceutical industries appear to violate the law more frequently than do other industries. Particular types of crime, such as collusion and anti-trust activity, may also be more common in highly concentrated industries (Coleman, 1987). A striking example of collusion in a setting that restricts competition is reported by Wayne Baker (1984). In a study of trading in the pits of securities markets, Baker observed that traders organized themselves in tightly knit social groups that jealously guarded their pits. As a result, they often did not "hear" better bids shouted by traders who visited from other pits, and they juggled trades to exhaust the capital of outsiders.

The weak role anti-combines legislation has played in restraining monopolistic practices in Canada will be discussed later in this chapter. *Maclean's* magazine has observed that Canada's competition laws are "among the weakest in the Western World and its economy among the most concentrated" (18 July 1983). This implies a significant amount of white-collar crime.

The scale of the crimes that access to corporate resources makes possible will now be considered. In an intriguing study, Wheeler and Rothman (1982) categorized white-collar offenders into three groups: those who committed offences alone or with affiliated others using neither an occupational nor an organizational role (individual offenders); those who committed offences alone or with affiliated others using an occupational role (occupational offenders); and those who committed offences in which both organization and occupation were ingredients (organizational offenders). The results of this study indicate in a variety of ways the enormous advantages accruing to those who use formal organizations in their crimes. For example, across a subset of four offences, the median "take" for individual offenders was $5279, for occupational offenders $17 106, and for organizational offenders $117 392. In a parallel Canadian study, Hagan and Parker (1985) report that securities violators who make use of organizational resources commit crimes that involve larger numbers of victims and are broader in their geopolitical spread. Why the organizational edge? Wheeler and Rothman (1982) answer with a example.

> Represented by its president, a corporation entered into a factoring agreement with a leading ... commercial bank, presenting it with $1.2 million in false billings over the course of seven months; the company's statements were either inflated to reflect much more business than actually was being done, or were simply made up. Would the bank have done this for an individual? Whether we conclude that organizations are trusted more than individuals, or that they simply operate on a much larger scale, it is clear that the havoc caused when organizations are used outside the law far exceeds anything produced by unaffiliated actors.

Just as the organizational form has facilitated economic and technological development on a scale far beyond that achieved by individuals, so too has this form allowed criminal gains of a magnitude that men and women acting alone would find hard to attain.

This section has sought to make the point that the structure of the modern corporation allows a power imbalance to prevail in which those individuals at the top experience a relative freedom, while those at the bottom often experience pressure applied from the top that encourages various kinds of white-collar crime. The point has also been made that the corporate form itself can be used effectively to perpetrate "bigger and better crimes" than can be achieved by individuals acting alone. Access to these corporate resources is a unique advantage of class positions involving ownership and authority in business organizations. It is in this sense that it can be said that the social organization of work itself is criminogenic in the world of the modern corporation.

WHITE-COLLAR CRIME AND LEGAL SANCTIONS

Given the distribution of freedom and pressure that has been identified within the structure of the modern corporation, and the power this gives to those who run it, the question that recurs is: What does the law do to remedy the potential for abuse? This question raises issues of legal liability and the enforcement of law.

"We have arranged things," writes Christopher Stone (1975), "so that the people who call the shots do not have to bear the full risks." This, in a nutshell, is the consequence of the limited liabilities borne by modern corporate actors.

> Take, for example, a small corporation involved in shipping dynamite. The shareholders of such a company, who are typically also the managers, do not *want* their dynamite-laden truck to blow up. But if it does, they know that those injured cannot, except in rare cases, sue them as individuals to recover their full damages if the amount left in the corporations' bank account is inadequate to make full compensation.... What this means is that in deciding how much money to spend on safety devices, and whether or not to allow trucks to drive through major

cities, the calculations are skewed toward higher risks than suggested by the "rational economic corporation/free market" model that is dreamily put forth in textbooks. If no accident results, the shareholders will reap the profits of skimping on safety measures. If a truck blows up, the underlying human interests will be shielded from fully bearing the harm that they have caused. And then, there is nothing to prevent the same men from setting up a new dynamite shipping corporation the next day; all it takes is the imagination to think up a new name, and some $50 in filing fees. (Stone, 1975)

It may be conceded that large corporations are not quite so free as the small corporation in the example to dissolve and reconstitute their operations. However, the separation of shareholder and management interests gives rise to a related problem of liability. Given that corporate officers gain their primary rewards through salaries, the effects of damage judgements are indirect, and judging from experience, limited. Stone (1975) reminds us that in 1972, for example, the Ford Motor Company suffered fines and penalties of approximately $7 million for a violation of the U.S. Environmental Protection Act. Yet the salaries of the chief executives of this company increased dramatically in following years. There is no record of shareholders successfully altering such patterns by changing management in the wake of lawsuits. There are also indications that companies such as the Johns-Manville Corporation have filed for protection under federal bankruptcy laws in the United States to limit their potential liability from lawsuits.

These discussions raise the broader issue of how and why the law is used to control white-collar crime. It has already been seen that civil remedies are not very effective. We turn now to criminal sanctions. How does the state decide what kinds of upperworld indiscretions will be called criminal? The most interesting work that has been done on this issue in Canada involves the development of anti-combines legislation. Given the powerful economic interests involved in forming the monopolistic enterprises this legislation presumably seeks to prevent, one might wonder how an anti-combines law would ever have been passed in the first place. Goff and Reasons (1978) indicate that the initiative for the original legislation in 1899 "came not from the general populace but from small businessmen, who felt their firms were at the mercy of big business interests." However, more recently Smandych (1985) has noted that a "Royal Commission on Labour and Capital" created for the purpose of investigating industrial conditions in Canada interviewed and recorded testimony from numerous trade-union representatives and workers. This testimony, cited in the report of the Commission in 1899, specifically sought legislation against monopolistic practices, and Smandych argues that "the possibility that worker demands for the elimination of combines went unnoticed by the government of the day is extremely doubtful."

Smandych goes on to conclude that "...the first flourishing of Canadian anti-combines legislation was the product of an essential confrontation between labour and capital, and of the state's effort to find an acceptable solution." None of this is to say, as later noted, that this legislation was strong or effective. Quite the contrary, as Snider (1979) observes. Efforts over the years to strengthen the legislation with "proconsumer and procompetition" amendments regularly "were weakened or eliminated in the face of business opposition." Smandych, Snider, Goff, and Reasons are all agreed that this legislation has done less than it promised to reduce monopolistic practices and to punish those who promote them.

But what of the white-collar offenders who are held criminally liable and processed through the criminal justice system? Are they liable to as severe sanctioning as individual actors? Notions of "equality before the law" are perhaps nowhere more subjective in meaning than in their application to the sentencing of white-collar offenders (Hagan and Albonetti, 1982). This is reflected in at least two kinds of comments made by judges about the sentences they impose for white-collar crimes. It is reflected first in the suggestion that white-collar offenders experience sanctions differently than other kinds of offenders, and second in the assertion that different kinds of sanctions are appropriate in white-collar cases.

The view, common among judges, that white-collar offenders experience sanctions differently than other kinds of offenders is well summarized in Mann, Wheeler, and Sarat's (1980) conclusions after interviewing a sample of judges who have tried such cases: "Most judges have a widespread belief that the suffering experienced by a white-collar person as a result of apprehension, public indictment and conviction, and the collateral disabilities incident to conviction—loss of job, professional licenses, and status in the community—completely satisfies the need to punish the individual." This belief persists in the face of findings from a recent study by Benson (1989:474) that "although they commit the most serious offences, employers and managers are least likely to lose their jobs after conviction for a white-collar crime." The argument for white-collar leniency endures in the minds of judges and others: the defendant, having suffered enough from the acts of prosecution and conviction, does not require a severe sentence.

What kinds of sentences, therefore, are judged appropriate for white-collar offenders? In white-collar cases, judges articulate what they see as a recurring problem—how the goal of general deterrence may be accomplished without doing (perceived) injustice to the individual offender. A judge interviewed by Mann et al. (1980) suggests the mental conflict this dilemma stimulates.

> The problem is the tension between use of incarceration for its deterrent factors, and the inclination not to use it because it is too excessive given the noncriminal record of the [white-collar] offender. From the individual standpoint there are good arguments against sentencing; from the societal interest of deterring crime there are some good arguments for using the sentence.... The tension between those two values is very acute.

Mann et al. (1980) conclude that most judges seek a compromise in resolving this dilemma. "The weekend sentence, the very short jail term, and the relatively frequent use of amended sentences (where a judge imposes a prison term and later reduces it) are evidence of this search for a compromise."

It is important to acknowledge the disputed role of fines in sentencing white-collar offenders. Posner (1980) asserts that "the white-collar criminal ... should be punished only by monetary penalties." His argument is that if fines are suitably large they are an equally effective deterrent and cheaper to administer, and therefore socially preferable to imprisonment and other afflictive punishments. It has already been noted that corporate entities are liable to little else than fines. However, Mann et al. (1980) find judges to be sceptical of the effectiveness of fines. They report

> a conspicuous absence of responses by judges that a fine was the appropriate sanction to be imposed on a defendant.... Where fines were used in conjunction with another sentence it was generally the other sentence ... that was thought to have the intended deterrent effect. Where the fine was used alone, the idea that the commencement of the criminal process against the defendant was the punishment seemed to be more important in the judges' minds than the fine itself.

This kind of ambivalence toward fines is reflected in Goff and Reasons' (1978) analysis of the history of prosecution and sentencing under the Canadian anti-combines legislation discussed previously. Goff and Reasons note that under this legislation, between 1952 and 1972, a total of 157 decisions were made against 50 corporations in Canada. These decisions were predominantly against small- and medium-sized businesses, rather than against the larger corporations. Nonetheless, more than half of Canada's largest corporations have been recidivists (that is, convicted more than once), with an average of 3.2 decisions registered against them. Most interestingly, however, Goff and Reasons report that no individual has ever been jailed for illegal activities under the Combines Act. Instead, the government has usually issued Order of Prohibition penalties, rather than fining the offender or issuing other penalties such as lowering the tariff duties on foreign products to compensate the Canadian consumer by way of increasing competition.

The sense that emerges is that judges are acutely aware of the issues of deterrence, disparity, and discrimination in the sentencing of white-collar offenders, and that they attempt to respond to these issues by fashioning sentences that combine sanctions in a compromise fashion. Consistent with this view, Hagan and Nagel (1982) find, in a sentencing study covering the period from 1963 to 1976 in the Southern District of New York, that judges attempted to compensate for the shorter prison terms given to white-collar offenders by adding probation or fines to their sentences. Similarly, fines were most frequently used in conjunction with prison and probation sentences. In any case, all of these findings suggest the likelihood that white-collar offenders are advantaged by the specific types and combinations of legal sanctions that are imposed on them.

However, both in Canada and the United States, there is some evidence that the mid-1970s brought a new and somewhat harsher attitude toward white-collar crime. Katz (1980) speaks of a "social movement against white-collar crime" that began in the United States in the late 1960s, and the evolution of public opinion documents an increasing concern with the occurrence of such crimes (Cullen et al., 1982; Schrager and Short, 1978). This new concern seems at least in part to have been a response to incidents such as the American experience with Watergate and the Canadian experience with Harbourgate. It was illustrated by the "proactive" prosecutorial policies of several U.S. attorneys (Hagan and Nagel, 1982), and in the increased prosecution of large-scale securities violations in Ontario (Hagan and Parker, 1985). In 1987, the Canadian government replaced the Environmental Contaminants Act with new legislation which provides for fines of up to $1 million per day and jail terms of up to five years for guilty executives. Further, the government of Ontario has increased the fine for insider trading of securities from $25 000 to $1 million, and has increased the possible jail term from one to two years.

CANADA'S "HARBOURGATE"
Politicians 'On the Take' Dredge Trial Tape Says

HAMILTON—"A very high percentage" of politicians are on the take, but it's hard to prove, according to former Hamilton Harbor Commissioner Kenneth Elliott in a conversation tape-recorded by Royal Canadian Mounted Police and played in court today.

The recording, made on May 8, 1974, in Charleston, S.C., was the third one heard in the trial of Elliott, 42, and Reginald Fisher, a business consultant.

They face 10 charges of fraud, conspiracy and uttering in connection with three Hamilton harbor projects.

The RCMP took former dredging company executive Horace "Joe" Rindress to Charleston and wired him to record conversations with Elliott.

Got $1.2 Million
Rindress, 48, former president of J.P. Porter Co. Ltd., a Montreal-based firm, says his company got a $1.2 million Hamilton contract after two other firms co-operated by rigging tenders.

He says he paid off Elliott on behalf of his company.

Early in the four-hour tape, which began this morning, the pair commiserated with each other about the nervous tension put on them by the Mountie investigation.

Elliott remarked: "How come the ... politicians are all the same, they've got everything of life and these assholes think they're going to nail me for any graft?"

Rindress: "A very high percentage of these guys are on the take but to prove it is something else again, eh?"

Elliott: "That's right."

Rindress: "It's funny when they die, they all end up with big estates and yet only make $20,000 a year."

Elliott laughed loudly and agreed. He remarked on the commissioner of Broward County in Florida who he said spent $1.25 million campaigning for a $22,000-a-year post.

After further discussion of this, Elliott remarked: "That's the democratic way."

Rindress: "Yeah, real democracy."

A few minutes later, Elliott remarked, when told that nine Quebec City women had won the $1 million first prize in the first Olympic lottery: "I think it's fixed, Joe."

Earlier in the conversation, Elliott spoke wearily of the "worry and aggravation" he had undergone through the RCMP investigation.

"I just made up my mind six months ago, f—— it. What can they really do. I've been all through it."

"The worst I can do is wind up with a fine and conflict of interest so they can criticize me in court and in the newspapers. F—— it. As far as the political payoff—they can kiss my ass. That's all he's after is political payoffs."

("He" was apparently a reference to RCMP Inspector Rod Stamler, to whom Elliott had referred a moment before.)

He added "if they want to put me in jail, then f—— them. They can put me in jail," he added with resignation.

Rindress, who is named as a co-conspirator but not charged, is testifying under the Canada and Ontario Evidence Acts. This means his testimony can't be used against him except in case of perjury.

Premier William Davis' name came up yesterday in a brief reference in a tape recording made May 7, 1974.

A voice identified as that of Elliot told Rindress that "Bill Davis overruled the environment people" on what was apparently a Stelco harbor-land project.

Elliott: "The shit hit the fan again. Peter Gordon ... told Davis you get off your ... and tell those people we're talking ..."

Rindress: "That meant a lot to those two companies."

"Big Kickback"

Elliot: "Oh, did it ever ..."

Gordon is Stelco's president and chief executive officer.

The Davis reference was not amplified.

> Elliott went on to laugh at a suggestion that he got a "big kickback" from Stelco, Hamilton's biggest firm.
>
> "Can you imagine ... All they got to do is pick up that phone to city council and say look it, tell that f——ing Elliot that we want that property ..."
>
> ———————————————
>
> Source: John Brehe. "Canada's 'Harbourgate'." *The Toronto Star* 4 June 1975. Reprinted with permission of The Toronto Star Syndicate.

So, there *appears* to be a move toward tougher legal sanctions for white-collar offences. Of course, charges must be laid before sanctions can be imposed, and the power of corporations and of persons in high social class positions makes the decision to prosecute problematic (see Benson et al., 1988). Wheeler et al. (1982) have sought to demonstrate that policies like those described above have led to the more severe sentencing of high-status white-collar offenders. Hagan and Palloni (1983) concur in reporting an increased use of imprisonment with white-collar offenders after Watergate, but also indicate that the length of these prison sentences was unusually short. The Canadian study of the enforcement of securities laws in Ontario (Hagan and Parker, 1985) reveals a similar pattern of tradeoffs in the severity with which white-collar offenders are treated. Overall, treatment of white-collar offenders seems to have been lenient in the past, and there is no unambiguous evidence that this situation has changed markedly.

SUMMARY

This chapter has sought to outline some of the important ways in which the study of white-collar crime alters our views of major issues in the field. It has sought to make the point that the relationship between class and crime is more complicated than frequently assumed, that fundamental aspects of the social organization of work have much to do with the kinds of white-collar crime that are experienced, and that the sanctioning of white-collar crime is unique in its purposes and often lenient in its consequences. The study of white-collar crime can bridge a gap that is too frequently apparent between the study of crime and other social processes. It can do so by bringing our attention to issues of stratification that are centrally involved in this kind of crime. It may well be that such issues are equally important to the study of other kinds of crime as well, and that the study of white-collar crime can in this way serve a further role in renewing our attention to fundamental processes that should focus criminological work more generally.

BIBLIOGRAPHY

Asch, P., and J.J. Seneca. (1969). "Is Collusion Profitable?" *Review of Economics and Statistics* 58:1–12.

Baker, Wayne. (1984). "The Social Structure of a National Securities Market." *American Journal of Sociology* 89:775–811.

Baumhart, Raymond. (1961). "How Ethical Are Businessmen?" *Harvard Business Review* 39:5–176.

Benson, M.L. (1989). "The Influence of Class Position on the Formal and Informal Sanctioning of White-Collar Offenders." *Sociological Quarterly* 30:465–79.

Benson, M.L., W.J. Maakestad, F.T. Cullen, and G. Geis. (1988). "District Attorneys and Corporate Crime: Surveying the Prosecutorial Gatekeepers." *Criminology* 26:505–18.

Braithwaite, John. (1981). "The Myth of Social Class and Criminality Reconsidered." *American Sociological Review* 46:36–57.

Brenner, S.S., and E.A. Molander. (1977). "Is the Ethics of Business Changing?" *Harvard Business Review* 55:57–71.

Casey, John. (1985). "Corporate Crime and the State: Canada in the 1980s." In Thomas Fleming (ed.), *The New Criminologies in Canada*. Toronto: Oxford University Press.

Clinard, Marshall, and Peter Yeager. (1980). *Corporate Crime*. New York: Free Press.

Coleman, James. (1974). *Power and the Structure of Society*. New York: W.W. Norton.

———. (1985). *The Criminal Elite*. New York: St. Martin's Press.

———. (1987). "Toward an Integrated Theory of White-Collar Crime." *American Journal of Sociology* 93:406–39.

Colvin, Mark, and John Pauly. (1983). "A Critique of Criminology: Toward an Integrated Structural-Marxist Theory of Delinquency Production." *American Journal of Sociology* 89(3):513–51.

Cullen, Francis, Martha Larson, and Richard Mathers. (1985). "Having Money and Delinquency Involvement: The Neglect of Power in Delinquency Theory." *Criminal Justice and Behavior* 12(2):171–92.

Cullen, Francis, Bruce Link, and Craig Polanzi. (1982). "The Seriousness of Crime Revisited: Have Attitudes Toward White Collar Crime Changed?" *Criminology* 20:83–102.

Daly, Kathleen. (1989). "Gender and Varieties of White-Collar Crime." *Criminology* 27:769–93.

Elliott, D.S., and Susan Ageton. (1980). "Reconciling Race and Class Differences in Self-Reported and Official Estimates of Delinquency." *American Sociological Review* 45:95–110.

Ermann, M. David, and Richard Lundman. (1980). *Corporate Deviance*. New York: Holt, Rinehart and Winston.

Fantel, Hans. (1989). "Tape-Copying Decks Improve Their Act." *New York Times* (July 9):2:27.

Farberman, Harvey. (1975). "A Criminogenic Market Structure: The Automobile Industry." *Sociological Quarterly* 16:438–57.

Franklin, Alice. (1979). "Criminality in the Workplace: A Comparison of Male and Female Offenders." In Freda Adler and Rita Simon (eds.), *The Criminology of Deviant Women*. Boston: Houghton Mifflin.

Geis, Gilbert. (1975). "Victimization Patterns in White Collar Crime." In Israel Drapkin and Emilio Viano (eds.), *Victimology: A New Focus, Vol. 5: Exploiters and Exploited: The Dynamics of Victimization* (pp. 89–105). Lexington, MA: Lexington Books.

———. (1984). "White Collar Crime and Corporate Crime." In Robert F. Meier (ed.), *Major Forms of Crime*. Beverly Hills: Sage.

Geis, Gilbert, and Robert Meier. (1977). *White Collar Crime.* New York: Wiley.

Goff, Colin, and Charles Reasons. (1978). *Corporate Crime in Canada.* Scarborough: Prentice-Hall.

Greenwood, Peter. (1982). *Selective Incapacitation.* Santa Monica, CA: Rand.

Hagan, John. (1982). "The Corporate Advantage: The Involvement of Individual and Organizational Victims in the Criminal Justice Process." *Social Forces* 60(4):993–1022.

Hagan, John, and Celesta Albonetti. (1982). "Race, Class and the Perception of Criminal Injustice in America." *American Journal of Sociology* 88:329–55.

Hagan, John, A.R. Gillis, and John Simpson. (1985). "The Class Structure of Gender and Delinquency: Toward a Power-Control Theory of Common Delinquent Behavior." *American Journal of Sociology* 90:1151–78.

Hagan, John, and Fiona Kay. (1990). "Gender and Delinquency inWhite-Collar Families: A Power-Control Perspective." *Crime and Delinquency* 36(3):391–407.

Hagan, John, and Ilene Nagel. (1982). "White Collar Crime, White Collar Time: The Sentencing of White Collar Criminals in the Southern District of New York." *American Criminal Law Review* 20(2):259–301.

Hagan, John, Ilene Nagel, and Celesta Albonetti. (1980). "The Differential Sentencing of White Collar Offenders in Ten Federal District Courts." *American Sociological Review* 45:802–20.

Hagan, John, and Alberto Palloni. (1983). "The Sentencing of White Collar Offenders Before and After Watergate." Paper presented at the American Sociological Association Meetings, Detroit.

Hagan, John, and Patricia Parker. (1985). "White Collar Crime and Punishment: The Class Structure and Legal Sanctioning of Securities Violations." *American Sociological Review* 50(3):302–16.

Hagan, John, John Simpson, and A.R. Gillis. (1979). "The Sexual Stratification of Social Control: A Gender-Based Perspective on Crime and Delinquency." *British Journal of Sociology* 30(1):25–38.

———. (1987). "Class in the Household: A Power-Control Theory of Gender and Delinquency." *American Journal of Sociology* 92:788–816.

Hartung, Frank E. (1950). "White Collar Offences in the Wholesale Meat Industry in Detroit." *American Journal of Sociology* 56:25–34.

Hill, Gary D., and Anthony Haris. (1981). "Changes in the Gender Patterning of Crime, 1953–77: Opportunity v. Identity." *Social Science Quarterly* 62(4):658–71.

Hindelang, Michael, Travis Hirschi, and Joseph Weis. (1981). *Measuring Delinquency.* Beverly Hills: Sage.

Kleck, Gary. (1982). "On the Use of Self-Report Data to Determine Class Distribution of Criminal and Delinquent Behavior." *American Sociological Review* 43:427–33.

Lewis, Peter. (1989). "Cracking Down on Computer Pirates." *New York Times* (July 9):2:10.

Maclean's. (1983). "Ottawa's Cautious Competition Bill." (July 18):36–38.

Mann, Kenneth, Stanton Wheeler, and Austin Sarat. (1980). "Sentencing the White Collar Offender." *American Criminal Law Review* 17(4):479.

Mills, C. Wright. (1943). "The Professional Ideology of Social Pathologists." *American Journal of Sociology* 49:165–80.

Nagorski, Zygmunt. (1989). "Yes, Socrates, Ethics Can Be Taught." *New York Times* (February 12):F2.

Nettler, Gwynn. (1978). *Explaining Crime.* New York: McGraw-Hill.

Posner, Richard A. (1980). "Optimal Sentences for White Collar Criminals." *American Criminal Law Review* 409–18.

Reasons, Charles, and Duncan Chappell. (1985). "Crooked Lawyers: Towards a Political Economy of Deviance in the Profession." In Thomas Fleming (ed.), *The New Criminologies in Canada*. Toronto: Oxford University Press.

Reasons, C., L. Ross, and C. Paterson. (1981). *Assault on the Worker: Occupational Health and Safety in Canada*. Toronto: Butterworths.

Reiss, Alberta. (1981). "Foreword: Towards a Revitalization of Theory and Research on Victimization by Crime." *Journal of Criminal Law and Criminology* 72:704–13.

Ross, E.A. (1901). *Social Control*. New York: Macmillan.

Schrager, Laura, and James F. Short. (1978). "Toward a Sociology of Organizational Crime." *Social Problems* 25(4):407–19.

Shapiro, Susan. (1980). "Thinking About White Collar Crime: Matters of Conceptualization and Research." In *Research on White Collar Crime*. Washington, DC: National Institute of Justice.

———. 1990. "Collaring the Crime, Not the Criminal: Reconsidering the Concept of White-Collar Crime." *American Sociological Review* 55:346–66.

Shearing, Clifford, Susan Addario, and Phillip Stenning. (1985). "Why Organizational Charts Cannot be Trusted: Rehabilitating Realism in Sociology." Paper presented at a Symposium on Qualitative Research: Ethnographic/Interactionist Perspectives. University of Waterloo (May 15–17).

Simon, Rita. (1975). *Women and Crime*. Lexington, MA: Lexington Press.

Simpson, Sally. (1986). "The Depression of Antitrust: Testing a Multilevel, Longitudinal Model of Profit-Squeeze." *American Sociological Review* 51:859–75.

Smandych, Russell. (1985). "Marxism and the Creation of Law: Re-Examining the Origins of Canadian Anti-Combines Legislation, 1890–1910." In Thomas Fleming (ed.), *The New Criminologies*. Toronto: Oxford University Press.

Smith, Douglas, and Christy Visher. (1980). "Sex and Involvement in Deviance/Crime: A Quantitative Review of the Empirical Literature." *American Sociological Review* 45(4):691–701.

Snider, Laureen. (1979). "Revising the Combines Investigation Act: A Study in Corporate Power." In Paul J. Brantingham and Jack M. Kress (eds.), *Structure, Law and Power: Essays in the Sociology of Law*. Beverly Hills: Sage.

———. (1980). "Corporate Crime in Canada." In Robert Silverman and James Teevan (eds.), *Crime in Canadian Society*. Toronto: Butterworths.

Steffensmeier, D. (1980). "Sex Differences in Patterns of Adult Crimes, 1965–77: A Review and Assessment." *Social Forces* 57:566–84.

Stone, Christopher. (1975). *Where the Law Ends: The Social Control of Corporate Behavior*. New York: Harper & Row.

Sutherland, Edwin. (1940). "White Collar Criminality." *American Sociological Review* 5:1–12.

———. (1945). "Is 'White Collar Crime' Crime?" *American Sociological Review* 10:132–39.

———. (1949). *White Collar Crime*. New York: Dryden.

———. (1983). *White Collar Crime: The Uncut Version*. New Haven: Yale University Press.

Swartz, Joel. (1978). "Silent Killers at Work." In M. David Ermann and Richard Lundman (eds.), *Corporate and Governmental Deviance*. New York: Oxford University Press.

Tappan, Paul. (1947). "Who is the Criminal?" *American Sociological Review* 12:96–102.

Thornberry, Terrence, and Margaret Farnsworth. (1982). "Social Correlates of Criminal Involvement: Further Evidence on the Relationship Between Social Status and Criminal Behavior." *American Sociological Review* 47:505–18.

Tittle, Charles, W.J. Villemez, and Douglas Smith. (1978). "The Myth of Social Class and Criminality: An Empirical Assessment of the Empirical Evidence." *American Sociological Review* 47:505–18.

Weisburd, David, Elin Waring, and Stanton Wheeler. (1990). "Class, Status and the Punishment of White-Collar Criminals." *Law and Social Inquiry* 15(2):223–46.

Wheeler, Stanton. (1976). "Trends and Problems in the Sociological Study of Crime." *Social Problems* 23:525–34.

Wheeler, Stanton, and Michael Rothman. (1982). "The Organization as Weapon in White Collar Crime." *Michigan Law Review* 80(7):1403–26.

Wheeler, Stanton, David Weisbord, and Nancy Bode. (1982). "Sentencing the White Collar Offender: Rhetoric and Reality." *American Sociological Review* 47:641–59.

Wolfgang, Marvin. (1972). *Delinquency in a Birth Cohort.* Chicago: University of Chicago Press.

FURTHER READING

Clinard, M.P., and P.C. Yeager. (1980). *Corporate Crime.* New York: Free Press. This book provides a thorough examination of corporate crime in the United States in terms of the corporate structure and economic milieu in which violations occur.

Coleman, J.W. (1989). *The Criminal Elite: The Sociology of White Collar Crime.* (2nd ed). New York: St. Martin's Press. Coleman focuses on the "culture of competition" as well as inequities of class and power to explain, and suggest remedies for, white-collar crime.

Ermann, M. David, and Richard Lundman. (1978). *Corporate and Governmental Deviance: Problems of Organizational Behavior in Contemporary Society.* New York: Oxford University Press. A collection of readings that combines classic papers by James Coleman, Albert Reiss, Edwin Sutherland, Gilbert Geis, Marshall Clinard, and Richard Quinney with more recent research and analysis.

————. (1982). *Corporate Deviance.* New York: Holt, Rinehart and Winston. This book provides a conceptual framework for the study of corporate deviance, a typology of corporate deviance, and a discussion of efforts to control corporate deviance.

Fleming, Thomas. (1985). *The New Criminologies in Canada: State, Crime and Control.* Toronto: Oxford University Press. This collection of articles brings together much recent Canadian theorizing about crime and criminal law and includes a number of papers on white-collar crime. Much of the work helps to place the topic of white-collar crime in theoretical context.

Geis, Gilbert, and Robert Meier. (1977). *White Collar Crime.* New York: Free Press. This collection of articles includes reports of original research on a variety of white-collar crimes, including corporate, business, commercial and political white-collar crime.

Goff, Colin, and Charles Reasons. (1978). *Corporate Crime in Canada.* Toronto: Prentice-Hall. The first comprehensive treatment of the development of anti-combines legislation in Canada, set in the broader context of issues surrounding corporate crime and criminological theory.

Reasons, C., L. Ross, and C. Paterson. (1981). *Assault on the Worker: Occupational Health and Safety in Canada.* Toronto: Butterworths. This book provides a critical analysis of the complicated issues surrounding death and injury in the workplace, with a particular emphasis on the Canadian experience.

Reiman, Jeffrey. (1979). *The Rich Get Richer and the Poor Get Prison.* New York: Wiley. An inquiry into the failure of the American criminal justice system—its causes, mechanisms, and moral implications. The causes as well as the consequences of white-collar crime are a part of this story.

Sutherland, Edwin. (1984). *White Collar Crime: The Uncut Version.* New Haven: Yale University Press. The original and still classic study of white-collar crime, including sections of the original manuscript that were originally suppressed.

INDEX

Aboriginal Justice Inquiry
    (Manitoba), 335, 343
Aboriginal peoples, 7, 12-13,
    31-32, 106-113, 274, 285-86,
    335-38
  school policy and, 335, 342
Acephalous societies, 5
  dispute settlement in, 10-14
Achievement Place, 223-24
Actus reus, 42-44
Adler, Freda, 154, 328
Admissibility of evidence, 50-51,
    53-54
Adolescence and age–crime
    relationship, 92-97
  see also Delinquency
Adoption studies, 190-94
  psychopathy and, 200
Adrenalin studies, 198
  of psychopaths, 202
Adultery, 10, 39
Advisor system of dispute
    settlement, 11-14
Age and criminal behaviour, 92-97
Agents of social control, 296-300
Ageton, S., 95, 116
Aggressive behaviour
  brain disease and, 187
  endocrine factors in, 188, 198-99
  glucose tolerance and, 198-99
  social learning theory and,
    220-22
Agnew, Robert, 254
Akers, R.L., 223, 332
Alcoholism
  case of Leroy Powell, 52
  legal defence of, 46
  Native criminality and, 112-13
  prohibition, 298, 413
  psychopathy and, 204
  public drunkenness, 52, 274
Alderton case, 137

Allis-Chalmers, 458
Allodi, F., 230
Amendolito, Salvatore, 410-11
American Motorcycle Association
    (AMA), 401
Amir, Menachem, 147
Anglo-Saxon law, 16
Anomic suicide, 316
Anomie theory, 148, 240, 243, 254
Anslinger, Harry, 26
Anti-Combines Legislation,
    278-79, 461, 465
  history of, 27
Antisocial Personality Disorder,
    200-201, 226-28
Aranda of Australia, 10
Argot, 173
Asbestos-exposure, 30, 453-55
Asch, P., 461
Ashford v. Thornton (1818), 50
Assaults, 359-70
    see also Sexual assault
Asselin, John D'arcy, judge, 404
Atavism, 150, 173
Attachment, 321
Attempt, crime of, 44-45
Attention Deficit Disorder, 196-97
Authorities and subjects, 273-74
Automatism, legal defence of, 47
Automobile theft, 376
Autonomic nervous system studies,
    197-98
  of psychopaths, 201-203
Aversive conditioning, 223

Badgley Report, 364-65
Baker, Wayne, 461
Balbus, Isaac, 279
Bandura, Albert, 220-22
Bank of Credit and Commerce
    International (BCCI), 284, 350
Battered women, 141-45

Beaver case (1957), 45-46
Beccaria, Cesare, 166-69
Becker, Howard, 26, 149, 299, 301
Behaviour disorders, brain disease
    and, 187-88
Belief, 322-23
Béliveau, André, 433-34
Bell-Rowbotham, B., 117
Bennett, Trevor, 375
Bernard, Thomas, 243, 256-57
Berton, Pierre, 429-30
Betrayal of the Poor (Rose), 261
Bias
    in crime statistics, 58, 86
    in IQ tests, 179
    in law enforcement of Natives,
        109-112
Bienvenue, R.M., 112
Binet-Simon intelligence test, 179
Biological factors in crime, 185-206
Biological theories (of crime),
        199-200
    early theories, 172-80
    Lombroso's theory, 172-76
Biron, L., 220
Black hand, 395
Black market, 408
Block, Alan, 256-57
Blood sugar levels and aggressive
        behaviour, 198-99
    in psychopaths, 202
Blumer, Herbert, 293
Bohannan, Paul, 25
Bohm, Robert, 334
Boldt, E.D., 111
Bourassa, Robert, 428
Bowlby, J., 216
Box, Steven, 106, 322
Boydell, C.L., 117
Boyle, 137
Brain disease, aggressive behaviour
        and, 187
Brain disorders, criminal behaviour
        and, 203-204, 229-32
Braithwaite, J., 113, 258-60
Branan, Karen, 29

Brant, Clare C., 7
Break and enter, 4, 59, 355, 374-75
BRICOLE (operation), 432
British Columbia Court of Appeal,
        138
Brodeur, Paul, 30
Brodsky, S.L., 228-29
Brown, W.A., 198
Buchanan, John, 443
Bundy, Theodore, 224-26
Burgess, R.L., 223
Burglary, *see* Break and enter
Byles, 117

CACSW, 128, 130, 141
Calley, Lieutenant, 47
Camorra, 395
Canada, political crime in, 419-47
Canada's Criminal Code, *see*
        Criminal Code of Canada
Canadian
    Advisory Council on the Status
        of Women (CACSW), 128,
        130, 141
    Anti-Combines Legislation,
        278-79, 461, 465
        history of, 27
    Association of Chiefs of Police,
        402
    Bill of Rights, 429
    Centre for Justice Statistics, 64
    Committee on Corrections,
        Report of (1969), 102
    Committee on Sexual Offenses
        against Children and
        Youth, 364-65
    Correctional Service, 305
    Criminal Justice Association,
        379
    General Social Survey (1988),
        354, 361, 366
    Royal Commission on Labour
        and Capital, 463
    Uniform Crime Reports, 58,
        68-79
        victimization surveys and, 80

Urban Victimization Survey (CUVS), 79, 89, 98, 361
Canadian Connection, The (Charbonneau), 390
Canadian Natives, *see* Aboriginal peoples
Canadian Pacific Railway, 434, 439-40
Cannabis offenses, statistics and, 72
Capitalist democracy, 425-27
Card hustlers, 301-302
Career criminality, 267-69
Car theft, 376
Casey, John, 278
Causation (crime)
    biological theories, 199-200
        early theories, 172-80
        Lombroso's theory, 172-76
    early theories, 165-81
    mainstream theories, treatment of women, 148-49
    psychological theories, 213-32
    see also Labelling theory, sociological theories
Causes of Delinquency (Hirschi), 321
Chaiken, Marcia R., and Jan M., 381-83
Chambliss, William J., 273, 280-82, 317, 392
Chan, Janet, 318
Charbonneau, Jean-Pierre, 390
Charter of Rights, 38, 51, 53, 54
Chase case, 137
Check, J.V.P., 221-22
Chesney-Lind, Meda, 154
Chicago Area Project, 338-39
Chicago School, 267
Chieftainships, 17-18
Child abuse, 221, 364-65
Chinese Triads, 397-400
Chromosome studies, 189
Clark, Lorenne M.G., 135, 362
Classical School, on crime causation, 166-71
Classification of crimes, 42
Clastner, D.S., 222

Cleckley, H., 227
Clement, Wallace, 425-26
Clinard, Marshall, 421, 452, 461
Clingempeel, W.G., 213
Cloward, R., 246-49, 250, 254, 255
Cocaine distribution, 400
Cohen, Albert K., 216, 251-52, 255, 271, 302
Cohen, Lawrence E., 352-54, 378
Colombian Mafia, 400
Colson, Elizabeth, 6
Comack, Elizabeth, 26
Commisso family, 406-407, 412
Commitment, 322
    to crime, 303-304
    reactions, 304-305
    of values, 296
Communities, Kobrin's types of, 244-46
Compensation legislation, history of, 27-28
Compulsion, legal defence of, 46-47
Comte, Auguste, 172
Conditioning theory, 222-24
Conduct norms, 267-70
Conflict theories, 149, 267-88
    critiques, 267-69, 271-72, 276-77, 286
    cultural, 267-69
    group, 270-71
    Marxist, 155-56, 277-88
    Weberian, 272-76
Conformity, 149
Conger, Rand D., 232, 332
Consensual crime, 408-409
Consent, 39-40, 47-48
    in rape, 135, 138, 140
Conspiracy, 45
Contagion of violence, 360
Containment theory, 320
Contract law, history, 22-25
Contradictions, Marxist theory of, 280-83
Control theory, *see* Social control theories
Conventional crime, 351-84

Conviction rates, 93-95
Cook, T.D., 221
Cooper, Tom, 336
Cormie, Don, 257
Corporate crime, 28-30, 281-82,
    453-56
  murder convictions for, 29
  petrochemical industry, 256-58
Correlates of criminal behaviour,
    91-121
  age, 92-97
  defined, 91-92
  opportunity structures, 244-56
  race, 106-113
  self-report studies and, 95, 98,
    115
  sex, 97-106
    theories, 104-106
  Shaw and McKay on, 316-18
  social class, 113-20, 193
Corruption
  in organized crime, 407
  political, 439-46
Cosa Nostra, La, 396
Costner, Herbert, 247, 249
Côté, G., 230
Cotroni-Violi Mafia family, 397
Courtis, M.C., 79
Court of the Star Chamber, 167
Cowie, John, 153
Cowie, Valerie, 153
Craddick, R., 228
Craven, W., 230
Crime
  categories, 70-71
  causation, see Causation
  classification of, 42
  control of, 52-53
  conventional, 351-84
  corporate, 28-30, 281-82, 453-56
  murder convictions for, 29
  petrochemical industry, 256-58
  definition of, 37-38, 186
  fear of, 84
  incidence, time of day, 355
  legal elements of, 37-55

and mental illness, 203-204,
    229-32
  organized, 401-405
  patterns of, 355-78
  prevention of, 378-83
  rate, definition of, 72
  reduction, strain theory and,
    258-61
  statistics, see Statistics
  unreported, 79-82
  white-collar, 451-68
Crime: Its Causes and Remedies
    (Lombroso), 174
Crimen laesae majestatis, 419
Crimes and Punishments, An Essay
    on (Beccaria), 166-67
Criminal Code of Canada, 38, 53,
    69-75, 135-36, 140, 361
  organized crime and, 415
Criminal identity, 307
Criminal intent, 42-46
Criminality of Women, The
    (Pollak), 150-52
Criminal justice statistics, 61-65
Criminal law
  general principles, 37-55
  history of, 38, 48-51
  morality and, 40
  versus social and penal policy, 54
Criminal liability, 42-45
Criminal negligence, 29-30
Criminal typologies, 380
Cross-fostering studies, 190-94
Cross, James, 427
Cullen, Francis, 249
Cultural conflict theories, 267-69
  critique, 269-70
Currie, Raymond F., 334

Dahl, Robert, 424
Dahrendorf, Ralf, 272-73
Dalton, K., 188
Dark figure of crime, 68, 80
Darwin, Charles, 172
Darwinism, social, 150, 180
Davis, Nanette, 307

Davis, William, 467
Death sentences in 18th century, 168
DeBeck, E. Paula, 378
Defences to criminal charge, 45-48
DeKeseredy, Walter, 282
Delinquency
    age–crime relationship and, 95
    control theory and, 154-55, 316-18
    the deviant career, 294-96, 380-81
    and family, 325
    Gluecks' study of, 178
    Kohlberg's theory of, 217
    learning theory and, 223
    psychophysiological factors and, 197-98
    and religion, 327-28
    Schoenfeld's psychoanalytical theory of, 216
    schools and, 325-26
    and self-concept, 320
    sequential model, 331-32
    sex difference and, 98, 154-55
    socio-economic status and, 116-18
    see also Social class
    and white-collar crime, 455
    see also Causation; schools and delinquency
Delinquency and Opportunity (Cloward and Ohlin), 246-48
Delinquent Boys: The Culture of the Gang (Cohen), 251
Demers, D.J., 111
Democracy in Canadian political system, 423-27
Democratic perspectives on political crime, 422-23
    capitalist, 425-27, 430-31, 434-35, 437-39, 446
    pluralist, 424-25, 430, 433-34, 437, 445-46
    representative, 423, 429-30, 432-33, 436-37, 445

table, 438
De Silva, S., 69
Deterrence
    classical theories of, 170
    control theory and, 233
De Verteuil, Jacques, 363
Deviance, 294-306
    the deviant career, 294-96
    Durkheim's model of, 240-41
    Lemert on, 294-95
    primary, 294-96
    secondary, 300-304
Diagnostic and Statistical Manual of Mental Disorder, 226-28
Diamond, Stanley, 25
Dickson, Donald, 26
Dietz, Park, 226
Differential association theory, 148, 306-307
    and control theory, 331-33
Discipline (parental), 323-24
Dispute settlement
    history of, 15-18
    in small-scale societies, 9-14
Division of Labour in Society (Durkheim), 239
Dobson, James, 225
Domestic assault, 141-45, 367-69
D'Orban, P.T., 188
Dowie, Mark, 29
Down's syndrome, 185
Doyle, Daniel P., 326
Dracula, Count, 174-75
Drapeau, Jean, 428
Driedger, Leo, 334
Drug legislation, history of, 26
Drug trafficking, 298, 408
    by Chinese Triads, 399-400
    by Colombian Mafia, 400
    control of, 298
    by ethnic-based groups, 405
    by motorcycle gangs, 404
    profitability of, 408-409
    statistics and, 72
Drunkenness, public, 52, 274
    see also Alcoholism

DSM-III R, 226-28
DSM-IV, 228
Dubro, James, 390, 394, 412
Duplessis regime, 440
Durkheim, Emile, 239-41, 242, 247, 254
    on social integration, 315-16
Dutil, Jean L., judge, 407, 409
Dyscontrol syndrome, 188

École Polytechnique, Montreal, 145-46
Ecological analysis, 316-18
Edison Penick, B.K., 79
Education, *see* Schools and delinquency
Egoistic suicide, 315-16
Eichmann, Adolf, 47
Elder abuse, 369-70
Elders' councils, 12, 16-17
Election Expenses Act (1974), 445
Electrodermal response studies, 197
    of psychopaths, 201
Elliott, D.S., 95, 116
Elliott, Kenneth, 466-68
Embezzlement, 41, 456
Empey, Lamar T., 95, 310
Employment for ex-felons, 260
Endocrine disorders, criminal behaviour and, 188, 198-99
English law and the Canadian Criminal Code, 38
English legal history, 18-24
Entrepreneurs, moral, 296-99
Epilepsy, 188
Equity Funding Corporation of America, 284
Ermann, M. David, 28, 454
Ethics of selective incapacitation, 383
Ethnomethodologists, 309
Evidence, rules of, 37, 50-51, 52-54
Executive influence, 460
Ex-offenders, 303
Extortion, 406-407
Extraversion, 219

Eysenck, Hans, 214, 218-20, 228-29
Eysenck Personality Inventory, 229
Eysenck, S.B.J., 219

Falardeau, Jean B., 402
False pretences, 41
Family relationships, control theory and, 323-25, 339-41
Family studies, 190, 221, 319, 334
Farberman, Harvey, 460-61
Farnworth, Margaret, 116, 250
Farrington, David, 213-14, 220, 324, 325
Felonies, 42
Felson, Marcus, 352-54, 378
Female criminality, 328-29
    endocrine disorders and, 188
    genetic predisposition and, 189
    patterns of, 97-106
    prostitution, 40
Female Offender, The (Lombroso and Ferrero), 150
Feminists, 280-81, 328, 362
    criminology, 155-58
    scholarship, 147-58
Ferrero, William, 150, 153
Ferri, Enrico, 172
Feudalism, 18-22, 165-66
Fidler, Richard, 430-31
Figlio, Robert M., 305
Fillmore, C., 104
Film violence and aggression, 221-22
Fines and white-collar crime, 465
Finkler, H.W., 112
Firearms, homicide due to, 357, 359
Firestone official, 452
Fisher, J., 103-104
Fisher, Reginald, 466
Flanagan, Timothy J., 363, 378
FLQ (Front de Liberation du Québec), 427-31
Ford Motor Company, 463
Ford Pinto accidents, 29

Forth, H. and Co. Ltd., 459-60
Fox, J., 105
Fraud, 41
Fréchette, M., 95
French penal code, 170
French, Richard D., 433-34
Freud, Sigmund, 215
Friedman, Lawrence, 27
Front de Liberation du Québec
    (FLQ), 427-31

Gabarino, James, 364
Gabor, Thomas, 373
Gabrielli, W.F., Jr., 190
Gang, The (Thrasher), 316
Gangs, 247-49, 300, 401-404
Garofolo, Raffaelo, 172
Gayme case, 140
Geen, R.G., 221
Gelsthorpe, Loraine, 149
Gemeinschaft, 9
Gender and sex, 152
Gender differences, 152-54, 361
General Electric, 457-58
Genetic factors
    criminal behaviour and, 189
    in psychopathy development, 200
Gess, Nick, 406
Gibbons, D.C., 121
Giffen, P.J., 102, 249
Giller, Henri, 324-25, 341
Gillis, A.R., 98, 318, 328, 334
Glaser, Daniel, 332
Glassner, Barry, 307-309
Glucose tolerance and aggressive
    behaviour, 198-99
Glueck, S. and E., 178, 320
Goddard, H.H., 178-79
Goff, Colin, 27, 278, 463, 465
Goffman, Erving, 300, 302
Gold, Martin, 320
Golding, S.L., 230
Gomme, I.M., 98, 117, 334
Gonthier, Charles, justice, 140
Gordon, David M., 278
Gordon, Peter, 467

Gordon, R.A., 113
Goring, Charles, 176-77
Gorsuch, Anne, 258
Gottfredson, 97
Gould, Stephen Jay, 173
Graham, James, 26
Grassy Narrows, 335-38, 343
Gravel, Marcel, 444
Greenberg, David, 96-97, 255, 262
Griffiths, G.B., 176
Grosman, Brian, 429
Gross (criminal) negligence, 44
Group conflict theory, 270-71
    critique, 271-72
Groves, W. Byron, 335
GSS, see Canadian General Social
    Survey
Guardianship, 378-79
Gudjonsson, G.H., 214
Guerry, Andre Michel, 114, 171
Gunn, J., 230
Guns, homicide due to, 357, 359
Guze, S., 229

Hagan, John, 26, 98, 102, 106,
    108-109, 111, 118, 154-55,
    274, 318, 328, 329-30, 334,
    461, 465, 468
Hakeem, M., 229
Hale, C., 106
Hall, Jerome, 22
HAM (operation), 432
Hamilton Harbour Commission,
    466-68
Handguns, homicide due to, 357,
    359
Harbourgate, 466-68
Hare, Robert D., 200-202, 227,
    382
Harris, S.L., 224
Hart, H.L.A., 54
Hartnagel, T.F., 105, 111-12, 221
Hartung, Frank E., 452
Hatfield regime, 442-43
Havemann, P., 108, 112-13
Hawkins, J. David, 342

Hawkins, William, 444
Health and safety legislation,
    27-28, 281-82
Heidensohn, Frances, 148, 152,
    156-57
Heilbrun, A.B. Jr., 228
Hell's Angels, 401-404
Henshel, Richard L., 276
Hepburn, John R., 278, 329
Heroin trafficking, 410
Hill, D., 198
Hinch, Ronald, 136, 280, 282, 286
Hindelang, Michael J., 113, 86-87,
    100, 216, 351-53
Hirschi, Travis, 86-87, 250, 324
    on age–crime relationship, 97
    on religiosity, 322-23, 326-27
    on social control theory, 149,
        321-23
History
    of Canadian Mafia, 395-97
    of contract law, 22-25
    of crime theories, 165-81
    of criminal law, 38, 48-51
    of dispute settlement, 9-14,
        15-18
    of drug legislation, 26
    of human social organization,
        4-32
    of jury system, 50-51
    of legal system in England, 18-24
    of occupational health
        legislation, 27-28
    of sex-differences in crime,
        100-104
    of sexual offenses, 39-40
    of trade unions, 435-36
Hodgins, S., 230
Hoebel, E. Adamson, 9
Hoffman-Bustamente, Dale, 153
Hollin, C.R., 214
Homicide, 355-59
    corporate, 453-55
    defined, 355-56
    lawful and unlawful, 39
    statistics, 74, 78, 356-59

Homosexuality, law against, 40
Homosexual rape, 361-62
    lesbian battery, 368
Hooton, Ernest A., 177
Hospitalization *versus*
    imprisonment, 54, 230-31
Hussein, Saddam, 350
Hutchings, B., 190
Hutton cheque-kiting scheme, 460
Hylton, J.H., 106, 109
Hyperactivity studies, 196-97
Hyperkinesis studies, 196-97
Hypoglycemia and aggressive
    behaviour, 198-99
    in psychopaths, 202

Illegally obtained evidence, 54
Imprisonment *versus*
    hospitalization, 54, 230-31
Incapacitation, 380-83
Inchoate (incomplete) crimes, 45
Indian Affairs and Northern
    Development Ministry, 106
Indian Conditions (1980), 112
Indians (Canadian), *see* Aboriginal
    peoples
Indictable offenses, definition of, 42
Industrial accidents, 27-30
Infanticide, 356
Inheritance of criminal behaviour,
    176-79
Inmates, *see* Prison, Prisoner studies
Insanity, legal defence of, 47
Instrumentalist Marxist theory, 278
Intelligence
    and crime, 176-79
    and psychopathy, 228
Interactionist theories, 293-311
    limitations, 307-309
Intoxication, legal defence of, 46
    see also Alcoholism
Inuit, 9, 12-13, 31-32
Involvement, 322
IQ tests and crime, 179
Italian immigrants in Montreal,
    268

Italian School on crime causation, 172

Jacobsen, D., 230
Jail, *see* Prison
James, J.T.L., 109
Japanese Yakuza, 399
Jeffrey, C.R., 19, 223
Jennings, W.S., 217
Jensen, Gary F., 320, 333, 342
Job injuries, 27-30
Johns-Manville case, 30, 453-55
Johnson, Holly, 98, 106, 157, 363, 372-73, 377
Judges on white-collar crime, 464-66
Jury, history of, 50-51
Justice system (criminal), statistics on, 61-68
Jutai, Jeffrey W., 382
Juveniles, crime rate of, 93-95
    see also Delinquency

Kallikak, Martin, 178
Keable Commission (Québec), 431
Kedward, H., 230
Kendzierski, D.A., 221
Kennedy, Mark, 278
Kennedy, Robert, 407
Kent, Lori, 327
Kickback schemes, 440
King, Joan, 175
King's Peace, 19-20
Kirby, Cecil, 407
Klein, Dorie, 153
Kobrin, S., 244-46, 249
Kockx, Ron, 139
Koenig, Daniel J., 378
Kohlberg, L., 217
Konpoka, Gisella, 153
Kornhauser, 254-55
Kuhn, Thomas, 287
Kung Lok, 399
Kushner, S., 230

Labelling theory, 60, 149

criminal identities, 299-300
interactionism and, 294, 297-300
limitations of, 308, 310
Labour disputes, 271
La Cosa Nostra (LCN), 396
Ladinsky, Jack, 27
Lamb, H.R., 231
LaPorte, Pierre, 427
LaPrairie, Carol P., 109
Larceny, 377-78
history of laws on, 40-41
LaSalle, Roche, 444
Latif, A.H., 112
Law enforcement against organized crime, 414-15
Law and morality, 40, 53
Law Reform Commission of Canada, 3, 41, 108
Law in society, 25-30
LCN, *see* La Cosa Nostra
Learning theory (social), 220-22
LeBlanc, Marc, 95, 98, 117, 220, 332-33
Leeson, Delbert, case, 139-40
Left realism, 283-86
Legalization of illicit goods, 413-14
Leiter, Kenneth, 309
Lemert, Edwin, 294-95, 300, 304-305
Lenski, 4
Leon, Jeffrey, 26
Leonard, Eileen, 148
Lépine, Marc, 145-46
Lesbian battery, 360
Levels of analysis, psychological, 214-15
Lévesque, René, 428-29
Levy, Madeleine, 23
Lewis, C.S., 54
Lewis, Debra J., 135, 362
Lewis, Dorothy, 226
Lewis, Stephen, 298
L'Heureux-Dubé, Claire, justice, 140
Liberty League, 299
Lieber, Michael, 250

Liebow, Elliot, 255
Lifestyle/exposure theory, 351-53, 370
Linden, Rick, 104, 328, 334
Liquor violations
    Native criminality and, 112-13
    see also Alcoholism
Liska, Allen E., 277
Lombroso, Cesare, 172-76
    on political crime, 420
    on women's crime, 150, 153
Luciano, Lucky, 396
Lundman, Richard, 28, 454
Lynch, Michael, 335
Lyon, J. Noel, 429

McCarthy, B., 118
McCord, Joan, 320, 325
McCord, William, 320
McCorrister, Lesley, 144-45
McDonald, Bruce, judge, 144
MacDonald Commission (Canada), 431
McGuire, Kathleen, 363-64, 378
Machiavelli, 419-20
McKay, Henry, 316-18
MacKenzie Commission Report (1968), 433
McLean, Walter, 444
Maclean's magazine, 461
MacLeod, Linda, 141, 143, 367
McPherson, L., 227
Mafia, 394, 410-11
    Canadian, 395-97, 406-407
    Colombian, 400
    history of, 395-97
Mahler, Russell, 257
Maine, Henry Sumner, 51
Malamuth, N.M., 221-22
Manitoba Aboriginal Justice Inquiry, 335, 343
Manslaughter, 356
Manson, Charles, 224, 226
Manticore, The (Davies), 252-53
Marchessault, Henri, case of, 308
Marsden, William, 410-11

Marx, Herbert, 429
Marx, Karl, 277
Marxist analysis, 24, 119, 308
Marxist conflict theories, 155-156, 277-86
    of contradictions, 280-83
    critiques, 286
    instrumentalism, 278
    left realism, 283-86
    structuralist, 278-80
Mask of Sanity, The (Cleckley), 227
Mass media violence and aggression, 221
Mataco of South America, 10
Maternal bonding, 216
Matthews, Roger, 283, 286
Maturational reform, 96-97
Matza, David, 294-95, 305
Maxwell, Ann, 145
Mayhew, Henry, 171
Mayhew, Pat, 375
Mediators, 16
Mednick, S.A., 190, 199-200
Meier, R.F., 117
Meighen, Arthur, 436-37
Mencken, H.L., 457
Mennonites, 334
Mens rea, 42-46
Menstruation, criminal behaviour and, 188
Mental illness, crime and, 203-204, 229-32
Merchant class, rise of, 20-24, 166
Mercredi, Ovide, 343
Merton, Robert, 148, 241-42, 243-44, 247, 250, 254, 255, 261, 421
Métis and Non-status Indian Crime and Justice Commission report (1978), 110, 112
Metropolitan Toronto Police, 135
Metro Toronto Action Committee on Violence Against Women and Children, 131-32
Michalowski, Raymond, 4-5

Mikel, D., 108
Miliband, Ralph, 24, 278-79
Mills, C. Wright, 457
Minimal brain damage studies, 194-97
Minnesota Multiphasic Personality Inventory, 229
Misdemeanours, 42
Mistake, legal defence of, 45-46
Mobilization for Youth Project, 260-61
Mob Rule: Inside the Canadian Mafia (Dubro), 390
Modelling, effects of on aggressive behaviour, 220-21
Mohawk, 7
Monahan, J., 229-30
Money laundering schemes, 409-413
Montreal Massacre, 145-47
Montreal Police Drug Squad, 308
Montreal Social Welfare Court, 95
Moral development, theories of, 217-18
Moral entrepreneurs, 296-99
Morality and criminal law, 40, 53
Morris, Allison, 128, 148-49
Morrison, Peter, 376
Morton, M.E., 98
Motorcycle gangs, 300, 307, 401-404
Motor vehicle theft, 376
Movie violence and aggression, 221-22
Muirhead, G.K., 109
Mulroney, Brian, 443-44
Murder, 355-59
    defences to charge of, 46-48
    rates in different countries, 187
Mutual conversion, 252
Myths about rape, 128-34

Naffine, Nadine, 148-49, 328-29
Nagel, Ilene, 465
Natalazia, E.M., 158
Nathan, P.E., 224

National Task Force on Suicide in Canada (1987), 305
Native Counselling Services of Alberta, 109
Native Offender and the Law, The (1974), 108
Natives (Canadian), *see* Aboriginal peoples
Native women, 157
Necessity, legal defence of, 46-47
Negligence, within criminal law, 29-30
Nettler, Gwynn, 92, 96, 244, 320, 360-61, 382
Neuroticism, 219
New Brunswick Court of Appeal, 137
Newcombe, Charles, judge, 144
New Criminology, The (Taylor et al.), 149
Newman, J.P., 229
Newman, Katherine, 10
New York Times, 452-53
Nidal, Abu, 350
Nietzel, M.T., 217
Nixon, Richard, 329-30
Nonsexual assault, 365-67
Noriega, Manuel, 350
Normandeau, André, 373
North West Mounted Police, 434
Nye, F. Ivan, 86, 115, 318-19

Occupation in white-collar crime, 451-52
Occupational deaths and injuries, 453-55
Occupational health legislation, 282
    history of, 27-28
October Crisis (1970), 271, 427-35
Ohlin, Lloyd, 246-47, 255
Oil company spies, 248
Ojibwa, 7, 12-13, 336-38
Okihiro, Norm, 79, 374
Olweus, D., 198
One-percenters, 401
Ontario Court of Appeal, 137

Ontario Workers' Compensation Board, 454
Operant conditioning, 222-24
Operation BRICOLE, 432
Operation HAM, 432
Opportunities for Youth, 261
Opportunity structures, 244-56
    illegitimate, 246-48
    marginal, 249
Orders, carrying out, legal defence of, 47
Oregon Social Learning Center, 339-40
Organization in white-collar crime, 451-52, 456-62
Organized crime, 389-416
    controlling, 413-15
    definition, 391
Osgood, D.W., 95
Outlaw bikers, 401-405
Overrepresentation of aboriginals in jails, 106-113

Pacific Railway scandal, 439-40
Pagelow, Mildred Daley, 368-69
Palloni, Alberto, 468
Pappajohn case, 46
Paramount chieftainships, 17-18
Parental
    bonding, importance of, 216
    criminality and delinquency, 190-94
    discipline, 43-44, 323-24, 340-41
    role model, 324-25
Parker, Patricia, 461
Parole of Native offenders, 111
Parti Québecois, 428, 432, 434
Passive avoidance learning, 203
Patterson, Gerald, 339-41
Peine fort et dure, 49
Pelletier, Gérard, 431
Penal policy and theory, 54
Penitentiaries, see Prison
Pennsylvania State Task Force on Organized Crime, 390

Personality and crime, theory of, 226-28
Personal victimization, see Victimization
Petersilia, Joan, 380
Petrochemical industry, corporate crime and, 256-58
Physical characteristics and crime, 176-78
Piaget, Jean, 217
Pillemer, Karl A., 369-70
Pinto accidents, 29
Pizza Connection, 411
Platt, Anthony, 26
Pluralist democracy, 424-25
Podnieks, Elizabeth, 369
Poison Stronger than Love: The Destruction of an Ojibwa Community (Shkilnyk), 336-38
Police
    arrests of mentally ill by, 230-31
    illegal RCMP Security Service activities, 431-35
    investigation of organized crime by, 414
    misconduct, 420-21
    statistics, 61-64, 68-72
        problems with, 57-60, 359
        on sexual assault, 362
    strikes, 333
Political crime, 275-76
    in Canada, 419-47
    defined, 421-22
    political protest, 271
    theories, see Democratic perspectives
    Watergate affair, 329-30
Political terrorism, 435
Polk, Kenneth, 341-42
Pollak, Otto, 150-53
Polsky, Ned, 61
Porter, J.P. Co. Ltd., 466
Positive School, on crime causation, 172-76
Possession offences, 44-45
Poulantzas, Nicos, 279

Powell, Leroy, case of, 52
Premenstrual syndrome, 188
Prevention of crime, 379
Principles of Criminology
    (Sutherland), 306
Prison
    aboriginals in, 106-113
    homosexual rape in, 361-62
    mental illness in, 229-31
    population of, 65-67
    suicides, 305
Prisoner studies
    problems of, 228
    self-report, 382
Proal, Louis, 420
Production and reproduction,
    155-56
Prohibition, 298, 413
Property offences, 40-41, 47-48
    age and, 93-94
    consent in, 47-48
    rates, 76-78
    sex differences and, 99-101, 157
Prostitution, 157
    alleged identity, 307
    the law and, 40
Provocation, legal defence of, 46
Prus, Robert C., 301
Psychoanalytic theory, 215-17
Psychological theories (of crime),
    213-32
    see also Labelling theory
Psychopath studies, 226-28, 382-83
    biological factors and, 200-203
Psychophysiological factors, 197-98
Psychoticism, 219
Public drunkenness, 52
    see also Alcoholism
Public welfare offences, 41-42
Pulkkinen, L., 195
Punishment (parental), 323-24

Quasar Petroleum, 453
Québec
    Crime Probe (1977), 396-97,
        408

Duplessis regime, 440
    nationalism and the October
        Crisis, 427-31
Queen's University, 132-34
Quetelet, Lambert A.J., 114, 171
Quicker, John, 250
Quinney, Richard, 259, 273, 278,
    421-22
    Marxian theory of, 119-20

Rabkin, J., 231
Race and criminal behaviour,
    106-113
Race and drug legislation, 26
Radzinowicz, Sir Leon, 175
Rafter, N.H., 158
Rand Corporation, 380, 381, 383
Rape, *see* Sexual assault
Rappaport, J., 214
RCMP, 429, 466
RCMP Security Service illegal
    activities, 431-35
RCMP: The Real Subversives (Fidler),
    430-31
Reaction formation, 252
Reasons, Charles E., 27, 29, 278,
    282, 453, 463, 465
Reckless, Walter, 319-20
Records (police), *see* Police statistics
Redress
    for asbestos-exposure, 30, 455
    self- or kin-based, 10-11
    Workers' Compensation
        legislation, 27-28
Reiss, Albert J., Jr., 318-19
Relativity of crime, 39-42
Religion and law, 37, 40, 49
    religiosity and criminal
        behaviour, 326-28
Reppucci, N.D., 213
Representative democracy, 423
Reproduction and production,
    155-56
Reverse-onus clauses, 53
Revolutionary Workers League,
    430, 432, 434

Richard, John Albert case, 144
Rindress, Horace, 466-68
Rivard, Jean, 441
Robbery, 370-73
    armed, 373
Roberts, Leslie, 440
Robertson, M., 230
Roebuck, Julian B., 380
Roesch, R., 230
Rojek, Dean G., 342
Ross, E.A., 451
Ross, Rupert, 7, 12-13
Rossi, Peter, 25-26
Rothman, Michael, 461
Rousseau, J.J., 168
Routine activities approach, 352-54
Rowbotham, Robert (Rosie), 406
Rutter, Michael, 324-25, 341

Sacco, Vincent F., 372-73, 377
Safety legislation, 27-28, 282
Sanborn, Michael, 406
Sarbin, T.R., 213
Sargent, W., 198
Sawatsky, John, 433
Scale of seriousness of crime, 63
Scaramella, T.J., 198
Schafer, Walter E., 341-42
Schoenfeld, C.G., 216
Schools
    aboriginal, 335
    and delinquency, 96-97, 117,
        325-26
    goal frustration and, 251-52
    social policy and, 341-43
Schutz, Alfred, 309
Schwartz, Michael, 320
Schwendinger, Herman and Julia,
    244, 255
Seaboyer case, 140
Security Service activities, illegal,
    431-35
Seidman, Robert, 273, 281-82
Self-concept and delinquency, 320
Self-defence, legal defence of, 46
Self-redress, 10-11

Self-report studies, 86-87, 117-18
    age–crime relationship and, 95
    of prisoners, 382
    sex ratio in, 98
    social class and, 115
Self-restraint, in small-scale
        societies, 6-7
Sellin, Thorsten, 26, 63-64, 267-70
    scale of seriousness of crime, 63
Seneca, J.J., 461
Serotonin, 197
Sex differences
    in criminal behaviour, 97-106,
        149, 193
    endocrine disorders and, 188
Sex and gender, 152
Sex hormones
    criminal behaviour and, 188
    premenstrual syndrome, 188
Sexual assault, 128-41, 361-65
    against children, 139-40, 364-65
    consent in, 39-40, 47-48
    cultural construction of rape,
        128-135
    evidentiary rules, 136
    failure to report, 80-82
    history of, 39-40
    new legislation, 135-41, 280-81
    rape laws, former, 26-27, 134-35
    situational theory, 364
    victims, 363-64
Sexual consent, age of, 39
Sharper, C.R.D., 301
Shaw, Clifford, 316-18, 338
Sheldon, William, 177-78
Shkilnyk, Anastasia, 336-38
Short, James F., Jr., 86, 115, 294,
    331-32
Silber, D.E., 229
Silverman, R.A., 69
Simon, Rita J., 105, 154
Simpson, John, 98, 328, 334
Simpson, Sally, 457
Simpsons-Sears, 459-60
Situational theory of rape, 364
Skinner, B.F., 223

Skogan, W., 85

Sky Shops affair, 440-42

Slang, criminal, 173

Slater, Eliot, 153

Small, Shirley, 26

Small-scale societies, 5-14
   dispute settlement in, 9-14
   transformation to the state, 14-25

Smandych, Russell, 27, 279, 463-64

Smart, Carol, 138, 148, 153

Smith, D.A., 104

Snider, Laureen, 26, 27

Social bond, 321

Social change, 343

Social class and crime, 109-111,
   113-20, 193
   opportunity structures, 244-56
   self-report studies and, 115
   Shaw and McKay on, 316-18

Social control, agents of, 296-300

Social control theories, 315-44
   criticisms, 329-38
   and differential association,
     331-32
   early, 318-21
   and motivation, 330
   and upperworld crime, 329-30

Social disorganization theories,
   315-18

Social inequality, history of, 15

Socialization into crime, 306-307

Social learning theory, 220-22

Social order, origins of, 4-32

Social policy and schools, 341-43

Societies, small-scale, 5-14
   dispute settlement in, 9-14
   transformation to the state, 14-25

Socioeconomic status and crime, see
   Social class and crime

Sociological theories (of crime)
   conflict theories, 267-88
   differential association, 148
   interactionist theories, 293-311
   moral development theory,
     217-18
   role theory, 153-55

social control theory, 315-44
strain theories, 239-62
   versus correlation, 92
women's crime, 150-58

Sociopath, 226

Solicitor General, Ministry, 79-85,
   108

Somatotype theory of Sheldon,
   177-78

Spatz Widom, Cathy, 228-29

Spencer, Herbert, 172

Spitzer, Steven, 426

Stark, Rodney, 326-27

Stark, Werner, 333

State
   eclipse of control, 28
   emergence of, 14-25

State in Capitalist Society, The
   (Miliband), 24

Statistical School, on crime
   causation, 171-72

Statistics (crime), 57-87, 97-103,
   354-55
   criminal justice, 61-65
   early pioneers of, 171-72
   homicide, 74, 356-59
   official, 68-79
   property crimes, 76-77
   reliability, 57-61
   self-report studies, 86-87
   sexual assault, 362-65
   sexual differences, 97-103
   victimization surveys, 79-86
   violent crimes, 75, 77, 355-73

Statistics Canada, 64, 79, 365, 374
   on homicides, 356-59
   victimization survey and, 79-86

Steadman, H.J., 229-30

Stebbins, Robert A., 302-303

Steffensmeier, D.F., 97, 102-104,
   105-106

Stelco, 467-68

Stone, Christopher, 29, 457-58,
   462-63

Strain theories, 239-62
   crime prevention and, 258-61

criticisms of, 253, 255-56
structural functionalism, 239-41
Strodtbeck, Fred, 332
Structuralist Marxist theory, 278-80
Subjects and authorities, 273-74
Suicide
Durkheim on, 240-41
in prison, 305
Suicide (Durkheim), 240
Summary offences, definition of, 42
Superior order, legal defence of, 47
Superstition, role of
in crime causation, 165
in criminal law, 49
Supreme Court of Canada, 45-46,
137, 140-41
Suspects, homicide, 359
Sutherland, Edwin, 256, 267,
269-70
on differential association,
148-49, 306-307, 331
on social disorganization, 269
on white-collar crime, 451-53
on women's crime, 148-49
Swartz, Joel, 454
Sykes, Gresham M., 286

Tangri, Sandra S., 320
Tappan, Paul, 269
TARP (Transitional Aid Research
Project), 260
Task Force on Aboriginal Peoples
in Federal Corrections, report
(1989), 108, 110
Tate, Sharon, 224
Tax havens, 410-13
Taylor, Ian, 269-70, 276
Teevan, J.J., 221
Television violence and aggression,
221
Temperance movement, 298-99
Teplin, Linda, 229, 231
Tepperman, L., 95, 103
Terrorism in Canada, 427-35
Testosterone studies, 198
Theft

history of laws on, 40-41
larceny, 40
motor vehicle, 376
Theories of crime, *see* Causation
Thomas, Charles W., 329
Thomas, S.V., 221
Thomas, W.I., 150-51, 153
Thorburn, H.G., 424, 430
Thornberry, Terence P., 116, 305
Tigar, Michael, 23
Tittle, C.R., 113-15, 117, 120
Tongas of Zambia, 6
Tönnies, Ferdinand, 9, 23
Torrance, Judy, 429
Torture, 49-50, 167-68, 276
Trade unions, history of, 435-36
Transitional Aid Research Project
(TARP), 260
Transnational corporations, 28, 30
Trasler, G., 203
Treason, 260, 419
definition of, 39
Triad societies, 397-400
Trial
by battle, 49-50, 165
by fire, 165
by jury, history of, 50-51
by ordeal, 49, 165
by water, 165
Tribalism, 6-9, 18
Tribble, Stephen, 118
Trudeau, Pierre, 427-31
Trudeau, Yves (Apache), 402-403
Turk, Austin, 273-77, 286, 287
on political crime, 420-21, 425
Twin studies, 190
Typologies, criminal, 380

UCR, *see* Uniform Crime Reports
Unadjusted Girl, The (Thomas), 150
Uniform Crime Reports, 58, 68-79
victimization surveys and, 80,
82, 85-86
United States
Bureau of Justice Statistics, 373
CIA, 350, 429

Congress, 413
Democratic National
    Committee, 329-30
Environmental Protection
    Agency, 257-58, 463
National Crime Surveys, 351,
    363, 365
National Security Council, 350
Standard Metropolitan Statistical
    Areas, 115
Supreme Court, 52
Uniform Crime Reports, 97, 100
Unreported crime, 79-82
Upper-class crime, 259-60
Upperworld crime, 329-30
    control theory and, 329-30
Urban Victimization Survey
    (Canadian), 79, 89, 98

Vallieres, Pierre, 427-31
Value commitment, 296
Van der Hoop, Peter, judge, 139
Vaz, Edward, 117
Velarde, Albert J., 332
Veltmeyer, H., 28
Verdun-Jones, S.N., 109
Victimization
    lifestyle/exposure theory of,
        351-53
    surveys, 79-86
Victim precipitation, 147
Victims, 79, 354
    of domestic assault, 367-69
    elderly, 369-70
    of homicide, 358-59
    of larceny, 377-78
    of nonsexual assault, 366-67
    of robbery, 372
    of sexual offences, 363
    of violent crimes, 354
Vilella, 172
Villemez, W.J., 113-15
Violence
    contagion, 360
    exposure and aggressive
        behaviour, 220-22

Violent crimes
    age and, 93-94
    by organized crime groups,
        329-30
    rate of, 74-75, 77
    sex differences and, 99-101
    victims of, 354
Violent predators, 381-82
Visher, C.A., 104
Voir dire, 140
Vold, George, 270-72
Volstead Act, 413
Von Hirsch, Andrew, 383

Waite, Emily, 25-26
Wall, Dale, 374
Waller, Irvin, 79, 374, 379
Walters, Vivienne, 28
Walton, Paul, 269-70, 276
War Measures Act, 271, 428-31
Warren, M.Q., 216
Watergate, 329-30
Watson, Mark, 300
Weapons
    homicide due to, 357, 359
    robbery and, 370-71
Weber, Max, 272
Weberian conflict theory, 272-76
    critique, 276-77
    nonpartisan, 273-76
Weis, Joseph G., 86-87, 342
West, W. Gordon, 26, 98, 117,
    305, 324, 325
Wheeler, Stanton, 461, 468
White-collar crime, 451-68
    legal sanctions, 462-68
White Niggers of America
    (Vallieres), 427
Wife battering, 141-45
    see also Domestic assaults
Wife Battering in Canada: The
    Vicious Circle (MacLeod), 141
Wilson, James Q., 170
Winnipeg General Strike (1919),
    435-39
Witchcraft, 167

Wolf, Rosalie S., 369-70
Wolfgang, Marvin E., 26, 63-64, 305
Women
    and crime, 127-59, 334
    in criminology, 148-58
    incarceration, 158
    as legal persons, 142
    as property, 10, 142
    as victims, 80-82
        of domestic assault, 141-45
        of sexual assault, 128-41
    see also Female criminality

Women's liberation thesis, 153-55
Wooton, Barbara, 54
Workers' Compensation legislation, 27-28
Wright, Richard, 375
Wynne, D.F., 111-12

XYY men, 189

Yakuza, 399
Yeager, Peter, 452, 461
Young, Jock, 269-70, 276, 300
Young Offenders Act, 170

To the owner of this book:

We are interested in your reaction to *Criminology: A Canadian Perspective,* Second Edition, edited by Rick Linden. With your comments, we can improve this book in future editions. Please help us by completing this questionnaire.

1. What was your reason for using this book?
    _____ university course
    _____ college course
    _____ continuing education course
    _____ personal interest
    _____ other (specify)
2. If you used this text for a program, what was the name of that program?
3. Which school do you attend?
4. Approximately how much of the book did you use?
    ___ 1/4 ___ 1/2 ___ 3/4 ___ all
5. Which chapters or sections were omitted from your course?
6. What is the best aspect of this book?
7. Is there anything that should be added?
8. Please add any comments or suggestions.

- -

(fold here)

**Business
Reply Mail**
No Postage Stamp
Necessary if Mailed
in Canada

POSTAGE WILL BE PAID BY
Heather McWhinney
Editorial Director
College Division
HARCOURT BRACE JOVANOVICH, CANADA
55 HORNER AVENUE
TORONTO, ONTARIO
M8Z 9Z9

(tape shut)